Britain since 1707

Britain since 1707

Callum G. Brown and W. Hamish Fraser

Longman
is an imprint of

Harlow, England • London • New York • Boston • San Francisco • Toronto • Sydney • Singapore • Hong Kong
Tokyo • Seoul • Taipei • New Delhi • Cape Town • Madrid • Mexico City • Amsterdam • Munich • Paris • Milan

PEARSON EDUCATION LIMITED

Edinburgh Gate
Harlow CM20 2JE
United Kingdom
Tel: +44 (0)1279 623623
Fax: +44 (0)1279 431059
Website: www.pearsoned.co.uk

_____

First edition published in Great Britain in 2010

ISBN: 978-0-582-89415-0

British Library Cataloguing in Publication Data
A CIP catalogue record for this book can be obtained from the British Library

Library of Congress Cataloging in Publication Data
A CIP catalog record for this book can be obtained from the Library of Congress

10   9   8   7   6   5   4   3   2   1
14   13   12   11   10

Set by 35 in 10.5/13pt Baskerville MT
Printed and bound in Great Britain by Henry Ling Ltd, Dorchester, Dorset

The Publishers' policy is to use paper manufactured from sustainable forests.

Contents

Focus on

List of timelines

List of tables

List of maps

List of figures

Acknowledgements

We are grateful to the following for permission to reproduce copyright material:

Alamy images for Figures 2.1, 13.1, 18.1 and 38.1; Yale University Pictorial Records and Collections, Lewis Walpole Library for Figure 2.2; Cambridge University Press for Figure 3.1, from Mitchell, B. R. and Deane, P. (eds), *Abstract of British Historical Statistics* (1962); Sir John Soane's Museum/ Eileen Tweedy for Figure 4.1; Mary Evans Picture Library for Figures 8.1, 9.1, 12.1, 14.1, 17.1, 20.1, 22.1, 23.1, 24.1 and 26.1; The Trustees of the British Museum for Figures 9.2, 10.1 and 11.1; Science & Society Picture Library for Figures 16.1, 28.1, 29.1, 32.1 and 34.1; Topfoto for Figures 27.1 and 36.1; RCAHMS Enterprises for Figure 30.1; the British Cartoon Archive, University of Kent (www.cartoons.ac.uk) for Figure 31.1; the Press Association for Figure 33.1; Getty Images for Figure 37.1.

Pearson Education Ltd for Maps 1 and 2, adapted from Evans, E. J., *The Forging of the Modern British State* (2001); Pearson Education Ltd for Map 4, adapted from Smith, Iain R., *The Origins of the South African War, 1899–1902* (1995).

Cambridge University Press for Tables 20.1 and 20.2, from Mitchell, B. R. and Deane, P. (eds), *Abstract of British Historical Statistics* (1962); Cambridge University Press for Tables 34.1 and 34.2, from Broadberry, S., 'The Performance of Manufacturing' in Floud, R. and Johnson, P. (eds), *The Cambridge Economic History of Modern Britain: Volume III – Structural Change and Growth* (2004).

Taylor & Francis for the poetry extracts on p. 125, from Davidoff, L. and Hall, C., *Family Fortunes: Men and Women of the English Middle Class*, (Routledge, 1987); Birlinn Ltd for the extract on p. 122, from Fraser, D. (ed), *The Christian Watt Papers* (2004); Edinburgh University Press for the extracts on pp. 199–200, from Flinn, M. W., *Report on the Sanitary Condition of the Labouring Population of Great Britain by Edwin Chadwick, 1842* (1965); Taylor & Francis for the extract on p. 208, from Bedarida, F., *A Social History of England, 1851–1900* (Routledge, 1991); the Birmingham Black Oral History Project for the extracts on pp. 583–5 (except the Esme Lancaster extract), from Price, D. and Thiara, R. (eds), *The Land of Money? Personal Accounts by Post-War Black Migrants to Birmingham* (Birmingham City Council, 1992); Pearson Education Ltd for the Esme

Lancaster extract on p. 584 from Brown, C. G., *Religion and Society in Twentieth-Century Britain* (2006); News International Syndication for the extract on p. 601 from *The Times*, 1 July 1967.

The extract on p. 493 from Orwell, G., *The Lion and the Unicorn* copyright © 1956 George Orwell. Reprinted by permission of Bill Hamilton as the Literary Executor of the Estate of the Late Sonia Brownell Orwell and Secker & Warburg Ltd (World, except USA); reproduced by permission of the publisher Houghton Mifflin Harcourt (USA only).

The extract on p. 505 from Sage, L., *Bad Blood: A Memoir* (Fourth Estate, 2001) © 2001 Sage, L., HarperCollins Publishers Ltd (UK); courtesy of Faith Evans Associates (Europe); copyright © 2000 by Lorna Sage, reprinted with permission of HarperCollins Publishers (USA and Canada).

The extract on p. 613 from de Beauvoir, S., *The Second Sex*, translation by Parshley, H. M., reprinted by permission of the Random House Group Ltd (UK and Commonwealth, excluding Canada) and Random House Inc. (US and Canada). A new translation by Shiela Malovany-Chevalier and Constance Borde was published by Jonathan Cape in 2009.

We were unable to trace one of the authors of extracts on pp. 391 and 440, and we would appreciate any information that would enable us to do so.

Preface

This book charts the history of Great Britain from the Treaty of Union of 1707 that united the parliament of Scotland with that of England and Wales, to the year 2009, when the power of that united parliament was looking challenged. It is a book that seeks to incorporate each of the constituent elements of Britain, including Ireland (until 1922) and Northern Ireland (since 1922). Amid current debates on Britishness, we seek to explore both the common grounds and the great varieties of experience within the British Isles over the three centuries for which the modern state of Britain has existed. We look at the tensions between a large England and its smaller neighbours in Scotland, Wales and Ireland, at the rise and fall of the Empire, and at the tensions of social class, religion and gender change as they too have risen and sometimes fallen. We look at the indirect paths from a rural agricultural nation to a post-industrial high-tech economy, from a Christian country to a multicultural, though largely secular, one, and from an undemocratic nation through the advent of the universal franchise to one in which loss of confidence in politics is causing voter apathy and even revolt. The agendas of the historian change through the three centuries, and we try to keep pace with those.

Our main hope for this book is that students find it accessible and useful. We try to assume no historical knowledge on the part of the reader so that it may suit the beginner in British history, whilst providing sufficient detail and elaboration to foster material for essay work. We have tried to focus on some of the central topics that are likely to arise in any course on modern British history. The book is organised into six main time periods, in each of which we offer around six chapters which discuss relevant themes of that era. Some themes crop up in each period: politics and government, overseas expansion and relations, war and empire, economy, and society and culture. But in addition there are special chapters dealing with topics like urbanisation, intellectual change, black Britain and youth culture when they become most relevant. Inserted in each chapter are special *Focus on . . .* sections which provide extracts from primary sources and guidance on special themes, and guides to *Further reading* appear at the end of each chapter. At the end of each part, useful dates are given in *Timelines*.

As with anyone involved in university teaching, the authors owe a debt of gratitude to those undergraduates and postgraduates at the Universities of Strathclyde and Dundee who over the years helped shape their ideas about history, and about teaching and learning. Colleagues have also – and perhaps unwittingly – contributed to our better understanding of different aspects of the past. To these we can only express our general thanks. Special thanks are due to David Brown, Irene Maver, David Ross and Jim Tomlinson for reading parts of the book and offering valuable advice and suggestions for improvements that were usually gratefully seized upon. However, the responsibility for the outcome is entirely our own. Thanks also to Timothy Hatton, Department of Economics at the University of Essex, for permission to quote the data cited in Table 37.1. Special thanks are due to Christina Wipf Perry, Jessica Harrison, Anne Henwood and Melanie Carter at Pearson Education for the care they have taken with editing. Any remaining errors are our own. Most of all, warm thanks go to our wives, Lynn Abrams and Helen Fraser, who, in addition to offering advice on many of the themes, have had to live with this book for such a long time and showed such toleration.

PART 1

Introduction

1

Approaches to Britain's history

Images of Britain

Historians do not work in a vacuum. Our knowledge of the past is influenced by the world in which we live and the way the past intrudes on us on a day-to-day basis. We see images of the past all around us – in paintings and, from the 1840s, in photographs and, more recently, through moving images on film and television. But the past is also interpreted for us in writing, whether in the fictional works of Daniel Defoe, Charles Dickens or Graham Greene, or the overtly non-fictional, though often self-justifying, accounts left by participants. All of these shape how we see the country. But so too does the language we use to talk about the past.

The rural landscape contains much about our past. In itself the countryside was in 1707 central to the economy, people's living and everyday existence. The very nature of country landscape tends to recall the past to us – a slower pace of life, fewer services, poorer houses and lower standards of education and culture. In the eighteenth century, the bulk of people lived in small labourers' cottages, most of which have long since been knocked down. However, the aristocracy and gentry moved out of the fortified structures or modest farmhouses of previous centuries and erected palatial and elegant country houses amid parkland and gardens which today (through visits to National Trust properties) dominate our appreciation of rural landscape and leisure.

The kinds of change that have taken place in the built environment reflect the changes in social structures, in politics and in economics that have taken place in Britain over the last 300 years. In almost all cities, there is an historic social division between east end and west end – one strongly middle-class and one working-class in composition. In all cities, suburbs grew in the nineteenth century based on social distinctions, with the better-off generally moving ever westwards to escape the smoke, the smells, the crowds, the dangers of the centre, while the less well-off moved east-wards. Within predominantly working-class areas, streets of the skilled and the clerical were separated from those of the 'rough', whilst middle-class homes became larger to accommodate servants. Although social divisions grew in British cities between 1707 and 1950, the geographies have been changing since then, with 'gentrification' of city centres and of some working-class suburbs, making our landscape history more complex.

A look at any townscape tells us other things about the past. The numbers of spires and church towers – many now put to secular uses – reveal a highly religious society in the last three centuries. A visit to any of the country's great cathedrals dramatically brings out the links between church and state – the battle standards of British Army regiments are still housed in the great Christian churches, alongside the memorials commemorating wars against French, Russians, Afghans, Zulus, Boers and Germans. Statues to heroes and (more rarely) heroines of the past still dot cityscapes. Military ones proliferate, with long-forgotten generals present in abundance; few now recall the importance of General Henry Havelock (statue in Trafalgar Square), General Colin Campbell (in Glasgow's George Square), or the relatively unsuccessful General Redvers Buller (in Exeter). Politicians and great aristocrats proliferate. Everywhere in statues and street names there are Queen Victoria and Prince Albert, although few other monarchs are so commemorated outside London. Most cities also have their splendid town halls. These are often extraordinary statements about local pride, wealth and power: Leeds town hall built in 1858 on woollen industry wealth, Manchester's of 1888 on 'king cotton', and Glasgow's, also of 1888, on shipbuilding and engineering.

The history of our islands also come to us through art. John Constable's painting *The Hay Wain* (1821), with its thatched cottages with flowers growing up the wall; Sir Edwin Landseer's *Monarch of the Glen* (1851), with hills and heather behind the mighty stag, and the darker social commentary of Hogarth's London scenes or Joseph Wright of Derby's paintings of industry and science in the eighteenth century provide the visual grammar by which we understand Britain's past. Artists, like historians, have had a tendency to idealise the British countryside for its rustic values, and to regard the cities that sprang up in the late-eighteenth and nineteenth centuries as dark and forbidding places to be condemned for their poor environment and health conditions. The idealisation continued with eighteenth-century paintings of individuals and families (by artists like Allan Ramsay, Joshua Reynolds or Thomas Gainsborough) that revealed a wealthy, peaceful elite, often with their country house in the background and evidence of their culture by their side. By the early nineteenth century, a wealthy middle class was also getting itself painted. However, it was photography that, from the 1840s, changed images of Britain – bringing not just the successful to our view but also the exotic (with scenes from the British Empire of native peoples and places), and the working classes and the poor at home. Photographs give us a strong sense of our family history – perhaps the most personal and universal way in which we each have an investment in the past. Moving images also bring us fictionalised versions of the past which have been extremely influential – especially of Britons at war in William

Wyler's *Mrs Miniver* (1942), Michael Powell and Emeric Pressburger's *One of Our Aircraft is Missing* (1942), Lewis Gilbert's *Reach for the Sky* (1956) and David Lean's *Bridge on the River Kwai* (1957). The idea of Britain still depends to a great degree on the notion of unity and heroism brought by the Second World War, lingering in television series as well as films.

Language of the past

Particular images of the past also come from phrases in regular use – 'a thousand years of British history', 'the mother of Parliaments', 'our island history', and 'democratic traditions and values'. The 1980s saw a lively debate on Mrs Margaret Thatcher's invocation of 'Victorian values', echoed in John Major's 'Back to Basics' campaign in the 1990s and Gordon Brown's promotion of 'Britishness' in the 2000s. Nostalgia for an undated 'lost age' of order, of politeness, of neighbourliness, of respectability, of deference and patriotism has been a major factor in creating what, if polls are to believed, is sometimes a discontented and unhappy society. The evidence on most of these is that such a lost age never did exist, but the narrative to the contrary remains the powerful one.

Of course, a great deal of the past that has been shown in paintings and films is pure invention. History is often 'false history' in the sense that it has been used to push a cause or strengthen an institution, or merely to make money from a people keen to celebrate its own virtues. This tendency to manufacture a past is particularly powerful when a national history is involved. Historians and others have argued long and hard over what a 'nation' is, and how the sense of national identity is fostered and developed. In a well-known study, the American Benedict Anderson argued that nations do not exist other than in the imagination, in what he terms 'imagined communities', invented and fabricated for political reasons – not least to keep us in order. In this argument, no one is born instinctively feeling English, Welsh or Scottish. It has to be instilled. The historian Linda Colley has shown the efforts that politicians and others went to in the eighteenth and early nineteenth centuries to generate a sense of Britishness, using anthems, flags, jubilees and parades. And this campaign to create a sense of Britishness worked by making England and Britain largely synonymous, with Welshness largely disappearing from the public view and the Scots rushing to identify themselves as North Britons. However, this imagining of Britishness has been faltering. In the 1920s, Ireland was partitioned between a 'British' north and an Irish republic in the south. In the 1950s and 1960s, the British Empire ended, leading to Britain becoming home to increasing numbers of black and Asian peoples, as well as, more recently, to East European migrants. And since the 1970s, there has been rising pressure for home rule and independence in Wales and Scotland, as the distinct identities of those countries emerge. In all sorts of ways, then, the unity of Britain and Britishness established in the first two centuries covered by this book has in the last century become vulnerable.

This means that the language of the past and present is not stable. 'Britishness' has changed meaning and resonance. It is a term which, by 2000, was being displaced by competing multicultural identities – of black, Asian, Scottish, Irish and Welsh, and also the re-mergence of English identity. Yet, the British state still perpetuates Britishness in parades, military regiments, national war memorials and pageants of royalty and celebrity. Though monarchy was, by 2000, much less influential than it had been even a hundred years before, it remains a symbol of political unity. As nationalism rises in Scotland and Wales, and devolved government returns in the 2000s to Northern Ireland, Queen Elizabeth remains a vital source of identity for most Britons, and confounds many predictions of the end of monarchy. More than any other single institution, the Royal Family is the nation's central vehicle for expressing its history. But, like monarchy itself, the nation's past is not a single, agreed under-standing. History is like politics – it is open to debate.

The disputed British past

History is dominated by debate, and historians of Britain are just as likely as any others to disagree over interpreting the nation's past. Sometimes, the debate is over what happened. New knowledge, new information about events, based on documents or other sources that have come to light, can change the basic knowledge of an episode or process in the past. Most of the time, however, historians are not disputing *facts* but debating the *significance* of events and processes, and how to interpret them. It is analysis and interpretation that drives forward new publications in books and history journals. Looking at history writing ('historiography', as it is called) is thus to consider different interpretations and approaches to the past.

Historians will argue from evidence as to what is the best way to explain episodes from the past. At the same time, though, there are different approaches. For example, there are political historians, economic historians, social and cultural historians, intel-lectual historians, historians of religion, historians of the labour movement, historians of science and of philosophy. With the rise of the feminist movement in the 1970s, the history of women become a major part of the writing of history. More recently, there has been a tremendous growth in environmental history, resulting from new knowledge about climate change and the impact that humankind has had upon the planet. On the other hand, with the decline of religion in Britain in the later twentieth century, the emphasis on religious history has waned (though not disappeared). These instances demonstrate that the way history is written tends to be strongly influenced by the concerns of the present time. With each decade, the past is re-examined to bring out modern agendas and understanding, contemporary concerns and perspectives.

Economic historians, rather more than other historians, are given to constructing their research around large questions that form the centres of debate. There are several examples of these. Was the Industrial Revolution really industrial or a revolu-tion? Did the British working classes benefit from industrialisation between 1760 and

1830? Did the late Victorian economy fail? Was the British economy regenerated in the 1930s? Was the British economy in decline from the 1960s? This book in part reflects this tendency, with a greater than usual focus on disputed interpretations in the chapters on economic matters. This reflects the way in which there is less emphasis on an agreed narrative of British economic history than on exposing the lines of debate. In other areas, historians are more prone to seek to produce consensus in their narratives, and to seek to influence the way in which this narrative is produced by introducing new areas of research and new angles on existing ones. Thus, topics like social and cultural history, gender history, and the history of immigration and race appear as part of the increasing diversity of the narrative of British history, rather than as subjects based around clearly defined disputes. Of course, there are disputes going on everywhere in the study of British history. But they are often complex and subtle, rather than structural to the study of each subject.

Political history: putting the Great in Britain

The earliest history of Britain, dating from the eighteenth century, was written mostly by men. As the Enlightenment evolved, the history they wrote moved further and further away from medieval conceptions of the role of religion. Rather than seeking religious lessons from the past, the Enlightenment prompted a rejection of the power of religion in interpretation while sustaining a place for religion as a stabilising social force. The Enlightenment encouraged a search for 'truth' and objectivity, and stressed the primacy of 'facts' and the creation of policy from facts as both possible and superior to any other method. Studying the past could teach lessons and release modern knowledge from the unwelcome power of religious fanaticism and superstition.

Nevertheless, behind the search for truth there lingered a strong romance about the developing 'greatness' of Britain. One consequence was a tendency to marry history with philosophy, as in David Hume's *History of England* of the 1750s. Britain was a nation envisaged as the culmination of intellectual and cultural progress, though in Hume's Tory/Jacobite view it lost merit because of the Hanoverian succession. Moreover, the way in which historians such as Hume and Edward Gibbon wrote placed emphasis on the creative imagination of events rather on documentary evidence and scrupulous attention to detail. A sceptic of historical writing, Samuel Johnson, wrote in 1775: 'We must consider how very little history there is; I mean real authentick history. That certain Kings reigned, and certain battles fought, we can depend upon as true; but all the colouring, all the philosophy of history is conjecture.'[1]

The romantic view of British greatness continued in nineteenth-century writing, but in the work of one of the great exponents, T.B. Macaulay, the Tory view was replaced by a Whig outlook of upward progress in a grand idealistic narrative. Here

---

[1] Quoted in M. Bentley, *Modern Historiography: An Introduction* (London, Routledge, 1999), p. 13.

the romance of British greatness focused considerably on Britain's constitutional monarchy from 1688, which seemed to have modernised its outlook and legitimacy whilst, in the *anciens régimes* of European nations, there seemed to be a rigidity that had led to revolution, the breakdown of social harmony and an end to progress itself. The British system was seen as far superior to anything elsewhere in the world. There was an assumption of the nationalistic uniqueness of the English and Scots as superior and well-adjusted peoples who had systems of law, education and rational religion that allowed for the dutiful acknowledgement of both the world of God and the world of man. The history of Britain was written as the story of the gradual extension of constitutional government since 1688 and resistance to any attempts to increase royal power. English historians had particular faith in a trait of English character that seemed to desire liberty, a desire they traced back to Anglo-Saxon times and which could never be totally suppressed.

Historians writing at the peak of British imperial progress in the nineteenth century found it difficult to avoid speaking in praise of the nation – its progress, its leadership and dominance, its superiority in religion, law, education and industry. This tendency is one that underscores much of the writing of British political history until the mid-twentieth century. Praise came for the absence of revolution and civil war on mainland Britain after the 1740s, often attributed to the unwritten constitution and the facility it allowed for change, together with the absorption of new elites into the hierarchies of power. Social mobility was seen as a benefit to civil progress. The emphasis was on the peculiar stability of Britain and its steady progress.

This gave rise to what is referred to as the Whig interpretation of British history, which sought to trace a centuries-long progress of constitutional change, leading to the present. The emphasis was on English exceptionalness because of the avoidance of revolution (other than what was regarded as an exceptional – and therefore Glorious – English Revolution in 1688) and the formation of an apparently free society. The focus was very much on political history, and such an approach came under attack from the 1930s, with demands for other areas of history to be studied. Even so, it was still very easy for historians to slip back into Whig interpretations that take the present as the starting point and look at how things arrived there, and for these interpretations to be embedded in other parts of the history discipline in ideas such as 'the rise of the welfare state' and 'the long march of labour'.

One of the strongest challenges to the Whig interpretation was in Sir Lewis Namier's study of *The Structure of Politics at the Accession of George III* (1929), which presented a picture of politics not shaped by ideas but by the narrow self-interest of individuals. Constitutional reform came about as a result of manoeuvres among the political elite, not as a result of pressures from outside. It encouraged the study of the minutiae of a period or of individual lives, rather than trying to devise some grand narrative. Influenced by such an approach, many historians of the mid-twentieth century rejected the influence of ideas in determining human progress. In their view, ideas did not cause history to change. On the contrary, ideas changed as a result of history changing – a vision of history matching what seemed the sensible, responsive, utilitarian and pragmatic political system of Britain itself. This outlook suited the imperial mentality of the time as the British Empire moved towards the liberation of the old colonies to constitute the British Commonwealth of independent nations. So, British historians, like British imperial elites, saw the British as not fixated on ideas and principles like the French or even the Germans. On the contrary in this outlook, Britons subordinated ideas to the need to get the job done.

This vision of the past has been overtaken by more complex and varied narratives in recent political history writing. Few historians now regard the British Empire or restricted voting rights as having been an unalloyed good thing, but they adopt more pragmatic criteria with which to judge the politicians and administrators who managed the country under those circumstances. Unlike Namier's history style, however, there is now a more nuanced understanding of the influence in previous centuries of ideas and ideologies upon the minds of the great leaders and their formulation and conduct of national policy. Significant in the origins of this trend was the emergence of labour and social history.

Labour and social history

The reputed 'greatness' of British history was challenged by emerging anti-industrial intellectuals of the nineteenth century. William Cobbett (1763–1835) wrote in a diary called *Rural Rides* of a trip around England in the 1820s in which he saw industrialism destroying the landscape and the yeoman people who were the backbone of the nation. Like many radicals of the time, he developed a critique of Britain's supposed greatness that was essentially conservative yet which saw radicalism as the maintenance of the tried and tested past. This established a tradition of combined scholarship and commentary that regarded worker-radicalism not as revolutionary but as essentially opposed to change; radicalism was seen as *protecting* the people from harmful change.

In the late nineteenth and early twentieth centuries, this tradition merged with the growing Labour movement of trade unions, radical political campaigns and pronounced revolutionary notions. With husband and wife historians, J.L. and Barbara Hammond, there emerged in the 1910s a concerted critique of the benefits of economic and constitutional progress for the plight of working people. The Hammonds wrote:

> The social system produced by the Industrial Revolution reflected a spirit that we may describe as a spirit of complacent pessimism, and this spirit has done more than any event in English history to create the 'two nations' of which Disraeli used to speak. . . . This age had taken for its aim the accumulation of economic power, and its guiding philosophy was a dividing force, because it regarded men and women not as citizens but as servants of that power. If the needs of that power seemed to conflict with the needs of human nature, human nature had to suffer. In its extreme form this theory made the mass of the nation the cannon-fodder of industry.[2]

---

[2] J.L. Hammond and B. Hammond, *The Town Labourer 1760–1832: The New Civilisation* (London, Longmans, Green & Company, 1920), p.vi.

In this way, capitalism itself became the target for historical criticism and, with Marxist historians, became openly the object of assault by those in pursuit of the proletarian revolution. Marxists looked upon Britain as the first industrial nation, which should produce, or have produced, the first proletarian revolution. That it did not aroused tremendous scholarly inquiry into what factors in Britain's past prevented this from happening. From the 1950s to the 1970s, the writing of British history was radically altered by a generation of left-wing writers. British Marxist historians, such as Christopher Hill, Eric Hobsbawm and E.P. Thompson, were originally members of the Communist Party and their scholarship of the 1950s and after grew out of what was termed 'scientific Marxism'. In this view, history was an ineluctable progression through the states of primitivism, feudalism and capitalism towards an ideal state of communal ownership (in which private possessions were reduced to the level of individual need). According to Marx, what caused history to progress was economic determinism, self-interest and the need to survive as social groups. As he and Engels wrote: 'The history of all hitherto existing society is the history of class struggles.'[3] So the work of these scholars combined economic history with a new strong social history, concentrating on the people, the downtrodden and the poor in an empathetic manner. As E.P. Thompson wrote in 1963: 'I am seeking to rescue the poor stockinger, the Luddite cropper, the "obsolete" hand-loom weaver, the "utopian" artisan, and even the deluded follower of Joanna Southcott, from the enormous condescension of posterity.'[4]

This group and others trained a generation of historians who, from the mid-1960s, took the surge towards social history to new heights. University history departments, especially in new and adventurous universities, were rapidly staffed with left-wing social historians. Many of these took up the ideas of the Italian Marxist theorist Antonio Gramsci to examine how the working people of Britain's past were held down not merely by economic oppression in the workplace, but also by what he called the 'hegemony' (or dominance) of the pervasive bourgeois culture in schools, colleges, churches and public affairs in general. This brought historians to re-examine the flaws of economic and political advance – the 'oppression' of the people through the loss of rights to control the work process, and through declining cultural freedom. Scholarship came also to look more directly at how the people resisted such pressures and came close to erupting in that supposedly inevitable revolution to overturn capitalism, but never quite did so. Indeed, much of British social history of the 1960s and 1970s was devoted to answering the question why Britain, the first nation to industrialise, failed to produce a proletarian revolution. This produced a vast explosion of historical investigation into British labour history, the history of social organisation and the social condition of the people.

---

[3] K. Marx and F. Engels, *The Communist Manifesto* (1848), which can be read at http://www.marxists.org/archive

[4] E.P. Thompson, *The Making of the English Working Class* (Harmondsworth, Penguin, 1968 edn), p. 13.

The rise of left-wing history writing was accompanied by a growing influence of sociological theory amongst historians. Sociologists in the mid-twentieth century developed a large and adaptable theory, the theory of modernisation, to explain the emergence of modern society, principally from the eighteenth century onwards. The theory positioned this transformation as a long-term one, incorporating intellectual and social movements which fostered modern social relations and outlooks, and claimed to explain much of the nature of the modern condition of a largely unreligious, socially stratified urban world with few social bonds of paternalism and deference. In this way, the rush to social history accompanied theories which seemed to permit historians – Marxist and right-wing alike – to explain the creation of the secular, alienated, urban consumerist society of the mid-twentieth century. One book typified this influence, Peter Laslett's *The World We Have Lost* (1965), which in its very title conveyed the hypothesis that there had been a golden age of social harmony and relative peace before the Industrial Revolution, when primitivism and naïveté dominated. Of that age, he wrote: 'All our ancestors were literal Christian believers, all of the time.'[5]

This represents a powerful thread running through much left-wing historiography – 'golden ageism' and the adverse impact of industrialism and urbanism upon the lives of the people. In many ways it is the opposite of a Whig approach in that the pre-industrial past (of the eighteenth century at least) is seen as one of good community relations, individual worker freedoms, a calm pace of life and what E. P. Thompson called a 'moral economy'. Social and labour historians do not deny that standards of living improved in more recent times, but they tend to look negatively at the impact of the Industrial Revolution.

Economic history

Underlying the rise of social history, though not always in agreement with it, has been economic history. With so many British historians viewing the progress of Britain's past in terms of material advance, it was understandable that economic conditions were often at the forefront of explaining important moments of historical change. At the same time, historians of the right, who favoured capitalism as the exemplar of modernity and progress, were keen to provide a more systematic and scientific understanding of what made Britain the first nation to industrialise and, from the late nineteenth century, the first nation to experience what seemed to be economic decline.

Economic historians from the late nineteenth century to the mid-twentieth century were optimistic and bullish. This was best seen in the influential work of an American historian, W.W. Rostow, who in the midst of the Cold War in 1960 argued that the British Industrial Revolution of the eighteenth century should be exported to the

---

[5] P. Laslett, *The World We Have Lost* (London, Methuen, 1965), p. 71.

developing nations of the world as a model for growth to counter the export of communism from the Soviet Union.[6] But whilst the British Industrial Revolution remained an exemplar of economic progress, much of the history written about Britain's recent economic past was, by the 1960s, about failure. This became even more pronounced in the 1980s when there was a challenge to what was perceived as a culture of decline in British politics, marked by the rhetoric and politics of the Thatcher Conservative government elected in 1979. Along with this came a great deal of historical writing that looked at the economic origins of British decline, suggested cultural causes and, in some cases, looked even for its moral origins. A few economic historians of the 1980s were strongly influenced by the outlook of the Thatcher government, taking the British economy to be in decline, and tracing the reasons for this in the negation of the conditions of individualism and weak state power that had caused the Industrial Revolution. History mattered politically.

From this arose the notion of a 'dependency culture' which, fostered by the welfare state after 1945, had eroded individuality, entrepreneurship and originality. It was claimed that insufficient numbers of people with drive and ambition, and willing to take economic risks, lay at the root of Britain's failure to move with the economic times. A continued reliance on manufacturing of older staple products, and the dominance in economic thinking of coal mining, shipbuilding, engineering and volume car production, were held to have diverted investment and risk-taking away from exciting new products like electronics, passing the baton of progress to countries like the USA and Japan. At the same time, decades of poor industrial relations between trade unions and company management were blamed for bad working practices; British manufacturing methods bred labour-intensive operations, low investment in new machinery and, above all, low productivity. On top of this, there was the so-called 'British disease' – strikes that were seen to have crippled the British economy from the 1950s onwards. In the 1970s, they argued, successive disputes caused high wage inflation, undermined savings investment, and produced immoral behaviour (including the strike of grave diggers in 1979), finally contributing to the fall of the Labour government of James Callaghan in that year.

Some economic historians trace these problems of Britain further back. The shedding of empire in the 1940s, 1950s and 1960s was seen as one cause, diverting excessive resources into the maintenance of overseas colonies in their declining years prior to independence, and undermining the sense of British national purpose. Blame now fell upon the Empire for a conglomeration of economic mistakes even earlier – notably, diverting investment overseas in the 1870–1914 period, just when it was most needed at home to re-invent manufacturing industry for new products and new markets. Whilst reliance on the closed imperial market was seen to have been a benefit to nurturing industry between 1760 and 1870, it became blamed for allowing British

---

[6] W.W. Rostow, *The Stages of Economic Growth: A Non-Communist Manifesto* (Cambridge, Cambridge University Press, 1960).

manufacturers to rest on their laurels thereafter, relying on imperial sales, and not keeping up with innovation by American, German and French manufacturers. This developed into a theory of an 'economic climacteric' in the late 1870–1914 period – a pinnacle of British progress from which British economic decline could be dated – which enjoyed considerable support amongst economic historians through the 1980s.

The cultural origins of Britain's supposed decline had developed as an intrinsic element in the economic story. But this cultural analysis pushed the origins of the problem further back to the very foundations of the Industrial Revolution. The argument here was centred on the idea that Britain never really accepted industrial capitalism. Supporters of this argument spotted various elements. First, British entrepreneurship was flawed by a constant preference for being 'gentlemen' rather than 'players' – for playing the game rather than playing to win. Secondly, there was talk of a generational decline in entrepreneurship. The original founders of big enterprises were innovative and risk-taking; the second generation began to turn away from the firm and involve themselves in public affairs; and the third generation were prepared to live off the profits of the firm but to take little interest in how they were made, instead partying their family's fortune away on the French Riviera. The third major argument was that the cause of this was a fundamental absence of a spirit of industrial capitalism. The American historian Martin Wiener asserted that the British were fundamentally hostile to industrial cities, to the grime and smog of such places, and to the factory. We examine the Wiener thesis in Chapter 20, but it is important to note here that this approach amounted to describing a failure of the industrial spirit in Britain, bringing in failure in education and religion, and an aversion to urban living.

The *moral* failings of Britain also entered the rhetoric of historians who argued for 'the decline of Britain' hypothesis. Led by Margaret Thatcher, there was a particular denigration of what the youth culture of the 1960s had done to British moral fibre. The rise of popular music, sexual promiscuity and drug-taking represented a loss of inhibition and restraint that was blamed for social breakdown and the rise of crime in Britain from 1957 onwards. With it, there was reputedly a decline of hard work and thrift, which were replaced by increasing reliance upon the state for social handouts. Whilst not all historians agreed with this analysis, there were scholars like Christie Davies who argued from the 1970s onwards that moral deviance had become the norm in British young people. A new moral right emerged in politics and, to some extent, amongst scholars.

In the 1990s and 2000s, historians have once again begun to reshape the under-standing of British economic history. With this, came reassessments of the post-war British economy. The first realisation was that during the period 1950–90, the British economy was not in decline. It was growing and, moreover, at a very healthy rate. At the same time, a series of myths that had developed were shown, under close exam-ination, to be untrue. It had been widely believed that British productivity and rates of investment had been low and that the 'British disease' – strike action – had been a massive problem that had distinguished British experience from that of the USA and most European countries. The new research showed these statements to be false.

The statistical hard data, when looked at dispassionately and closely, showed that Britain was either at the top or pretty near to the top of the economic performance of advanced industrial nations, with other west European nations catching up with the British position.

The second realisation was that the reason this account of the British past had developed was that a 'culture of decline' pervaded the British elites – the top echelons of government, including the civil service and political parties – and was commonly found in the British press, in overseas images of Britain, and amongst many historians. This realisation led to the 'culture of decline' itself becoming an interesting object for study: just why did British commentators becomes so pessimistic about British economic and cultural life in the 1960s and 1970s? Part of the answer, the pessimists averred, was the loss of empire, and the loss of a role. Other explanations lay in a desire to see failure in a period of change. The economy was adjusting to a post-manufacturing age. There was cultural revolution in the air and these developments were seen to be undermining British traditional values and experience. It thus became vital to look at cultural explanations of economic history analysis and to think about the different ways in which the nation's economic past had been branded.

Cultural history

One of the powerful trends in the writing of British history since the 1980s has been the rise of cultural history. This developed mainly within social history, but was to spread across the whole discipline, and brought British historiography more closely in line with historians' ideas from Europe and elsewhere.

At the root of cultural history lay a series of concerns with social history. This was seen as too dependent on sociological theories (like modernisation) which compelled thinking in terms of progress or its reverse, as too obsessed with studying Marxist-driven ideas about class struggle and the chances of worker revolution, and as too little concerned with thinking about gender, race, religion and other categories. The reliance on social science methodology supposed the past could be understood with the certainties of science itself, creating the prospect of historians only ever being chroniclers of modernisation. For some in the 1980s and 1990s, a new cultural history grew directly out of Marxism – a new cultural history of the left. But others traded the theories of Marx, Gramsci and sociology for those of Barthes, Foucault and Derrida – for a modern cultural theory (sometimes referred to as postmodernism and poststructuralism).

Cultural historians had a significant impact on the way British history was studied. Poststructuralism raised doubts about the validity of historians' structures like social class. Class came to be regarded as increasingly problematic for study because of its variable and indeterminate meanings, and because too much reliance had been placed on it by left-wing historians to explain British history. In its stead, many women's historians placed gender as a category of analysis that was of immense and underrated importance, while historians of colour looked to race and ethnicity as categories that required to be examined intensively in British domestic and imperial history.

These impulses fostered amongst historians a cultural understanding of Britain's past. This has had a number of key characteristics. First, it has encouraged reflection on the 'historians' gaze': how factors in our own time determine what aspects of the past interest us, and how our interpretations of the past derive from present concepts, beliefs and ideologies. This starts with reflecting on the language we use to write our historical narrative – our use of terms (ranging from 'nation' and 'empire', to 'Industrial Revolution', 'social class' and 'inequality') and what we are implying by them. When we use these words, we must immediately consider whether the peoples of Britain in the eighteenth and nineteenth centuries used them and, if so, whether they understood them in the same way as we do today. History as a written account is conjured by the words we invoke, and we carefully consider our meaning and the meanings of past peoples. This interest is not limited to understanding individual words, but encompasses wider representations. The cultural historian gains much by reflecting on the meaning of entirely commonplace things, peoples and identities. For example, what place did material things like cutlery, bowls and bed-sheets have in the eighteenth-century world of status? How did a man foster a sense of masculinity in industrialising Britain of the early nineteenth century? Why did so many married women of the mid-twentieth century adopt 'housewife' as a self-description? How were arriving Afro-Caribbeans and Asians looked upon by a predominantly white society in the 1950s? To answer these questions, the historian essentially explores the differences in meaning between then and now. Looking at representations of such objects in daily life results in a deeper appreciation of how each age understood itself.

A key device of the cultural historian, then, is to look at representations – often referred to as 'discourses'. A discourse is an injunction or interpretation being expressed by a representation to which people adhere in daily life. Discourses tell us what, in a given time and culture, was considered to be ideal behaviour and what was considered deviant or unacceptable. For example, we will see later in the book how, from around 1800 to 1960, it was considered by most of the British middle classes that a woman's proper desire was to be married and that her place was in the home, without a job, bringing up children, whilst her husband worked; to be a spinster was seen as undesirable – 'on the shelf', having failed to 'catch a man'. Though very large numbers of married women (especially of the working classes) did, in fact, go out to work, this discourse was approvingly represented for many centuries in the word 'housewife'. However, in more recent times, notably since the 1960s, the term and its discourse have fallen from universal popularity; the approving meaning of 'housewife' has become more ambiguous (sometimes implying a woman who has missed out on a career and worldly excitement), though it retains a greater power and significance amongst some ethnic groups.

The study of a term like 'housewife' and what it has represented in different times and for different people is one example of how cultural history has changed ways of viewing the past and has expanded the agenda of issues for study. This technique is sometimes referred to as discourse analysis, and we will see its influence in a variety of chapters in this book (including in sections on gender, sexuality and black Britain).

In this way, the former notion that British history is about the nation only, about what powerful men did, and what irrefutable single visions can be used in writing it, is no longer acceptable. Historians bring different skills to studying different themes, and the nation has developed a rich, eclectic and multicultural history that has only recently been more fully recognised. This book reflects the trend towards diversifying the angles of approach to the history of Britain.

Further reading

Bentley, M., *Modern Historiography: An Introduction* (London, Routledge, 1999)

Brown, C.G., *Postmodernism for Historians* (Harlow, Pearson Longman, 2005)

Burke, P., (ed.), *New Perspectives on Historical Writing* (Cambridge, Polity Press, 2001)

Cannadine, D., *What is History Now?* (Basingstoke, Palgrave Macmillan, 2004)

Colley, L., *Britons. Forging the Nation 1707–1837* (New Haven, Yale University Press, 1992)

Green, A. and Troup, K. (eds), *The Houses of History: A Critical Reader in Twentieth-century History and Theory* (Manchester, Manchester University Press, 1999)

Tosh, J., *The Pursuit of History: Aims, Methods and Directions in the Study of Modern History* (London, Longman, 2000)

PART 2

An uncertain stability 1707–79

2

The political system

The making of Great Britain

'A thousand years of British history' is a phrase much used by commentators and politicians, but the United Kingdom of Great Britain did not emerge until 1 May 1707, when the Acts of Union between Scotland and England came into force. It had taken long and hard negotiation to bring it about. Although there had been a single monarchy since 1603, when Scotland's James VI succeeded Elizabeth, Scotland retained its separate Parliament. In the last years of the seventeenth century and the early years of the eighteenth, relations had on occasion deteriorated so much that conflict seemed possible. Most of the tensions arose over trade, but there was also a refusal by the Scottish Parliament to accept, without some concessions, the English Act of Settlement of 1701, guaranteeing a Protestant succession to the throne. This did not mean that most of the Scottish politicians were supportive of the exiled Stuarts. They were committed Presbyterians and had no desire to come under French Catholic influence, but they wanted any closer union with England to bring real advantages.

Among the main concerns was a desire to retain access to English markets (threatened by an Aliens Act, that would have treated the Scots as aliens) and to open up access to English colonies. An attempt to establish a separate Scottish empire in Darien in central America in the 1690s had collapsed, with considerable financial losses for leading figures in Scotland, and with much recrimination about England's role in the failure. There was a powerful sense that Scotland was falling behind an England that was already experiencing rapid economic growth. From the point of view of English politicians, union would remove an irritating and potentially danger-ous threat in the north. The restoration of a pro-French Stuart on the throne was strategically unacceptable, and there were those in England who were prepared to invade to prevent such an occurrence.

There was no great enthusiasm for the union among Scots in general and accusations of bribery of key political leaders to persuade them to go along with the union have persisted ever since. Most recent work, however, accepts that most of the Scottish politicians genuinely believed that Scotland's economic future was dependent upon merger with England, and that it was necessary to safeguard Protestantism. The arrangement negotiated was a good one. Although Scotland lost its independent Parliament, it retained a separate church and distinct legal system, and, although the economic benefits took some time to work through, they did eventually come.

Politics and power

The new state was run by the aristocracy and their associated landed gentry. The English aristocracy had put the monarchy firmly in its place in the seventeenth and early eighteenth centuries. It was they who put Charles II on the throne in 1660, after a decade of experimentation with republicanism. It was they who carried out the *coup d'état* against James II, in 1688, and summoned William, the Dutch Stadtholder and his wife, Mary, James's Protestant daughter by his first wife. It was they who decided on Anne, Mary's younger sister, to succeed William in 1702 and it was they who chose the descendants of Elizabeth, the daughter of James VI and I in 1714, now the electors of the German state of Hanover, as Anne's successors. Any remnants of the idea that monarchs were there by divine right had gone. Reputedly, there were 58 people with a stronger claim to the throne in terms of birth than the Elector of Hanover.

The Hanoverians were identified as heirs under an Act of Settlement of 1701 that specified that the monarch had to be Protestant and, indeed, had to become Anglican and could not marry a Roman Catholic. The Act also made clear that it was a limited monarchy, not an absolute kingship, ensuring that the Hanoverians could be firmly kept in check by Parliament. The post-1688 settlement had ensured that the monarch was not financially independent, but had to turn annually to Parliament for an adequate income. This did not mean that the Crown was lacking in power, however. Crown, Lords and Commons were seen as separate but interdependent, and there was great admiration for what was regarded as the balance of this constitution between the three parts. All politicians appealed to the constitution, claiming that their rivals were trying to knock it off balance, and to tilt it too much in the direction of one part.

Ministers were the monarch's servants. The monarch appointed them and could dismiss them and, in theory, ministers were all equal. The monarch could also create peers, so that this gave added power through the House of Lords, which had just over

200 members. The Crown, by which is meant the monarch and the government, also had tremendous patronage in positions, commissions, pensions and sinecures that could be distributed to those who showed their devotion by doing as they were instructed in Parliament. Any ambitious politician had to learn to work in both the royal court and in Parliament. The monarch was obliged to work with Parliament, because the House of Commons controlled the supply of money and, in practical terms, that meant that the monarch had to find ministers who could command a majority in Parliament, and Parliament, in both its Houses, was controlled by the aristocracy.

Political power, in the eighteenth century, was in the hands of a clique of propertied aristocratic families – around 70 mainly Whig families with extended marriage links and remarkably closed to new blood. By the Property Qualifications Act of 1711, membership of the House of Commons was restricted to those who possessed land worth £600 per annum in the counties or £300 per annum in towns – very large sums indeed. Land ownership was at the root of aristocratic power, although many had already tapped into the world of trade and finance. Land produced wealth, but it also brought prestige, authority and time to engage in public affairs. Aristocrats clung to their exclusiveness and to political power, and members of the landed elite continued to make up three-quarters of the membership of the House of Commons until after 1867. This relatively small, family-linked political world also generated a relatively closed social world. Politics were not just about what went on in Parliament. There was a social dimension to them, carried on in visits, in balls and in correspondence. Despite political rivalry, most of the time there was a substantial level of harmony among the elite. The politically active met in the clubs and coffee houses of London and in the town houses and country houses of the leading families. In this world wives, mothers and mistresses played their part, acting as hostesses, passing on political information, gathering political gossip. Social situations were utilised for political purposes.

We do not know exactly how many people actually had the vote in the early eighteenth century. What calculations there have been suggest around 300,000 out of a population of fewer than ten million – about one in four of the adult males – and during the eighteenth century that proportion shrank. Although direct bribery of voters was rare, nonetheless, to have the vote was a valuable asset. All voters expected to get something for their vote. It was a piece of property, to be bought and sold. At the very least, voters would expect to be entertained and, in key constituencies, they could expect to be able to trade their vote for the patronage of a powerful magnate. The complaints about doubtful electoral practice are legion but, in more popular constituencies, there were numerous signs of electors responding to the issues of the moment, and an increasing number of newspapers, pamphlets and propaganda sheets is testimony to the liveliness of political debate.

The 558 Parliamentary constituencies were of two kinds: counties and boroughs. The vote in the 40 counties of England, where each county returned two Members of

Figure 2.1 Hogarth election print III – *The Polling*. Published by William Hogarth between 1755 and 1758, this is the third of his series of engravings illustrating the chaos and corruption of elections. In this one, voters make their way to the hustings to cast their vote, with candidates still canvassing and non-electors gathered in the background.
Source: Alamy Images

Parliament, and in the 13 Welsh counties, which returned one MP each, went to those in possession of freehold property valued at 40 shillings. This meant a relatively large electorate in most county seats – perhaps around 4,000 voters on average, although Yorkshire had nearer 20,000. In Scotland, where there were 30 single-member county seats, the electorate was much more limited and the vote probably went to fewer than 2,000 voters, who had land worth £130 per annum. No Scottish county had more than a couple of hundred voters and the county of Sutherland had merely ten in mid-century. Landowners with what was called an 'interest' in the counties in which they had their estates expected to be involved in decisions on all jobs that gave people influence: in the selection of Members of Parliament, of local magistrates, of clergy and of excise officers. It was their right as hereditary landowners, and there was an acceptance that it was perfectly justified to get offices and jobs for friends, relatives and constituency supporters. Within counties there could be competition between landed families, and politics was often about a struggle for local influence. This gave central government some leverage, since it could buy support by using powers of Crown patronage to give a landowner the appointments that he wanted, thus extending *his* powers of patronage.

Borough constituencies – 203 in England, 12 in Wales and 12 in Scotland – varied tremendously. In some cases, the vote was attached to particular pieces of property, a 'burgage'. The extreme example was Old Sarum in Wiltshire, where five electors who owned little more than pieces of wall returned two MPs. In other boroughs, the vote lay with the town council, the corporation, generally an unelected, self-perpetuating body. Many of these were notoriously corrupt and their support could be cheaply purchased. The Scottish burghs, which, with the exception of Edinburgh, were combined in groups, each chose a delegate to select the member and, in many cases, merely took turns to nominate the MP. Alongside these, there were some quite popular constituencies where an electorate could consist of the freemen, the recognised merchants and craftsmen of the town. There were even a few constituencies with a very broad franchise. In Preston in Lancashire, anyone who was in town overnight before the election could vote. In other places, all could vote as long as they paid poor rates and had not been dependent upon poor relief ('Scot and lot'). In yet other places, the vote was confined to those with a hearth: 'potwallopers'. The variations were numerous and the reasons for them often lost in the distant past. Constituencies did not follow population. The declining towns of the south-west of England were grossly overrepresented, while some of the growing towns in the north and Midlands of England had no representation other than as part of their counties.

Elections were seen as a useful check on executive power and, in 1694, popular pressure had brought triennial Parliaments, which meant an election roughly every two years. After 1716, however, a government with a safe majority was able to push through an act by which elections were required only every seven years, and that remained the position until 1911. In practice, fewer than a fifth of the constituencies usually experienced a poll at election time, most candidates being returned unchallenged. It was relatively easy to get agreement, with two members being returned in many constituencies, and conflicting interests could be represented.

One should not assume that non-electors had no influence. The process of election was a public affair and elections were spread over two or three weeks, in order to minimise the danger of public disorder. Both voters and candidates were expected to present themselves at a public hustings, where both were vulnerable to public disapproval. It was not uncommon for an unpopular candidate to be chased through the streets by a mob. In a few urban constituencies, battles between opposing bands of thugs, bribed and lubricated by the candidates, were a feature. Local elites had to be aware of local sentiments and, for most of the time, attitudes to local individuals and local issues seem to be what mattered in elections. However, from time to time there is evidence of national issues having an effect throughout the country, with this becoming more pronounced as time went on and communications improved. But elections were not about deciding the fate of governments. It was relationships between the monarch and different groups in Parliament that decided governments and elections largely confirmed in power those who already had that power.

In his classic study of *The Structure of Politics at the Accession of George III*, Sir Lewis Namier looked at the kind of people who went into Parliament. There were what he called the 'inevitable Parliament men', the eldest sons of politically active peers. Then there were 'the country gentlemen', who were not particularly politically ambitious, but who saw themselves as representing their community. Thirdly, there were the politicians who were ambitious for office and who participated in government, if they could. These were the core of activists who competed for office and around whom political debate flowed. Men went into Parliament because of what they hoped they would get out of it and there were plenty who were mere social climbers, 'placemen' keen to collect the income from the numerous sinecures and appointments available to those who would unquestioningly support the government. There were legal, military and naval people who saw a seat in Parliament as the easiest road to advancement in their services. And there were the merchants and bankers anxious for a share of government contracts. In many cases, these sat for a constituency with which they had no real connection other than having bought it, or for which they had cultivated the influence of an aristocratic patron. But that is not to say that Parliament was unresponsive to the demands of communities. Members of Parliament had to respond to the petitions that poured into them from their constituencies over issues concerning roads, bridges, markets, harbours and industry, and a great deal of Parliamentary time was taken up with local acts.

Whigs and Tories

Namier's influential work tended to encourage a view that politics were largely about the pursuit of self-interest and generated a history of Parliament that focused primarily on individuals and their particular interests and influences. It is true that many of the political divisions among politicians were between those who were in power and in favour with the monarch and those who were out of power, but there were also ideological divisions. The terms 'Tory' and 'Whig' had been in use since the last quarter of the seventeenth century. Broadly, Tories were those who generally defended royal prerogatives and the Anglican establishment. They believed that the Established Church and the state had to be closely interlinked. The Tories were strongest in pressing for the maintenance of the Test Act of 1673, which excluded Catholics, Protestant Dissenters and Jews from public office, and the Corporation Act of 1661, which limited membership of municipal corporations to Anglicans. They were hostile to rights being given to non-Anglicans and slightly uncomfortable at Parliament laying down the royal succession. Many had a hankering for the Stuart line as the rightful monarchs and a few continued to toy with Jacobitism through until the 1750s. The Whigs too were defenders of the Anglican establishment, but readier to tolerate Protestant Dissenters.

They were warier than the Tories about the extent of monarchical power and could present themselves as the stronger supporters of a parliamentary system.

There was nothing resembling the discipline of a modern party system and the terms encompassed a relatively wide spectrum of opinions. Patronage and attachment to some great man's interest could readily lead to factionalism. But 'Whig' and 'Tory' did indicate differing perceptions of the history of the previous century and particularly of the civil wars and the 1688 revolution. Such divisions went down to quite a low social level: Tories and Whigs drank at different coffee houses, attended different social clubs, backed different race meetings and read different newspapers. The Whigs had at their head some of the most powerful of the aristocratic families. The Tories, broadly, came from the ranks of lesser landowners. The Whigs were deeply hostile to French ambitions in Europe, while the Tories were warier about being pulled into conflicts which they saw as less in the interests of Britain than those of first Holland, then Hanover.

There was also a division between what has been called a 'court party' – the politically ambitious, jockeying for power – and a 'country party' – the country gentlemen, who were in Parliament out of a social duty to represent their local interests, representing the small squires and yeomen who prided themselves on their independence and were often more Tory in their attitudes. These disliked the growing dominance of London and were suspicious of a metropolitan lifestyle. They also saw themselves as bearing the brunt of taxation, but losing their influence to courtiers and government office-holders. They were generally unenthusiastic about involvement in continental wars that pushed up taxation and required an increase in the size of the standing army. Country gentlemen gained little from these wars, unlike many of the financiers, government contractors and merchants, and they tried to ensure, with limited success, that membership of the Commons was confined to those who had income from land. These 'country' attitudes brought with them what has been called a 'country ideology', with its roots in the seventeenth century, which involved being constantly on guard against the extension of executive power in a way that would threaten the rights and privileges of the gentry. They wanted the House of Commons to act as a check on government and were wary of the power that came from the patronage at the disposal of the executive. Superimposed on these divisions were the personal attachments of MPs to particular figures, attachments that could depend on 'interest', on family connection or on expectation of future advancement. Faction and party and interest and historical perception existed side by side and it is this that made the politics seem relatively unstable at times. On the other hand, all of these could be 'managed' by the most successful of political operators.

Monarchs, of course, did not want to feel themselves to be totally in thrall to politicians and parties and would use their influence to try to curb the power of the over-mighty by trying to create more broadly-based governments. They wanted to maintain the royal prerogative of being able to choose the best men, regardless of party, and intrigue around the court frequently created instability in government.

Focus on

The constitution of England

This extract comes from a widely used textbook by William Paley (1743–1805) based on the lectures that he gave at Cambridge University in the 1760s and 1770s. It reflects his conservative views of the existing political system.

Every district of the empire enjoys the privilege of choosing representatives, informed of the interests and circumstances and desires of their constituents, and entitled by their situation to communicate that information to the national council. The meanest subject has some one whom he can call upon to bring forward his complaints and requests to public attention.

By annexing the right of voting for members of the House of Commons to different qualifications in different places, each order and profession of men in the community becomes virtually represented; that is, men of all orders and professions, statesmen, courtiers, country gentlemen, lawyers, merchants, manufacturers, soldiers, sailors, interested in the prosperity, and experienced in the occupation of their respective professions, obtain seats in parliament.

The elections, at the same time, are so connected with the influence of landed property as to afford a certainty that a considerable number of men of great estates will be returned to parliament; and are also modified, that men the most eminent and successful in their respective professions, are the most likely, by their riches, or the weight of their stations, to prevail in these competitions.

The number, fortune and quality of the members; the variety of interests and characters amongst them; above all, the temporary duration of their power, and the change of men which every new election produces, are so many securities to the public, as well against the subjection of their judgments to any external dictation, as against the formation of a junto in their own body, sufficiently powerful to govern their decisions.

The representatives are so intermixed with their constituents, and the constituents with the rest of the people, that they cannot, without a partiality too flagrant to be endured, impose any burden upon the subjected which they do not share themselves; nor scarcely can they adopt any advantageous regulation, in which their own interests will not participate of the advantage.

The proceedings and debates of parliament, and the parliamentary conduct of each representative, are known by the people at large.

The representative is so far dependent upon the constituent, and the political importance upon public favour, that a member of parliament cannot more effectually recommend himself to eminence and advancement in the state, than by contriving and patronizing laws of public utility.

Source: William Paley, *The Principles of Moral and Political Philosophy* (London, 1785), pp. 389–90.

Queen Anne's government

When the new United Kingdom came into being in 1707, a predominantly Whig government had been in office since 1702. The Earl of Godolphin had proved an extremely effective administrator who had found the means to raise the credit necessary to pursue European wars, while his associate, John Churchill, the Duke of Marlborough, had won military victories over France that ensured popular support (see Chapter 6). Railing at control by a tightly-knit 'junto' of Whigs, the Queen looked for alternatives and turned to the manipulative Tory, Robert Harley, who had played a crucial part in negotiating the treaty of union with Scotland. Harley believed that he could give the Queen what she wanted and create a coalition of moderates from amongst both Whigs and Tories, together with those who were dependent on royal patronage. The Tories were also able to present themselves as the peace party, ready to seek a compromise settlement of a war that was becoming increasingly expensive. The Tories' defence of Anglicanism attracted much support in the election of 1710 and Dissenters' churches were attacked. Within the year, the Occasional Conformity Act was passed, making it an offence to attend Dissenting services after having been appointed to office in local corporations or an office under the Crown, thus penalising those religious Dissenters who went through the motions of accepting the Anglican Establishment by attendance at the Anglican Church only on official occasions. An even more discriminatory Schism Act of 1714 was intended to ban separate schools run by Dissenters. It was never put into practice and it was repealed in 1719, but it is important to remember that religion was central to much of the politics of the eighteenth century at all levels of society.

The immediate issue for the government was achieving a peace treaty with France, and allies were abandoned in favour of a rapid settlement. Peace proved popular, and the Tories had another success in the election of 1713. However, their success concealed deep divisions. One of the two secretaries of state, Henry St John, Viscount Bolingbroke, started to undermine Harley and, more dangerously, to hint at the possibility of a Jacobite succession to Queen Anne. Coupled with direct assaults on the rights of religious Dissenters and even talk of disenfranchising them, his actions appeared to many to be dangerously unsettling.

Since Queen Anne had no surviving children, the question of succession had long been critical. A few among the leading politicians favoured another Stuart succession, to bring in James Edward, the 'Old Pretender', son of the deposed James II. However, he would not renounce his Roman Catholicism, although he was prepared to guarantee the maintenance of the established Church of England. 'Whig' politicians gave their backing to Sophia of Hanover, granddaughter of James VI and I, and, after her death just before Anne's in 1714, to her son George Ludwig, the Elector of Hanover. When, as George I, he came over in 1714, it was the Whigs who were brought into office, ushering in 40 years of Whig domination. Too many of the Tory politicians prevaricated. Those who were seen to have dallied with the Stuarts were impeached, locked up or exiled. Among the last was Bolingbroke, who had to flee to France.

As the Jacobite uprising of 1715 to win the throne for the Stuarts indicated, the threat was real enough, but was largely confined to parts of Scotland, embittered or disenchanted by the union of 1707; to gentry in the north of England and the far south-west; and to Oxford dons. It was eventually contained by an army under the Duke of Argyll, using reinforcements of Dutch and Swiss troops, at Sheriffmuir in April 1716. But there were further panics and abortive risings in 1717, 1718, 1719 and again in 1722, so the Jacobite threat was persistent. The dynasty and the Whig governments were conscious of the threat to their security. Tories, therefore, had to tread cautiously so as not to be smeared as Jacobites, and the Whig hold on both the main offices of government and subordinate offices was tightened. Many an instinctive Tory abandoned principle and friends and began to identify with the party in power. Within a decade, the Tory party had become marginalised from the political establishment, but fears of Jacobitism remained.

It was a measure of the confidence in the political situation that, after the 1715 uprising, George I headed back to Hanover and this left plenty of room for intrigue and factionalism. In his absence, tensions among Whig politicians led to splits in the government, with politicians who were out of power conspiring with the Prince of Wales. (One recurring feature of the Hanoverians was to be their detestation of their children!) However, unity was restored in the aftermath of financial crisis. The bursting of the South Sea 'Bubble' in 1720 (an investing mania in which some made huge sums while others lost out badly) threatened both a financial and a political disaster and this helped rally the political class. The wars with France since the 1690s had involved heavy government borrowing at high rates of interest. The South Sea Company, originally established in 1711 to develop trade with South America, offered to take over the largest part of the national debt. Holders of government stock were persuaded to exchange this for shares in the company. To persuade the public, ministers and courtiers that this was a good idea, the company embarked on widespread bribery and deception. In the first six months of 1720, the value of shares in the company increased sevenfold. It triggered a mania in share buying, into which a number of even more fraudulent companies tapped. Since trade with South America was largely non-existent, the 'bubble' eventually burst (as there was no genuine income), and the price of shares plummeted faster than it had risen. The losses went from the King down to lowly country squires and hapless widows, many of whom had been dabbling in the stock market for the first time.

The Walpole era

After much jockeying for position among the leading politicians, in 1722 power fell firmly into the hands of Robert Walpole and his brother-in-law, Charles, Viscount Townshend. Although Walpole had initially been caught up in the mania, he had been critical of some aspects of the scheme, and managed to escape the opprobrium that fell upon others. Walpole was to be the controlling genius of the political and fiscal system for the next 20 years. Rough, foul-mouthed, weighing over 20 stone, and personally venal, he was a shrewd and devious political manager and is usually regarded as the first Prime Minister – a term first used in the 1730s, although sometimes in a critical way, implying that too much power lay with Walpole. He had made a reputation as a sound financial manager and in the aftermath of the losses that many people had made as a result of the 'Bubble', such skills were seen as necessary.

Although he presented himself as the defender of Whig principles, once in power Walpole watered down many of these. There would be no attempts to restrict who could sit in the Commons, no attempts to exclude government placemen, no concessions to Dissenting churches. Walpole and his associates ruthlessly replaced their enemies in offices and exploited the system for their own benefit and that of their friends. All jobs in government, in the army, navy, in the law, at court went only to their friends, relations and useful allies. Those who did not identify with the Whigs were branded as Jacobite, although Walpole was wary about antagonising too many of the independent country gentry by purging them as justices of the peace. Using the secret service fund, the government bought many of the MPs, creating placemen by giving them government jobs, or jobs to distribute in their localities in return for votes. Anglicans' fears about the advance of dissent were assuaged, and the 'country' opposition was kept contented most of the time by keeping the land tax low, avoiding costly wars and clamping down on local crime and misdemeanours against property with the Black Act of 1723 that made poaching and stealing timber a hanging offence. Walpole was able to reduce the size of the army and bring down taxes. Taxation was increasingly switched from the land to indirect taxes on consumption: on beer, salt, candles, leather, paper and soap, through the excise, and on imports, through customs. Under Walpole, an oligarchy of loyal leading ministers ran a formidable political machine, which gave political stability for 20 years. His great strength lay in his ability to manage Parliament so that the King's business could be carried out. His enemies bitterly described Walpole's governments as 'Robin's reign' or the 'Robinocracy'.

George I died unexpectedly in 1727 and his son, George II, ascended the throne. Walpole might have expected to be ousted – after all, he had served the hated father – and there were attempts to unseat him. But he had charmed the new Queen Caroline and he survived. It helped that he increased the civil list, the money that Parliament granted the King, to unprecedentedly high levels. He also shrewdly remained in the House of Commons, the arena of politics that was the most difficult to control, and used very effectively the powers of patronage that being the main servant of the Crown gave him.

There were occasional misjudgements. In 1733, an attempt to extend the curb on smuggling and provide the resources to cut the land tax further caused a tremendous, nationwide uproar. The plan was to reduce fraud by replacing the customs duties on tobacco and wines collected at the ports with excise duties collected at the warehouses of merchants. It was easy to portray it as an extension of the state's interference with the liberty of the subject and an opportunity for increasing government bureaucracy by the creation of an army of excise officers. Walpole was forced to withdraw it in the face of popular protest in pamphlets, demonstrations and petitions. Despite the power and control that Walpole had, he could be blocked. In the 1734 election, the government lost ground to Tories and to dissident Whigs. The King stuck with him, but Walpole never had quite the same confidence again and was now dependent on royal backing rather than on popular support.

It was a vulnerable position to be in, since there was widespread antipathy to George and Queen Caroline. Also, by the end of the 1730s, the adult Prince of Wales, Frederick, was at war with his parents. Frederick's court became the focus of opposition politicians. They held out the prospect of less corrupt, more principled government that could unite the nation. To make matters worse, Walpole, much against his instincts, found himself drawn into continental wars over the Austrian succession, because that was of some importance to Hanover. The result was that he could no longer keep his traditional supporters contented with tax reductions. He had made too many enemies; too many of the powerful were excluded from the fruits of office. Independent members began to swing to opposition, election results turned against his friends, and pamphlets and protests outside Parliament demanded that Walpole should go. There were demands for an inquiry into the conduct of the war, which it was argued he was incapable of running successfully. Despite the efforts of the King to keep him, and after many months of division within the ministry, in 1742 Walpole resigned and went to the Lords on a pension of £4,000 a year (worth about £600,000 at 2008 prices).

There was much glee at the fall of 'poor Cock Robin' and a belief on the part of some that it would bring an end to a corrupt system. Walpole had, however, been immensely significant. He had more or less decided who his fellow ministers were going to be. Though they were all appointed by the King and could be sacked by the King, Walpole had managed to ensure he was consulted. But his fall was also significant. He had fallen from power, not because he had lost the confidence of the King, but because he had lost the support of the House of Commons. Ministers had to retain somehow the support of the Crown and the Commons if they were to survive for any length of time, and that was not easy.

Pelham to Pitt

In the aftermath of Walpole's fall some new faces came to the fore, but the old system of sharing power among the ruling families remained, and the government was merely broadened to bring in some opposition peers, to give it what was called a 'broad bottom'. From 1743 until his sudden death in 1754, Henry Pelham, with his brother, the Duke of Newcastle, ran an effective, efficient and substantially less corrupt government than his predecessor. But broad-based coalitions were difficult to maintain, especially when the King was hostile to some of the members. However, the inclusion of some Tories ensured that there was no significant focus of support for Jacobitism.

Prince Charles Edward, grandson of James VII and II, landed in the Western Isles in July 1745. In September, Edinburgh surrendered to him and on 4 December his army reached Derby. There was more to the rising than what is usually presented as wild or romantic Highlanders descending on the south, but support in Scotland was patchy and mainly from anti-Presbyterian Anglicans. Once across the border into England, the Jacobites found sullen resentment or worse. While secret sympathy with the Stuarts may have been wider than sometimes allowed, few amongst a relatively prosperous gentry in England, with substantial sums invested in the property of their fine, unfortified, country houses, wanted the destruction of civil war. None of those town-dwellers in both England and Scotland with interests in commerce and trade wanted a disruption to business, and they resented the heavy requisitions imposed on them by the Jacobite army. Without effective French aid, the Jacobites stood little chance. At Culloden in April 1746, the depleted army could only charge against the guns and numbers of the Duke of Cumberland's force, including three Scottish battalions, backed by years of experience on the battlefields of Europe. In Glasgow and other Scottish towns the bells were rung in celebration.

The Jacobite rising raised the suspicion, once again, that there were pro-Stuart elements among some of those who had been most hostile to Walpole. The effect was to revive party distinctions and, by 1746, Walpole's old cronies, the 'Old Corps' were largely back in power. The lesson was that political stability was relatively fragile.

Once the 1745 uprising had been crushed, the government pursued a fairly conciliatory policy towards suspect Tories. In the Highlands of Scotland, however, there was a determination to eradicate any future threats and to bring the Highlands into line with the rest of Scotland. With the Whig Duke of Argyll in effective charge, arms and tartans were forbidden and, with the abolition of heritable jurisdictions, the powers of the clan chiefs were essentially eradicated. The military built an effective road system for the first time, together with a row of forts. The Highlands were encouraged to participate in the 'modern' agricultural, fishing and manufacturing economy that was beginning to take hold in the rest of Scotland and, as never before, became integrated into the rest of the nation.

Pelham and Newcastle were fortunate in that Frederick, Prince of Wales, had died in 1751, so there was not an immediate focus for opposition. His son was, as yet, too young for political intrigue. For a time, Pelham was able to bring together the Whig factions, skilfully manipulating the various interests. On his death, Newcastle took over, but he lacked his brother's political skills. The government survived a peace treaty at the end of a war in which they had been largely defeated, except in North America. Internal feuds, often over personal differences, mounted, with William Pitt, a politician who was growing increasingly critical of government policy, especially condemning what he saw as an ineffective pursuit of a new war with France, the Seven Years' War, in 1756 (see Chapter 6). Pitt presented himself as the great patriot, who could unite different shades of political opinion, who was against getting caught up in continental wars, but happy enough to take on the French at sea and in the colonies, to loot the French empire. He was immensely popular in the City of London and with the merchants in the main trading towns, who expected to do well out of imperial expansion, and he was able from 1757, despite royal hostility, to dominate the ministry in coalition with Newcastle.

George III and Lord Bute

After 1745, anyone with political ambitions called themselves a Whig. Only a few obscure country gentlemen might use the term 'Tory' to describe their politics. But 1760 marks a major turning point with the accession of George III, the grandson of George II, and just 21 years of age. He was an earnest, well-read young man of simple tastes and a religious outlook. He was determined to make England, rather than Hanover, the base of his kingdom and keen to play a more active role in politics. He seems to have had hopes of broadening support by welcoming some new faces into the inner circles of government from outside the ranks of the usual Whig leaders. In a well-meaning way, he may have genuinely hoped to introduce a new kind of politics. In any case, the call for change was timely, since many independent gentry had lost their enthusiasm for Pitt's colonial wars, with the land tax staying persistently high. Egocentric in the extreme, Pitt was antagonising and exhausting his colleagues. Now bent on war with Spain, he found himself outvoted in the Cabinet and resigned in October 1761. A few months later, the Duke of Newcastle, who had held some form of government office for 40 years, was also pushed into resignation. Many whose advancement had depended upon Newcastle's patronage found themselves ousted or sidelined in the election at the end of 1762.

George's dependence on a Scottish outsider, his friend and tutor John Stuart, Lord Bute, as the main conduit between ministers and himself, and then his appointment of Bute to lead the government, inevitably affronted the old guard. The appointment of Tories to positions at court confirmed their worst suspicions. Bute, ponderous and pompous in manner, was blamed for being a Stuart who was pulling power away from Parliament and back into the hands of the King. Bute, and therefore the King, was accused of trying to restore absolute government and to undermine the Act of Settlement. Bute was an easy target. In the aftermath of the 1745 uprising, loyal Scottish aristocrats had been encouraged to tap into the gravy train of power and profit, and they did so with enthusiasm. They brought in their wake other Scots who saw, as Dr Johnson declared, 'no finer prospect' than the high road to England. At all levels of London society there was hostility to penurious Scots 'on the make'. Bute did not help by appointing so many of his fellow countrymen to positions around the court, to the extent that Buckingham Palace, the new house to which the King had recently moved, was dubbed 'Holyrood', after Edinburgh's royal palace.

The peace settlement with France in 1763, against the advice of Pitt, proved unpopular and although Bute resigned in April 1763, he was seen to continue to guide the King from behind the scenes. Political hostility towards Bute and wider hostility towards Scots were the background to an intervention by the roguish Member of Parliament and journalist, John Wilkes, proprietor of *The North Briton*. The son of a prosperous distiller, Wilkes was a man whose physical ugliness was more than compensated by his wit and conversation. He had married a wealthy heiress, ten years his senior, and this gave him both money and links into political society. He was a friend of Pittite politicians. His paper, *The North Briton* combined animosity towards Scots, with

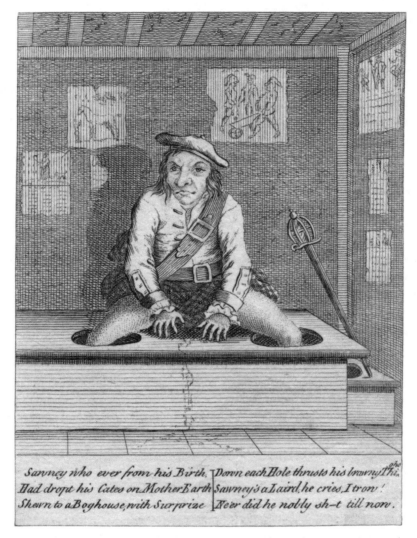

Figure 2.2 *Sawney in the Boghouse*, 1745. One of the many hostile cartoons of Scots published in the aftermath of the Jacobite risings until the 1780s. In this one, the ignorant Scot has no understanding of the intricacies of English plumbing.
Source: Yale Pictorial Records and Collections, Lewis Walpole Library

hostility to Bute and, therefore, to the government. In issue number 45 on 23 April 1763, Wilkes accused Bute of having bribed the Commons to get ratification of the Peace of Paris, bringing the Seven Years' War to an end. The new government under Pitt's brother-in-law, George Grenville, anxious to maintain the crucial royal support, determined to act. Wilkes was arrested, charged with seditious libel and held in the Tower of London for three days. But there were doubts about the legality of arresting a Member of Parliament for sedition and even more doubts about the use by the authorities of a general warrant, which merely authorised the apprehension of the printers and publishers unnamed. Wilkes launched a civil lawsuit against the government, the outcome of which was that general warrants were declared illegal. However, a pornographic *An Essay on Women* – a parody of Alexander Pope's *An Essay on Man* – which Wilkes had published privately for his associates in the decadent Hell-Fire Club, brought new charges of obscene libel. Taking no chances, Wilkes absconded to France and was expelled from the House of Commons, with only one dissenting voice. He was found guilty in his absence and was outlawed.

The next seven years brought shifting political alliances and a jockeying for power between rival groups of politicians. There were five Prime Ministers as George struggled to find people whom he regarded as acceptable and who could, at the same time, command a majority in an increasingly factional Parliament. Whig unity had broken up in acrimony. The King, disliking the idea of party government, persisted in trying to create a broadly-based ministry. Government patronage was used to build up a circle of what came to be called 'King's Friends', who were attacked as Tories by Whig polemicists.

The government was faced with a national debt that had risen to over £133 million and there was concern about the ability to service this debt. Military and naval expenditure were sharply reduced, but the level of debt prompted demands for the colonies to contribute to the costs of their own defence. These in turn led to growing discontent in the American colonies (see Chapter 6). It also encouraged efforts to make the gathering of taxation more efficient, which, in turn, produced tensions at home. Dislike of the burden of taxation, which was borne by the mass of consumers, added fuel to political discontents. Grenville's ministry collapsed in 1765 and a new ministry, dominated mainly by Newcastle Whigs, came in under the leadership of the wealthy Yorkshire landowner, the Marquis of Rockingham. This did not last long, however, and in July 1766, the King swallowed his antipathy and persuaded Pitt to form a ministry. He hoped Pitt would be able to restore political stability and keep the nation happy with successful imperial escapades. But age, ill-health and mental instability had taken their toll and, having moved to the Lords as Earl of Chatham, Pitt proved unable to control the fractious Commons. The man who had for so long presented himself as the 'Great Commoner' now lacked the diplomacy and energy to create stable support from among the various political factions. By the end of 1767 he was having almost no contact with his ministers and little with the King. There was a growing assumption that Pitt was now insane, yet it was not until the autumn of 1768 that he finally resigned to be succeeded by the Duke of Grafton.

Ousted after such a short time in office, the Whig group around Rockingham now grew ever louder in their criticism, not just of the personality of Bute, but of the whole system of politics that gave power to the court and to what they called 'secret influence'. They presented themselves as defenders of the traditional balance between monarch and Parliament, which, they argued, had become weighted too much towards the monarch. The case was most clearly articulated by Rockingham's secretary, Edmund Burke, in his *Thoughts on the Present Discontents*, published in 1770. Here he condemned the attempt which had been going on, at least since the start of the King's reign, to create a party of 'King's Men' which would carry out the royal will separate from the administration that emerged from Parliament. He saw it as a bid to subvert the role of party in government, meaning specifically the aristocratic Whig party that had checked royal power since the seventeenth century. The call was for some limited measure of constitutional reform by the reduction of Crown influence on elections.

To add to the political difficulties, John Wilkes, his financial resources depleted, returned from France early in 1768. Immediate action was not taken against him, and he stood in the general election in the City of London, coming bottom of the poll. He immediately offered himself for another constituency, Middlesex – something that was quite easy when elections were spread over two or three weeks. Middlesex had the attraction that it had a broad electorate of potwallopers. To almost everyone's astonishment, Wilkes was returned at the head of the poll. He now presented himself to the authorities to face the sentences outstanding against him and was fined £1,000 and sentenced to 22 months' imprisonment.

Wilkes' election had triggered off riots, with crowds chanting 'Wilkes and liberty', while Thames watermen and coal heavers linked their demands for higher wages to support for him. At the beginning of 1769 the decision was made, at the King's behest, to expel Wilkes from the Commons once again and to call a by-election in Middlesex. This time, 137 voted against his expulsion and many abstained. Yet again, Wilkes offered himself for election and, since no one stood against him, he was declared returned, only to be expelled the following day. On 10 March, another by-election produced the same result and a further expulsion, accompanied by a declaration that Wilkes was ineligible to be elected. Ignoring this, he stood again and, this time, the government put up a candidate against him, one Colonel Luttrell. He received only 296 votes to Wilkes 1,143, but, having ruled that Wilkes was ineligible, the Commons voted to seat Luttrell. However, the House of Commons did not have the authority to decide who was to be a Member of Parliament. Without legislation, there was no law to prevent Wilkes taking his seat. It was, it could be argued, the tyranny of the House of Commons, but it was easy for opposition members to pin the blame on government with its backing of 'King's Friends'.

The significant thing was the extent to which Wilkes was able to tap into wider discontents that generated a popular movement of criticism of government. A spread of newspapers in most towns of any size was widening participation in politics to include the middle ranks of society. A Society for Supporters of the Bill of Rights, led by John Horne Tooke, provided Wilkes with financial backing, paying off his considerable debts, and there were scores of petitions to Parliament in support of him from around the country. The financial and commercial interests of the City of London backed him and he was elected first an alderman in 1769, then Sheriff in 1771 and eventually Lord Mayor in 1774.

Lord North

The man who had ensured the majorities for Wilkes' expulsion was the leader of the Commons since 1767, Lord North. It was North who, at the beginning of 1770, emerged as a Prime Minister of whom the King fully approved and who could control Parliament. North, who was able to hold power until 1782, had been a protégé of the Duke of Newcastle. He was a man of few pretensions and considerable wit and charm who was able to use Whig divisions and Crown patronage to create a government that excluded some of the most powerful Whig politicians.

Whatever government was in office, it faced the problem of growing agitation in the 13 American colonies. With open hostility to troops stationed there, the drift to war gathered momentum. North tried conciliation and, when that failed to curb unrest, swung to coercion. The colonies eventually declared their independence in 1776 and more direct conflict broke out. For many this was a civil war, that ought not to have happened. Chatham and the Rockingham Whigs all argued for conciliation. Others accepted the right of the colonists to secede. North, perhaps, did not at first entirely comprehend what the war was about. If anything, he saw it as upholding the rights of Parliament to tax its territories. The danger was that the conflict in America encouraged those in Ireland who also wanted to secede, and that always caused great anxiety, since it was closer to home. Defeats in war led to mounting criticism of the King's government and there was a demand for reform of the political system.

Opposition to the policy of trying to crush the colonists grew. In Parliament, the Rockingham Whig, Charles James Fox, proved a powerful advocate of the right of the Americans to choose their own form of government. Fox had the oratory to stir Parliament and the Dublin-born philosopher and political theorist, Edmund Burke, added his literary skills to the American cause. Outside Parliament, there were renewed signs of discontent amongst the landed gentry at the cost of the war and at what they regarded as the extravagance and corruption of government. A meeting of Yorkshire gentry, called by the Reverend Charles Wyvill, called for an enquiry into government expenditure, for the reduction in payments being made to individuals out of public money and for the abolition of 'sinecure places and unmerited pensions'. Within weeks, similar petitions began to emerge from other meetings of country squires. In 1780 a motion was passed in the House of Commons, by 233 votes to 215, moved by the Whig lawyer, John Dunning. Dunning's motion was 'that the influence of the Crown has increased, is increasing and ought to be diminished'. Soon afterwards, his fellow Whig, Edmund Burke, introduced an 'economical reform' bill that would have substantially reduced the number of sinecures and court and government appointments. The threat to the constitution was seen as coming from above, from the excessive power of the King's government over the Parliament. The difficulty was how to get out of the American War. To the King, conceding independence was unacceptable. As he announced to a Cabinet meeting which he, not the prime minister, summoned in the summer of 1779, 'It was his resolution to part this life rather than suffer his dominions to be dismembered'.

Walpole and his immediate successors had succeeded in entrenching the often unpopular Hanoverian monarchy and, by careful manipulation of Parliament and the court, had created a political stability that encouraged commerce to flourish. At the same time, the political elite had limited the extent to which the landed interest, from which the politicians came, was affected by the encroachments of the state. There had been relative success in war and in commercial rivalry. The 20 years after 1760, when the old ideological division between Whig and Tory had largely disappeared, had brought instability at the centre that pointed to the need for political realignments. The defeat in America and the issues raised by the new language of liberty coming from there speeded that up and pointed to new challenges for the ruling elite. The balance of power between Parliament and monarch and between the government and the Commons was increasingly being challenged.

Further reading

Black, Jeremy (ed.), *British Politics and Society from Walpole to Pitt 1742–1789* (Basingstoke, Macmillan, 1990)

Black, Jeremy, *The Politics of Britain 1688–1800* (Manchester, Manchester University Press, 1993)

Hoppit, Julian, *Land of Liberty? England 1689–1727* (Oxford, Oxford University Press, 2000)

Jupp, Peter, *The Governing of Britain 1688–1848: The Executive, Parliament and the People* (London, Routledge, 2006)

Langford, Paul, *Eighteenth-Century Britain. A Very Short Introduction* (Oxford, Oxford University Press, 1984)

Langford, Paul, *A Polite and Commercial People* (Oxford, Oxford University Press, 1989)

3

Power and society in rural Britain

Population and economy

At the beginning of the eighteenth century, British people were more modern than we sometimes appreciate. Perhaps 60 per cent of families were in receipt of wages, and even if some of those still had some rights to land, it suggests that a waged economy was already well on the way to abolishing subsistence farming. This process was hastened during the course of the century as small freeholders in England were dispossessed, often by the forced enclosure of common land by parliamentary act, and landlords eliminated formerly secure leases of land. Large farms absorbed the small, and all across England, Wales, Scotland and Ireland ownership was consolidated in the hands of an increasingly wealthy class of large landowners. The great estates became bigger, representing in most places the emergence of the three-class structure of rich landlord, large tenant farmer and landless labourer.

With these changes to the land came greater mobility for people and for goods. It has been estimated that in 1715, passenger traffic within Britain amounted to 67,000 passenger miles, but by 1765 this had almost doubled to 123,000.[1] There was a quickening to the pace of life due, in part, to growing numbers of people. The population of England in 1706 has been estimated at 5,334,000; by 1781, it had risen to 7,206,000. After a seventeenth century of relative stasis in total population, this was a significant rise. It marked the beginning of the demographic growth that was to accompany British economic development over the long period from the eighteenth to the early

---

[1] S. Ville, 'Transport,' in R. Floud and P. Johnson (eds), *The Cambridge Economic History of Modern Britain: Volume I: Industrialisation, 1700–1860* (Cambridge, Cambridge University Press, 2004), p. 298.

twentieth century; indeed, it signalled that population rise was in itself to be an important driver of economic growth. The early eighteenth century was the last time, too, in which a significant demographic crisis occurred on mainland Britain. The late 1720s was the final period in peacetime in which the death rate exceeded the birth rate, as a result of a series of bad harvests. But in the midst of that setback, there was a dramatic surge in the marriage rate, and this led to an increase of births in the early 1730s which, although not sustained, did introduce the long period of strong population growth from the 1740s through to the 1840s.

Several things were happening to cause population growth. In England, about two-thirds was due to an increased birth rate – or fertility, as it is called – which rose from 28.5 births per 1,000 people in 1706, to 35.8 in 1776. This was caused by a mixture of related developments: women were getting married younger (a mean of 26 years of age in 1700–9, dropping to 24 in 1780–9), thus bearing more children in their lifetime; the numbers of stillborn children were declining (the result of better diet and health of mothers); and, though less important, the intervals between giving birth were decreasing whilst illegitimacy was rising (from, in England, 1.8 per cent of all births in 1675–99 to 6.2 per cent in 1700–25). Behind it all lay economic experience. In England between the 1540s and the 1840s, there was a strong linkage between harvests and wage rates on the one hand and the number of marriages on the other: years of better harvest produced higher wages, more marriages and live births (and, incidentally, fewer adult deaths), and thus population growth. Falls in the death rate, by comparison, were less important for growth. The overall death rate was largely static over the period 1700–80 (at around 25–27 deaths per 1,000 of population), whilst deaths amongst infants (in the first year of life) were high in the first half of the eighteenth century and, after improvement, were to rise again in industrial England in the late nineteenth century.[2]

The situation in Scotland was a little different. Scotland's union with England and Wales in 1707 came at a low point in its economic history. Terrible economic crises of the late sixteenth century were followed by periodic crises in the seventeenth, culminating in the so-called 'Scottish Famine', or Lean Years, of 1693–7, when a series of harvest failures brought about severe hunger in many parts of Scotland. Through the combination of death and emigration, this may have reduced Scotland's population by as much as 15 per cent. The stimulus of population growth is less evident in Scotland, and it may be, indeed, that it was the burden of existing population that prompted large landowners north of the border to make stark moves to increase efficiency, consolidate their holdings, and innovate in production. In this way, it is possible that whilst opportunity fostered agricultural improvement in England, it was crisis that caused it in Scotland.

---

[2] E.A. Wrigley, 'British population during the "long" eighteenth century, 1680–1840', in R. Floud and P. Johnson (eds), *The Cambridge Economic History of Modern Britain: Volume I: Industrialisation, 1700–1860* (Cambridge, Cambridge University Press, 2004), pp. 57–95.

Focus on

Population

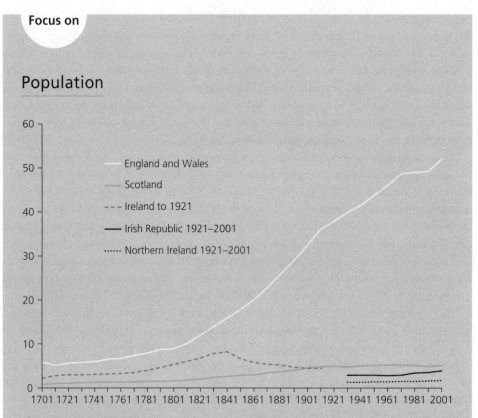

Figure 3.1 Population of England and Wales, Scotland and Ireland, 1701–2001 (millions)

Notes:
1. For 1701–91, this graph shows for the total population for England and Wales the Brownlee estimates at nearest adjacent year, for Scotland the Webster figure for Scotland in 1755 entered at 1751 and estimated values for remaining years, and for Ireland the figures give by Connell for nearest adjacent years.
2. For 1801–2001, the graph shows the total population for each country at census dates (with 1941 figures for England and Wales and Scotland using the 1939 mid-year estimates).

Sources: B.R. Mitchell and P. Deane (eds), *Abstract of British Historical Statistics* (Cambridge, Cambridge University Press, 1962), pp. 5–7; http://vision.edina.ac.uk/census/; http://en.wikipedia.org/wiki/Irish_Population_Analysis; http://www.scrol.gov.uk/; http://www.nisranew.nisra.gov.uk/census/censusstatistics/index.html

This graph shows the growth of population for each of the constituent countries of Britain and Ireland from 1701 to 2001. It shows various important features of the history of demographic change.

First look at the graph line for England and Wales. This shows that, after rather little change in the early 1700s, there followed a fairly steady rise in population for the rest of the eighteenth century, followed by a rapid acceleration around 1800–20 which was sustained until the 1870s, when it became even more rapid. Around the 1910s, a slowing down in population growth is evident – though the figures continued to rise until the 1960s, when there was a significant slowing of population growth for the next 20 years. Only in the 1990s was there a resumption of very rapid population growth (the result mainly of rising immigration from Europe).

The graph line for Scotland seems to follow a similar trend until around 1900, but at a slower rate of growth than in England and Wales. But after 1900, Scotland's population fails to grow like England's, and is indeed quite stagnant – the product of high rates of emigration in various decades.

Lastly, look at the graph lines for Ireland. The graph for 1701–1921 shows that population growth was fairly strong growth until 1841, indicating a trend very similar to that for England and Wales during those decades. But then in the 1840s the total population of Ireland plummets – the result of the demographic disaster resulting from the Irish potato famine of 1845 (see Chapter 13), which led to large-scale mortality and sustained levels of emigration, which caused the total population to maintain its downward trend until the 1930s. At this point, Ireland splits into the Irish Republic in the South and Northern Ireland (which stayed within the UK). The total population of each of these remained relatively stable for much of the twentieth century, but started to rise from the 1970s, especially in the Irish Republic (the result in part of immigration).

The demographic development of Britain in the eighteenth century was truly remarkable. Its rate of population growth was higher than most of Europe (only Scandinavia matched it) and contributed to a massive rise in the total output of the economy, almost all of it coming from what has been described as the traditional 'organic' economy based on agriculture and textiles, rather than the mineral-based 'inorganic' economy that was to become so important in the nineteenth century. Britain was pulling away from her neighbours in the rate of economic change, but this was being produced largely by changes in scale, small-scale innovation and improvement in conventional activities, not by a major leap into new modes of production. During the eighteenth century, there was what historians call 'proto-industrialisation', in which the intensification of labour, the growth of domestic manufacturing, and the dynamic quality of economic growth laid down an infrastructure for intensive economic development. One of the main economic developments of the century before the Industrial Revolution of the late eighteenth century was the marked growth of regionally concentrated rural domestic industries based in country homes, but serving distant markets. This occurred especially in cotton, woollen and linen textiles, in hosiery, lace and many metal wares. Frequently, artisans producing these products ran small businesses on their farms, and undertook both farming and manufacturing processes, using the labour of their own family or a small number of live-in workers.

Most commonly, merchants who had markets for such products distributed raw materials to domestic workers who would work on one part of the process, such as spinning or weaving, and the merchants would collect their output and take it to another domestic worker for the next stage of production. When the items were finished, the products were sold on for sale or export to distant markets.

One interesting characteristic of this development is that a good deal of it occurred in the north of England and the Midlands, across much of central Scotland, and in many parts of Ireland. In places, there was a strong association between the development of rural industries and farming. The Pennines formed a focus for development between linen, cotton and wool cloth-making in the seventeenth and eighteenth centuries; on the western slopes in Lancashire and the eastern slopes in Yorkshire there was strong development of textile-working in the home. But these proto-industries were also to be found in non-upland areas – woollen manufacture in East Anglia, silk in Essex, and pillow lace and straw plait industries in Buckinghamshire, Bedfordshire, Hertfordshire and Huntingdonshire. In Ireland, the linen industry dominated, with most of its output exported to mainland Britain, providing an important source of cash revenue to the Irish economy.

What produced this industrial surge in certain parts of the countryside? First, there was cheap labour in farming districts, particularly upland arable farming areas, where income from animal husbandry was low and where the seasonality of labour provided the basis for domestic labour: farm workers had spare time at parts of the year, and industrial work in the home provided much-needed family income. Second, rural industry in the home tended to do well where co-operative farming was weakest, where the individual tenants and freeholders had the greatest freedom to take on additional labour in the home. Third, rural industries tended to take off where partible inheritance (division of land between surviving male children) was strongest, as there was a greater need for extra sources of income for those families that failed to inherit land. Fourth, common rights of workers (to common land, to mining rights, and to squatting rights) enabled rural workers in some areas to organise and exploit resources in ways restricted elsewhere. Fifth, fertile farming areas often had the most advanced artisan structure, which tended to restrain entry into manufacturing and generally provided obstacles to new manufacturing.

Specialisation of production was often highly localised. In some places, workers came together to co-operate in planning development and exploiting resources. In others, such as Birmingham, absence of controls and religious freedom contributed to a culture of proto-industrial expansion. Yet, not all proto-industrial regions became industrial zones in the late eighteenth and nineteenth centuries. Perhaps only half did so, the most important being south and west Yorkshire, south Lancashire and the west Midlands, and certain parts of Scotland. With more sustained industrial development after 1800, the location of coalfields was important to the further development of these areas. Meanwhile, some places where there had been strong proto-industrialisation actually de-industrialised in the nineteenth century and suffered poor economic development – two examples being East Anglia, which lost out to Yorkshire where cloth was produced more cheaply, and the Weald of Kent, whose charcoal-based iron industry was overtaken by that of the coal-using Midlands.

Women and children were important to most eighteenth-century proto-industrial manufacturing in rural areas. In Yorkshire, women workers in the home lived in households where the men were often employed in different sectors, such as farming or mining. In some areas, such as the Midlands and the south-west, it was the impossibility of men making enough wages in farming for enough of the year that led to women taking low-wage, labour-intensive work in the home (in knitting and candle-making, for instance), while children worked too at picking stones from fields, and scaring birds from seeds and crops. Proto-industry encouraged earlier marriage and also a modest rise in births outside of marriage. With industrial earnings giving younger people the greatest opportunity to leave home, start families, and, indeed, have more children, population growth was fastest in these areas.

During this period, Britain experienced broadly two agricultural systems. The first was the open-field system (dating from the medieval period, when more than half of farm land was in open fields and commons), in which the village land was divided into arable for growing crops and pasture for keeping animals like sheep and cattle. The arable was subdivided into large fields which were then split into strips which rotated in use from wheat or rye in year 1, barley oats, beans or peas in year 2, and fallow in year 3. Rotation in use would extend also to pasture, and all would be managed by the community as a whole, while large areas of marginal outfields and hillsides were left for rough pasture and wasteland. This system had been diminishing slowly for centuries because it was a relatively inefficient way of farming, leaving too much land unused, with too few economies of scale. There was little incentive to innovation, and slow and unresponsive management by groups of men. Its decline continued in the modern era: in 1700, 29 per cent of England was open or common land; by 1914 the proportion had dwindled to 5 per cent, where it remains today.[3] The open-field system was passing away in much of Britain, including in the Scottish Lowlands, but in the Highlands the improvement was much slower and, indeed, less successful. In the Highlands open-field farming was known as *runrig*, in which the rigs or strips of land were farmed for oats – a less valuable crop than wheat or barley, but all that it was possible to grow. The soil was poor and stony, with little advanced technology available to improve drainage and effective ploughing, while the climate was generally cold and wet and most unsuited to arable farming.

The second and more efficient type of agriculture was enclosed farming, in which landowners replaced strip farming, using large numbers of farmers, with a few large farms run by tenant farmers selected for their innovation and enterprise. These employed farm labourers (known in Scotland and some other places as 'farm

---

[3] R.C. Allen, 'Agriculture during the Industrial Revolution', in R. Floud and P. Johnson (eds), *The Cambridge Economic History of Modern Britain: Volume I: Industrialisation, 1700–1860* (Cambridge, Cambridge University Press, 2004), p. 99.

servants') to introduce more specialised systems of farming, including advanced animal husbandry; crop rotation around four-field systems; improved drainage; and enclosing these new fields with stone dykes, hedges or (in the nineteenth century) with fences. Instead of three-year rotation came the Norfolk four-year rotation of turnips, barley, clover and wheat, and since there was no fallow year, there was a dramatic increase in overall output. With this regime, pioneered in Norfolk by Charles Townshend (the brother-in-law of the Prime Minister, Robert Walpole), enclosure of common land speeded up in the late eighteenth and early nineteenth centuries in the English Midlands and lowland Scotland. Land was resurveyed and the pattern of medieval strips gave way to compact modern farms held by individual tenants. This type of farming was more efficient and increasingly favoured by landowners as it allowed them to increase the yield from renting to ambitious tenant farmers. It fostered innovation, specialisation and, increasingly in the eighteenth century, regional specialisation in farming produce. Certain parts of the country became noted for certain types of farming: the flatlands around London for grain; the uplands of Scotland for black cattle for meat; the south-west of England for fruit; and areas close to large population concentrations for dairying. Animal husbandry improved from the end of the seventeenth century, with the wider use of fodder crops and the use of turnips and clover on a large scale. With these developments, farms got larger and investment grew. All of this was encouraged by a general upward trend in food prices; except for the second quarter of the eighteenth century, food prices rose until the 1790s, giving landowners and innovative tenants the prospect of increasing prosperity.

Rural society was also transformed between 1700 and 1780 by the improvement of transport. It was traditionally seen as the responsibility of local government, the quarter sessions of justices of the peace, to control and monitor the roads, but in the eighteenth century the government stepped in repeatedly to make right the deficiencies of local authorities. In 1706, government allowed landowners and entrepreneurs to form turnpike trusts which, for renewable periods such as 20 years, could improve roads in return for exacting tolls. Transport by road, river and canal grew as improvements to road surfaces, river navigation (by dredging, for example) and canal construction transformed the means of movement. Canal construction boomed from the 1760s, notably in Lancashire, Cheshire and central Scotland. This linked regions together and benefited bulk cargoes like coal, cotton, brick, chalk, stone and other quarried materials, opening up rural economies to the shock of new forms of enterprise and the beginnings of urban development. This could take a long time and huge investment: the Act of Parliament authorising the construction of the Forth and Clyde Canal connecting the east and west coasts of Scotland was passed in 1768, but it was not completed until 1790, whilst the Leeds and Liverpool Canal took from 1770 until 1816 to build. Meanwhile, coastal trade had a long heritage in an island nation, and it allowed pretty regular movement of people and goods in the eighteenth century.

There were massive disparities in wealth and standard of living both between and within Scotland, Ireland and England. Economic progress was neither uniform nor universal. In Ireland, the agricultural sector was bifurcated. In the seventeenth century, plantations of mostly Protestant farmers from Scotland and England had created a farming community, most of it in Ulster in the north-east, in which modern techniques and the opportunity for reasonable prosperity existed. Elsewhere in central and eastern Ireland, there was considerable sustained growth in the rural economy in the eighteenth century, though in much of the rest of rural Ireland (such as in Connemara, in the west) small Catholic tenants subsisted by mixed farming, growing oats and potatoes, and perhaps rearing a few animals. There was a growing dependence on potatoes as a food crop, and this created amongst the poorest tenants in the least advanced areas a long-term problem of major significance. Food shortage and famine became an habitual feature of the Irish economy, especially in the West. Regular harvest failures created periodic famines – in 1740–1, 1755, 1766 and 1782–3 (to be followed by more in 1801, 1816–18, 1822 and 1831), presaging the major Irish famine of 1845 (see Chapter 13). So, there were elements of strong economic growth in this period. Yet, similar to the Scottish Highlands, Hebrides and Northern Isles of Orkney and Shetland, there remained places of great fragility in the rural economy of Ireland, and these were susceptible to economic disaster, social dislocation and community division.

Although parliamentary union in 1707 did not immediately create a unified economy, the Scottish rural economy fared much better than that of Ireland. Calamities such as those of the 1690s became rarer and less severe in the eighteenth century (with major crises only in 1709, 1724–5 and 1740–1). But compared to England, Scotland was a poorer nation by far, and remained so for some time. In the 1730s, an English mason or carpenter averaged money wages almost 50 per cent higher than a Scottish one.[4] So, union with England created both gains and losses for the Scottish economy. On the plus side, Scottish merchants had access to what was now the largest free trade area in Europe, and to the growing colonies of England that now formed the beginnings of the British Empire. Scots were to become major contributors to imperial growth, with younger members of gentry families, hurt in economic downturns at home, emigrating to establish business concerns in North America, the Caribbean and India. Scottish urban commerce was to benefit even more. But the advantages to Scotland were only really evident after 1750, when Scottish merchants came to dominate the Virginia tobacco trade and become strong in the Caribbean sugar plantations. When profits from expatriates in India started to be brought home and invested in land and enterprise, they contributed to agricultural improvement and, to some extent, to mineral extraction and transport innovation. On the debit side, grain and meal exports from Scotland doubled during the first decades of the Union, leading to higher prices and some shortages at home that caused violent demonstrations. As Scottish fiscal policy was brought in line with that of England, some taxes

---

[4] T.M. Devine, 'Scotland', in R. Floud and P. Johnson (eds), *The Cambridge Economic History of Modern Britain: Volume I: Industrialisation, 1700–1860* (Cambridge, Cambridge University Press, 2004), p. 395.

rose (such as those on salt and malt used to make beer), resulting in riots and popular opposition to the Union itself. The economic gains of the Union only started to be felt strongly in Scotland after about 1750.

Church and religion

Religion was an important part of the social and economic fabric of England, Wales, Scotland and Ireland. Each country had a state or established church – respectively the Church of England (in England and Wales), the Church of Scotland, and the Church of Ireland. All three were Protestant churches which had emerged at the sixteenth-century Reformation, but they had different doctrinal and organisational forms: the Church of England and the Church of Ireland were Episcopal (ruled by bishops) whilst the Church of Scotland was Presbyterian (managed by annually elected assemblies). Despite these differences, they had an equally important place in each country.

The established churches were dominated by the landed and urban elites and by the Crown. Each country was divided into parishes in which there was normally at least one church building and one clergyman, invariably selected by the landed classes or the Crown, exercising the role of the church in keeping the moral behaviour of parishioners in line. Church courts and lay helpers ensured that the rules of the church and of the state were equally enforced at local level. The parish church was thus an important institution of social order, and was looked upon by the state as an active arm of government. In societies still without police forces or, in many cases, effective local courts of justice, a great deal of store was placed on the churches imposing discipline through moral control. However, the position of the Church of Ireland was unique in that it represented only a tiny minority of the population – often the elite, some of whom adhered to it because it was politically convenient.

In part because of these circumstances, the established churches in the eighteenth century were riddled with abuses. In the Church of England and Church of Ireland, many parsons did not live in their parishes, but often resided in London, living off the earnings of their church, and employing poorer curates to perform religious functions. Abuse also included pluralism: holding more than one parish at a time to increase income. As many as 60 per cent of English clergy did not live in their parishes (though some lived just outside). In the Church of Ireland, less than half of the clergy resided in their parishes. The system involved corruption: advowson, the right to appoint the clergyman in a parish, was often bought and sold between wealthy figures, resulting in more than two-thirds of parishes being held in private hands rather than in the hands of the church. Meanwhile in Scotland, where landowners were legally responsible for providing a church, manse and parish school, and for paying the minister's stipend, the greatest scandal was over the patronage system (reintroduced in 1712) which gave a landowner a right to select the minister, but which allowed the costs to be passed onto the poorest people – the peasant farmers and labourers – by way of taxing harvests of crops and fish, rents for pews, charges for marriages and baptisms, rent of coffin cloths, and other charges.

Though there had been opponents of these abuses in the established churches in the seventeenth century, it was in the eighteenth century that hostility became significant. First, there was the growth of religious dissent. Dissenters were Protestants who left the established churches in pursuit of a more evangelical or fervent form of religion, free of state and elite control and financial abuse, and from interference by landowners and gentry. They were characterised by a desire to meet in their own churches, with ministers and preachers more to their liking. This gave rise to the pursuit of congregational democracy – most marked in Nonconformist groups in England, like the Independents (who later divided into the Baptists and Congregationalists), the Unitarians, and Presbyterian Dissenters in Scotland, like the Seceders. Of growing importance in this period were the Methodists, followers of John Wesley and his acolytes, who started a movement in the 1730s to found a more 'methodical' faith, free from the perceived corruption and lukewarm religion of many in the established church. With time, the Methodists drifted from the ambit of the Church of England, growing rapidly everywhere (except in Scotland and Catholic areas) and attracting rural labourers and the landless, fishermen and, towards the end of the century, significant numbers of miners (notably in the Cornish tin mines). Those who were striking out with independent lives, or in dangerous occupations, or those most alienated from employers were attracted to the vibrancy of the Methodist chapel. In these circumstances, religion became an important source of social identity.

In addition, the Roman Catholic Church, which had been overturned at the Reformation in mainland Britain, was regaining influence through a policy of toleration that spread from England in the 1660s to Scotland in the eighteenth century, and, though many restrictions on Catholics remained, priests were starting to move more freely. This revived the Catholic faith – notably in western and southern rural Ireland, in north-western and north-eastern Scotland, in Lancashire and in towns and cities like London. In these parts, many aristocratic and gentry families had remained Catholic, and they provided protection for Catholic tenants and priests. In Ireland, however, the Protestant Church of Ireland was the official church of the state, and the Catholic majority were in an inferior economic, social and ecclesiastical position. More than that, to be a Catholic in Ireland showed that you belonged to an opposing political culture to the government, and had a conflicting view of history. The eighteenth century witnessed the continuation of what was called the 'Protestant Ascendancy', which affected all parts of life. In 1729, the right to vote was removed from Catholic freeholders, and the Irish Assembly in Dublin was Protestant only. Despite this, Catholic life was deeply embedded in the eighteenth century, in the form of religious orders, the saying of Mass (which was illegal in Scotland), the building of new churches and, from the 1750s, the training of priests in seminaries. With a small Catholic gentry, notable especially in the West of Ireland, Catholics were in some positions of economic and civil influence in many Irish towns, despite the anti-popery laws.

In all, between 1700 and 1780, there was a significant development of religious worship outside the established churches. In England by 1780, there were 38,000 Methodist Church members (and many more adherents and family members), which when they are added to other dissenting groups probably meant that around 15 per cent of the people were in association with dissent. In Scotland somewhere in the region of a fifth of Protestants belonged to one dissenting church or another, whilst in Ireland it seems likely that under 20 per cent of people adhered to the Church of Ireland, another 10 per cent to Presbyterianism and other Protestant churches, whilst probably 70 per cent or more were Roman Catholic. But it is important to remember that the choice of which church people attended was not merely a religious matter; it was also a question of civil loyalty and obedience to social elites.

Social relations

The eighteenth century gave to British heritage the large and elegant country houses that still dot some of the country's finest landscape. They bear witness to the impact of the rising wealth of large landowners, with regular gardens and artificial lakes, by designers like Lancelot 'Capability' Brown (known for his informal country settings and serpentine-shaped water features) surrounding massive stone and brick mansions. Some of these were of extraordinary proportions. Chatsworth House in Derbyshire, the seat of the Dukes of Devonshire, had 126 rooms, mostly built during its eighteenth-century expansion, whilst Holkham Hall in north Norfolk, the seat in the nineteenth century of the Earl of Leicester, had a severe exterior but sumptuous interior rooms. The country houses were of increasing grandeur and lavishness, all equipped with large numbers of public rooms for the entertaining of aristocratic guests in their finery, for spectacular meals eaten off the best modern china, at tables made by craftsmen like Chippendale. The levels of consumption grew throughout the century, defining an age in which, more than any other, wealth and status were marked by a decadence and extravagance in food and wine.

The estate owner was the instigator of agricultural change, usually starting with enclosure, the removal of small tenantry, and the granting of leases to approved tenants with potential for implementing new farming techniques. The commonest and most admired of these was known as the 'Norfolk system' and was associated particularly with Charles, second Viscount Townshend (1674–1738), nicknamed 'Turnip' Townshend for his advocacy of turnip as a fodder crop, and Thomas William Coke (1754–1842), the first Earl of Leicester, of Holkham Hall. Their determination to improve farming techniques led to rising productivity, increased rents charged to tenant farmers, and a new wealth, which they spent on ever larger country mansions and town houses in London. This led, amongst other things, to a great increase in the demand for skilled artisans and craftsmen. In Coke's case at his estate in north Norfolk, rental income had already increased 44 per cent between 1718 and 1758 alone, helping to fund the construction of Holkham Hall. The house was modelled on the Palladian style, which a previous owner had admired on a Grand Tour of Europe in the early decades of the century, and as the wealth grew, the Hall was built between the 1730s and 1760s. It was constructed to regal standards of opulence, with a sumptuous marble hall and statue gallery, a 'receiving saloon' and many luxurious and comfortable bedrooms – all built with the best marble and stone, and decorated with the finest carvings, wallpapers and paintings. As with many country houses of the century, a private chapel for the family was added at the side. Virtually everything for miles around the British country house belonged to and was controlled by the estate. At Holkham in the later eighteenth century, some 30 new farm buildings were created and homes erected for the labourers. Typically, local shops and inns were also owned by estates, and almost no activity was free from their influence. The landowner was effectively the employer of everybody and the owner of every scrap of land and home. This was a new centralisation of power.

The irresistibility of the economic power of the improving large landowners meant that other forms of power accrued to them too. Landowners were usually the patrons of the parish church of the Church of England or Church of Scotland, and there was an expectation in many rural parishes that the tenantry and employees would pay homage to the church and its vicar and usually attend every Sunday. The deference owed extended from the weekday to the Lord's Day, and honoured the earthly lord as much as the heavenly one. Churches had pews that were let or assigned to worshippers in patterns that reflected the social order. In England, it was customary for the higher social ranks to have family pews close to the altar, with the estate stewards, tenantry and labourers ranked behind. In Scotland, the layout was usually different, with the landowner and his family assembled in either the front rows of a large rear gallery, or at the side in an isolated and elevated 'loft', often with their own comfortable seats and private fireplace to keep them warm during the service, and in many cases with their own staircase external to the church to emphasise their private route to God's house. In some parishes, the landowners believed in the importance of self-help, and insisted that their tenantry even pay rents for the privilege of sitting in an assigned pew; the system of pew renting became ever more widespread in the eighteenth century, and in Scotland was to last into the twentieth century.

To the power of the church in the rural estate must be added the other institutions of civil society which, almost equally, fell under the effective patronage and control of the landowning family. Schooling and charitable work were aspects of life that were utilised by the elites as part of their civic responsibilities, extending an often genuine concern for the wellbeing of the less well-off. Rural justice was also strongly influenced by landowners, who were often justices of the peace, or who passed responsibility for justice on a day-to-day basis to estate stewards. As justices of the peace, meeting in quarter sessions, landowners had powers over local military activity (the militia) and over the regulation of wages. They also tended to act as toll pike trusts and bridge commissioners, and operate the Poor Law for the relief of poverty. The larger landowners might not take personal responsibility in such bodies, but their estate managers and stewards often did. In this way, the idea of separated civil and private powers in the countryside was often fictional; in reality, power was highly centralised.

Power was also political in form. The larger landowners in the eighteenth century aspired to spend at least some of the year in London, the seat of political power and the centre of social display. Typically, they had large town houses, and many of the regal Georgian houses in the capital were the products of the rental income from improving country estates of this period. As with both Coke of Holkham and 'Turnip' Townshend, there were political careers to pursue. Coke was elected to be a Member of Parliament for Norfolk in the same year as inheriting the family estates. He took a great interest in agricultural matters, and was a great publicist of the technical innovations which he oversaw on the home farm at Holkham. Coke was the archetypal great improving landlord of the period, combining agricultural improvement with the maintenance of a close paternalistic concern for the tenantry and workers on the estate.[5]

Though rural professional classes existed (including clergy and teachers), the reality of rural social life was the economic, political and ecclesiastical power of the landowning class. So much of the future of the land depended on it.

Further reading

Floud, R. and Johnson, P. (eds), *The Cambridge Economic History of Modern Britain: Volume I: Industrialisation, 1700–1860* (Cambridge, Cambridge University Press, 2004)

Foster, R.F. (ed.), *The Oxford History of Ireland* (Oxford, Oxford University Press, 1989)

Gilbert, A.A., *Religion and Society in Industrial England: Church, Chapel and Social Change 1740–1914* (London, Longman, 1976)

Hay, D. and Rogers, N., *Eighteenth-Century English Society. Shuttles and Swords* (Oxford, Oxford University Press, 1997)

Martins, S.W., *Changing Agriculture in Georgian and Victorian Norfolk* (Cromer, Poppyland Publishing, 2002)

Rule, J., *Albion's People: English Society 1714–1815* (London, Longman, 1992)

---

[5] J.V. Beckett, 'Coke, Thomas William, first earl of Leicester of Holkham (1754–1842)', *Oxford Dictionary of National Biography* (Oxford, Oxford University Press, September 2004); online edn, January 2006 [http://www.oxforddnb.com/view/article/5831, accessed 11 September 2007].

4

Urban life

Town and city

A key development of Britain between 1707 and the present day has been urbanisation. Towns grew in number, in size and in diversity. They became the engine of the economy, of consumption and of culture. This process began in earnest in the eighteenth century.

The proportion of people living in towns was very low in 1700. In England and Wales, 13.3 per cent of the people lived in towns of over 5,000 people, but only 5.3 per cent in Scotland and 3.4 per cent in Ireland. This compared with 33.6 per cent in the Netherlands, 23.9 per cent in Belgium, more than 13 per cent in Italy, 11.5 per cent in Portugal and 9.2 per cent in France.[1] Unlike Europe, with its relatively high proportion of urban habitation, its metropolitan cities (like Paris and Berlin) and large regional cities (like Cologne and Lyons), Britain was little urbanised before the Industrial Revolution. So, when urbanisation got under way it was fast and frenetic, and, apart from London, there was little experience of urban living, regulation of growth, and coping with larger conglomerations. European cities already had structures of government and a heritage of urban law upon which to draw when faced with town growth. But Britain would make some fumbling mistakes.

One estimate is that there were only 28 towns with a population of more than 5,000 in mainland Britain in 1700, the largest being London with over 310,000 people, the second largest being Edinburgh with just over 50,000, and only a further nine with between 10,000 and 50,000 citizens.[2] Some parts of the British Isles – like

[1] J. De Vries, *European Urbanisation 1500–1800* (London, Methuen, 1984), p. 39.
[2] J. Langton, 'Urban growth and economic change c. 1688–1841,' in P. Clark (ed.), *The Cambridge Urban History of Britain: Volume II 1540–1840* (Cambridge, Cambridge University Press, 2000), p. 463.

the Scottish Highlands, southern Scotland and most of Ireland – had very little town living at all. Most towns that did exist were centres for agricultural markets, places for sales of farming produce and providers of service functions, labour hiring and suchlike for the farming communities in the neighbourhood. Medieval towns had developed with a mixture of artisan trades, butchers, bakers, merchants and ecclesiastical leaders. But specialism was growing in the seventeenth and eighteenth centuries. Some markets were of national importance – such as those at Falkirk, in central Scotland, where the cattle market attracted beasts brought for sale from all over the Scottish Highlands and onward droving to Cambridgeshire and the London meat market. The eighteenth century also saw the rise of resorts for holidays and fashionable living – like Bath and Harrogate with their spas, and Brighton with its seaside holidays for the fashionable London set. After 1760, many towns developed chic Georgian quarters – Clifton in Bristol, the new towns of Edinburgh and Glasgow, and Bath. Merchants of the commercial revolution and improving landowners, who sought access to the ranks of Britain's aristocracy through property acquisition, were important in fuelling this boom in town houses and gracious living.

From the 1770s, urban change brought by industry was being felt in many places. Regions, towns and villages of every size were developing specialisms of one kind or another. In the Belfast area, linen developed as the basis of textile manufacturing, with total Irish exports (largely from Ulster) rising from 2 million yards in 1715 to over 40 million yards in the 1790s.[3] The five towns of the Potteries in the Black Country (now known as Stoke-on-Trent) specialised from the seventeenth century in pottery, which in the mid- and later eighteenth century became fashionable, with special processes and styles pioneered by family firms like those of Josiah Wedgwood and Josiah Spode. At the other extreme, the tiny village of Doune in Perthshire became home between the 1690s and 1780s to a specialist pistol-making industry, creating ornate, high-status pairs of pistols for clan leaders, army officers and the gentry. Throughout Britain, increasing numbers of people in villages and small towns were working in the home or in sheds as cotton, linen or woollen handloom weavers, and new industrial villages were being erected for power spinning machines close to fast-flowing water in Lancashire, Yorkshire, Lanarkshire and on the edges of the Scottish Highlands. Industry became seen as the instigator of urban improvement, just as new farming techniques brought improvement to the countryside.

Nevertheless, there was a price to pay for urban growth. Even by the 1770s the adverse effects of industry on towns were starting to be noted. The opening of new coalfields in the mid-eighteenth century, and the use of steam engines to pump up water from deeper pits, produced ever-cheaper coal for burning in the domestic hearth. This not only made urban living warmer, but was less expensive than wood from diminishing forests. However, it created a fog of smoke (later called 'smog') in the

---

[3] P. Ollerenshaw, 'Industry 1820–1914', in L. Kennedy and P. Ollerenshaw (eds), *An Economic History of Ulster, 1820–1940* (Manchester, Manchester University Press, 1985), p. 67.

centre of larger towns like Manchester and Glasgow, the ill-effects of which were already leading some town councillors to seek restrictions. Industrial cities became dominated by coal burning, both in the home and, from the 1790s, in steam engines, contributing to the trend for gentry and upper-middle-class families to escape urban pollution in out-of-town residences.

A large proportion of towns were ports, especially those on the east coast, which served the coastal and European trades. In 1750, Britain was the world's greatest trading nation, with a wide variety of textiles and hardware goods being exported, and mostly organic products (ranging from Baltic timber to North American grain) being imported. The American trade was highly significant. From the sixteenth century, the colonies were peopled by English, Scots, Welsh and Irish settlers and, in the eighteenth century, they became a large trading block with which British traders conducted a huge amount of commerce. Sugar from the West Indies and tobacco from Virginia and Maryland were more valuable than all of Britain's trade with the East. Bristol, Glasgow and Liverpool were especially important in the transatlantic trade, but large numbers of small inlets and ports along the western coast of Britain played host to trading ships that plied across the Atlantic. With little regulation, an entrepreneurial spirit and a less than effective customs and excise administration, coastal communities traded in legal and illicit goods almost without distinction. The Channel Islands specialised in smuggling goods between France and Britain, and tea was smuggled from the East, while, at the other end of the British Isles, the Shetland Isles were notorious for smuggling Scandinavian timber as well as Rotterdam gin. For such communities, smuggling was a tremendous source of long-term financing of local business (in Shetland's case, contributing to the capitalisation of inshore fishing fleets in the 1800s and 1810s). However, for the rest of Britain, it was the legal and larger-scale trading in tobacco and sugar that constituted the engine of commercial development. Each of these was an *entrepôt* trade, dependent to a great extent on re-export of imports from North America. About one-third of sugar was re-exported, and two-thirds of tobacco imports in the 1710s, but by the 1770s, tobacco re-exports had risen to 85 per cent, mostly to mainland Europe.[4] Though of less value, trade in goods like tea from India and China also rose in the eighteenth century. The American connection was also vital for the export trade. Around two-thirds of the products of new industries (often metal goods) went to North America by the 1770s.

British ports were buzzing with growth. Glasgow, Bristol, Liverpool and London grew with enormous speed in the eighteenth century, fuelled by the expansion of transatlantic trade. The peopling of the American colonies, the rise of the slave trade, and the development of the key farmed products of cotton, tobacco and sugar in plantations, both on the mainland of America and, in the case of sugar, in the West Indies,

---

[4] C. Knick Hartley, 'Trade: discovery, mercantilism and technology', in R. Floud and P. Johnson (eds), *The Cambridge Economic History of Modern Britain: Volume I: Industrialisation, 1700–1860* (Cambridge, Cambridge University Press, 2004), p. 183.

fed self-sustaining growth that fostered the economic life of the home ports. Glasgow and Bristol benefited greatly from this. In the case of Bristol, slave traders from the city became important in the triangular trade between Britain, Africa and America, shipping slaves to America, tobacco and other produce to Britain, and mixed goods to Africa (see Chapter 6). Glasgow was the base of the so-called 'tobacco lords' of the Virginia trade: Virginia was virtually owned by Glasgow merchants, who provided lands to planters and reaped the benefit in bringing the tobacco to Glasgow and other UK ports, from where it was sold both at home and throughout Europe. And Glasgow, more than any other port, was to exploit eighteenth-century commercial expansion as the basis for industrialisation after 1780.

By the end of the eighteenth century, modern patterns of urbanisation were established, though the scale of towns and cities was still small. By the time of the first national census of population in 1801, greater London had 1.1 million inhabitants, but there were still only six other towns with more that 50,000 people (and these all had populations under 100,000) – Bristol, Birmingham, Manchester, Liverpool, Glasgow and Edinburgh. But there were now increasing numbers of towns of over 5,000 people, many clustered around the larger cities in zones of industrial urbanisation. In Lancashire and Lanarkshire especially, almost continuous urban districts – or conurbations, as they became called – were already developing, with interdependence between towns in the various branches of the cotton textile industry, engineering and coal-mining. By 1801, the urbanisation of the British people in towns of over 5,000 was more rapid than anywhere in Europe, involving 20.3 per cent of the population in England and Wales, 17.3 per cent in Scotland and 7.0 per cent in Ireland. This rate of change was outstripping Europe where (with the exceptions of Spain and Poland) the proportion of the population living in cities was either static or declining. Britain was rapidly emerging as the first urban nation to be founded not primarily on commerce, but on manufacturing. And behind this lay a dramatic growth in the consumption of goods.

Luxury and consumption

The eighteenth century was the turning point in the rise of consumer society. Though this was not a society of mass consumerism (as in the twenty-first century), luxuries and their ownership became more widespread than in any previous age. Moreover, access to luxury was no longer restricted to the landed elite but extended also to the growing middling ranks of society. Material culture became the talk of the day, with people becoming very conscious of consumption, of buying and acquiring things, of displaying them in the home (and having rooms dedicated to display), and of passing these on to friends and relatives when they died. Material things entered people's sense of self and their identities much more starkly in the eighteenth century. For this reason, it would be wrong to see the rise of consumption facilitated by the new wealth of the middle orders all over Britain as merely regional emulation of the metropolitan or aristocratic elites. Complex patterns of consumption by region and by class were forging the identities of the new social order.

People of this century talked about luxury and its importance to the economy, morality and civilisation. Amongst the rich and intellectuals there were so-called 'luxury debates', in which they identified the rise in luxury items and talked about a change in their nature. Whereas, in previous centuries, luxuries had been primarily associated with the body (clothing and jewellery, for instance), now domestic luxuries were to be found all around the home. This was an important transition. Before 1700 there had been sumptuary laws that had forbidden the wearing of special types of cloth and gold and silver lace by all but prescribed elites, as they were seen as evidence of corruption. Like Elizabeth I's Statutes of Apparel of 1574, they reinforced social hierarchies, and limited any challenge by a rising bourgeoisie to the aristocracy. Now in the eighteenth century, morality started to be located in cleanliness, comfort, decency and convenience, and luxury items for the home provided the means to achieve these qualities, to achieve a higher state of being. Such items were not just to be found amongst the rich. The economist Adam Smith argued that the wealth of a nation was to be found in the extent to which the peasantry might acquire 'necessaries and conveniences', and he noted in 1759 the fascination of British people with trinkets and toys: 'What pleases these lovers of toys is not so much the utility, as the aptness of the machines which are fitted to promote it. All their pockets are stuffed with little conveniences. They contrive new pockets, unknown in the clothes of other people, in order to carry a greater number.'[5] Things gave delight to the people of all ranks.

Tea and coffee were two articles of consumption that defined the century. The British East India Company imported 9 million pounds (or 4.08 million kilos) of tea in the 1720s, mostly from China, rising to 87 million in the 1750s, representing 60 per cent of the total value of imports.[6] Tea became the embodiment of middle-class sobriety, decorum and respectability, the etiquette of the female-centred episode of tea drinking contrasting with the male-centred flamboyance and clubbiness of the Restoration coffee house of the late seventeenth century. By 1750, tea was well entrenched in the life of many working families, certainly in England. Along with it came rising consumption of sugar, and together these marked the important transition in the British diet from one based on oatmeal, milk and cheese to one based on bread, tea, sugar and butter.

Luxury also affected clothing and domestic wares. Vast dinner services in heavily decorated Chinese and Japanese porcelain became the rage and, later in the century, were mimicked by the British china industry, led by Josiah Wedgwood in the Potteries.

---

[5] Smith quoted in M. Berg, *Luxury and Pleasure in Eighteenth-century Britain* (Oxford, Oxford University Press, 2005), p. 22.

[6] M. Berg, 'Consumption in Britain', in R. Floud and P. Johnson (eds), *The Cambridge Economic History of Modern Britain: Volume I: Industrialisation, 1700–1860* (Cambridge, Cambridge University Press, 2004), pp. 366, 368.

Printed calicoes and other imported cottons from the East provided light and fashionable cloth for ladies' wear and these too, in due course, were copied and mass-produced by the cotton textile industry in Britain. With further ideas brought back by the well-to-do from their Grand Tour of fashionable Europe, the demand for luxury fostered new trade and manufacture.

The setting for luxury and consumption in the eighteenth century was the home. Luxury and consumption were domestic pleasures, to be shared with guests not just in the public rooms like the parlour, but also in private bedrooms. It was in her bedroom that the woman of a household often played host to her lady friends for gossip, tea and material display, and these were furnished to a high standard with chairs and tables. The dining room became an important venue for conspicuous consumption amongst the middle orders, entertaining friends and family with food, tableware and furnishings of rising quality as well as quantity. In addition to the shift from consumption-display by the body to consumption in the house, there was an increasing role for women (including in gender-mixing at meals to reduce the older excesses of male-only dining and drinking). The household was a women-centred place in the eighteenth century. Even in well-to-do houses cooking was undertaken by the wife or housekeeper for much of the century, and the decorous plates and serving utensils indicated a rich material culture and complex eating and tea-drinking rituals. At death, crockery and cutlery were usually assigned in wills by women rather than by men, indicating close female identity with such goods, which they often left to members of an extensive network of women friends and family. By contrast, men left few details in their wills or inventories of their clothing and furnishings, and they tended to leave their goods only to close family members.

Just as the home became feminised, shopping became much more women-centred. Shopping was especially fashionable on Saturdays, allowing for a feast of consumption in splendid shops in the new towns and streets of the British Isles. Shopping was dominated by the rage for style, for the commodities which came into and fell out of 'fashion', for the latest designs on clothes and china from the East, and, in the case of men especially, for the latest gadgets and toys. This was to start the surge of retail development in Britain, leading quickly to the establishment of large shops catering for luxury and display.

The sensibility of this consumer society was not averse to sexual connotation. A language of sensual display was located in fine clothes and furnishings, whilst tea drinking customs offered a vocabulary for courting rituals and female exchange of indiscretions. All forms of sexuality could be masquerading as consumerism. There was a taste for pornography amongst some of London society, and prostitutes could participate in the culture of display. This world of display and sex was captured in the engravings of Hogarth – the very term 'Hogarthian scene' becoming resonant with debauchery amidst finery. Moralists denounced luxury spending amongst the poor as amongst the rich, with even tea parties being seen as a possible sign of decadence. Luxury had the capacity to debase. The poet and dramatist, John Gay wrote in 1725 of a lady with a 'passion for old china':

China's the passion of her soul;
A cup, a plate, a dish, a bowl
Can kindle wishes in her breast,
Inflame with joy, or break her rest.[7]

Luxury thus became the object of an ethical tension, with the added concern that many of the most sought-after items were imported from the still-mysterious Orient, where excessive luxury was being perceived as potentially corrupting (see Chapter 6). On the one hand, many criticised this culture for the abandonment of proper decorum, a licentiousness that undermined the moral virtues, and left women rather more than men prone to an indulgence and frippery that diluted seriousness. And if the eighteenth century was the century of culture of consumption, the nineteenth was to be the century of seriousness. On the other hand, luxury and consumption were the products of an increased pace to the economic life of many households of the middle ranks, artisans and even many of the poor classes. This combined with falling prices for overseas goods as trade grew to make access wider. And the growth of luxury defined the rising numbers of the middle classes. They wielded a spending power that drove much of the burgeoning demand for foods, fostering manufacturing, trade and commerce. To give one indication of the economic importance of middle-class purchasing power, purchase of household goods like earthenware, pewter, clocks, pictures and curtains probably rose by as much as five-fold between 1670 and 1725, as did the ownership of knives and forks. Homes increased in size, with more having parlours in which conspicuous consumption could be displayed, thus giving stimulus to the building industry, furniture-making and ancillary trades.

Focus on

Hogarth

William Hogarth (1697–1764) was a painter, cartoonist and satirist most famous (or infamous) for his depictions of bawdy life in London. In 1731–2, he made six paintings and engravings of *A Harlot's Progress*, in which a girl from the country, Moll Hackabout, was shown coming to London, starting a life as a prostitute, and falling relentlessly in moral worth until she died of a sexually transmitted disease.

---

[7] Quoted in M. Berg, *Luxury and Pleasure in Eighteenth-century Britain* (Oxford, Oxford University Press, 2005), p. 234.

He followed the popularity of this in 1732–5 with eight scenes in *A Rake's Progress*, which depicted a rich heir, Tom Rakewell, coming to London and spending all his wealth on betting, prostitutes and rich living, ending up in debtors' prison and then in the madhouse. Hogarth continued to produce moral tales and scenes of contemporary life, intended to satirise and amuse at the same time. He used parodies of other art forms: works showing moral decline formed something like a strip cartoon to invert the upward religious progress of Bunyan's novel *The Pilgrim's Progress* (1678), and mimicked the religious paintings of Leonardo da Vinci and Albrecht Dürer. The London scene and the life of the upper classes were favourites for his sharp eye and wit, and his prints were widely sold and enjoyed. It was in the spirit of the times that those being mocked enjoyed the mockery, and became amongst his biggest fans.

Figure 4.1 William Hogarth's *Rake's progress 3: The Rake at the Rose Tavern*, 1734. The third of eight paintings and engravings made between 1732 and 1735 depicts the spendthrift son of a wealthy merchant wasting his inheritance at the Rose Tavern in London's Covent Garden, a well-known pub and brothel.
Source: Sir John Soane's Museum/Eileen Tweedy

How much did the working people participate in this bonanza? In the eighteenth century, there appears to have been great regional variation; the wealthier agricultural counties in the south and east seem to have fared well, whilst some of the regions (like Cornwall) may have seen a decline of working-class consumption. Moreover, as we will see in a later Chapter 8, there is considerable disagreement amongst historians as to whether the coming Industrial Revolution was to benefit the working classes materially in the short term. Yet it seems clear that, even before the onset of strong industrial expansion in the 1780s and 1790s, expenditure on so-called non-essential items grew. Behaviour may have been changing, with clothing and style developing a stronger premium in the construction of an individual's life than had hitherto been the case. Clothing in particular became socially more widely distributed; servants, making up a sizeable proportion of working people, were clothed in purchased gowns. Clothes were more elegant and worn by many social groups for display as well as out of necessity, indicating that there was a broad move underway from living by subsistence standards to living in a more prosperous manner. Yet, it is important to stress that not all benefited equally. Much of the rise of conspicuous consumption was to a great degree socially limited – notably to the elites who, in town and country, were able to display their wealth, their standing and their aspiration. Consumption divided society, marking groups by wealth, and providing on a local basis a firm place for each family in society.

Social rank and culture

Although society was divided into status ranks, defined by economic income and wealth, there was a general sharing of many common values. Indeed, some historians tend to see the eighteenth century as the last in which there was a series of common social aspirational values, shared by all or nearly all people, based on aristocratic stewardship in both town and country. Property and patronage, coupled to the protection by the strong of the weak in exchange for the deference of the latter to the former, may have held pre-industrial society together. What was true of the country areas also pertained to the towns, in large part because most towns, most of the time, existed on the fruits of the land being brought to urban markets. Equally, social leadership fell to rural elites who, when residing in their town houses, acted as merchants and major consumers. Much of economic wealth was rural in origin, and most towns depended on it.

Though urban people were rarely as subject to a single authority as rural people were to the landowner, they nonetheless belonged to a culture that contained a common set of customs, beliefs and practices in which all town dwellers participated to greater or lesser extents. The elites might have an exclusive culture, based on wealth, multiple homes and the ability to feed their consumption mania, but they still participated with the lower orders in socially bonding common activities. These common activities were often masculine. Gentlemen and plebeians would share in the enjoyment of watching sports – horse-racing, pugilism, pre-rules football matches, cock-fighting – of gambling, and, above all, drinking. Masculinity was classless in many respects, dominated by ideals of physical strength, bravery, assurance and financial independence. So too for women, in that qualities of beauty and attractiveness were fairly common sought-after qualities – though the role of conspicuous consumption tended to divide women's culture according to economic means.

Bonding by gender across social ranks had always existed, though before industrialisation there was less social segregation but quite strong sexual segregation. For instance, the relative smallness of towns meant that there was strong mixing of social classes in the same streets and even in the same houses; in Scotland, multi-storey tenements were famously home to persons of all social ranks, with a certain segregation by height – the upper social ranks tending to be located higher up in the building. Moreover, in the case of craft industries, home and workplace were often shared spaces in which the master craftsmen provided board and lodging for journeymen and apprentices. In this way, proximity forced a high degree of shared culture.

Segregation of the sexes was common in the eighteenth-century town, however. Inns and coffee houses were the preserve mainly of men, whilst wives and daughters sought amusement in parlours and some tea houses. Inter-class association was emphasised when ranks were part and parcel of life. In the army and the Royal Navy, for instance, the officers and ranks may have been separated – marked by different conditions, pay, uniforms and the discipline required by brutal punishment of the one by the other. But at the same time, the military experience was a shared one, where the values forged by valour, deprivation and hardship bonded brothers-in-arms and excluded most women. Some women still followed their menfolk on military expeditions in the eighteenth century, though this did not undermine the ability of war to unite British men across social backgrounds in common endeavour for the kingdom and the emerging Empire.

Nevertheless, town life did involve some degree of social distinction, and these were to become more accentuated during industrial expansion. As in every age, social distinction was marked not just in work and residence but in recreation. The eighteenth century witnessed considerable innovation in this regard. For the gentry and the highest of the professional classes from 1700, there was a major growth in venues for pleasures: coffee houses, balls, masquerades and 'assemblies'. To mark the rise of Enlightenment, there were science clubs for medicine, debate and astronomy. For gentlemen there were venues for various types of sports, including racecourses. The St Leger was run at Doncaster from 1776 and the Derby was started at Epsom in 1780, whilst the Jockey Club provided an important centre for a gentleman's social life from 1750. There were billiards and cards clubs and old-fashioned cockpits where cocks were put to fighting each other with considerable wagering on the outcomes. The rise of this 'society' was fastest in London, though by the 1760s and 1770s regional towns like Edinburgh, Bath and Harrogate had assembly rooms and concerts, and gardens for the fashionable to walk and be seen in. Drinking houses continued, as in every period, and the favoured tipple in most places was gin. Theatres and operatic music grew in significance, not just in London but in provincial market towns like Norwich, Bristol and Edinburgh. Painting and galleries were a rage of the eighteenth century, especially portraiture and landscape painting, which were widely used by urban and rural elites to show wealth and status. Books became a fashionable accessory, most often borrowed from through subscription libraries.

Religion was an extremely important source of identity and meaning in town, as it was in the country. In England and Wales, the Church of England, as the state church, was vital as the fulcrum of parish life, controlling access to baptism, marriage and funerals, and as the default church for social gathering and access to charity, to letters of introduction, and social networking. For instance, those migrating from country to town in search of work in the eighteenth century invariably required testimonials from the parish clergyman, both to provide an introduction to church contacts in towns and as proof of the reliability of the bearer. The same applied to the Church of Scotland, the state church there. Through its Presbyterian structure, it stressed the importance of church courts – from the parish kirk session to the district presbytery to the national general assembly – to the structure of national life, and these courts tended to meet in towns and to be important occasions for social and business transactions. Churches sought hard to continue to operate in towns as they did in rural parishes, coping with growing numbers of migrants whose behaviour often seemed alienated from that of a sincere Christian. As we shall see in later chapters, both the Church of England and the Church of Scotland very quickly came to realise that modern towns, with their temptations of the flesh, represented a special problem for ecclesiastical operations.

One of the factors affecting the power of the established churches in towns was the rise of religious Dissenters. Older dissenting churches in England – Congregationalists, Baptist and Quakers – were already strongest in a few towns, but in the eighteenth century they lost growth in favour of the Methodist Church. Founded by John Wesley (1703–91), Methodism led the evangelical revival of the later century, representing the development of a more serious, disciplined and puritanical form of Christianity than was common in the Church of England. It attracted those from the state church who sought or experienced a 'second birth' – a realisation of a new personal faith. Methodists and other evangelical Dissenters represented a move from shared social pleasures to the creation of new groups of people, many from the lower orders, who saw in a serious evangelical Protestantism a righteousness that provided a way not merely to religious redemption but to social betterment. This was to grow even more after 1780 to become, by the Victorian period, a powerful culture in British society. But between the 1740s and 1770s, Methodists were seen as a troublesome minority, and became the object of both elite and popular opposition throughout Britain and Ireland. Methodism was distrusted for its itinerant preachers who bypassed the parish system and disturbed the power and prestige of local clergy. Mobs of local people were persuaded that no law existed for the Methodists and they set about disturbing their preaching events. Wesley became the object of stone throwing and verbal abuse in many towns the length of Britain, but he and his followers behaved with meekness and humility, gathering support from increasing numbers of urban and rural working people. In a similar vein, Scotland had its own Dissenters, starting with Episcopalians who won freedom of worship in 1709; numbers grew considerably from 1733 with dissenting Presbyterians called Seceders, who objected to Church of Scotland ministers being chosen by landowners. The eighteenth century witnessed considerable growth in dissent, much of it in the countryside, but this led inevitably to urban growth as migrants came from the countryside and as churches became easier to organise away from the stranglehold that landowners exerted on their estates.

The Dissenters were often critical of pleasures – of drinking to excess, theatre-going and gambling, of gaudy display in clothes, and riotous gatherings. The concern extended beyond the Dissenters. Though towns and cities owed much to the customs and rituals of the countryside brought by migrants, urban life developed its own character and ambience. Urban authorities down to 1780 were still pretty much in control of town dwellers, but there were hints of change on the way. Moral behaviour was changing in towns faster than in the countryside. Extra-marital sexual behaviour, excessive drinking and social disturbance were more common, and there was particular concern with gin houses and the behaviour of people at race meetings and theatres. The state and local elites in this period started to get anxious about the way in which the people of towns and cities could dissolve in disorder. Riot, which, in the countryside, had often been a ritualised warning of discontent, in the towns could become a direct threat to people and property. There was less readiness to tolerate potentially disorderly gatherings. This produced parliamentary legislation in 1741 against proliferating small race meetings, and in 1751 against small retailers of gin who were providing numerous places of consumption, especially in London and other English towns. In 1752 an Act sought to bring theatres under control through a licensing system, because, as it stated in the preamble:

> the Multitude of Places of Entertainment for the lower Sort of People is another great Cause of Thefts and Robberies, as they are thereby tempted to spend their small Substance in riotous Pleasures, and in consequence are put on unlawful Methods of supplying their Wants, and renewing their Pleasures . . .[8]

Concern was slowly growing that, as the Act put it, a 'Habit of Idleness, which is become too general over the whole Kingdom, and is productive of much Mischief and Inconvenience' was undermining the wealth and progress of the kingdom. So, the social bonds of patronage and deference seemed to be under a little strain by the middle decades of the eighteenth century. This tendency was to grow even more after 1780 with the rise of industrialism.

By 1780, it was clear to most observers that towns and cities were becoming more and more significant in the economic life of the nation. Despite the fact that the development of manufacturing in country areas had been most important, urban areas were

---

[8] Places of Public Entertainment Regulation Act, 1752.

consuming increasing amounts of wealth in building, in leisure activities and in commerce. Ports were booming, with the rise of international trade, and infrastructure developments like canals were moving bulk cargoes around with greater ease. From Georgian spa towns like Bath to the emerging textile mills of Manchester, it was clear that the nation was gearing up more and more to cater for and to exploit urban life. Though hints were already surfacing of the problems that might accompany uncontrolled urban growth, yet there was little systematic fear that the town was going to become a major social concern for the nation.

Further reading

Berg, M., *Luxury and Pleasure in Eighteenth-century Britain* (Oxford, Oxford University Press, 2005)

Borsay, P., *The English Urban Renaissance: Culture and Society in the Provincial Town, 1660–1770* (Oxford, Clarendon Press, 1989)

Borsay, P., *A History of Leisure* (Basingstoke, Palgrave Macmillan, 2006)

Clark, P. (ed.), *The Cambridge Urban History of Britain: Volume II 1540–1840* (Cambridge, Cambridge University Press, 2000)

Kent, S.K., *Gender and Power in Britain 1640–1990* (London, Routledge, 1999)

Langford, Paul, *A Polite and Commercial People* (Oxford, Oxford University Press, 1989)

Whatley, C.A., *Scottish Society, 1707–1830: Beyond Jacobitism towards Industrialisation* (Manchester, Manchester University Press, 2000)

5

The Enlightenment and gender

The nature of the Enlightenment

The Enlightenment was one of the defining developments of the modern world. It fostered the forms of reasoning in science and social science, created the possibilities of most modern ideologies, and promulgated the principles upon which government works today. The Enlightenment did much to make our world what it is. Its heritage is everywhere, not least in the way we study History and in the education system of Britain and most of the world – including colleges and universities. Much of the Enlightenment is associated with continental *philosophes*, especially from France (such as Rousseau, Voltaire, Montesquieu, Diderot and many others), and its influence grew in Britain as members of the British elites undertook the Grand Tour – visiting the continental centres of learning and antiquity. This increased British awareness of European ideas and literature. But at the same time, there were distinctive contributions to the Enlightenment from Britain.

The Enlightenment, at heart, was about knowledge – about expanding, verifying, and spreading human knowledge. The German philosopher Immanuel Kant gave the Enlightenment its best motto – *sapere aude* – dare to know! Daring was an apposite description, because knowledge was previously a restricted commodity, held in the hands of the Christian Church and perceived as God-given. The pre-1700 world had imposed restrictions on how far scientific and philosophical information could overturn the role of the divine, and on who might possess knowledge. The pre-modern European world had seen the dominance of the Christian Church, both Catholic and Protestant, over what constituted knowledge and, indeed, what knowledge could be accepted. There had been vetoes on the discoveries of astronomers and others about the nature of the solar system; Galileo had been under close criticism from the Papacy from 1616 for advocating heliocentrism (the theory that the earth orbited the sun, not vice versa, as was the orthodoxy), and was tried for heresy in 1633, ending up under house arrest until his death. The Enlightenment overturned this outlook: from around the 1660s there was mounting distrust of ecclesiastical authority and its role in censoring what was known, who knew it and even, in many countries, what books might be published. Theology and knowledge had been inextricably linked before 1650, and breaking this was the victory of the Enlightenment.

From the late seventeenth century, many thinkers, scientists, clerics and politicians across Europe were driven by a desire to establish knowledge on new foundations. There was a new concern for understanding based on facts – on empirically verifiable, provable facts, facts that could be supported with evidence and evidence alone, free from theology and divinity and the intervention of clergymen and of rulers who saw themselves as divinely elected. This movement was highly controversial, and there were major struggles in the seventeenth and early eighteenth centuries over Church interference in knowledge; this interference was especially strong in Scotland, where the power of the Church was considerable. But in the main, from 1700 there was clear evidence that a new approach to understanding the physical world was emerging. Superstition was being rejected as an answer to the known, seeable and touchable world. In a drive for facts, three key words emerged to characterise the movement of the Enlightenment – improvement, progress and reason. It became accepted that facts made it possible to improve society and the human condition, to progress European civilisation and government, and to use reason, based on facts, to extend forms of thinking founded on logic and deduction, not upon divinity and prayers. New institutions came into being. The Royal Society was established in London in 1662 as a centre 'for Improving Natural Knowledge', followed in 1731 by the Royal Dublin Society 'to promote and develop agriculture, arts, industry, and science in Ireland', and in 1783 by the Royal Society of Edinburgh for 'the advancement of learning and useful knowledge'. The acquisition of knowledge and application of reason were the aims of the new age of science and reason.

One of the major impacts of the Enlightenment was on political ideas. A leading light was the Englishman John Locke (1632–1704), who argued that all knowledge is the result of experience, including the knowledge of government. Government and rulers were not divine but man-made, forged by social experience. Government therefore had to be by a civil contract between rulers and the ruled. Locke wrote that reason 'teaches all mankind, who will but consult it, that being all equal and independent, no one ought to harm another in life, health, liberty and possessions'.[1] So a political society was a voluntary agreement to protect life and property. One of the foremost philosophers of the time, and arguably the best that Britain has ever produced, the Scot David Hume (1711–76), argued in modification of Locke that human society and government, and indeed the course of history, were not the products of reason but of

---

[1] J. Locke, *Two Treatises of Government* (orig. 1690, London, C. & J. Rivington, 1824), p. 133.

self-interest. Understanding self-interest and, indeed, managing the competing claims of groups and persons with conflicting self-interest, was the key to the well-ordered society. Hume's work covered more than this, including controversially denying the existence of God and the necessity for thinking of the human mind as in some way pre-mapped by a mind of God. His work has in many respects stood the test of time, and is much studied by philosophers today.

The Enlightenment also challenged the political order. It argued for the better ordering of the world on a rational basis. Government should be on rational principles, not on issues of divine order as in the thinking of the medieval world. This would, of course, upset the notion of the divine right of kings and the right of the aristocracy to rule over the rest of society. Herein lay the intellectual origins of notions of government behind the American Declaration of Independence (1776) and the French Revolution (1789), and that from the 1790s were called 'democratic'. For this reason, the Enlightenment had immense implications for the future of the political order all across the world, though initially in Europe and the United States.

For all its philosophical and political implications, the Enlightenment in Britain is probably most associated with scientific discovery and invention. One of the great scientists was Isaac Newton (1643–1727), best known to us for his development of ideas concerning forces – about actions and reactions, and about the nature of gravity (although that has remained a mystery ever since and is not fully explained even today). Newton exemplified the Enlightenment mind. He argued that everything was explicable in a rational way and there was no need to involve divine mystery or intervention to explain the current workings of the physical world. However, he did believe in the existence and supremacy of God in the creation of the universe and its laws, though he considered that human beings were masters of their own destiny, that nothing was pre-ordained in this world, and that we can change and remake the world as a better place. He believed in the development of a scientific method – indeed, he was a major contributor to understanding the way in which scientific method should work. As a definer of science as a system, he argued for the role of hypothesis or argument being followed by observation and experimentation, and thereby described scientific method as a movement to resolve the truth or falsity of any hypothesis. One major consequence of this was that scientific method became transferable to topics outside science itself – to social science and government policy – and this was one of the great legacies of the Enlightenment period.

In the wake of Newton came many other eighteenth-century scientists based in Britain who made great discoveries. Henry Cavendish (1731–1810) discovered hydrogen; Joseph Black (1728–99) discovered carbon dioxide; Joseph Priestley (1733–1804), a dissenting clergyman, discovered oxygen; Caroline Herschel (1750–1848) discovered many comets; and John Hutton (1726–97) virtually invented the science of geology by spending time examining strata, including on the Salisbury Crags seen from his window at the University of Edinburgh. A key characteristic of science in this era was the combination of developing theory with discovering practical application. Many inventions developed from first principles, and led to innovations in industry and the military, as well as in medicine, where great strides in knowledge of the human body were made. Universities, notably in Scotland, became centres of exploration and investigation of knowledge, expanding horizons of understanding at an electric pace. With all this scientific discovery came a clear challenge to religion – to the excesses of doctrine, violence and bigotry of the sixteenth and seventeenth centuries that had turned Europe upside down through the Reformation, Counter-Reformation and the great witch-hunts that had put so many people to death. There was a growth of moderation in religion, and of toleration of different viewpoints, and a growth of deism (or belief in a personal God detached from the physical world, which was governed by its own scientific laws). So, though science and religion did clash in some ways, in the main there was a movement to accommodate reason and faith through a separation of their spheres of intellectual influence.

An important change of the era was the increase in reading materials. New books and, especially, newspapers became more widely available and were greedily read by men and women of learning all over Britain. In the early eighteenth century came periodicals like Daniel Defoe's tri-weekly *A Review of the Affairs of France* (1704) and Richard Steele's *The Tatler* (1709), followed by Steele's and Joseph Addison's *The Spectator* (1711–12). Satire became an important form of pamphleteering and journalism, especially in the work of the Irishman Jonathan Swift (1667–1745), who set the standard for political writing in the early part of the century. Following periodicals and pamphlets came newspapers like Edinburgh's *Caledonian Mercury* (1736), the *Glasgow Journal* (1741), the *Aberdeen Journal* (1748), *The Times* of London (1788), and *The Observer* (1791). The French started a mania for listing knowledge in a cross-reference format, known as the *Encyclopédie* (its initial version was published in 28 volumes during 1751–72), followed by an Edinburgh-based version, the *Encyclopaedia Britannica* in 1768–71. This format proved to be enduringly popular, and forms the basis for online as well as print encyclopaedias in the twenty-first century. Through widening publications, the Enlightenment ensured that knowledge was accessible to all, and was not restricted by Church, government or elites. Its ideas led to a fashion for learning – for the creation of libraries and public lectures, for new societies for learning and debate, and, from the 1790s, for new institutions dedicated to the spread of access to knowledge for women and for artisans (notably in the mechanics' institutes of the 1820s).

The Enlightenment may have challenged the pre-medieval religious hold on knowledge, but it is too easy to characterise the emergence of the Enlightenment as an attack on religion. The advancement of science from the eighteenth century to the present was not a grand victory of reason over religion. For one thing, by the eighteenth century, the churches embraced the Enlightenment. Religious knowledge itself became more and more grounded on scientific rules of reasoning, and evidence-based argument became important in theology. More broadly, a rational Christianity became popular, in which it was felt that Christian doctrine and the Christian church should be put on a rational foundation commensurate with the facts of science. Science and religion had to be welded together in a way that permitted both to flourish. This was a movement with considerable support in the British Isles in the eighteenth century and beyond. Many clergymen of the Church of England, the Church of Scotland and the Church of Ireland became devoted followers of the Enlightenment, developing their own interests in scientific investigation – notably in areas such as archaeology, botany and wildlife. A good example is the Revd Gilbert White (1720–93), a Church of England vicar in Hampshire. His book based on his parish, *The Natural History and Antiquities of Selborne* (1789), gave a new understanding of ecology (including of his own garden) and the interaction between animals, plants and soil. White's diaries provide one of the earliest accounts of the emergence dates of plants and animal species during the year. Vicars, priests and ministers proved to be astute recorders, their diaries mimicking scientific laboratory books, and even used methods of scientific note-taking to record the effects of religious movements upon their parishioners.

In this way, the Enlightenment was not merely concerned with the advancement of a science narrowly defined, but with the extension of scientific method into new areas of human endeavour. Science had previously been something thought of in very limited terms, often determined by religious ideas. It had been about understanding metals and compounds, about the place of man at the centre of the universe, and about the power of man over all other species. But the Enlightenment extended the meaning of science to cover the study of humankind as a science. Alexander Pope (1688–1744), poet, essayist, satirist and translator, stated that 'the proper study of mankind is man'. This reflected the growing interest in using scientific method to study humankind. This was the beginnings of social science, of the subjects of sociology, social history and psychology. For example, Thomas Malthus (1766–1834), another Church of England parson, made a famous prediction that population growth could outrun food supply, meaning that 'premature death must in some shape or other visit the human race'.[2] This is a forecast that has haunted science ever since, cautioning us about any expectation of endless expansion of world resources. Other clergy explored the impact of industrialisation and urbanisation upon human behaviour. Among them was a Church of Scotland minister, Thomas Chalmers (1780–1847), who predicted the possibility of the breakdown of law and order amongst the very poor of industrial communities. In these ways, the Enlightenment opened up the study of the modern human world.

The most highly developed and enduring of the studies of social science was the work of the Scottish philosopher, economist and friend of David Hume, Adam Smith (1723–90). Smith was a lecturer in philosophy at the University of Glasgow, and moved the world of philosophy into the practical world of government and economies. His most famous book was *The Wealth of Nations* (1776), which today is for many right-wing economists and politicians the bible of the free market system, whilst for others it represents a balanced understanding of the principles of economic and social relations.

---

[2] T. Malthus, *An Essay on the Principle of Population . . . volume 2* (orig. 1798, Washington DC, Weightman, 1809 edn), p. 74.

In it, Smith accepted Hume's arguments about the motivation of self-interest and described economies as operating according to principles of competition. Individual entrepreneurs worked through self-interest and yet, 'led by an invisible hand', they promoted unintentionally the public interest of increased wealth. This worked best when government interfered as little as possible in the process. Through his description, he made the study of economics akin to the study of science, with the same interest in observation and measurement, and laid down an argument (which became hotly disputed) that the free market is morally neutral. Smith wrote in another book that the rich 'consume little more than the poor; and in spite of their natural selfishness and rapacity, though they mean only their own conveniency, . . . they divide with the poor the produce of all their improvements'.[3] In essence, he described the operation of the free market as an economic system that operated much like a scientific system. There were laws of economics which, if allowed to develop, created greater efficiency, productivity and new wealth (and did not merely steal wealth from others), fostering a spread of income and happiness throughout a population. Smith argued that the way in which industry and commerce improved was through the expansion of production and the creation of new markets. This involved using new techniques, dividing up the process of production into specialist work, and reducing the need for skilled labour so that all might be employed in unskilled work. He described essentially what was then happening in Britain in the 1770s, and about to expand tremendously in the Industrial Revolution – namely, the subdivision of the process of production.

Focus on

Adam Smith

Adam Smith suggested that at the root of the improvement in productivity in manufacturing lay the subdivision of labour. In his *Wealth of Nations* (1776), he argued his case from the manufacture of the simplest product imaginable – the pin. He noted that 'a workman not educated to this business (which the division of labour has rendered a distinct trade), nor acquainted with the use of the machinery employed in it (to the invention of which the same division of labour has probably given occasion), could scarce, perhaps, with his utmost industry, make one pin in a day, and certainly could not make twenty'. But in the modernised industry, even of the 1770s, he noted how the work has become 'a peculiar trade':

[I]n the way in which this business is now carried on, not only the whole work is a peculiar trade, but it is divided into a number of branches, of which the greater part

---

[3] Adam Smith, *The Theory of Moral Sentiments* (London, Bohn, 1853), pp. 264–5.

are likewise peculiar trades. One man draws out the wire, another straights it, a third cuts it, a fourth points it, a fifth grinds it at the top for receiving the head; to make the head requires two or three distinct operations; to put it on, is a peculiar business, to whiten the pins is another; it is even a trade by itself to put them into the paper; and the important business of making a pin is, in this manner, divided into about eighteen distinct operations, which, in some manufactories, are all performed by distinct hands, though in others the same man will sometimes perform two or three of them. I have seen a small manufactory of this kind where ten men only were employed, and where some of them consequently performed two or three distinct operations. But though they were very poor, and therefore but indifferently accommodated with the necessary machinery, they could, when they exerted themselves, make among them about twelve pounds of pins in a day. There are in a pound upwards of four thousand pins of a middling size. Those ten persons, therefore, could make among them upwards of forty-eight thousand pins in a day. Each person, therefore, making a tenth part of forty-eight thousand pins, might be considered as making four thousand eight hundred pins in a day. But if they had all wrought separately and independently, and without any of them having been educated to this peculiar business, they certainly could not each of them have made twenty, perhaps not one pin in a day; that is, certainly, not the two hundred and fortieth, perhaps not the four thousand eight hundredth part of what they are at present capable of performing, in consequence of a proper division and combination of their different operations.

The result was increased efficiency and output. Smith also argued that individual freedom was not only an economic necessity but a political one too. He argued that the end of regulations of wages and prices, the end of craft controls over who could enter the professions, would lead to a more efficient economy.

Source: A. Smith, *An Inquiry into the Nature and Causes of the Wealth of Nations* (orig. 1776, London, Methuen, 1904 edn). Online version http://econlib.org/library/Smith/smWN1.html, book I, chapter 1, para. 3.

The Enlightenment was immensely influential. It affected the way in which the world was perceived, how knowledge and debate were approached, and how the political system was to be changed. It created much reaction in British religion. One was the rise of evangelicalism in Christianity – characterised by conversionism that changed lives, activism in evangelism, biblicism in holding to Scripture, and crucicentrism which stressed Christ's sacrifice on the cross. John Wesley in England was influential in his foundation of the Methodists who, more than any other group, assisted the spread of evangelicalism in the later eighteenth century. There were political reactions to the Enlightenment. It generated debate amongst conservatives like Edmund Burke, who argued that most people were not rational but that good government came from experience, tradition and stability (see Chapter 11). And the

Enlightenment provoked a reaction amongst those who saw it as too rational, too scientific and thus too lacking in soul and feeling; this was the romantic movement of the early nineteenth century, exemplified in the romantic poetry and novels of William Wordsworth (1770–1850), Lord Byron (1788–1824), Percy Bysshe Shelley (1792 –1822), John Keats (1795–1821), Sir Walter Scott (1771–1832) and Charlotte Brontë (1816–55). The romantic movement was to colour the British reaction to the Enlightenment and the rise of industry; it was preoccupied with a sense of the unknowable, the sublime, and conduct divorced from discipline and constant method. This romantic reaction to science was to become a permanent feature of British culture.

The greatest political consequence of the Enlightenment was the rise of liberalism – the belief in a liberal economy with a political system that allowed what we now call democracy to foster invention, happiness and the progress of society at large. Liberalism emerged from the Enlightenment to cultivate the power of reason and rational debate within political life – to come up with solutions to social and political problems. Liberalism held it as a self-evident ideal that freedom for the individual was good, and that the role of government should be kept to the minimum. Religion was still important to liberalism, though. Religion was necessary to sustain the morality of the individual by internal discipline and self-control, and for the good order of society at large. But religion should be tolerant, moderate, personal and principled. It should not be intolerant, bigoted and divisive.

The Enlightenment casts a very long shadow over modern Britain, from 1700 to the present. It is virtually impossible to reject the advances in knowledge, and in the ways of thinking about knowledge, that the thinkers of the eighteenth century started. But it is worth observing that in the twentieth and twenty-first centuries there has been a reaction to the Enlightenment even stronger than that of the romantic movement. In art and literature, there have been those who criticised the obsession with science, progress and reality that the Enlightenment created. It has been criticised as being Eurocentric in its view of knowledge and ways of thinking about the world in general, and as marginalising the achievements in knowledge of other civilisations and nations (notably from Africa, the Arab world, India and China). For some, the Enlightenment was white-centric, promulgating a view of the world within which racism was sustained and intellectualised in the British Empire and its suppression of native peoples. It was seen, in short, to commend and admire a European vision of science, society and economics that was overwhelmingly white, Christian and male. Indeed, it was in its impact upon relations between men and women that the Enlightenment was to have one of its most immediate consequences within British society.

The Enlightenment and gender

From 1700 to the present the Enlightenment has played a significant part in influencing changes in male–female relations in British life, in their respective rights, and in the nature of marriage. Gender change was not instigated by the Enlightenment alone, as powerful economic and cultural factors were at work. Yet, Enlightenment writers debated a great deal about the nature of the roles held by men and women, and this was to influence lawmakers and society.

Until 1735, witchcraft was still a criminal offence in Scotland: Janet Horne, the last 'witch' to be executed in Britain, was burned to death at Dornoch in 1727 for allegedly turning her daughter into a pony. This was a final remnant of how, for more than two centuries before that, Europe had vilified mainly women as guilty of entering pacts with the devil. This represented a wider understanding that women, much more than men, were inherently capable of social disorder, of disrupting the smooth running of families, and of needing special supervision and scrutiny. Without restraint, women could cause immense social damage and the corruption of children. They needed to be constantly 'tamed', and the responsibility for that rested with fathers and husbands, backed up by church courts and, if necessary, by the civil state. Women were characterised as socially and even spiritually inferior to men. This outlook still lingered into the early eighteenth century and, far from being quickly overturned by Enlightenment thought, it was to be cemented into aspects of British law.

Men in the early eighteenth century justified their political power *as men* from ideals of virtue. Religious piety was exemplified in manhood, and a man was judged on his ability to control the morally and emotionally dangerous passions of womanhood. Landed property allowed men to express their independence from state or other patronage and, since ownership of land was severely restricted to men (and in England was legally a man's alone in marriage), this made citizenship and virtue itself masculine qualities. To be in debt, for instance, was a shameful state, and one associated in popular culture with feminine qualities. Daniel Defoe, author of the famous novel *Robinson Crusoe*, likened having financial credit to being an irrational woman: 'This is a coy Lass . . . If once she be disoblig'd [offended], she's the most difficult to be Friends again with us.'[4] This linked to the notion that a man who spent too much time in women's company would weaken his masculinity – in the sense that the sensibilities and pleasures of women would undermine men's strength and ability to order society. Even to be active in commercial affairs in the early eighteenth century was felt to court weakness. There was a danger that, being represented as a female passion, commercialism might alienate men who feared loss of traditional masculinity. Indeed, it was because women were so important as consumers in the century, and helped to fuel the early commercial revolution, that masculinity was conceived as the antithesis of commerce and consumption. Pleasures were located in feminine culture, fostered by social events of all sorts, and broadcast by novels – a creation of the century that from the start (as still today) appealed more to women than to men.

Early in the century, it was difficult for men to lead a commercial life without being thought touched by feminine qualities. But this changed. The passion of commerce was reconceived by philosophers and economists of the era like David Hume and

---

[4] Quoted in S.K. Kent, *Gender and Power in Britain 1640–1990* (London, Routledge, 1999), p. 58.

Adam Smith into a system – an economic machine that operated according to masculine laws and order. Women's role in commerce, so great in the expansion of consumption in the century, was increasingly displaced, with women's tasks being linked to the home rather than to the world of commerce. Women took on significance as the source of new qualities – a capacity for sympathy, gentleness, submissiveness to men, and as home-makers. A popular guide to female manners of 1765 said that women should 'expect to command by obeying . . . and by yielding to conquer'.[5] These virtues were no better attested in the eighteenth century than by the memorial stones to rich women, which spoke at length of these new qualities in womanhood. Phrases such as 'amiable and virtuous wife' recur in memorials of the period. A good example is the memorial stone to a woman who died in 1760 in Galway City, on which it was said of her:

> She was a loving and obedient Wife, a careful and indulgent Mother, affable and courteous to her Acquaintance. Her *Piety, Prudence* and well-disposed *Bounty* to the Poor, Giving Bread to the Hungry and Cloathing the Naked made her a worthy Example to her Sex.[6]

This shows how a switch was under way in the eighteenth century, from virtue being masculine to being feminine. The French philosopher Jean-Jacques Rousseau popularised this shift in his widely read novel *Emile* (1762) in which the role he advocated for women was exemplified in classical Greece:

> As soon as Greek women married they were no longer seen in public. Within the four walls of their home they devoted themselves to the care of their household and family. This is the mode of life prescribed for the female sex both by nature and by reason. These women gave birth to the healthiest, strongest, and best proportioned men who ever lived, and except in certain islands of ill repute, no women in the whole world, not even the Roman matrons, were ever at once so wise and so charming, so beautiful and so virtuous, as the women of ancient Greece.[7]

Feminine virtue was located in domestic roles as daughter, wife and mother – what has come to be known as the ideology of separate spheres. In this process, women's work outside the home became, in bourgeois sensibilities, increasingly frowned upon; work corrupted women's virtue. So, even if Rousseau assisted the Enlightenment to rehabilitate women in both intellectual and public regard from being naturally troublesome to being naturally virtuous, he did not advocate equality between the sexes. On the contrary, he believed that men and women were fundamentally different, suiting each

---

[5] Quoted in S.K. Kent, *Gender and Power in Britain 1640–1990* (London, Routledge, 1999), p. 69.

[6] St Nicholas Church, Galway City.

[7] J.J. Rousseau, *Emile, or On Education* (1762), trans. G. Roosevelt, Book 5, para 1286, accessed at http://projects.ilt.columbia.edu/pedagogies/rousseau

to the opposing spheres of the world of work and that of domesticity. In essence, Rousseau believed girls were born to please men and their education should prepare them for this task. Rousseau distinguished the male hero from his wife Sophie:

> Sophie's mind is pleasing but not brilliant, and thorough but not deep; it is the sort of mind which calls for no remark, as she never seems cleverer or stupider than oneself . . . her mind has been formed not only by reading, but by conversation with her father and mother, by her own reflections, and by her own observations in the little world in which she has lived . . . In a word, she endures patiently the wrong-doing of others, and she is eager to atone for her own. This amiability is natural to her sex when unspoiled. Woman is made to submit to man and to endure even injustice at his hands.[8]

From this Rousseau argued that a woman's education should be planned in relation to a man – to make her 'pleasing in his sight, to win his respect and love, to train him in childhood, to tend him in manhood, to counsel and console, to make his life pleasant and happy, these are the duties of woman for all time, and this is what she should be taught while she is young'. This view was to be challenged by some people from the 1790s, but it was to dominate European culture for most of the next two centuries, becoming embedded in the institutions, the law, the education system and the intellectual life of virtually all western countries.

The empowerment of women in ideals of piety and domesticity did little, perhaps nothing significant, to create gender equality. Men remained privileged in law, career and institutional control. What the Enlightenment did was to intellectualise such gender inequality, including in the law. The English legal scholar William Blackstone offered a commentary on marriage in 1756 that was to codify existing presumptions and provide a moral basis for the continued legal subjugation of women. His commentary became much quoted in legal judgments. He wrote: 'By marriage, the husband and wife are one person in law; that is the very being or legal existence of the woman is suspended during the marriage, or at least incorporated and consolidated into that of the husband; under whose wing, protection and *cover*, she performs everything.' His approach reinforced the notion of the *femme covert* – meaning that a woman was protected by a husband – a simple yet profound concept that was to have far-reaching consequences. In this approach, a married woman did not possess an independent legal existence. She was taken to be part of the property of her husband, implying that she was both a possession of his and that he had the unstoppable opportunity to abuse her. Blackstone wrote: 'The husband also (by the old law) might give his wife moderate correction. For, as he is to answer for her misbehaviour, the law thought it reasonable to intrust him with the power of restraining her, by domestic chastisement.' Thus it was that, until the late twentieth century, there was no concept in law of rape within marriage and, more broadly, there was little legal restraint upon a husband's abuse of his wife. Only in the extreme cases of major physical injury or murder was a man to be

---

[8] Ibid.

held to account in practice for his actions towards a wife. This harsh and seemingly barbaric legal view was, in the eighteenth-century context, seen as enlightened and eminently self-evident. Blackstone himself wrote: 'These are the chief legal effects of marriage during the coverture [a husband's protection of a wife]; upon which we may observe, that even the disabilities which the wife lies under, are for the most part intended for her protection and benefit. So great a favourite is the female sex of the laws of England.'[9]

If gender inequality became cemented in codified laws produced by the Enlightenment, scientific and medical discovery had much the same effect. The eighteenth century witnessed a change in the way the female body was understood. As science replaced church understandings, a woman's body was not seen as derivative of man's body (as in the Christian Bible, which stated that Eve was born of Adam's rib), but as a different body and a site of different qualities. Anatomical understanding grew in the century through medical dissection, and through this it became ever more clear that women's bodies were constructed in very different ways from men's. The notion that a woman's reproductive capacity dominated her mind was taken seriously by some in the medical profession, so that women's so-called nervous complaints – often labelled 'hysteria' – were treated as if they were the result of a malfunction of the womb rather than the consequence of boredom, restraining corsets or post-natal depression. The 'rest cure' of seclusion and a denial of stimulants of all kinds from reading to exercise was popular treatment in some quarters. But some renegade doctors offered more interventionist cures, including hysterectomy (removal of the uterus or womb). Generally, a woman's mental and physical health was seen as dependent on her menstrual cycle; she was a prisoner of her reproductive functions. In this way, the Enlightenment's medical revolution was double-edged for women; on the one hand, it affirmed women were physiologically different from men, yet, on the other, new medical knowledge justified women's difference and weakness.

If the Enlightenment was used to justify female subordination on legal and medical foundations, the popular conduct books of the period placed greater emphasis on women and men having mutual respect within marriage. One author of 1846 recommended that marriage should resemble a 'limited monarchy', but recognised that 'marriage was never intended to be a state of subservience for women . . . the very word "union" implies a degree of equality'.[10] Separate spheres for men and women were being forged in the culture of ideals. Men's role in the world was one of order and economic affairs, whilst women's was in the home. Hundreds of thousands of plebeian women went out to work, and played a leading role in the Industrial Revolution. But in the middle ranks of society, work for wages outside of the home was severely criticised. Women's industriousness was devalued in favour of women's motherhood.

---

[9] William Blackstone's *Commentaries on the Laws of England* can be searched at http://www.yale.edu/lawweb/avalon/blackstone/blacksto.htm

[10] Quoted in R.B. Shoemaker, *Gender in English Society 1650–1850* (London, Pearson Education, 1998), p. 102.

Women's work became negatively portrayed in polite society, and from this was to emerge the concept of the ideal woman as an angel in the house.

In this way, the eighteenth century witnessed one of the most important gender changes of any period. From being pious, virtuous and independent, ideal masculinity was recast as open to moral temptation and needing the moral stability of domestic femininity. From being morally dangerous, with a piety inferior to men's, ideal femininity was reshaped in the image of the angel in the house, free from worldly distraction. In the nineteenth century, these separate spheres were to be further cemented in the social and civic fabric of British society.

Further reading

Hyland, P. with O. Gomez and F. Greensides (eds), *The Enlightenment: A Sourcebook and Reader* (London, Routledge, 2003)

Kent, S.K., *Gender and Power in Britain 1640–1990* (London, Routledge, 1999)

Munck, T., *The Enlightenment: A Comparative Social History 1721–1794* (London, Hodder & Arnold, 2000)

Porter, R., *Enlightenment: Britain and the Creation of the Modern World*, 2nd edn (Harmondsworth, Penguin, 2001)

Porter, R., *The Enlightenment* (Basingstoke, Palgrave Macmillan, 2001)

Shoemaker, R.B., *Gender in English Society 1650–1850* (London, Longman, 1998)

6

The British abroad

These decades saw both the rise of Britain to the pre-eminent imperial nation and the loss of a major part of an older empire. The developments of this period were to lay the basis for British supremacy as a world power. What started as a search for markets and raw materials was transformed into pressure for a control of territory. What happened in remote corners of the globe was increasingly a two-way process affected by what was happening in British politics but also profoundly influencing these politics.

Early imperial expansion

The process of expansion had begun much earlier than 1700. A great deal of sixteenth-century English effort was devoted to seeking a northern route to China, the fabled land of Cathay. In 1577 the English pirate, Drake, found his way to the East Indies by way of Cape Horn, becoming the first Englishman to circumnavigate the globe. A starting point for empire is generally taken as 1583, when the island of Newfoundland was claimed. England had incorporated Ireland with difficulty and brutality into its empire by the early seventeenth century. Cromwell's army had crushed resistance in 1649, decimated the population and left the way open for English and Scottish settlers to colonise. Elsewhere, the pressure of colonial settlement came from commercial companies. From the early seventeenth century, colonies had been established by English settlers in Virginia and in Massachusetts, some encouraged by hopes of trade, others, like the Pilgrims who arrived in the *Mayflower* at Cape Cod in 1620, seeking religious freedom. There were already Dutch and Swedish settlements, but in 1664 the Dutch surrendered New Amsterdam to the English and the colony in time became New York. The 1680s saw the creation of yet another colony at Pennsylvania by the Quaker, William Penn and, further south, between Virginia and the Spanish settlements in Florida, a charter was granted to various proprietors to develop what were called the Carolinas. Settlements were not confined to the mainland of North America. Colonies were established in Bermuda, Barbados, Nevis, Antigua and Montserrat in the 1620s and 1630s. Jamaica was seized from the Spanish in 1655.

By the 1640s, sugar was replacing tobacco as the key crop in Barbados. The back-breaking work of sugar production could not be met by native labour and, increasingly, the West Indies became dependent on indentured labour, by which some-one was bound to a master for a specific length of time in return for shelter, clothing and food, and on imported black slaves, who were bound for life. The first African slaves had arrived in Virginia in 1619. By the second half of the seventeenth century, black slavery was a central feature of Caribbean and North American society. It has been calculated that, over the next two centuries, something like two million Africans were imported into North America and the Caribbean, where life expectancy was short and a constant renewal of supplies was necessary. British shipowners, who shipped half the slaves across the Atlantic, thrived on the lucrative trade that encom-passed Spanish America as well as the British Empire.

By the second half of the seventeenth century, the English became more predatory and exclusive towards European rivals. Navigation laws from the 1650s laid down that all colonial products had to be transported in English ships. This was not only about achieving a monopoly of trade, but it also ensured a pool of trained seamen who could be utilised by the navy in time of war. Sugar millionaires from the West Indies and the Nabobs of the East India Company were assimilated into landed society and formed powerful pressure groups to defend their interests. The exclusion of the Scots from these fruits of empire helped precipitate the Union of 1707.

Despite its transatlantic interests, Britain remained a European power, pulled into conflict with France by William III and into central European struggles by the arrival of the Hanoverians. The prospect of eventual unification of the crowns of France and Spain led to British entry into the War of the Spanish Succession against France in May 1702. The military skills of the Duke of Marlborough at Blenheim in 1704 helped to drive the French out of the German states. At Ramillies, in 1706, the French advance in the Netherlands was halted. A further victory at Oudenarde in 1708 did not, however, lead to an advance into France and a speedy end to the conflict and, despite tentative peace overtures, the war dragged on. Eventually, war weariness led to a change of government in Britain and the abandonment of the Dutch and other allies in 1713.

The war had provided opportunities for territorial expansion and produced a debate over strategy. Should Britain be involved in battles in continental Europe which were largely about defending and advancing Dutch interests against France? Or should Britain be concentrating on what was called a 'blue water' strategy of building up naval supremacy and concentrating on defending and expanding trade routes and markets? Increasingly, the tendency was to lean to the latter. Gibraltar was seized from Spain in 1704, Menorca in 1708, thus allowing the navy to blockade the French and

Spanish coasts and protect and foster Britain's commercial interests in the Mediterranean. British armies moved into the French territories in America, and French Acadia became the new British province of Nova Scotia.

By the Treaty of Utrecht of 1713, Britain secured firm control of Hudson Bay and of Newfoundland. More significant than either of these was the grant to Britain of the *asiento*, the right to supply the Spanish colonies in South America with 4,800 slaves per year. Free trade in slaves replaced the monopoly once held by the Royal Africa Company. This necessitated strong West African bases as places for trading with the indigenous slave merchants. Cloth, alcohol and arms were traded for slaves, and the slave ships returned from the West Indies and South America with sugar, rum and tobacco. By 1730 Britain was the world's major slave trader, taking around 45,000 slaves a year from Africa. The wealth of London, Bristol and later Liverpool became increasingly dependent upon the slave trade.

Attitudes to empire were shaped by what the political economist Adam Smith called the 'mercantile system' or 'mercantilism'. This assumed that national power came from increased wealth in the shape of gold and silver bullion and by maintaining a favourable balance of trade. It was assumed that the world's supply of raw materials and its markets were finite and that the most successful nation would ensure that it obtained the greatest share of these resources at the expense of rivals. Prosperity would increase through maximising foreign, rather than domestic, trade and, therefore, as many trading outposts as possible needed to be acquired, to the exclusion of rivals. The Navigation Laws and the granting of monopolies of trade to chartered trading companies were all part of the same thinking. As Smith complained in *The Wealth of Nations* in 1776, 'nations have been taught that their interest consisted in beggaring all their neighbours'.

Marauding on Spanish possessions and even more extensive smuggling were carried on by British merchants, desperate to penetrate the lucrative markets of the Spanish Empire in the Americas. The seizure of British ships by the Spanish authorities regularly led to tensions between the two countries and in the 1720s there was, to all intents, an undeclared war between Britain and Spain, with Gibraltar under lengthy siege. For a decade and more, pamphleteers called for the renewal of war with Spain and opposition politicians took up the cry. The apparent excising of the ear of one such privateer, Robert Jenkins, by Spanish coastguards in 1731 provided a suitable excuse for further attempts to undermine the Spanish Empire.

Seven years after the supposed incident, encouraged by the immensely wealthy West India merchant, William Beckford MP, Jenkins produced his ear, pickled in brandy, before a House of Commons Committee and helped stir a war-fever against Spain. William Pitt led the call for a vigorous defence of British trading interests. War was presented as being about British freedom of the seas against Spanish oppression. Pitt held out the prospect of Britain becoming a world power. He offered a vision of an expanding commercial empire in the western hemisphere. But the story of the war was rather one of defeat and humiliation, with little gained in the way of territory and hundreds of soldiers dead from fever in the West Indies. Thomas Arne's *Rule Britannia* with Britain 'ruling the waves' was timely but inaccurate when performed before the Prince of Wales in 1740. Britain was, as yet, far from dominant.

Yet another war of succession broke out in 1740, this time over the Austrian throne. Pitt declaimed against going to war only for the good of the 'despicable Electorate' of Hanover and called for a wider attack on France and Spain, using Britain's increasing naval dominance. A French victory at Fontenoy in May 1745, coupled with Jacobite rebellion at home, ended British involvement on the European continent. The Duke of Cumberland was recalled to crush the Jacobite army at Culloden.

Despite the peace settlements, clashes between the British and French, with their amerindian allies, continued on the frontiers of America. The renewal of wider conflict was only a matter of time. The Seven Years' War (1756–63), with some justification regarded as the first global war, was more productive of results, although it began badly with the capture by the French of Menorca, the main British base in the Mediterranean. The result was the execution by firing squad of Admiral Byng – not, as Voltaire had it, *pour encourager les autres*, but to mollify a popular outcry against the government and the ruling aristocratic order, increasingly criticised for being profligate with the nation's resources and steeped in 'unmanly luxury'. The demand was for manly heroes, not for shrewd tacticians, like Byng, who knew when attack was futile. French ports were blockaded with only limited success and French squadrons were able to break out. Early assaults on French West Indian possessions were generally repulsed. The Duke of Newcastle's government was attacked bitterly by Pitt for committing Britain to war on the continent at the cost of potential imperial gains.

In this war, Britain and Hanover were lined up alongside the rising power of Prussia against France and Austria. Frederick the Great of Prussia was presented as a Protestant hero fighting for the preservation of Protestantism in the German states and, thanks to Frederick's remarkable victories, the French advance was stemmed and the tide gradually began to turn. The British and Hanoverians were victorious at Minden in Westphalia in August 1759 and, within days, Admiral Boscowen, off the coast of Southern Portugal, had destroyed the French Mediterranean fleet, intended for an invasion of Britain. A few months later, Admiral Hawke smashed half the French Channel fleet in a stormy Quiberon Bay in Britanny. The British navy had, to all intents, secured control of the Atlantic, thus ensuring that reinforcements could not be sent to the French in North America. The British now became masters of the Caribbean, gaining Dominica, Grenada, St Vincent and Tobago, and turned to North America.

Canada

French settlers were well-established along the St Lawrence River in Canada from early in the seventeenth century. Further south, they controlled the area of Louisiana and were trying to link the two by controlling the Ohio valley. Around Hudson's Bay, there were British fur traders. Small skirmishes between the French and British, using local Indian tribes as proxies, went on intermittently. By the mid-eighteenth century, the French in the St Lawrence were seen as an irritating blockage to linking British possessions along the whole east coast of North America, and their activities further west were seen as a barrier to western expansion.

Initially, the French were successful in resisting British advance but, by 1758, the tide had turned and the British began to gain control of forts. The capture of Louisbourg, the strongest French fort in the New World, which commanded the mouth of the St Lawrence River, opened the way. French-Canadian opposition on both sides of the St Lawrence was met with brutality, the burning of farms, the locking up of inhabitants and the scalping of those Indians who had sided with the French. The efficient, if neurotic, James Wolfe, with a successful military career on the battle-fields of mainland Europe and at Culloden behind him, was able to capture Quebec in 1759. Montreal surrendered a year later and all of French Canada passed into British hands.

With the Treaty of Paris in 1763, the French ceded to Britain all their territory east of the Mississippi, having already ceded territories west of the Mississippi to Spain. The Spanish had already handed control of Florida to the British in return for the restoration of Havana. Settlers began to expand westwards beyond the Appalachian mountains from the 13 colonies. But this was a new empire – a territorial empire and not just a sea empire. It also brought in a new French-speaking population. Before then, there had been an assumption in the rhetoric that the Empire was about free-born Britons living overseas. Now there was an empire that contained a growing number of non-British settlers alongside the indigenous population. It was an empire that was scattered across the world and, as the Duke of Newcastle said, ministers had now to 'consider the whole globe'.

The territorial gains from the Seven Years' War opened up immense opportunities for merchants, shipowners, administrators, soldiers, speculators and settlers. The Scots were among the most avid at seizing these opportunities. The expanded army had proved an attraction for Scottish Highlanders, Pitt's 'intrepid race of men' from 'the mountains of the North'. After decades of simmering hostility to the 1707 Union, increasing reconciliation can be seen from the 1750s, as the gains of Union become more apparent and widespread. The most lucrative honey-pot was in the East.

India

In India, commercial competition between France and Britain was underway by the end of the seventeenth century, with the East India Company, which had operated in India since the early seventeenth century, being challenged by the *Compagnie des Indes Orientales*. The main settlements where the East India Company had a presence were Bombay (now Mumbai), Madras (now Chennai) and Calcutta (now Kolkata). From these, cotton cloth was exported to meet a growing British demand for cheap, washable fabrics. The Mughal domination of India was beginning to disintegrate, with local governors increasingly asserting their independence. This encouraged the rival trading companies to interfere in Indian politics and to court the states that were emerging from the break-up of the Mughal Empire. In their turn, local rulers were willing to work with Europeans to aid their struggles with rivals and with the Mughals. European companies were also able to take advantage of internal divisions within many states where new commercial elites were arising to challenge the old military orders. The very presence of Europeans created instability. Servants of the East India Company engaged in private trade with Indian merchants, often playing off one group of merchants against another, evading customs duties and undermining the authority of existing rulers who once had the monopoly on such items as tobacco and opium.

The wars in Europe brought armed conflict between the armies of the French and British companies, but it also brought direct government involvement, with troops and ships being sent to the East. Success went to the British when, by 1754, Robert Clive had effectively gained control of southern India. The seizure of Calcutta in 1756 by the Nawab of Bengal, Suraj-ud-daula, who, with French backing, was trying to reassert his authority over different elites of merchant-bankers, landowners and military factions, met with very little resistance. It led to the imprisonment of some European residents. In the excessive heat and confined space, anything from 18 to 43 of them died. When accounts reached London many months later, the figures had become exaggerated to as high as 250 and an English woman had been added to the victims of the 'Black Hole of Calcutta'. Yet the events aroused only limited popular interest in Britain and it was only in the Victorian period that this incident was raised into a key moment on the road to empire.[1]

Clive was despatched from Madras on Royal Navy ships to reassert British prestige in Bengal and to guard European investments. At Plassey in 1757, Clive's forces, at the cost of only 18 of his troops, overwhelmed an Indian force of nearly 50,000 and drove French influence from Bengal. A satellite ruler was installed, but Clive became the *Diwan*, the collector of revenue, emerging as a skilful manipulator of divisions within the Bengali elites. In 1765 the East India Company took direct rule over Bengal, with Clive as governor.

There was a blurring of the distinction between what was East India Company business and responsibility and what were national state concerns. Regular British regiments combined with the Company's Indian forces to extend control over various Indian states. Pitt had wanted to bring all the Company territories under British Crown sovereignty, but was blocked in the Cabinet. From 1767, the Company was required to make an annual contribution of £400,000 to the national exchequer, much of it used to buy out foreign creditors of the national debt. But territorial control also brought administrative costs and, coupled with a disastrous famine in Bengal in 1769–70, there was near-complete collapse of the Company. The rising costs led to attempts to get Indian rulers to fund the Company's army. When that did not happen, there was yet more pressure for direct intervention and annexation.

The period until the 1780s was one when many of the British were full of admiration for the brilliant culture that they discovered in both Islamic and Hindu India.

---

[1] Linda Colley, *Captives: Britain Empire and the World 1600–1850* (New York, Anchor Books, 2004), p. 255.

There was a considerable amount of intermarriage between senior British officers and administrators and Indian women. Hindu and Islamic customs and law were sustained in British-supervised courts. Nevertheless, there were many who had reservations about the impact on Britain of imperial expansion. Those who returned from India from the middle ranks of society but with lavish wealth, the so-called 'Nabobs' like Clive, were seen as having a corrupting influence on British politics and society. There was a feeling that many of the successes in India involved moral corruption and military despotism. Clive, suffering growing criticism over how his fortune had been acquired, eventually committed suicide. Chatham in 1770 talked of the riches of Asia pouring into Britain, but warned that 'Asiatic luxury' was bringing 'Asiatic principles of government'. In return for a loan to the East India Company to save it from collapse, in a remarkable intrusion into the rights of a private, chartered company, the Regulation Act of 1773 required a measure of political control. Warren Hastings, who became Governor of Bengal in 1772, became the first crown-appointed Governor-General in 1774. Hastings resisted schemes to impose English law on the Indian states, but attitudes towards indigenous cultures gradually changed as the century moved to its close. Hastings was to pay the price of these concerns and for offending powerful interests within the Company, with an investigation and trial that spread over more than a decade.

This territorial expansion was driven not by the prestige that came from controlling territory but by the prestige and power that came from trade. Increasingly, Britain presented itself as the greatest trading nation. The largest markets remained those in continental Europe, but the growth areas in the early eighteenth century were in the Empire (see Chapter 4). Anything beyond trade was seen as alien and there were considerable fears that the expansion of empire would have a corrupting influence at home. Thanks to a classical education, empire was suspect. Had not imperial expansion eventually corrupted and destroyed the noble values of the Roman Republic? This was particularly the case with expansion in the East. The initial reaction, well into the eighteenth century, was to be wary of too much involvement with the Orient. It was presented as excessively luxurious, as sensual and effeminate and, therefore, a threat to Protestant virtue.

It was in these years that images of the Orient, stretching through the Arab world to India and China, began to enter the popular imagination. The Qur'an (Koran) was translated into English in 1734 and studies of Islamic culture and of Oriental languages began to appear. The Arabic folk tales, *One Thousand and One Nights*, were translated into English from a French compilation in the early eighteenth century and were merely one of many translations and fictional accounts which generated a sense of the exotically different East. An increasing number of travel accounts looked at the East through the prism of these tales and detected despotism and brutality alongside hedonism and sensuality. The argument was that the exceptionalist nature of the British, their inherent love of freedom, meant that they should not conquer other people, but merely form trading links with them. If they did conquer, then they, in time, would be corrupted. But, if the arguments of Edward Said's highly influential study, *Orientalism* (1978), are accepted, it is in these years of the eighteenth century that the image of the Orient as 'the other', the contrast with the West, emerges and the ground was being laid for the eventual domination of the East.

The Pacific

The Pacific also became a centre of attraction and shaped attitudes. The Dutch, Spanish and French had been there earlier, but the first serious British encounter with the Pacific was John Byron's voyage in 1764, after claiming the Falkland Islands in passing. Distance had always been a great obstacle to Pacific exploration, but the mastering of the task of measuring longitude by means of Nevil Maskelyne's naval almanac and John Harrison's chronometer meant that exact positioning was possible. A recognition that scurvy was a dietary problem also reduced the death toll among seamen that long voyages had always occasioned.

It was the voyages of Captain James Cook that brought the Pacific firmly into public consciousness. During his first voyage of 1768–71, he circumnavigated New Zealand and observed the west coast of Australia before continuing round the world. During the voyage not a single one of his crew was lost through scurvy, thanks to the mixture of sauerkraut and malt on which they were fed. It brought a new enthusiasm for the exotic aspects of empire. Joseph Banks, the wealthy naturalist, who had been on Cook's *Endeavour*, publicised the strange aspects of the Southern Seas round the salons of the rich. Tahiti in particular, with its beauty, its hierarchical society and its apparently welcoming women, enthralled. The South Seas were presented as mankind in its pure, innocent, natural state.

In 1772, Cook embarked on a second voyage, which took him further south than any European had been before. But the great southern continent which he had hoped to find, proved elusive. The second voyage, however, brought to Britain the young Polynesian, Omai. For two years he was shown off by Joseph Banks. He had the manners, the dignity and bearing of the 'noble savage' and balanced the concerns raised by tales about free love and infanticide among the Tahitians. But the tone changed. By the end of the decade, Banks was much readier to describe the indigenous population of the South Seas as 'naked, treacherous' and 'extremely cowardly'. Cook's death on Hawaii in 1779 was seen as confirmation of these altered attitudes. The change in perception had begun even earlier. The early evolutionist Lord Monboddo, drawing on information from Cook's first voyage, saw European influence not as something that would corrupt primitive society, but something that would bring progress. Progress would lead to man becoming 'a rational political animal', different from 'the brute or savage'. His fellow Scot, John Miller, a few years later wrote of the need to bring 'the seeds of improvement' to primitive societies. An introduction to the report on the third of Cook's voyages talked of the Pacific islanders recognising their 'extreme inferiority', but deciding that they would try to escape from that and try 'to rise nearer to a level with those, who left so many proofs of their generosity and humanity'.

It was Cook's voyages that brought the Pacific into British consciousness, and the decision in 1786 to establish a penal colony at Botany Bay perhaps reflected a new determination to replace the Spanish as the dominating power in the Pacific.

American rebellion

The end of the Seven Years' War, with the removal of the French threat, had major implications for the 13 American colonies. The anglicised leaders of American society had regarded themselves as free-born Britons, partners in the Empire. There were networks that spanned the Atlantic, religious links, business links, family links and political links. Colonists looked to London for credit; as a market; as the entrepôt for their goods; as the source of their laws, instructions, information, ideas and styles. Leading colonial figures spent time in Britain, mixing with both the intellectual and political elites. Before 1774, when the first Continental Congress was held, more of its members had visited London than Philadelphia. There were colonial agents in London who pressed the case of the colonists over a whole variety of issues, and systems of political patronage worked in America, just as in Britain.

The distances involved and the contrasting environments were, however, generating a distinctive colonial life. Although there were royally appointed governors and appointed councils, most colonies had elected assemblies, that legislated for the day-to-day running of the colony. The colonies were very diverse and the role and status of the assemblies and other focuses of authority were often rather undefined. The wars with the French were seen by British politicians as being about defending the colonists, which was the same as defending British trading interests. However, the wars had also brought out the limitations on the extent to which the interests of Britain and the colonies were seen as mutual. Most of the colonial assemblies voted fewer war resources than were being sought by the government. In other cases, colonial troops refused to fight outside their own colony and colonial merchants continued to trade with the French West Indian islands. The British found that they had to furnish troops largely from Britain or using mercenaries, and they met fierce protests as cases of impressment of colonists into the navy increased. Many British officers did little to hide their contempt for colonials. General Wolfe made his views clear: 'The Americans are in general the dirtiest, the most contemptible, cowardly dogs that you can conceive. There is no depending upon them in action. They fall down in their own dirt and desert by battalions, officers and all.' Many colonials felt that they were given only the most demeaning roles. George Washington had resigned his military commission at the end of 1754 because he resented the discrimination in pay between British and American officers.

The Seven Years' War altered much. Until then Britain had seen the colonists in America as allies and partners in the Empire. They were largely Protestant and English-speaking and they had played their part in the defeat of the French. The American Benjamin West's iconic painting of the death of Wolfe before Quebec, displayed at the Royal Academy in 1771, had Scots Highlanders, Amerindians,

Americans and Englishmen surrounding the dying Wolfe; this seemed to say that a united Britain at home, united with the British abroad, had brought victory.

After the war, however, there was much less reticence about territorial expansion and the belief was that this now diverse Empire – and the term 'British Empire' began to be increasingly used – needed to be brought more closely under the control of London. There was a widely held view that colonies had become too independent. Merchants complained bitterly about Americans ignoring the Navigation Acts and illicitly trading directly with France, Spain and the Netherlands. Administrators and military commanders complained about unscrupulous traders and settlers causing tension with the Indians on the frontier and adding to the costs of defence. The colonists, in their turn, resented attempts by Parliament in London to legislate for them. There was talk of oppression, as the British authorities tried to apply taxation, restrict areas of settlement, curb smuggling and impose military discipline. The increased number of troops and of customs and excise officers was a constant irritation. The British, with the vast debts generated by the Seven Years' War to pay off, believed that the colonies had not borne enough of the costs of their own defence, while the colonists argued that, in proportion to population, they had contributed more than the mother country. Expectation that there would be rewards for loyalty and support during the war were not met.

Some prominent colonists, keen to speculate in land – among them George Washington – resented the attempt to block settlement in the west, beyond the Appalachian mountains. Intellectuals, influenced by the ideas of the Enlightenment, argued for more rational and consistent systems of law enforcement. Increasingly self-confident American colonists became hostile to what they saw as growing supervision and control from London, and governors did not have enough imperial patronage available to buy off new elites. Fervent religious revivalism, in what is called the 'Great Awakening', was also gaining ground among the Presbyterians, Baptists and Congregationalists of New England. In part, it was a challenge to the Anglican elite in the colonies, but it was also something foreign and undesirable to the increasingly relaxed Anglicanism of the British ruling class. There was less of a sense of Britishness when a third of the population was not of British stock.

Grievances over the implementation of the Sugar Act of 1764, that reduced the duty on sugar and molasses from the West Indies but implemented it more strictly, were further inflamed by the Stamp Act in 1765, which placed a duty on newspapers, pamphlets, playing cards and legal documents. Colonial opposition was instant and almost universal, and an inter-colonial congress was summoned in New York. It issued a declaration of rights claiming that, if they were not represented in Parliament, then they could not be taxed without consent. 'No taxation without representation' was to prove a powerful slogan. Rockingham's government backed down and repealed the Stamp Act, but passed a Declaratory Act, affirming that Parliament had the right to make laws binding the colonies. As Edmund Burke warned in 1769: 'Americans have made a discovery, or think they have made one, that we mean to oppress them; we have made a discovery, or think we have made one, that they intend to rise in rebellion against us.'

An interlude of relative peace followed, until in 1773 the East India Company, in financial difficulty, was given the right to send tea directly to the colonies without paying the duty of one shilling in the pound. This was a blow to those merchants who had made a living importing tea illicitly from the Dutch. When 342 tea chests were dumped in Boston harbour, the harbour was forcibly closed by troops until the tea was paid for. The condemnation of this attack on property was general in Britain. The coercive measures against Boston were seen as mild compared with the criminality of the act, while the punishment of Boston caused huge anger in the colonies.

The Quebec Act of 1774 was to deal with the fact that the Empire now included 60,000–70,000 French settlers, something like 99 per cent of the total population of Canada. The Act meant abandoning the idea that the French population in Canada had to be anglicised. It accepted the Catholic Church in Quebec, granted Catholics equal civil rights, allowed the continuation of French civil law, and set up an appointed, not elected, colonial council. In the view of many American colonists, the principles of the Act threatened a civil society based on Protestantism and challenged the right of popular government. Alexander Hamilton, soon to be one of the founding fathers of the American republic, believed that London was paying more attention to the concerns of 'a superstitious, bigoted, Canadian Papist' than to the Protestants of New England. To these concerns was added the fact that Quebec included the entire area west of the Appalachians up through the Great Lakes to Hudson Bay. Powerful merchants and planters in the 13 colonies saw themselves being excluded from the land and valuable furs of the west. Events moved to a climax, when royal governors dissolved colonial assemblies that protested, and were defied. Governmental control in Massachusetts and elsewhere began to collapse. The first Continental Congress was evenly divided between radicals and moderates, but demanded the removal of what were called the 'Intolerable Acts' and the dismissal of the King's 'designing and dangerous ministers'.

The colonists were able to approach rebellion by drawing on that country ideology that they had learned from Britain (see Chapter 2). This accepted the right of freeborn Englishmen to resist an overpowerful executive that was threatening their liberties. As was common among the country party, the argument was that the King's ministers were corrupt and undermining traditional rights. Therefore, for many, the focus became the monarch and a handful of ministers. In Britain, the Whig assumption had been that Parliament, and, in particular, the House of Commons, was the ultimate check on potential royal tyranny. Legal commentators focused upon the sovereignty of Parliament as the central aspect of the British constitution, so a challenge to it was difficult to condone. Taxation was central to Parliament's role and American suggestions that they could bypass Parliament and deal directly with the Crown had the potential to undermine the advances against royal prerogative that had been made since the 1640s. For many colonists, the fact that Parliament was asserting its rights to control the colonies meant that Parliament itself must be corrupt. Americans had, therefore, to draw on an earlier ideological tradition from the days of the Commonwealth in the seventeenth century, which allowed for a republican alterative. On 4 July 1776 the Continental Congress issued the Declaration of Independence. The 'rights of Englishmen' had given way to the 'natural rights' of free men.

Focus on

American republicanism

This extract comes from Thomas Paine, *Common Sense*, a pamphlet written in January 1776. Paine (1737–1809) originally a staymaker from Thetford in Norfolk, emigrated to America in 1774 and was soon writing in support of independence. Here are his 'Thoughts on The Present State of American Affairs':

> I know it is difficult to get over local or long standing prejudices, yet if we will suffer ourselves to examine the component parts of the English constitution, we shall find them to be the base remains of two ancient tyrannies, compounded with some new republican materials.
>
> First. The remains of monarchical tyranny in the person of the king.
>
> Secondly. The remains of aristocratical tyranny in the persons of the peers.
>
> Thirdly. The new republican materials, in the persons of the commons, on whose virtue depends the freedom of England.
>
> The two first, by being hereditary, are independent of the people; wherefore in a constitutional sense they contribute nothing towards the freedom of the state.
>
> To say that the constitution of England is a union of three powers reciprocally checking each other, is farcical, either the words have no meaning, or they are flat contradictions.
>
> To say that the commons is a check upon the king, presupposes two things.
>
> First. That the king is not to be trusted without being looked after, or in other words, that a thirst for absolute power is the natural disease of monarchy.
>
> Secondly. That the commons, by being appointed for that purpose, are either wiser or more worthy of confidence than the crown.
>
> But as the same constitution which gives the commons a power to check the king by withholding the supplies, gives afterwards the king a power to check the commons, by empowering him to reject their other bills; it again supposes that the king is wiser than those whom it has already supposed to be wiser than him. A mere absurdity!

Source: The full text of *Common Sense* can be found at http://www.earlyamerica.com/earlyamerica/milestones/commonsense/text.html

A skirmish at Lexington, as General Cage tried to size the arsenal of the local militia, heralded the outbreak of open warfare in April 1775. This was soon followed by an abortive attack on Quebec by an American army, but they found little enthusiasm there for getting caught into another war so soon after the Seven Years' War. A year later, the British had pulled out of Boston in the face of George Washington's forces and General 'Gentleman Johnny' Burgoyne, trying to bring a British force from

Canada to capture Albany in New York, found himself surrounded at Saratoga in October 1777 and surrendered his entire force. Within months, the French had signed an alliance with the new United States. A year later, Spain, hopeful of recovering Gibraltar and Florida, joined in.

Difficult as the situation was, the entry of the European powers into the war usefully allowed it to be presented as a foreign war rather than a civil one. A peace offer from Lord North in February 1778, overcoming bitter objections from the King and the reservations of a reluctant Cabinet, included a willingness to renounce the right of taxation. It was rejected by the American Congress and an increasingly brutal, largely guerrilla war continued. American victory was by no means assured. As late as April 1781, George Washington was writing that: 'We are at the end of our tether.' But, in the summer of that year, the largest British army in America, under Cornwallis, found itself cut off in the Yorktown peninsula of Virginia by an army of Americans, led by Washington, and 7,000 French. The appearance of the French West Indies' fleet effectively closed the trap and Cornwallis surrendered in October. To all intents the war was over.

The government in London accepted the reality of the situation. The country's military resources were overstretched. Also, diplomatically, Britain had allowed herself to become completely isolated. British attacks on neutral shipping heading for French or Spanish ports had long been resented and, by the end of the war, Russia, Sweden, Prussia, Austria, Denmark and Portugal were all united in an 'armed neutrality' against Britain. Lord North resigned in March 1782 and negotiations with the United States began at once, leading to a separate peace with them before the settlement with France and Spain. Britain recognised the independence of the United States and accepted the Mississippi as the western boundary. 50,000 loyalists headed for Canada; others fled to the West Indies and the Bahamas, while a few returned to Britain. In the formal Treaty of Paris, Spain had Florida restored and was ceded Menorca. France recovered St Lucia and Tobago and her West African base in Senegal. Ceylon was restored to the Dutch. Britain held on to the West Indian Islands of Dominica, St Vincent and Grenada. The defeat was clearly of huge significance.

To many it was a surprise, but, with hindsight, it is easy to see how impossible was the task of trying to retain by force such a huge area as the 13 colonies. As some had warned as early as 1775, given the size of the British army, trying to conquer America 'was like driving a hammer into a bin of corn – the biggest risk was that the hammer would get lost'. Despite its size, the navy was in relatively poor condition. Ships were not being replaced as quickly as necessary; experienced seamen were in short supply. But there were also deep divisions within Britain on the war itself. British army commanders were reluctant to wage an all-out war against fellow-Englishmen. The Duke of Richmond had told the House of Lords in December 1775 that American independence 'was neither treason nor rebellion, but it is perfectly justifiable in every possible political and moral sense' and sailed his yacht with an American pennant on it through ships of the Royal Navy. Like many Whigs, he was critical of the situation having reached the position that generated rebellion in North America. Parliament had the

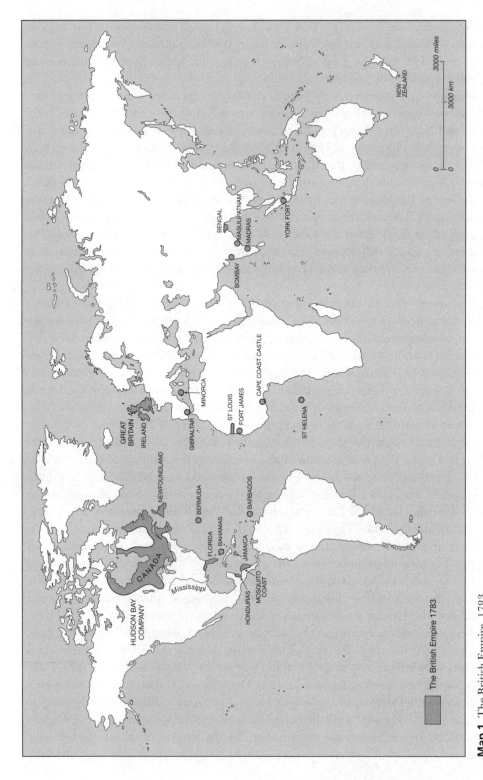

Map 1 The British Empire, 1783
Source: adapted from Evans, E.J., *The Forging of the Modern British State* (Pearson Education Ltd, 2001)

right to tax the colonists but generally it had been felt unwise to force the issue by exercising that right.

There were similar pressures to those that led to rebellion in the American colonies on the Caribbean islands, and the same discourse on the rights of free-born Englishmen was apparent. The Jamaican assembly passed a resolution in support of the American resistance to the Stamp Act. It was, however, a very heterogeneous society of Scots, Irish, English, Jews, Creoles (Caribbean-born), mulattos, free blacks, rebel ex-slaves (known as maroons) and slaves. Many of the planters were absentees and had a limited sense of being part of a distinct community. More importantly, however, they lived in permanent fear of a slave uprising. Jamaica alone in 1776 had almost 200,000 slaves in its 775 estates and had some 75 slave rebellions during the century.

That is not to say that the authorities were not anxious about how the West Indies might react. For many, the West Indies seemed more important that the 13 colonies as a source of wealth for Britain, and sugar duties were a major source of government revenue and a guarantee of the government's credit. The very powerful West Indian lobby of merchants, planters and members of parliament was able to squeeze concessions from the government. Admiral Rodney's defeat of the large French fleet at the Battle of the Saintes in 1782, too late to save Cornwallis, eradicated the French threat to the West Indies and gave Britain naval supremacy in the Caribbean.

Ireland

Ireland was regarded by the British state as in large part a 'colonial' issue, and one of the fears roused by the American rebellion was the impact this would have there. The nobility and gentry who had created the Anglican Protestant Ascendancy over the previous century and more had their own reasons for resenting interference by the Westminster Parliament. Yet at the same time they were conscious that they were a minority surrounded by a large Catholic Irish population and, in the north, with some difficult Presbyterian Dissenters.

The defeat of James II's forces at the Battle of the Boyne in 1690 had ensured the triumph of the Protestant Ascendancy over the majority Catholic culture in Ireland. The lands of active Jacobites were confiscated. Attempts in the Treaty of Limerick to be more conciliatory towards the Catholic population were blocked by the entirely Protestant Irish Parliament, that refused to ratify the treaty and enacted penal anti-Catholic legislation. Catholic bishops and priests were banished, intermarriage between Catholic and Protestant was a ground for disinheritance, and even the value of horses that Catholics could keep was restricted. As in all colonies, there was often flexibility in how such laws were actually applied, and formal conversions to Protestantism to gain access to Parliament were tolerated. However, in 1728, an Act deprived Catholics of the right to vote. There was constant resentment at the requirement of all to pay tithes to the Anglican Church of Ireland. Presbyterian Dissenters, largely settled in the north-east of the island, also resented the restrictions on their rights. Power was to be firmly entrenched in the hands of an Anglican minority.

The Irish Parliament operated under Poynings' Law of 1494, which required all Irish legislation to get approval from Westminster, and made English law applicable in Ireland. The executive in Dublin Castle focused on the Viceroy. Central to his task was the management of the Irish Parliament which, like its counterpart at Westminster, worked through connections, interest, families, factions and, of course, patronage. There was also an Irish House of Lords. The ruling elite, although keen to maintain loyalty, were prepared to resist the government if they felt that Protestant interests were threatened. A 'Declaratory Act' of 1720 had reiterated that Ireland was a 'dependant kingdom', but much of the stuff of politics was about opposition to London authority and there was a vibrant Irish press with some 160 newspapers by 1760.

There were also growing links between Ireland and America in the mid-eighteenth century, with a great deal of emigration to the American colonies, particularly from Ulster. Irish merchants were involved with trade to the Americas and to the West Indies, but resented their exclusion from the East Indian markets. Inevitably, the American revolt had huge repercussions. The Quebec Act, with its rights for Catholics in Canada, was paralleled by an Act that allowed Irish Catholics to take an Oath of Allegiance. Catholic families, dispossessed from land, had begun to make inroads into trade and the professions. Such advances raised the ever-present fears amongst the Ascendancy. The restrictions on trade resulting from the war caused a great deal of resentment and, indeed, financial crisis. The right to import directly from the colonies was withdrawn and exports were restricted. It led to widespread protest and the establishment of a volunteer corps, which was ostensibly to defend the country from any possible French invasion, but which began to be hinted at as a possible basis for unconstitutional action. The central demand was for an end to restrictions on Irish trade, but it was coupled with the demand for an independent Parliament.

Although the main pressures came from Anglican gentry, merchants and professionals, talk of constitutional change also stirred activity among the substantial Catholic middle class. The Catholic Relief Act of 1778 removed restrictions on Catholic landholding. Lord North's attempt in 1778 to remove some of the restrictions on Irish trade led to a storm of protest from manufacturers and traders in Britain. Protestant gentry and merchant discontents with government were, as ever, both increased and curtailed by fears that more concessions might be made to Catholics. Like many Americans, they saw themselves as *both* British and Irish and the 'patriots', as oppositionists termed themselves, just like their American counterparts, used the 'country party' arguments familiar in Britain. However, some went beyond that and argued for natural rights and talked of the Irish nation.

Powerful local interest groups began to feel themselves being marginalised by the government, as Westminster tried to exert more direct control over this corner of the Empire. New politicians were being brought into the inner political circles. The sweet-tongued lawyer, Henry Grattan, emerged as leader of the 'patriot' group. In 1780 Grattan made a powerful 'Declaration of Irish Rights', although he soon

Focus on

Irish demands

This comes from a speech delivered by Henry Grattan on 19 April 1780. Grattan was a Dublin lawyer and Member of the Irish Parliament who, in this speech, was demanding the repeal of Poynings' Law of 1494, reaffirmed by the Declaratory Act of 1720, by which all legislation of the Irish Parliament had to be approved by the Westminster Parliament. The Irish Parliament of 1782–1801 was labelled Grattan's Parliament.

> Sir, we may hope to dazzle with illumination, and we may sicken with addresses, but the public imagination will never rest, nor will her heart be well at ease – never! so long as the Parliament of England exercises or claims a legislation over this country: so long as this shall be the case, that very free trade, otherwise a perpetual attachment, will be the cause of new discontent; it will create a pride to feel the indignity of bondage; it will furnish a strength to bite your chain, and the liberty withheld will poison the good communicated.
>
> The British minister mistakes the Irish character: had he intended to make Ireland a slave, he should have made her a beggar; there is no middle policy; win her heart by the restoration of her right, or cut off the nation's right hand; greatly emancipate, or fundamentally destroy. We may talk plausibly to England, but so long as she exercises a power to bind this country, so long as the nations are in a state of war; the claims of the one go against the liberty of the other, and the sentiments of the latter go to oppose those claims to the last drop of her blood. The English opposition, therefore, are right; mere trade will not satisfy Ireland – they judge of us by other great nations, by the nation whose political life has been a struggle for liberty; they judge of us with a true knowledge of, and just deference for, our character – that a country enlightened as Ireland, chartered as Ireland, armed as Ireland, and injured as Ireland, will be satisfied with nothing less than liberty.

parted company with many of his fellow 'patriots' by supporting the admission of Catholics to Parliament. The fall of Lord North's government and the coming into office of Lord Rockingham's administration in 1782, peopled by Whigs who had used Irish grievances as a stick with which to beat the government, brought a response. The Declaratory Act was repealed and Irish parliamentary bills could no longer be amended by Westminster. For the next 18 years Ireland had what goes by the name of 'Grattan's Parliament'.

Despite the loss of what is sometimes called the first British Empire, there were few signs that British governments had given up a desire to capture markets. How far this involved a coherent imperial policy is much more difficult to assess. Much of the expansion was left to traders and private companies, with only the pressures of war pulling in the government. Some historians see signs of a new sense of creating a territorial empire from about the 1760s and certainly Parliament is much more involved in discussions of empire issues. There were signs that the American experience had taught them to rule with a light touch, and Ireland briefly gained from this. Elsewhere, however, there are contrary signs that the aftermath of 1783 brought a tighter grip on colonial government. It is often asserted that the Empire 'financed' the Industrial Revolution, with talk of the profits from slave economies, but the part that the expansion of empire played in stimulating industrialisation in Britain is difficult to prove. Individual traders and officials did well from the loot of India, but for the state there were huge costs, just as there were in North America. There is not a great deal of evidence that imperial wealth found its way into stimulating new industry in Britain, and Europe and the independent USA were much more important as markets for exporters than any colonies. But empire and British identity and British self-perception were undoubtedly becoming ever more closely linked. Indeed, the wars with France were probably helping to shape that British identity. As Linda Colley has argued, national identity requires an enemy, an 'other'. In the British case this was Catholicism. Britain was a Protestant state and the 'other' increasingly was France. The British knew they were British because they were *not* French.

Further reading

Bayly, C., *Imperial Meridian. The British Empire and the World 1780–1830* (London, Longman, 1989)

Brewer, John, *The Sinews of Power: War, Money and the English State, 1688–1783* (London, Unwin Hyman, 1989)

Colley, Linda, *Britons. Forging the Nation 1707–1837* (New Haven, Yale University Press, 1992)

Conway, Stephen, *War, State and Society in Mid-Eighteenth Century Britain and Ireland* (Oxford, Oxford University Press, 2006)

Dickinson, H.T. (ed.), *Britain and the American Revolution* (London, Longman, 1998)

Foster, R.F., *Modern Ireland 1600–1972* (London, Penguin, 1988)

Lawson, Philip, *A Taste for Empire and Glory. Studies in British Overseas Expansion, 1660–1800* (Aldershot, Ashgate, 1997)

Moody, T.W. and Vaughan, W.E. (eds), *A New History of Ireland: Vol. 2, Eighteenth-Century Ireland 1691–1800* (Oxford, Clarendon Press, 1986)

Walvin, James, *Slaves and Slavery. The British Colonial Experience* (Manchester, Manchester University Press, 1992)

Wilson, Kathleen, *The New Imperial History. Culture, Identity and Modernity in Britain and the Empire, 1660–1840* (Cambridge, Cambridge University Press, 2004)

Timeline 1707–80

Year	Government and politics	War and empire	Economic and social	Cultural and intellectual
1706			Population of England, 5,334,000; London's population 310,000; Edinburgh 50,000	
1707	1 May – Union of Parliaments of Scotland and England			
1708	Whig 'Junto' in power; 'Old Pretender' lands in Scotland			
1709			Abraham Darby smelts iron ore at Coalbrookdale; food shortages	
1710	Tory majority; government of Harley and St. John; trial of Dr Sacheverell for Ultra-Tory views			
1711	Occasional Conformity Act against Dissenters	South Sea Company incorporated		Addison and Steele publish The Spectator periodical
1712			Thomas Newcomen's steam pump	Patronage re-introduced in Church of Scotland
1713		Treaty of Utrecht; Britain gets Gibraltar, Menorca, Hudson Bay, Nova Scotia and Newfoundland		
1714	Death of Queen Anne; accession of George I			
1715	Whig election victory; Bolingbrooke flees; Jacobite rebellion		Riot Act passed	

Year	Government and politics	War and empire	Economic and social	Cultural and intellectual
1716	Septennial Act extending life of parliament to 7 years; splits in Whig government; Stanhope and Sutherland dominant			
1717				
1718	Attempted Jacobite invasion	War with Spain	First transportation of convicts to Barbados	
1719				Daniel Defoe, *Robinson Crusoe*
1720			South Sea 'Bubble'	
1721	Robert Walpole First Lord of the Treasury			
1722				
1723			'Black Act' makes many more crimes capital offences	
1724			Famine in Ireland	
1725				
1726				Jonathan Swift, *Gulliver's Travels*
1727	Accession of George II	Spain besieges Gibraltar		
1728			Food riots	John Gay, *The Beggar's Opera*
1729		Treaty of Seville with Spain; Gibraltar retained		
1730				
1731				Royal Dublin Society founded; Hogarth paints *A Harlot's Progress*

1732	Salt tax introduced	
1733	Kay's 'flying shuttle' patented; Secession Church formed from defection from Church of Scotland	Protests against Excise Bill
1734	John Harrison's marine chronometer allows calculation of longitude	General election
1735	Witchcraft stops being an offence in Scotland	
1736	Porteous riots in Edinburgh; John and Charles Wesley form evangelical societies; *Caledonian Mercury* newspaper founded in Edinburgh	
1737	Act for licensing plays appoints Lord Chamberlain as censor	
1738		
1739	David Hume, *A Treatise on Human Nature*	War of Jenkins' Ear until 1748; Admiral Vernon captures Porto Bello
1740	Food riots; potato famine in Ireland; 'Rule Britannia' published	
1741	David Hume, *Essays Moral and Political*	
1742	Handel's 'Messiah' performed in Dublin	Resignation of Walpole
1743		Henry Pelham First Lord of the Treasury
1744		War with France over Austrian Succession, until 1748

Year	Government and politics	War and empire	Economic and social	Cultural and intellectual
1745	Arrival of Charles Edward Stuart, 'the Young Pretender'; Jacobite rebellion	Capture of Louisbourg		
1746	Defeat of Jacobite rebellion at Culloden			
1747				
1748		Treaty of Aix-la-Chapelle		
1749				Henry Fielding, *Tom Jones*
1750				Jockey Club founded
1751	Death of Frederick, Prince of Wales	Robert Clive captures Carnatic		
1752				Gregorian calendar adopted; Places of Public Entertainment Regulation Act
1753	Death of Pelham			
1754	Duke of Newcastle becomes First Lord of the Treasury			
1755			Potato famine in Ireland	Samuel Johnson, *A Dictionary of the English Language*
1756	Elder Pitt in ministry	Start of Seven Years' War; loss of Menorca	Food riots	William Blackstone's legal approval of women's subjugation in marriage
1757	Pitt–Newcastle ministry	Battle of Plassey; Clive captures Calcutta; Admiral John Byng shot for 'failing to do his utmost' at battle for Menorca	Militia riots	

Year				
1758		Strutt's stocking frame		
1759	British Museum opens	Wedgwood pottery introduced	Capture of Quebec	
1760				Accession of George III
1761		Brindley's Bridgewater Canal opens	War with Spain	Bute made Secretary of State; Pitt resigns
1762	J-J Rousseau, *Emile*			Bute becomes Prime Minister
1763			Treaty of Paris ends Seven Years' War; France cedes Canada, Grenada and control of India; Spain cedes Florida	Resignation of Bute; Grenville Prime Minister; John Wilkes publishes *The North Briton*, no. 45.
1764		Hargreaves' 'spinning jenny' invented		Wilkes expelled from House of Commons and flees
1765		James Watt's steam condenser	Stamp Act	Rockingham ministry
1766	Hydrogen discovered	Potato famine in Ireland; food riots	Stamp Act repealed, but Declaratory Act passed	Rockingham resigns; Chatham Prime Minister
1767	Adam Ferguson, *An Essay on History of Civil Society*	Joseph Priestley experiments with electricity		
1768	*Encyclopaedia Britannica* begins publication in Edinburgh	Arkwright opens his first factory in Nottingham; Forth and Clyde canal started	Cook's first voyage to the Pacific	Wilkes elected for Middlesex; Chatham resigns; Grafton Prime Minister
1769		Wedgewood's Etruria pottery opened; Arkwright's water frame		Wilkes expelled and re-elected
1770	Edmund Burke, *Thoughts on the Present Discontents*	Leeds and Liverpool canal begun	Boston massacre	Lord North Prime Minister
1771				
1772		Food riots; Lord Mansfield's judgement on slavery	Cook's second voyage	

Year	Government and politics	War and empire	Economic and social	Cultural and intellectual
1773		Boston 'Tea Party'		
1774		Port of Boston closed; Continental Congress; Quebec Act	Priestley discovers ammonia and isolates oxygen	
1775		American rebellion; battles of Concord and Lexington	Boulton and Watt's steam engine	
1776		American Declaration of Independence		Adam Smith, *Wealth of Nations*; Tom Paine, *Common Sense*; John Cartwright, *Take Your Choice*; Richard Price, *Observations on Civil Liberty*; Edward Gibbon, *Decline and Fall of the Roman Empire*; St Leger first run at Doncaster
1777		United States formed		
1778	Death of Chatham; Catholic Relief Act in Ireland	War with France	Bramah's water closet	
1779		War with Spain; Captain Cook killed in Hawaii	Penitentiary Act to set up state prisons; Iron bridge constructed at Coalbrookedale; Crompton's spinning mule	
1780	Wyvill's Yorkshire Association; Dunning's motion; Society for Constitutional Information formed; Gordon Riots against Catholic Relief Bill	Henry Grattan's 'Declaration of Irish Rights'		Derby first run at Epsom

PART 3

The industrialising nation 1780–1829

7

The Industrial Revolution

Economic change

Britain experienced the world's first industrial revolution. The period 1780–1830 has long been seen as the period of its classic revolution, which propelled the country from being predominantly agricultural to predominantly industrial. This image of economic change is not, however, wholly true. Research is constantly changing the perception here, and historians disagree to some extent on how to interpret the character and performance of the economy. Yet, the trend is now to downgrade considerably the status of the Industrial Revolution during these 'classic' years of economic change. Instead, the emphasis is on placing British economic performance down to 1830 as little different *in kind* from what had been going on for a century and more before, but rather different *in pace*.

The British economy did grow significantly in this period. But growth needs to be carefully defined. There was little growth in the average economic output of the average person; this figure is known as the growth in Gross Domestic Product per person (or GDP per capita), and the most recent research shows this to have moved little between 1760 and 1830, and what little movement there was occurred after 1800. Growth was slow, and limited to certain sectors of the economy. These were relatively small sectors, such as the cotton and woollen industries, the iron industry and machinery manufacture. Most of the rest of the economy experienced little increase in growth until after 1830. Moreover, even in the case of industries experiencing growth, there were major parts which were static. The most dynamic industry in Britain, the cotton industry, had many parts dominated by manufacture in the home, where there was no sign of the new methods of production developing in factories. New technology was thus not reaching everywhere. Some developments saw growth in productivity, though with little change in technology. In the area of transport, for instance, there was growth in inland and coastal shipping from more intensive working rather than major technological change; steam engines were only introduced in coastal ships in the 1820s and 1830s, and were not used in canal traffic until the mid-nineteenth century.

Across the economy as a whole, rather than technology changing the economy dramatically, it seems that even more change may have come from the fact that British workers and their families started to work harder – and worked for the market (to sell their wares) and not merely for subsistence (consuming within the home). This has been termed the 'industrious revolution'.[1] For example, people were working longer hours; some historians have argued that average working hours for men in prime years of life rose by between 20 and 35 per cent between 1750 and 1850. There is also considerable evidence that men worked on more days of the year, as holidays like the tradition of St Monday and calendar customs like fairs and religious holy days were being squeezed out.[2]

There was strong regional variation in economic performance. Scotland, Wales and Ireland were coming from more economically backward starting points than almost all of England. Farming in each of these was generally less productive, manufacturing more limited in scale, and the levels of wealth and income markedly lower (especially in the case of Ireland). Even within England and Ireland, there was tremendous variation, however. Indeed, it may be wise to some degree to think of the period as one in which distinct economic regions emerged. If the national economy was still hampered by transport and economic divisions, one thing the Industrial Revolution did was to unite the local communities within regions and undermine localism. Industrialisation, insofar as it occurred, was more an intense economic change to a small number of areas of Britain. Between 1760 and 1830, these areas were limited mainly to Lancashire and parts of Cheshire (around Manchester), Lanarkshire, Renfrewshire and Dunbartonshire (around Glasgow), and west Yorkshire (around Leeds and Bradford). The Manchester and Glasgow zones were led by the ascendancy of the brand new cotton industry, whilst Leeds and Bradford dominated in worsted production based on wool (eclipsing older worsted manufacturing zones around Norwich, north Essex and Exeter).

To these need to be added other types of regional development. There were larger zones of less intense industrial change (in the English south-west, for instance). There were some small zones of narrow industrial economies (such as tin mining in Cornwall, and coal mining in the English north-east around Newcastle). And smaller industrial changes were to be found in many parts of Britain (ranging from industrial workshops, arsenals and shipyards in London, to the development of slate and stone quarries in the West Highlands of Scotland).

---

[1] It was first coined in J. de Vries, 'The industrial revolution and the industrious revolution', *Journal of Economic History*, 54 (1994), pp. 249–70.

[2] H.-J. Voth, 'Living standards and the urban environment', in R. Floud and P. Johnson (eds), *The Cambridge Economic History of Modern Britain: Volume I: Industrialisation, 1700–1860* (Cambridge, Cambridge University Press, 2004), p. 277.

In Ireland, the late eighteenth century witnessed a growing economic and social crisis. Rapidly rising population destabilised rural life, putting pressure on scarce land resources of land, and all were badly affected by trade fluctuations. Popular protest over taxation fostered rural unrest, contributing to the full political union with Britain in 1801 (see Chapter 9). This seemed to help the Irish economy by drawing it into the British free trade area, but from the 1810s economic development remained unstable, with sustained periodic potato famines. Yet patchy rural development progressed, with cotton factories established in both the Belfast area and in centres like Waterford. But some industries could not cope with the superior and cheaper products of British industry, and suffered badly, throwing more pressure back onto farming, where overpopulation and land hunger were leading many areas towards a demographic catastrophe.

Each region of the British Isles had its distinctive development characteristics, and, for this reason, it is difficult to generalise about the character of industrial change. But if our concern is for leading sectors of the national economy, then it is important to identify the significance of textiles (mainly cotton and worsted, though including linen). In this regard, 90 per cent of all English textile workers were located in 1810 in three areas – the largest being Lancashire, Yorkshire and Nottinghamshire, the second in the English south-west around Bristol, and a third much smaller area in north Norfolk. Scotland contributed a high density of cotton workers in west central Scotland, but handloom weaving was spread over many towns and villages of that country, whilst the linen industry became concentrated in a small area in Perthshire, Angus and Fife. In Ireland, linen had dominated, especially in Ulster, but in the 1790s it gave way there to a brief expansion of cotton spinning and handloom weaving, which were important till the contraction of that industry in the 1840s.

Yet, despite regionalism, there were few – arguably no – areas of mainland Britain which were untouched by the impact of change. Market forces provided the impulse to new industries, new ways of working, the failure of older industries, and the arrival of new products. There were regional casualties in all of this. East Anglia suffered badly from the decline of the worsted industry, beaten by the greater efficiency of west Yorkshire. By the 1790s, the industry was collapsing in rural Norfolk and, by the 1830s, in the city of Norwich itself. With agriculture in Norfolk in a poor state by the 1820s and 1830s, there was great economic hardship, large-scale poverty and widespread unrest. Even in areas of economic growth overall, there could be sharp downturns in trade in some years, causing great distress to large numbers of families. In short, the period 1780–1830 was one of dramatic economic changes in many communities, but these could be of fluctuating or detrimental character.

The urban transformation of Britain and Ireland accelerated between 1780 and 1830, taking cities in new directions of development resulting from economic change. The proportion of the people living in cities of over 5,000 inhabitants rose appreciably – reaching by 1850 40.8 per cent in England and Wales, 32 per cent in Scotland and 10.2 per cent in Ireland. Mainland Britain was now the most urbanised part of Europe, with Scotland rising from almost the least urbanised place in 1700 to the second most urbanised in 1850. The cities and large towns that were being created were characteristically cramped, with the spread of poor-quality housing for the working classes and the poor. Cities like Manchester, Liverpool and Glasgow were modest-sized towns of around 10,000 people in 1700 but, by 1800, each had populations in excess of 70,000 and, by 1851, in excess of 300,000. They were attracting increasing numbers from rural areas, where overpopulation, land enclosure and poor economic prospects encouraged migration. Cities concentrated the factors needed for industrial production (which we look at in 'Causes of change', below), but also provided markets for the many hand-made products of day-to-day life, such as boots, shoes and clothes, each of which employed thousands of people in large and medium-sized cities, and which were to remain little changed until the later nineteenth century.

Yet, cities were also experiencing change. The arrival of large-scale coal-burning in the late eighteenth century (fostered by canals in many places) brought pollution, exacerbated by steam engines and the general increase in economic activity. In the absence of general planning laws that might separate industry and commerce from residential areas, city centres were becoming increasingly unhealthy, polluted places. Above all, towns were becoming places dominated by manufacturing and not by markets. People were buying more things at home and abroad, and British towns and cities were becoming more important to the manufacture of these. The economy was shifting its centre of importance from country to town.

Causes of change

The Industrial Revolution was the product of no single factor, but of several acting in unison. These factors of production needed to operate in a beneficial interaction. For an economy to grow, it requires labour (a workforce freed from other economic activity); demand (a population with disposable income with which to buy products); capital (growing sources of funds to invest in fixed machinery and premises, and in working capital to buy raw materials and extend credit to customers); technological improvement (ranging from large inventions to minor improvements to existing machines); transport (to allow for the movement of goods in and out of a place of work); and entrepreneurship (risk-taking business people willing to exploit new opportunities for making and selling goods). Some parts of Britain had all of these factors in abundance and were to flourish (at least for a period of time), whilst other parts were hampered because some factors were absent. The factors operated in a predominantly free market, in which the laws of supply and demand operated largely unrestricted. However, when considering the causes of change, we must ask whether the British state played any significant role in the Industrial Revolution.

The important backdrop to the Industrial Revolution was a tremendous growth in the number of British people, fostering both labour and demand (see Focus on Population, p. 40). The population of England and Wales rose from 6.7 million in 1760 to 13.9 million in 1830 – by far the greatest growth since the fifteenth century. With growth in Scotland as well, the rise in the number of people stimulated the economy as a whole. With more people, more things were being cultivated and more things were being made. Britain was becoming more crowded, and contemporaries noted that there was a quickening of the life of the nation. This was a distinctively British experience. Most other nations in Europe had either static or very slow growth in population at this time.

What caused population growth on such a rapid scale? The period of most rapid increase in England was between 1791 and 1831, when the annual rate stood at 1.32 per cent per annum; compare this with the tiny figure of 0.2 per cent per annum growth between 1681 and 1741. Over the long term, about two-thirds of this indigenous British population growth was caused by increasing birth rates, and only the remaining third by declining death rates. Life expectancy did improve in England, but only marginally; in 1781, life expectancy at birth was 35.4 years, and by 1801 this had risen to 40.0 years, but it remained stubbornly at that level through to the 1830s with no improvement. In general terms, the increasing proportion of the population living in towns and cities exposed more and more people to ever-worsening sanitary conditions which caused high mortality rates, notably amongst the industrial working classes. Yet, over the whole period, British mainland population did not suffer a demographic crisis. From the 1750s to the 1810s, the marriage rate stayed at a reasonably high level, and, with no major mortality crises, population went into a spiral of growth uninterrupted by major disease or famine.

More people also meant more demand. But like growth in output, the growth of demand was not straightforward. The amount of money, food and goods that people made, bought and consumed followed a very similar pattern to that of output. The income that each person made changed very little between 1780 and 1830. Historians measure this by estimating as accurately as possible what is known as the 'real wages' of the people. 'Real wages' means the buying power of people's wages and salaries – what they could buy – or the cash wage in relation to the cost of living. The evidence points to very little movement in real wages during these years. Indeed, it is perfectly clear that agricultural day labourers, who made up the largest single group of British workers, were earning less in real wages in the eighteenth century than they were in the early 1500s. Moreover, during this period, their wages were dropping. In 1800–09, a farm labourer was earning on average 7 per cent less than in 1750–59, largely as a result of the rising cost of living (which almost doubled between those years).[3] So, as a period of economic change, it was for most people one of economic loss, not gain. This makes the Industrial Revolution sound like regression rather than advance. In some ways this is true, and we examine the social consequences of economic change in the next chapter.

Despite this apparent lack of significant improvement in income nationally, some historians argue that the consumer boom in the eighteenth century (notably after 1775, and certainly in England) fuelled demand for manufactured products, creating

[3] G. Clark, 'The long march of history: farm wages, population, and economic growth, England 1209–1869', *Economic History Review*, 60 (2007), pp. 97–135 at p. 109.

what one has described as 'an orgy of spending'.[4] Economic growth was, then, linked to the rise of consumption and the culture of luxury in the first three quarters of the eighteenth century (discussed in Chapter 4), which heralded a more widespread demand for goods, notably for cotton clothing available to most ranks in society by 1800. One way this occurred, it has been suggested, was by the notion of the 'industrious revolution' we noted earlier: firstly, families bought cheap goods like cotton clothes instead of, as previously, making woollen or linen fabrics at home; and secondly, by working longer hours in domestic manufacture of goods for sale, women in particular were able to accrue more funds to spend on consumer products like china, glassware, dresses and soft furnishings, as well as on food and drink. In this way, women are seen by some scholars as central to both the manufacturing and the demand-led nature of the Industrial Revolution. However, women's role should not be overstated. Women only bought a limited range of domestic consumer products, and few metal goods, for instance. Moreover, it was only certain women who had significant purchasing power. Since overall incomes rose little between 1780 and 1830, working-class women continued to make a limited range of purchases over that 50-year period. More broadly, the working classes could not afford many luxuries by 1830 or 1840, and those they did get were often second-hand. The growth of demand is therefore traceable to the middle classes, whose numbers and wealth were rising very rapidly.

Capital was vital to the economic change of the late eighteenth and early nineteenth centuries. But the usual sources with which we are familiar today (banks, building societies, loans companies) did not exist in the same way then, and sources of capital were not so well organised or willing to lend to people. Indeed, as in the early nineteenth century, the vast bulk of capital investment came through borrowing from people who knew the entrepreneur. Most was obtained through the simple device of partnerships, involving often only two or a handful of people, who entered an agreement to undertake an enterprise and for one of their number to manage it. Those who invested had to have some money. In 1787, a list of 230 cotton-mill owners shows that 90 per cent of them were from upper social groups.[5] Some enterprises were large-scale and involved greater organisation. The building of canals involved very large sums of money, required the co-operation of very many people (such as the landowners over whose property canals were to be constructed) and, by the 'Bubble' Act of 1720 (see Chapter 2), businesses of this type – known as joint-stock companies – had to be formed by a separate Act of Parliament. That was time-consuming and expensive, but in time this type of operation became freed from close parliamentary scrutiny to form the model for modern business organisation. During the period 1780–1830, however, obtaining working capital was of greater importance. This was often obtained by bills of exchange, signed between a supplier of goods and a firm buying them, which

---

[4] Neil McKendrick, 'Introduction', in N. McKendrick, J. Brewer and J. Plumb (eds), *The Birth of a Consumer Society* (London, Longman, 1982), p. 6.

[5] S. King and G. Timmins, *Making Sense of the Industrial Revolution: English Economy and Society 1700–1850* (Manchester, Manchester University Press, 2001), p. 117.

delayed payment until an agreed date, perhaps three months hence, in return for a rate of interest. The supplier then used such a bill to pay for his or her own purchases, thereby creating a trade in bills of exchange as a substitute form of money. This allowed business to function and trust to develop between merchants and manufacturers, leading, in regions like the north of England, to the transfer of funds between industries and then, from the 1810s, to the formation of many regional banks.

The role of invention in the Industrial Revolution is hotly debated. Inventors like James Watt, James Hargreaves and Thomas Newcomen are much praised in British culture for developing machines and ideas that, deriving from Enlightenment science, created the spark of industrial innovation, new products, deeper digging of mines, swifter production methods, and moved the economy from working with small machines in the home to working with giant machines in factories. And there *were* some genuine breakthroughs, notably in the cotton industry. Yet most of these occurred in the period 1760–1800, while the great advances in cotton production were actually after 1800.

A general point is worth stressing. Scientific revolution did not cause the Industrial Revolution. There were various reasons for this. Firstly, scientific innovations were frequently of pure or abstract knowledge; these did not have immediate impact upon production methods in industry or agriculture, but rather required long-term technical innovation taking up to a century. Secondly, scientists had less impact upon the economy than improvers – those craftsmen who applied new methods of working with one metal to another, or transferred techniques from wood to metal – and entrepreneurs and landowners who introduced new ways of organising production. Thirdly, much of the increased production of the Industrial Revolution was the result of switching from one material to another – for instance, burning coal rather than wood, in both home and workshop. Fourthly, a tremendous part of the effect of economic change came from the wider dissemination of new ideas in technical journals and societies, in agricultural shows and competitions. And fifthly, what allowed these first four factors to operate in a benevolent way to foster an Industrial Revolution was the free market. As we shall see shortly, the role of government was limited to particular areas, and did not induce nor limit the dissemination of new knowledge. Still, science was the object of praise and emulation and provided the culture and language of technical innovation, forging a bridge between science and industry. Scientists like Joseph Black and James Watt had feet in both camps, making Britain a nation of innovative engineers.

Entrepreneurs were needed to bring the factors of production together in business. These were men and, more rarely, women, who saw an opportunity to make or sell a product, were willing to take a risk by borrowing money or seeking partners, and established manufacturing or warehousing facilities to get started. Entrepreneurs could come from a variety of backgrounds, though they were often from grammar schools or dissenting families, and many were already merchants who made money from trading in goods during the commercial expansion of the third quarter of the eighteenth century. Such entrepreneurs often became celebrities. Two examples are Josiah Wedgwood (1730–95), who founded a porcelain tradition in the Potteries in the 1760s, and whose fame was built on the fashion for his plates and dishes with their distinctive patterns and colours. A second was David Dale (1739–1806), whose cotton-spinning factories in Glasgow and Ayrshire in the 1770s formed a model that many of the Scottish propertied classes begged him in the 1790s to bring to their own neighbourhoods, so that the spirit of enterprise and improvement could be spread. Entrepreneurs were seen as combining innate moral qualities with dynamism and a self-improving credo that was regarded as ethically and even spiritually improving, and their factories were regarded as epicentres of a public-spiritedness that could transform idle and poverty-stricken country people into industrious workers (see Focus on the Factory, p. 112).

In all of this, what role for the state? In the great upsurge of economic activity between 1780 and 1830, the role of the state was lessening, not increasing. In the seventeenth and eighteenth centuries, there had been a mass of legislation passed that regulated trade and manufacturing, and local authorities added to this burden under their own rights to impose regulation of trade and to control entry to crafts. There was very far from a free market in the eighteenth century, and the market in foodstuffs became more, not less, controlled by Corn Laws, which imposed tariffs on imports of grain in order to protect British landowners and farmers by keeping prices high. After 1800, state regulation went into reverse, however. Wage fixing and apprenticeship regulations were repealed in 1812–13; the Poor Law of England and Wales was replaced in 1834, removing wage subsidies; the monopoly of the East India Company was removed in 1813; restrictions on the forming of joint joint–stock companies were removed in 1826; the Corn Laws were repealed in 1846; usury laws regulating interest rates charged by lenders were repealed in 1854, and the Navigation Acts were abandoned in 1850 and 1854.[6] But though government restriction lessened, there was considerable government investment. One way was in the expenditure on armed forces, with the Revolutionary and Napoleonic Wars of 1793–1815 and the growing British Empire leading to major contracts for ships (many built in the vast naval dockyards at Chatham and Portsmouth), for iron for armaments, and for uniforms. As one historian has said, 'The British state between the years 1700 and 1850 was indeed a warfare state, not a welfare state.'[7] Yet, compared to the modern state, levels of expenditure by government remained low.

In this sense, the Industrial Revolution was about improvements in different sectors in the economy. More often than not, improvement did not need science or invention, but application and better organisation, and the spread of ideas. However, after 1830 there was a period of renewed invention, in which application of ideas became very much quicker – notably in metalworking, steam-engine making and transport. Pragmatic and experimental knowledge was much more important than science or major invention. Knowledge was sought out wherever it lurked, including on the continent, where entrepreneurs sent artisans for training in new techniques.

---

[6] R. Harris, 'Government and the economy', in R. Floud and P. Johnson (eds), *The Cambridge Economic History of Modern Britain: Volume I: Industrialisation, 1700–1860* (Cambridge, Cambridge University Press, 2004), p. 206.

[7] Ibid., p. 219.

Patterns of work

Much of the development of the period involved the intensification of trends in manu-facturing that had been underway in the eighteenth century. Most important of these was the continued growth of domestic industry – of families, especially in rural areas, taking work into the home. This type of work was commonly related to the textile industry, but varied by textile (in the cotton, linen, straw and woollen industries) and by process (in spinning, weaving, plaiting and bleaching). The greatest growth during this period was in handloom weavers in the cotton industry. Their numbers in main-land Britain rose from 75,000 in 1795 to 224,000 in 1820, before a sharp decline to 60,000 by 1835, when there was a surge in powerloom weaving in factories. Handloom weavers would characteristically have a loom located in their home – sometimes on the second floor, where the light through the windows could be maximised – and the loom was worked principally by the man of the household but also, to some extent, by women and even children. One of the key characteristics of this period was the way in which handloom weaving increasingly became a full-time occupation for domestic workers. In the eighteenth century, it was common for handloom weaving to be com-bined with agricultural work, but the decreasing cost of food and the difficulties of securing employment on the land, plus the huge growth in demand as the spinning side of the industry developed in factories, led to weaving in the home becoming a more important part of the life of the rural working class.

A great deal of the Industrial Revolution was to do with the persistence and growth of what has been called 'hand technology'.[8] This can be seen in three ways – in the use of hand-held tools (saws, hammers and scissors) and hand-powered machines (includ-ing new inventions like the spinning jenny for cotton, and the handloom for weaving cotton), and the manufacture by hand of porcelain china and even iron (which involved hand-stirring of molten iron and shaping by hammer and anvil). Much of the growth of industrial output, the diversification of product ranges, and improve-ment in the products were due to advances in hand technology. The bleaching of cloth was improved by the development in 1799 by Charles Tennant of Glasgow of a system of obtaining chlorine concentrate which bleachers dissolved in water to obtain the strength they required, thereby reducing bleaching times greatly. Hand technology often staved off the introduction of new machines when low-paid workers beat the costs of capital investment in expensive and sometimes unreliable machines. Hand technology could produce higher-quality work to lower tolerances. It was observed in 1843 that, in a shipyard, 'it might at first thought be imagined that machine-worked saws would be used; but the curvatures and angles of the timbers are so extremely varied . . . that the precision and regularity of machinery would be here thrown away'.[9]

---

[8] S. King and G. Timmins, *Making Sense of the Industrial Revolution: English Economy and Society 1700–1850* (Manchester, Manchester University Press, 2001), pp. 70–9.
[9] George Dodds, quoted in S. King and G. Timmins, *Making Sense of the Industrial Revolution: English Economy and Society 1700–1850* (Manchester, Manchester University Press, 2001), p. 75.

Hand technology often pushed the costs of 'tooling-up' a manufacturing process onto the ordinary worker, and this relieved the entrepreneur of risk. It remained cheaper for many merchants to have workers in the home rather than in an expensive factory.

Cotton spinning factories were the most famous and numerous of the factories of the early Industrial Revolution. The earliest ones were erected in Lancashire in the 1770s and in Lanarkshire in the 1780s and, by the 1800s, they were being built with great speed in many parts of north-west England, Yorkshire, central and Highland Scotland, and in the English south-west. Initially, factories were most often located beside fast-flowing rivers to provide water power, but close enough to existing villages which could provide a labour force to start production and could expand to house a migrant population coming to work at the factory. Early examples of factory villages include Josiah Wedgwood's pottery factory at Etruria in Staffordshire from 1769, and Jedediah Strutt's cotton mill works at Belper in 1778. From the 1780s the numbers of such villages mushroomed as industry boomed. By 1835, there were 1,330 woollen mills, 1,245 cotton factories, 345 flax mills and 238 silk mills in Britain and Ireland. Many of these were small. Woollen mills had an average work force of fewer than 60 even in 1851.

The steam engine was to prove an important aspect of the Industrial Revolution, though it was to be of far greater importance after 1830 than before. Indeed, the deployment of steam engines was heavily restricted between 1760 and 1830. One of the major reasons for this was that the patent on James Watt's version of the steam engine

Focus on

The factory

Large factories only employed perhaps 6 per cent of the British labour force by the 1830s and 1840s, but where they existed they were extremely influential in changing patterns of work and leisure, in attracting workers to migrate from country to town, and could generate enormous profits for their owners and managers. This newspaper description from the 1830s is a eulogy to factories, giving a sense of the novelty of their scale, organisation and machinery. It praises aspects which later in the nineteenth century were condemned and banned – such as the employment of children for up to 11 hours per day in factory and school work. Note the lack of any criticism, and the way economic and moral benefits are attributed to factory work. The Deanston works featured undertook both spinning and weaving to make cloth, and was located in Perthshire, on the edge of the Scottish Highlands from which flowed a river which powered the mill's machinery. The cotton arrived in bales from the United States, and what happened to it is described below:

Deanston Cotton-Works employ perhaps 1,100 persons, young and old, and contain the most perfect machinery in the kingdom . . . The whole of the works are lighted with gas, and they possessed this advantage so early as 1813, before any of our towns could boast the same brilliant light. Tunnels are made all underground, by which communication can be had with the different departments without going out of doors . . .

The process of manufacture may be described as follows: – The bags of cotton, containing each about 300 pounds weight [c.150kg], are laid upon the floor in rows, taken out and thrown into a machine called a *Willow*. This willow is a revolving cylinder with iron teeth, which divides and breaks down the masses. The material is then conveyed to another machine – *the Angel*. The cotton is then weighed in small portions, spread out, and put into a machine which determines and regulates the grist of the thread. Pasting through pairs of rollers, the cotton is struck by iron beaters (as in a thrashing-mill) at the rate of six thousand feet per minute! . . . The cotton is now in the form of a web – is next wound on rollers – and put to the carding machines, whereby the fibres of the cotton are completely separated, and any remaining lumps or refuse are taken out . . .

The next process to which the material passes, is the drawing machine, wherein the fibres are drawn into a parallel and longitudinal position, by means of successive rollers . . . The material is carried to what is a called a *roving frame*, where it is drawn to a much smaller grist, and then twisted unto a thready form, and is wound upon bobbins. These bobbins are carried to spinning machines, when the grist is still more reduced, until the thread reaches its desired size, when it is twisted sufficiently firm to become thread fit for weaving . . . The bobbins, by the movements of which the twist is thrown into thread, go at the amazing velocity of 8,000 revolutions per minute! The effect is magical. These machines are attended by children, chiefly little girls, who are singularly dexterous, and they are superintended by grown-up women – one male superintendant having the general charge of the department. The work is light and easy, but requires constant attention and great cleanliness and order, and thus it may be said to form an excellent school for training the young to habits of attention and industry. These little girls follow the employment with spirit and cheerfulness, from eight to twelve hours a-day. The yarn intended for woof or weft [weaving] is upon the *mule jenny* . . . Hitherto such machines have generally been worked by men of great strength and skill, who acquired high wages, and were the chief movers in all the combinations of the cotton trade. To obviate the inconveniences of these strikes, . . . [the] invention of [a new] machine removes the only laborious and slavish employment that remained in the cotton manufacture . . . It has created a demand for young females' labour . . . [After preparing the warp for the weaving process] it is carried to the power-loom, where the whole operations are performed by mechanism; the young women, who attend two looms each, having merely the supply of woof from time to time, and mend such threads of the warp as may break in the process . . . These looms, to the number of about 300, are arranged in rows, with alleys between, in a most spacious apartment, which, when lighted with gas, has a most magnificent effect.

In going over the vast establishment, it seemed to us like entering an illuminated village, and we shall not soon forget the effect of 300 gas lights in one apartment . . . There is a head or superintendant to each department – every one has his own allotted part – and in most cases they are paid by the piece, not in weekly wages. They receive the amount of their earnings every Thursday morning (that being the market day); and the youngest individual about the works is paid his or her wages into their own hand, which seems to give them an idea of personal consequence. They have the privilege of leaving any moment they choose, without previous warning; and we were informed that this is found to insure a more steady, agreeable, and lengthened service . . . There is no fine or punishment, excepting for damage to the works through evident carelessness. The order of the establishment is preserved by the dismissal of offending individuals, or their banishment for a limited period. By 'stopping the supplies,' every member of the family is interested in the good conduct of the whole, and a banished child, man, or friend, finds no rest at home. The morals of the people are in general very correct; no drunkard is permitted within the establishment.

Immediately adjoining the works is a handsome little village, built and founded by the company, which contains about 1,200 inhabitants. The houses are neat, built in one long street parallel to the water course, and are two stories high, with attics. They are most exemplary patterns of cleanliness, and to each house is attached a small piece of garden ground, and a range of grass plot for bleaching. A school-room is united to the establishment, capable of containing 200 children, and a teacher is paid by the company. The young children generally go to school when about five years of age; and as none are admitted into the works until they are nine, they are mostly good readers, and able to write and cypher before they enter the works. The children employed in the works from nine to thirteen years of age, must, according to the Factory Act, work only eight hours per day, and about three hours are devoted to the school-room. The number of this amounts to 100, and they are divided into relays of 33 each; so that while two relays are at work, one is attending school. The youth above thirteen years of age and under sixteen are expected to attend an evening school four nights in the week; and a Sabbath school in the village contains about 150 pupils. Thus the works at Deanston seem to possess every facility and recommendation; they have changed the aspect of the country – beautiful and romantic as it is – by introducing into it habits of industry, order, and the highest mechanical genius and dexterity; they cause a circulation of money to the extent of about [£]20,000 per annum; they furnish employment for the people of all ages; they have called forth the spirit and activity of the agriculturalists to meet the ever-recurring demands of the place; and in all respects they are a splendid monument of British enterprise, skill, and perseverance.

Source: J. Gordon (ed.), *The New Statistical Account of Scotland* (Edinburgh and London, Blackwood and Sons, 1845), volume 10, pp. 1233–9, accessed at http://stat-acc-scot.edina.ac.uk/link/1834–45/Perth/Kilmadock/

was in force until 1800, restraining expanded production by other manufacturers. But equally, the application of steam engines to processes depended on other technological breakthroughs or perfecting of technique. The first major use was in pumping water, especially from mines. As flooding was one of the major factors restricting mine operations, this was to be a significant advance, notably in allowing mines to go deeper. A second major use was in transport. Steam engines were first used in small ships in the 1810s, starting with the 'Comet' built on the River Clyde, but the application was not widespread until the 1840s and 1850s. Railways were to be just as important, with the Stockton to Darlington railway of 1825 using George Stephenson's 'Rocket', and by 1830 there were the beginnings of steam-powered travel along a number of routes. The third major use was in powering static machinery in manufacturing, and this was held back until after 1850 in many industries by the lower costs of both water-powered production and of domestic manufacture.

These were the exceptions, however. Whilst bringing workers together under one roof allowed the use of mechanical rather than human power, there were factors that restrained the physical size of most factories. For one thing, factory workers were often more expensive in terms of wages, and more difficult to recruit, than domestic workers labouring in their own homes. With markets for products being so given to rapid fluctuation – even more so during war and imperial expansion – it was risky for manufacturers to invest heavily in large-scale works. Another reason was the nature of organising work. A common way was subcontracting by factory owners – whether within or outside the factory. In Birmingham, the gun-making industry relied on small master craftsmen who received subcontracts from merchants. This happened in many of the metal trades, lowering the need for investment and reducing the risk to entrepreneurs. Where factories did win over home production was in reducing transport costs, flexibility in changing product ranges, and some better control over embezzlement.

Among the important characteristics of the Industrial Revolution were the training of labour, the transition of skills and the collective innovation of the workforce. In many cases, the factory was an ideal location for these developments. The factory was a place where training could be intensive, where the work culture was imposed forcibly and very quickly upon new workers, many of whom in this period might be employed in some capacities from as early as 9 years of age. Certainly, by the age of 12 or 13 many might be operating machinery. This was a process that involved the deskilling of the workforce – substituting machines for human skill, a process that was to grow in significance during the nineteenth and early twentieth centuries. Outside of the factory, there were still opportunities for training, with networks of women workers exchanging information through mutual aid and providing technical education to each other. This was especially common in knitting and other textile working where women worked in the home, in the fields, or even as they were walking, training each other in new techniques.

The ownership of industries in this period was concentrated in families, common-law partnerships, and partnerships between merchants and the technically competent engineer. Family firms were dynamic, flexible and cost-efficient, tending to be free from much cheating and illegality and thus efficient and effective. Family and friendship-based partnerships were common, and some involved wealthy landowners who had made considerable money from agricultural improvement and the selling of mining or transport rights. If a firm needed more money, it took on more partners.

The evidence is growing from recent research that the extent of the factory, of large-scale production, and of major technological invention have each been overstated as elements in economic change between 1780 and 1830. Much of the economy was sustaining older characteristics, but doing so with more people and greater output. In other ways, things were changing, and with very profound consequences for the strength of the nation and for the long-term prosperity of the people. The mere fact that the British economy survived in its strength by the 1790s – let alone the 1830s – is indicative of its resilience. It had survived colonial wars with France, with the colonists in the American War of Independence and, between 1793 and 1815, the Revolutionary and Napoleonic Wars with France.

Despite these pressures, and that of population growth, Britain was able to sustain reasonable living standards and avoid the crises of scarcity that had bedevilled earlier centuries. It was this sustained growth that was distinctive to Britain between 1760 and 1830. Nowhere in Europe, nowhere in the world, was able to match this experience at that time. Britain started the major economic mismatch between the first and third world, between developed and undeveloped countries, the division between East and West, the creation of a gap in economic performance that in the twenty-first century is known as the gap between North and South. What the Industrial Revolution did was to introduce the possibility that growth was standard and continuous, not unusual and episodic.

Agriculture

Increasing population and the rising demand of manufacturing workers who were no longer working in full-time farming caused food prices to rise very dramatically during the Napoleonic Wars, before sliding from the 1810s to the 1850s. This made agriculture very volatile and, in places, led by the end of the period to serious crisis.

The total numbers employed in agriculture changed remarkably little during the period 1700–1850, staying relatively stable in England and Wales at around 1.40–1.55 million. However, within this total there was a sharp fall in the numbers of boys and of women, reflecting the extent to which farming became increasingly hierarchical and professionalised, and dominated by men; in 1700, men made up only 39 per cent of the farming workforce, but by 1850 the proportion had risen to 64 per cent.[10] This

---

[10] R.C. Allen, 'Agriculture during the Industrial Revolution', in R. Floud and P. Johnson (eds), *The Cambridge Economic History of Modern Britain: Volume I: Industrialisation, 1700–1860* (Cambridge, Cambridge University Press, 2004), p. 105.

showed the decline of family labour, of smallholding farming, and the rise of erratic farm employment. Hundreds of thousands were, by the 1810s, itinerant harvesters – mostly from Ireland, but others from the Highlands of Scotland – who moved round the British mainland during the summer months to bring in the harvest. Jobs in agriculture were becoming more specialised, leading to increased productivity, but also to marginalisation of some groups, such as local casual labourers and women workers.

Productivity continued to rise as in the eighteenth century, largely because the amount of land under farming grew, encouraged by the high prices during the war years, but the workforce stayed roughly constant. Put another way, the number of workers per acre decreased as the larger farming methods introduced economies of scale. Moreover, the agricultural products improved in quality. New strains of corn proved more resistant to disease, stockbreeding introduced new varieties of cattle, and new breeds of sheep and pigs weighed more.

The tendency to enclose open fields continued in this period with increasing intensity, and spread to more marginal agricultural areas. But a different type of land use emerged in the upland estates of the north of England and the Highlands of Scotland. On such marginal land from the 1770s, landowners found that conventional farming reaped insufficient rentals, and they turned instead to clearing huge swathes of hillside of all inhabitants and using a combination of large-scale sheep-farming and, on country estates, sport shooting of deer, pheasant and grouse for the very rich. In the Highlands and Islands of Scotland, the creation of large estates based on sheep-farming and deer-hunting for the elites led to the removal of the common people in vast numbers either to poor coastal settlements where small parcels of land, known as crofts, were intended to provide a subsistence living supplemented by coastal fishing, or to new weaving or factory villages. These clearances caused intense social distress, leading to a feeling of great bitterness and resentment that was to spill over in the later nineteenth century into protest and a schism in the social fabric unmatched on mainland Britain.

These changes in agriculture, though deep and profound for many people, were insufficient to continue to meet the demands of the whole economy. From the 1790s, British self-sufficiency in food ended, and imports of grain from overseas became critical to domestic diet. Moreover, the agricultural sector failed to provide a good diet to Britons, and those working in farming earned so little that they did not form a good market for the industrial output of the manufacturing sector. In addition, whilst many landowners made huge profits from farming during this period, relatively little made its way into investment in industry. A great deal was directed into the construction of stately homes.

The end of the Napoleonic Wars in 1814–15 exposed Britain to increased competition from exporters elsewhere, notably in agriculture. Grain imports were rising, including, importantly in the long term, from North America, where highly productive wheat and corn growing was developing on vast farms in the flatlands. To save the revenue from rental incomes, the landowning class lobbied intensively for the passing of the Corn Laws in 1815, which put tariffs on the importation of grain from overseas.

This effectively sustained the price of home-grown cereals, saving the agricultural sector from the premature effects of cheap imported food. However, the cost was high food prices for the impoverished in Britain. Some rural farm workers benefited from rising prices, but the urban and industrial poor did not. This helped to foment popular protest in the late 1810s and 1820s amongst the urban and industrial working classes. It also underpinned the growing consensus amongst the middle classes that the ideal economic arrangement was free trade. The result was a longer-term unease in urban and industrial Britain that the rural elites were receiving preferential treatment from the British state.

Further reading

Daunton, M.J., *Progress and Poverty: An Economic and Social History of Britain, 1700–1850* (Oxford, Oxford University Press, 1995)

Floud, R. and Johnson, P. (eds), *The Cambridge Economic History of Modern Britain: Volume I: Industrialisation, 1700–1860* (Cambridge, Cambridge University Press, 2004)

King, S. and Timmins, G., *Making Sense of the Industrial Revolution: English Economy and Society 1700–1850* (Manchester, Manchester University Press, 2001)

Mathias, P., *The First Industrial Nation: The Economic History of Britain 1700–1914* (London, Routledge, 2001)

Pope, R. (ed.), *Atlas of British Social and Economic History since c.1700* (London, Routledge, 1989)

Whatley, C., *The Industrial Revolution in Scotland* (Cambridge, Cambridge University Press, 1997)

8

The social revolution

The birth of class

The Industrial Revolution did more than change the structure of the economy. It did much to change the structure of society too. Though this change started in the countryside, it was the spread to the towns and cities that was to cause the greatest impact. The changes were often subtle, to be observed in manners or relations between people of different ranks as well as between people of the same station in society. In the 1780s, 'stations' and 'ranks' were the main words used to describe the society of Britain. By 1830, 'class' was the new term of choice. A new world of social classes was born in the minds of contemporaries.

In a very basic way, this has often been described by historians as the 'birth of class' – the increasing separation of society by large horizontal divisions into the working classes, middle classes and upper classes or, in rural society, into farm labourers, tenant farmers and landlords. With political radicalism and the spread of trade unionism between the 1790s and 1820s, social classes were being forged in increasingly oppositional social relations, created by the new modes of economic production, ideas induced by the French Revolution and by growing social distance. The relations between classes became increasingly dominated by money – by wages. Landowners in the countryside held to values of inherited wealth, stewardship of land and ostentatious consumption. The new very rich merchants, manufacturers and higher professionals in urban areas were distinguished by having made their wealth through risk-taking, entrepreneurship and hard work; but many of these also bought into the values of the landed classes, acquiring landed properties in the countryside to mark their new standing. This served an additional purpose of offering escape from the unhealthy living conditions of even the richer quarters of industrialising cities like Manchester or Glasgow.

The social revolution brought in a large social stratum of the middle classes which, in urban and industrial districts, was composed of medium-sized merchants, larger shop-keepers, clerks, and professionals like bankers and lawyers. This group might aspire to escape to a gentrified country house, but characteristically settled for new suburban houses to rent. Their values were less represented in ostentatious consumption; they deprecated the idleness of many of the rich who lived off rental income, dallied in foreign travel and conducted a decadent social life. Rather, their values rested in a puritan outlook of restraint, thrift and sobriety, no better expressed than in assiduous church-going. Holding this group of interlocking values together was the emerging notion of 'respectability', which lay behind this group's pressure by 1830 to attain the vote.

The working classes, in turn, had – or were compelled to adopt – different values: of collective solidarity and mutual support. Isolated from middle-class paternalism, they were forced to create their own cultural traditions. In the late eighteenth century, they experienced an intensification of labour, as well as hardening lines of exploitation in workshop and factory, and diminishing control over property, as land and homes became either rented to them or tied to their jobs. This pushed them to rely upon their own resources and to find strength through unity. They formed friendly societies, benefit clubs and burial clubs, into which they put regular savings in return for benefits when they were sick or died. This collective spirit also contributed to the formation of combinations or trade societies to resist periods of wage reductions or falling working conditions. Older established groups of craftsmen, who were organised in guilds or trade incorporations, deprecated the influx of new workers, often with fewer job skills, into their protected craft, but all felt the new time discipline being imposed by merchant manufacturers.

Workers also resisted the increasing attack on pleasures. Industrial employers and urban elites saw in traditional forms of play and recreation challenges to the order and discipline needed for continued economic development. This led to much play, leisure and recreation being considered 'irrational' and not 'useful' either to the individual or to society. Popular culture was squeezed by controls upon working-class time between Monday and Saturday, and by the shut-down of all leisure on the Christian Sunday. The traditional half-work day of St Monday (a jokey informal saint's day that had existed in the eighteenth century) came under attack from employers, who wanted every working day to be fully utilised and not have expensive machinery lying idle. Middle-class obsession with Sabbath profanation meant it was virtually impossible to undertake sport or other forms of play. Going to church was one of the few organised Sunday activities left in many communities.

One of the consequences of the new regime of industrial capitalism was that the workplace fell more under the control of the employer, the foreman and overseer. In pre-industrial society, group identities had developed to a considerable extent in the place of work. Work time had traditionally involved artisans indulging in play, ritual and leisure – such as cards, drinking in the workshop and games of various kinds – thus linking work with cultural identity very strongly. But with the development of industrial society between 1780 and 1830, the factory offered less respite from work. The pace of work was no longer in the worker's control, whilst timekeeping became a focus of friction, with the factory hooter marking the working day and some workers

Focus on

The birth of class

These extracts illustrate how contemporaries in the early nineteenth century noted the beginnings of social class relations. These were becoming evident in the breakdown of former paternalism by elites and deference by lower social ranks and in the reduced power of both rural peasants and urban artisans to control their working conditions.

The first extract is a song written by strikers in the Sheffield cutlery trade in 1787. A master cutler by the name of Joseph Watkinson had created a large firm, and started to demand increased production from his workers. He paid his workers by the dozen knives they made. In 1787, he demanded 13 knives for the wages of a dozen. The workers went on strike, and made up this song:

> That offspring of tyranny, baseness and pride
> Our rights hath invaded and almost destroyed.
> May that man be banished who villainy screens
> Or sides with big Watkinson and his thirteens.
>
> And may the odd knife his great carcass dissect:
> Lay open his vitals for men to inspect
> A heart full as black as the infernal gulf
> In that greedy, blood sucking, bone-scraping wolf.

Faster production brought control of time. A witness to a parliamentary committee reported on life in a mill:

> There we worked as long as could see in summer, and I could not say at what hour it was that we stopped. There was nobody but the master and the master's son who had a watch, and we did not know the time. There was one man who had a watch . . . It was taken from him and given into the master's custody because he had told the men the time of day . . .

Things in the countryside were becoming just as divisive. John Ramsay (1736–1814) was a major landowner who owned significant amounts of farming land in central Scotland to the west of Stirling. He had invested heavily in improvements by removing small tenants, giving leases to better tenants, and he reaped the benefits of improved rental income with which he built himself a large mansion. But he noted in his diary around 1800 that a big change in attitudes came, especially with many of his tenants no longer going to his own parish church of the Church of Scotland, but going instead to a dissenting meeting house of what were called 'Antiburghers' (so-called because they refused to take burgess oaths of loyalty to the Church of Scotland):

Not many years ago, in walking upon the highroad, every bonnet and hat was lifted to the gentry whom the people met. It was an unmeaning expression of respect. The first who would not bow the knee to Baal were the Antiburghers when going to church on Sunday. No such thing now takes place, Sunday or Saturday, among our rustics, even when they are acquainted with the gentleman. It is connected with the spirit of the times.

Christian Watt, a fisherwoman from a village called Broadsea near Fraserburgh in north-east Scotland, was on the receiving end of this agricultural improvement. She too noted that most of the common people in her community became religious Dissenters, but in her memoir she explained the economic circumstances that led to this:

And then the whole world changed. It was not gradual but sudden like lightening. Whole gangs of men came in to reclaim the land, they ploughed bogs and stanks, everywhere was the smell of burning whins. Suddenly huge big parks were marching up the side of Mormond hill, so greedy did they become for land. Around Cairnbulg and St Combs what had been large tracts of bents suddenly became farmland. You could make a good bit of money at drystane dyking if you had the skill, for all the parks were enclosed. New steadings and farm houses were going up everywhere . . . In the new order the cottar was hardest hit. Formerly he was a tenant at will with the same rights as a free man, for he could sell his little holding or leave it to his son. Now he was a slave, with a shilling or two to break the bond . . .
    After this prosperity farmers started to marry out of their own class and often took professional men's daughters as wives who were not brought up in the country and did not know the land. They looked down on their employees and aped the gentry, they looked down on us fishwives. We were no longer welcome and part of the family as before. But cottars and croft wives remained the same.

The loss of paternalism by the elites was called by the historian Thomas Carlyle in 1839 the 'abdication on the part of the governors'. Though families might move up or down the social scale according to changes in their wealth, society had become split into major horizontal classes, with considerable loss of personal acquaintance and empathetic understanding between people in each.

Sources: http://www.lyrics007.com/PLM%20Lyrics/Watkinsons%20Thirteens%20Lyrics.html accessed 13 September 2007; E.P. Thompson, *Customs in Common* (London, The Merlin Press, 1991), p. 389; J. Ramsay, *Scotland and Scotsmen in the Eighteenth Century, vol. II* (Edinburgh and London, William Blackwood, 1888), p. 557; D. Fraser (ed.), *The Christian Watt Papers* (Collieston, Caledonian Books, 1988), p. 47.

being deprived of watches on arrival. The casual expression of social identity became more difficult in places of labour characterised by control and occasional industrial dispute – including Luddism in the 1810s, when wool and cotton mills were attacked and machine breaking spread over the introduction of new looms that were undermining employment. The workplace was becoming contested territory. Foremen and overseers so drove the workforce that cultural development and identity had to be constructed outside of work.

In this, religion played an important role for many workers. What went on outside hours of labour became very important to working-class identity. And with a long working week, this meant increasing attention focused on Sundays, the one day of rest for most workers. Religion and play on Sundays became equally important to identity for both middle and working classes. The Methodist Church in England, Wales and Ireland, and the Presbyterian churches in both Scotland and Ireland, became sites where groups could cultivate their social identity at Sunday worship and weekday church meetings – so much so, that tensions erupted within these religious groupings, leading to repeated splits from the 1810s to the 1840s. Within Methodism, for instance, prosperous middle-class congregations developed – in part from prospering artisan families and in part from rising commerce – leading in many towns in the north of England to congregations removing from one church to another, and sometimes relocating to the comfortable suburbs. Many congregations developed an air of social exclusivity to middle-class families, enforced through dress codes, high levels of pew rents, and a cultural ambience that deliberately distanced worshippers from those of lower social standing and affluence. The result was ecclesiastical schism; in Methodism, working-class denominations came into being from the 1810s, including the Primitive Methodists and the Bible Christians. By the 1840s, Methodism had nine different branches, and Scottish Presbyterianism had a similar number, representing heightened stratification in large part by social class.

The process of class formation in these decades was not an end in itself. Every society is constantly in flux, and the sharper class divisions of this period were to change and hybridise. The social structure of industrial Britain was never completely solidified into one form, but kept changing.

Gender relations

The social revolution was not just about sharper class division. Between 1780 and 1830, political and intellectual affairs introduced radically different visions of women's role. At the same time, there were important implications for the conception of what it was to be a 'true man'.

Britons were intrigued by the influence of the French Revolution upon women. In 1789, the women of Paris marched upon Versailles in a famous demonstration in search of bread. The English political commentator Edmund Burke made much mileage of this episode in his denunciation of the Revolution as a whole:

[T]he heads of two of the kings bodyguards were stuck upon spears and led the procession; whilst the royal captives who followed in the train were slowly moved along amidst the horrid yells, and shrilling screams, and frantic dances, and infamous contumelies, and all the unutterable abominations of the furies of hell, in the abused shape of the vilest of women.[1]

In 1793, Marie Antoinette was guillotined in front of a cheering crowd of Parisians. Her execution marked the beginning of a new order – not just a new political order but a new way of conceptualising relations between men and women. One of Marie Antoinette's 'crimes' had been her alleged failure in her motherly duties. So, one of the messages was that the age of the idle aristocratic woman was at an end. In the post-French revolutionary world the serious and responsible mother was to receive the highest adulation. Yet, when the Declaration of the Rights of Man and the Citizen was published in 1789, women had been disappointed that they were not included in the term 'man'. And the 1791 Revolutionary Constitution defined as active citizens independent men over 25 (with women's rights supposedly taken care of by men). Political women were viewed as dangerous and as symbols of disorder.

In Paris at the time was an Englishwoman, Mary Wollstonecraft, attracted by the romance of the revolution, but soon disillusioned by the exclusion of women from revolutionary reforms and the definition of citizens as men. In 1792, she wrote: 'It is vain to expect virtue from women till they are in some degree independent of men; nay, it is vain to expect that strength of natural affection which would make them good wives and mothers. Whilst they are absolutely dependent on their husbands they will be cunning, mean and selfish . . .' In her critique, marriage itself lay at the root of women's problems:

> . . . nor will women ever fulfil the peculiar duties of their sex, till they become enlightened citizens, till they become free by being enabled to earn their own subsistence, independent of men . . . Nay, marriage will never be held sacred till women, by being brought up with men, are prepared to be their companions rather than their mistresses; for the mean doublings of cunning will ever render them contemptible, whilst oppression renders them timid.[2]

Wollstonecraft denied the condemnation of women's emotions and inner difference from men. In essence, she crafted, almost single-handedly, a manifesto of feminism. In the short term, it had little positive impact. She became immediately notorious as 'unnatural and rebellious', depicted (even by her husband, the radical William Godwin) as a wild and uncontrollable woman. In truth, Wollstonecraft's ideas were too radical

---

[1] Quoted in E.J. Payne, *Burke Select Works*, Volume 1, new edn (Oxford, Clarendon, 2005), pp. 84–5.
[2] M. Wollstonecraft, *A Vindication of the Rights of Woman* (orig. 1792, online version at http://www. cartage.org.lb/en/themes/GeogHist/histories/histdocs/biblio18/A18/Woolstonecraft/mw-vind.html), Chapters 9, 12.

for her time, and were often ridiculed after her death. By the 1860s and 1870s, however, her ideas were being taken up by the first organised feminists as they campaigned to increase women's legal and political rights.

Until the 1860s, at least, it was ideas such as those of Rousseau and of medical men of the Enlightenment that held sway. The notion that women were biologically predetermined to pregnancy and motherhood, that they were the moral heart of domestic bliss, and that they were unsuited to a wider role in worldly affairs, came to dominate in the nineteenth century. Literature of the time expressed these ideas. In 1802, the English poet Ann Taylor Gilbert penned a poem in praise of her mother:

> Who fed me from her gentle breast
> And hush'd me in her arms to rest
> And on my cheek sweet kisses prest?
>   My Mother.
> When sleep forsook my open eye,
> Who was it sung sweet hushaby
> And rock'd me that I should cry?
>   My Mother.[3]

The beginnings of what some might regard as a gushy sentimentality emerged from the romantic movement of the period, placing motherhood and femininity at its heart. Below is William Wordsworth's influential 1807 poem eulogising women:

> I saw her upon nearer view,
> A spirit, yet a woman too!
> Her household motions light and free,
> And steps of virgin liberty;
> A countenance in which did meet
> Sweet records, promises as sweet;
> A creature not too bright or good
> For human nature's daily food;
> For transient sorrows, simple wiles,
> Praise, blame, love, kisses, tears and smiles.[4]

This approach to women was not all negative in its results. There was an immediate gain for women in the recognition of their important role as mothers and educators, leading to improvements in access to higher educational lectures for small numbers of women at institutions such as Anderson's College (1796) in Glasgow and Birkbeck College (1823) in London. However, this did not open educational qualifications or

---

[3] Quoted in L. Davidoff and C. Hall, *Family Fortunes: Men and Women of the English Middle Class, 1780–1850* (London, Routledge, 1987), p. 459.

[4] 'Perfect woman', originally from W. Wordsworth, *Poems in Two Volumes* (1807), quoted in *Christian Miscellany*, 1890, p. 394.

professional careers to women. On the contrary, as the professions expanded for men, it became harder for women as their economic roles were increasingly narrowed to so-called 'women's work', charitable activity, or domestic confinement. Few at this time believed that women should have equal political rights.

In turn, men's role in the state, the family and society became more clearly marked out by these definitions of women's roles. Men were the political rulers and the key workers. Industrialisation brought a spread of opportunities for artisan specialisation, for, with declining control of entry to the professions and guilds, there were more jobs, with new trades, new products and, in some cases, new working conditions in larger factories or large workshops. Attendant upon this was increasing insecurity. Trade depressions and the possibility of being laid off in bad times made skilled workers more economically vulnerable. This had cultural consequences. Male artisan culture prized the man's ability to fend for his family, but this became difficult in periods of low wages or underemployment. Domestic violence by artisans upon their wives and children was one result, growing rapidly in the 1790s and 1800s in industrial towns like Glasgow, fostering a long-term problem that was to stretch through into the twentieth century. Male machismo developed a sharper edge in the midst of such economic vulnerability, with public house and illegal drinking shebeens developing in industrial cities, from which men might arrive home, reeling drunk, to cause fear in their families. Civil leaders, the churches and others became increasingly concerned with this, promoting a moral panic that men were the social problem of the new urban society. One result in 1828 was the inauguration of the British temperance movement, which propagandised men to take the pledge of abstinence from strong alcoholic beverages and thereby improve the conditions of their families.

The new artisan culture was to prove influential in the evolving conception of masculinity in British society. There was nothing new, of course, in the importance of physical prowess in the conception of manhood. But in the midst of industrialisation and the creation of large cities in which the working class and the poor were beginning to be seen as alienated from other social classes, the conception grew that men's temptations to drink, dissipation, violence and anger were the causes of major social problems and family breakdown. Men were seen as 'heathens' whose threat to society needed to be confronted by evangelisation by the churches. From the 1810s, massive efforts were being made in what became known as 'the home missions', using Sunday schools and temperance organisations to bring the gospel to young men and husbands, to bring them to church and thus good behaviour. In this situation, women's God-given role to be mother and homemaker offered the hope for society and moral betterment. Whereas in the seventeenth and eighteenth centuries, women had carried the stigma of being disorderly and slatternly, they matured in the early nineteenth century into 'the angel in the house'. Men were now depicted as the problem of society, and women were the solution.

One outcome of this was increased gendering of work. Industrialisation brought more marginalisation of women in the workplace. Women were relegated to low-paid, low-status and what were seen as low-skilled jobs. In the middle classes, women were regarded as not being part of the workforce at all – women's place was in the home (though many did develop professional and charitable activities). In the working classes, exploitation of women rose; women (as well as children) were assumed to be the key group of workers for whom new manufacturing methods were designed, with work processes subdivided in order to allow child and female workers to do them easily and skilfully – for example, the spinning jenny was first invented for a young girl to use.[5]

Women's lives changed in other ways. They were marrying younger, and were getting pregnant before marriage to a much greater extent, resulting in both high marriage rates and rising illegitimacy rates. Significantly more women gave birth between the ages of 15 and 29 in the 1780–1829 period than in the previous 100 years. Teenage pregnancy was on the increase, as well as teenage marriage. This was in contrast with France at that time, and seems to signal a significant British change in the nature of sexual relations and the taking of sexual partners. Moreover, an increasing proportion of pregnancies were going to term and producing live births.[6] Women's domestic roles also worsened among the working classes and the poor. Households seem to have become larger with the onset of the Industrial Revolution. Housing pressure was one factor, forcing families and lodgers to co-habit in small and cramped dwellings, sometimes many persons to a room, in order to afford the rent, heat and light. Live-in servants in agriculture were to remain important through the Victorian period, but of rising significance in middle-class urban homes was the live-in domestic servant. The middle-class home, in a vital and important way, was becoming the dominant cultural ideal, and after 1830 it was to become one that was impressed upon the working classes. But one of the key factors restraining this from developing before 1830 was the standard of living amongst the working classes. As the next section discusses, the Industrial Revolution was to prove extremely detrimental to the overall standard and quality of life of the vast majority of the working people of Britain.

The standard of living debate

There has been no longer-standing, more hard-fought or more controversial dispute in the economic and social history of Britain than the standard of living debate. It grew out of contemporary and political debate in the nineteenth century, to emerge into universities in the 1910s and the 1920s. Since the First World War, historians have been engrossed with this question.

What is at stake in the debate is simple to describe. Did the British working classes benefit from the early industrialisation of the economy between 1760 and 1830? The

---

[5] M. Berg, 'What difference did women's work make to the Industrial Revolution?', in P. Sharpe (ed.), *Women's Work: The English Experience 1650–1914* (London, Arnold, 1998), p. 161.

[6] E.A. Wrigley, 'British population during the "long" eighteenth century, 1680–1840', in R. Floud and P. Johnson (eds), *The Cambridge Economic History of Modern Britain: Volume I: Industrialisation, 1700–1860* (Cambridge, Cambridge University Press, 2004), p. 70.

issue is much less controversial after 1850. It is generally agreed that, in the second half of the nineteenth century, though poverty, low wages, poor housing and ill-health were still prevalent, nearly all social groups experienced rising standards of living. But where Britain's first period of rapid economic change between 1780 and 1830 is concerned, the answer is much disputed. The debate is a fairly straightforward one in conceptual terms, but the empirical study, involving different types of evidence, sometimes interpreted in different ways, is highly complex.

The standard of living debate is structured by the ideological considerations of the protagonists. There are, in general, very clear battle lines. There are essentially two sides, each characterised by different ideological backgrounds, different methodologies of research in the debate and, of course, different answers. The two sides are known as the optimists and the pessimists. The optimists consider that, on balance, the British working classes did benefit from the Industrial Revolution, while the pessimists conclude that, overall, they did not. The optimists are frequently economic historians, and argue using economic evidence. Sometimes, they have been politically right-wing, and their arguments were boosted by work conducted during the supremacy of right-wing economic thinking during the Conservative government of Margaret Thatcher in the 1980s. By contrast, the pessimists tend to be social historians, are often more left-wing and sometimes Marxist, and their arguments tend to blend qualitative social evidence with economic data.

The battle lines of the debate have shifted considerably over the decades. In the late nineteenth and early twentieth centuries, the orthodoxy was that the working classes had suffered badly during early industrialisation. Socialist intellectuals and those making new headway in social science in the 1890s and 1900s were rediscovering the extent of poverty in their own time and, as part of their analysis, they projected their pessimistic interpretation back to the 1760–1830 period. The most famous treatment of this view, *The Town Labourer*, published in 1917, was by a husband and wife team of historians, J.L. and Barbara Hammond, whose moral indignation at the suffering of the working classes and the poor in early industrial England deeply affected their interpretation of the benefits of industrialisation. Their book concluded with a long passage on the ideological and economic oppression of the proletariat, and the final sentence stated: '. . . amid all the conquests over nature that gave its triumphs to the Industrial Revolution, the soul of man was passing into a colder exile, for in this new world, with all its wealth and promise and its wide horizon of mystery and hope, the spirit of fellowship was dead.' The Hammonds deprecated the surge in social inequality from the late eighteenth century. The Industrial Revolution, in their view, shifted the balance of power, wealth and earning capacity away from the working classes towards the landed elites and the class of large industrialists. They were quite sure that 'real wages fell rapidly', saying:

> The wage earners employed in these industries did not obtain any part of the new wealth. They received more money in wages when employment was good than when it was bad, but the expansion of industry did not in itself increase their share in the wealth

of the nation . . . The industries that were making the new wealth were not supporting their workpeople . . . The general feature of the times was the rise of a class of rich employers and the creation of a large and miserable proletariate.[7]

The theme that the Industrial Revolution witnessed 'the fall of man' was taken up by an influential commentator of the inter-war period, the Christian and socialist R.H. Tawney, and this was to persuade many British intellectuals in the twentieth century of the correctness of the pessimist case.

The right-wing response to the Hammonds was the emergence in the interwar period of a new economic history, led by John Clapham, followed by T.S. Ashton. They placed greater emphasis on what statistics of the level of workers' real wages revealed about their standard of living, arguing that whilst some workers suffered, the majority benefited from the new industrial age because prices were falling in the long term, making food and housing cheaper, and because employment became more regular and more widely varied with the arrival of the new industries. In the 1950s, this surge by the right-wing, using the statistical evidence of workers' wages, was pursued by newcomers like Max Hartwell, but it also came under attack from the new left, notably Eric Hobsbawm and E.P. Thompson.

Hobsbawm took up the cudgels of the Hammonds, making much headway in criticising the statistical techniques of the optimists. He pointed out that workers in the early Industrial Revolution were frequently unemployed and underemployed, and that, no matter what falls in prices might have occurred, the supply and quality of food and housing was extremely variable between the 1760s and the 1840s. Amongst the many minor points he made, Hobsbawm showed that the growth in the amount of beef and mutton in London between 1801 and 1851 did not keep pace with population growth in that city, clearly indicating the likelihood of a fall in the standard of diet for the low-income groups in the capital. E.P. Thompson added his indignation to that of Hobsbawm, placing greater emphasis on the quality of life of the people, drawing on the evidence of Royal Commissions, autobiographies and commentaries which described the deterioration in condition of the working classes. Thompson said that even if the real wages of the workers increased (and he did not necessarily concede that), the working classes nonetheless suffered. He wrote: 'People may consume more goods and become less happy or less free at the same time, [suffering] a catastrophic experience [of] intensified exploitation, greater insecurity, and increasing human misery.'[8]

Then, in the 1980s, a new breed of economic historian emerged on the back of the rise of the new right in economics. These went back over the old ground to re-assert the virtues and benefits of unbridled capitalism that, in their view, had instigated the Industrial Revolution and brought widespread benefits to the people. This was an

---

[7] J.L. Hammond and B. Hammond, *The Town Labourer* (London, Longmans, 1920), pp. 95–6, 329.

[8] E.P. Thompson, *The Making of the English Working Class* (Harmondsworth, Penguin, 1968 edn), p. 231.

important issue; if the most famous era of unbridled capitalism in the early Industrial Revolution had *not* benefited all the people, then no period was likely to. P.H. Lindert and J.G. Williamson went over the wage and prices data and concluded that real wages may not have moved much before 1800 or even 1820, but from 1820 to 1850 they improved so much (they argued by over 80 per cent) that 'the debate should be over'.[9] Williamson also asserted, amongst other things, that the industrial towns of the 1760–1830 period could not have experienced such an explosion of population if the people moving to them had not been experiencing the benefits of the new economic age. People would not have migrated from country to town if the towns had not been better places to live than the countryside. In this way, Williamson moved into the quality of life aspects of the debate to square up to E.P. Thompson. Another right-wing historian, Nicholas Crafts, revisited the wages' statistics, continuing to argue for the financial benefits that the working classes experienced during this period. But, in an indicator of less progress, Crafts argued that civil and political rights constituted an important aspect of any debate about standards of living, and he calculated that there was no change in political rights, but a deterioration in civil liberties (with repression during the Napoleonic Wars, and the crackdown on the Luddites in the 1810s and the Captain Swing Riots of the 1830s), though there was an improvement from the 1840s.

In the 1990s and 2000s, the debate has been invigorated by new data and new concepts amongst historians. Real wages have been revised significantly because of new data on prices from the period after 1800, when it had been previously assumed that the cost of living declined by 51 per cent (between 1809/14 and 1849/51). A new figure calculated by Charles Feinstein, covering a bigger range of everyday goods, showed that this decline was only 37 per cent. This meant that the overall 80 per cent rise calculated by Lindert and Williamson is reduced by Feinstein to just over 30 per cent as an average and, for the whole period from 1778/82 to 1848/52, may have been within a range as low as 19 per cent or as high as 55 per cent; in either case, much lower than the optimistic figures generated by historians in the 1980s.[10] Other historians have offered even more pessimistic readings. G. Clark has suggested that even Feinstein's data is too optimistic about improvement in the real wages of the working classes. For agricultural workers, he said, there was a marked deterioration in farm day wages between 1750/9 and 1800/10 (the damage caused by a doubling in the cost of living for this group between 1750/9 and 1810/19) before a slow improvement to 1850.[11]

New forms of measurement have emerged later in the debate, but with disputed results and value. One was of the height of British army recruits of 20–23 years of age,

[9] P.H. Lindert and J.G. Williamson, 'English workers' living standards during the Industrial Revolution: a new look,' *Economic History Review*, 361 (1983), pp. 1–25.

[10] H.-J. Voth, 'Living standards and the urban environment', in R. Floud and P. Johnson (eds), *The Cambridge Economic History of Modern Britain: Volume I: Industrialisation, 1700–1860* (Cambridge, Cambridge University Press, 2004), pp. 272–3.

[11] G. Clark, 'The long march of history: farm wages, population, and economic growth, England 1209–1869', *Economic History Review*, 60 (2007), pp. 97–135.

where height is argued to be a good indicator of physical well-being and standard of living. But because height restrictions were imposed on recruiting at certain times, historians employ different techniques to compensate, and this can cause different results. One research project showed the recruits increased in average height from 167.4 cm in 1760 to 170.7 cm in 1830, before falling markedly in the 1840s to 165.3 cm in 1850; another project showed opposite results – that heights of those recruits fell from 171.1 cm in 1760 to 165.6 in 1830 and to 164.7 in 1850. Meanwhile, some historians argue that height is not that good an indicator of well-being since many so-called primitive societies have been known to have giant heights, and economic growth can cause height reduction. Yet, despite these problems, we know that in the twentieth century, British heights shot up markedly because of improved health, diet and standards of living: between 1900 and 1950 males grew by 1.6 cm per decade. The fact that, even at best, army recruits declined by a total of 2 cm (or approximately 0.2 cm per decade) between 1760 and 1850 would tend to suggest that there was negligible movement in standard of living (except perhaps in the 1840s), and certainly no height evidence of great improvement.[12]

Another measure of well-being is volume and intensity of work. Working hours appear to have increased for most workers between 1750 and 1850, possibly by between 20 and 35 per cent, the product largely of disappearing holidays like local festivals and St Monday. If the working day was largely unaffected for most workers, some, notably those in larger textile factories, experienced greater intensity of work, combined with environmental deterioration and the introduction of long hours. Evidence from the level of piece-rates (wages per product made) in relation to their weekly wages indicates that factory workers worked up to a third harder and agricultural workers at least 40 per cent harder between the eighteenth and mid-nineteenth centuries. The arrival of factory working created a marked deterioration in the lives of children. For them, as for adults, injuries and death were another element to be factored into the standard of living debate.

A final area reflecting on standard of living is consumption of luxuries and leisure. Whilst consumption of clothing increased (the product of rapidly falling prices), most items showed little increased consumption by most workers in the late eighteenth and early nineteenth centuries. The same applies to studies of food consumption, which advanced little and may have declined for some groups of people, bearing out Hobsbawm's early research on this in the 1950s.

Standards of living were not the same across all of Britain. Rural Ireland, Wales and Scotland were distinctly poorer than almost all of England, whilst within England there could be major differences between regions. During 1765–95, carpenters in Aberdeen and Edinburgh had, at most, 45 per cent of the wages of London carpenters and only two-thirds of those in Manchester.[13] Moreover, these differences changed at

---

[12] H.-J. Voth, 'Living standards and the urban environment', pp. 271, 273–6.
[13] T.M. Devine, 'Scotland', in R. Floud and P. Johnson (eds), *The Cambridge Economic History of Modern Britain: Volume I: Industrialisation, 1700–1860* (Cambridge, Cambridge University Press, 2004), p. 395.

varying rates. For instance, it is generally observed that, in the early nineteenth century, standards of living fell for agricultural workers in the south and east of England compared to those in the north. The near availability of industrial work meant that farmers had to pay more to keep their workers.

Looked at in economic terms, in many ways life did not improve all that much for the British people and their economy between 1750 and 1850.[14] The weight of historical opinion in the standard of living debate has veered since the 1980s towards the pessimistic view, and the bold revisionism of the right-wing, Thatcher-era historians has retreated significantly. Where workers were better off in 1830 than in 1780, they had achieved this often by more intensive working, by a longer working year, and by involving more of their family in production (not necessarily for more wages). Moreover, gains were often qualified by a deterioration in the living conditions.

Housing and health

The condition of cities became increasingly varied, both between and within cities. Elegant inner suburbs and new towns were built in some places – London's Regent Park, Edinburgh's New Town, Cheltenham, and the spa centre of Bath. These catered for the rich, with grand sweeping terraces, spacious rooms with elaborate internal decoration, paved streets and gated gardens for residents to walk in, and palatial churches with ornamentation and increasingly comfortable pews, often boxed and paid for privately. Seaside resorts emerged for this class of people too, operating from the 1800s the new-fangled bathing machines to allow men and women to swim in head-to-ankle bathing suits in reflection of the rapid puritanisation of manners of that time.

For the majority of British people, however, cities represented experiences different from these. Cities expanded with enormous speed. Liverpool, Manchester and Glasgow each grew from around 60,000 people in 1780 to around 250,000 people in 1830. This growth was crammed into a remarkably small area, with each of these places remaining largely 'walking cities' that could be crossed on foot in under an hour. For the inhabitants, conditions were worsened by the intensity of building. Vacant lots and spaces were filled in by the construction of new houses, streets became narrower, and many houses built for the well-off ended up being 'made down' into tinier houses for the working classes. Toilets as we know them today did not exist. Ash pits were the norm – holes in the ground with rudimentary toilet benches or seats above, into which human excrement was tossed and periodically covered by ash. They were emptied by scavengers, whose job it was to scoop out the contents onto open carts that were pulled to the countryside where it might be sold to farmers as manure. The collection of

---

[14] J. Mokyr, 'Accounting for the Industrial Revolution', in R. Floud and P. Johnson (eds), *The Cambridge Economic History of Modern Britain: Volume I: Industrialisation, 1700–1860* (Cambridge, Cambridge University Press, 2004), p. 2.

Figure 8.1 Libberton's Wynd, Edinburgh, c.1840. Living conditions in the medieval heart of many cities deteriorated rapidly with increased population and the spread of industry in the early nineteenth century.
Source: Mary Evans Picture Library

waste made cities really smelly places. Even the continuation of the conditions of the pre-industrial period might have meant a decline in the quality of life. One socialist historian of the early twentieth century wrote: 'Twelve insanitary houses on a hillside may be a picturesque village, but twelve hundred are a grave nuisance, and twelve thousand a pest and a horror.'[15] And this does not acknowledge what came along

---

[15] G.D.H. Cole, quoted in E.J. Hobsbawm, *Labouring Men* (London, Weidenfeld and Nicolson, 1964), p. 117.

with urban concentration: oppressive policing and the control imposed on ordinary families by rack-renting landlords and factory owners. In short, the sheer concentration of people in industrial towns transformed bearable poverty into unbearable poverty, disease and oppression.

The poorest conditions of life were often at work. It is a truism to say that much of the British Industrial Revolution was facilitated by the labour of women and children. They worked for lower wages than men, in many cases could operate intricate machinery better or get to places (under machines, for instance) men found difficult, and they also tended to be more biddable and less likely to strike or join trade unions. The employment of children in factories was considered to be right and proper, to be part of the process of working-class children learning industrious habits, good discipline and training for their future economic life (see Focus on the Factory, p. 112). There was no real concept of childhood as a period separate from work; education was thought important, but had to be balanced with the need for families to become self-supporting. Thus it was that children went down mines, worked long hours in new cotton spinning factories, worked in domestic situations collecting waste from underneath handlooms and re-threading the shuttlecocks, and, as a result, developed adverse health conditions that were to stunt their life expectancies. Children were the most vulnerable in society, but the prevailing outlook of the period was that children needed the discipline and inculcation of a work ethic that could only be provided through economic labour. One result was a reduction in the extent of education of young people in the late eighteenth and early nineteenth centuries, with evidence that rates of literacy dropped considerably. Instead, more and more children were working in economic roles outside the family – including pauper children.

In these various ways, the standard of living of the vast majority of the people between 1780 and 1830 probably declined in terms of economic income. In terms of health and in terms of education it certainly did. The Industrial Revolution's short-term impact was one of loss, not gain, for most.

Further reading

Floud, R. and Johnson, P. (eds), *The Cambridge Economic History of Modern Britain: Volume I: Industrialisation, 1700–1860* (Cambridge, Cambridge University Press, 2004)

Kent, S.K., *Gender and Power in Britain 1640–1990* (London, Routledge, 1999)

Perkin, H.J., *The Origins of Modern English Society 1780–1880* (London, RKP, 1969)

Rule, J., *The Labouring Classes in Early Industrial England* (London, Longman, 1986)

Smout, T.C., *A History of the Scottish People 1560–1830* (London, Collins, 1969)

Taylor, A.J., *The Standard of Living in Britain in the Industrial Revolution* (London, Methuen, 1975)

9

Running the state

During the 50 years from 1780 to 1830, the world of aristocratic politicians had to face growing demands for change. Some of these demands came from within their own ranks, but there were also new voices coming into the political arena and challenging aristocratic dominance. Growing numbers from the middle ranks of society, the merchants and manufacturers of expanding industry, were demanding a greater say in the running of affairs in their own localities and looking for government policies that were in tune with their business needs. But skilled craftsmen who were finding their work conditions altering dramatically were also getting a voice. Both groups came round to demanding changes in the political system. The struggle for politicians was to find ways of responding to these pressures and of managing the process of change. To this was added the crises of the long war with first revolutionary France and then Napoleonic France.

From North to Pitt

Sensational as it was in parliamentary terms, there was no great follow-up to Dunning's motion of 1780 condemning the extent to which government power had increased at the expense of the Commons, or to the calls for what was called 'economical reform' (see Chapter 2). The Crown's patronage was utilised to the full, the dissidents were cajoled back into line and the opposition momentum ran out. Nonetheless, the war in America, defeats in India, Ireland restless and disorder at home had all created a sense of crisis, doubt about the future and a feeling that changes of some kind were necessary.

The Prime Minister, Lord North, as ever, was keen to resign but was pressed to remain by the King, who was appalled by the alternatives of the various Whig factions who blamed the North government, and therefore implicitly the King for provoking the American revolution. Brief talk of a coalition in the summer of 1780 showed the extent of Whig divisions and North and the King could confidently call an election. Terrified of stirring up more demands for reductions in government patronage, the dominating patrons in most counties went out of their way to avoid a contest. Where there were contests, the Whigs generally lost out, with Edmund Burke losing his seat at

Focus on

Election to Parliament

The following comes from a manuscript Memoir of Henry Beaufoy, MP 1783–95. Beaufoy was a Quaker businessman and, after various attempts, was elected MP, first for Minehead and then for Great Yarmouth.

> I was now for the first time in my life at liberty to attempt the execution of the plans I had formed; and to avail myself of the earliest opportunity that should offer of obtaining a seat in the House of Commons.
>
> With this view, I applied to those attorneys of whom there are several in London, that consider a knowledge of the state of parties in boroughs, and a particular acquaintance with the commanding interest in each, as an important branch of their business. But these applications served only to convince me of the hazards to which a new man, who, without political connexions, endeavours to obtain an independent seat in Parliament, is unavoidably exposed; for, in the first place, he is generally excluded from all chance in such elections as are principally influenced by considerations of public good; the title to favour being naturally one of which he is not possessed, that of services performed and of patriotism already tried. If Wilberforce had not acquired a splendid reputation by his conduct in the former Parliament, he would not in the year 1783 [sc.1784] have been chosen for the County of York.
>
> In the next place, if he engages in a contest, he is exposed to the hazards of sacrificing his fortune, and with it his independence, to the acquisition of his seat in Parliament; by which means he loses in the pursuit, that which alone, if he has honest views, can give value to successes. Or, if in order to avoid this risk, he attempts to procure for a specific sum, the possession of a quiet seat, he not only finds himself engaged in competition with several individuals who have the same object in view, and among whom those from the East are frequently indifferent to the price they give; but he is also obliged to outbid the Treasury itself, for the disposal of such seats is always of consequence to the Minister.

Source: A. Aspinall and E.A. Smith, *English Historical Documents, XI 1783–1832* (London, Eyre & Spottiswoode, 1959) pp. 241–2.

Bristol. Fortunately for him, his patron, the aristocratic Marquess of Rockingham, was able to find him one of his pocket boroughs.

In October 1781, the last substantial British army in America surrendered at Yorktown. Although the King's speech at the opening of Parliament in November implied that the war would go on, most were aware that the game was up. In March 1782, votes of censure were passed and North resigned. The King had no alternative but to send for the opposition and Rockingham took the Treasury, while the rakish Charles James Fox was Secretary of State for Foreign Affairs and Lord Shelburne for Home and Colonial Affairs. The Whigs accepted office on the condition that the King would agree to accept American independence and a minor piece of economical reform, the exclusion of government contractors from Parliament.

Peace negotiations began with the now *de facto* independent America and with France, but, with Shelburne and Fox having a deep mutual antipathy, disputes quickly appeared. The unexpected death of Rockingham led to the King asking Shelburne to take charge. Fox, petulantly and damagingly to his reputation, suggested that Shelburne's appointment was unconstitutional. Fox also now identified with the hard-drinking, high-playing group around the Prince of Wales, now of age, thus, in true Hanoverian fashion, earning the undying hatred of the King. Meanwhile, Shelburne was bringing the American negotiations to an end. Influenced by the ideas expressed in Adam Smith's *Wealth of Nations*, published in 1776, he no longer believed that colonies were essential for British prosperity, and was prepared to concede to the United States most of its territorial demands in the old French territories. Shelburne saw a good free trade agreement with the new state as being the way to future prosperity. But such views were far too radical for most of Parliament. Mercantilist thinking was deeply ingrained and a landowning class instinctively wanted to retain restrictions on the importation of food and had little interest in the new imports of cotton that were making their way to the industrial areas. American ships continued to be excluded from Britain and from the West Indies.

As Shelburne's majority began to break up, Fox refused to rejoin the government. Instead, to the general astonishment, Fox and Lord North, in February 1783, entered an agreement to bring down Shelburne. A vote of censure on the peace terms was carried and Shelburne resigned. The King went to great lengths to try to avoid a government with Fox in it. He, like many others, regarded the coalition as entirely amoral, and contemplated abdication. After all, Fox and the Rockingham Whigs had been denouncing North and his associates both publicly and privately for the last decade as responsible for the American war and its failures, as a threat to British liberties and as dishonest manipulators of a corrupted system. While personal animosities no doubt played their part in the Fox–North coalition, there were also rational political arguments. Both disliked Shelburne's reforming zeal, both were opposed to parliamentary reform, both were prepared to think in terms of cross-party collaboration in order to achieve political stability in the post-war world. Fox cynically defended himself, declaring 'my friendships are perpetual, my enmities are not so' and explaining that the end of the American crisis meant the end of the cause of his differences with North.

In the end, the King could find no alternative combination to provide a majority in Parliament and reluctantly accepted Fox and North as Secretaries of State, with the amenable Duke of Portland as First Lord of the Treasury. When Fox insisted that the King should have no say in the composition of the Cabinet, the King again threatened abdication, but had to give in. He still, however, retained the power to create peerages and this he refused to do at the behest of the new government. The return of North was also a provocation to Americans and destroyed Shelburne's hopes of a peaceful domination of transatlantic trade.

The end of Shelburne's ministry had brought the fall from office of the young William Pitt, son of Chatham. The precocious young man had entered Parliament in 1781 at the age of 21 and had been made Chancellor of the Exchequer, and, effectively, leader in the Commons. He quickly made his name as an able administrator with a quick grasp of detail. Pitt took the lead in the opposition to the coalition, playing on the divisions within it over issues of parliamentary reform.

Where there *was* general agreement was on the need for reform of the East India Company. There had long been dislike amongst the older political elite for the way in which returned nabobs, company servants who had made their fortunes in India, had been able to use their often fabulous wealth to purchase seats in Parliament. What was proposed was the transfer of the government of India to a commission, sitting in London, of seven government appointees and nine members appointed by the company. When the list of commissioners was published, it contained four of Fox's associates and three loyal followers of North, including his own son. Here was the supposed enemy of Crown influence apparently creating his own patronage system, greater than the Treasury ever had. Although the India Bill sailed through the Commons, the King, with doubtful constitutionality, but encouraged by Pitt, made it clear to the House of Lords that 'whoever voted for the India Bill were not only not his friends but he would consider them as his enemies'. In December 1783, the Bill was thrown out and, to widespread amusement, the King asked Pitt to form a government, which many thought, 'like mince pies', would barely survive over the Christmas festivities.

But royal power was still formidable. Peerages were granted to three of the largest controllers of borough votes in return for ensuring that their clients delivered for the new government. The second step was to dissolve Parliament and to hold an election when all the influence of government patronage could be brought to bear. The ground had been well laid. The issue was presented as a choice between the King and Fox, but this was a King who after 24 years on the throne, and despite many vicissitudes, had begun to attract public affection. The backlash against North and Fox was massive. One hundred and sixty of the supporters of the coalition, 'Fox's Martyrs', lost their seats. Pitt was able to command a working majority of over 200, as public opinion among the gentry and financial community and Treasury patronage delivered. What Fox had failed to appreciate was the extent to which the political world was changing, and public opinion, outside the closed circle of an aristocratic Parliament, was having to be taken into account. Pitt was the one who was given the freedom of the City of London and a dinner, presided over by John Wilkes.

Pitt the Younger

Pitt was to retain office, as both First Lord of the Treasury and Chancellor of the Exchequer, for the next 17 years. To the end of his life he regarded himself as an independent Whig in politics. He saw his role as the maintenance of the King's government and, most of the time, was prepared to uphold the royal prerogative – certainly, in the last analysis, he was not prepared to challenge it. In that sense, his opponents had a case in describing his government as a Tory one. His reforming instincts did not entirely desert him, but the direction of them was different. He surrounded himself with able administrators and set up processes to keep track of the public finances. Given the rising cost of government, and a national debt approaching £250 million, it was more and more necessary to ensure that government revenues were collected as fully as possible and that government costs were kept under control. Pitt continued to trim the number of sinecures and, slowly, continued a process, begun under North, of ensuring that senior civil servants were paid salaries rather than receiving fees. Customs and excise were reorganised for greater effectiveness and offices were amalgamated. He managed to push through excise duties on wine, tobacco and spirits – a feat that had eluded Walpole back in 1733 (see Chapter 2). He also found ways of raising new revenue, with the extension of the existing tax on windows, and the introduction of new taxes – on horses, on personal servants, on hackney carriages and later on dogs, clocks and watches, among other things. The window tax, in particular, was a useful wealth tax based on the number of windows and was one that could easily be assessed. Pitt paid a great deal of attention to the actual running of Whitehall departments and brought in numerous steps to increase their efficiency and reduce their costs. In a remarkably short time, he had succeeded in bringing some stability and order into the public finances.

Pitt made tentative moves towards free trade, obtaining in the treaty of 1786, negotiated by William Eden, a mutual reduction of tariffs between Britain and France. Duties on French oil, vinegar and wine were reduced but, in return, the French market was opened up to British textiles and pottery. With the Commutation Act of 1784, Pitt set out to increase government revenue and, at the same time, to solve imperial problems. Duties on China teas were reduced from 120 per cent to only 12.5 per cent, immediately lowering the attraction of smuggling. The Act encouraged increased consumption, moving tea from being a high luxury item, and this in turn boosted the demand for sugar (see Chapter 8). In a stroke it strengthened the government's tax base, bailed out the East India Company, which did the importing, and helped the West Indian sugar planters.

Although there were occasions when Pitt misjudged the mood of the House of Commons, generally he was able to be confident in his secure majority. He also bought political support and backing in the Lords by the creation of some 87 peers – not counting Scottish and Irish peers – between 1783 and 1801, increasing membership of the House of Lords by 40 per cent. This weakened the old landed aristocracy and brought in some of the new wealthy and some able administrators. The Whigs, around Fox, were relatively powerless. Fox, as always, was erratic in the attention which he gave to issues. There was not, at this time, any sense that the other party's role was that of constant opposition to government policies. Fox identified himself with the people around the Prince of Wales, hopeful that when the time came for succession, the Whigs would come into their own.

The succession soon emerged as an issue. Towards the end of 1788, there were increasing signs in the King of the effects of what has now been identified as porphyria, a physical illness which produces mental disability in the form of delirium. To contemporary observers, it looked like insanity. Fox was hopeful that the Whig moment would not be long delayed. Pitt, for his part, was determined to play for time, in the hope that the King would recover. He proposed a commission to look at precedents, which unleashed upon him a speech from Fox, declaring that, to all intents, the Prince of Wales was Regent already, the succession was automatic and that it was not for the House of Commons to interfere. Coming from the supposed defender of the Whig tradition, this was an astonishing speech, which had Pitt delightedly declaring: 'I'll un-Whig the gentleman for the rest of his life.' Pitt now proposed that there should be restrictions on the power of the Regent, the most significant of which was a ban on the creation of new peers. Fox and his associates argued that the Regent ought to have the full powers of the monarchy and were, reputedly, already planning on the distribution of offices and peerages. Instead, the King recovered and Fox's reputation was further damaged.

Pitt's increasingly conservative stance became apparent in his reaction to proposals to repeal the penal laws against Dissenters. In response to a proposal in 1787, he accused some Dissenters of holding dangerous opinions, not short of calling for disestablishment of the Church of England. Renewed efforts by Dissenters were again blocked in 1789 and 1790, with Pitt firmly identifying with defence of the established church. He did, however, give support to the campaign against slavery that Quakers and evangelical Christians on both sides of the Atlantic had been pressing since before 1783, when a Quaker anti-slavery committee was formed. The movement found a powerful propagandist in 1786 in Thomas Clarkson. Clarkson was an indefatigable letter-writer and gatherer of information and statistics on the trade. In May 1787, the Quaker committee, together with Clarkson and Granville Sharpe, an older campaigner who had taken up the case of individual slaves as early as the 1760s, formed the Society for the Abolition of the Slave Trade. Over the next few years, the Society pioneered what were to become the tactics of nineteenth-century pressure groups and a new kind of politics, mobilising public opinion by writing letters, producing pamphlets and statistics, giving lectures, packing committees, lobbying members of Parliament and occupying the moral high ground. They were joined by the diminutive William Wilberforce, MP for Hull and a recent and ardent convert to evangelicalism. In Wilberforce they found a voice in the House of Commons, with the added advantage of his being a close friend of Pitt.

Wilberforce annually brought in a bill that went down to defeat amid celebrations in Liverpool and Bristol. After the defeat of the measure in 1791, Quaker activists

Figure 9.1 William Pitt the Younger addressing the House of Commons, c.1793, based on a painting by Karl-Anton Kickel. Charles James Fox is on the far right and Henry Addington, later Lord Sidmouth, is Speaker.
Source: Mary Evans Picture Library

launched a boycott of West Indian sugar, against the advice of the conservative Wilberforce, who was increasingly anxious about the rise of radical sentiment in the country. It has been calculated that between 300,000 and 400,000 gave up sugar in their tea, dubbed by the poet Robert Southey 'the blood-sweetened beverage'. Abolition committees spread throughout the country, attracting many women supporters, and petitions flooded into Parliament. In April 1792, Pitt made a passionate speech in favour of abolition, although he had declined to make it a government policy, and the trade survived for another 15 years. As ever, Pitt had shown himself sympathetic to aspects of reform, but immensely cautious in challenging any powerful vested interests.

War with France

The fall of the Bastille, in July 1789, was seen by most British politicians as a likely precursor of the emergence of a constitutional monarchy in France. Fox enthused, 'How much the greatest event it is that ever happened in the world! And how much the best!' Pitt was neutral and probably welcomed the fact that it weakened France and removed the need for further great expenditure on defence. As late as the beginning of 1792, he was envisaging a situation when the country could 'reasonably expect fifteen years of peace' in Europe. For the Whigs, however, it was more problematic. Fox's enthusiasm for the new France was countered by the Whig Edmund Burke, who had long supported economical reforms but who set his face against popular democracy. His polemics against the threat of the multitude, 'a mere multiplied tyranny' became ever more strident. Fox tried to curb Burke's invective, but to no avail and, in May 1791, in a dramatic confrontation in the Commons, Burke severed his connection with his long-term friend, who wept. By then there were signs that the events in France were firing the enthusiasm of many outside the ranks of the political classes (see Chapter 11). Pitt made clear his view that any further attempt at political reform in Britain would produce 'anarchy and confusion'.

War began to seem an increasing possibility – not because of what was going on in France, although large numbers of émigrés fleeing the executions in France were urging intervention – but because Britain was committed to the defence of the United Provinces against a French attack. Pitt was different from Burke: he did not see the Revolution as a threat to the European order as long as it did not move beyond the boundaries of France. In February 1793, the French declared war on Britain, anticipating a British response to their invasion of the Low Countries (see Chapter 11).

The war allowed a further clampdown on radical critics and appeals to national patriotism. Criticism of government, both within and outside Parliament, became less acceptable. Individuals and then groups of Whigs, anxious to indicate their patriotism, broke with Fox and voted with the government, declaring themselves a 'Third Party'. They were unable to accept Fox's opposition to war and his nonchalance at the increasing violence of events in France, and were worried about the spread of 'levelling doctrines'. It was something that Pitt had been working for since before the outbreak of war, dangling before frustrated Whigs the prospect of government offices in a coalition government.

The repression of radical movements, now dangerously linked with popular protests against rising prices and unemployment as trade was disrupted, continued with increased harshness. Meetings of more than 50 persons without the permission of the magistrates were banned, and magistrates were given the authority to arrest speakers or writers who were critical of the constitution or were trying to coerce Parliament. Foxite Whigs saw this as all part and parcel of a Tory conspiracy to increase the influence of the Crown, but Fox's protests met with little support in the Commons, against Pitt's 'patriotic' justifications for the measure. The evidence was that popular support lay with the government. After the general election of 1796, Pitt was able to command a massive majority, with some 424 Pittites against 95 Whigs and 39 independents and, in May, Fox announced that he would no longer attend a Parliament that he regarded as 'deaf and blind'.

Mutinies in the navy in the spring of 1797 were a new threat. When patriotic harangues by admirals had limited effect and even promises of pay rises seemed to fall on deaf ears, the government took more drastic action. With supplies to the fleet at the Nore cut off, the mutiny collapsed and 29 leaders were hanged. Army loyalty was secured with a substantial pay rise after a short-lived army mutiny at Woolwich, and the death-penalty was to be applied to anyone abetting the mutiny.

Ireland and Union

Long-simmering unrest in Ireland had broken out into open rebellion and, to all intents, civil war in the summer of 1798. In June, Pitt's cousin Lord Grenville, who was Secretary of State for Foreign Affairs, and Henry Dundas, the third member of the triumvirate that effectively controlled government policy, made the decision to incorporate Ireland in Britain. They were anxious about a possible French landing in Ireland and concerned as to whether there were sufficient troops available to prevent it. Pitt was willing to make concessions of political rights to Catholics as a price for support, while Grenville argued that Catholic relief would help with recruitment for the war effort. The original plan was to proceed with Union and Catholic Emancipation together, but they faced the opposition of the Protestant Ascendancy, in no mood to make concessions after the violence of the summer. As a result, it was decided to separate the two issues. In January 1799, the House of Commons voted for Union by 149 votes to 24, while the Irish House of Commons rejected it. The task then was to persuade the Irish to change their position. Opinion in Ireland was deeply divided. Some were in favour of Union, but opposed to Catholic Emancipation; others were for Union and Emancipation. Some, like Henry Grattan, favoured Emancipation but were against Union, while yet others set their face against both Union and Emancipation. Cornwallis, the viceroy, was encouraged to undertake the necessary 'dirty work', as he called it, and to allow the Catholic leadership to believe that Catholic Emancipation would accompany the Union. Others were persuaded that only after the Union had brought stability would the Catholic issue be addressed and that the Irish Catholics would have little effect on an all-British Parliament. Bribes, threats, cajolery and compensation for lost office no doubt also played their part and, in June 1800, the Irish Parliament had come round to accepting it, with the Union coming into force in January 1801. The Irish Parliament was abolished, but an executive remained in place at Dublin Castle. Ireland received 100 seats at Westminster and 28 peers could be elected to the House of Lords, together with four bishops.

The King had made clear in 1795 that Catholic Emancipation was a subject 'beyond the decision of any cabinet of ministers'. In 1801, he was even more explicit, announcing that 'no consideration would ever make me give my consent to what I look upon as the destruction of the Established Church; which, by the wisdom of Parliament, I, as well as my predecessors, have been obliged to take an oath at our coronations to support'. The Cabinet was already breaking up over both foreign and domestic issues, and Catholic Emancipation merely added to the divisions. The bulk of Pitt's parliamentary supporters were hostile. Faced with military failure, bad harvests, and popular discontent, Pitt was keen to find a peace settlement, and was prepared to agree to huge territorial concessions to the French. But, Grenville, the

Foreign Secretary, and the King were both in favour of continuing the war. The French Directory rejected the approaches, and Pitt, finding his options blocked by the King's intransigence and showing signs of physical and mental weariness after so long in office, resigned in March 1801. There was remarkably little public reaction to his departure.

Addington to Liverpool

On Pitt's recommendation, Henry Addington, the rather colourless Speaker of the House of Commons, was asked to form a government. Those closest to Pitt, who seemed to idolise him and who had been committed to Catholic Emancipation, declined to continue in government, many of them adopting an aristocratic hauteur towards Addington, the son of a doctor and the first member of the professional classes to become Prime Minister. The result was a Cabinet thin on parliamentary debating talent, although not lacking in administrative skill. Addington also enhanced the power of the Prime Minister by getting the King to accept that he would not deal directly with other ministers but only through Addington. Nonetheless, to those out of office it was the dull, stolid 'Dumplin' Ministry'. Very quickly there were moves by his friends to try to restore Pitt to office. It may have been with this in mind that Pitt sent a message to the King promising that he would not raise the issue of Catholic Emancipation again during the King's lifetime.

Both Pitt and Addington were clear that the country's finances were overstretched and that a peace treaty was vital. Predictably, there was much criticism of the terms of the Treaty of Amiens from former ministers and from the King, but it was popular in the country at large. Addington responded to popular expectations by abolishing Pitt's income tax and, instead, increased the taxes on malt and beer and the excise on exports and imports. The reward was a general election where the pro-government forces remained huge and the opposition Whigs made little advance.

By the end of 1802, however, there was renewed tension with the French. There were also clear signs that a revived Pitt was keen to regain office. In a debate on the renewal of war in May 1803, Pitt gave a bravura performance in marked contrast to Addington's uninspired ramblings. Talk of a broadly-based ministry that might even include Fox came to nothing, but once war was declared, it was only a question of how much longer the administration could survive. Additional resources were necessary for what many now assumed might be a long war with Napoleon, with an invasion expected. Addington, therefore, re-introduced an income tax. Pitt used the budget debates to snipe at Addington's government, while his associates condemned the inertia of the government's war policy, that was basically a defensive one. In April 1804, Addington resigned, overwhelmed by the levels of personal hostility towards him. Pitt returned as Prime Minister on the day that Napoleon was proclaimed Emperor. But he failed to achieve the political unity that many had expected. Factionalism remained prevalent and old perceived grievances were harboured. Nelson's victory at Trafalgar in October 1805 ensured Britain's continuing dominance of the sea, but the news of his victory was followed within weeks by the crushing defeat of Russian and Austrian forces at Austerlitz (see Chapter 10) and, within another month, Pitt was dead. To the end he remained something of an enigma and, even now, historians find it difficult to resolve the apparent contradictions in his career. Clearly, in many of his attitudes he became conservative, not prepared seriously to challenge the status quo, and Conservatives have therefore felt able to claim in his governments the roots of the modern Conservative Party. On the other hand, he was not a religious believer, was firmly on the Whig side in supporting Catholic Emancipation and had none of Burke's horrors about the French Revolution.

With Pitt gone and the Pittite faction split, the King had no choice but to turn to the opposition, and Grenville became Prime Minister, with Fox as Foreign Secretary and the dominant personality in the government. It was predominantly Whig in composition, but with Addington, now Viscount Sidmouth, added. This gave the false impression of a 'broad-bottomed' administration, which was dubbed, with heavy irony, by the Pittite George Canning as a ministry 'of all the talents'. Given the mix of the government, the room for manoeuvre on controversial measures was limited. Grenville and Fox, keen to attract cross-party support from abolitionists, succeeded in getting a resolution condemning the slave trade passed in 1806 and, in 1807, a bill was carried for its abolition. This brought to a conclusion more than 20 years of campaigning both in and out of Parliament, but could also be presented as part of the struggle with Napoleon, who had reintroduced slavery in the French Empire in 1802. The 1807 bill was a government measure and they were able to deliver a majority of 283 to 16. Success was probably due to the highly effective campaigning of the abolitionists, and abolition had been an issue in the 1806 general election. But minds were also altered in Parliament by concern about the dangers of slave rebellion. At huge cost in lives and resources, the military had failed to crush a slave revolt in St. Dominique (Haiti), which had been seized from the French in 1793, and there was constant fear of trouble in Jamaica and other islands.

Fox, at the moment of his success had not lived to relish it, having died in September 1806. His reputation as a reformer had been undermined by his erratic career, his attachment to the increasingly gross Prince of Wales and his association with the aristocratic and acquisitive clique around Grenville. Without Fox, the coalition government was precarious. Grenville favoured Catholic Emancipation, which gave him common ground with most Whigs, and the ministry was broken by an attempt to allow Roman Catholics in Britain to hold commissions in the army, where there was a huge number of Irish recruits, and in the navy. Ireland was again in a state of unrest and the government was desperate to find some concessions to make. Sidmouth and the King saw this as a step towards Emancipation and Sidmouth resigned, precipitating the government's collapse. The last predominantly Whig government for 23 years came to an end and Sidmouth became firmly entrenched in Whig demonology.

The new administration, under the doddering Duke of Portland, included the young and clever George Canning, who regarded himself as Pitt's true heir and called himself a Tory, and who was given the Foreign Office. It included others of Pitt's acolytes, capable administrators, who were to dominate politics over the next few years. Secretary for War and the Colonies was Lord Castlereagh and at the Home Office was Lord Hawkesbury, soon to be Earl of Liverpool.

Portland's government was quickly beset by scandals and accusations of corruption in high places. There were revelations that the former mistress of the commander-in-chief of the army, the King's brother, the Duke of York, was pretending to sell army commissions, whilst a 'Delicate Investigation' was carried out into the colourful love life of Princess Caroline, the estranged and loathed wife of the Prince of Wales. Military failure did nothing to help. However, the Whigs were not united enough to be able to sustain an effective assault on the government and were wary of being too outspoken during wartime, with Napoleon now spanning the continent.

A dispirited Portland resigned in 1809, to be succeeded by Spencer Perceval, the Chancellor of the Exchequer, a fierce opponent of Catholic Emancipation and, there-fore, acceptable to the King. He was faced, at the end of 1810, with another bout of the King's illness. Much had changed in attitudes to the monarchy since the early days of the King's reign. From the 1780s, the King had become a focus of popular patriot-ism. His advisers had come to appreciate that royal ritual had an appeal that could be usefully utilised to help create national unity. The celebrations of the golden jubilee of his accession in October 1809 had brought unprecedented celebrations throughout the land and in the Empire. The King's longevity had helped engender affection and a sense that his presence somehow guaranteed stability in an unstable world. There was none of that residue of affection for the now bloated Prince of Wales who became Prince Regent. It might have been expected that he would bring in a new government, but his views had become decidedly Tory. Perceval's government survived. Perceval himself did not, however, earning the dubious distinction of being the only British Prime Minister to be assassinated. His assassin, Bellingham, had been ruined as a result of the economic warfare between Napoleon and Britain and had been seeking some compensation from government.

The Liverpool ministry

After some weeks of manoeuvring, in June 1812, Lord Liverpool emerged as First Lord of the Treasury, an office that he was to hold for the next 15 years. With even greater vigour than its predecessor, Liverpool's government took steps to crush the popular disaffection and disorder that was apparent in various parts of the country. Any concession to Roman Catholics in Ireland was minimal and it was agreed that Emancipation should be an issue on which members of the government could agree to disagree. At the Home Office, Sidmouth encouraged brutal reprisals against the Luddite workers who had been protesting across the Midlands and Yorkshire. Machine smashing was made a capital crime. He swept away the Elizabethan Statute of Artificers that had regulated the number of apprentices in various trades and removed the last vestiges of wage regulation permitted to justices of the peace. It was a reflection of the way in which the ideas of Adam Smith, albeit modified and simplified, were finding their way into the thinking of someone even as conservative as Sidmouth. There was a growing acceptance that a market system, in which state intervention was kept to a minimum, was best.

At the same time, the Cabinet, landowners as all of them were, was happy for government to intervene to maintain the price of corn. Corn prices had fluctuated dramatically during the war years but, with the war drawing to a close, they had plummeted, nearly halving between January 1813 and January 1815. There had been some intervention in 1804 to prevent importation should the price fall under 63 shillings a quarter. But, under the powerful pressure of the farmers, the Corn Law of 1815 restricted imports until the price of home-grown wheat had reached 80 shillings a quarter. It was a recognition that agriculture was still, by far, the country's largest industry, and that coercion of part of the population had to be paralleled with concessions to others. It also reflected a determination to ensure that the country maintained what Sidmouth called 'an ample and independent supply' of grain. This could only be done, it was argued, by protecting the property of landowners and their farmers from foreign encroachment. Others, including Liverpool, held that the laws were not entirely out of line with the increasingly fashionable *laissez-faire*. After all, by supporting home agriculture, output would be increased and, in time, the price would fall – an argument that generally proved correct. Hardly any member of the Commons spoke in favour of free trade in grain. Popular protest against the legislation was quickly suppressed, but resentment against the measure, which in practice failed to maintain farm incomes, continued.

June 1814 brought a temporary end to the war and the government basked in the glory of victory parades. But eight months later Napoleon was back in France for one final sally that only ended at Waterloo. The government was able to enjoy the ultimate defeat of Napoleon, but it failed to meet the much-inflated expectations of what peace would bring. Debts generated by the war were huge. The national debt stood at £846 million (something like £60 billion at 2008 price levels) in 1816 and, because the income tax was ended after a huge outcry by petitions and press and a government defeat, taxation on consumption, particularly through excise duties, remained high. There was widespread unrest and food riots in different parts of the country. A secret committee of 1817 concluded that there was an organised conspiracy through a network of clubs and societies that, while ostensibly seeking parliamentary reform, was actually fomenting sedition and revolution. The government became fixated with law and order. Habeas corpus was again suspended and legislation against radical activities extended and consolidated (see Chapter 11).

Trade with Europe was slow to revive and there was growing pressure for further modification of tariffs to stimulate business and bring an increased volume of trade. The gradual return to the gold standard after 1819 and a phasing out of paper currency met some of the demands of the financial community, although it was all done too rapidly, resulting in a sharp deflation and a rise in unemployment. The government had begun the process of reducing age-old restrictions on certain imports from as early as 1816 and the moves in this direction received a great deal of support from the talented younger members of the government, who operated under the rather mediocre members of the Cabinet. William Huskisson, son of a minor Midlands' landowner, Robert Peel, son of a successful Lancashire calico printer, and the more aristocratic Frederick Robinson were all enthusiasts for a liberalisation of trade and industry. These men gradually came into their own, and were backed by Liverpool.

Castlereagh, after failing to push through Parliament the King's divorce from Queen Caroline, and suffering from depression and paranoia, took his own life in August 1822. His successor as Foreign Secretary was his long-time rival, Canning, to whom many of the younger 'Liberal' Tories looked for leadership. Soon afterwards, Robinson came in as Chancellor, Peel succeeded Sidmouth at the Home Office and Huskisson took the Board of Trade. These last years of Liverpool's government have generally been dubbed the years when 'Liberal Toryism' held sway and, by some definitions, it did. Robinson in his first budget swept away Pitt's old taxes on windows, male servants, wheeled vehicles, occasional servants and gardeners, ponies and mules among other things. These were all taxes which fell on the better off, but the theory was that their expenditure would have a trickle-down effect on the less prosperous. In the following year, a range of essentially prohibitive import tariffs was reduced – on rum, wool and silk among other things. Inland duties on coal were removed. Robinson and Huskisson continued the process of chopping tariffs in 1825. More effective gathering of the remaining tariffs and taxes ensured that there were annual surpluses. The effect of allowing more foreign goods, and especially raw materials, into Britain was to provide the means for other countries to buy British manufactured goods. Peel, at the Home Office, embarked on a programme of consolidation and reform of the criminal law, of police reform that led to the formation of the Metropolitan Police in 1829, and of prison reform, influenced by the campaigning of the Quaker Elizabeth Fry.

Catholic Emancipation

The relative harmony of the Cabinet began to break during 1824, when the Catholic question once again came to the fore. The Cabinet had always been divided on the issue, particularly when Canning, whose 'Catholic' stance was best known, came in. A majority was opposed to concession, including Liverpool and Peel. The latter had, from 1812 until 1818, been Chief Secretary for Ireland and had been dubbed 'Orange Peel' due to his Protestant sympathies. However, what brought the issue to the forefront was the formation of Daniel O'Connell's Catholic Association.

Since the failure to deliver Emancipation in the wake of the Union there had been regular petitions from Catholic Ireland for action. There was particular resentment at a parliamentary oath that described Catholicism as 'superstitious' and 'idolatrous' but also, of course, at the exclusion of Catholics from so many public offices. In 1813 the elderly Henry Grattan proposed a Catholic Relief Bill in the Commons, that had various 'safeguards' built into it to limit Catholic influence. O'Connell, a Catholic lawyer, and his supporters rejected the proposal and the Catholic Committee in Ireland, that had hitherto provided leadership, split. In the aftermath, O'Connell emerged as a popular and populist leader, linking religious freedom to political equality, with his demand for 'unqualified emancipation'. He resented the assumption that his religion was something to be tolerated rather than a fundamental right.

In May 1822, Canning's bill to admit Roman Catholic peers to the House of Lords passed the Commons by 12 votes, only to be rejected by the Lords. O'Connell now tapped into widespread social discontent in rural Ireland to form a new Catholic Association, a nationwide organisation aiming for a mass membership and levying a penny a month 'Catholic rent'. With its large income of more than £20,000 in the first nine months, the Association did not confine itself to Emancipation. Backed by Catholic priests who helped collect the 'rent' at Sunday Mass, it took up issues of tenants' rights and any other matters affecting members of the Catholic community. A network of local leaders emerged at parish and county level. But, most significantly, the Association began to force commitments from parliamentary candidates, using the clout that Catholic 40-shilling freeholders had in Irish elections. With a commanding appearance, coupled with a magnificent voice and skilled oratory, O'Connell was able to attract huge loyalty. He was careful to argue that change could be achieved through the moral force of public opinion. He talked of a 'moral electricity' that came from focusing public opinion on a single issue. On the other hand, he was ready to hint that the alternative could be civil war: 'Nations have . . . been driven mad by oppression.'

In 1825, the Catholic Association and all other political associations were banned. Catholic rent collection had to be suspended. Another Catholic Relief Bill was proposed with the 'safeguard' of disenfranchising 40-shilling freeholders, thus excluding the poorer Catholic peasantry. The Bill passed the Commons but the peers threw it out. O'Connell now reorganised the Association and the general election of 1826 saw its pressure being applied very effectively. Opponents were put up against those candidates who would not commit to support Emancipation. Contests were forced in counties that had not had elections in decades. There was talk of Irish politics having been revolutionised, with the Catholic Association dictating the politics of the future. As against that, the chants of 'no-popery' had played well in English constituencies and the number of committed Protestants in the Commons had increased at the election. The Whigs' support for Emancipation was a central belief that made them far from popular in the country.

In February 1827, Liverpool had an incapacitating stroke and negotiations between his colleagues went on for seven weeks, with no agreement on a successor. Canning was asked by a very reluctant King, who had never forgiven him for being one of the many lovers of his former wife, to form an administration. Canning's 'pro-Catholic' position allowed him to attract some Whig support, although he was against any parliamentary reform, and Lord Grey, the Whig leader, made it clear privately that anyone whose mother was an actress, as Canning's had been, should never be Prime Minister. In deference to the King, Canning again left Emancipation as an 'open question'. However, for some Ultra-Tories, for whom Protestantism was the central tenet of their politics, Canning was unacceptable. An uneasy coalition struggled on over the summer months. After a mere hundred days in office, in early August, Canning died and the King sent for Robinson, now Viscount Goderich, who, with difficulty, sought to maintain the Canningite coalition. But Robinson lacked the force of personality to maintain a diverse Cabinet and it quickly became factionalised around other ambitious politicians. Attempts to maintain the coalition failed and, in January 1828, the Duke of Wellington and the Tories came in. Wellington and Peel, the leader in the Commons, were known as strong 'anti-Catholics', and hopes of Catholic Emancipation seemed at an end. But both Wellington and Peel were ready to compromise, and many of the Ultra-Tories, to their chagrin, were excluded from the Cabinet.

Events now began to gather a momentum of their own. Since 1823, there had been a revival of political activities by Dissenters, calling for repeal of the Test and Corporation Acts. The Whig Lord John Russell introduced a bill in February 1828. Against the government's advice, it passed the Commons, with many anti-Catholics voting for it in the expectation that it might delay Emancipation, and Wellington got it through the Lords. Huskisson got through a bill adjusting the Corn Law to a sliding scale so that when prices rose duty fell, but within a short time he had resigned and most of the Canningites in the government followed him.

In his restructured government after the departure of the Canningites, the 'pro-Catholic' Irish MP, Vesey Fitzgerald, was given the Board of Trade and, as was the custom, had to stand for re-election. O'Connell announced that he would stand against Fitzgerald in County Clare, finding a way around the law that forbade a Catholic to sit in Parliament but not to stand for Parliament. Catholic Ireland exploded with marches and demonstrations in support. O'Connell was duly elected by 2,057 votes to 982.

The decision to concede Emancipation seems to have been made soon afterwards. The Commons had made it clear that they saw conciliation of the Irish as the only way to silence the agitation in Ireland. Wellington wanted the earlier 'safeguard' of getting rid of the 40-shilling freeholders in Ireland who, just as in County Clare, could outvote 'Protestant' candidates, but this could not be done before Emancipation. He broke the news to the King in a memorandum in August, when he warned of impending rebellion in Ireland. He worked to convince Peel and, in January 1829, Peel conceded, fearful of civil war.

The King's speech at the opening of Parliament in February promised Emancipation, to the shock and consternation of many on the Tory backbenches. Peel made the case in the Commons, earning forever the accusation of treachery from elements within his party. Petitions of protest flowed in from all corners of the country. Peel, sensitive to the attacks on him, offered himself for re-election to his Oxford University seat and was duly defeated. In March 1829 the bill passed the Commons with a majority of 178 and the Lords by 213 to 109. A reluctant monarch had no option to give his assent. A new oath of allegiance was drafted that was acceptable to Catholics,

Figure 9.2 *The Apostates and the Extinguisher*, by Williams. This cartoon reflecting fierce hostility to Catholic Emancipation has the Duke of Wellington kissing the toe of the Pope, while Sir Robert Peel offers both the crown and the Anglican liturgy to the Pope. In the lower right corner the papal bull gores the docile English dog. Many never forgave Peel for what was seen as treachery to his 'Orange' past.
Source: © The Trustees of the British Museum

and state offices, with the exception of the offices of Lord Chancellor, Lord Lieutenants and any future Regent, were opened to Catholics. The price paid was that 40-shilling freeholders in Ireland were disenfranchised, and replaced by £10 property holders, having proved their lack of deference to local landlord influence and their attachment to the Catholic Association. County voters in Ireland fell from 216,000 to 37,000.

If the expectation was that Emancipation would defuse tension, Wellington and Peel were profoundly wrong. Political radicals in Britain had noted events in Ireland and their result. In Birmingham, the radical banker, Thomas Attwood, noted that victory had been achieved 'by union, by organisation, by general contribution, by patriotic exertion, and by discretion, keeping always within the law and the constitution'. It was a model to be followed. On the other side, to many Ultra-Tories the passage of Catholic Emancipation was proof that the system was corrupt and unrepresentative of popular feeling and, therefore, parliamentary reform was necessary.

A bitter winter produced widespread distress in many parts of the country and much rural discontent. Radicals and Ultras combined to denounce the ministry. In June 1830, George IV died and his brother the Duke of Clarence succeeded as

William IV. As was customary, an election followed. There was a swing against the ministry and on 16 November, the government went down to defeat and, after nearly a quarter of a century, the Whigs found themselves in office.

After 1830 and well into the nineteenth century, Whigs and their successors, the Liberals, went out of their way to present Liverpool's government and, to an extent, Pitt's as 'reactionary' Toryism in contrast to 'enlightened' nineteenth-century Liberalism. Liberal Toryism was regarded as something of an oxymoron. In recent decades, however, the record of the Liverpool governments has been reassessed and Liverpool himself has emerged as someone who, perhaps for the first time in a Prime Minister, had a clearly thought-out economic policy moving towards free trade. The repression of popular disorder in the years after Waterloo was harsh, though it was mild compared with what contemporaries were doing in the rest of Europe. Peel's reforms of the police and of prisons were sophisticated, modern methods of maintaining order. Since 1780, Liverpool and his predecessors had successfully pulled power away from the monarch into the hands of Parliament with few of the threats to stability that had shaken the rest of Europe for half a century. They had been able to mobilise the state successfully to win a great war. They had responded – reluctantly no doubt, but also quite effectively – to many of the demands coming from those who were increasingly referring to themselves as the middle classes. On the other hand, the fact that the overriding issue that divided politicians from the 1790s until 1829 was Catholic Emancipation reveals how far an older politics, based on religion, still held powerful sway, and the wariness of politicians to tackle the issue until it was forced on them is an indication of how far they believed that the defence of the established churches was crucial to the maintenance of social stability.

Further reading

Colley, Linda, *Britons. Forging the Nation 1707–1837* (New Haven, Yale University Press, 1992)

Hilton, Boyd, *A Mad, Bad and Dangerous People? England, 1783–1846* (Oxford, Clarendon Press, 2006)

Hochschild, Adam, *Bury the Chains. The British Struggle to Abolish Slavery* (Basingstoke, Macmillan, 2005)

Mori, Jennifer, *William Pitt and the French Revolution 1785–1795* (Keele, Keele University Press, 1997)

O'Gorman, Frank, *The Emergence of the Two-Party System 1760–1832* (London, Hodder and Arnold, 1982)

O'Gorman, Frank, *The Long Eighteenth Century: British Political and Social History 1688–1832* (London, Hodder and Arnold, 1997)

10

Britain at war

With only limited interludes, Britain had been at war with France since the 1680s. These wars had initially been about trying to prevent French domination of Europe in the Netherlands and in the German states. First a Dutch King, William III, and then a Hanoverian one ensured that the preoccupations of mainland Europe had to be taken into account. But there had also been the British desire that the important trading links with the Low Countries and in the Mediterranean should not be hampered by rival powers. In other words, commercial concerns had always been a factor. From the 1730s, these became even more important and governments, pressed by powerful trading interest groups and with a relatively small army and therefore limited ability to intervene in the Continent, saw the wars as a way of protecting and, hopefully, increasing British markets and trade routes. This had been done most successfully during the Seven Years' War, when control of Canada and much of India had been gained, together with domination in the West Indies. Defeat in America by a union of other powers might have made it look as though the balance of influence in the world had shifted sharply against Britain.

Out of isolation

Britain's prestige was badly damaged and there were those in Europe who felt that recovery would take a long time. With France, Spain and the Netherlands aligned with the Americans in 1780, Britain seemed very vulnerable. In the English Channel, hostile ships greatly outnumbered the British, and there were fears of an invasion. The French invasion plans fell through, and Gibraltar withstood a lengthy siege, but Menorca was lost to Spain and the French captured Tobago. On the other hand, naval setbacks encouraged a large ship-building programme by the British, a programme that continued through the 1780s. In contrast, French governments lacked the resources to do this and, by the end of 1782, British naval superiority had been re-established. It was too late to save Lord North's ministry. The government resigned in March 1782, after it was defeated on a motion to continue the war, and negotiations for peace were launched. American independence was finally recognised in the Treaty of Versailles in September 1783.

Although the American colonies were gone, most of the British gains from the Seven Years' War were retained. Hopes of maintaining a free-trade relationship with the United States were not fulfilled and American merchants were actively excluded from trade with the West Indies. British importers were encouraged to look for alternative sources of supply to replace American timber and foodstuffs. American reneging on aspects of the Versailles Treaty, over the treatment of loyalists and compensation to British merchants, ensured cool relations for the next decade and more. But the French failed to make great inroads into the American markets and although, for a time after 1783, sugar, coffee and cotton from French colonies dominated the market of colonial re-exports in Europe, they were not able to sustain this dominance. By the 1790s, British exports to the United States were back to the level of the colonial era.

The younger William Pitt's precarious government after 1783 (see Chapter 9) was conscious of the need for peace, to give time for a military, naval and economic recovery and to stabilise its own political position. It was also very aware of Britain's diplomatic isolation. When France signed a treaty with the United Provinces of the Netherlands in 1785, Britain was more isolated than ever. Britain was not in a position to resist French pressure to work out new commercial arrangements, something that was part of the 1783 Versailles Treaty. The result was the Eden Treaty of 1786, by which both countries agreed to reduce duties on a range of items. The treaty, skilfully negotiated by the diplomat, William Eden, is generally seen as being to Britain's advantage, the French having underestimated the rate and extent at which British manufacturing was growing.

Tension within the United Provinces, with Dutch 'Patriots' challenging the domination of the Prince of Orange, provided the route out of diplomatic isolation. The British helped subsidise Orange resistance, as a way of weakening French influence, which was strong among the Patriots. Offence caused to the Prussian monarch's sister, who was married to the Prince of Orange, provided an excuse for Prussian intervention and, with British approval, Prussian troops invaded the United Provinces in September 1787, crushed the Patriot regime and restored Orange authority. The French could do little. Political and financial crises were paralysing France and the Dutch Patriots were left to their fate. Prussia and Britain agreed to defend the Orange dynasty. It had long been a fundamental doctrine of British foreign policy that no hostile Power (which largely meant France) should be allowed to control the coastal area between the rivers Rhine and Scheldt.

Rebellion in the Austrian Netherlands (roughly present-day Belgium) against the centralising reforms of Joseph II saw Britain and Prussia again determinedly backing the *status quo*. A strong, Austrian-dominated province was seen as vital to resist French encroachments. There was, however, a price to pay for the Prussian alliance. Prussia's real interests lay in eastern Europe. The Prussians had joined with Russia and Austria in seizing parts of Poland in 1772 and they were determined to ensure that they received their share of any further partition. Prussia was also concerned with Russian and Austrian advances into the Ottoman Empire. Russia was not prepared to give up its gains from the Turks on the north coast of the Black Sea and, for a time, it looked as if Pitt, in the spring of 1791, might be prepared to try to use force to persuade the Russians to surrender the Black Sea fortress of Ochakov, captured in 1788. There was, however, little support for such involvement outside the Cabinet and Pitt was forced to abandon his plan.

While maintenance of the Prussian alliance had probably been the main consideration in involvement in the east, there were signs of the emergence of a new strategy that involved broadly supporting the Ottoman Empire against Russian and Austrian predations. With the ever-growing importance of India to Britain, the routes to the East, by both land and sea, were becoming of crucial concern. Ottoman dominions bestrode the short land route and Russian encroachment towards the eastern Mediterranean began to be seen as a threat.

Turmoil in France in the aftermath of the 1789 Revolution left Spain without an ally and gave Britain an opportunity to deal with a recurring irritation. There was sporadic Spanish harassment of British traders and merchants along the Pacific coast around Nookta Sound, a good natural harbour on the west coast of Vancouver Island. The threat of war was enough to force the Spanish to renounce their claim to control of the Pacific coast north of the fiftieth parallel. Pitt's determined stand on this matter was an indication that, like his father, his prime consideration was the defence of British trading interests.

French events were watched at first with detachment and a certain pleasure that the French position in the world would be seriously weakened. But soon there was a growing anxiety. There was a wariness about any direct interference because of the extent of sympathy for the revolution that was apparent among many groups within Britain. Nor did they wish to see French revolutionary sentiment spread to the United Provinces or to the Austrian Netherlands. Stability in the Low Countries remained a prime British concern, since the alternative was sure to encourage French involvement there. Pitt was also keen to see military and naval expenditure brought under control after a decade of growth, with signs of popular disquiet at the levels of taxation.

When the French declared war on Austria in April 1792 the British government declared its neutrality. No doubt there was an expectation that Austrian forces could quickly crush the French army. Instead the result was French victories, leading to the French seizure of the Austrian Netherlands. The French opened the River Scheldt to international trade, undoing a closure that had survived for nearly 150 years, much to the advantage of London and Amsterdam and at the expense of the port of Antwerp. By the end of 1792, strategic concerns, together with Edmund Burke's increasingly chilling warnings about the dangers unless the French Revolution was crushed (see Chapter 11), were pointing in the direction of war. France's declaration of its readiness

Figure 10.1 *British Liberty and French Liberty*, James Gillray cartoon, 1793. Gillray (1757–1815) was one of the most effective of British caricaturists. Although many of his cartoons lampooned the King and the Prince Regent, during the 1790s he took an anti-revolutionary stance and published in the *Anti-Jacobin Review*.
Source: © The Trustees of The British Museum

to support the cause of liberty wherever it arose seemed to be confirmation of the perils. The British indicated that they would be prepared to accept the French Republic on condition that the French withdrew behind their 1789 frontier in the north. It soon became clear that this would not happen. The execution of Louis XVI on 21 January 1793 led to the expulsion of the French ambassador and, in anticipation of British action, the France declared war on Britain on 1 February.

The first coalition

It was a country that was ill-prepared for a war in Europe. In the aftermath of the American War, partly because of the traditional suspicion of too large a standing army and partly for reasons of economy, the army had been sharply reduced in size. Fewer than 14,000 troops were actually stationed in the British Isles, with the remaining two-thirds garrisoned overseas, mainly in India and the West Indies. A local militia in England undertook little training and was purely for homeland defence. As always, therefore, there was no desire to get caught up in a land war in Europe and the strategy was to support by means of subsidies those continental powers that were prepared to resist France. Prussia was initially the main recipient, but subsidies also went to Piedmont in the north of Italy, and to the Kingdom of Naples, with its important naval bases in the Mediterranean. Mercenaries were also bought, as in the past, from Hanover and Hesse and these made up the bulk of the forces under the Duke of York that were despatched to Flanders to join the Austrians. But there was a lack of any clear strategy. After some initial success, British forces were driven back by French

Focus on

Opposition to the war with France

The following are the Resolutions against the War in France put before the House of Commons by the Whig, Charles James Fox, 18 February 1793.

1. That it is not for the honour or interest of Great Britain to make war upon France on account of the internal circumstances of that country, for the purpose either of suppressing or punishing any opinion and principles, however pernicious in their tendency, which may prevail there, or of establishing among the French people any particular form of government.
2. That the particular complaints which have been stated against the conduct of the French Government are not of a nature to justify war in the first instance, without having attempted to obtain redress by negotiation.
3. That it appears to this House, that in the late negotiation between H.M.'s Ministers and the agents of the French Government, the said Ministers did not take such measures as were likely to procure redress, without a rupture, for the grievances of which they complained; and particularly that they never stated distinctly to the French Government any terms and conditions, the accession to which, on the part of France, would induce H.M. to persevere in a system of neutrality.
4. That it does not appear that the security of Europe, and the rights of independent nations, which had been stated as grounds of war against France, have been attended to by H.M.'s Ministers in the case of Poland, in the invasions of which unhappy country, both in the last year and more recently, the most open contempt of the Law of Nations, and the most unjustifiable spirit of aggrandisement has been manifested, without having produced, as far as appears to this House, any remonstrance from H.M.'s Ministers.
5. That it is the duty of H.M.'s Ministers, in the present crisis, to advise H.M. against entering into engagements which may prevent Great Britain from making a separate peace whenever the interests of H.M. and his people may render such a measure advisable, or, which may countenance an opinion in Europe that H.M. is acting in concert with other Powers for the unjustifiable purpose of compelling the people of France to submit to a form of government not approved by that nation.

Source: Cobbett's Parliamentary History, XXX, pp. 431–2.

armies and beat an ignominious retreat. The opportunity to expel the French from the Low Countries and limit Britain's involvement in the war was lost. By July 1794, the French had control of the Dutch fleet. There was no coherent British strategy on support for internal rebellions within France and generally help was given too little and too late. In addition, Prussia had largely lost interest and was much more concerned with obtaining its share of the final partition of Poland.

In contrast with the army, the navy was well prepared and substantially larger than it had been in 1783. The war was seen as an opportunity to cripple French overseas trade and seize further territory. Admiral Howe's destruction of seven French ships of the line on 1 June 1794 was greeted with wild enthusiasm as a 'glorious' victory, although he failed to prevent the convoy of grain ships getting through. However, initial advantage was lost here too by uncertainty over strategy and war aims. Expeditions to the West Indies resulted in the capture of French-held islands but at huge cost and they drew troops from the European arena. They also resulted in disastrous casualties. Something like 40,000 perished in the Caribbean over the next three years, mainly from yellow fever (more than were to die in five years of war in the Iberian Pensinsula), while another 40,000 were rendered unfit for service. Thirteen thousand slaves were purchased to support the military.[1] Meanwhile, the first coalition against France was crumbling. France had control of the Netherlands and the now republican United Provinces signed an alliance with France. Spain made peace with France in February 1795 and, in the following year, declared war on Britain. Despite its British subsidies, Prussia signed a peace with France and threatened British access to the Baltic. Austria was now Britain's only ally but she had lost interest in the area that was closest to British concerns, the Netherlands. Austria's attention was on the French threat to its territories in northern Italy. The 27-year-old General Bonaparte captured these in 1796 and the British could do little to assist. The navy largely withdrew from the Mediterranean and Austria soon concluded its own peace with France. Only adverse weather in Bantry Bay prevented a French force of some 15,000 landing in Ireland in December 1796, but substantial numbers of troops had to be kept there to suppress rebellion. Little wonder that Pitt felt it necessary to put out feelers for a compromise peace, but an insistence on the restoration of the Bourbons ensured that the republican government of France would reject these overtures.

In February 1797, the Bank of England had to suspend cash payments and abandon the gold standard because of a run on the banks. Instead, low-denomination notes began to be issued in increasing quantities. The only good news was Admiral Jervis's victory at Cape St Vincent, which prevented the Spanish fleet linking up with the French fleet at Brest, and Admiral Duncan's capture of 11 Dutch ships at Camperdown. Unfortunately, this was almost immediately followed in April by the mutiny of the Channel Fleet at Spithead, which refused to put to sea, and by similar trouble

---

[1] Mark Philp (ed.), *Resisting Napoleon. The British Response to the Threat of Invasion, 1797–1815* (Aldershot, Ashgate, 2006), p. 30.

at the Nore with the North Sea fleet. Nonetheless, confidence in government was sufficient to ensure that the British credit system survived and the government was still able to raise substantial loans to carry on the conflict. Also, with much talk of a possible French invasion, Pitt felt confident enough to introduce income tax.

Britain's great advantage over all other powers was the ability of government to raise loans and taxation with which to finance the war effort. The readiness of people to accept taxation and the ability of government to gather it had given the country the resources to carry out more than 100 years of more or less continuous warfare since 1689. The need of the government to raise loans had led to administrative and financial changes over a century that allowed the creation of what has been dubbed a 'military-fiscal state'.[2] The changes involved the development of a sound credit and banking system. From early in the eighteenth century, a credit system was in place that allowed government to borrow on an entirely new scale and at manageable rates of interest. To a much greater extent than in other countries, there was confidence that interest on loans to government would be regularly paid. Parliament's control of the nation's money was the guarantee of that. Pitt was able to impose taxes on both luxuries and necessities and, although there was resentment at the intrusiveness of the income tax, people paid up. It gave the government the huge resources needed to buy support from European powers. At the same time, rising taxation was producing increasing social tension (see Chapter 11) and Pitt was keen to try to get a settlement with France. He found little support for this in either Cabinet or court. The King found a settlement with a revolutionary government unacceptable and Pitt's colleagues were unwilling to give up the opportunities for dismantling more of the French maritime empire.

The second coalition

With domination on land more or less complete, the French were in no mood to negotiate a compromise peace. Instead, Napoleon Bonaparte, now one of the Consuls running France, prepared to challenge the British in India. Rebellions were encouraged by French agents and, in 1798, Napoleon set off with a force of 31,000 on an invasion of Egypt, as the first step in the partition of the Ottoman Empire. Napoleon's invasion force was able to avoid Nelson's fleet and to capture Malta, run by the Knights of St John, before moving on to Egypt. By July 1798, Napoleon was in Cairo but, within days, Nelson had found the French fleet in Aboukir Bay and annihilated it, thus isolating Napoleon's army.

The French were still strong enough to seize Naples a few months later, but, nonetheless, the setback to Napoleonic ambitions in the east revived the possibilities of a second anti-French coalition and Pitt rejected peace overtures. Russia was

---

[2] The term is John Brewer's in *The Sinews of Power: War, Money and the English State, 1688–1783* (London, Unwin Hyman, 1989).

concerned by French ambitions in Turkey and offended by the seizure of Malta, over which the Tsar claimed a Christian protectorate. British subsidies encouraged him to promise military aid if the Prussians could be persuaded to assist also and, although the Prussians proved recalcitrant, Russian troops were sent to the west. This persuaded the Austrians to renew hostilities against the French and, once again, France was thrown on to the defensive, defeated in Italy and in Switzerland by Austro-Russian forces.

In August 1799 a British-Russian force landed in the Netherlands, confident that the Dutch would rise in support against French domination. But no rising materialised and, within months, the army had to be evacuated. Austria had failed to move at the same time in southern Europe to deflect French forces from the Low Countries. When it did move, it went down to a massive defeat – first at Marengo in June 1800 and then at Hohenlinden at the end of the year. Austria sued for an armistice. With the French threat to Turkey also removed, there was little motivation for the Russians to continue their involvement and there was resentment that a Russian army had been left without allied support in Switzerland, where they were defeated by the French.

Russia, with other Baltic states, objected to the British policy of intercepting and searching the merchant ships of neutral states to blockade trade with France. The Armed Neutrality, which Russia had contrived during the American War in 1780 to resist British interference with neutral ships, was now revived with Sweden, Denmark and Prussia at the end of 1800. The British took this as nothing short of a declaration of war, seized their ships in British ports and encouraged privateers to pillage neutral shipping heading in and out of the Baltic, while Prussia, Denmark and France invaded Hanover. Concerned that the Baltic fleets might link up, Admirals Parker and Nelson sank the Danish fleet at Copenhagen in April 1801. It was too late to save Pitt's government. In February, he had resigned, with little to show for eight years of war other than survival. By a combination of force and diplomacy, the French had largely outmanoeuvred Pitt, who had failed to develop any coherent war strategy.

A fortunate twist of fate, however, had resulted in the assassination of Tsar Paul of Russia a few weeks before, and his successor, Alexander, reversed the previous policy and made overtures to Britain. The crises of the last two years had been survived. Napoleon and the French were unassailable in Europe but, with the possibility of access once again to the Baltic area, so essential for the timber needed by the navy, British command of the seas was secure. Malta had been recaptured in September 1800 and the French army, long since abandoned in Egypt by Bonaparte, was finally driven out in the summer of 1801, by British troops backed up by an Indian army and the Turks. A stalemate on land and sea encouraged both Britain and France to embark on preliminary peace talks. The demands for peace in Britain were growing among the business community, who were finding themselves excluded from traditional European markets. Napoleon's emissary at the preliminary peace negotiations was cheered by a London crowd. After many months of negotiation, it was agreed at Amiens in March 1802 that Britain would hand back most of its colonial gains with the exception of Trinidad, which had been seized from Spain, and Ceylon, which had again been taken from the Dutch. The French were left in control of the Low Countries. Grenville, who had been Pitt's Secretary of State, raged in vain against the surrender of hard-won colonial gains and the abandonment of attempts to create a new anti-Bonaparte alliance.

The third coalition

Peace did not persist for long. British merchants still found themselves largely excluded from areas of Europe under French influence. There were tales of French intrigue from different quarters and growing evidence of a French naval building programme. As a result, Addington's government refused to hand over Malta, which had been part of the Amiens agreement, and, in May 1803, war resumed. There were immediate fears of a French invasion. Pitt returned and set about creating a third coalition with subsidies to entice allies to put men in the field. Russia was promised Malta, and Austria came in when Napoleon declared himself King of Italy. British and Russian forces landed at Naples but pulled out and fell back on Sicily. It had the effect of persuading Napoleon to abandon his invasion plans and to dash eastwards to smash the Austrians at Ulm on the Danube in October 1805 and an Austrian-Russian force at Austerlitz on 2 November. Between the two battles, on 21 October, came Nelson's victory at Trafalgar, when 18 French and Spanish ships were destroyed. Although Nelson's funeral was turned into a massive celebration of the Trafalgar victory, as Pitt himself recognised, the defeat of the Russians and Austrians at Austerlitz was, in the short term, of far greater importance. However, the fact that the British retained domination of the seas weakened Napoleon's ability to bring the rest of Europe firmly within his control. He lacked the ability to exclude Britain entirely from European markets.

There was no British military activity on the continent to reduce the pressure on the allies, and a growing sense amongst them that Britain was taking the opportunity to expand its domination of world trade. There was some truth in it. Britain already controlled three-quarters of the world's sugar trade. A force of 6,500 had seized the strategically important Cape of Good Hope from the Dutch and Castlereagh, the Secretary at War, also turned his attention to the Spanish territories in South America. Like others before him, he envisaged this as a potentially huge market for British goods at a time when British trade was largely excluded from the Mediterranean. A force from the Cape of Good Hope captured Montevideo and, in June 1806, British forces seized Buenos Aires. The assumption that the local population would greet the British as liberators proved, not for the last time, to be wishful thinking and, in January 1807, the British garrison at Buenos Aires was forced to surrender after a popular revolt.

After Pitt's death in January 1806, Fox and his associates in the 'ministry of the talents' did not hide their unwillingness to get embroiled on the continent and peace negotiations made allies suspicious. Not surprisingly, the third coalition fell apart and

Russia rushed to make its peace with France at Tilsit in 1807. A central British fear was that the French would manage to create a navy large enough to challenge British control of the sea. Rumours emerged of secret articles in the Tilsit agreement that involved the creation of a maritime league against Britain, which would incorporate the navies of neutral Denmark and Portugal. When the Danes declined to hand over their fleet to Britain as a 'sacred deposit' and give up their neutrality, an expedition was despatched. The British bombardment of Copenhagen in September 1807 resulted in more than 2,000 civilian deaths and the destruction of about a third of the city's buildings. The fleet was surrendered. The King, for one, had no doubt that it was an immoral act and, on mainland Europe, it confirmed perceptions of 'perfidious Albion' and completed Britain's isolation.

Napoleon sought to emphasise this isolation by his 'Continental system', excluding British trade from Europe. It had a severe effect on Britain for a short time in 1807–8 and remained an irritation and a disruption until 1812. The British responded with Orders in Council that tried to regulate the trade of neutral states by forcing them to send their vessels via Britain, where they had to pay duties and receive a licence before proceeding.

It was Napoleon's demand that Portugal close its ports to British vessels that brought the Iberian peninsula into the picture. The French invaded in October 1807 and the royal family, together with the Portuguese navy, fled to Brazil. Napoleon, however, overplayed his hand in Spain, peremptorily deposing the King and replacing him with his brother, Joseph Bonaparte. In May 1808, there was a popular uprising against the invaders. A British force under Arthur Wellesley was sent to Portugal to stimulate an uprising there, and Wellesley defeated the French at Vimeiro. Lisbon was retaken, but it was a measure of the sense of weakness that existed at this time, that under the Convention of Cintra, in return for the French commitment to withdraw from Portugal, the British agreed that the captured French garrison at Lisbon, complete with their loot, would be returned to France on British ships. There were no restrictions on their participating again in the war.

There was much euphoria about Wellesley's initial success, despite the general condemnation that followed the news of Cintra. Reports from Spain were initially also good. Joseph Bonaparte had to withdraw from Madrid after only 11 days, but by the autumn, in the face of a powerful French onslaught, Spanish resistance had collapsed and their British support, in a force led by Sir John Moore, had to beat a hasty retreat in appalling winter conditions through harsh country to the port of Corunna and evacuation. Moore himself was fatally wounded and the half-starved battered and ragged survivors were shipped home.

Enthusiasm in Britain for the war was waning, but Castlereagh persuaded Parliament to agree to send Arthur Wellesley back to Portugal to launch an offensive against the French in Spain. Success proved elusive. An initial, but bloody victory, at Talavera on the road to Madrid in July 1809 resulted in the loss of a quarter of his force. Wellesley was created Viscount Wellington but, when the French regrouped, his army was soon driven back to the defensive positions of Torres Vedras to the north of

Lisbon. Equally disastrous was the expedition to Walcheren Island in the mouth of the River Scheldt in July 1809. Forty-four thousand troops were landed amid gales and storms, but failed to make it to their goal of Antwerp before French reinforcements arrived. Thousands died of disease before the force was eventually withdrawn in November 1810.

There was also growing tension with the United States. The British policy of stopping and searching neutral ships was always an irritation. The United States' attempt to maintain neutrality by restricting trade with both France and Britain was much more to the disadvantage of the latter. When the British also began to seize crew from American ships, claiming that they were British deserters, as no doubt many were, the protests from Washington grew sharper. In June 1812, the United States declared war, with some in the American government keen, as ever, to take the opportunity to seize Canada. But there was little enthusiasm for this amongst most New Englanders, who depended on trade with Britain. The Americans captured York (as Toronto was called) in 1813, but soon abandoned it, and the British succeeded in burning the White House in Washington in 1814, but failed in an attempt to capture New Orleans as a route to the West. Generally, the war, which gradually became a stalemate, was a series of rather desultory and unconnected actions, but it drained troops from the European arena.

The turn of the tide in Europe came in June 1812 with Napoleon's ill-judged invasion of Russia. Troops had to be pulled out of Spain and Wellington, at long last, was able to begin an advance. The battles were hard fought and the victories generally brought brutal rapine and looting, but, after smashing Joseph Bonaparte's army at Vitoria in June 1813, Wellington's forces were across the Pyrenees by the end of the year. With the victory in Spain and with Napoleon's Grand Army in untidy retreat from Russia, on the run from 'General' winter and marauding Cossacks, a new boldness returned to European states. Britain helped to provide the financial resources of resistance and to generate yet another coalition effort. Lavish financial aid and armaments were sent to Russia, Prussia, Sweden and Austria. It paid off at the Battle of the Nations at Leipzig in October 1813 and, by March 1814, the Prussian and Austrian armies had crossed the Rhine, while the Russians were in Holland, although without Britain, which lacked the troops to add to the allied forces. Wellington's efforts were still concentrated in southern France. In April 1814, Napoleon abdicated and set off for Elba. The allied leaders gathered at Vienna to decide the shape of the post-war world.

The return of the Bourbons to control of France did little to endear the post-war settlement to the French population. It was not entirely surprising that, when Napoleon returned in March 1815, he was greeted with considerable enthusiasm. The allies meanwhile were in deep quarrels about the spoils of war. The British troops in Flanders that Wellington now commanded were of very doubtful quality, with many of the best despatched to North America to finish the American war. Napoleon showed much of his old skill in dividing Wellington from his Prussian allies. Fortunately, at Waterloo in June 1815, Blücher and his Prussians arrived to take the pressure off Wellington's depleted red squares.

With France's power curbed, Britain had undoubtedly emerged from the war as the dominant world power, with much extended territory in Africa, the West Indies and in India, and with a control of the sea that gave her influence in every corner. Her economic strength and the financial resources upon which she could draw were apparent to ally and foe alike. Her financial subsidies and armaments were what had proved vital, along with a navy that kept France blockaded. Britain's actual military contribution, compared with the huge losses suffered by Austria, Russia and Prussia, was limited, although Wellington's Peninsular campaign had kept the flame of resistance to Napoleonic dominance alive in the dark years of 1808–12. His and Blücher's victory at Waterloo was an assertion that Britain still mattered in Europe and was prepared, when necessary, to interfere directly to prevent domination by a single power. Most striking, though, had been the ability to raise huge resources and maintain high levels of taxation in order to win the war against Napoleon. With the war ended, however, there was a determination to reduce commitments.

Congress of Europe

At the Congress of Vienna in 1814–15, the victorious allies laid down the new frontiers of Europe. From the British point of view, the main concern was to ensure that there were strong enough buffers on France's eastern frontier to block any future expansionism. In the Low Countries, a new larger Netherlands was formed, incorporating the French-speaking areas of Flanders. Prussia was given control of the Rhineland. Savoy became a larger Piedmont and Austria controlled the northern Italian plains. Castlereagh, the Foreign Secretary, while attracted by the idea of European Congresses as a way of dealing with international problems, kept well clear of the Tsar's schemes for a 'Holy Alliance' to defend conservative Europe against the forces of change. He did, however, concede the Quadruple Alliance with Russia, Austria and Prussia, which he saw as essentially about defending the established frontiers.

At Aix-La-Chapelle in 1818, France was included in the Congress as an equal, and Castlereagh succeeded in blocking the Tsar's proposal for the creation of an international army. During 1819, there were Liberal disturbances in a number of the German states and open rebellion against reactionary governments in Spain, Portugal, Naples, and Greece. The Tsar called for an interventionist policy, particularly in Spain, where the King had been forced to accept a democratic constitution. Castlereagh issued a state paper in which he sought to define the limits of Britain's role in mainland Europe. He rejected the idea that the Quadruple Alliance had ever been intended to be a 'union for the government of the world or for the superintendence of the internal affairs of other states'. He did not reject the possibility of intervention in some circumstances: it was always 'a question of the greatest possible moral as well as political delicacy'. The alliance had come about to ensure that no power used military force to disturb the equilibrium of Europe and, therefore the peace of the world. Only when that balance of power was threatened was there a right to intervene. The alliance was not concerned with the nature of the internal government of nations. Castlereagh spelled out the arguments against intervention – the costs; the fact that no army could remain in occupation indefinitely; the constant danger of the members of the intervening army being 'contaminated' and bringing home dangerous ideas. 'We shall be found in our place,' he concluded, 'when actual Danger menaces the System of Europe, but this Country cannot and will not act upon abstract and speculative Principles of Precaution.'

By the time the last Congress met at Verona in 1822, Castlereagh was dead and Canning was at the Foreign Office. He himself did not go to Verona, but sent Wellington in his place. Wellington, in stormy meetings, made clear that there would be no British involvement in the affairs of Spain, which the French, for their own reasons, were about to attack, or of Greece, which was starting a struggle for independence from the Turks. At the same time, in the succeeding months there was much diplomatic intervention at Madrid to persuade the Spanish to make concessions that would stave off French or any other intervention. When that failed, the government declared its neutrality, but was not averse to selling arms to the Spaniards – something that had been banned since 1814. Indeed, Canning went to so far as to declare, sensationally for a Tory minister, that he hoped that Spain would 'come triumphantly out of this struggle'.

In defending the government from its critics, Canning aligned himself with Castlereagh's state paper and helped establish the perception that Britain was different from the authoritarian powers of the rest of Europe. Nonetheless, there were plenty in Tory circles, including Wellington, who began to have doubts about where Canning was taking them with his 'Liberal' foreign policy, particularly when he at times was receiving praise from Whigs.

The rejection of interventionism in the internal affairs of other countries was confined to Europe. It did not apply to the non-European world. The war years and the turmoil in Spain gave the Spanish colonies in South and Central America the opportunity to rebel. British volunteers had participated in the initial revolts and British commercial interests had been quick to move in. Canning believed that Britain's dominant position needed to be consolidated by recognising the independence of the new states. He also saw this as a step towards curbing the privateering that went on against British merchantmen in the Caribbean. The French invasion of Spain in the spring of 1823 and the restoration of absolutism posed the threat of European intervention in South America. Canning sought a joint declaration with the United States against this, but, such was the American suspicion of British intentions, that they insisted that, as a first step, Britain recognise the new states, as America already had done. This Canning could not yet deliver because of hostility among his Cabinet colleagues, but they were prepared to agree that it should be made clear to France that the British navy would, if necessary, be used to prevent any attempt to retake the former colonies. The Americans, still suspicious of British motives, issued their own statement, in President Monroe's message to Congress in December 1823. This warned against any further colonisation within the American continent, a warning that was aimed at Russia and Britain, both of whom had territorial claims on the western seaboard of North America, as much as against France and Spain, with their claims in South America. But Canning, always with an eye to a wider audience, went out of his way to make clear that the reality was that the possible use of the British navy was what, in practice, ensured that the new states survived. It was not, however, until early in 1825 that royal objections to recognition could be overcome. Mexico, Columbia and Buenos Aires were recognised and, as Canning wrote, 'the New World established, and if we do not throw it away, ours'. Once again, commercial considerations had been paramount in shaping British policy, although there were also the political considerations of balancing French advance in Spain and keeping the United States firmly in check. Both were necessary to reassert British standing in the world.

There has always been a tendency to contrast Canning's 'liberal' foreign policy with Castlereagh's readiness to deal with reactionary European powers, but as the problems of settling international relations in the aftermath of war became more apparent in the twentieth century, Castlereagh's reputation has grown. He saw the Congress system as a means of keeping a check on French aggression and that meant at times going along with the other great powers of Russia and Austria, but he resisted where he could the efforts of these powers to turn the system into a suppression of all liberal reform. Canning's policies were little different. There was only so far that Britain was prepared to go in European entanglements and Castlereagh was already distancing himself from the direction the European powers were taking before Canning took over.

Further reading

Black, Jeremy, *Britain as a Military Power 1688–1815* (London, UCL Press, 1999)

Byrne, Michael, *Britain and the European Powers, 1815–1865* (London, Hodder & Stoughton, 1998)

Cookson, J.E., *The British Armed Nation 1793–1815* (Oxford, Oxford University Press, 1997)

Hall, Christopher D., *British Strategy in the Napoleonic War 1803–15* (Manchester, Manchester University Press, 1992)

Jones, J.R., *Britain and the World 1689–1815* (Brighton, Harvester, 1980)

Mori, Jennifer, *William Pitt and the French Revolution 1785–1795* (Keele, Keele University Press, 1997)

Stone, Laurence (ed.), *An Imperial State at War. Britain 1689 to 1815* (London, Routledge, 1994)

11

Challenges to the political system

Pressures for reform

Protest and demands for change coming from below were not new. The rich and powerful were vulnerable to popular pressure. The forces of law and order were scarce and thinly spread and riot and disorder were not uncommon as a way of expressing discontent. It has been calculated that there were 275 significant riots in the 65 years between 1735 and 1800, an average of four a year. Riots were often part of the ritual of politics. They were the way in which those in power could be reminded of their duties and responsibilities. It was not the poor who participated in such demonstrations, but tradesmen, shopkeepers, innkeepers, small businessmen, and it was rare for property and people to be violently assaulted. The powerful were pelted and jostled, but generally not much more. The ruling groups in town and country had to pay the price for the deference, or at least the acquiescence, of the lower orders by accepting that they had some paternal responsibility. Also, politicians excluded from office were not averse to using the crowd for their own political purposes

Remaining supporters of the Wilkesite campaigns (see Chapter 2) continued to press for parliamentary reform. Year after year, bills were brought in to shorten the duration of Parliament. The American war generated intense political debate on individual and political rights. There were small groups of intellectuals who kept alive the more radical traditions of the seventeenth-century Commonwealth. In 1774, John Cartwright, a landed proprietor and major in the Nottinghamshire militia and the brother of the future inventor of the powerloom, regenerated the argument of the 'Norman Yoke': that there had been a time before 1066 when an Anglo-Saxon England had had a democratic constitution and individual freedom that the Norman conquest had nipped in the bud. In 1776, in his pamphlet *Take your Choice*, he called for universal manhood suffrage as the ultimate goal, annual parliaments – the traditional check on government – equal single-member constituencies, payment of Members of Parliament to free them from dependence on government patronage, and the abolition of property qualifications for sitting in the House of Commons, to bring in those who had resources other than land. It was a programme, reinterpreted over time, that was to remain at the core of radical demands for the next three-quarters of a century.

John Horne Tooke, who had been active in Wilkes's struggles in the 1760s, joined with Cartwright and others in forming the Society for Constitutional Information in April 1780. It was not, in any sense, populist. Members were elected by ballot and membership cost a guinea. Its pamphlets, however, were free. The intention was to educate 'the community at large' politically on the nature of and the dangers to the constitution and to give them 'a knowledge of their lost Rights'. Although the language of these circles sounds very democratic, there were limitations on how far democracy should extend. Manhood suffrage usually meant suffrage confined to male householders and ratepayers. The poorest, the mobile, the dependent were not expected to participate. The members of such bodies were from the middling ranks of society, people who resented landowner domination of the political system.

Yet another of the circle was the Welsh dissenting minister, Richard Price, who had been one of the strongest defenders of the Americans and, indeed, saw in American liberty signs of the 'lost constitution' that had been corrupted in Britain. At the same time, however, he used the American argument that all men had a natural and inalienable right to life, liberty and property, and, to ensure this, required the right to elect their representatives.

The fact that reformers drew their inspiration from the levelling republicanism of the Civil Wars antagonised Whigs. What most of those politicians who, in 1780, were talking of reform meant was economical reform – the elimination of sinecures and patronage that had led to the corruption of the constitution. Edmund Burke rejected the idea of there being natural rights. He was a determined campaigner for reforms that would eradicate bribery and Crown patronage, but vehemently resisted parliamentary reform involving changes in the composition of Parliament or of the franchise. Christopher Wyvill in the Yorkshire Association saw economical reform, together with annual parliaments and more county (and therefore gentry) members, as enough to purge the system of its main faults and restore its pristine purity.

Between 7,000 and 8,000 Yorkshire freeholders signed Wyvill's petition in 1780, indicating a high level of discontent among the gentry. The calls for change beyond this group, however, were limited. Indeed, the instincts of many lower down the social scale were strongly traditional. The Gordon Riots of June 1780 silenced many potential supporters of wider reform. What had begun as a demonstration led by Lord George Gordon, leader of the Protestant Association, against the lifting of some of the penal laws against Catholics in Britain and Ireland developed into six days of anti-Catholic rioting. Nor was it confined to London. By the end of the week, chapels were going up in flames in Bath, Bristol and elsewhere. Nearly 300 rioters were killed and hundreds wounded when the troops moved in. Not surprisingly, there was anxiety about forces which could be so readily released.

The Rockingham Whigs showed no enthusiasm for constitutional reform. In May 1782, William Pitt the Younger raised the issue of parliamentary reform in a discussion in the House of Commons, suggesting the need for 'establishing a more solid and equal representation of the people, by which a proper constitutional connection could be revived'. It was couched in the vaguest of terms to attract as many Whigs as possible, and all that Pitt had in mind was a reorganisation of the existing electorate. But it was still further than most were willing to go. Burke denounced a proposal for shorter parliaments with what was described as 'a scream of passion'.

Once in office as Prime Minister at the end of 1783 and with a majority in the election of 1784, Pitt returned to the issue of parliamentary reform. In 1785 he brought in an extensive reform bill that would have reduced bribery, extended the county franchise, disenfranchised 36 rotten boroughs and created 72 additional seats for some counties, for London and for a few of the larger cities. There was massive hostility to his proposals both at the court and in Parliament and little sign of wider enthusiasm for them. Wyvill did his best to stir the county associations, but the last thing Pitt wanted was to generate populist agitation. His bill was defeated in the Commons and Pitt never again took up the issue. The reform impetus amongst the gentry and within the Society for Constitutional Information petered out.

What brought a revival of interest in the issues was the celebration of the centenary of the 1688 Revolution. Dinner clubs and celebrations throughout England toasted English liberties and rights. Also, groups of Dissenters, especially in provincial towns, began to campaign for repeal of the Test and Corporation Acts. In practice, these acts were rarely utilised to prevent Nonconformists from getting public office. They were largely ignored and, from time to time, indemnity acts were passed, suspending the measures. But to the growing numbers of the middle ranks who were Dissenters these acts were an affront to their social position. To older elites, on the other hand, the rise of dissent was a challenge and there were 'Church and King' clubs in Manchester and elsewhere, resisting the campaign to repeal the Test Act. Many of the Dissenters and intellectuals who had been involved in the campaign went on to be active in reform politics, while many of the 'Church and King' people hardened their resistance to change.

The impact of the French Revolution

The outbreak of the French Revolution, with the fall of the Bastille in July 1789, occasioned little immediate alarm amongst the political class. Whig intellectuals welcomed the Revolution and, with their French contacts, hoped to influence its course. Reformers were galvanised. Richard Price at the Revolution Society of London welcomed events in France as a 'glorious example' with universal implications 'to encourage other nations to assert the *unalienable* rights of Mankind, and thereby to introduce a general reformation of the government of Europe and to make the world free and happy'. In November 1789, he preached a sermon on the 'Love of Our Country' that was published as a pamphlet. Price argued that a country was a community of the people and it was the people who ultimately were the governors. Free men had the right 'to chuse[sic] our own governors; to cashier them for misconduct; and to frame a government for ourselves'. Thanks to the events in France: 'I see,' he declared, 'the ardour of liberty catching and spreading; a general amendment beginning in human affairs; the dominion of kings changed for the dominion of laws, and the dominion of priests giving way to the dominion of reason and conscience.'

It was the publication of Price's sermon that brought, a year later, Edmund Burke's *Reflections on the Revolution in France.* He was angered by the suggestion that events in France had implications for Britain. Burke's stance was important because he was seen as a guardian of the Whig tradition. To Burke, the French Revolution was 'a foul, impious, monstrous thing, wholly out of the course of moral nature', a revolt against the Almighty, against nature, against property, against order and against rational liberty, attempting 'to methodise anarchy'. Burke rejected the idea that one generation had the right to reject past tradition and to claim that it had some monopoly of the truth that it could impose. Good government had to be built on past experience: 'When ancient opinions and rules of life are taken away the loss cannot possibly be estimated. From that moment we have no compass to govern us, nor can we know distinctly to what port we steer.' Society, in Burke's view, was held together not because men made rational choices, but by the maintenance of traditional morality and force of habit. Civilisation was a delicate flower whose existence was always precarious and which needed social order, imposed by state, church and family, to maintain it. He rejected also the idea that government had to respond to popular pressure. Good government was what mattered and that required caution and wisdom, not bidding at 'an auction of popularity'. The starting point for any political system was, he argued, 'the ignorance and fallibility of mankind'. British liberties, according to Burke, were '*an entailed inheritance* derived to us from our forefathers and to be transmitted to posterity'. 'Good order is the foundation of all good things,' he declared, and for that to happen the people must be 'tractable and obedient . . . They must respect that property of which they cannot partake.' The world, by its nature, was unequal and, if people found it unjust, then they must be taught to seek consolation in prayer. It was the aristocracy and the church, working in harmony, that were the guarantee of social order and, indeed, of civilisation itself. If that were to disappear then both order and learning would 'be cast into the mire and trodden down under the hoofs of a swinish multitude'.

By far the most striking and popular response to Burke came from Thomas Paine, now returned from the United States, where his pamphlets had played a huge part in encouraging American moves to independence. Paine's *Rights of Man*, echoing the French National Assembly's 'Declaration of the Rights of Man and the Citizen', was published in March 1791. Paine dismissed the much-vaunted British Constitution as a fraud.

> Can then Mr Burke produce the English Constitution? If he cannot, we may fairly conclude, that though it has been so much talked about, no such thing as a constitution exists, or ever did exist, and consequently that the people have yet a constitution to form.

He declared that there was little that was 'Glorious' about the Glorious Revolution of 1688 and, anyway, 'the vanity and presumption of governing beyond the grave is the most ridiculous and insolent of all tyrannies'. He was, he declared, 'contending for the rights of the *living* and against their being willed away . . . [by] the manuscript assumed authority of the dead'. The existing monarchical and aristocratic system, based on heredity and precedent, was an irrational system that was incapable of reform from within. Only a system that gave 'equal representation to the people' would change the situation.

Focus on

Thomas Paine

This is an extract from *Rights of Man*, by Thomas Paine (1737–1809). Paine returned to England from the United States in 1787 and made regular visits to revolutionary France. He returned to the United States in 1802 and died there in 1809.

> What we formerly called Revolutions, were little more than a change of persons, or an alteration of local circumstances. They rose and fell like things of course, and had nothing in their existence or their fate that could influence beyond the sport that produced them. But what we now see in the world, from the Revolutions of America and France, are a renovation of the natural order of things, a system of principles as universal as truth and the existence of man, and combining moral with political happiness and prosperity.
>
> I. *Men are born, and always continue free and equal in respect of their rights. Civil distinction, therefore, can be founded only on political utility.*
> II. *The end of all political associations in the preservation of the natural and imprescriptible rights of man; and these rights are liberty, property, security, and resistance of oppression.*
> III. *The Nation is essentially the source of all sovereignty; nor can ANY INDIVIDUAL, or ANY BODY OF MEN, be entitled to any authority which is not expressly derived from it.*
>
> In these principles there is nothing to throw a Nation into confusion by inflaming ambition. They are calculated to call forth wisdom and abilities, and to exercise them for the public good, and not for the emolument or aggrandisement of particular descriptions of men or families. Monarchical sovereignty, the enemy of mankind, and the source of misery, is abolished; and sovereignty is restored to its natural and original place, the Nation. Were this the case throughout Europe, the causes of wars would be taken away.

Source: Thomas Paine, *Rights of Man, Part 1* (1791).

Paine published a second part of the *Rights of Man* in February 1792. This was much more radical than the earlier part. In Part 2 there was a direct call for the establishment of a republic: a hereditary succession was 'a burlesque'. Like America, Britain required a proper written constitution with representative government. Paine analysed how the nation's taxes were raised and spent and argued that resources needed to be concentrated upon the old and the young. He claimed that there was more than enough raised from taxes to provide for a quarter of a million poor families, to educate 1,030,000 children, to make provision for 140,000 old people, to provide birth, marriage and funeral allowances and ensure full employment for the casual poor in London and Westminster. In a reformed Britain there would be no place for a monarchy, a nobility or an established church.

By early 1792, there were signs of a stirring among groups who had hitherto been outside the political nation. In December 1791, a handful of tradesmen in the Sheffield Constitutional Association, that had met to complain about the price of foodstuffs, called for universal suffrage and annual parliaments, having read the *Rights of Man*. Within three months, there were about 2,000 members, organised in groups of ten, discussing the writings of Paine and others. The London Corresponding Society, formed by Thomas Hardy, a Scottish-born shoemaker working in Piccadilly, was modelled on the Sheffield group. Horne Tooke helped Hardy draft an initial statement that linked the discontents about prices with the need for parliamentary reform. A network of societies across the country, linked by correspondence, had been one of the features of the American revolution. The London Corresponding Society issued its first public statement in April 1792 and by then it had some 70 members. 'The nation', it declared, 'is unrepresented . . . the present system is totally unconstitutional.'

A group of young Whig aristocrats tried to keep control of the agitation by founding, in April 1792, the Society of the Friends of the People, calling for a moderate measure of parliamentary reform to avoid the kind of unrest that had caused revolution in France. But, with the second part of the *Rights of Man* selling like hotcakes and reform societies of tradesmen, shopkeepers, mechanics and journeymen appearing in towns throughout the country, the government acted. On 21 May 1792, a royal proclamation was issued against seditious writings. Far from curbing matters, it had the opposite effect and, according to a Scottish soldier turned politician, 'acted like an Electric shock' and stimulated debate on the nature of society and government: 'It set people of all ranks a-reading . . . farmers, ploughmen, peasants, manufacturers, artificers, shopkeepers, sailors, merchants.'[1]

Numbers in the popular reform associations began to increase. In marked contrast to earlier reform movements, the London Corresponding Society deliberately set out to attract 'unlimited numbers' with a subscription of only one penny a week. In Edinburgh, a local newspaper claimed that 'the peasant seems to be equally knowing about politics as the peer' and there were reports of a Gaelic version of the *Rights of*

---

[1] Norman Macleod, quoted in Edward Hughes, 'The Scottish Reform Movement and Charles Grey 1792–94: Some Fresh Correspondence', *Scottish Historical Review*, 35 (1956), p. 31.

Man circulating in the Highlands. Enthusiasm for developments in France seemed to be on the increase. Trees of liberty, bedecked with candles and apples, were planted in many provincial towns and occasionally *God Save the King*, increasingly becoming accepted as the national anthem, was shouted down by the more popular, revolutionary chorus of *Ça Ira*, which included the chilling lines calling for aristocrats to be strung up:

> Les aristocrates à la lanterne!
> Ah! ça ira, ça ira, ça ira,
> Les aristocrates, on les pendra!
> Le despotisme expirera,
> La liberté triomphera.

But there were also signs of a reaction to reform demands. In Birmingham, a Unitarian meeting house was set on fire by a loyalist crowd, the Unitarians being seen as the most radical of the dissenting groups. The mob then turned on the house of the town's best-known radical, Dr Joseph Priestley. Priestley, a scientist of considerable repute and a writer who had questioned such Christian beliefs as miracles and the fall of man, had been a passionate upholder of the American cause in the 1770s and had been quick to hail the French Revolution. He had long argued that the object of government needed to be the 'the good and happiness' of the majority of the population. Burke had attacked him in the Commons for his dangerous views. Priestley's manuscripts and furniture were pitched from the windows, his wine cellar emptied and his laboratory sacked. It was a riot deliberately stirred by established church people who resented the increasingly powerful dissenting interest in Birmingham. Priestley left the country for the United States and the Dissenters in Birmingham were effectively silenced.

In September 1792, 186 Manchester publicans signed a pledge to exclude from their premises those they regarded as Jacobin supporters of the French Revolution. Cambridge publicans followed, declaring their intention to report conversation, pamphlets and books 'of a treasonable or seditious tendency' to the local magistrates. In November, John Reeves, a government lawyer and probably with ministerial approval, launched the 'Association for Preserving Liberty and Property against Republicans and Levellers', and there was an extensive anti-radical literature in pamphlet and press warning of the dangers of French influence. The *Anti-Jacobin Review* very effectively turned individual radicals into popular hate figures.

With an invasion scare in December and the calling out of militias, many in the middle ranks began to back away from too direct involvement in reform movements. There were concerns about the spread of the 'democratic spirit' and, with industrial unrest and complaints about rising prices being linked to the demands for political reform, many manufacturers, as Pitt's ally, Henry Dundas, gloatingly pointed out, began to repent their earlier championing of reform.

As preparations for war with France intensified, so did the pressure on people and organisations to declare their loyalty. Individual tradespeople with reform sympathies found it increasingly difficult to get work, while others found credit from their bank drying up. Radical booksellers found it wise to disappear rather than to risk imprisonment. At a Convention of Scottish reformers in April, many of the more 'respectable' names were missing. There were signs of a more radical tone. William Skirving, the

Focus on

The trial of Thomas Muir

The following is an extract from Lord Braxfield's address to the jury in the trial of Thomas Muir for sedition before the High Court of Justiciary, Edinburgh 30–31 August 1793. Muir, an Edinburgh advocate, was sentenced to 14 years' transportation. He eventually escaped from Australia and made his way to France, where he died in 1799.

There are two things which you should attend to, which require no proof. The first is, that the British constitution is the best in the world; for the truth of this, gentlemen, I need only appeal to your own feelings. Is not every man secure in his life, liberty and property? Is not happiness in the power of every man, except those, perhaps, who from disappointment in their schemes of advancement, are discontented? Does not every man enjoy unmolested the fruits of his industry? And does not every man sit safely under his own vine and his own fig-tree, and none shall make him afraid? The other circumstance, gentlemen, which you have to attend to, is the state of the country during last winter. There was a spirit of sedition and revolt going abroad which made every good subject seriously uneasy. I observed the reflection of the master of the Grammar School of Glasgow, who told Mr Muir, he conceived that proposing reform then was very ill-timed. I coincide in that opinion, and I leave it for you to judge whether it was perfectly innocent or not in Mr Muir, at such a time, to go about among ignorant country people, and among the lower classes of the people, making them leave off work, and inducing them to believe that a reform was absolutely necessary to preserve their safety and liberty, which if it had not been for him they never would have suspected to have been in danger . . .

Mr Muir might have known that no attention could be paid to such a rabble. What right had they to representation? He could have told them that the Parliament would never listen to their petition. How could they think of it? A government in every country should be just like a corporation; and, in this country, it is made up of the landed interest, which alone has the right to be represented; as for the rabble, who have nothing but personal property, what hold has the nation on them? What security for the payment of their taxes? They may pack up all their property on their backs, and leave the country in the twinkling of an eye, but landed property cannot be removed.

Source: State Trials, XXIII, pp. 229–31.

secretary, declared that there would be no more petitioning and that, while earlier movements with their aristocratic membership had been about working for the good of the people, at this Convention 'we are the people themselves', a much more revolutionary concept. The young Glasgow lawyer, Thomas Muir, who had been active in the earlier movement and then had gone to France, returned to Scotland in July and was immediately arrested. Overly confident in his own legal skills, he defended himself, but he was quite unprepared for the bias of the trial judge, Lord Braxfield. Muir's crime, in Braxfield's eyes, was to have gone 'among ignorant country people, and among the lower classes of people, making them leave off work, and inducing them to believe that a reform was absolutely necessary for their safety and liberty'. He was sentenced to 14 years' transportation – the kind of sentence reserved for the severest crimes against people and property, not for political activities. Other court cases followed. The Dundee Friends of Liberty issued a paper that warned that the House of Commons was no longer a check on executive power but was part of an aristocratic tyranny against the people. The implication was that petitioning 'a wicked ministry and a compliant Parliament' was pointless. The author, an Etonian Unitarian preacher, Thomas Fyshe Palmer, was sentenced to seven years' transportation.

Despite the hostile atmosphere, a small group of radicals held yet another Convention. The 'British Convention of the Delegates of the People, associated to obtain Universal Suffrage and Annual Parliaments' met in Edinburgh in early December. Maurice Margarot and Joseph Gerrald represented the London Corresponding Society. The authorities were prepared, and the proceedings well-infiltrated with informers. Members addressed one another as 'citizen' and there was an assumption that, should the situation become critical and the government act to ban meetings and suspend habeas corpus, then the Convention could be converted into a revolutionary Parliament. Gerrald denounced the war and appealed to the working classes: 'It is the blood of the peasant and the manufacturer which flows in the battle; it's the purse of the tradesman and the artificer which is emptied in the contest.' Margarot and Gerrald were quickly arrested, together with Skirving. At their trials in the spring of 1794, they conducted their own defence before Lord Braxfield. In response to Braxfield's well-known statement at the trial of Thomas Muir that the British constitution was the best in the world and that required no proof, Gerrald claimed that what the reformers sought was the restoration of the purer, democratic constitution of pre-Norman days. With juries including many who were active in loyalist associations, and Braxfield advising the jury that Gerrald's eloquence was 'enough to persuade the people to rise in arms', the three were duly sentenced to 14 years' transportation.

There were protests in London, Sheffield and elsewhere at the harsh sentences. In May 1794, the chance discovery of a dozen pikes, spearheads and battleaxes in a house in Edinburgh led to reports of arming among reformers in other Scottish towns. Faced with a number of military failures and with signs of discontent from many different directions, Pitt acted. Hardy and John Thelwall from the London Corresponding Society were arrested, together with six middle-class members of the Society for Constitutional Information, including the veteran John Horne Tooke. A few days later habeas corpus was suspended, with only 12 MPs supporting Fox's protests. The charges against the reformers were for high treason. Horne Tooke subpoenaed Pitt to attend as a defence witness and compelled him to admit that he had attended a meeting of parliamentary reformers in 1782 and, in spite of an attempt to suggest that the London Corresponding Society was part of an armed conspiracy, Hardy, Thelwall and the others were acquitted, amid scenes of jubilation in the streets of London.

During 1795, the London Corresponding Society continued to hold regular meetings and to tap into popular discontent at taxation and food shortages, and anger against recruiting officers and press gangs. Attendances at its meetings seem to have peaked in the autumn of 1795 and, from what limited information we have on membership, it is clear that the society attracted considerable numbers of artisans and tradesmen alongside lawyers, doctors, booksellers, clerks and shopkeepers. There were also signs of a growing peace movement. Reputedly, as many as 100,000 turned out in Copenhagen Fields in north London to hear John Thelwall and other reformers call for peace and political reform. During the state opening of Parliament, the King's coach was waylaid by a crowd carrying tiny loaves wrapped in black crepe, shouting 'No war! No King!' The government rushed through the 'Two Acts' or the 'Gagging Acts', as they became known. The 'Treasonable Practices' Act made all criticism of the King or his heirs and successors high treason, punishable by death. The 'Seditious Meetings' Act banned public meetings of more than 50 people 'for the alteration of matters established in Church and State' and required lecture halls to be licensed.

There was still some defiance. The young Samuel Taylor Coleridge, who had denounced the 'Two Acts' at meetings in Bristol, continued to talk admiringly of the Scottish martyrs, 'that small but glorious band, whom we may truly distinguish by the name of thinking and disinterested Patriots'. His fellow poet, Robert Southey, hailed the 'Martyrs of Freedom' who stood 'For justice, liberty and equal laws'. Even the more cautious Wordsworth dared to visit the circle of intellectual radicals that gathered at the home of William Godwin and Mary Wollstonecroft.

But, there were no more mass meetings after December 1795. Reformers had to act with great circumspection. Much of what was going on after that was carried out in secret and, therefore, is difficult to disentangle. The London Corresponding Society broke up during 1796, beset by a lack of finance and by differences over tactics. As Napoleon led French troops into Italy and the Balkans, enthusiasm for things French waned. However, there is no doubt that there was a radical underworld of conspirators in different places, and there were loose links between these. From the government's point of view the most serious threat came from Ireland.

Ireland

Inspired by events in France, the Society of United Irishmen had been formed in Belfast in 1791, thanks to William Drennan, a Belfast-born Presbyterian doctor, and a group of prominent Presbyterian merchants. The secretary was the Dublin Protestant lawyer, Theobald Wolfe Tone. Tone aimed at convincing Dissenters 'that they and the Catholics had one common interest and one common enemy' and that Catholics could be trusted not to use their political power to try to unpick the seventeenth-century land settlement. The movement launched a campaign for parliamentary reform that would embrace 'all the people of Ireland'. The government was already contemplating moves in the direction of Catholic Emancipation, but had to neutralise powerful Ascendancy opposition and ensure that there were no moves for a Protestant-led break with Britain. Some concessions to Catholics were made in 1791 and 1793, giving Catholics the right of public worship and the freedom of erecting their own schools. Propertied Catholics were also given the vote in parliamentary elections, although still excluded from sitting in Parliament. Talk of repealing all the laws limiting Catholic rights met with a predictable outcry.

Although, initially, the Society of United Irishmen had envisaged a constitutional dual monarchy with an independent Parliament, by 1794, many had come round to considering a complete break with Britain, 'the never-failing source of all our political evils', and the establishment of a republic. In April, Tone was telling French agents who were active on the island that the government of Ireland would tumble 'the moment a superior force appears' since it had 'no base in either the interests or the affections of the people'. Tone, now calling for 'open war' with Britain, petitioned the French Directory to give assistance to a rebellion and, in December 1796, a French fleet with some 15,000 troops set sail for Ireland with Tone on board. Storms scattered the fleet and it was forced to abandon a landing in Bantry Bay and return to France.

Discontent in Ireland continued to rise as new war taxes began to bite. 1797 brought a financial crisis and the end of subsidies to the grain trade. Arrests spread – as many as 600 in Ulster during 1797. Open rebellion broke out around Dublin in May 1798, but widespread rumours quickly arose of sectarian massacres and expected French landings. What had been intended as a movement that would cross the sectarian divide became reduced in most people's minds to a Catholic–Protestant struggle. Wolfe Tone had hoped to substitute the 'common name of Irishman, in the place of the denominations of Protestant, Catholic and Dissenter', but it was not to be. Protestant businessmen in the north were already anxious at the entry of Catholic merchants into the linen industry and Protestant farmers resented the admission of Catholics to farm tenancies. Atrocities were perpetrated on both sides. It was not until four months after the start of the rising in May 1798 that a relatively small French force of about 1,000 landed in County Mayo, but was quickly surrounded by British troops. By the end of the summer of 1798, it was estimated that as many as 30,000 had perished in the civil unrest. Tone was captured and sentenced to death, but took his own life. By the standards of the time, the retribution was restrained. Two hundred and thirty-one were sentenced to death but about fifty or more of these sentences were commuted to imprisonment or transportation. Two hundred and forty were sentenced to transportation, while others managed to escape to France.

During 1796, the United Irishmen clearly felt that it was worth their while to try to re-establish links with the underground groups in Scotland and England. By the spring of 1797, there were at least 26 societies of United Scotsmen, consciously modelled on the United Irishmen. In England, 29 branches of United Englishmen were identified by the Home Office, mainly in Lancashire and part of London, where there were growing Irish communities. The extent of support that such groups had is difficult to gauge, because of their secret nature and because of the fact that we have to rely largely on the reports of government spies for details. Also, there was a wariness about committing statements to paper since this could lead to arrest for sedition. Communications from the United Scotsmen and the United Irishmen were also found in the papers seized in the aftermath of the naval mutinies at the Nore and the Spithead, which shook national confidence in 1797. Long-running discontents amongst men who, in many cases, had been impressed into the service made fertile ground for political agitation and the United Irishmen had contacts among the 15,000 or so seamen of Irish extraction in the fleet.

The unrest in Ireland led to mass arrests in London and elsewhere of radicals who often had no connection with events in Ireland. Most of the surviving members of the Committee of the London Corresponding Society were rounded up in April 1798. With habeas corpus again suspended, most remained in prison until the spring of 1801. As part and parcel of the same repression, but also as a sop to middle-class businessmen, trade unions were banned by the Combination Acts of 1799 and 1800. While talk of this as a 'reign of terror' by the government may be an exaggeration, there is no doubt that harassment, imprisonment and intimidation were all effectively used to break the popular radical movement. The government certainly remained mightily anxious about the possibility of insurrection.

Radicalism revives

Rising prices, food scarcities, changes in workplace organisation and erratic employment all frequently produced protests. There has been debate among historians as to how far these could be channelled into political demands. Certainly, government informers frequently thought that there were political aspects to industrial movements. The Luddite disturbances in Lancashire, Yorkshire and Nottinghamshire in 1811–12, when there was a series of incidents of machine-smashing, were triggered by the severe economic conditions of the time coming on top of longer-term grievances among workers in the hosiery trade of the east Midlands, the woollen trade in Yorkshire and the cotton trade in Lancashire. Frame-work knitters, weavers and cloth dressers in these industries were losing their status, finding their living standards cut and facing an uncertain future (see Chapter 8). Machine-breaking was an effective way of bringing pressure to bear on their employers. But the Luddites quickly found that they were also up against the state. On more than one occasion, the local militia was called in to defend mills against protesting workers. By the summer of 1812, there was again talk of the possibility of a general rising of the people. The retribution on machine-breakers was brutal.

Small groups of reformers, both old and new, committed to working within the existing system, did continue to be active, Particularly after the death of Pitt, there were signs of a revival in radicalism. In 1807, thanks largely to the efforts of the tailor, Francis Place, and other former members of the London Corresponding Society, the committed parliamentary reformer, Sir Francis Burdett, won the Westminster constituency, which had the largest electorate in the country. In dissenting and business circles – frequently the same – there were increasingly loud demands for an end to the war and, at the very least, for an end to the Orders in Council that were restricting British exports being traded through neutral ports.

The argument that parliamentary reform was about restoring the purity of the constitution was still the usual case put forward by those who were pressing for reform in these years. William Cobbett in the *Weekly Political Register* raged against what he called 'Old Corruption' that was sweeping away the good things of 'Old England'. But a younger generation of Whigs was finding a voice in the pages of the *Edinburgh Review*, launched in 1802. It sought to 'design political institutions suitable to the needs of a modern commercial society' and the foundation of this new political order would be 'the middling order' of society, which Francis Horner, one of the founders of the *Review*, defined as those with 'the opinions, interests and habits of those numerous families who are characterised by moderate but increasing incomes, a careful education in their youth and a strict observance of the great common virtues'. Terrors inspired by hints of revolutionary conspiracies and possible insurrections were enough to moderate the demands of most of the middle ranks, but the discontent at the continuing wars, including that with the United States, was apparent.

Even before the war ended, the elderly reformer, John Cartwright, was travelling the country trying to arouse interest in another reform campaign. Cartwright's arguments had not altered a great deal. He continued to argue that only annual parliaments, manhood suffrage and vote by ballot could restore 'the true principles of the English Constitution' and create, once again, a representative House of Commons freed from the overweening influence of Crown and Lords. The end of the war allowed more open criticism of government without risking the accusation of giving succour to the French.

Initial protests focused on the Corn Laws and on the income tax. The Treaty of Vienna seemed a poor recompense for 20 years of war. In Glasgow, at the largest political meeting hitherto held in Scotland, an old reformer of the 1790s declared that it seemed to have been fought 'for no other object than the restoration of whatever was detestable, bigoted and despotic . . . the reestablishment of the despicable family of Bourbon, the restoration of the pope in Italy and of the Jesuits and the Inquisition in Spain'.[2] The government was forced to repeal the income tax, but had to compensate for the loss of revenue by maintaining, and, indeed, extending the taxes on consumption that fell most heavily on the less well-off.

For the Whigs, the answer was retrenchment, the reduction in government expenditure by extensive economic reform and the elimination of corruption. In the view of

---

[2] *Glasgow Herald*, 1 November 1816.

many others, including increasingly vocal campaigners amongst the working classes, only more drastic reform bringing universal suffrage could solve the problem. Although the Hampden Clubs that had emerged as a result of John Cartwright's lecture tours initially attracted merchants, small businessmen and shopkeepers, with economic distress exacerbated by army demobilisation, support widened. During 1816, there were strikes and food riots in many parts of the country. A younger generation of reformers began to make a more direct appeal to the working class. Among the most influential was Henry Hunt, who had already earned the sobriquet 'Orator Hunt'. It was Hunt who was the main speaker at a mass meeting in London's Spa Fields on 15 November 1816 to approve the carrying of a petition to the Prince Regent, calling for the radical programme of universal male suffrage, annual parliaments, and vote by ballot. In the following month, a meeting in London of delegates from petitioning groups and Hampden Clubs in different parts of the country that included many working men debated whether to confine the petition to a demand for household suffrage, but on the motion of a young Lancashire weaver, Samuel Bamford, the meeting came out in favour of universal suffrage.

All through 1817, there were protest marches, renewed organisation and nascent uprisings. From Manchester, weavers set off on a hunger march to London. In June, Derbyshire working men from Pentrich in Derbyshire set off for Nottingham in the expectation that there was to be a general uprising. In Scotland there were mass arrests and charges of sedition were laid, only for the accused to be acquitted in most cases. A good harvest in 1817 and an improved economy eased the pressure in 1818, but there were numerous strikes as workers tried to regain some of the wages lost in previous years. A climax of protest came in August 1819, when an attempt was made to arrest Henry 'Orator' Hunt at a huge meeting in St Peter's Fields in Manchester. Local yeomanry were sent in to disperse the meeting and 17 were killed, including 3 women, with 650 wounded, a quarter of whom were women and children. The affair was quickly labelled Peterloo. The Home Office had been urging the use of force against radical meetings and the government's response was the Six Acts, that further curbed radical activities and muzzled the press. Training and drilling became an offence, as did marching with flags and banners. Justices were given permission to search for and seize arms; meetings of more than 50 without official permission were banned; stamp duties on newspapers were raised and the definition of blasphemous and seditious libel was broadened. Hunt was sentenced to two years in prison.

Two months later, the government were able to claim that their repressive measures were essential when a group of London ultra-radicals, whose activities had been under constant surveillance by the police, were seized in Cato Street as they plotted the assassination of the Cabinet as a prelude to a general insurrection. This group had been arguing for some time that a real revolution which would bring distribution of property was what was required, if the position of the mass of the people were to be improved. Their plans were pretty well-known and in a 'sting operation' by an informer in their midst they were exposed. Six members were hanged and beheaded and another five were transported.

Figure 11.1 *A many-headed monster in a pile of emblems – Universal Suffrage or the Scum Uppermost,*
George Cruikshank cartoon, 1819. George Cruikshank (1792–1878), Gillray's successor as
leading caricaturist, shows little sympathy for popular aspirations for democracy in this cartoon.
Source: © The Trustees of The British Museum

In April 1820, after weeks of rising tension and rumours about a general rising
beginning in Manchester, groups of workers in various towns in the West of Scotland
responded to a call to arms. An attempt to seize the Carron Ironworks in Falkirk,
where the famous 'Carronade' artillery was produced, was intercepted by a troop of
hussars. Mass arrests followed and, in the end, three, identified doubtfully as ringleaders,
were executed for treason.

How serious the post-war unrest was will continue to be debated. Clearly, a government determined to reject demands for even moderate constitutional reform had a
vested interest in exaggerating the extent of treasonable activity. The police and the

Home Office depended on spies and informers for their information and these had an interest in overstating the importance of what they had to report. There can be little doubt that there was a handful of people who were ready to consider armed rebellion and perhaps even a network which could be regarded as maintaining an underground revolutionary tradition, awaiting the moment when they might link into mass protests. The remarkable thing is that there were people – albeit perhaps just hundreds – in different places who at different times were gathering arms and preparing for an expected uprising. The language of London ultra-radicals can be heard, only slightly modified, in Lancashire and in Scotland. Inevitably, there were debates about tactics and timing and plenty of people who still believed that patient, peaceful petitioning would convince politicians, who constantly spoke of the glories of British liberty, who considered that further constitutional change was necessary. The language of most public meetings was still rooted in constitutionalism, talking about traditional rights and the ancient constitution that had been corrupted. Therefore, in theory, by eradicating corruption, the constitution's purity could be restored. The Paineite case about the natural right of people to democratic representation was rather muted. Change still seemed possible without the terrors and dangers of revolution.

Events such as Peterloo came as a shock to the increasingly prosperous and confident middle classes. The killing of civilians at a peaceful public meeting was something that was not expected to happen in Britain. It was the method of reactionary continental governments. There were signs of renewal of agitation from amongst the middle ranks of society. Since early in the century, a younger generation of Whigs, outside Parliament, had been seeking to adjust Whig thinking to respond to the social changes which they saw around them. Such people were horrified by the radical unrest of the post-war years and were careful to distance themselves from it. At the same time, they were appalled that a reactionary government was contributing to the conditions that could threaten the existence of a 'modern commercial society'. The *Edinburgh Review* and other journals began to argue for a measure of middle-class enfranchisement. There was increasing talk of 'a middling class', a group that lay between the upper and lower orders, who would eradicate the worst abuses, but, at the same time, present no threat to property and stability. The writer, James Mill (1773–1836), at the centre of a group of 'philosophical radicals' associated with Jeremy Bentham (see Chapter 17) began to write of a middle-class mission 'to counteract the despotic tendencies engendered in other classes by the progress of improvement'.

The 1820s have generally been seen as a period of quiescence after the turmoil of the post-war years and, certainly, the prosperity of the early 1820s took the sting out of the working-class agitation. Nevertheless, it was a decade of ideological debate and ferment. In 1823, remnants of the old slavery abolition committee that had created the conditions for success in 1807 re-formed in the cautiously named 'London Society for Mitigating and Gradually Abolishing the State of Slavery Throughout the British Dominions'. Quaker-dominated, it reflected a new stirring among the ranks of different groups of Nonconformists (as Dissenters were increasingly called) that soon involved demands for an end to the continuing discrimination of the Test and Corporation Acts.

Fox's former acolyte, Charles Grey – now Earl Grey – had lost much of his enthusiasm for political reform as the decades passed. He saw universal suffrage as a 'mischievous absurdity'. However, in the 1820s, the issue of parliamentary reform began to attract the attention of the young Whig, Lord John Russell, of the great Whig family of the Dukes of Bedford. He started with calls for the disenfranchisement of corrupt rotten boroughs, campaigned for repeal of the Test Acts and then took up the cause of wider parliamentary reform. Thanks to such people, the Whigs, despite the fact that they contained some of the grandest and richest of aristocrats, began to be able to present themselves once again as reforming 'friends of the people' and to take advantage of the break-up of the Tory party.

How far the radicalism of these years was revolutionary at moments and posed a serious threat to government continues to be debated by historians. Edward Thompson's classic work argued that the combination of radical political ideas and the actual experience of industrial change in these years brought about the 'making of the English working class'. Workers became conscious of themselves as a class against other social classes. Concepts of class and how far one can talk of a common experience of industrialisation have been much challenged since the 1960s. In their politics, working-class radicals continued to use the language of eighteenth-century radicalism about eradicating the corruption in what was basically a sound constitution. It was a common language with middle-class reformers rather than a language that challenged the capitalist economic system into which workers were being caught. On the other hand, there were signs of elements of the middle classes who saw their future not as part of a wider movement of the people against the aristocracy but as a property-owning group who could be threatened by working-class radicalism and whose future lay in alliance with the landed class.

Further reading

Dickinson, H.T. (ed.), *Britain and the French Revolution 1789–1815* (Basingstoke, Macmillan, 1989)

Dickinson, H.T., *The Politics of the People in the Eighteenth Century* (Basingstoke, Macmillan, 1995)

Elliott, Marianne, *Partners in Revolution. The United Irishmen and France* (New Haven, Yale, 1982)

Emsley, Clive, *British Society and the French Wars 1793–1815* (Basingstoke, Macmillan, 1979)

Epstein, James A., *Radical Expression. Political Language, Ritual and Symbol in England, 1790–1850* (Oxford, Oxford University Press, 1994)

Royle, Edward, *Revolutionary Britannia? Reflections on the Threat of Revolution in Britain 1789–1848* (Manchester, Manchester University Press, 2000)

Thompson, E.P., *The Making of the English Working Class* (Harmondsworth, Penguin, 1968)

Timeline 1780–1830

Year	Government and politics	War and empire	Economic and social	Cultural and intellectual
1781	Petitions for parliamentary reform	Cornwallis surrenders at Yorktown	Population of England, 7,206,000; life expectancy at birth in England & Wales 35.4 years; Cort's pudding and rolling process	
1782	Rockingham and Fox ministry; Rockingham dies, succeeded by Shelburne; Pitt the Younger Chancellor		Boulton and Watt rotary motion engine	
1783	Fox–North coalition; Pitt the Younger becomes Prime Minister	Treaty of Paris (Versailles) ends American War	Potato famine in Ireland; food riots	Royal Society of Edinburgh founded
1784	General election gives Pitt a majority	India Act gives control of East India Company		Arthur Young's *Annals of Agriculture*
1785				Foundation of *The Times* newspaper
1786			David Dale founds New Lanark cotton mill	Caroline Herschel discovers first of 8 comets; Thomas Clarkson's *An Essay on the Slavery and Commerce of the Human Species*
1787			First transportation of criminals to Australia	Society for Abolition of Slavery founded
1788	Discussion of Regency			
1789		French Revolution		Revd Gilbert White's *The Natural History and Antiquities of Selborne*

Year				
1790				Edmund Burke's *Reflections on the Revolution in France*
1791	Joseph Priestley's house attacked by loyalist mob	French Revolutionary Constitution		Thomas Paine's *Rights of Man, Part 1*; death of John Wesley; *The Observer* newspaper established
1792	Formation of London Corresponding Society, and Society of the Friends of the People	Sierra Leone as home for former slaves		Mary Wollstonecraft's *A Vindication of the Rights of Woman*; Thomas Paine's *Rights of Man, Part 2*
1793		War with France; Louis XVI and Marie Antoinette guillotined		
1794	Trial of Thomas Hardy and others from LCS; Portland Whigs join government		Suspension of habeas corpus	
1795	Treasonable Practices and Seditious Meetings Acts		Food riot; 75,000 handloom weavers in cotton industry	
1796		War with Spain		Anderson's College founded in Glasgow
1797			Naval mutinies at Spithead and the Nore	
1798	Revolt of United Irishmen	Nelson's victory at the Nile; French troops invade Ireland	Habeas corpus suspended	Thomas Malthus, *An Essay on the Principle of Population*
1799			Income tax introduced; Combination Act makes trade unions illegal; Charles Tennant of Glasgow perfects chlorine concentrate bleaching method	
1800			Food riots in London	

Year	Government and politics	War and empire	Economic and social	Cultural and intellectual
1801	United Kingdom of Great Britain and Ireland formed; resignation of Pitt; Addington Prime Minister		Life expectancy at birth in England and Wales 40.0 years; first decennial census; potato famine in Ireland	
1802		Peace of Amiens	Health and Morals of Apprentices Act	
1803		Renewal of war with France; Third coalition		
1804	Pitt returns as Prime Minister			
1805		Battle of Trafalgar	Grand Junction Canal completed	
1806	Death of Pitt; 'Ministry of all the Talents'; death of Fox		Continental system against British trade	
1807	Portland Prime Minister		Abolition of slave trade	
1808		War in Iberian peninsula		
1809	Spencer Perceval Prime Minister			
1810	Regency established			
1811			Luddite unrest	
1812	Perceval shot; Liverpool Prime Minister	War with United States	Paddle steamer 'Comet' begins passenger service on River Clyde	
1813			Robert Owen's *A New View of Society*	Jane Austen's *Pride and Prejudice*
1814		Defeat of France	Repeal of Statute of Artificers	Walter Scott's *Waverley*
1815	Corn Law established	Battle of Waterloo; Congress of Vienna; British control of Cape of Good Hope confirmed		

Year			
1816	Hampden Clubs; reform meeting at Spa Fields	Abolition of income tax; potato famine in Ireland	
1817	Blanketeers' march; Coercion Acts	Pentrich Uprising; widespread economic distress	David Ricardo, *Principles of Political Economy*
1818			
1819	Peterloo Massacre; Six Acts	Raffles in Singapore	John Keats writes 'Ode on a Grecian Urn'
1820	George IV; Cato Street conspiracy; radical war in Scotland	224,000 handloom weavers in cotton industry	
1821			*Manchester Guardian* launched
1822	Death of Castlereagh; Canning becomes Foreign Secretary	Potato famine in Ireland	
1823		Huskisson reduces duties on some imports	Birkbeck College founded in London
1824		Repeal of Combination Acts	
1825		Stockton to Darlington railway	
1826		Economic Crisis	
1827	Resignation of Liverpool; Canning Prime Minister in February; death of Canning in August; Goderich Prime Minister		University College, London founded
1828	Wellington Prime Minister; O'Connell wins Co. Clare election	Repeal of Test and Corporation Acts; revision of Corn Law	
1829	Catholic Emancipation Act	Formation of Metropolitan Police	King's College, London founded
1830	Accession of William IV; Wellington resigns; Earl Grey Prime Minister	'Captain Swing' protests	

PART 4

The dominant nation 1830–79

12

The making of an urban society

Urban conditions

Cities lay at the heart of Victorian Britain. They grew with enormous speed, transforming the landscape and the lives of millions of people. By 1851, the majority of mainland Britons lived in towns and cities, and cities were far and away the most important economic centres of the nation. But it was not just a change of scale. Urban society was developing distinctive characteristics that distinguished it from the countryside and from earlier towns. A new mode of life was being forged.

Manchester was a prime example of what happened. Built on the power of one industry, from which it derived its nickname of 'Cottonopolis', by the 1840s the city buzzed to the power of cotton mills. Mill-workers' housing spread out in many directions, with satellite towns and villages built around available water-power, and ancillary trades thriving on the factors of production that the city brought together. Though 'king cotton' was a central driver of the economy, Manchester developed a wide range of industries, ranging from engineering to chemicals and financial services. Its growth was rapid. In 1801, it had a population of 75,000 people, rising to 182,000 in 1831, and 462,000 by 1881.[1] Its municipal government, though struggling to keep pace with need, was nonetheless amongst the most advanced in the country. In the 1840s, it was the first city to lay proper water-borne main sewers, and to bring plentiful fresh water supply from the countryside. Yet, it was a city of pollution, ill health and low life expectancy. In the 1840s, the average age of death in Manchester of mechanics,

---

[1] B.R. Mitchell and P. Deane (eds), *Abstract of British Historical Statistics* (Cambridge, Cambridge University Press, 1962), p. 24.

labourers and their families was 17 years, compared to 38 years for a similar group in the rural county of Rutland.[2] In the 1840s, the German businessman and associate of Karl Marx, Friedrich Engels, surveyed one area of central Manchester and found it difficult 'to convey a true impression of the filth, ruin, and uninhabitableness, the defiance of all considerations of cleanliness, ventilation, and health which characterize the construction of this single district'. He challenged anyone to come and 'to see in how little space a human can move, how little air – and such air! – he can breathe, how little of civilization he may share and yet live'.[3]

This starts to convey the way in which the nature of the urbanism that Britain pioneered between 1830 and 1880 was new to the world. It was an intense mixing of manufacturing, commercial and unregulated cultural activity, accompanied by a fantastic diversity of lifestyle, wealth and health. Cities became the breeding ground of a type of inequality that was really unknown before. Middle-class families moved out in large numbers, escaping the overcrowded, smelly, noisy, and deeply unpleasant streets and thoroughfares of city centres. The result was that cities became increasingly socially ghettoised into separate areas with distinctive class characters. For those who could afford to get out, the suburbs were, in most English, Welsh and Irish towns, of considerable terraced splendour, with back and front gardens, two- or three-storey properties with separate bedrooms, living rooms, drawing rooms and indoor toilets, but still generally rented rather than bought. In Scotland, middle-class suburbs also contained terraced housing, but in addition there were superior stone tenement buildings of four or five stories, each containing up to ten flats with high-ceilinged rooms and interior bathrooms. Each home was large enough for not just the family but for at least one live-in domestic servant known as a general maid; detached homes for upper middle-class households were able to keep two or more servants. Living in suburbs meant for the first time commuting to work for middle-income groups; this stimulated the first urban transit systems – initially horse-drawn omnibuses and trams (motorised with electric power from the 1880s) and suburban railways that were pioneered in London.

This removed the middle classes from the dwellings and environs of the working classes and those of the very poor. The areas they left became cheaper housing, characterised in most cases by overcrowding, social deprivation, rising crime, and deteriorating sanitary and health conditions, bringing epidemics of disease such as cholera which struck British towns with severity in 1831–2, 1848–9, 1853–4 and 1865–7. Social segregation led to a gulf in knowledge and understanding of the conditions the middle classes were leaving in their wake, so that, in the 1840s and 1850s, investigations into conditions in working-class districts by parliamentary investigators and private social commentators (often doctors) became bestselling publications in

---

[2] M.W. Flinn (ed.), *Report on the Sanitary Condition of the Labouring Population of Great Britain by Edwin Chadwick, 1842* (Edinburgh, Edinburgh University Press, 1965), p. 223.

[3] F. Engels, *The Condition of the Working Class in England* (Harmondsworth, Penguin, 1987), p. 92.

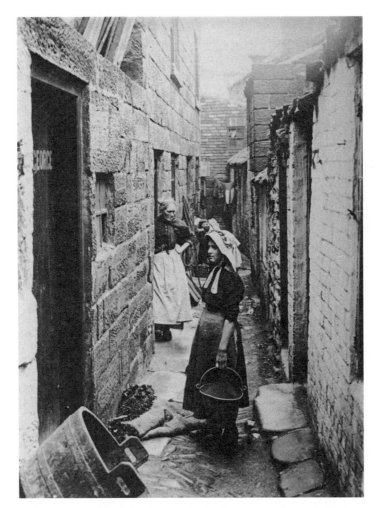

Figure 12.1 Back-to-back housing at Staithes in Yorkshire in the late nineteenth century. Despite growing awareness of the problems of public health, much of the housing built in industrial towns and villages, often by employers, in the second half of the nineteenth century was of poor quality. These were in a village near Whitby.
Source: Mary Evans Picture Library

middle-class circles. With worsening air pollution from coal fires and steam engines, and with excessive building in vacant plots in central areas, daylight was reduced (causing medical conditions like rickets, produced by vitamin D deficiency). Night-time was but poorly illuminated by the new gas street lighting that developed in these decades. It was in this period that British cities developed a reputation as increasingly dark and dangerous places into which the middle classes feared to tread.

With inadequate local government and mounting structural problems, cities became a central problem of Victorian Britain. At the heart of the urban condition was housing. In the East End of London, the industrial Midlands, north of England, Northern Ireland and South Wales, and in coal-mining villages everywhere, working-class housing was characteristically brick terraces of one room upstairs, one room downstairs, or, for the slightly better-off, two up, two down. The very worst of this type were back-to-back houses, which took up the smallest possible area, thus maximising the profits for speculative builders and the middle-class *rentiers* (many of them single women) who lived off the rental income. These houses suffered from poor through ventilation and were renowned for the high incidence of tuberculosis and other re-spiratory chest conditions. This situation was aggravated by growing housing density, caused by population growing faster than the city area. Liverpool and Glasgow, in particular, both faced a huge wave of migration in the aftermath of the Irish famine of 1845–6. Open spaces in towns were built on by a process that was known as 'in-filling', leaving fewer gaps for light and air, whilst homes for the working classes and the poor became smaller, sometimes by 'making down' a large house vacated by a middle-class family into three or more homes for the working classes.

In Scotland and in parts of some English cities like London, Liverpool and Manchester, the characteristic housing type was the tenement of from four to six storeys with (especially in Liverpool and Manchester) basement houses below ground level. In Scotland, house overcrowding peaked in the five- or six-storey tenements, where a family of six or more could live in one room (known as a single-end) or two rooms (known as a room and kitchen). Scottish housing was widely acknowledged as the worst in the industrialising world, the product of low wages, remnants of a feudal system of land dues that encouraged high-density building, and rapid urban growth on small pockets of land. The second half of the nineteenth century saw an increasing proportion living in one- and two-roomed tenement houses: by 1901, 48 per cent of people in Edinburgh, 70 per cent in Glasgow, 72 per cent in Dundee and about half of all Scots, compared with a mere 20 per cent in London.[4]

Almost everywhere, urban sanitary conditions were poor. Until the 1850s, most houses relied on external ashpits for toilets and, even after that, for most of this period only the middle and upper classes could afford internal plumbing and water closets (WCs). Legislation to improve housing came very slowly with the emphasis in the Public Health Act of 1848 being upon creating water-borne sewage disposal and water-supply for new houses. That Act did not apply in Scotland, and individual cities there tried novel solutions; Glasgow in 1862 sought vainly to reduce overcrowding by ticketing houses with a plaque stating the permitted occupancy, and employing night searches to evict excess residents. In the later 1860s, larger cities with the worst slum problems like Birmingham, Glasgow and Edinburgh obtained private parliamentary Acts allowing the town corporations to widen streets and clear slums, whilst general Acts of 1868 and 1875 permitted some limited building of local authority housing

---

[4] J. Butt, 'Working-Class Housing in the Scottish Cities 1900–1950', in G. Gordon and B. Dicks (eds), *Scottish Urban History* (Aberdeen, Aberdeen University Press, 1983), pp. 234, 248, 260.

for the working classes across British cities. By 1880, the greatest improvements had largely been made at the behest of commerce, with city-centre terminus stations being created for railway companies in the 1860s and 1870s, along with the formation of fashionable shopping streets, both of which required the demolition of many of the worst houses. Slum clearance became a mania in the 1870s before the building of good cheap houses really started, dispersing slum-dwellers to make overcrowding worse in other houses. Smaller towns with fewer financial resources made the least headway against the problems. This was especially the case in Scotland where Britain's worst conditions were to be found; the most overcrowded houses were in towns like Linlithgow, whilst Stirling was probably the most insanitary, with human and slaughter-house effluent running down the castle hill into the town.

Industrial suburbs grew up around factories, shipyards or coal pits, with housing often owned by the company. It was a useful but not always effective way of controlling the workforce; if a worker joined a strike, his family would lose their home. A handful of benevolent employers saw the importance of reasonable housing as necessary for moral improvement as well as economic efficiency, building model communities such as Titus Salt's Saltaire near Bradford (erected 1851–76), George Cadbury's Bournville (1893–1901) and W.H. Lever's Port Sunlight (1899–1914). However, most of the working classes and the poor were left behind in inner-city houses, many of medieval vintage and unimproveable, or else made-down (or subdivided) large houses deserted by the bourgeoisie or jerry-built terraced houses thrown up by speculative builders wanting to make quick profits. In the cotton county of Lancashire, parents and their married children and other kin were often crammed together in the same small house. The more industrial the town, the more crowded together were in-migrants, their off-spring and dependants. Extended families were the norm in many booming industrial towns, with grandparents and grown-up children often living in adjacent houses or streets. Lodgers were very common; in Preston, 23 per cent of homes had them in 1851.[5]

Urban households were far from uniform. Industrialisation and urban growth brought different local traditions; some cities, like Dundee, Preston and the Potteries towns saw large numbers of married women working for wages (in jute, cotton and porcelain industries respectively). But in most communities, an informal 'marriage bar' dominated, whereby women around their wedding time gave up paid work outside the home because of pressure from family, workmates, employers and what was seen as the 'proper thing' to do. With incomes low, this led in towns like Preston and Oldham to large numbers of married couples staying with parents, making for an increase in the incidence of extended families in industrial cities.

Live-in domestic servants, almost exclusively young women, became a vital part of the urban landscape in the Victorian period. With the rise of the middle classes in

---

[5] J. Humphries, 'Household economy', in R. Floud and P. Johnson (eds), *The Cambridge Economic History of Modern Britain: Volume I: Industrialisation, 1700–1860* (Cambridge, Cambridge University Press, 2004), pp. 244–5.

suburban homes in the middle decades, domestic servants were a major status symbol, living in back rooms or garrets, or sometimes even in back-blocks or over stables. By 1881, one in eight of all waged people in Britain was a domestic servant, the vast majority of them women. Most were aged 12–18 years of age, in their first and perhaps only job away from home, at the beck and call of a household from 6 a.m. to 9 p.m., with usually only every second Sunday afternoon off (and very often that only to attend a special servants' service at the parish church). This was a hard life, with little independence from employers, and few friends, and though around a third of all women tried domestic service at least for a short time, vast numbers gave it up in favour of what was seen in comparison as the 'freedom' of factory work.

Health conditions in both town and country saw a clear deterioration between 1830 and 1880. Clean water, still in the hands of private companies in many places, was in short supply, and most cities relied on wells or gravity-fed open channels that supplied brackish and often polluted water sold for profit. Sewage disposal in the 1830s and 1840s was characteristically by open channels, funnelling into rivers from which communities downstream took water. Such conditions fed the ills of the city. Contagious diseases spread very easily in the overcrowded, insanitary conditions: typhus, whooping cough, measles, and the new killer of the nineteenth century, cholera. Water-borne Asiatic cholera first arrived in Britain in 1831–2, being brought ashore at Sunderland off a rat-infested ship from Riga in Baltic Russia. It spread very fast through Britain, striking both middle- and working-class areas of towns and cities, but causing high mortality amongst the poor. In England alone, 82,528 became victims, of whom 31,376 died.[6] It kept coming back, notably in 1848–9, 1853–4 and 1865–7. The threat of cholera caused great fear – partly because of the awfulness of the symptoms and partly because of the uncertainty as to where it would strike. The cotton towns of Lancashire were largely untouched by cholera, although their normal death rate was high. There was almost no cholera in Birmingham, although it was rampant in the Black Country. London had escaped comparatively lightly in 1832, but thousands died in 1849, when 54,000 perished in England. Meanwhile, the outbreak of 1853–4 was largely confined to the north of England and Scotland.

Other diseases also took their toll. Typhus, carried by lice as 'an unerring index of destitution', lingered in the poorest streets and rookeries. Typhoid, scarlet fever and smallpox all came in regular waves. Chronic illnesses like tuberculosis, pneumonia and bronchitis left many incapacitated, and measles, whooping cough and diphtheria were deadly for children. Life expectancy plummeted. During the 1820s a Glaswegian who had survived to the age of 10 could expect to reach 42 for a man and 45 for a women. By 1841 these figures had fallen to 37 and 40. Even worse was Bradford, where 59 per cent of the population died before reaching the age of 20.

One of the most sensitive barometers of social wellbeing in any society is the infant mortality rate (IMR) – the proportion of children who die in the first year of life. This

---

[6] P. Sharpe, 'Population and society 1700–1840,' in P. Clark (ed.), *The Cambridge Urban History of Britain: Volume II 1540–1840* (Cambridge, Cambridge University Press, 2000), p. 512.

provides some indication of the diet and health of the mother as well as that of the child. The IMR was highest in cities, especially in the poorest quarters, and in counties with more urbanisation and coal villages, where conditions in miners' rows were very poor. In 1841, both urbanised and rural counties had very high rates – in excess of 170 infant deaths per 1,000 live births – Cambridgeshire (175), Lancashire (178) and the East Riding of Yorkshire (184), but few counties had fewer than 140 deaths per 1,000. In the next few decades, some agricultural counties like Cambridgeshire and Gloucestershire were improving, but in industrial villages and manufacturing towns conditions were getting worse. In Durham, IMR rose from 156 in 1841 to 179 in 1872, and in Leicestershire from 151 to 186. England was becoming more deadly for infants, with an average IMR of 150 in 1872; curiously, Scotland, despite its very poor housing, was a little better at 124, and stayed so until the 1930s. Remarkably, perhaps, the infant mortality rate reached its peak in England in 1899 at the astonishingly high level of 163.[7] Why did city life remain so bad?

Tackling urban problems

The period 1830–80 was the critical first phase of British urban improvement. These were the decades in which British local government (town councils and corporations) and the British Parliament turned their attention seriously to investigating and beginning to try to solve the major problems of urban living. The cholera epidemic of 1831–2 first drew attention to cities as harbingers of disease, leading to the creation of temporary local boards of health to impose rudimentary barriers to its spread, though the sense of urgency for action rarely lasted longer than the epidemic. However, in the 1840s, a broader feeling that 'something must be done' started to form in British political culture.

There were two major hurdles to tackling the urban condition. The first was ideological, with the philosophy of *laissez-faire*, that had done so much to breed the Industrial Revolution in the first place, dominating attitudes to public expenditure by town councils. Where town councils existed, they had powers to raise rates (equivalent to today's council tax) to pay for urban improvement schemes. Councils had existed in many older towns for centuries, but newer industrial towns did not have them at all to begin with, and some had to wait for a number of years or decades before creating them. The Municipal Corporations Act of 1835, and the more limited Burgh Reform (Scotland) Act of 1833, made the formation of town councils easier, extended the vote to the middle classes, and increased powers of urban improvement. But the development of such powers, experience and electoral backing was a slow process. Improvement cost money, paid for by the ratepayers of each town, and as voters they tended to resist rates increases. There were few powers to allow or encourage building

[7] C.G. Brown, 'Urbanisation and living conditions', in R. Pope (ed.), *Atlas of British Social and Economic History since c.1700* (London, Routledge, 1989), pp. 180–1.

control, proper layout of streets, tackling poor water and sewage disposal. Resistance to the extension of municipal powers remained very strong in the 1830–80 period, and those far-sighted individuals who saw the absolute necessity for intervention had to fight long and hard battles to win the approval of middle-class voters. This they did, usually in the weeks and months following an outbreak of cholera or typhus that had carried off middle-class as well as working-class victims. Disease put voters in a mind for spending money.

The second big hurdle to improvement was management. There was hostility to centralisation and direction from Whitehall, and to compulsion by Parliament. So piecemeal treatment became widespread, based on voluntary legislation (known as permissive acts). There developed a tradition, set by London, that, for each new undertaking of municipal government, a separate organisation with separate rate-levying powers was needed – often for individual urban parishes. What were called variously 'improvement commissioners' and 'watch committees' mushroomed, with their own powers to levy rates and undertake improvements, leading to a lack of joined-up government and poor overall control. Gradually, in the 1860s and 1870s, such problems eased, certainly outside of London, but they left a legacy of poor co-ordination. In London, these difficulties were only properly tackled in 1889 with the formation of the London County Council, which started to co-ordinate the capital's improvement. Ideology and management issues remained constant headaches for urban government, and never totally went away in this period and for some time after.

From the 1840s to the 1860s, the principal initial forms of improvement that middle-class electors could be persuaded to approve were usually to do with two things – sanitation (water supply and sewage disposal) and immoral housing conditions. Immorality was important to the respectable voters, and sanitary campaigners like Edwin Chadwick played on this in his campaigning reports on sanitation. His famous 1842 *Report on the Sanitary Condition of the Labouring Population of Great Britain* was packed with allusions to the immoralities produced by human sewage in houses and back courts (which he spoke of as reducing humans to the state of beasts), and by over-crowded housing and the lack of clothes amongst the poorest, which led to boys and girls and related adults sharing beds (in a strong suggestion of sexual impropriety and incest). Such conditions were partly caused by very poor people having to go to bed during the day because they shared clothes with others who were out. The Chadwick Report, like many others of the time, included accounts by medical doctors of conditions in their own town and city, medicalising both illness and the immoral conditions that urbanisation had fostered.

This mobilised consent for some state action (see Chapter 17). The 1848 Public Health Act for England and Wales required that new houses should include water closets; Scotland only obtained a similar Act in 1867. In addition, many town councils of the bigger cities (including most in Scotland) obtained private improvement Acts of Parliament in the 1850s and 1860s which allowed them to bring in bye-laws covering many issues: sewage removal by street scavengers, lighting of city streets and alleys, and measures to combat house overcrowding. Manchester was the first city to lay a

Focus on

The condition of towns in the 1840s

Here is the testimony of two witnesses who submitted evidence to an inquiry, and which was published in Edwin Chadwick's *Report on the Sanitary Condition of the Labouring Population of Great Britain* (the Chadwick Report), published in 1842.

Report of Mr. Riddall Wood, an agent of the Manchester Statistical Society, on the overcrowded housing he found in north of England towns:

> In what towns did you find instances of the greatest crowding of habitations? – In Manchester, Liverpool, Ashton-under-Lyne, and Pendleton. In a cellar in Pendleton, I recollect there were three beds in the two apartments of which the habitation consisted, but having no door between them. In one of which a man and his wife slept; in another, a man, his wife and child; and in a third two unmarried females. In Hull I met with cases somewhat similar. A mother about 50 years of age, and her son I should think 25, at all events above 21, sleeping in the same bed, and a lodger in the same room. I have two or three instances in Hull in which a mother was sleeping with her grown-up son, and in most cases there were other persons sleeping in the same room, in another bed. In a cellar in Liverpool, I found a mother and her grown-up daughters sleeping on a bed of chaff on the ground in one corner of the cellar, and in the other corner three sailors had their bed. I have met with upwards of 40 persons sleeping in the same room, married and single, including, of course, children and several young adult persons of either sex. In Manchester I could enumerate a variety of instances in which I found such promiscuous mixture of the sexes in sleeping-rooms. I may mention one; a man, his wife and child sleeping in one bed; in another bed, two grown-up females; and in the same room two young men, unmarried. I have met with instances of a man, his wife, and his wife's sister, sleeping in the same bed together. I have known at least half-a-dozen cases in Manchester in which that has been regularly practised, the unmarried sister being an adult.

An idea of the unregulated insanitary practices, resulting from the absence of sewage pipes, inadequate water supply and sheer poverty, is obtained from evidence of Dr Laurie, a GP, on the state of Market Street in the centre of industrial Greenock:

> In one part of the street there is a dunghill, – yet it is too large to be called a dunghill. I do not mistate its size when I say it contains a hundred cubic yards of impure filth, collected from all parts of the town. It is never removed; it is the stock-in-trade of a person who deals in dung; he retails it by cartfuls. To please his customers, he always keeps a nucleus, as the older the filth is the higher is the price. The proprietor has an extensive privy attached to the concern. This collection is fronting the public street; it is enclosed in front by a wall; the height of the wall is about 12 feet, and the

dung overtops it; the malarious moisture oozes through the wall, and runs over the pavement. The effluvia all round about this place in summer is horrible. There is a land [tenement] of houses adjoining, four stories in height, and in the summer each house swarms with myriads of flies; every article of food and drink must be covered, otherwise, if left exposed for a minute, the flies immediately attack it, and it is rendered unfit for use, from the strong taste of the dunghill left by the flies. But there is a still more extensive dunghill in this street; at least, if not so high it covers double the extent of surface. What the depth is I cannot say. It is attached to the slaughter-house, and belongs, I believe, to the town authorities. It is not only the receptacle for the dung and offal from the slaughter-house, but the sweepings of the street are also conveyed and deposited there; it has likewise a public privy attached.

Source: M.W. Flinn (ed.), *Report on the Sanitary Condition of the Labouring Population of Great Britain by Edwin Chadwick, 1842* (Edinburgh, Edinburgh University Press, 1965), pp. 119, 192.

proper system of main sewers, and in 1846–51 built a chain of reservoirs, aqueducts and pipes to bring a plentiful clean water supply over 15 miles from a series of reservoirs in the Longdendale Valley in the Pennines. In 1853–61, Glasgow copied this scheme, but over a more ambitious distance of 26 miles, bringing water from Loch Katrine in the Trossachs. The same engineer, J.F. Bateman, designed both schemes, and went on to design the water works for Dublin, Belfast and Halifax. In the 1860s, both Glasgow and Birmingham pioneered slum clearance schemes, led by a series of religiously inspired businessmen who formulated a 'civic gospel' of improvement. Glasgow's scheme of 1866 took almost 30 years to complete and knocked down virtually the whole of central Glasgow, leaving only the cathedral, the market cross, an ancient prison and one medieval house untouched. Birmingham's scheme of driving wide streets and railways through the worst slums was led by Joseph Chamberlain, who built a national political career in the Liberal Party on the basis of his municipal work as improving mayor (see Chapter 23). What Glasgow and Birmingham did was soon copied, with a general Act of Parliament in 1867 allowing town councils all over Britain to start slum clearance, and places like London and Liverpool, as well as scores of smaller towns, followed suit from the 1870s. In many of these cases, the immediate impetus to slum demolition was an offer from a railway company to construct a city-centre terminus station and associated approach tracks; town councillors were persuaded (sometimes corruptly) of the financial and social benefit to their city, and rapid change to the layout of city centres resulted.

It was a hard struggle for campaigners for change. To pay for the Loch Katrine water project in the 1850s, Glasgow town council charged an extra rate for several years, but when no water appeared in city pipes during the construction phase, there was a ratepayers' revolt at the cost; it was only stopped when, in 1859, councillors made the scheme seem 'patriotic' by asking Queen Victoria to come at short notice from Balmoral Castle to open the yet-unfinished project. Similarly, in the same city seven years later, the Lord Provost responsible for the slum clearance scheme lost his town council seat when he imposed a 6d. (2.5 pence) rate on every pound of house rental, although nothing was actually demolished for another three years.

This kind of problem remained for urban improvement, with waves of voter reluctance to pay for better facilities. Nonetheless, the example of Birmingham helped generate a new civic confidence in other towns and gave momentum to urban reform. By 1880, civic improvement was accepted and in fashion, and civic pride was starting to overcome the resistance of ratepayers to funding such massive and expensive schemes of urban regeneration. There was a readiness to confront vested interests and for the municipality to buy out private gas and, later, tram companies, make profits from both, and use them to pay for urban improvement in the public interest. However, there still remained complex sanitary, housing and health problems to overcome, and it would not be until after the First World War that major change was to come in the most critical matter – the improvement of working-class housing.

Poverty, policing and children

The life of British people was affected in various, sometimes contradictory, ways by the rapid economic and social change of the Victorian period. Just as the fabric of towns and cities was affected, so too the pace of change caused enormous dislocation to individuals and families – and notably to children.

All the evidence suggests that, for the vast bulk of people, the standard of living started to rise from the 1850s to the end of the nineteenth century and beyond. But the 1830s and the 1840s were notable decades of struggle for many people. The 'Hungry Forties', as they were known, brought large-scale underemployment, low wages, hunger and increased mortality. The poor relief system was strained to meet the needs of the population, and there was a real fear amongst some of the elites that there would be insurrection and a challenge to the government.

Until the 1830s, the relief of poverty was sustained by a mixture of charity and statutory forms of relief. In England and Wales, this was based on a system of alms-giving dating back to sixteenth-century principles, but supplemented from the 1790s by the Speenhamland system, designed for farming districts, which forced the wealthy to supplement the wages of the poor. This became regarded as burdensome in the economic crises of the 1820s and 1830s, and gave way to the Poor Law Amendment Act of 1834, which abolished 'out relief' (essentially giving of cash or other aid) and instituted relief only in workhouses. Parishes were united to form Poor Law Unions to organise workhouses in which the principle of 'less eligibility' was established – that fewer of the poor were to be eligible for this relief. They were to be dissuaded from entering the poorhouse by making its conditions of work, diet and ruling regime worse than the worst conditions experienced by the poorest labourer outside. In this way, English poor law reform was designed to reduce relief being given out.

In Scotland, a different legislative framework existed, based largely on voluntary giving at churches and paid out by kirk sessions in each parish. These prohibited aid to the able-bodied and confined it largely to the aged, the infirm, and to single mothers and their children. This system was strongly supported by many churchmen as encouraging family responsibility and self-reliance. But in the crisis of the Hungry Forties, and large-scale immigration of Irish and Highland paupers to places like Glasgow and Edinburgh, the Poor Law (Scotland) Act 1845 was passed to increase relief, with compulsory levies of ratepayers. However, Scotland did not suddenly become overly compassionate. Its own poorhouses were a cross between prisons and hospitals, frequently with poor conditions of health, and few chose to go there unless in dire need. As a result, from 1860 to 1880, Scotland acknowledged fewer official 'paupers' per head of population than England; in 1870–4, for instance, there were 35.6 paupers per 1,000 population in Scotland, compared to 41.6 in England, at a cost 44 per cent higher per head than in England.[8] The poor relief system of Victorian Britain was not generous to the poor. Poverty was regarded as the product of weakness – invariably of drinking, dissipation, gambling and general lack of self-help. The poor were expected by the social philosophy of *laissez-faire* to help themselves.

Little regard was given to cities as places where social breakdown was a product of environment, misfortune and exploitation. Urban working lives were for very many people unwholesome, dangerous and a serious threat to health. Workshops and factories often experienced extremes of temperature: cold in winter, and stifling heat in summer or near to furnaces and braziers. Protective clothing was rare, and workers were expected to suffer such vicissitudes. Danger came in the form of unguarded machinery, precipitous climbs or descents into mines, where rock falls, flooding and fires were common and the cause of often large-scale catastrophes. Even in smaller workshops, only brought under regulation in the 1870s, conditions were usually poor. Work for many was long, sometimes 12 or 16 hours at a time, although skilled workers had generally managed to achieve a Saturday half-holiday by the 1860s and were campaigning for a nine-hour working day and, by the 1880s, for eight-hour days. Although legislation gradually improved the position, child labour was still much used, particularly in the textile industry, but also as delivery boys, cleaners, scavengers and, in the case of girls, as all-purpose domestics.

Concern about children was one of the most powerful motivations for charitable giving. This grew hugely in the years from the 1850s to make philanthropy one of the notable features of Victorian life. It was perceived as essential in a society where state help was almost non-existent. In working-class communities, people had to look to family and neighbours for help in minor crises but, for longer-term problems, charities were vital. However, charitable dependence was not confined to the working classes. There were societies for decayed gentlewomen; for the sons of officers; for the widows

---

[8] M.A. Crowther, 'Poverty, health and welfare', in W.H. Fraser and R.J. Morris (eds), *People and Society in Scotland: Volume II 1830–1914* (Edinburgh, John Donald, 1990), p. 269.

of clergy; for the orphans of merchants; for indigent gentry; for aged artists and for old Etonians.

Much charitable giving was motivated by Christian concern at the plight of the less well-off, but there were also elements of fear, since giving seemed to rise in times of social tension. Much emphasis was laid on the importance of direct personal contact between giver and receiver, and visiting the homes of the poor to assess need was something that both men and women could do. It was also a way of ensuring that charitable giving was not dissipated in drink. In the 1860s, there was concern that charitable giving was getting out of hand and that groups of people were becoming dependent on charity and eschewing the need for self-help. There was also ample evidence of 'clever paupers' defrauding charities by appealing to different ones under a variety of guises. The result was the formation of the Charity Organisation Society (COS) in 1869, to provide 'the machinery for systematizing, without unduly controlling, the benevolence of the public'. Local committees were to investigate all cases and decide whether an applicant deserved help, before passing him or her to a charity or to the Poor Law. The COS developed the beginnings of modern social case-work by regular systems of visiting and directed assistance to restore families to a position where they could rely upon themselves. It was the product of a concern to close the gap between classes and to restore what was seen as an essential charitable relationship of obligation and subordination. Personalised aid was seen as more important than the amount of material aid. According to the COS, 'charitable relief is of true and lasting benefit only when it has to do with individuals and their families; when it is grafted on to personal sympathy; without this, it were often better for the recipient that it were not given at all'. Critics often saw this as an unwelcome intrusion by middle-class do-gooders into the lives of the poor, an attempt to impose middle-class norms upon the behaviour of people and to distinguish between the 'deserving' and the 'undeserving' poor. No doubt there was also an element of voyeuristic prying for some of the fashionable who went 'slumming'. Nonetheless, many men and women, particularly from the professional classes, devoted time and energy and took risks in entering the alleys and closes of the slums in order to carry out charitable work.

The rapid growth of towns also brought concerns about crime. Unlike in the eighteenth-century village, cities were full of strangers and constantly changing. Physical division between social classes was widening; the well-off in their new suburbs saw less of the poor than once they had. There was much anxiety in the early nineteenth century that crime was on the increase. The very fact of urbanisation was seen by many as the cause of moral degeneracy, rising crime figures and increasing numbers of juvenile delinquents. It was added to the many other fears about a potentially dangerous working class, about the rise of pauperism and about the breakdown of family life that troubled the middle classes. Policing became a priority, and the Victorian beat policeman was a device to watch for potential trouble before it happened.

The state increasingly took upon itself the maintenance of public order. There was no longer confidence that it could be left entirely to local decision-making and supervision. Peel had established the Metropolitan Police in 1829. These were full-time professionals, with Scotland Yard at the forefront of developing new strategies for handling crime. Parliamentary reform riots in Bristol and elsewhere in 1831 (see Chapter 18) convinced some politicians that provincial towns needed policing. Other cities soon followed London, but in most areas the army was still called in at moments of tension. Troops were used extensively to intimidate Chartist demonstrators and striking workers in the north of England in the 1830s and 1840s. However, the use of the army was costly and problematic (people got shot) and smacked of continental authoritarianism. Sending Metropolitan 'Peelers' to control events in provincial towns did not go down well either. Pressure mounted for the expansion of police forces to rural areas. In 1856 the County and Borough Police Act required all counties and towns to establish permanent police forces, overseen by local committees, but inspected and financed by central government.

Most police action tended to be against the poorest elements in society and the young. Vagrants, hawkers and prostitutes were among the most liable to arrest and the concept of a criminal underclass that needed to be curbed and controlled was embedded in general perceptions. Gatherings of youth for disorderly games in public areas were seen as threatening. Fears of the 'dark and dangerous classes' emerging from the rookeries became increasingly pervasive among the middle classes. Distrust of the new police forces was widespread among the working classes. Much police activity, often directed by magistrates and councils with evangelical concerns about moral improvement, seemed to be geared against popular pastimes like drinking, gambling, cock-fighting or dog-fighting, boxing and other unregulated sport. The police presence was increasingly noticeable at fairs and horse-races – anywhere that crowds gathered, but including political meetings and industrial disputes, which they attended to protect strike-breakers. The arrival of new police in Lancashire in the 1840s led to outcries in the working-class press against the 'blue devils' and 'blue bottles'. In some northern towns there were riots on the arrival of the new police, while even some middle-class ratepayers regarded them as an unnecessary expense. Even in the 1880s, in Flora Thompson's Candleford Green, the police were still seen as 'a potential enemy, set to spy on them by the authorities'.[9]

More policing required more prisons. From the 1780s, many convicts had been sent to Australia, but the colonial administration there was showing reluctance at this trade. As a result, many prisoners found themselves incarcerated in rotting ship hulks on the Thames and other estuaries, but in the 1840s more than 50 new prisons were started. A model for many was Pentonville prison in London, opened in 1842, which followed a pattern recommended by the philosopher, Jeremy Bentham, some decades before – the 'panopticon', with five blocks radiating from a central point so that all

---

[9] F. Thompson, *Lark Rise to Candleford* (Oxford, Oxford University Press, 1954), p. 553, quoted in R.D. Storch, '"The Plague of Blue Locusts": Police Reform and Popular Resistance in Northern England, 1840–57', *International Review of Social History*, 20 (1975), p. 90.

wings could be kept under observation. Prisoners were in single cells and communication between prisoners was kept to a minimum. Prisoners were given often pointless tasks like walking on a treadmill or turning a screw for a specified number of hours. Prison was no longer seen as merely a mechanism to take people out of society, but a place where order and discipline would be taught.

At the same time there were efforts to keep people out of prison. Linked with general concerns about crime, was concern about children and young people. Children begging or just wandering in the streets were to be rescued from a life that might lead to crime. Sheriff Watson in Aberdeen in 1841 started one of the first industrial schools, known as 'ragged schools', which spread around the country. These provided both moral and religious instruction, along with training in practical skills useful for employment – girls were taught sewing, knitting, cooking and cleaning, boys building trades. The regimes for children sent by magistrates to church reformatories were often harsh, and for some children this became worse when 'farmed out' to private homes for training and education. The Victorian moral and criminal code did not allow much leeway for fun for children, and neither did the charities and police services of the period.

Children continued to be seen as part of the workforce until 1870. Children's employment was widely promoted and defended by some of the most respected economists and social commentators of the day. Edward Baines, MP for Leeds, wrote in his *History of the Cotton Manufacture in Great Britain* (1835) that 'factory labour is far less injurious than many other forms of employment', and argued against the Factory Acts that sought progressively to reduce child labour. For some campaigners, the issue was not that children worked, but that they might work excessive hours in bad conditions.

Having some measure of schooling was considered important, and the 'half-time system' – of a child spending half the day at work and half the day in a factory school – was prevalent in parts of the textile industry. However, much informed opinion came, little by little, to oppose child labour entirely. Many in the churches viewed it with hostility, and it was through the work of ecclesiastical educational reformers that the case for state schooling and, separately, for compulsory schooling gained traction in the 1850s and 1860s. In England and Wales, state schools were created by the 1870 Elementary Education Act to fill the gaps in the church school system to ensure a place for all children. Scotland followed with its Education (Scotland) Act of 1872. This set up a more developed system of school-board schools everywhere in Scotland, incorporating virtually all Protestant schools, and established compulsory education for 5–10 year olds (a measure only enforced for England and Wales in 1880). By 1880, the British state was starting to ensure the closer protection of children from exploitation.

Further reading

Clark, P. (ed.), *The Cambridge Urban History of Britain: Volume II 1540–1840* (Cambridge, Cambridge University Press, 2000)

Daunton, M., *The Cambridge Urban History of Britain: Volume III 1840–1950* (Cambridge, Cambridge University Press, 2000)

Emsley, C., *Crime and Society in England, 1750–1900*, 3rd edn (London, Longman, 2004)

Lee, R., *Unquiet Country: Voices of the Rural Poor, 1820–1880* (Macclesfield, Windgather Press, 2005)

Morris, R.J., *Cholera 1832: The Social Response to an Epidemic* (London, Croom Helm, 1976)

Morris, R.J. and Rodger, Richard, *The Victorian City. A Reader in British Urban History 1820–1914* (London, Longman, 1993)

Murray, P., *Poverty and Welfare 1815–1950* (London, Hodder Murray, 2006)

Rees, R., *Poverty and Public Health 1815–1948* (London, Heinemann, 2001)

13

The Victorian economy

The steam age

Between 1830 and 1880, the British economy developed its dominant position in the world. Indeed, to a very great extent, the world economy came into being during this period, as international trade developed rapidly through merchant shipping, and as many European nations (including Britain) developed empires. British investors became important in capitalising business overseas, both within the Empire in Canada, Australia, Africa, India and South East Asia, and in the United States and South America and even in mainland Europe. Much of the investment went into railway building, but exports were not confined to capital: machinery, rails and locomotives came from Britain. The value of exports went up almost threefold between 1854 and 1873. And although there were numerous economic and financial crises – in the early 1840s, in 1857–8, in 1866–7 and after 1873 – this was the heyday of British economic prominence. Britain developed new products and new ways of manufacturing, and re-organised modes of living around its application of technology.

Economic self-confidence came of age in this period, matching the confidence in imperial acquisition and dominion over other races, and the feeling of military and naval supremacy. After almost a century of difficulties with royalty, there was also a pride in the new strong monarchy in the person of Queen Victoria and Albert, her Prince Consort. This was nowhere more apparent than in an idea of Albert's – the Great Exhibition of 1851. In a massive Crystal Palace erected in Hyde Park, the strength and might of the British Industrial Revolution was on display, with companies displaying their working engines, textile machine and engineering achievements, and with displays of wares and costumes (as well as peoples) from the nations of the British Empire. Other nations had exhibits, but it was Britain's greatness as the workshop of the world that was on display.

Focus on

The 1851 Great Exhibition

In 1848 Europe had been gripped by fear of revolution. Very quickly, that fear of revolution was dispelled in Britain by the success of industry, technological innovation, entrepreneurship and Empire. This new feeling of success was evoked most powerfully in the Great Exhibition of 1851 – an event that was a symbol of Britain in the half-century that followed.

Its proper title was 'The Exhibition of the Works of Industry of All Nations'. It was the brainchild of Prince Albert, Queen Victoria's husband. He chaired the organising committee and, through his powerful position, was able to create the world's largest and most-visited spectacle to date. The Exhibition's centrepiece was a breathtaking glass and iron building, like a vast greenhouse, under which there were thousands of exhibits from around the world, but dominated by British firms, which brought their manufacturing technologies and products, and by items from the British Empire. The Exhibition was supposed to be international, and indeed there were exhibits from European nations. But it was, in reality, a statement about British prowess in every field of endeavour. Britain was the workshop of the world, and the exhibition showed this.

The very building in Hyde Park was a new wonder of the world. Designed by Joseph Paxton, it was known as the Crystal Palace, being an enclosure made of wood, iron and glass that extended to 564 metres long and 33 metres high, and created a spectacle of space and light. The Exhibition opened on 1 May 1851 when 30,000 people – the invited guests and hangers-on – were able to enter the building to see Queen Victoria open the event and tour the stands. A further half a million people crowded outside in the park. By the standards of the day, it was a truly mass event, which not only raised the profile of the Exhibition nationally, but also raised the Queen in public esteem and prominence. The occasion was a glorification of the union of Britons in world endeavour. It praised the artisan and technologist, the entrepreneur and capitalist, the Christian missionary and the artist. With 14,000 exhibitors, the event was a nation in microcosm, a mirror to a glorious people and their exploits in all fields of activity. The Exhibition song captured the mood:

Gather, ye Nations, gather! From forge, and mine, and mill!
Come, Science and Invention; Come, Industry and Skill!
Come, with your woven wonders, the blossoms of the loom,
That rival Nature's fairest flowers in all but their perfume;
Come with your brass and iron, your silver and your gold,
And arts that change the face of earth, unknown to men of old.
Gather, ye Nations, gather! From ev'ry clime and soil,
The new Confederation, the Jubilee of toil.

This account given by the writer Charlotte Brontë (1816–55) evokes the response of the ordinary visitor.

> Yesterday I went for the second time to the Crystal Palace. We remained in it about three hours, and I must say I was more struck with it on this occasion than at my first visit. It is a wonderful place – vast, strange, new and impossible to describe. Its grandeur does not consist in *one* thing, but in the unique assemblage of *all* things. Whatever human industry has created you find there, from the great compartments filled with railway engines and boilers, with mill machinery in full work, with splendid carriages of all kinds, with harness of every description, to the glass-covered and velvet-spread stands loaded with the most gorgeous work of the goldsmith and silversmith, and the carefully guarded caskets full of real diamonds and pearls worth hundreds of thousands of pounds. It may be called a bazaar or a fair, but it is such a bazaar or fair as Eastern genii might have created. It seems as if only magic could have gathered this mass of wealth from all the ends of the earth – as if none but supernatural hands could have arranged it thus, with such a blaze and contrast of colours and marvellous power of effect. The multitude filling the great aisles seems ruled and subdued by some invisible influence. Amongst the thirty thousand souls that peopled it the day I was there not one loud noise was to be heard, not one irregular movement seen; the living tide rolls on quietly, with a deep hum like the sea heard from the distance.

By the time the Exhibition closed in October 1851, over 6 million people attended. Of these, 4.5 million visited on cheap-entry days when the admission was one shilling (5 pence). The main railway network was in the process of completion, and all lines led to London. For hundreds of thousands of people, coming to the Great Exhibition was their first railway journey and their first visit to London. Never before had the nation's capital become so familiar to the people. The event cemented their sense of being a part of one nation, one Empire, one monarchy, and one great industrial nation.

Sources: poem quoted in F. Bédarida, *A Social History of England 1851–1990* (London, Routledge, 1991), p. 7. Brontë quotation from Clement Shorter, *The Brontës: Life and Letters* (1907), quoted at http://www.mytimemachine.co.uk/greatexhibition

A key component of the growth of the British Victorian economy was the railways. Starting in 1825 with the Stockton–Darlington line, and expanding with some vigour in the 1830s, the explosion of railway-building erupted into a 'railway mania' in 1845–7 in which tens of thousand of miles of line were laid down. Railways represented one of the important ways in which the Industrial Revolution involved both private and public investment and ownership. Railway-building was permitted, mostly on a line-by-line basis, by separate acts of Parliament, granting to businesses the right to buy land, construct railways, and provide a service. From 1844, the Railway Act allowed a strengthened Board of Trade Railway Department to supervise the construction and operation of railways, requiring railway company reports, with further powers added from 1868. In this way, the state played a key role in infrastructure provision, keeping a system of regulation in its pocket that provided a useful method of guiding the construction of the nation's transport network.

The rate of railway growth was staggering. In 1830 there were a mere 157 kilometres of track in Britain; this had grown to 9,797 km after the railway mania of 1846–50, and to 25,060 in 1880. After this, there was only marginal growth, and usually only of branch lines. The railway transformed economic activity and the movement of people; it cut many journey times across Britain from days to hours and, even in the 1860s and 1870s, commuter journeys in the London area had started, allowing people to live very much further from their jobs. The impact on city size was immense, heralding the end of the 'walking city'. The railway transformed the landscape, creating huge engineering projects to make embankments, cuts (through hillsides) and tunnels, and railways had to be brought into the new inner-city termini constructed in the 1860s and 1870s, either underground or, more often, by great arched viaducts above houses. The technical problems were great, leading to new techniques of construction by engineers like Isambard Kingdom Brunel. In the 1840s, many Britons' first experience of railways was in excursions by Sunday schools and other church or community groups to the seaside (leading to the development of mass tourism to Blackpool, Brighton and similar resorts), but with parliamentary legislation forcing railway companies to include cheap (third class) carriages, by the 1880s experience of rail travel had grown. In 1842, 25 million passengers were carried on railways; by 1880 the figure was 597 million.[1]

Did the railways instigate the Victorian industrial boom? Historians have been divided on this issue. On the one side there are historians who argue that railways were the leading sector of the economy, driving increases in demand, capital formation in the stock exchange, earnings by investors, technical innovation, increasing efficiencies in transport of goods, and integration of the British economic market. For example, the contribution of transport to the fixed capital formed in Britain – that is, invested infrastructure – was falling from the 1790s (when it stood at around 20 per cent) to 15 per cent in the 1820s, then it shot up to between 30 and 38 per cent in the 1840s and 1850s.[2] This would point to the immense importance of railways in those critical decades to the creation of a dispersed, high-technology economic resource (track, stations, rolling stock), backed by Britain's largest and most dynamic companies. On the other side of the argument lie historians who undertook 'cost savings analysis' in an attempt to calculate how much extra it would have cost the economy to move people and goods (by road and water) in this period if railways

---

[1] S. Ville, 'Transport,' in R. Floud and P. Johnson (eds), *The Cambridge Economic History of Modern Britain: Volume I: Industrialisation, 1700–1860* (Cambridge, Cambridge University Press, 2004), p. 307.
[2] Ibid., p. 321.

Figure 13.1 Isambard Kingdom Brunel and launching chains of the *Great Eastern*, 1857. Brunel (1806–59) was one of the greatest Victorian engineers, responsible for the Thames Tunnel, the Clifton Suspension Bridge, the Great Western Railway and Bristol Docks. His *Great Eastern* ship, the largest yet built, launched just before his death, was not a great success.
Source: Alamy Images

had not existed. This is known as a 'counterfactual' exercise, since it puts forward a 'what-if' scenario that did not actually take place. The evidence offered here was that, in moving cargo, railways saved the economy only 4 per cent of national income over other forms of transport, but that, in addition, they saved as much as 20 per cent in a social rate of return by promoting growth in other industries, many of which were facilitated by railway transport (such as national newspapers and perishable industries like market gardening and dairy). In general, most historians would argue that railways were critical to economic development during this period.

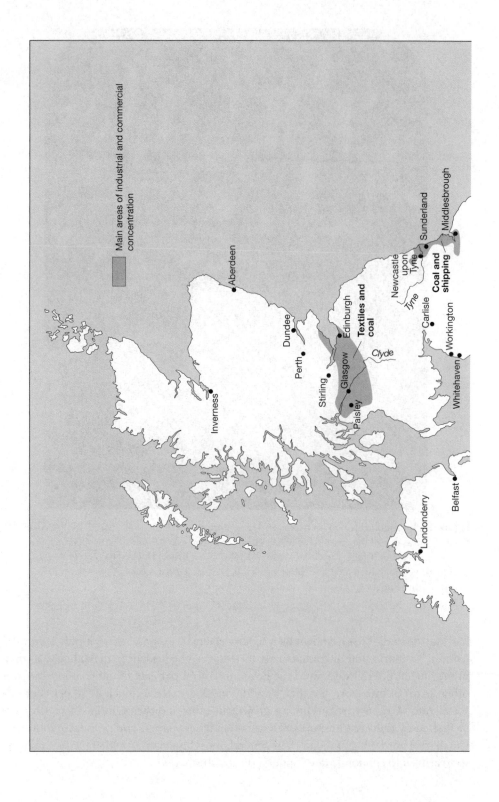

Main areas of industrial and commercial concentration

Aberdeen

Dundee

Perth

Stirling

Inverness

Glasgow

Paisley

Edinburgh

Textiles and coal

Clyde

Newcastle upon Tyne

Tyne

Sunderland

Middlesbrough

Coal and shipping

Carlisle

Workington

Whitehaven

Londonderry

Belfast

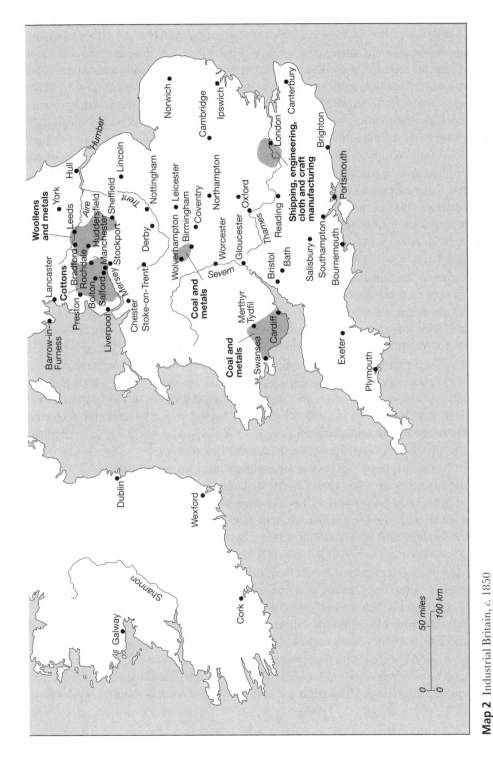

Map 2 Industrial Britain, *c.* 1850

Source: Evans, E.J., *The Forging of the Modern British State* (Pearson Education Ltd, 2001)

It was not just railways that were changing the nature of transport. Steam-powered coastal shipping of the 1820s and 1830s moved on in the 1840s and 1850s to steam-powered sea-going ships; these grew larger in a short period of time as engines became more powerful and as ship-construction started to move from wood to metal. In 1830, there were 18,876 sailing ships registered in Britain, but only 298 steamships; by 1880, the figures were 19,938 and 5,247 respectively, but with larger metal ships, steam's capacity was almost equal to that of sail.[3] These developments increased speed, reliability and capacity, though sailing ships remained important to navigation until the late nineteenth century – for instance, in the tea trade, where the clipper ship *Cutty Sark* excelled. Yet, it was the sheer scale and total tonnage of steam ships that were to create vast new centres of wealth and employment. Belfast, for instance, was transformed from 1860 to 1914 by the rise of shipbuilding in the Harland and Wolff shipyard, which constructed ships notably for Liverpool shipping companies. Harland and Wolff alone employed 14,000 workers by 1914, as well as having a major yard on the River Clyde west of Glasgow.

Central to the demands of the railways and the shipping industry was the huge expansion of the iron industry. In the 20 years after 1850, the numbers involved in the production of iron rose from 80,000 to 180,000. In Lanarkshire there were 16 blast furnaces belonging to the Baird Company alone, in South Wales 18 blast furnaces at the Dowlais Works, and from a first furnace in Middlesbrough in 1851 there were 122 within a 20-mile radius in 1871. The Bessemer process gradually allowed the production of cheap steel to replace wrought iron, and Barrow-in-Furness, which had the right kind of coal for the process, grew from a village of around 700 in 1850 to a steel town of 35,000 inhabitants in 1873. There was a huge demand for iron and steel from throughout the world, and vast quantities went for export, particularly to the United States, until America's own output began to grow in the 1870s.

By 1830, steam power was becoming strongly associated with the cotton industry; over the next two decades, the industry in Lancashire and Lanarkshire was transformed by this new power source. Textiles were easily the country's main export, with cotton making up the biggest part. It was, however, an industry very vulnerable to cyclical demand and to increasing foreign competition, with a tendency to over-production when markets seemed good. It was also vulnerable on the supply side, being dependent on imported cotton from India and the United States. This came out most clearly in the early 1860s, when supplies from the southern states of America largely dried up during the Civil War. Some speculators and blockade runners did well, but the brunt of the 'cotton famine' was borne by the Lancashire and west of Scotland workers who had to endure the hardship of extended unemployment. The Poor Law could not cope with mass unemployment and the state had to, rather unwillingly, step in to help finance public works schemes. The Lancashire industry recovered quite quickly after 1865, although it increasingly looked for raw cotton supplies from

[3] Ibid., p. 303.

Egypt and India, the latter rapidly becoming its main market. In Ulster, the cotton industry largely failed in the 1840s, the result in part of unsuitable factories converted from the linen industry, but linen itself remained important. The number of flax mills rose from 35 in 1839 to 78 in 1871, using steam power fuelled by coal imported from mainland Britain.[4] Steam power assisted such specialisation, especially where coal was locally mined, and where engineering expertise was available to build and maintain the engines. This allowed for the adoption of steam power in other industries also. Even by the mid-1820s, steam horse power (by which the engines were rated) was heavily concentrated: 5,460 in London; 4,800 in Manchester; 4,500 in Glasgow; 2,300 in Leeds and 1,200 in Birmingham.[5]

Economic organisation

Steam power lay behind the rise of iron ships, railways and large-scale factory production. Steam became the symbol of the age and the driving force of economic development. It was also important to the way in which capitalism itself developed. For steam power – especially in railways – was expensive and demanded large-scale investment, and for this sophisticated forms of organisation were required. The stock exchange and dealing in company shares developed rapidly from the 1840s, allowing people with money to locate businesses needing investment. This period saw the birth of the 'disinterested investor' – that is, someone willing to put money into a business in order to take profits back, but unwilling to take any part in its management.

Investment in the Victorian period continued to rely extensively on either the family firm or the partnership. But from 1826, joint-stock banks developed in the industrial regions of Britain, offering another route to investment. Though there was some 'blind investment' of the type we know in the twenty-first century (in which the bank invests in enterprises in which the bankers have no experience or family involvement), more typical was access through social and business circles in which industrialists moved, in which formal and informal contact overlapped. Bankers knew their local industrialists personally and socially, and came to treat them as people who could be entrusted with bank investment. Indeed, bank partners and shareholders, their families and immediate business clients were frequently the most favoured borrowers.[6]

With the development of the insurance industry, too, the financing of manufacturing became more complicated. As a result, there were frequent crashes and business

---

[4] P. Ollerenshaw, 'Industry 1820–1914', in L. Kennedy and P. Ollerenshaw (eds), *An Economic History of Ulster, 1820–1940* (Manchester, Manchester University Press, 1985), p. 71.

[5] S. King and G. Timmins, *Making Sense of the Industrial Revolution: English Economy and Society 1700–1850* (Manchester, Manchester University Press, 2001), p. 85.

[6] P. Hudson, 'Industrial organisation and structure', in R. Floud and P. Johnson (eds), *The Cambridge Economic History of Modern Britain: Volume I: Industrialisation, 1700–1860* (Cambridge, Cambridge University Press, 2004), pp. 53–5.

bankruptcies. Bankruptcies could have a domino effect, and entire communities could be thrown into despair with finance running out, business collapsing, large numbers of workers losing work (or not being paid for work done) and families becoming destitute, hungry and thrown upon charity and the parish for some form of relief. At the same time, this networking of credit and inter-reliance created strong bonds within communities and regions, with high degrees of trust and reciprocity between businesses and between workers and their employers. Most of the time, it worked well. But in times of crisis, caused by a downturn in trade, overseas war, loss of raw materials supply or any number of factors, this trust could break down. Social unrest could result and the relations of production could become fraught. But things changed perceptibly with the rise of limited liability firms, which started to be permitted by Acts of Parliament of 1844 and 1855, reducing the financial burden on investors should a business collapse. This encouraged risk-taking by entrepreneurs and investors alike, and was to become one of the hallmarks of modern capitalism.

The workplace remained diverse in character in the Victorian economy, but the large-scale factory was starting to become more significant. In part this was due to the increasing significance of heavy industry, with shipyards for large iron ships, engineering works, railway engine yards, iron and steel works, and all sorts of factories making diverse metal goods. Parts of the country became specialists in such heavy industry – Belfast, Glasgow and Tyne and Wear especially. The growth of chemical manufacturing (in large part to produce dyes and bleaches for textiles) also encouraged large-scale production. Production techniques started to change more rapidly as a result. Machines became ever more important in the subdivision of labour, and in reducing labour costs through deskilling. But there were limits to this. The subdivision of jobs intensified skills in the workers; they might learn fewer skills, but the machines and equipment they were being asked to use required greater application and training. This was very much the case in heavy industry. In shipyards, for instance, the range of jobs boomed, with boiler-makers, carpenters, plumbers, shipwrights, engineers, riveters, rivet-catchers, and so on. Trade unions became stronger in such trades during this period, to defend the rights of skilled workers to control entry to the trade, to protect their wages and conditions, and to prevent dilution of skills. One way in which such skill groups were defended in some industries was through the widespread practice of subcontracting. This was widely used, even within large factories, where masters developed specialisation of certain aspects of production, bidding for work from the factory owner, and employing his men and women to manufacture one stage of the production process. In this way, the small-factory production technique was incredibly influential within British manufacturing, and was to remain so, in some cases, well into the twentieth century. Some workers continued to work at home with a central power source piped to their house; in the 1840s and 1850s, silk weavers could work at home with a steam engine at the end of the street.[7]

---

[7] Ibid., p. 39.

The factory is often considered the key characteristic of the Industrial Revolution. It was certainly an iconic institution by the 1830s. The arrival of a factory in a locality signalled, as few other edifices did, the coming of large-scale capital investment, organised labour, large machines and great power sources. The factory represented a new economic order and a new philosophical order of grand scale in semi-rural districts. It also represented the coming of a new type of social order, with the imposition of work discipline and a culture of improvement in an effort to end lawlessness, idleness and irreligion amongst an expanding and shifting population. Many middle-class people and landowners longed for well-known entrepreneurs to come to their district to establish a factory; it brought business, a spirit of improvement and a sense of modernity.

The mid-Victorian years saw the British state take an increasing interest in regulating the operation of the economy. The conditions of work in factories and mines were a major focus of attention, especially as they related to women and children. There was a great deal of concern about both physical and moral conditions of work for women. In the middle-class ideology of the period, women's place was in the home, not in sordid workplaces; if they had to work, it should be in 'becoming' occupations like those of domestic servant, milliner or dressmaker. There was concern that factory work, which tens of thousands did, exposed women to crude male banter, unchaperoned liaisons, and sexual temptation. Christian moralists were especially alarmed about mill girls – an occupation taken by some to be little short of prostitution. The benefits of industrialism were thus perceived to be, in some regards, offset by ethical issues which remained to be solved. Overall, the state was to take an ever-greater role in controlling and regulating the economy, and especially the place of work.

Blight and depression in Ireland and Scotland

In Ireland, the Scottish Highlands, the Hebrides and the Northern Isles of Orkney and Shetland, there were successive and intense crises of subsistence for very large numbers in the population. These were brought on by structural problems in the economy, population pressure on the free resources of the countryside, and the fragility of the food supply. But underlying them were fundamental social-structural issues. In each case, the society was divided between, on the one hand, a class of large landowners who sought to maximise income from economic activity and, on the other, the bulk of the population who were mostly poor tenants eking out an existence from land and sea. Moreover, in the case of Ireland, there was very clearly a relationship of colonial exploitation by the British government on behalf of an often absentee landlord class, in which the bulk of the people were Roman Catholic and the bulk of the gentry were Protestant.

In rural Ireland, living conditions were probably the worst of any place, in any decade, of the modern era. Ireland was struck by a potato blight, caused by a pathogen that spread across all of Europe between 1845 and 1849, causing mass starvation and mass emigration. The death toll was in the region of one million deaths (above the normal death rate) or about one-ninth of the population, largely from disease resulting from undernourishment, and estimates suggest that a further million or more fled to Britain, the United States and elsewhere.[8] The famine had such savage consequences because of a dependency on the potato and because of the policies of landlords and the British government. The agricultural system of Ireland had been bifurcating since the plantations of Protestant Scots and English in the early seventeenth century; Protestant lands were allowed to consolidate into large farms, whilst Catholics lands were continuously subdivided, resulting in small and poor-quality plots of land upon which, by the time of the famine, Catholic families had to subsist. With potatoes a seemingly 'natural' subsistence crop for the soil and climate of Ireland (as of the Scottish Highlands), the result was successive catastrophes as potato crops failed in many years, notably in the early 1830s in the west of Ireland and in the mid-1830s in Ulster. However, the crisis of 1845–9 was by far the most general and the most severe.

The situation was exacerbated by the reaction of landlords and government. Many of the landlords were absentees, living in England or Scotland, and they and their large tenant farmers made their livings from food exports from Ireland. Exports of cattle were continued, and some exports increased during the famine years. The British government refused to ban exports although this might have made it possible to redirect surplus food to relieve famine conditions. In addition, with non-payment of rents during the famine, large numbers – again mostly Catholic families – were evicted by landlords. Government assistance was neither significant nor timely. The response was slow and mostly passive – notably the repeal of the Corn Laws in 1846, which permitted the importation of foreign grains to Ireland and Britain to relieve the general high prices of home-produced corn (see Chapter 16). There were subsidised public works projects, but these were problematic in that they demanded heavy labour when men were weakened by malnourishment. By the later 1840s, emergency provisioning was still causing emigration, notably through the harsh operation of the Irish Poor Laws, which forced many from their small tenancies. Even then, local poor relief often stopped for lack of funds and, although a special tax was instituted, the island remained in the grip of poverty, deaths from disease and mass emigration. There was some voluntary aid, notably from Quakers and from relief agencies formed in Britain in 1847, with individual donations often trying to supply food through soup kitchens for the worst hit. But the scale of the problem was too great for the level of help offered.

The result of the Irish Famine went way beyond social division and social protest. The failure of landlords and the British government, the sheer neglect, was seen as a wilful response by a Protestant establishment to the plight of Catholics. It was – and continues to be – seen by many as a colonial act of neglect, and the culmination of

---

[8] C. O'Gráda, *Ireland Before and After the Famine: Explorations in Economic History, 1800–1925* (Manchester, Manchester University Press, 1993 edn), pp. 104–5.

religiously discriminatory policies that had scarred Ireland since the seventeenth century. The famine was a defining moment in Irish Catholic consciousness, one that was carried into the newly inflated Irish diaspora that spread around the world as a result of the famine. The effects of the famine were to prove critical to the intensity of future growth in Irish nationalism, and to the desire to be free of British colonialism in Ireland. It also led to transformation in Irish agriculture, with a dramatic fall in numbers working the land, and a shift in produce from crops to livestock – though, after an initial decline until 1908, potato output substantially recovered, doubling by 1928.

The potato famine also afflicted Scotland, largely the Highlands and the Hebrides. This area had suffered political and military repression after the failed Jacobite rebellions of 1715 and 1745, but had benefited from various government and charitable activities that had built model villages and established fishing enterprises such as that at Ullapool on the west coast. There was a growing recognition of the long-term economic fragility of the region, caused by poor land, overpopulation and economic exploitation by many landlords. By the 1840s, as in Ireland, there was a dependence on the potato, supplemented by fishing, and the blight of 1845 caused a heightened death rate. Again, there is evidence of a slowness in government's response, and also of some lowland Scots blaming the Highland Gaels for their own predicament. But the Highland Famine bore no comparison to the Irish Famine. There is no evidence of mass starvation or death, and though there was growth in emigration, it was more due to the clearance of the land than to the famine itself. On top of that, there were significant efforts by some well-to-do people to provide assistance. The Free Church of Scotland, newly formed in 1843, had strong support amongst the Gaels, and the wealthy lowland congregations of the Church were quick to assist Highland brethren. In this regard, it does seem that the largely Protestant Highlanders received assistance when in Ireland Catholics received comparatively little.

The experience of Ireland and the Scottish Highlands during the famine years scarred those places, leaving an indelible mark on politics, culture and emigration. It was a defining period for these areas, sometimes referred to as the Celtic parts of the British Isles. The sense of bitterness engendered by these events would come to threaten the constitution of Britain and its continued existence.

Agricultural improvement and society

England, Wales and lowland Scotland did not experience the same severity of rural poverty as Ireland and the Highlands. Yet there was some distress and significant protest. In 1831, agriculture accounted for 23 per cent of British national income; by 1881, this figure had fallen to just over 10 per cent.[9] Behind this decline lay a number

---

[9] Figures from A. Howkins, *Reshaping Rural England: A Social History 1850–1925* (London, HarperCollins, 1991), p. 9.

of different experiences. Between 1830 and 1850 in England, most of Wales, and central and southern Scotland, there was severe turbulence in both economy and society (the culmination of developments since the 1790s); this was followed from 1850 to 1872 by a calm period of rising general prosperity and improvement, after which, from 1873, came a new crisis.

In these areas, there were mixed fortunes for farming. In upland zones, the farm-centred community dominated in southern and north-eastern Scotland and the north of England. Here, groups of cottages crowded round a farm to form inward-looking and isolated communities, self-sustaining and often bound together by kinship ties. Often, one landowner owned all the land and homes. These communities developed from 1850 as highly migratory, with a rapid turnover of families. In some places, like Northumberland, the hiring of entire families was common, whilst in others, such as Aberdeenshire, young men migrated from home to work in a male-dominated farming culture, living in bothies and cradled by a strong popular culture of music and drinking. Conditions and wages were good compared to the south of England, with much payment in kind. Relations between master and servant were often close, with a strong harmony relatively little affected by unionisation of farm workers. Overall, the relationships between social ranks was stable.

Contrasting with this was the experience of the more lowland areas of England, including the vast flatlands of Lincolnshire, Cambridgeshire and the East Anglian counties of Norfolk, Sussex and Essex, plus the Scottish counties of East Lothian, Fife and Ayrshire. Here, the village community dominated, characterised by open landownership, based round ancient settlements and including parish churches with some of the land forming the glebe of the Church of England or the Church of Scotland. In some villages, a very large landowner could control virtually everything, from church to shops to public houses to homes and farms. Here social relations tended to be tightly controlled, with tenants vetted and nearly all attending the one church, but sometimes, where there was an absent landowner, poor relations could exist between social ranks. One product of this style of community was often a reliance on labourers and harvesters from adjoining communities of a different type – places of diminished control and prosperity – resulting in topsy-turvy social relations during the farming year. The most famous social disruption of rural society occurred in the years 1830 to 1832 during what are called the 'Captain Swing' riots.

In the south and south-east of England by the 1830s, the agricultural system was in turmoil. Farm labourers faced reductions in wages and excessive demands from clergy of the Church of England for the annual tithes to pay the vicars' stipend. They directed their fury against the clergy, magistrates and poor-relief administrators, and against new threshing machines, which they considered as contributing to their plight. The Swing riots of 1830 were a notable explosion of social breakdown in many parts of the south, especially in Sussex and East Anglia. 'Captain Swing' was the name on anonymous threatening letters sent to farmers and others during the disturbances. Captain Swing was probably a mythical figure, but whether there was or was not such an actual person is impossible to verify. Certainly, the mythology was very strong, and large numbers of farm workers came out in open revolt, beginning in Kent, and spreading throughout Sussex and East Anglia, attacking new threshing machines and Church of England priests. Bands of farm workers moved with military discipline through farming districts, calling at the houses of the tenant farmers, the landowners and the priests, making demands with the threat of physical violence. There were short-term benefits – many farmers refrained from using or buying new threshing machines, and wages rose in many places in the south of England. But there was little threat of the revolt turning into anything like a revolution. There was no revolutionary ideology amongst the Swing rioters, and even the extreme methods used to quell the disturbances did not cause a more violent reaction.

In all, across England, some 600 rioters were imprisoned, a further 500 were transported to Australia, and 19 were executed. The causes of the Swing riots were not just temporary, but deep-seated and long-lasting. Indeed, the breakdown of social relations in the southern countryside continued for much of the century. It reared its head in opposition to landowners enforcing new laws against poaching of rabbits (which rural people regarded as a traditional right), and clergymen dispensing with traditional payments to choirs and bell-ringers, which, both symbolically and financially, had helped hold local parish communities together. In Walsingham in Norfolk, one of the worst-hit areas of unrest, a newly installed organ in the church was blown up in 1867 in seeming protest at the loss of income to working people in the choir.[10] Another result was the development in the Victorian period of unions for agricultural workers. In all of these cases, the aim of labourers' protests was not to overturn the existing order, but to restore it in the face of change. Equally, farmers and landowners fought hard against the campaign in the 1840s to repeal the Corn Laws (see Chapter 18), but fears of a disaster after 1846 were not realised. Overseas supplies of grain did not exist in sufficient quantity to swamp the British market and a growth in demand gave farming an opportunity to adjust. Many of the landed class reaffirmed their faith in the value of land by investing in drainage and other improvements. There was increased use of artificial fertilisers and in better quality seed. Machinery was being used much more. Cyrus McCormick's reapers had been one of the hits of the Great Exhibition and the horse-drawn reaper began to replace the scythe and sickle in the harvest field.

There was considerable social and ideological fallout from the new techniques and from the social antagonisms in England's flatlands between 1830 and 1880. One was the impact on the Church of England, previously the social cement between the families of landowners, farmers and farm labourers, which became identified as the church of the elite, of exploitation and oppression. From the 1760s, Methodism had developed considerable strength in the rural counties of the east, south and south-west, offering an ecclesiastical form of social protest which, to a great extent, was translated

---

[10] R. Lee, *Unquiet Country: Voices of the Rural Poor, 1820–1880* (Macclesfield, Windgather Press, 2005), pp. 119–21.

into something harsher and more political in the troubles of the 1820s and 1830s. From then, parsons became seen in most places as creatures of the elites, rarely speaking up for the protesters or the poor – a situation exacerbated by the tithe system of church taxes which made the church into an oppressive institution. However, in the 1830–80 period, the Church of England put considerable effort into meeting the challenge of Methodism, building new churches and chapels nearer to villages, and requiring clergy actually to live in their parishes and minister to local needs. The Church of England became more committed, better organised and increasingly successful in tackling the challenge of Methodism and the Dissenters and, for the first time in a century, the relative position of the Church of England started to improve. Instrumental in this was the fact that, from the 1850s, churchmen in rural areas pressed for reformation of traditional calendar customs, associating them with religious observance and church services. One such custom was harvest home, which since at least the sixteenth century had been a highly bawdy celebration as the last stook of corn was transported from the fields to the village, attended by harvesters and families. This was re-invented by many clergy in these decades as an event that ended in the church, attended by elites as well common people, with much reduced drunkenness, thus reinforcing traditional institutions and social relations. In this way, the Church started to re-impose itself on popular ritual, and to make ritual a much greater part of religious worship. This latter move was controversial in a theological sense, as ritual was strongly opposed by Evangelicals in the Church and by most Protestant Dissenters, and the ritual controversy stored up problems ahead for the Church. But for rural villages, a new paternalism was being established, involving the church to a very great extent.

But rural society was never wholly calm in the Victorian period. The countryside became used to increasing numbers of strangers. Harvesters came from Ireland and Scotland, great armies that swept around the country, following the harvest as it was collected from July to September. Navvies came too – from the 1840s, in vast numbers – again Irish and Scots predominantly, building railway tracks that criss-crossed the nation. Roads and bridges were constructed, especially during the depression of the late 1840s in massive work schemes – the 'destitution roads' – to rescue the poor from near-starvation and crime. Criminality was more often than not economic crime, or protest crime, or a mixture of both. Poaching – for fish and for rabbits most commonly – was increasingly prosecuted. The Night Poaching Act of 1828 and the Game Act of 1831 facilitated readier prosecution and harsher sentences – up to transportation for life. The Poor Law Amendment Act of 1834, which cut the practice of giving cash and kind handouts to the poor and forced claimants to accept life in deplorable workhouses, added to the sense of rural grievance. These were seen as ancient rights by local people, and their poaching was driven by the sense that a common law right had been removed.

Some parts of British rural society thrived. Market towns – communities to be found all over Britain – were larger settlements somewhat adrift from other farming districts, including the hinterlands that they served as places for provisions, sales and hiring fairs. Market towns were more diverse and prosperous, with segregation of social classes and highly organised social and cultural activities, constituting places where calendar customs, balls and parties were common throughout the year. They were favoured by the fashionable middle classes here, something that was encouraged by the arrival of the railways in the 1850s and 1860s, bringing an intercourse between rural middle classes and those of the larger cities and of London. Market towns also often had legal and ecclesiastical status – hosting assizes or sheriff courts, or touring High Courts, which made them centres for the legal profession – and cathedrals, like York, Winchester, Salisbury and Durham. Places like Lewes in Sussex and Banbury in Oxfordshire enjoyed fashionable reputations, and larger towns (in some regards, cities) like Norwich were sites of both industry and agriculture, whilst towns like Oxford, Cambridge, St Andrews and Durham had universities, which added to rural status.

The numbers employed in agriculture reached a peak in the 1850s. In 1851, there were 2 million employed in farming, and this then fell to 1.6 million in 1881. At the same time, the *proportion* of the population in agriculture fell more steeply from about 30 per cent in 1830 to 13 per cent in 1881.[11] From 1860, for most of mainland Britain we can see rural population decreasing. In large measure, this was due to two main trends. The first was the increasing regional specialisation of agriculture, where the flatlands of England were turned over to large-scale cereal production, and the uplands were increasingly turned over to animal husbandry. This reduced the need for permanent farm workers: cereals needed harvesters, hired for short periods in late summer, whilst animal husbandry required relatively few shepherds and herders. The second trend was that of country workers, in the light of decreasing demands for the traditional year-round crafts and skills, leaving for towns and cities, and some emigrating to the Americas and, later on, to Australia. Even harvesters became harder to come by from the 1870s in many places, and this drove farmers to increasing mechanisation to replace the disappearing country worker.

In addition to these trends was the general crisis coming upon British agriculture during the 1870s. This is traditionally known as the Great Depression, lasting from around 1873 to 1896. The central feature of this was the rise of cheap food imports – cereals from the USA and Canada, which between 1870 and 1880 climbed from 1.5 metric tons to 2.2 million metric tons[12], and refrigerated meat from New Zealand, Australia, the USA and Argentina. Exacerbating the problems were poor harvests in eastern England during 1877–9. These events caused many changes to the countryside. With wheat prices tumbling, and the growth of urban populations with increasing standards of living, there was a move to market gardening in East Anglia, southern and south-west England, and a rise in dairy farming producing milk, cheese and butter. Increased specialisation helped ease the Great Depression.

In any event, it was not as severe as previous recessions or the potato famines in Ireland and Highland Scotland. The long-term trend was for increasing prosperity

---

[11] Figures from A. Howkins, *Reshaping Rural England: A Social History 1850–1925* (London, HarperCollins, 1991), p. 8.

[12] Metric figures calculated from imperial measures in Howkins, *Reshaping Rural England*, p. 138.

in rural Britain, but with smaller numbers of people and even smaller numbers of agricultural workers.

Further reading

Floud, R. and Johnson, P. (eds), *The Cambridge Economic History of Modern Britain: Volume I: Industrialisation, 1700–1860; Volume II: Economic Maturity, 1860–1939* (Cambridge, Cambridge University Press, 2004)

Howkins, A., *Reshaping Rural England: A Social History 1850–1925* (London, HarperCollins, 1991)

Kennedy, L. and Ollerenshaw, P. (eds), *An Economic History of Ulster, 1820–1940* (Manchester, Manchester University Press, 1985)

O'Gráda, C., *Ireland Before and After the Famine: Explorations in Economic History, 1800–1925* (Manchester, Manchester University Press, 1993 edn)

14

Class, gender and religion

Class

Victorian society was one in which social division seemed to be represented in every aspect of life. In education, work, home, leisure, sport and popular culture, people's activities were sharply distinguished by which social class they belonged to. Though social class is a vital concept in understanding the nature of society in Britain in these years, it is a difficult concept, and one that needs to be seen as evolving into different forms. Whilst the later period, 1850–80, witnessed a maturing of social division within generally improving economic conditions, the 1830s and 1840s were difficult decades for many of the less well-off.

Social classes were perceptions of division within society into major groupings. In the early modern period before about 1800, society had been seen in the form of gradations of ranks or orders. Around the 1790s and 1800s, a society of social classes was perceived by contemporaries to come into being, with classes more sharply divided from one another in terms not just of their occupations and wealth, but of their cultural activities and identities. Broadly, there were three classes – the landed classes, the middle classes, and the working classes.

The landed aristocracy and the associated gentry remained together the dominant social group. A survey of landholding in 1871 revealed that a quarter of the land of England was held by 1,200 people; half the land of England was held by fewer than 8,000. They were losing some of their political influence, but continuing power stemmed from deference and from the continued great wealth of a few. Many had gained from the transformation of Britain into an urban society. The value of land around the growing towns rocketed. A look at London street names gives a clear idea of who was making money from its growth. The Russell family, the Dukes of Bedford, had between £70,000 and £80,000 a year from their Bloomsbury estates. Away from London much the same was happening. The Duke of Devonshire shaped the development of Eastbourne as a holiday resort and Barrow-in-Furness as an industrial town. In Liverpool, the gainers were the Earls of Sefton and Derby. In industrialising Cardiff, it was the Earls of Bute.

The aristocracy and the gentry below them remained a relatively narrow circle, only occasionally admitting people from outside their class. The grandson of the great eighteenth-century cotton manufacturer, Jedediah Strutt, was created Lord Belper in 1856, but by then the family had been in land for three generations. Not until the 1880s did more people who had made their money in business begin to get peerages. However, with farming facing severe difficulties in the 1870s and 1880s, there was a greater readiness to look for new money. Surplus town houses could be sold off and the new rich began to buy some fine mansions. Some turned to the wealthy of the United States for marriage partners. Jennie Jerome, daughter of an American financier, was a good catch for the younger son of the Duke of Marlborough, Randolph Churchill. Others were prepared to swallow their pride and find a bride amongst the daughters of rich industrialists or offer their name as directors of industrial enterprises. Despite this, most country estates were no longer able to support traditional patterns. Rents had to be cut if farms were to survive and there was, by the 1880s, a powerful sense of the landed class in retreat.

The middle classes, sometimes referred to as the bourgeoisie, were far more numerous and ranged considerably in wealth and occupation, from well-off merchants, bankers, shopkeepers and entrepreneurs, to less well-paid teachers, accountants, clerks and others in the rising number of professional occupations. Among the political and social leaders were some of the big industrial families, like the Dixons and Chamberlains of Birmingham, the Rathbones of Liverpool, the Tennants of Glasgow, the Peases of Darlington and the Palmers of Reading. But the salaried and fee-charging professions of education, government administration, the law and medicine were growing fast and new professions, like civil engineering and surveying and business management, were appearing. Middle-class power and influence lay in the towns and, although some of the wealthiest might purchase property in the country, they continued to involve themselves in civic affairs. But what tended to give identity to the middle classes was their sense of respectability and high moral standing, their belief in hard work and individual endeavour, and the strength of their support for *laissez-faire* and low taxation. Equally, they were united as 'the servant-keeping class' – from the grand household with four or more live-in servants (including butler, cook, nanny and maids), to the most modest of lower-middle-class households with one poorly paid general maid. The middle classes regarded themselves as the shapers of the spirit of the age, the social grouping that was creating the wealth and Christian strength of the British Empire. They projected the spirit of self-help and individual improvement, and clamoured for the political and social recognition which they felt their importance warranted.

Most numerous of all were the working classes – a term that covered families ranging from the poor to the prospering skilled artisans. In the 1830s and 1840s, the economic fortunes of many skilled artisans suffered as a result of trade depression, agricultural protest and new machinery; most notable were the cottage-based handloom weavers, who suffered from the advent of power looms and factory-based production. But in the 1850s and 1860s, the growth of heavy industry, railway working and international trade led to increased numbers of both traditional crafts (like carpentry) and new trades (like that of engineers in shipyards and locomotive works). This change in fortunes was marked by rising prosperity and declining worker radicalism; industrial conflict persisted, but after 1850 it was essentially over hours and wages and not about changing society by challenging capitalism. The craft unions of skilled workers that were growing in number and size were not about revolutionary change, but about protecting one group of workers from other workers who might be threatening their jobs by taking work at a cheaper rate or by ignoring apprenticeship rules. Some historians have looked closely at the development of skilled trades between 1830 and 1870, examining the role of the elite manual workers, the 'labour aristocracy', who were usually organised in craft unions, were better paid, better housed, better treated and more secure than the mass of workers. These were aspirational workers who sought to distance themselves from the unskilled proletariat whilst, at the same time, proclaiming their independence from middle-class-sponsored institutions of self-improvement and the propaganda of church, school and popular literature, which all emphasised the importance of hard work, respectability, thrift and self-help. These were values held by many of the elite manual workers, but they sought to express them through their own organisations and activities (see Chapter 15).

The respectable working man went to the mechanics' institute or the friendly society, had the security of investing in a savings bank, lived in a house in a 'respectable' neighbourhood. He kept clear of pubs and the whole popular culture associated with drink. Instead, there were concerts and soirées consisting of popular songs, recitations and monologues, with tea and soft drinks as refreshments – entertainments provided by temperance societies, church bodies or the Working Men's Club and Institute Union (far removed from the present-day working men's club). Many after 1859 joined the popular Volunteer Movement (the predecessor of today's Territorial Army). Organisations became in themselves a mania of working-class men, willing to show through committee work, ordered public meetings, the recording of minutes and letter books, that they were as able as any to co-ordinate sophisticated social structures. Coupled with this was the popularity of benefits and temperance organisations, such as the Independent Order of Rechabites (formed in Salford in 1844) and the International Order of Good Templars (founded in Britain in the 1860s). Self-improvement societies, providing educational lessons, classes in advanced subjects, and access to libraries, were also an important characteristic of this period. Self-improvement and advancement through self-help and emulation of the great engineers became extremely popular amongst skilled workers. Whilst trade unionism was important, it was the extension of self-improvement into so many aspects of plebeian life in these decades that marked an important stage in the maturing of class identity.

Poorer than the skilled artisan was the large section of the working class involved in casual labour or as labourers to the skilled. These unskilled manual workers earned less and their struggle was one of maintaining subsistence and a perpetual battle to find adequate accommodation. They lacked security and were vulnerable to the trade cycle, the seasons and the fickleness of employers, as well as to sickness or accident. In contrast to the values of 'respectability' associated with the highly skilled, the unskilled were looked down upon (often unfairly) as the 'rough', a class whose men frequented the public houses or illegal drinking dens (the shebeens).

In some ways, many women were poorer still – especially those who were unmarried or widowed, who because of their sex were excluded from men's skilled work and confined to so-called 'women's work' – washing clothes, cleaning coal at pitheads, or cleaning shops and factories. Even patently skilled work, like being a seamstress or milliner, was lower paid than men's comparable work as tailors. At the bottom of society financially were the very poor – dwellers in lodging houses, the homeless, and orphaned street boys and girls eking out existences in selling newspapers, shining boots and shoes, or begging.

The mid-Victorian decades from the 1830s to the 1870s witnessed these class identities being cemented into British life. Whilst economic circumstances did much to dictate class affiliation, institutions and cultural activities grew up in these years to confer strong social identities. The Rechabites and Good Templars were important from the 1840s to the 1910s, but some other inventions of this period lasted very much longer, to endure in British society for over a century.

One major development of class identities occurred in the field of sports and recreations. The English public schools, which, contrary to their name, were elite institutions providing boarding education for boys, expanded rapidly in this period from serving children of the aristocracy to the male offspring of the upper middle classes. Grammar schools too proliferated in major towns and cities. In both types of school there was, by the 1850s and 1860s, an important revolution in ideals towards the inculcation of a sports ethic through games, mainly games of football and cricket.

Football came in a variety of forms, involving different degrees of use of feet and hands, varying according to local and, indeed, school tradition. With increasing desire for competitive games, there was a need to standardise rules, and this took place in a flurry of activity in the 1860s across various sports. In 1863, the Football Association was formed by former public school boys and they drew up the first basic rules of soccer. In 1866, the rules of boxing were standardised in the Queensbury Rules; and in 1870, the rules of rugby football (the handling game) were drawn up to distinguish it from soccer. In each of these sports, there was initially a strong domination by public school and former public school pupils. But each game appealed to many in the working classes, and the challenge to public school dominance grew as fitness and money became more available to allow for specialisation and training. Working-class teams were formed in the 1870s, aspiring to beat the polished amateur gentlemen of the elites. A memorable milestone was reached in 1883 when the FA Cup was won for the first time by a non-public schoolboy team when Blackburn Olympic from Lancashire defeated Old Etonians at the Oval by 2–1.

At the same time, however, there was the continued popularity of the sheer delights of drink, bawdy entertainment, gambling and escapism. Drinking in pubs and illegal drinking houses grew during this period, with an increasing consumption of alcohol. Controls over drinking were lax in the 1830s and 1840s, and only started to become more strict as the churches and the temperance movement campaigned for parliamentary and local authority action. Scotland was the first place to start restrictive licensing, with an Act of 1853 which closed pubs on Sundays and imposed a strict licensing regime. England only followed suit in the 1870s and, over the next few decades, there was increasing pressure upon magistrates to curb drinking – with measures like testing of publicans to see if they were 'fit and proper persons', age restrictions on buying drink, and closing off of pubs from street gaze. But drinking remained popular, largely with men, and though Sunday closing extended to Wales late in the century, there was little threat to the continued importance of the public house in the culture of all four countries.

The Victorian period saw the rise of the 'free and easies' that combined drinking and cheap stage shows, followed, from the 1870s, by the music halls that created the first form of mass entertainment. During this period, these were widely regarded as dangerous and unrespectable places, characterised by rolling programmes of comics, dance-troupes, short drama productions and sing-along sketches, which attracted many men of the working classes and the more 'adventurous' middle classes. Even more popular in many ways was gambling, which grew with organised sports of all kinds, and which, despite increasing criminalisation in the Betting Houses Act of 1853 (and another in 1874), became widespread and entrenched in most towns and cities in the country. Gambling was most often upon horse racing, where on-course betting was legal. Betting everywhere else was made progressively illegal, however, resulting in bookies operating furtively in back alleys and public houses, with teams of lookouts and runners.

The widening forms of sport and entertainment of the Victorian period were marshalled to the defining of social class. The aspirational middle and working classes developed a keen sense of what was 'respectable' and what was not, and though there were hypocrites galore (especially amongst men), British society was increasingly dedicated to class differentiation.

Gender

Behind virtually all of these developments was the continuing gendering of behaviour. By the 1830s, changes in the nature of the relations between men and women, which had been slowly developing for four or five decades, had become quite strongly ingrained in society. Where men and women had each undertaken similar, though not identical, roles in the family, in the economy and society before 1800, these roles became increasingly segregated. A series of very significant shifts in the functions of men and women, in expectations of each, and in the law, increasingly segregated their roles. This was to be immensely important for the shaping of modern society throughout the nineteenth and the twentieth centuries.

Four fundamental changes in gender relations developed. Firstly, there was a slowly increasing female access to equal rights to men under the law; secondly, an increasing separation of home and work; thirdly, the development of an ideology of domesticity and separate spheres; and fourthly, a gendered division of labour in the employment market. Each of these involved complex developments, and all interacted in a way which established new social conventions and experiences for men and women in British society.

The Victorian period witnessed a slow enactment of law reform that began to grant some women's rights. In the eighteenth century, the legal subordination of the married woman to her husband was enshrined in law, and the early feminists like Mary Wollstonecraft had railed against the failure of revolutionary ideology to grant the same human rights to women as to men (see Chapter 5). The Victorian period witnessed long years of campaigning to get the law in England and Wales to recognise women's right to a divorce (in Scotland, women had held that right for some centuries). Important measures were: the Infant Custody Act of 1839, which allowed a woman separating from her husband to have custody of a child under 7 years of age (extended to under 16 years in 1873); the Divorce and Matrimonial Causes Act 1857, which allowed divorce in England and Wales without an act of Parliament, and allowed a woman to instigate divorce proceedings if she could prove her husband guilty on two of the three counts of cruelty, desertion or adultery;[1] the Married Woman's Property Act of 1870, which allowed a married woman to retain ownership of wages, investments, gifts or inheritance, and the similarly titled Act of 1882, which allowed a married woman to buy, sell and own property. Other legal restrictions upon women were many and varied, however, and were to continue well into the twentieth century. Equally importantly, there were vast areas of work, education and leisure in which there was no legislation defending the rights of women. Even with a woman's right to own property, social convention led fathers to bequeath property to daughters through trusts composed of male lawyers and relatives. Despite the legislative advances, then, society held profoundly gendered conceptions of rights and privileges.

One example of this was Victorian society's perception that the home was a woman's domain and the world of work a man's. The ideology of separate spheres developed alongside this. A belief increasingly pervaded the middle class and skilled male artisan classes that men's and women's worlds were distinct. The masculine world was seen as embracing work, politics, public affairs and organised forms of leisure, which were strongly dominated by male activities. Women, on the other hand,

---

[1] The husband needed only prove one ground for divorcing his wife.

Focus on

Women and domesticity

The ideology of separate spheres is summed up by a verse from a poem by Alfred Lord Tennyson:

> Man for the field and woman for the hearth:
> Man for the sword and for the needle she:
> Man with the head and woman with the heart:
> Man to command and woman to obey;
> All else confusion.

In 1890, a religious magazine wrote in its 'Hints for Home life' column:

> Order conserves energy, and does away with the friction of spirit and temper caused by irregularity and uncertainty. A young woman with a well balanced mind and definite will, who so guides her house that there is a time and place for everything, and yet an elastic, facile adaptation of rule to unforeseen circumstances, will realise that order creates and ministers to happiness, and a practical arrangement of time makes every day thirteen hours long. She is the architect of home, and it depends on her skill, her foresight, her soft arranging touches whether it shall be the 'lodestar to all hearts', or whether it shall be a house from which husband and children are glad to escape either to the street, the theatre, or the tavern.

Sources: Alfred Lord Tennyson, *The Princess, A medley* (1847) Canto V, lines 437–441; *The Christian Miscellany and Family Visitor* (1890).

were increasingly confined by a very sharp ideology of domesticity, which argued that a women's place was in the home. These ideologies were circulated through everyday culture, philosophical writings, popular journals and daily discourse. They became accepted as universal laws of human activity, as ideals which described the appropriate activities for men and for women.

Leading these developments was the culture of the rapidly expanding middle classes. The woman's domain was the home, a haven from the frenetic public world of factory, office, business and politics. The home developed in the Victorian period to symbolise this ideology – with soft furnishings, cascading drapes and curtains creating cosy rooms that restrained the sight and sounds of the outside streets, cocooning the family. The middle-class female's dress matched her home, emphasising her separation from the world: long flowing fashions, covering skin from neck to ankle, but accentuating femininity and motherhood functions, with corsets, crinolines and hoop-skirts exaggerating the hips, the buttocks and the breasts. Home-making, giving birth and child-rearing were the roles for women, and the home was dedicated to those, and was not conceptualised as a place of economic production. Marriages were no longer the economic partnerships that were found across many social ranks in the seventeenth and eighteenth centuries, and rooms in the house were now distinguished by social rather than economic functions. Domestic servants had separate spaces for cooking, cleaning and living. The good woman was now a dependant, and submission to that state of reliance on the husband was the source of a middle-class lady's respectability.

Women of the Victorian middle classes spent more time with their children than their predecessors. They were more likely to breast-feed, play with and educate their children, and to incorporate them into the day-to-day life of the home. Motherhood was a key virtue, and those women who failed to have children, whether through choice or through inability to do so, were seen as odd and as contravening normal behaviour. Those who did not marry were viewed as pitiable female creatures condemned to be 'left on the shelf' as spinsters (a word loaded with derogatory meaning). Marriage was seen as a woman's natural state by the age of 20 or 25 years. Novels like Jane Austen's *Pride and Prejudice* clearly showed that a young woman's destiny was marriage.

These values were reflected in the ideal woman of the period, Queen Victoria. Reigning from 1837 to 1901, she was the longstanding symbol of respectable femininity and motherhood. Just as her monarchy established stability after decades of turbulence in the royal family, widely distributed images and, from the 1840s, photographs of her provided the most potent symbols of domestic virtue and marital constancy. With a large number of children, she was seen as 'the mother of the nation', whilst her marriage to Albert represented the ideal of marital harmony. After he died in 1861, duty and devotion were symbolised in her lifelong mourning in black dress and widow's cap – a mourning that lasted virtually undiminished for four decades. Victoria seemed to personify the qualities of the ideal women broadcast by both secular and religious magazines. Deviation from the model she offered was dealt with harshly by many social classes. Above all, a woman had to be chaste and virtuous. To know about sex, let alone to lose her virginity before marriage, would damn the respectable woman without hope of redemption. Children born to single girls and women were often put by relatives into homes for unmarried mothers run by church charities, from where they were swiftly removed and farmed out to households – sometimes for money – or sent to orphanages from where many were forcibly emigrated to Canada and Australia. Society condemned children for the transgressions of parents; women paid the most, and the absent fathers often got off scot-free.

A man's functions and roles were considered very different from those of a woman. Man's clothing became the antithesis of those of the eighteenth century. Instead of flamboyant cloaks, tight breeches, cocked hats and large powdered wigs, from the 1780s men's clothes started to become markedly more restrained. By the 1810s, men were wearing loose-fitting jackets and trousers, invariably black and plain, with short hair and a black top hat – an ensemble emphasising the restraint of masculine excess, and even the desexualisation of the male body in comparison to the female. The home, for a man, was a place of moral nourishment after the vicissitudes of business and worldly affairs. The successful wife and mother regenerated affection, emotion, spiritual redemption and contentment. In 1850, Hippolyte Taine summed up the predominantly English view of home and family: 'Every Englishman has, in the matter of marriage, a romantic spot in his heart. He imagines a "home", with the woman of his choice, the pair of them alone with their children. That is his own little universe, closed to the world.'[2]

Masculinity was a contested virtue, where success in the world of business and work, and strength in physical endeavour and sport, were balanced against the dangers of male temptation. Central to these was drink, which could lure a man into dissipation and unhealthy conversation with other men and unvirtuous women:

> O lift the workman's heart and mind
> Above low sensual sin!
> Give him a home! the home of taste!
> Outbid the house of gin![3]

Books and magazines on good conduct for men appealed through Victorian idols – the scientists, engineers, inventors and entrepreneurs. The author Samuel Smiles became famous for a long series of books about male heroes – great engineers and industrialists like George Stephenson, Matthew Boulton, James Watt and Josiah Wedgwood, as well as best-selling books on virtues such as *Self-Help* (1859), *Character* (1871), *Thrift* (1875), and *Duty* (1880). In such uplifting stories, scientists were models not of science but of upright and Christian lives, pursuing inventions which brought moral benefit to society. In the same way, the good man had to combine the qualities of strength with homely qualities. This was a delicate balance for the Victorian male; even pushing the pram (the perambulator for babies) was seen by many men as effete and a step too far; child-minding was a woman's task.

Nevertheless, there is plenty of evidence that many Victorian men were strongly attached to their children and spent time with them, though this was probably easier for the wealthier middle-class man than for the artisan or labourer working long hours. Fatherhood obviously proclaimed a man's masculine status; men without children were pitied for having no son and heir. Fathers grieved hard at the loss of their young ones. A Birmingham banker was distraught when his daughter died, writing: 'I am so overwhelmed with the sudden loss of my precious child, that I scarcely know

[2] Hippoltye Taine, quoted in J. Tosh, *A Man's Place: Masculinity and the Middle-class Home in Victorian England* (New Haven and London, Yale University Press, 1999), p. 28.

[3] Ebenezer Elliott, quoted in H.N. Fairchild, *Religious Trends in English Poetry, Vol. IV: 1830–1880: Christianity and Romanticism in the Victorian Era* (New York and London, Columbia University Press, 1957), p. 88.

how to write. The dear girl just entering a time of life . . . She is constantly before me in every movement I take, remembering how joyfully she met me on my return from Town on the omnibus, was the first to open the door, and come to meet me . . . I cannot express the sorrow it has brought over my mind.' [4]

In the area of work, the gendered segregation of society was most stark. Women of the working classes had to work out of economic necessity. It was much more difficult for them to conform to the ideal of the leisurely homemaker, and with larger families, no servants, and men whose wages were often susceptible to trade depression or unemployment, women's earnings were vital. But here the inequality between men and women loomed large. In the early stages of industrialisation, the sexual division of labour in the workplace became much more pronounced than in previous centuries. Of the thousands of new jobs generated by industrialisation, of the new occupations with their varying skills and requirements, it is notable that the best-paid, the most prestigious and the most celebrated went invariably to men.

There were sexual hierarchies of labour. In textile production in the home in the eighteenth century, it had been commonly the case that the woman had been the spinner and the man the weaver. Yet, with factory production, the reverse developed: machine spinning became a male occupation, while power-loom weaving was commonly undertaken by women, though with male supervisors. There were several arguments made in support of such segregation. The first was that there was a natural sexual difference, such that only men could garner high work skills to operate large and complex machinery, whilst women were suited to work using their nimble fingers and dexterity. A second argument was that mechanisation caused an exclusion of women because the machines required the strength of men to operate. Male trade unionists, protecting the jobs and wages of their mainly skilled male membership, sought to exclude women from the labour force because they drove down wage rates and thus threatened 'male' jobs. Men workers aspired to a position of being able to afford to keep a wife at home. One speaker at the Trades Union Congress in 1877 supported restrictions on women's work, saying:

> It was their duty as men and husbands to use their utmost efforts to bring about
> a condition of things where their wives should be in their proper sphere at home,
> seeing after their house and family, instead of being dragged into the competition
> for livelihood against the great and strong men of the world.[5]

Women workers, still burdened with housework and waged work, also aspired to stay at home. Thus, a predominantly middle-class ideology came to be adopted by many of the working classes. Married women were increasingly marginalised from

---

[4] Quoted in L. Davidoff and C. Hall, *Family Fortunes: Men and Women of the English Middle Class, 1780–1850* (London, Routledge, 1987), p. 331.

[5] Quoted in D. Simonton, *A History of European Women's Work, 1700 to the Present* (London, Routledge, 1998), p. 174.

the industrial labour force, while the conditions for working men were marginally improved.

Work and home were not the only gendered aspects of social life in Victorian Britain. Popular culture was suffused by gender. In poetry, novels, magazines, biography and autobiography, notions of gender difference based around distinct roles for men and women were given open and common expression. Like any society, the Victorian middle classes continuously circulated representations of how the ideal woman and the ideal man should behave. Reading was a great female pursuit in the middle classes, and from the 1840s there was a vast literature in book and, especially, magazine format for them. Girls and young women read magazines which portrayed the woman in the domestic setting. Female readers were targeted with stories of romance and thoughts on how to reach fulfilment, and these invariably depicted the contented woman as seeking a husband, having children, and creating a comfortable and sedate home life without work. As far as entertainment was concerned, women's opportunities in the middle classes were severely restricted. Charitable activities, Sunday-school teaching, 'at homes' for afternoon tea were common, as were musical evenings, or soirées, and learning to play musical instruments. Religious activities were very important. Indeed, the Victorian church was a major centre for female middle-class activity in charitable and good works.

Religion

One of the important sources of class identity at this time was religion. During the years before 1830, Methodism had started to develop an important identification with working-class families in many mining, industrial and fishing communities in parts of England, and, in Scotland, Presbyterian Dissenters became strongly associated with farm servants. But from the 1840s, in both England and Scotland and, from the 1870s, in Wales, dissenting churches became increasingly important sources of identity. At the same time, there were new trends within the Church of England and the Church of Scotland.

In the midst of agricultural change, protest at elites who worshipped in the state Church of England and the Church of Scotland led to increasing popular identification with dissenting groups. In England, this led to a significant growth of Nonconformist churches – Baptists and Congregationalists, as well as Methodists – in rural communities undergoing economic change, notably in the East Anglian counties of Norfolk, Sussex and Essex, and in Cambridgeshire and Lincolnshire. In mining areas such as Cornwall, Methodism continued to be a very strong source of identity, whilst in coal-mining areas of Durham and the North-east, the Midlands and South Wales, Methodist chapels and new sects like the Plymouth Brethren became a vital sanctuary in communities feeling themselves estranged from employers and state parish churches alike. Meanwhile, in fishing communities all round Britain, from Cornwall to Shetland, evangelical churches like the Methodists and Baptists developed a very strong support. Strengthened by the arrival of Dissenters from the countryside during these decades, Nonconformist denominations were also strong in industrial cities and larger towns of the north of England, South Wales, and in the variegated Protestant culture of the north-east of Ireland. In Scotland, the Free Church of Scotland emerged in 1843 after a schism in the Church of Scotland, attracting 40 per cent of the clergy and perhaps half of the adherents. On the surface, the split was over the issue of patronage in the appointment of ministers, but it reflected deeper social tensions between old and new elites in urban society. In the Highlands and Hebrides, the Free Church attracted about 90 per cent of the small crofters and fishermen who were alienated from the landowners and their parish church.

Religion was a vital ingredient in family, community and class identities. The churches provided a focus for Sunday worship, of course, and, in the dissenting churches, the observance of the Sabbath as a day of no work or play was strong. Attendance at two and even three services on a Sunday was common, including for children, who might attend Sunday school in the morning, and worship with one or other of their parents in the afternoon and evening. Women tended to go to worship more in the evening in England and some parts of Wales – the result of the need to prepare Sunday lunch as an important festival of family faith and unity. In Scotland and many parts of Wales, the observance of the Sabbath prevented the heating of cooked Sunday lunch, so mothers often attended morning service. Religious activities were not confined to Sundays. On weekday evenings, children were faced with an increasing plethora of organisations with high moral and religious purpose. These included the temperance movement, which, from the 1850s, offered children the pledge of total abstinence from alcohol, and weekly lectures and demonstrations on the consequences of drink upon the human body and the moral state of the individual. For parents, mothers' prayer meetings, mill girls' meetings, policemen's religious societies and hundreds of similar organisations offered religious activities on a week-day evening, so that organised leisure became for many dominated by religious and moral activities.

The Church of England remained the largest single denomination in England. The centre of its strength was more rural than urban; more in the south of England than the industrial north; but it had a particular strength amongst citizens of London, where dissent was generally weak. The Church of England remained the default church of choice for large numbers of middle- and working-class people. It was the main source of baptism, marriages and funerals, and, for these rites of passage, it fought to retain a hold over law and the people's affection. It was the church of the state for occasions of an official nature, and was the official church of the armed services. In this sense, it is important to note that it had a strong association with the landed and political elite and retained the loyalty of very large numbers of English people. Dissenters, on the other hand, became during this period more complex socially. The Methodists, Baptists and Congregationalists had, by 1830, already developed a strong ideology of self-improvement through hard work, sobriety and application, and they tended to be highly socially mobile, moving up the social scale in

Figure 14.1 Baptist preacher Charles Spurgeon preaching to a massive crowd at Crystal Palace, London, 1857. His popularity was so great that his Metropolitan Tabernacle at the Elephant and Castle had seating for 6,000 people.
Source: Mary Evans Picture Library

urban industrial society. For this reason, even before the 1830s, the Methodists in England and the Seceders in Scotland had become, in many medium and larger towns, wealthy congregations, who sought to express the obvious benefit of their faith by building ever larger and more ornate churches. Between the 1830s and 1880s, congregations became even more mobile, relocating sometimes as many as three times in 50 years to allow the church building to follow the members as they moved to the suburbs.

In towns like Harrogate, Leeds, York and Manchester, the large Wesleyan Methodist congregations of the mid-Victorian decades were centres of social refinement, pretension and segregation. Admission to the church was carefully vetted, with the respectability of families monitored closely for signs of wayward behaviour (especially by men). The costs of membership were high in terms of annual money 'givings' to the congregation; the good works of the denomination; pew-rents to seat the family; and the finest Sunday-best clothes with which to attend. One consequence was a degree of social tension within national denominations, which resulted in schism along social divisions. In England and Wales, the Methodists split into as many as nine different denominations and sects in this period, whilst in Scotland those who left the Church of Scotland had equally as many from which to choose. Religion became highly fractured. In 1851, even tiny villages could have many competing churches. In the village of Doune in Perthshire, a community of around 2,000 adults and children staffing an adjacent large cotton spinning mill, there were nine separate denominations. This was a common experience in industrial villages around Britain.

Each religious denomination was also subject to social variation. This was particularly the case with the Church of England, often described as a 'broad church' of people with different theological leanings – some towards the evangelical views of the Dissenters, and others of the 'High Church' favouring the Roman Catholic tradition. In the 1830s and 1840s, the Oxford Movement, based at the university, became an influential trend-setter for the High Church wing. It opposed liberal trends, and tended to reassert the historic links of Anglicanism with the older Catholic and Orthodox branches of Christianity, leading to the creation of religious orders for men and women in the Church. This presaged a resurgence of High Church liturgy and doctrine – including in the Church of Scotland, which, from the 1860s, had a group advocating practices like stained glass windows and hymn singing, previously felt to be antithetical to Presbyterianism. Some of those attracted to the Oxford Movement in the 1840s made the decision to join the Roman Catholic Church – the best-known of them, John Henry Newman, rose to become a cardinal – but for others, such a move was a source of scandal and, in some cases, destroyed careers and broke families.

In Ireland, the religious complexion was very different. More than 70 per cent of the people of the island were active or passive adherents of the Roman Catholic Church, with the remainder divided between the Protestant Church of Ireland, the Presbyterian Church, and the Methodist, Baptist or other Protestant churches. This was one part of the British Isles where the established or state church, the Church of Ireland, was clearly in a small minority. It was the church of the Anglo-Irish gentry, whilst the other Protestant churches tended to be strongly associated with the urban, artisan and industrial working classes of Dublin and Belfast, and the tenant farming community of the north-east. In Ireland, religion split the community in ways which were to be more potent than elsewhere, with all branches of life, work and politics falling into confessional divisions of Church of Ireland, Roman Catholic and Presbyterian which, to a major extent, mirrored respectively the divisions of gentry, peasantry and urban artisans.

Despite the vibrancy revealed by church dispute and schism, Victorians worried about the impact of urbanisation upon religion. It became an axiom of many churchmen – and many in political and civic life generally – that the growth of cities undermined faith. In particular, there was a strong belief that the working classes were alienated from the beneficial effects of Christian religion and churchgoing in the same way that they were alienated from the beneficial effects of familiarity with the elites. Cities produced social and religious distance. The notion was rife that the working classes were becoming 'heathens'.

There seemed to be plenty of evidence to support this view. Cities grew so fast that insufficient church buildings were available to house the people at Sunday worship. Panics developed from the 1810s through to the 1880s that people were avoiding church because of lack of pews on a Sunday and too few clergy. But the evidence for this was probably misleading. It was only in the nineteenth century that statistics of religious adherence and practice were gathered for the first time, and it was easy to make false assumptions about change over the century before. Equally, there was an underlying belief that rural society was 'more religious' than urban society; this belief was most strongly held by clergy who, in this century, were often born in the countryside and moved to urban areas, thereby developing an adverse view on the religiousness of urban factory workers and slum-dwellers.

By 1880, the panic was subsiding. This was in large measure because of massive church-building programmes by virtually all denominations during the 1850s, 1860s and 1870s that resulted in a great increase in space to accommodate the people in the pews. At the same time, the number of clergy trained by the churches rose, recruited especially among the Protestant Dissenters by a series of religious revivals in 1859 and 1873–4. In reality, churchgoing in the Victorian period was very high compared to the eighteenth and twentieth centuries. The 1851 census of churchgoing in mainland Britain showed that somewhere in the region of 40 per cent of the population attended church at least once on a Sunday, and many attended twice and even three times. If anything, church attendance may have risen until 1880, when there were probably the beginnings of a decline. However, even so, the place of religion was very strong in the society and culture of this period. It defined identity, united families in rituals like Sunday lunch, and divided communities (notably between Protestant and Catholic) in equal measure. The majority of the people may not have gone to church every Sunday, but most attended at least a few times per year. Most who went were working class, though large numbers of the middle classes also attended.

Religion was also central to identity in less becoming ways. Sectarian hostility between Protestants and Catholics was aroused in many parts – not just in Ireland but also in Liverpool, Manchester, Glasgow and many smaller industrial towns. There were anti-papal demonstrations involving a large number of the working class in 1851 on the restoration of the Catholic hierarchy in Britain and, during 1866–67, Murphy, an anti-Popish lecturer, was able to stir up riots in Birmingham, Liverpool, Newcastle and elsewhere. For generations in Lancashire and in Glasgow, the Conservative Party was able to use the anti-Catholic theme to get working-class voters to turn out for it.

It is difficult to overstate the importance of religion in the mid-nineteenth century. People often voted as they prayed. The Church of England, it was said (with only mild exaggeration), constituted the Conservative Party at prayer, whilst the Nonconformist churches were strongly aligned with the Liberal Party, its *laissez-faire* ideology and its many moral reform causes, like temperance. The churches were major providers of 'respectable' recreation, supported philanthropic endeavour, and in overseas work provided an important religious dimension to the expansion of the British Empire.

Individual Victorians were highly motivated by religious impulses – to hard work, to charitable giving, and even to scientific research. With much higher levels of religious observance than in the twentieth century, in most parts of Victorian culture religion had, in some way, a part to play.

Further reading

Davidoff, L. and Hall, C., *Family Fortunes: Men and Women of the English Middle Class, 1780–1850* (London, Routledge, 1987)

Fraser, W.H., *A History of British Trade Unionism 1700–1998* (Basingstoke, Macmillan, 1999)

Gleadle, K., *British Women in the Nineteenth Century* (Basingstoke, Palgrave Macmillan, 2001)

McLeod, H., *Religion and the Working Class in Nineteenth-century Britain* (London, Macmillan, 1984)

Reid, A., *Social Classes and Social Relations in Britain 1850–1914* (Basingstoke, Macmillan, 1992)

Thompson, F.M.L., *The Rise of Respectable Society: A Social History of Victorian Britain* (London, Fontana, 1988)

Tranter, Neil, *Sport, Economy and Society in Britain 1750–1914* (Cambridge, Cambridge University Press, 1998)

15

Responses to industrial change

Resistance to change

Giving his maiden speech in the House of Lords in February 1812, the poet Lord Byron turned his irony on those who were calling for the death penalty for the smashing of machines. He had witnessed some of the riots among the stocking makers of Nottinghamshire against the improved machines for knitting stockings, which would drive some of them out of work.

> Considerable injury has been done to the proprietors of the improved frames. These machines were to them an advantage, in as much as they superseded the necessity of employing a number of workmen, who were left in consequence to starve . . . The rejected workmen in the blindness of their ignorance, instead of rejoicing at these improvements in arts so beneficial to mankind, conceived themselves to be sacrificed to improvements in mechanism. In the foolishness of their hearts they imagined, that the maintenance of the industrious poor were objects of greater consequence than the enrichment of a few individuals by any improvement in the implements of trade, which threw the workmen out of employment, and rendered the labourer unworthy of his hire.[1]

He failed to convince the Tory government and the death penalty was introduced for the crime of machine-smashing. This was a fairly ruthless way of overcoming resistance to change, but the ruthlessness was evidence of how seriously the authorities took the opposition.

---

[1] *The Works of Lord Byron* (Paris, A. & W. Galignani, 1828), p. 554.

These Luddite riots of 1811 and 1812 are the best-known incidents of machine-breaking, but they are by no means unique. In the early 1830s, agricultural labourers were using the same techniques against threshing machines being introduced in the south and east of England. Twenty years later, the shoemakers of the Midlands fought a rearguard action against the introduction of sewing machines in the 1850s. Elsewhere, a 'spanner in the works' was always a tactic of protest. However, in general, workers' response to industrial change has always been rather more complex and less direct than lashing out at the machine.

It may not be altogether self-evident that workers will protest at industrial change unless one bears in mind that the transition from a traditional, rural society to a predominantly industrial society involves a social revolution that affects all sections of the population (see Chapter 8). Any society tends to be conservative. There is a built-in resistance to change and, for industrial change to take root, various barriers had to be overcome. With increasing knowledge and better communication, people become aware that there are alternatives to the existing way of work, but in addition there is an understandable and quite rational fear of the unknown. Change brings insecurity. But, mobility was essential to industrial change and new ways of working, as well as new social relationships, had to emerge.

Industrialisation also involved a certain loss of freedom. The pre-industrial craftsman laid great stress on his independence, but the industrial system required a discipline and control that destroyed much of this. To take one example, there was the discipline created by the larger market. No longer concerned just with satisfying the orders of fellow villagers, the craftsman had to think in terms of larger markets and greater production. This brought in middle men to organise distribution and to instruct the craftsmen on what to produce. Workers found that they had now to work to the timetable set down by the merchant capitalists. Reward had to become more important than freedom. Finally, industrialisation meant a breakdown in many traditional crafts. New skills became important, while mechanisation destroyed the need for certain crafts or made the tasks more widely accessible to workers with reduced skills. Such division of labour also created opposition to change.

There were numerous pressures pushing against such barriers to change. Firstly, there were economic pressures – particularly the pressure of population on land resources that forced many to look for alternative ways of surviving. Undoubtedly, the threat and reality of famine were a great force breaking down barriers to industrialisation. Most peasants from the Scottish Highlands and rural Ireland quickly learned to abandon their inhibitions over factory labour when the alternative might be starvation. Economic pressures continued when the demand for a particular skill or for traditional products declined. Secondly, there were political pressures, such as limiting the amount of help that could be obtained from poor relief, which meant that people were deprived of alternatives if they did not work. Thirdly, and more intangible, were the social pressures that pushed people out of their traditional community or family. In Britain, the laws of primogeniture ensured that only first sons could inherit the family land and this meant that the others had to move out and seek a living elsewhere.

Alongside these push factors, there were pull factors. Some people were undoubtedly attracted by monetary incentives in industry, without any great process of re-education. If money bought the goods and services that were desired, then people tended to expend the effort to procure money. There was also the appeal of acquiring new skills. The village millwright might be attracted by the challenge offered by new machines, not just by the rewards. Many desired individual mobility, perhaps to escape from a stultifying social, religious or cultural milieu. Industry became synonymous with progress, and progress was increasingly presented in school, pulpit and community expectation as what individuals should strive after. Taking part in industry could be made to seem exciting. Also, for most people, industrialisation meant work in a city, which had the appeal of the new, the thrilling and the dangerous.

Once workers had been induced to abandon agricultural pursuits, they had to be convinced of the benefits of remaining in the new urban and industrial society. They had to be persuaded to work with the necessary diligence and efficiency. This proved to be more difficult. Many workers retained their ties with their old life and this produced high labour turnover and absenteeism. A lack of commitment to the industrial system could take other forms. Drunkenness and bad time-keeping were problems for employers during early industrialisation; factories needed the discipline of set working hours and daily attendance. All this was difficult for people who had been accustomed to gearing their life to the sun, the weather and the seasons. It was also necessary to make workers committed enough to industrialism to go to the trouble of learning new skills. In these ways, the process of industrialisation was not just an economic process, but involved social, cultural, political and psychological dimensions.

The British experience

Lack of knowledge about alternatives to a traditional way of life was not a major barrier in Britain. Thanks to its small size and the ease of sea transport, it had long had a relatively mobile population. Even before an effective road system developed, London had been the 'great wen', pulling people into its orbit. It was very much the national capital on which Parliament, court, trade and much industry and banking centred. Before 1750, around one person in six probably went to London at some time in their lives, gaining knowledge of the riches and fashions of the world. From the 1820s, steamships were opening up even the most remote parts of the Scottish Highlands, while from 1825 the railway network started to spread, allowing people to travel more easily.

Early industrialists had recognised that the loss of traditional forms of security were a barrier to persuading people to work in their factories. They responded to this by attracting whole families to their industrial villages. The cotton industry was able to establish itself very quickly because women and children were needed to work alongside men. Whether in the home, workshop or factory, cotton spinning and weaving gave economic roles to men, women and their children. Access to farming land could still be important, though. The importance of land and a hostility to 'wage slavery' remained an extremely important part of workers' tradition, so numerous schemes emerged to allow families to opt out of the industrial work and create their own co-operative system, usually based on agriculture. Sometimes this took the form of allotments for cultivation. But more ambitious and persistent ideas for worker land-based communities were associated with the cotton employer and social idealist, Robert Owen, in the 1820s and 1830s, whilst the Chartists of the 1840s also had a land plan which envisaged a land-based society as the road to freedom.

There were other values that had to be accepted. Discipline of character by hard work, industry and self-denial was a central message that had to be got across. But considerable evidence shows that, in the eighteenth century, the concept of work discipline, intense working and tightly controlled hours of work were largely unknown. Instead, work patterns were more relaxed, both in agriculture and in manufacturing by handloom weavers, where the worker controlled the process and pace of work, with the aim of earning a decent living and enjoying good leisure time, but not expecting significant advancement in riches. One product of this was a distinctive concept of the working week. The eighteenth-century week often involved a weaver or other worker labouring intensively for three or four days, working 18 hours a day to get a job done, and then spending a leisurely time on Saturday, Sunday, and what was called 'St Monday' (in a mock suggestion of a saint conferring a holiday once a week). Such a casual pattern of work was unacceptable in a factory situation, but throughout the early nineteenth century the practice of 'St Monday' absenteeism was common. Slowly, factory owners from the 1820s to the 1860s negotiated the end of 'St Monday' – in many cases, offering workers a half day on Saturday in return, leading to the convention of football matches kicking off at 3 p.m.

Complaints at the loss of freedom brought by the intensification of work and competition for work were legion among craftsmen. Many of the early trade unions appearing in the eighteenth century sought to maintain customary rules in crafts that were being threatened by new patterns of organisation. Groups of shoemakers, tailors, cabinetmakers and others united to try to keep control over entry into their craft, and to maintain ideas of a 'fair price' and a 'just wage' for goods and services arrived at by mutual agreement between masters and men in the same craft. Traditional standards were being eroded by newcomers among employers, who charged what the market would bear for a product, and who were prepared to employ workers not fully trained and at lower rates of pay.

The actual breakdown of many craft skills came with mechanisation. Resistance to machinery was not blind destruction. Any new machine was likely to displace workers and resistance was perfectly rational. Some machine-breaking was what the historian Eric Hobsbawm called 'collective bargaining by riot'. It was a very effective means of putting pressure upon employers where it hurt. It could also help to ensure worker solidarity. This was one of the things behind the tactics of the 'plug strikes' in Lancashire in 1842, when striking workers moved from factory to factory removing plugs from the boilers, thus preventing the steam engines working. Small masters sometimes joined with workers in attacking machines that threatened them too by being too expensive for all but the biggest industrialists to install. But in the final analysis, it was fruitless to oppose new machines forever. Handloom weavers could not halt the increased use of powerlooms with their much greater productivity, and often worked by women workers who would accept lower pay. A growing urban population meant a rising demand for goods of all kinds, and to satisfy it traditional methods had to give way to new techniques.

The political pressures forcing change were many. In 1813 and 1814, the laws that had required workers in key crafts to have served an apprenticeship were swept away, as were laws that allowed justices of the peace to fix what were regarded as fair wages. Employers' attempts to impose discipline by means of fines for absenteeism were backed up by legislation such as the Master and Servant Acts, which made it a criminal offence for a worker to break the terms of his contract. The Poor Law Amendment Act, introduced in England and Wales in 1834, ensured that the alternative to work was more unpleasant than any kind of work. Resistance to change was actively discouraged by laws against workers' unions. The Combination Laws of 1799 to 1824 declared illegal trade unions formed to raise wages or shorten hours and, even after 1824, there were limits placed on trade-union activities. Social and ideological pressures in favour of industrialism came from all directions. What was needed from the working class, said Edmund Burke, were 'patience, labour, sobriety, frugality and religion', and these qualities were what educational, religious and cultural forces in society set out to achieve. Holidays, games and amusements associated with a traditional society were frowned upon. Morality was called upon in defence of the factory system. Andrew Ure, one of the most active propagandists of the new manufacturing system, argued that bad time-keeping, wastage of material and careless work were all signs of a lack of moral discipline. The churches of the period seemed to encourage worker discipline and their striving for social betterment; the historian E.P. Thompson argued that the complexities and subtleties of Methodism in parts of England turned the worker into 'his own slave driver'. Industry, prudence and thrift, all shibboleths of the growing middle class, were pressed on workers in lectures, articles, sermons, songs, on wayside pulpits and embroidered samplers. Though workers might resist the middle-class messenger, the message of improvement was already one with a strong resonance in many working-class homes.

Industrialism came through mere immersion in the bustling activity of the nineteenth-century city. To a rural worker, cities offered the possibility of new jobs and higher earnings. Housing rents would be higher, but a family was usually better off labouring in a town than working on a farm – though farm wages were higher near to cities, in an attempt to retain the agricultural workforce. For the young, jobs in industry offered the chance of economic independence at a much earlier age than waiting for a cottage or plot of land in the countryside. Friedrich Engels, writing of conditions in Manchester in 1844, found that it was fairly common for the young to pay a sum of money to their parents for board and lodging and to keep the rest of their pay for themselves, or for single people to set up house on their own or with friends of their own age. Steady jobs in industry also offered the opportunity of earlier marriage, which, at least for some, must have had an appeal.

Once in an industrial setting, such as a factory, discipline could be achieved in a variety of ways. Most early factories had a long list of rules and regulations – no whistling, no singing, no looking out of the window – in other words, nothing to remind workers of the casual aspects of a traditional rural life. Lateness for work, absenteeism and bad time-keeping were heavily penalised by fines or, in the case of child workers, often by beatings. There was a limit to how much could be done through fining, and piece work was widely sought by employers, so that a worker was paid for each item of output actually made. This was something that produced a great deal of worker resistance, but it had huge advantages for the employers. The elimination of drinking at work proved very difficult to achieve, since many craft rituals centred around drink. The temperance movement, gathering pace from the end of the 1820s, not surprisingly, received much approval from employers, but it also achieved considerable support from married women who suffered, along with their children, from loss of household income through husbands' expenditure in the public house.

Industrialisation was a traumatic experience for those caught up in it. It clearly involved protests of different kinds by those affected. Marx and those influenced by him argued that workers would become increasingly militant. Marx asserted that the 'accumulation of wealth at one pole, is therefore at the same time the accumulation of misery, agony of toil, slavery, ignorance, brutality, mental degradation, at the opposite pole'[2] and that the result would be the growth of discontent and protest. But the British workers' response to industrialisation during the mid-Victorian years was to become less, not more, militant. This did not mean that workers were opposed to combination into trade unions, however. Rather, workers started to develop unions into a system of effective collective bargaining for improvement of their pay and conditions.

Owenite unionism

Standing against the prevailing ethic that advancement would come through individual effort, there was, among some workers, still a widely held view that mutual responsibility mattered. The ethic of their trade unions and their friendly societies was that the individual needed mutual support at work, in sickness and old age. Throughout the 1820s, there had been a number of schemes to establish co-operative workshops, the argument being that the competitive system destroyed the craft spirit. It destroyed pride in work, it alienated men from their work and, therefore, it should be replaced by a system where people co-operated, shared the profits, and where workers gained as much as their employers from their contribution to producing goods. This viewpoint was often accompanied by a continuing suspicion of machines that displaced labour to the advantage only of the employer, and there was a rather naïve faith in hand labour. All of this was very much the product of the thinking of urban artisans under pressure

---

[2] K. Marx, quoted in E.K. Hunt (ed.), *History of Economic Thought: A Critical Perspective*, 2nd edn (New York, M.E. Sharpe, 2002), p. 244.

from industrialisation. Some were attracted by the possibility of opting out of the changes in work methods by means of co-operative communities, and many of the co-operative stores which appeared in the 1820s and 1830s were intended to be a means of raising money to eventually establish a co-operative, agriculturally based community.

A key figure in spreading such ideas was Robert Owen. Although he had been a cotton mill-owner at New Lanark near Glasgow, he believed that the capitalist system would only lead to social conflict, and he harked back to an older tradition of mutual responsibility, where there was concern about provision for the poor. But Owen always tended to assume that those in power could be convinced to change their views, abandon the new capitalist system and return to a sense of mutual responsibility. Most workers tended to hold out few such hopes. They had seen the way in which the landed ruling class had helped along the growth of capitalist society. They, therefore, looked rather to themselves to change society.

Opposing this outlook were working-class leaders, like the London tailor, Francis Place, who believed that the workers would gain from the creation of a *laissez-faire* society. The propaganda for the new society was undoubtedly having its effect. Place argued that the expansion of industry would bring increased prosperity and this would be to the advantage of all. Industry must expand, new machinery must be brought in to produce cheaper goods, so that all could gain. Place's argument was that the working class and the middle class should co-operate against the common enemy of the landed aristocracy. However, many of the writers in the illegal unstamped newspapers that flourished in the early 1830s aimed at a working-class readership and spoke in class terms. James Morrison, the editor of *The Pioneer*, wrote 'trust none who is a grade above our class, and does not back us in the hour of trial – orphans we are, and bastards of society'.

These two opposing views were to divide the working class from the 1820s onwards, but in the early 1830s it tended to be the views of the Owenites that were most influential. The early years of the 1830s saw a burgeoning of trade unionism in many crafts and talk of generating unions among all workers as an alternative to the individualism of capitalism. This was the ideal behind the creation in February 1834 of the Grand National Consolidated Trades Union, but the reality was far from the ideal. The GNCTU was intended as a federation of existing unions, divided by trade. It was strongest amongst tailors and shoe-makers in London, but though it had contacts with unions in the Potteries and Scotland and attracted some 11,000 dues in April 1834, it failed to attract general support. The constant complaint of the leaders of the movement was that the workers were not prepared to sacrifice their separate craft interests for the greater good. The Operative Builders' Union attempted to respond to the emergence of general contractors in the building industry by uniting masons, joiners, painters and general labourers, but struggled to maintain unity. Many other groups of workers tried to take advantage of a rising demand for labour by seeking to recover some of the wage reductions that they had experienced in the 1820s. Cotton spinners in Lancashire had bitter and often violent confrontations with employers and strike breakers until their union was broken in 1831.

Focus on

Trade unions in 1831

This is from a *Lecture on the Nature and Advantages of Trades' Unions* delivered by G. Kerr, a member of the Trades' Committee of Greenock, 26 December 1831. This committee was one of a number of attempts throughout the country in the early 1830s to draw together unions of different trades.

> Whoever has been observing the passing events around them, and throughout the United Kingdom, will easily perceive, that since the termination of the late war between France and Great Britain, that the latter country, to say nothing of the former, has been marching forward with gigantic strides in the attainment of science and literature; mechanism and the arts have flourished to an extent unparalleled in the annals of history. – Now one would be apt to suppose that the operatives, the productive classes, would have been benefited by these improvements; but has this been the case? Alas! For the sake of humanity I must answer, no! Look at the various and exorbitant reductions of wages that have been made, and still are making [sic] throughout the United Kingdom; and if that will not suffice to prove what I have said, ask the thousands of unemployed operatives who have toiled hard in order to complete these improvements, and who know not at present where to find a single day's sustenance for themselves and families. – Look also to the exorbitant taxation which is rung from the proceeds of our labour, for the support of a host of men, (I should have said *locusts*,) who give us nothing in return but their scorn and ingratitude; and when they hear us complain, they inform us that the evils are owing to a redundancy of population – not a word, by the bye, of a redundancy of *taxation*. In addition to the foregoing, only look to the different monopolies, both in machinery and manual labour, that have enriched a multitude of capitalists, and ruined and impoverished a dense multitude of the working population. These circumstances are, I trust, sufficient to prove that the operatives have been greatly the sufferers, and ever will be the sufferers, so long as they neglect to unite themselves, with hearts firm to the cause, for repelling, by every praise-worthy and lawful effort, the storm of monopoly which threatens to grasp, with its envenomed fangs, the little comfort which some of the operatives yet retain, if not timeously checked.

Source: W. Hamish Fraser, *British Trade Unions 1707–1918, Volume 3* (London, Pickering & Chatto, 2007), pp. 141–2.

The Owenite movement fell apart in a spate of strikes and in the pursuit of sectional interests. But what destroyed most unions was the strong response by employers, who used the lock-out and a 'document' (which required workers to abandon union membership) to break a union's hold. There was also sharp action against the movement by the government, which feared it might spread to agricultural workers. News that a small group of agricultural labourers at the village of Tolpuddle in Dorset had actually formed a trade union in 1834 revived aristocratic fears of a resumption of the 'Swing' protests of four years earlier. Though trade unionism was now legal, the 'Tolpuddle Martyrs', as they were dubbed, were sentenced to 14 years' transportation to Australia under a 1797 act against naval mutinies that had banned the taking of secret oaths. But after the GNCTU organised a demonstration in London that attracted 40,000 people, and following further campaigning, the Martyrs were released in 1836, in what became seen as a victory for trade-union rights. However, in Glasgow in 1837, the authorities took action to break the powerful cotton spinners' association by pinning the blame for the murder of a strike-breaking 'blackleg', on limited evidence, upon the association's committee and sentencing them to seven years' transportation. In this way, trade unionism still faced barriers to acceptance and growth.

New attitudes

There was little opportunity for effective trade-union action in the economically harsh years of the early 1840s, although in 1842, in the trough of the worst depression of the century, when more than a million people were on poor relief, something very close to a general strike spread among factory workers in Lancashire, Cheshire and parts of the Midlands. At the same time, attempts were being made to pull together local coal miners' unions into regional and national organisations. These struggles were not just about wages, but were over the new patterns of work that were being imposed. Skilled coal hewers, just like skilled cotton spinners, were conscious that they were losing much of their control over the pace and organisation of their labour.

Other groups recognised that a weakness in the past had been a lack of resources to maintain a lengthy strike, and unco-ordinated action in different firms. The highly skilled steam engine and machine builders took the lead in trying to bring together smaller local societies into a national union and to impose a certain amount of central control. Boilermakers, printers and ironfounders all succeeded in forming national organisations in the late 1840s. Coupled with the need for central control was a recognition that direct confrontation had had little effect in halting the advance of capitalism. It had generally led to defeat and the break-up of nascent unions. There were those who argued that what was needed instead, was an effective and stable organisation that would protect groups of workers within the capitalist system.

The most effective of the new unions to emerge was the Amalgamated Society of Engineers (ASE) in 1850, which linked together a number of regional societies of millwrights and machine builders. It started with only 5,000 members, but by the end of its first year, this had more than doubled. Its aim was to control entry into the trade, to ensure that only those who had served an apprenticeship and could earn an acceptable level of pay were employed. Like all workers, they were very aware of the plight of handloom weavers whose earnings and status had been devastated in the years after

1815 by the uncontrolled influx of numbers into the trade. The ASE was also concerned to ensure its own survival and stability. Early unions had all suffered from workers flocking into them at a time of dispute, but just as quickly dropping out afterwards. By requiring members to contribute for friendly society benefits, they ensured that members had a vested interest in remaining in the union. For their weekly one shilling contribution (5 pence, equivalent to 5 per cent of income), members could get unemployment and sickness benefit, a disablement or funeral allowance and even emigration assistance. Finally, in order to protect funds, most control lay with the London-based executive with a full-time general secretary.

To the early historians of trade unionism, Sidney and Beatrice Webb, the ASE was a 'new model' for modern unionism. This was true only to an extent. Thousands of small societies continued to exist and even many of the larger ones continued to operate along much more traditional lines. Nonetheless, there is no doubt about the importance of the ASE because it covered vital workers in key industries. One of

Focus on

Trade unions in 1852

This is taken from an article published in *The Bookbinders' Consolidated Union Circular* in 1852. The London bookbinders were one of the best organised groups of workers.

> Trades unions, if properly managed, are the grand corner-stone upon which rests the great fabric of 'man's elevation'. They are the working man's only hope, and his most faithful friend. Being composed entirely of working men, consulting each other's welfare, they can have only the good of the working man at heart . . .
>
> What, then, it may be asked, do the trades unions of the present day seek to accomplish? They seek the independence and happiness of the workman. It is well known that if employers were left entirely uncontrolled, the most abject tyranny would be brought to bear against the men. I don't mean to say that it would be so with all employers, but there are some who would not stand at anything for their own aggrandisement and wealth. The workmen would, in many cases, be subject to the most glaring insult and degradation – to every vicissitude – a prey to every designing knave, and the tool of every ambitious tyrant. Both boy and unskilled labour would be brought to bear against them. Their position would be unworthy of *freemen*, in a *free country*.

Source: 'Trades Unions, What they were, what they are and what they ought to be', *The Bookbinders' Consolidated Union Circular*, 12 August 1852.

the new unions that did model itself on the ASE was the Amalgamated Society of Carpenters and Joiners, formed in 1860 through the amalgamation of a number of small local woodworkers' unions. The general secretary was a very capable Hull joiner, Robert Applegarth, and he, together with his counterpart in the ASE, William Allan, was determined to bring new tactics into play.

To achieve the goal of controlling entry into their trade, they needed to get employers to accept their rules about who could be employed. This involved persuading employers and the wider public that unions, far from posing a threat, could offer employers a skilled and stable workforce. Some of the larger employers were attracted by the prospect that an effective union would prevent their being undercut by small firms, paying less than standard wages. Others recognised that it was easier to negotiate alterations in work patterns with trade-union officials than with a mass meeting of workers. There was, however, still plenty of hostility and unions were attacked as destructive of British competitiveness, as tyrannical towards both employers and workers, as run by agitators, and as being 'for the protection of the dunce, the drunkard and the unskilful', as one Manchester employer put it. They were accused of trying to maintain a protective system when the spirit of the age urged the removal of barriers to the free market.

Leaders like Allan and Applegarth worked, with some success, through middle-class allies to combat such views. The leading Liberal political economist and philosopher, John Stuart Mill, revised his classic text, *Principles of Political Economy*, to recognise the role trade unions had in 'enabling the sellers of labour to take due care of their own interests under a system of competition'. Union leaders also began to develop links with influential Liberal-Radical politicians, who were looking for allies in their struggles against continued aristocratic dominance. They associated in various radical causes in the 1860s, successfully convincing many that they were 'respectable' and 'safe'.

Such allies were essential when unions found their funds threatened as a result of a court decision against a branch of the Boilermakers' Union in 1867 which decided that the union, although it was officially registered as a friendly society, could not take action against a defaulting treasurer because of its rules on apprenticeship and on who could be employed. This, according to the courts, made the union 'in restraint of trade', which in common law was illegal. The case was closely followed by evidence that older forms of union method persisted when a cask of gunpowder was dropped down the chimney of a Sheffield scissors grinder who had failed to pay his union dues. Attacks on non-unionists and the destruction of their tools had a long history in the small craft societies of Sheffield, but this episode was seized on, with widespread condemnation of the 'Sheffield outrages'.

From some quarters there were calls for a renewed curb on unions, and the government set up a Royal Commission to enquire into trade unions and employers' associations. Unions were able to use their political contacts to ensure that they had at least two sympathetic voices on the Commission. Robert Applegarth and William Allan, with others, were very impressive witnesses, arguing that there was much more to modern unions than being mere strike weapons. Indeed, they claimed that, far from instigating strikes, their unions were a restraint on these, imposing discipline on the membership and ensuring that strikes were only a last resort. Whereas the majority report was fairly bland, a powerfully argued minority report reiterated the unions' case and called for legislation to protect their funds. The result was the Trade Union Act of 1871, which gave some protection to registered unions, although it was accompanied by a Criminal Law Amendment Act that put tighter restrictions on the actions that workers could take during a strike to keep out strike-breakers. It allowed hostile judges to interpret almost any action 'that caused an unjustifiable annoyance and interference with the master in the conduct of his business' as 'molestation' or 'intimidation' (key words in the legislation) and, therefore, illegal.

This and other legislation convinced union leaders that they needed a political voice. Although there had been earlier national union conferences on specific issues, the Trades Union Congress (TUC) held its first recognised meeting in Manchester in 1868. The concern aroused by the Criminal Law Amendment Act led to the appointment in 1871 of a permanent Parliamentary Committee of the TUC to lobby Parliament; it managed to obtain the Act's replacement in 1875 by a milder Conspiracy and Protection of Property Act that permitted peaceful picketing. That same year, the much-disliked Master and Servant Act was replaced by the Employers and Workmen Act, which no longer made breach of contract by a worker a criminal offence, and the 1876 Trade Union Amendment Act extended the protection of union funds.

Most of the trade unions were unions of the most skilled workers, one of whose main concerns was to ensure that their members did not face competition for jobs from people with less skill. Indeed, contemporaries, as well as historians, talked of an 'aristocracy of labour'. It was claimed that they looked down on those with less skill. Some historians have argued that, by ensuring that there was a section of the working class that was better paid and better treated than the mass of workers, those in power effectively kept the working class divided and prevented an effective challenge to their authority. By this argument, the potentially revolutionary situation of the 1830s gave way to a docile acceptance in the 1860s. In reality, the potential for revolution was much less in the 1830s and 1840s than has sometimes been suggested and the extent of docility in the 1860s and 1870s can easily be exaggerated. There was certainly no unquestioning acceptance of the *status quo* and, despite the protestations of the leaders, industrial conflict in individual workplaces could be sharp and bitter.

A spectacular economic boom in the early 1870s, thanks largely to a rapidly expanding American market, gave opportunities for substantial wage advances for many workers. It also encouraged previously unorganised groups to set up trade unions. Dock workers, shop assistants, postal workers, bus workers, gas stokers, builders' labourers and railwaymen were among those who formed unions in these years. What caught public attention more than anything was the spread of unionism among groups of farm workers. The Methodist lay-preacher Joseph Arch formed the Warwickshire Agricultural Labourers' Union in 1872, and similar bodies followed in Lincolnshire,

Huntingdonshire, Kent and Sussex. In 1874, Emma Paterson founded the Women's Protective and Provident League to organise women bookbinders and exploited women shirtmakers in the East End of London. Few of the unions of the unskilled survived the economic downturn of the second half of the 1870s, although most never entirely disappeared.

Of course, most workers were not members of trade unions – indeed only around one in ten was unionised. The rest responded to changes in a variety of ways. Many accepted the prevailing orthodoxy that somehow the market would produce the 'right' level of wages. Miners in many areas went along with wages being settled by a sliding scale related to the price of coal. Thousands of others sought to improve their position by emigration. Most struggled to maintain 'respectability' on what were often erratic and uncertain earnings. The plight of most workers and their families was precarious and subject to seasonal and economic cycles and to the whims of the market.

Further reading

Fraser, W.H., *Trade Unions and Society. The Struggle for Acceptance 1850–1880* (London, Allen & Unwin, 1974)

Fraser, W.H., *A History of British Trade Unionism 1700–1998* (Basingstoke, Macmillan, 1998)

MacRaild, D.M. and Martin, D.E., *Labour in British Society, 1830–1914* (Basingstoke, Macmillan, 2000)

Royle, Edward, *Revolutionary Britannia? Reflections on the Threat of Revolution in Britain 1789–1848* (Manchester, Manchester University Press, 2000)

Wright, D.G., *Popular Radicalism. The Working-Class Experience 1780–1880* (London, Longman, 1988)

16

Politics in transition

The issue of Catholic Emancipation broke up what is sometimes called the 'second Tory party' that Liverpool and his associates had created over the previous 20 years. It had grown from Pittites and from conservative Whigs. Defence of the established church remained central to the thinking of many of them. How this could be most effectively done was what divided them. The Whig party, too, had begun to regroup from its nadir in the 1790s and by the 1820s they were united by support for Catholic Emancipation, the removal of restrictions on Dissenters and as critics of the repressive measures of 1817–1820. They were ready to consider parliamentary reform. By the end of the 1820s, the Whigs seemed to moderate Radicals to offer the prospect of peaceful constitutional change.

Whig reform

Wellington's refusal to accept that parliamentary reform was necessary or that there was genuine demand for it brought down his government in 1830. There was a groundswell of opinion among the political classes that something needed to be done. The revolution in France that overthrew the reactionary government of Charles X concentrated minds. Many interpreted its cause as the alienation of the middle classes and were ready to derive lessons for Britain.

The Whig leadership was conscious that the legitimacy of the existing system was being challenged and that some 'temperate, gradual and judicious' (in Lord Grey's words) corrections of defects that time had produced were necessary. They also had concerns about the erosion of deference towards the traditional social leaders. This they put down to the fact that too many town dwellers, beyond landowner influence, could vote in county seats. They also recognised that new wealth was able to buy its way into Parliament by the purchase of rotten boroughs, again challenging traditional local community loyalties.

In addition, many Whigs had been influenced by three decades of argument put forward by influential, opinion-shaping journals, like the *Edinburgh Review*, that there was a middle class in society that could be won over to support the existing aristocratic order. What the Whigs and their allies were not going to do, as *The Scotsman* newspaper pointed out, was to 'enable those who possess neither money nor lands, nor any ostensible community of interest with them, to tax them at pleasure, and in effect render those who have nothing, masters of the property of those who have much'.[1] It was agreed to disenfranchise tiny boroughs to release seats that would be redistributed to large boroughs and to London and the counties and to give the vote to those who held property to the value of £10 per annum in the boroughs.

On the morning of 23 March 1831, the Reform Bill, which to many Whigs seemed a shockingly bold measure, passed its second reading in the House of Commons by a majority of one. The small majority encouraged the anti-reformers and, at the committee stage, these began to emasculate the Bill. An election was called and a reform majority was returned. The Bill again passed the Commons, only to be rejected by the Lords. Continued obstruction by the House of Lords and the King's unwillingness to create enough new peers to get the measure through the Lords led to the resignation of the government in May 1832 and to Wellington's attempt to form an alternative government. When Wellington's efforts failed, Grey forced a commitment from the monarch to create the necessary number of peers if the Lords still obstructed the passage of the Bill. After a circular from the King, the hardline opponents of reform in the Lords withdrew and, in June, the England and Wales Bill was passed, with Scottish and Irish measures following in August.

The aim of the measure was to bring into the borough franchise a relatively small group of respectable, worthy property-owners. Those who occupied property of a yearly value of not less than £10 were seen as falling within this grouping. Older, in some cases more democratic, franchises, such as 'scot and lot', where male ratepayers had the vote, were gradually to be phased out as the holders died, so that, in a handful of boroughs, the franchise became *more* limited. In the counties, the 40-shilling freehold in England and Wales was left untouched, but the vote was also given to those in different kinds of rented property. £10 copy holders and £50 leaseholders were those tenants who had a substantial measure of security of tenure and whose holding could be passed on from father to son. The Chandos clause, so called after its proposer, also gave the vote to much less secure tenants-at-will on land worth £50 per year. While ministers argued that these were bound to vote at their landowner's bidding, Radicals who wanted as wide a franchise as possible combined with Tories to get the clause accepted. In practice, the clause proved to have little effect on elections.

---

[1] *The Scotsman*, 19 January 1831.

The outcome was a desperately complicated system, with neighbours who had slightly different landholdings voting in different constituencies. Someone who held a 40-shilling freehold in a borough voted for the county members. If, however, he had a house worth £10, then he lost his county vote and had to vote in the borough constituency. On the other hand, if he had a house only worth £5 in the borough, but land worth £45 outside the borough boundary, that made him a £50 county voter. It made the registration of voters, another change brought in by the Act, exceedingly complicated and provided a field day for lawyer agents of politicians working to keep their opponents off the electoral register. By 1841, around one in five adult males was eligible to vote.

The most intense debates during the passage of the Act were over the redistribution of seats rather than over the level of the franchise, as parliamentarians battled to defend their own particular areas of territorial influence. Some tiny boroughs lost their seats and these were transferred to English and Welsh industrial towns, and to other boroughs. Eight new seats were given to Scottish boroughs, four to Irish boroughs and one to Trinity College, Dublin. Twenty-six new county seats with two members were created and seven counties received an additional member. The increase in county seats ensured that landowner influence through the counties more than balanced any new pressure from the boroughs.

The Whigs were concerned not to do something dramatically new, and certainly not to make the Act a first step to further reform. The aim was to give legitimacy to the existing system. For the Whig politicians the measure was as little reform as they felt they could get away with and they were reasonably confident that they had strengthened the position of the landed interest. Popular pressure may have pushed the Whig government further than it had intended, but the Reform Act was a Whig measure. The essence of Whiggery was that property had to have a dominant voice in politics.

As soon as the Reform Bill was passed, an election was fought on the new franchise and the Whigs reaped their reward with what, on the surface, seemed a reasonable majority. But there were also 38 unreliable Irish repealers and 40 or so radicals who could not be guaranteed to support the government. Amongst the Whigs there were various shades of opinion and a great deal of independence. Although a case can be made for saying that, over the next decade, something resembling a two-party system did begin to emerge, groupings were fluid and often lacked a consistent political philosophy to bind MPs. There was also still a suspicion of 'party' and an unwillingness to accept the need for grass-roots organisation of potential supporters, that might be seen as encouraging the erosion of deference to local landed elites. There were those who recognised that post-reform politics would require a different approach and better organisation of the new voters, but the Whig leadership in particular was slow to accept this.

The Whig leadership itself was far from united and Grey's problem was to satisfy some of the expectations that were raised by reform – to keep the radicals quiet, without antagonising the more traditional Whigs. Party structures were weak and the government was not always able to control the Commons. Most of the Whig leaders much preferred to find compromises that would get them Tory support, rather than have to succumb to Radical pressure. One cannot talk of a 'Radical party', as they were a very small, very diverse group of individuals without a leader, each pursuing their own particular fad. But they represented ideas that were in the air and were influencing how people outside Parliament viewed the world. Also, individual Radical politicians were generally part of important pressure groups pressing their ideas on other politicians. Their influence on opinion, through the ever-expanding press, was out of all proportion to their numbers in the Commons. There was no one corpus of Radical ideas. Most, however, were in favour of reducing the length of parliaments, introducing the secret ballot, redrawing electoral boundaries to give greater representation to the newer more populous areas, reforming the Church of Ireland and, increasingly, repealing the Corn Laws.

Initially, there were some rapid responses to middle-class demands. The Poor Law Amendment Act of 1834 dealt with long-standing complaints by the middle class about the subsidising of rural earnings. The need for reform of urban government had often been the factor that drove the middle class into demanding parliamentary reform. An Act for Scotland, where notorious cases of civic corruption and mismanagement had been exposed over the previous 20 years, came first in 1833. In England a Royal Commission identified more than 200 corporations running boroughs. The structure of these varied. Some were elected by a handful of electors, others were unelected, self-perpetuating bodies, with new members co-opted on. In many instances, the evidence of corruption was obvious as local funds were dissipated. In other cases, the concern was to keep local expenditure to a minimum, with little done to clean or light the streets. The measure proposed was to have town councils elected by local ratepayers and to ensure that all local funds were used for the benefit of the community. The Bill was considerably amended by the House of Lords, introducing a property-qualification for councillors and allowing the appointment of unelected aldermen, to check democratic pressures. The Act, as finally passed, is a good example of Whig compromise, succumbing to public demand and to pressure from radical groups, but at the same time anxious to place a check on democracy.

The factory legislation of 1833, on the other hand, can be seen as something of a tit-for-tat by landowners against the industrial middle class. If they were to have power, the argument went, then they had to accept their obligations. It was never quite as crude as this and, like most of the reform measures, the pressures for reform came from extra-parliamentary movements able to rally cross-party support (see Chapter 18). As in almost all cases, the government was pushed reluctantly to accept reform. Their main concern was to keep down public expenditure.

One striking example of the gradual impact of public pressure on government was the Slave Emancipation Act of 1833. It was the culmination of a campaign that had lasted for more than 60 years. The anti-slavery campaign, that included many women activists, had achieved partial success in 1807, with the ban on the slave trade, but for many, the continuing existence of some 800,000 slaves in the West Indies meant that the work was unfinished. A crucial factor, that brought matters to a head, was the slave rebellion in Jamaica in 1830–1, which planters (as slave owners preferred to call themselves) blamed on the anti-slavery movement's agitation. The measure that emerged in 1833 was a compromise, with slavery replaced by a system of what was called 'apprenticeship', by which freed slaves were compelled to work for their former masters for the next seven years. They could still be punished for absenteeism by flogging and imprisonment and, in many ways, the condition of the freed slaves was worse than before, with the number of floggings increasing. Revelations of this led to a further campaign until, in 1838, the apprenticeship system was abolished. The planters were compensated with a grant of some £20 million (about £1.4 billion at 2008 prices) and the importation of indentured labour from India was permitted. How far the abolition was largely the result of a half-century of campaigning by supporters of the anti-slavery campaign, or whether it was a reflection of the decline in the economic importance of the West Indies and the loss of West Indian political influence in London, is still debated.

After two years, the Whig ministry was creaking. Disunity had come to a head over Ireland. Catholic Emancipation had not brought the expected or hoped-for tranquillity, with the administration of Ireland remaining firmly in the hands of Protestants. Embittered by disappointed aspirations, Daniel O'Connell and his group of Irish MPs moved for repeal of the Act of Union and the restoration of an Irish Parliament. As so often, the government was divided on the extent to which agitation should be mollified by concession or crushed by coercion. There was also the additional problem of the Church of Ireland – Anglican and established – to which all had to pay tithes. This was an intolerable burden for many Catholics and there was a growing refusal to pay. Yet, to do anything about it had implications for sensitive religious issues on the mainland. If establishment was threatened in Ireland, would not the established churches in Scotland and in England and Wales be similarly challenged? Also, anti-Catholicism was far from dead. For a number of Whigs, the settlement of 1688, reinforced in 1714, was a Protestant settlement. An attempt to make concessions, by suggesting that some of the Church of Ireland's considerable wealth should be utilised to provide education, led to resignations and, when Grey discovered that some of the rest of the Cabinet were negotiating with O'Connell, he too resigned.

His successor, Lord Melbourne, had a distinctly decadent air about him. The government seemed weak and the King, anxious about Radical influence, pressed for a coalition with Tories, which Melbourne refused. William IV disliked the direction that the government's Irish church reform seemed to be taking and now asked for the government's resignation – the first time a monarch had done so since 1783, and it was to be the last. On Wellington's advice, he sent for Sir Robert Peel. Attempts to stir up agitation against royal 'despotism' generated little interest. Peel tried to avoid an Ultra-Tory government and, instead, to create a broadly based *Conservative* one. The word begins to appear in political vocabulary around 1833. Parliamentary reform might have been a mistake, he argued, but there could be no going back. Conservatism was not to oppose all change but to ensure that change was gradual and controlled. The new policy was enunciated in Peel's address to his constituents in 1834, the Tamworth Manifesto. The Reform Act was 'a final and irrevocable settlement of a great constitutional question'. He would go along with the spirit of the Act if it involved merely 'a careful review of institutions, civil and ecclesiastical, undertaken in a friendly temper combining, with the firm maintenance of established rights, the correction of proved abuses and the redress of real grievances', and did not involve perpetual agitation. Peel, whose father was a successful industrialist, was trying to find a way by which a Tory tradition could be made relevant to new and powerful middle classes.

The Conservatives made gains in the 1834 election, but not enough to secure a majority against the united Whigs and Irish. O'Connell now firmly aligned himself with the Whigs in return for promised concessions short of repeal, and the alliance voted out Peel's government. Sensing that the electorate was swinging to the right, Melbourne rejected Radical demands for a programme of further bold reforms. Rather, he determinedly sought to circumvent the Radicals by attracting Conservative backing.

Church issues loomed large. In the years after Waterloo, the Church of England, and to a lesser extent, the Church of Scotland and the Church in Wales, had been subject to criticism. The Church of England had lost its political monopoly with the repeal of the Test Acts and with Catholic Emancipation. Radicals saw the established churches as part of the corrupt system that they were attacking. Dissenters – Presbyterians, Baptists, Methodists, Unitarians, Quakers, Congregationalists – while far from united among themselves, could unite in a dislike of the privileges that establishment gave. The bulk of dissenting support came from the ranks of the middle classes and the clash between Church and dissent came to represent the clash between the new, assertive middle class and the traditional landed society and older urban elites. Dissenters still had numerous specific grievances. Only an established church marriage ceremony was regarded as legal. Dissenters were liable for church rates for the upkeep of established churches and they were excluded from the universities of Oxford, Cambridge and Durham. Melbourne's government in 1836 passed the Dissenters' Marriage Act and registrars' offices were set up in England and Wales to allow registration of births, death and marriages, something which had formerly been done by Anglican priests. An attempt to abolish church rates, however, was defeated by Whig and Tory gentry, and hopes of substantial educational reform perished in sectarian rancour.

Melbourne's one source of strength was that no one wanted the government to fall. Radicals and Irish had no desire to see Peel back in power, while Peel wanted time for his Conservatism to take firm root. Melbourne's position was strengthened in 1837 by the change of monarch. George III and Queen Charlotte had 15 children but there were few legitimate heirs. The Prince Regent had done his regal duty with Caroline of Brunswick and then determined never to go near her again. The offspring of that brief union, Princess Charlotte, died in 1817. With her death, the royal dukes, most of whom were living with their mistresses, were summoned to provide an heir. Only one obliged: the Duchess of Kent produced Princess Victoria. In 1837, the new Queen was an impressionable young woman of 18, charmed by the avuncular Melbourne, and did nothing to hide her partisan enthusiasm for the Whigs. As was usual at the accession of a new monarch, an election was quickly held. The Whigs did no more than hold their own. Conservatives made gains in county seats, while Radicals fared badly. Little was achieved by the government and, after a near-defeat in 1839, Melbourne, overriding the Queen's sobs, resigned. Peel stipulated that the Queen had to get rid of the Whig courtiers and ladies of the bedchamber with whom she had surrounded herself. When she refused, Peel declined office and Melbourne returned.

In February 1840, the Queen found a substitute for Melbourne in the shape of her new husband, Prince Albert of Saxe-Coburg, who rather disapproved of Melbourne's decadent ways and admired the 'modernism' of Peel. Victoria began to warm to Conservatism. The government looked for uncontroversial measures. Pressed by Rowland Hill, at the end of 1839 they accepted a bill to establish the penny post that was launched in 1840. Some progress was made in Ireland, when, with Peel's acquiescence, the Irish Municipal Reform Act was passed.

The Whig government fell in 1841, as a result of a hostile vote on fiscal proposals. With the Chartist movement very active (see Chapter 18), the electorate's swing to the right was reaffirmed in the general election and the Conservatives were returned with a majority of 80. It was the first time that a government had been defeated in a general election by an organised opposition.

Peel's government

The Conservative-Tory government that Peel formed in 1841 was one of the most effective governments for decades. Peel was determined that he himself would be the *prime* among minsters. The government came to power in the midst of economic and social crises. Peel's policy was to get an expansion of trade by freeing it from regulation. Like Pitt, in order to replace the income lost when duties on imports were lowered, Peel turned to income tax. This he reintroduced in his budget of 1842 with a tax of 7d (3 pence) in the pound. From the surplus that this gave him, he reduced the duties on 769 articles, in particular those on raw materials. He continued this policy in later budgets and it was successful. Trade rapidly expanded and quickly made up for any loss of revenue. In 1844, Peel abolished the duty on raw cotton and allowed an expansion of the cotton industry, thus dealing with the dangerous social disorder in Lancashire.

An instinctive desire for better administration caused Peel to turn to banks and companies. The Bank Charter Act of 1844 cut through age-long controversies, pegging the amount of notes that the Bank of England could put in circulation to gold reserves. It provided a stability that had hitherto been lacking. The Companies Act of 1844 sought to eliminate the worst features of speculation and fraud by companies, making registration necessary and requiring companies to publish prospectuses and balance sheets. Although the immediate effects of both these measures were limited, they laid the foundations for future, modern administration.

The government also undertook a number of social measures, but as the Whigs before them had found, these required pressure from groups outside Parliament. Lord Ashley, himself a Conservative, took the lead in some of these, but the leaders of the government were not Tories, who hankered after a paternalistic society. Rather they were enthusiasts for *laissez-faire*, who rejected state interference with industry. The Coal Mines' Regulation Act of 1842 was passed with only lukewarm support from the government. A Factory Reform Act of 1844 fell short of what reformers had been demanding and it was not until 1847 that a Ten Hours Act was passed (see Chapter 17), motivated – if Ashley is to be believed – 'not by love of the cause, but by anger towards Peel and the Anti-Corn Law League'.[2]

Meanwhile, Ireland continued to bedevil politics. The success of monster meetings in Ireland in 1842–3, once again calling for repeal of the Union, led to the arrest of O'Connell and his fellow leaders. The courts in Dublin sentenced them to imprisonment for sedition but, at the end of 1844, the Law Lords quashed their conviction. By then, however, the heat had gone out of the campaign and the government could once again try to balance coercion with conciliation. A Royal Commission was appointed to examine Ireland's agrarian problems and a bill was introduced to allow Catholics to hold other official posts. Finally, Peel proposed to treble the annual government grant (a grant of the pre-Union Irish Parliament) of £9,000 to Maynooth College, a college that included a seminary for the training of Catholic priests. Once again, the Catholic issue unleashed an unholy row.

Within the Church of England itself, new forces were at work. Since the end of the eighteenth century, the dominant influence in the Church had been Evangelicals, who believed in personal conversion and personal responsibility for salvation, with fairly broad views on doctrine. From the 1820s, groups within the Church began to react against this and to stress the Catholicism of the Church of England. The movement became associated with a group of Oxford clerical scholars. This Oxford Movement, in a series of tracts, pressed for a restoration of ritual – some even suggesting the restoration of confession. To most Protestants, this smacked of popery and of a threat to Protestant traditions. The fact that such ideas seemed to be making advances within the Church, with some of the Tractarians crossing to Rome (as the phrase went) strengthened dissenting fears.

With religious feelings running high, Ireland was a highly sensitive issue. Many Whigs and Conservatives wanted to improve the state of education in Ireland and they recognised that this involved some concession to the Roman Catholic Church there, but Protestants were not in the mood for concession. Hostility to Peel's proposal to increase the grant to Maynooth came from different directions. Anglicans feared for the position of the Church of Ireland; Dissenters were hostile to concessions to Rome and also to state aid being given to any church body. More than 2,000 petitions against the proposal flooded into Parliament. Ultra-Tory Protestants saw this as yet another

---

[2] J.T. Ward, *The Factory Movement 1830 to 1855* (London, Macmillan, 1962), p. 110.

instance of Peel sacrificing the constitution, as he had, in their eyes, done over Catholic Emancipation. Well over 100 Tories voted against the measure and it got through only with Whig support.

These divisions were far from healed when the issue of the Corn Laws came to a head. Peel's economic policy had been a progress towards the eradication of tariffs. But the laws also had symbolic importance in the struggle between land and industry. The country gentlemen claimed that they saw ruin facing them and their tenants if protection on corn were abandoned. What they also saw was the sacrificing of landed society to the demands of the new industrial society. In the country at large the Anti-Corn Law League had been waging a powerful campaign for repeal since 1838 (see Chapter 18). Addressing the landowners who dominated in Parliament, Richard Cobden, Manchester businessman and radical politician, talked of the new era which existed:

> It is the age of improvement, it is the age of social advancement, not the age for war or feudal sports. You live in a mercantile age, when the whole wealth of the world is poured into your lap. You cannot have the advantages of commercial rents and feudal privileges, but you may be what you always have been, if you will identify yourselves with the spirit of the age.[3]

This 'spirit of the age' was in favour of commercial expansion through economic freedom.

Peel found it difficult to respond to such an argument because, although emotionally he identified with agricultural society, his intellect told him that Britain had passed the point of no return into an industrial society. Yet, he had a party to run and the debates over Maynooth showed the strength of feeling within the party. It was one of those unanswerable questions whether Peel would have been able to educate his party to accept the decisive step towards free trade. But time was not allowed. The failure of the potato in Ireland and in the Highlands of Scotland brought starvation on a massive scale and Peel feared that it would lead to food shortages in England. He suggested to the Cabinet that the laws be suspended to allow the free flow of corn into Ireland. The Cabinet split on the issue.

Peel eventually decided that there could be no half measures and that there had to be total repeal. At the beginning of 1846, he brought in a repeal bill and was greeted with an icy silence from the benches behind him. The most exotic and strangest of Tories, the young Benjamin Disraeli, led the attack on Peel. When the crucial vote came in the Commons, 242 Conservatives voted with Disraeli, and only 112 voted with Peel. The Bill was passed with the votes of Whigs and Radicals and left a residue of bitterness that split Conservative families and friendships for a generation. Peel was traduced as the man who had betrayed his party and his principles. Surprisingly, the

---

House of Lords proved more amenable and in June 1846 the Act to repeal the Corn Laws was passed, although it was not until 1850 that the final duties disappeared – long after the worst effects of famine in Ireland had passed. Set on revenge, the protectionists soon joined the Whigs to defeat another measure and Peel resigned. The Queen sent for Lord John Russell.

Why did Peel do it? As an ambitious politician, he had always recognised the need to adjust to the moods of the time. While country gentlemen who had no desire for office were willing to take a stand on principle and accept the political wilderness, this was not what Peel and ambitious younger politicians were prepared to contemplate. The Conservative option that Peel took was to try to create an alliance of landed class and middle-class business as defenders of property against Radical and democratic pressures. He accepted Cobden's argument that old institutions could survive if they were responsive to the 'spirit of the age', although he was appalled by the class hostility of Cobden and the Anti-Corn Law League. If reform had to be undertaken it was better that it be undertaken by a Conservative party rather than by Whigs in thrall to Radicals. A concession on corn might protect the aristocracy and other institutions from further radical assaults. He had always felt that the social order was fragile.

Politics without cohesion

The election of 1847 gave the Whigs a majority. But there was little unity, and politics entered two decades of transition when stable majorities proved difficult to achieve and political parties were in danger of breaking up. Russell, the leading Whig, was ready to support limited reforms, but only on his own terms, not in response to democratic demands. He believed in government by an aristocratic class, who alone had the necessary education, leisure and financial independence to have the breadth of vision to lead the nation. Their duty was to provide good government and that did not mean individual voting rights; what it meant was ensuring that all interests were represented in Parliament. Others were attracted by the former Canningite, Lord Palmerston, who, unlike the typical Whig, was learning to court public opinion through the use of the press. Civilised and intellectual in reality, he managed to project himself as in tune with popular wishes and as a hearty defender of British interests again 'the foreigner'. Both needed support from the diverse collection of Radicals who hoped that the 1832 Reform Act was the preliminary to further reform of the church, the economy, foreign policy and administration. There was now also a group of Peelites, reduced to around 50 by the election of 1847, held together by loyalty to Peel but containing most of the brightest former Conservative leaders. Many returned to the Conservatives after 1852, when protectionism was abandoned, but there were a number with liberal sympathies who were held back from aligning with the Whigs by a deep suspicion of Russell and Palmerston.

To maintain Radical support, Russell was ready to embrace further parliamentary reform. What he was hostile to was reform that was forced by popular pressure or pointed towards universal suffrage. At the Foreign Office, Palmerston was a law unto himself, consulting neither Russell nor the Queen on key decisions. When criticised for aggressive posturing against small states, he ruthlessly played the patriotic card – the defence of British interests. At the end of 1851 he went over the score by welcoming Louis Napoleon's *coup d'état* in France against the National Assembly, without consultation with the Cabinet. Russell dismissed him, but he soon got his 'tit-for-tat' in February 1852 when Palmerston and his followers voted down the government.

The Earl of Derby – the former Whig, Lord Stanley, now leader of the Conservatives – went ahead and formed a minority government. Over the previous three years, Disraeli and Stanley had managed to win round enough of their supporters to recognising that protectionism had to be abandoned and free trade accepted. In the election of 1852, the Conservatives were still in the minority, but they were allowed to continue in office largely because Palmerston, Russell and Peelites would not co-operate. Disraeli made a brave attempt at a budget that would reduce the burden on agriculture without threatening free trade, only to have it demolished line by line by the Peelite, William Gladstone, rapidly showing financial mastery. It was the first time that Gladstone and Disraeli had clashed as two masters of parliamentary rhetoric and, ironically, they both regarded themselves as defenders of different kinds of Toryism.

Since neither Russell nor Palmerston would serve under the other, the Queen sent for the distinguished elder statesman, the Peelite, Lord Aberdeen, who, with difficulty, formed a Whig-Peelite government. Russell came in as Foreign Secretary, Palmerston went to the Home Office and Gladstone to the Exchequer. At the Exchequer, Gladstone continued the policy of Peel, getting rid of many of the remaining customs duties and unpopular taxes. Duties on soap were abolished and those on tea halved. The tax on newspaper advertisements, long resented, disappeared. Government expenditure was tightly curbed and, indeed, in 1851, government expenditure of £51 million was £10 million *less* than it had been in 1826. Gladstone's hopes of cutting government expenditure further were doomed, however, because a new European war was looming. Over the next five years, government expenditure rose by 25 per cent.

The Crimean War with Russia grew out of the perennial Eastern Question: what was to replace the vacuum created by the decline of the Ottoman Empire? Aberdeen and his government were faced with conflicting considerations about how far Russian expansion against the Ottoman Empire should be resisted. The Cabinet was split, with Aberdeen working for peace and Palmerston keen for confrontation. Increasingly, public opinion, whipped up by a press encouraged by Palmerston, was urging war. Aberdeen was, very unwillingly, pushed to a declaration of war against Russia in March 1854.

Serious fighting in the Crimea did not begin until the autumn. Alas, little had altered in the military sphere since 1815. The leaders in the Crimea were veterans of the Napoleonic Wars. The administration and supply side were little improved. Stores never got off the beach; ships sank; summer kit was provided for winter wear. There was nothing particularly new in such military blunders; the difference was that in the

Figure 16.1 'Valley of the Shadow of Death', Crimea. Roger Fenton produced some 500 photographs of the Crimean War. The title of this one of the aftermath of battle, but with the bodies removed, echoes Tennyson's poem 'The Charge of the Light Brigade' at Balaclava in October 1854:

> Half a league half a league
> Half a league onward
> All in the valley of Death
> Rode the six hundred.

Source: Science & Society Picture Library, Photo by Roger Fenton

1850s they were exposed. It was the first war in which war correspondents figured, and there were even photographs. *The Times* sent W.H. Russell, who wrote about the blunders and the inefficiencies and the suffering that these brought. There was also the powerful presence of Florence Nightingale, turned into a heroic figure by *The Times*, adding her voice to the revelations.

Criticisms mounted against a Prime Minister who was half-hearted in engaging in the war. Radical MPs forced an enquiry into the running of the war and Aberdeen resigned in February 1855. He was replaced by Palmerston. Palmerston never for one moment accepted the criticisms of aristocratic rule, but he was able to quieten them as the war moved on to victory. Sevastopol fell in September 1855 and peace was signed at Paris in February 1856.

Palmerston's government

The end of the war allowed the old tensions and rivalries within government to reappear. Groups were constantly shifting their allegiance; individuals were ready to trade their vote in return for office or favours. The ideological differences seemed to be slight and, with relative social stability in the more prosperous 1850s, there was little in the way of extra-parliamentary popular politics to encourage unity among the political class. The middle-class leaders, Bright and Cobden, who had stood out against the war, were effectively isolated and the working class had shown itself largely supportive of the war. The demands for change seemed muted. When in 1857, Russell, Gladstone, Cobden, Disraeli and Radicals combined to censure the government over its aggressive policy against China, Palmerston dissolved Parliament and was able to achieve a comfortable victory in the subsequent election. Parliamentary reform and the rise of a successful business middle class had not, it seemed, led to dramatic changes in politics. An aristocratic ruling elite still held sway and the reformed electorate had given support to someone who held them in contempt and who was a survivor of the days of the Prince Regent.

Palmerston's post-war popularity outside Parliament was more secure than his majority in Parliament, but his strength there lay in the fact that there was not an obvious alternative who could command enough support. Palmerston now proceeded to act as a major barrier to any further parliamentary reform. He did not believe that aristocrat rule was yet done. He had little but contempt for the middle classes and yet he managed to persuade them that he stood for something different. He did not believe that the working class was fit for the vote since they were open to bribery and intimidation. He was reflecting a widely held Liberal view that the ideal voter was a man who had property and intelligence that would give him the ability to form an independent and reasoned judgement.

A majority in the Commons was still not easy to maintain. Palmerston's government was, in fact, defeated in 1858, when, in the aftermath of an unsuccessful attempt by an Italian nationalist to blow up the French emperor, Napoleon III, Palmerston sought to make it a criminal offence to manufacture 'infernal machines' in Britain, with the intent of murdering foreign politicians. Some 80 Liberals rebelled and another minority Conservative government under Lord Derby came into power, although it was outnumbered three to one in the Commons. It kept going until March 1859, as a result of the tacit support of those who were opposed to Palmerston's return. It was a measure of how pragmatic the Conservatives had become that they actually brought forward a Reform Bill in 1859, but it was defeated as, once again, the Liberals were ready to unite.

Another thing that middle-class Radicals had always wanted was a moral foreign policy. Richard Cobden, particularly, had argued that Britain should not adopt the role of the world's policeman or use the strength of the navy to interfere in all parts of the world. He had been especially critical of Palmerston's bluster. However, foreign policy issues actually united Whigs and Radicals. The first issue was the Italian

Risorgimento of 1859, when the small state of Piedmont, assisted by Napoleon III, led the struggle against Austrian domination. The Conservative government tended to be suspicious of Napoleon's intentions and, like the court, pro-Austrian in attitude. Liberals, on the other hand, were pro-Italy. Palmerston and Russell could unite on this; so could most of the Radicals. Then there were the leading, remaining Peelites, in particular Gladstone. Gladstone, once the 'hope of the stern, unbending Tories', had become a firm supporter of Italian nationalist ambitions. Although the term 'Liberal Party' was, from the 1830s, used to describe the combination of Whigs and Radicals, it was a most unstable and unreliable combination. There is a strong case for arguing that it is from the summer of 1859 that one can date the formation of the Liberal Party in Parliament, reflecting a process that had been going on in the country through various voluntary organisations and through the expansion of a Liberal provincial press. Whigs, Radicals and the few remaining Peelites united around a number of key beliefs – free trade, limited government intervention in domestic affairs, a Liberal foreign policy. Such was the euphoria that Russell even agreed to serve under Palmerston. The government lasted until 1865 and solidified the grouping into the Liberal Party.

To a large extent, the Radicals found their foreign policy accepted. Palmerston did not interfere in the various international issues that arose. Gladstone at the Exchequer pinned his hopes on the motto: 'peace, retrenchment and reform', and set his face against rising state expenditure. He continued to extend free trade by removing duties, including, in 1861, the excise duty on paper – one of the notorious 'taxes on knowledge'. Palmerston was no enthusiast for a cheap press and resisted the abolition of paper duties, but Radicals were not going to destroy the new-found Liberal unity. Consequently, the first five years of the 1860s were in many ways a marking of time, with people taking sides for or against further constitutional change, which, it was felt, was bound to follow Palmerston's departure. Palmerston held on until the last. He did not resign, but called an election in July 1865. The Liberal majority again increased, but Palmerston never met the Commons. In October, he died and all were agreed that 'the quiet time was over'. The demand for a further extension of the franchise that had been bubbling beneath the surface of politics burst forth again (see Chapter 18).

Liberals, Tories and reform

Palmerston had always rejected the argument that everyone had a right to the vote: 'what every man and women too has a right to is to be well governed and under just laws, and they who propose a change ought to show that the present organisation does not accomplish those objects'. But some of his colleagues were changing their attitude. Most important of all was Gladstone, until now very much a figure of the political right in all except his free-trade economic policies. However, in a debate in 1864 on a private member's reform proposal, Gladstone made what was regarded as a sensational statement:

> And I venture to say that every man who is not presumably incapacitated by some consideration of personal unfitness or of political danger is morally entitled to come within the pale of the Constitution.

Gladstone's motives, as always, are cloudy. He was undoubtedly impressed by the deputations of working men whom he had met. He had also been impressed by John Bright's arguments that Lancashire workers were supporting the Northern cause in the American Civil War, despite the unemployment created by cotton shortages. These had shown 'self-command, self-control, respect for order, patience under suffering, confidence in the law, regard for superiors', all criteria in Gladstone's eyes for the franchise. There were also narrower partisan concerns. Gladstone had, by now, a deep distrust of Disraeli and he feared a situation where the Conservatives might start outbidding the Liberals on reform and turn it into a party issue. At the same time, he can be seen as putting down a marker for radical support for the future leadership. He could count on Whig, right-wing support since he was seen as a conservative figure, but to be sure of the leadership he had to attract Radicals. He was no democrat. He was a landowner, a high churchman and a strong defender of the Anglican establishment. But in 1864 he had his eye on the future leadership.

Russell, once again leader of the Liberals, arrived at Downing Street, as always, with a reform bill in mind, but facing an anti-reform Parliament. Russell had the usual task of all Liberal leaders of trying to satisfy the Radical wing of the party without antagonising the Whig wing. Gladstone was given the job of working out the details of a bill and, in March 1866, he proposed a very moderate measure of giving the vote to those men in borough constituencies who paid £7 per annum rates or rental for their houses. It would have added little more than 150,000 to the electorate. Not surprisingly, it aroused no enthusiasm amongst Radicals, but it was enough to antagonise a group within the Liberal Party that became focused around Robert Lowe, a group dubbed 'the Cave of Adullam' by John Bright.[4] Lowe was an intense, rather embittered character, an albino, not from a landed background, but largely self-made. In most ways he was an archetypal Liberal, no defender of hereditary privilege and a firm believer in a *laissez-faire* state. He put the anti-democratic case with great effect. Men, he argued, were unequal in ability: 'It is the order of Providence that men should be unequal, and it is the wisdom of the State to make its institutions conform to that order.' He questioned the assumption that reform was inevitable and the belief that it was for the good of the country. What had to be shown, he argued, was that reform would make the government better or more stable. What was needed was government of the educated, the most intellectually able, not of the masses. The Adullamites united with the Conservatives to defeat the government's measure.

---

[4] The reference is to the first Book of Samuel in the Bible, Chapter 22, where David was in hiding from King Saul: 'All those who were in distress, or in debt or discontented gathered round him, and he became their leader.'

Focus on

The claims of the working classes in 1866–7

This is taken from a speech of Robert Lowe, the leader of the group of Liberals opposed to parliamentary reform and dubbed 'the Adullamites' by John Bright.

> I would point out that the working classes, under the modest claim to share in electoral power, are really asking for the whole of it. Their claim is to pass from the position of non-electors to the position of sovereign arbiters in the last resort of the destinies of the nation. They who set up such a claim must show that they are masters of themselves before they can hope to be masters of others. One of the first qualifications of power should be a willingness to hear both sides – those who say what is unpleasing, as well as those who say what is smooth. They must not seek to limit the field of discussion by their own susceptibilities. They must expect to be critically surveyed and canvassed before they can persuade the present depositaries of power to abdicate in their favour. If it is competent for me to argue that with a little self-denial the franchise is already within the reach of many of them; that they will swamp the less numerous classes; that the expenses of elections will be increased, and the character of the House of Commons impaired; it is also competent for me to urge that since corruption and the other electoral vices prevail most in the lower ranks of the present constituencies, it is unwise and unsafe to go lower in search of virtue.

Source: Robert Lowe, *Speeches and Letters on Reform* (1867), p. 16.

The Conservatives under Lord Derby, with Disraeli leading in the Commons, returned with yet another minority government. They were faced with the problem of what do about reform, since the resignation of the government and Lowe's remarks had unleashed a more intense popular agitation. Clearly, there was anxiety about the size of the street demonstrations taking place, but there was also the argument that a Conservative government could keep control of any measure and make sure that it was a modest one. As usual, the Conservatives, although in a minority, wanted to hold on to office as long as possible. If they took up the reform issue, then the divided Liberals might allow them to continue in office. There were always attractions in keeping the Liberals divided and perhaps even a chance of wooing some of the Adullamites permanently into the Conservative ranks. It would also show that Conservatives were capable of dealing with the foremost issue of the moment. Derby declared that he had no intention of his government again being 'a mere stopgap until it should suit the convenience of the Liberal Party to forget their dissentions'.

Disraeli's proposals of March 1867 would have added about 500,000 extra, mainly working-class, voters in the boroughs. However, any increased working-class influence would be counteracted by a system of plural voting, whereby the wealthy would have another vote. Both Gladstone and Lowe were appalled by the proposals, believing that the safeguards against working-class dominance would prove unworkable. The Liberals were deeply at odds on how to respond. Disraeli's proposals went as far as many radicals really wanted and, therefore, were difficult to oppose, but Gladstone was determined to resist. When the bill reached the committee stage, almost all the proposed safeguards against democracy disappeared as radical amendments were accepted. Many reasons have been put forward for the transformation of a moderate measure into one that went further than most politicians had contemplated. Undoubtedly, there was not always clarity about the implications of what was being decided and there was a sense of the parliamentary game of 'dishing the Whigs' taking over. Although there was fear of popular unrest, the tactical struggle of keeping the Liberals divided seemed to drive the changes. Also, the Conservatives could be reasonably relaxed about what they were proposing since reform of the franchise was confined only to the boroughs; the county franchise remained the same, with more seats given to the counties, which were good Conservative territory. The largest cities of Glasgow,[5] Birmingham, Leeds, Liverpool and Manchester were each given a third member, but voters had only two votes. There was a chance that Conservatives could perhaps squeeze in as third member by 'plumping' for a single Conservative candidate. The large boroughs were not Conservative territory and granting the vote to the working class in the towns was not going to alter the political balance dramatically. The second Reform Act did not usher in democracy, although it added 88 per cent to the existing electorate: 938,000 voters. But for some towns it made a dramatic difference. The electorate of Birmingham went up four-fold; that of Leeds, six-fold and the new borough of Merthyr Tydfil now had ten times the number of voters.

Gladstone's first ministry

Lord John Russell resigned the leadership of the Liberal Party at the end of 1866 and Gladstone took over. In the election of 1868 the Liberals had a majority of 106 over the Conservatives. Liberals gains, however, were mainly in Wales and Scotland, with the Conservatives doing well in industrial Lancashire, where hostility to the Irish was strong. Gladstone had made a commitment to tackle some of the Irish issues.

In the aftermath of the famine, a nationalist movement had revived, not among the people of rural Ireland but among the urban middle class. An attempted uprising by the Young Ireland movement in 1848 was defeated. One of the rebels, James Stephen, founded the Irish Republican Brotherhood – quickly dubbed the Fenians – at the end

---

[5] There were separate Reform Acts for Scotland and Ireland in 1868.

of the 1850s. The Fenians rejected constitutional action and kept Irish discontents in the public eye with occasional atrocities and by stirring declarations. There were bomb explosions in a number of mainland cities. An attempt to rescue some Fenian prisoners being transferred to Manchester gaol resulted in the shooting of a prison guard. Three Fenians were convicted of the murder and executed, quickly being transformed into 'martyrs' for nationalism.

The attempts to suppress unrest involved the usual harsh coercion during 1866–7, but also produced pressure for conciliation. The Anglican Church of Ireland, to which only about a tenth of the Irish population belonged, was disestablished in 1869. Although the Church lost its endowments, thanks to pressure in the House of Lords it was well compensated. Some of the remaining income was diverted into poor relief, agriculture and education and even into donations to the Presbyterian and Catholic Churches for church building. Land reform in Ireland was less easily dealt with, and although the Land Act of 1870 gave some rights to tenants who were evicted to compensation for improvements made, it fell well short of their demands. There was, however, some recognition of tenants' moral rights to land – much to the outrage of many landlords, who saw the act as an infringement of the rights of property.

The measures did little to 'pacify' Ireland. In the summer of 1870, Isaac Butt, a Tory in politics, had formed the broad, interdenominational Home Government Association, calling for a Dublin Parliament to deal with Irish domestic affairs. The aim was a limited devolution of power within Britain. Soon numbers of the more moderate Fenians in Britain began to pin their hopes on this organisation. Home Rulers won 60 seats in the 1874 election.

Elsewhere, able ministers pushed ahead with reforms and the government, in a manner that had not existed in the past, saw the main measure of its success as getting through legislation. At the War Office, Edward Cardwell instituted extensive changes. To encourage recruiting, shorter enlistments were introduced and regiments were given a territorial identity. Troops were pulled back from the dominions. Flogging was abolished, as was the purchase of commissions. There is no evidence that the last measure made the officer corps any less exclusive. Entrance to Sandhurst, even at the end of the century, still exclusively depended on a public school or university background. The arcane legal system, so powerfully lampooned by Dickens in *Bleak House*, was modernised, with the reorganisation of the courts. Reform of the civil service, first embarked on in the 1850s, was carried a little further by opening the most senior civil service posts (except in the Foreign Office) to competitive examinations, though ones very much geared to the pattern of education offered in private schools and at Oxford and Cambridge. To please John Bright, rather than because of public demand, secret voting was introduced by the Ballot Act of 1872.

Trade unions and their allies had been remarkably successful in getting across their case before the Royal Commission on Trade Unions and Employers' Associations between 1867 and 1869. A Trade Union Act of 1871 gave protection to the funds of registered unions and removed the illegality of being 'in restraint of trade'. However, as a result of employer pressure within the Liberal Party, it was followed by a Criminal

Law Amendment Act, which drastically limited the actions that unionists could take during a strike. The Home Secretary, H.A. Bruce, sought to respond to temperance pressure with a Licensing Act in 1872, that brought restrictions on the hours of drinking in English and Welsh public houses. It was deeply unpopular and led to rioting in some towns. The Bishop of Peterborough, responsive to the popular mood, declared, 'England free better than England sober'.

There was educational reform, with the opening up of most academic posts at Oxford and Cambridge to Nonconformists in 1869. The Endowed Schools Act of the same year allowed charitable foundations to be reformed to create grammar schools for the middle classes, while the Elementary Education Act of 1870 in England and Wales and the Elementary Education (Scotland) Act of 1872 in Scotland ensured elementary education was provided for all (and in Scotland was compulsory). The state, in England, did not take responsibility for all schools and education was not free.[6] Church schools were allowed to continue and local school boards were established with the sole task of filling gaps in the voluntary system. The Bill was passed only with the help of Conservative votes, while, in the country at large, the National Education League, which had been campaigning for non-denominational education, organised protests and generated what has been dubbed the 'Nonconformist revolt'.

Disraelian Conservatism

Important as many of these measures were, they had limited popular appeal and their effect would take time to be properly felt. There were still only limited efforts by the Liberal leaders to connect with the new, popular electorate. The 'Nonconformist revolt', along with trade-union discontent, probably played its part in the Liberal defeat in the election that Gladstone called suddenly in January 1874, although Gladstone blamed the brewers and the pub landlords. For the first time since 1841, the Conservatives swept to power, with a majority of 83. In a speech at the Crystal Palace in 1872, that became famous largely with hindsight, Disraeli had sounded the keynote of future Conservatism. He identified its policies as 'the maintenance of our institution, the preservation of our empire, and the improvement in the condition of the people'. There were signs in 1874 that the Conservatives were able to attract both working-class voters and recruits from within business who were anxious about Gladstone's radicalism.

Disraeli's government, which was keen not to have any more constitutional reform, quickly responded to its new working-class constituency with social legislation. The Criminal Law Amendment Act was replaced by the Conspiracy and Protection of Property Act, which specifically permitted peaceful picketing. The Employer and Workman Act replaced the long-established terminology of 'master' and 'servant' and

---

[6] Education in England became largely compulsory in 1880 and elementary education was free after 1891.

Focus on

Disraeli and the Conservative Party

This is taken from a speech by the leader of the Conservative Party, Benjamin Disraeli at Crystal Palace on 24 June 1872.

> The Tory party, unless it is a national party, is nothing. It is not a confederacy of nobles, it is not a democratic multitude; it is a party formed from all the numerous classes of the realm – classes alike and equal before the law, but whose different conditions and different aims give vigour and variety to our national life.
>
> A body of public men distinguished by their capacity took advantage of these circumstances. They seized the helm of affairs in a manner, the honour of which I do not for a moment question, but they introduced a new system into our national life. Influenced in a great degree by the philosophy and politics of the Continent, they endeavoured to substitute cosmopolitan for national principles; and they baptized the new scheme of politics with the plausible name of 'Liberalism' . . . But the tone and tendency of Liberalism cannot be long concealed. It is to attack the institutions of the country in the name of Reform, and to make war on the manners and customs of the people of this country under the pretext of Progress . . .
>
> I have always been of the opinion that the Tory party has three great objects. The first to maintain the institutions of the country – not from any sentiment of political superstition, but because we believe that they embody the principles upon which a community like England can alone safely rest. The principles of liberty, of order, of law, and of religion ought not to be entrusted to individual opinion or to the caprice and passions of multitudes, but should be embodied in a form of permanence and power. We associate with the Monarchy the ideas which it represents – the majesty of the law, the administration of justice, the fountain of mercy and of honour. We know that in the Estates of the Realm and the privileges they enjoy, is the best security for public liberty and good government. We believe that a national profession of faith can only be maintained by an Established Church, and that no society is safe unless there is a public recognition of the Providential government of the world, and of the future responsibility of man . . .
>
> There is another and second great object of the Tory party. If the first is to maintain the institutions of the country, the second in my opinion is to uphold the Empire of England. If you look to the history of this country since the advent of Liberalism – forty years ago – you will find that there has been no effort so continuous, so subtle, supported by so much energy, and carried on with so much ability and acumen as the attempts of Liberalism to effect the disintegration of the Empire of England.

Source: T.E. Kebbel (ed.), *Selected Speeches of the Earl of Beaconsfield*, Volume II (London, 1882), pp. 527–9.

gave employer and employee equality before the law in breach of contract cases. The need for better working-class housing was pushed and Disraeli talked of the state's responsibility to provide pure air, pure water, pure food, healthy houses and public recreation. How far it was mere political expediency that produced the reforms is difficult to assess. Disraeli himself largely left it to individual ministers to take up issues that came to their attention. There was little sign of a coherent policy.

In foreign policy, however, there was a break with the past. There were signs of imperial ambition with the purchase, from the bankrupt Khedive of Egypt, of a large block of shares in the Suez Canal Company, and the transformation of the Queen into Empress of India. Little was done to restrain expansionist policies in southern Africa against both Zulus and Boers (see Chapter 19). There was also a growing determination to resist Russian advance in Central Asia and against the Ottoman Empire. An invasion of Afghanistan ended in disaster, but it was the decision to back the Turks to the extent of threatening war against Russia that divided the nation. On one side there was the jingoism of the music halls: 'We don't want to fight but, by jingo if we do, we've got the men, we've got the ships, we've got the money too.' On the other side there was Gladstone, who had largely withdrawn from politics after 1874, returning to the scene and taking up the issue, that some of the Radical journals had been pursuing, of Turkish atrocities against Christian subjects on the edges of the Ottoman Empire in Bulgaria. With an election looming, in 1879, he widened the criticisms into a general denunciation of the expansionist and aggressive policies that the Conservatives had been encouraging. In a series of powerful speeches in the constituency of Midlothian in 1879 and 1880 he denounced 'Beaconsfieldism'[7] and called for morality in foreign policy. He denounced the use of force as a means of settling international differences and the readiness to attack weaker countries under the pretence of defending British interests. The rights of all nations needed to be recognised, disputes should be settled by 'the concert of Europe' and 'needless and entangling' engagements should be avoided. In Scotland, at any rate, these speeches had a powerful appeal.

Despite the reforms and changes that had taken place, British politics in 1880 still remained dominated by the aristocracy. Reform acts might come and go, but the Cavendishes, the Cecils, the Stanleys and others continued to exercise immense power and influence. An analysis of 652 MPs made in 1865 found that 326 were members of the peerage or the baronetage or connected to these by marriage,

> They have a common freemasonry of blood, a common education, common
> pursuits, common ideas, a common dialect, a common religion and – what more
> than any other thing binds men together – a common prestige, a prestige growled
> at occasionally, but on the whole conceded, and even, it must be owned, secretly liked
> by the country at large.[8]

---

[7] Disraeli had been created Earl of Beaconsfield in 1878.

[8] *Essays on Reform*, no. vii, quoted in W.L. Burn, *The Age of Equipoise* (London, Allen & Unwin, 1964), p. 313.

Much the same could still have been said of the Parliament of 1874, in spite of the huge advances in middle-class wealth and power. But, by the end of the decade, there were signs of crisis as the returns from agricultural land began to shrink rapidly and the aristocratic hold on power gradually began to weaken. The Liberal Party was now seen as, to a large extent, the voice of the middle class while, at the same time, able to attract support from the organised working class. The strength of Liberalism was its breadth: it embraced a movement and a wide variety of voluntary organisations, held together by the idea that political and social progress was possible. It embraced all those who believed in crusading for change. But, as ever, this was an uneasy alliance and, in the Conservative victory of 1874, there were already signs of elements of the middle class feeling too many concessions were being made to the working class.

Aspects of politics had changed markedly since 1832. New studies of political change have argued that, rather than becoming progressively more democratic, in some senses, Britain became less so. Politics became much more structured and the political arena more narrowly defined. In the eighteenth century, a riot had been part of the political process, a way of sending messages of discontent to those in authority. By the nineteenth century, it was unacceptable as a form of protest. Politics after 1832 were increasingly organised through political parties, broad coalitions of all social classes, and these created their own identity by the language they used and how they interpreted the past. After the Ballot Act of 1872, politics for most people were merely something one read about in the newspaper, not something that involved real participation.

Further reading

Briggs, A., *The Age of Improvement 1783–1867* (London, Longman, 1979)

Hilton, Boyd, *A Mad, Bad and Dangerous People? England, 1783–1846* (Oxford, Clarendon Press, 2006)

Hoppen, K.T., *The Mid-Victorian Generation 1846–1886* (Oxford, Oxford University Press, 1998)

Jenkins, T.A., *The Liberal Ascendancy 1830–1886* (Basingstoke, Macmillan, 1994)

Newbould, I., *Whiggery and Reform, 1830–41. The Politics of Government* (Stanford, California, 1990)

Parry, J.P., *The Rise and Fall of Liberal Government in Victorian Britain* (New Haven and London, Yale University Press, 1993)

Vincent, J.R., *The Formation of the British Liberal Party* (London, Constable, 1966)

17

The growth of the state

How the state grew

A great paradox of this half-century is that, while *laissez-faire* was everywhere declared the prevailing philosophy of the age, in practice, the role of the state continued to expand. The transformation to an industrial and increasingly urban society put an immense strain on the older institutions that administered the state. From the 1830s, most politicians accepted that the government had some responsibility for policing and some welfare and that these could not be left entirely to voluntary effort. Legislation was passed bringing state regulation into factories, mines, education and public houses. Aspects of the economy were shaped by railway acts, banking and company regulation; the Post Office was reformed; the telegraph nationalised; the contents of food regulated; and measures taken to improve public health. The civil service and the police force expanded and municipal authorities extended their control of markets, docks, water and gas. In other words, there was at least the start of a 'revolution in government' in these years, although it was fitful and halting. How far this came about as a result of ideological conviction, administrative momentum, external pressure groups, the work of key individuals, or political circumstances continues to be debated.

Oliver MacDonagh presented a persuasive five-step model.[1] First, some social evil was exposed by a mining disaster, or a ship sinking, or by some written exposé. A humanitarian, largely Christian-driven, concern led to a demand for action and this produced a hurried piece of legislation in response. The second stage was a recognition that the legislation was not working well and, therefore, some mechanism was

---

[1] O. MacDonagh, 'The Nineteenth-Century Revolution in Government: A Reappraisal', *Historical Journal*, I (1958).

necessary to ensure its efficacy, such as the appointment of inspectors. The third stage was that the inspectors were able to expose the areas where legislation was not working and state how it could be improved. The fourth stage was the realisation that there needed to be a continuing use of executive powers in response to change. This led finally to a bureaucratic momentum for reform.

This model, in its turn, has been attacked as one that belittled the role of men and ideas. The assumption that social evils would somehow inevitably be righted by a society once they were exposed was particularly challenged. Social reforms, it was argued, had to be won in battles against vested interests, obscurantism and timidity. Committed reformers were central, not only because they came up with practical solutions to specific problems, but because they provided the justification for social action to improve the conditions and the morality of people. Individual reformers played key roles in shaping government policy and in propagating ideas of centralisation and inspection. Yet others have focused on the influence of Christian evangelicalism that was ready to combine state involvement and voluntary effort in its concern for the plight of the less well-off. Governments, both Whig/Liberal and Tory, tended to be relatively pragmatic in their approach, responding to pressure, doing what seemed easiest and always having to justify any expansion of the state's role.

The Poor Law

Justices of the peace, who administered the counties, had long been involved with the plight of the destitute, as much from worries about the dangers of vagabonds as from altruism. As a result of the social disruption caused by industrial and agricultural change and the prolonged depression in farming after 1813, the problem of pauperism was growing. With an increasingly mobile population, it was no longer possible to expect people to rely on family, neighbours, church and parish of birth for charity. The existing Poor Law in England came under attack from a number of directions. Some argued against any state involvement and that the poorest should be taken care of by private, Christian charity. The example of Scotland was frequently cited, where responsibility largely lay with the established Church of Scotland, and where Revd. Thomas Chalmers claimed that only charity delivered through the churches could maintain the essential personal relationship between giver and receiver. Yet others insisted that state provision of poor relief only encouraged dependency and discour- aged the poor from helping themselves. Another clergyman, Thomas Malthus, and his followers warned that resources would be overwhelmed unless population growth among the poorest was checked by moral restraint, and any system of poor relief was likely to undermine that restraint and encourage the poor to breed. Political economists reasoned that the more that went on poor relief, the less was the sum available for wages. They recommended that people should be encouraged to move to areas of economic growth, providing labour for the new factories. Existing laws that tied people to the parish of their birth in order to get relief were a barrier to labour mobility.

Finally, there were the complaints from those who were bearing what was perceived as a growing burden of poor rates, with businessmen in some areas particularly critical of a Poor Law that taxed them so that farmers could keep wages low by having them supplemented with poor relief.

Perhaps the last, together with fears triggered by the 'Captain Swing' disturbances of 1830, was the factor that persuaded the Whig government to act, and set up a Royal Commission on the Poor Laws in 1832. The great influence and source of ideas on the Royal Commission was Edwin Chadwick, who had been secretary to the philosopher, Jeremy Bentham in the last years of his life. Bentham had long argued that the old trappings of government and administration should be swept away, since institutions survived long after they were past their use-by date. Bentham's extensive writings were a great fount of ideas that others took up, propagated and developed, particularly in the publications of the philosophical radicals associated with the journal the *Westminster Review*.

The best-known summary of what Benthamism, or utilitarianism, was about is the phrase: 'the greatest happiness of the greatest number'. That should be the aim of society. It could be achieved by combining the maximum amount of freedom with the maximum amount of social responsibility. In other words, government intervention had to be kept to a minimum, but, in dealing with certain social problems, *laissez-faire* was not possible. Nor, Bentham had argued, could such matters be left to the vagaries of local bodies. Efficient administration demanded centralisation, so that an agreed policy could be carried out correctly and uniformly. This was the blueprint on which Edwin Chadwick and other Benthamites built over the next 30 years or so.

The report of the Royal Commission contained a sweeping – and to some extent unjustified – condemnation of the existing system, that left responsibility to local justices of the peace. The report sought to formulate a new policy to meet the needs of an industrialising society. It proposed a central board to administer a uniform Poor Law across the country. Under the board would be local boards of guardians from groups of parishes. These unions of parishes would allow for greater efficiency and the means to afford permanent officials and to build the workhouses that were essential to the new system.

The Commission had been particularly agitated by the amount of poor relief that seemed to be going to able-bodied men and their families. Under the new system, no help would be given to the able-bodied without their working in return, and such work would be carried out in workhouses. These, in turn, were intended to act as a deterrent to pauperism. The principle of 'less eligibility' was laid down. The position of the able-bodied pauper would always be 'less eligible', less congenial, than that of the lowest-paid independent labourer: 'Every penny bestowed that tends to render the condition of the pauper more eligible than that of the independent labourer is a bounty to indolence and vice.' People had to be deterred from looking to the state and the destitute had to be separated from the merely poor.

The recommendations of the report were translated into legislation by the Poor Law Amendment Act of 1834. A Central Board, with Chadwick as its secretary, oversaw the introduction of the new provisions. For the next 70 years, the principles laid down in the 1834 Act – with an Irish Act following in 1838 and a Scottish one in 1845 – were the ones by which pauperism was treated. There is evidence of the persistence of local variations, but the harsh conditions of the 1834 Poor Law left huge numbers who had to live in conditions of deepest poverty. The structure of the Poor Law Unions meant that the highest poor rates were in the poorest areas, often in the heart of cities from which the middle classes were moving out to the suburbs. Those left were the small shopkeepers and tradesmen whose concern was to keep down rates. Since these were often the people who ran the boards of guardians, they tended to be fairly frugal with the distribution of aid.

Although workhouses remained among the most hated institutions of the Victorian era, it would be quite wrong to see policies on the relief of poverty as static or uniform. The administrators in charge responded to changing circumstances. Concern about orphans led to the creation of some comparatively reasonable schools for pauper children. The need to deal with sick paupers led to the creation of Poor Law hospitals that, in time, were to become the main hospital provision for many beyond the ranks of the destitute. In dealing with long-term unemployment, various schemes were tried, including the establishment of what were called 'labour colonies', where the long-term unemployed would be re-introduced to the discipline of work and outdoor relief for the able-bodied continued to be provided at times of crisis.

Public health

Directly related to the question of the Poor Law was the issue of public health. The linking personality was Edwin Chadwick. Chadwick was alarmed by the economic wastage involved in disease and death and concerned at the burden placed on poor rates by those with ill health. On Chadwick's initiative, the Poor Law Commission called on three campaigning doctors in 1838 to examine conditions affecting health in a number of London parishes. Their report showed that masses of the population were living in physical conditions that made healthy life impossible. Many houses were unfit for human habitation in the overcrowded, undrained, uncleaned, unregulated wynds and 'rookeries' of central London. Water supplies were inadequate and fevers were rampant among the 77,000 or so paupers. The work was confined to London, but in 1839, the Bishop of London (a friend of Chadwick) moved for a national inquiry into the sanitary condition of the labouring classes. No money was granted and the inquiry was only carried out by the sheer determination of Chadwick. The result was the *Report on the Sanitary Condition of the Labouring Classes of Great Britain and Ireland*, published in 1842. It was largely Chadwick's own work and the Poor Law Commissioners declined to be associated with it, but its influence was to be great.

Chadwick's analysis of the causes of disease was quite erroneous, blaming 'atmospheric impurities' generated by decomposing animal and vegetable matter, though he linked this to the damp and filth that existed in closely packed, overcrowded

Focus on

The Poor Law

This is an extract from the *Fourth Report of the Poor Law Commissioners* (1838).

In general, all epidemics and all infectious diseases are attended with charges immediate and ultimate, on the poor-rates. Labourers are suddenly thrown, by infectious disease, in a state of destitution, for which immediate relief must be given. In the case of death, the widow and the children are thrown as paupers on the parish. The amount of burthens thus produced is frequently so great as to render it good economy on the part of the administrators of the poor laws to incur the charges for preventing the evils, where they are ascribable to physical causes, which there are no other means of removing. The more frequent course has been, where the causes of disease are nuisances, for the parish officers to indict the parties for nuisance, and to defray the expenses from the poor-rates. . . .

We have eagerly availed ourselves of the opportunity of making the present Report to submit to your Lordship the urgent necessity of applying to the Legislature for immediate measures for the removal of these constantly acting causes of destitution and death. All delay must be attended with extensive misery, and we would urge the consideration of the fact, that in a large proportion of cases the labouring classes, though aware of the surrounding causes of evil, have few or no means of avoiding them, and little or no choice of their dwellings. The Boards of Guardians have now the services of an efficient body of officers, including experienced medical officers, to guide them in the application of sanatory measures more efficiently than was practicable by the overseers of single parishes under the old system. Until more complete measure could be obtained, and even as a temporary measure, we should recommend that the guardians should be empowered to exercise the like powers that have heretofore been irregularly incurred by parish officers; that they should be empowered to indict parties responsible for such nuisances as those described, and to make arrangements with the owners of property, or take such measures, according to circumstances, for the removal of the causes of disease in cases where there is no ostensible party who can be required to perform the duty. So extreme has been the social disorder, and so abject the poverty of some of the places which are now the seats of disease, that great numbers of dwellings have been entirely abandoned.

Source: Fourth Annual Report of the Poor Law Commissioners for England and Wales, 1838, BPP 1837–38, XXVIII, 145.

dwellings. A wrong analysis came with a reasonably correct solution. There was a need for better drainage, for the removal of refuse from the streets and for the improvement in the supply of water, all of which would eradicate the things that caused people to succumb to disease. Such reforms, he argued, should be carried out by the public authorities because, in the end, it 'would be a pecuniary gain, by diminishing the existing charges attendant on sickness and premature mortality'. He also stressed the need for uniformity and for a national system developed by trained and knowledge-able civil engineers.

The outcome was a Royal Commission on the Health of Towns, that reported in 1844. Meanwhile, Parliament began to take other steps, with a committee recommending changes in legislation to allow towns to proceed with improvement measures without the expense of having to get private acts of Parliament. Also, on the initiative of the Poor Law Commissioners, free public vaccination against smallpox was offered, without any of the stigma of pauperism and loss of civil rights that attached to other aspects of the Poor Law. The Royal Commission's report itself did not make an immediate impact, but it was followed by the formation of a pressure group, the Health of Towns Association, the brainchild of Dr Southwood Smith, another Benthamite. It spread from London to many of the larger cities. The reformers' efforts came up against powerful apathy and hostility from vested interests, such as the water companies and the factory owners, and the opposition of the Home Secretary, the former Whig, Sir James Graham.

In spite of the apathy, the propaganda did begin to have some effect. In 1846, Liverpool Corporation got a Sanitary Act passed which allowed it to take control of drainage, paving and cleansing out of the hands of small local commissions. It also allowed for the appointment of the country's first Medical Officer of Health. The city of London appointed its first MOH, John Simon, in 1848, but most other cities were slow to follow: Glasgow in 1862, Leeds not until 1866, Manchester in 1868, Birmingham in 1872, and Newcastle in 1873.

After a number of abortive efforts, an act was eventually passed in 1848, incorporating some of the suggestions of earlier reports. This Public Health Act, which covered England and Wales, was the first national public health measure, although it was, in fact, a rather patchy compromise and did not provide the kind of comprehensive sanitary system for which Chadwick had hoped. He wanted to bypass the municipal authorities, as too small, too much in the hands of often conflicting vested interests and lacking the necessary expertise. What Chadwick wanted was an overarching directing central body, but what emerged was largely a permissive measure. The Act allowed the local authorities, if they wanted, to raise a rate to lay sewers and drains and improve water supplies. The General Board could only step in where the death rate in an area had reached a figure of 23 per 1,000. Otherwise it was dependent upon a petition signed by a tenth of the ratepayers. In these circumstances the General Board could inspect the area and then take the necessary action. Against Chadwick's advice, town councils, where they existed, were made the public health authority. Elsewhere, a new elected local Board of Health could be established. The appointment of a MOH

Figure 17.1 Deepening the sewer beneath Fleet Street, 1845. From the 1840s, there was growing concern abut public health and the beginning of efforts to eradicate smells and, with that, perhaps disease. Nonetheless, as late as 1858, London was still affected by 'the Great Stink' from the River Thames.
Source: Mary Evans Picture Library

was not obligatory. The Act did not cover either London or Scotland, which had to wait until 1867 for similar legislation.

It was a compromise, but it contained a certain amount of centralisation. Limits were laid on the independence of local authorities. For the first time, some kind of minimum standards were laid down for drainage and water supply. Chadwick appointed, as his superintending inspectors, engineers who were largely free from association with vested interests or tainted by patronage. One of the main agencies in ensuring the passage of the Bill was the cholera epidemic. Cholera frightened people. The randomness of an outbreak in 1832 had been disconcerting. No one knew how it was caused and most clung to the Chadwickian view that it was something in the atmosphere resulting from bad odours. It did mean that the attack on open cesspools and middens continued. There was some suggestion that contaminated water might have something to do with it, but the Board never pursued this. The cholera outbreak of 1847–9 killed some 54,000 in England alone. The disease returned in 1853–4, mainly confined to Scotland and the north of England. It was in 1855, after the outbreak, that Dr John Snow came up with pretty definite evidence that the disease was carried by a water supply contaminated by faeces. Although he was initially attacked as a defender of smells, his suggestions were gradually taken up,

Chadwick's interference – invited or uninvited – with local authorities built up resentments, which developed into a full-scale assault on Chadwick and the Board. The extension of the 1840 Vaccination Act in 1853, largely due to medical pressure, to make compulsory the vaccination of all infants in England and Wales, within three months of their birth, was perceived as a huge infringement of individual rights. The private water companies financed what Chadwick's biographer called 'obscure and sinister societies' as pressure groups. They were able to tap into a well-entrenched country and radical tradition of suspicion of central power. Many saw the root of the nation's problems in the erosion of local power and local self-government by central government bureaucracy. Palmerston, the Home Secretary in 1854, who was an advocate of sanitary reform and wanted to extend the Public Health Act, sacrificed Chadwick and Southwood Smith to his critics. *The Times* and others rejoiced at the fall of someone who was denounced in the Commons as the 'autocrat, pope, grand lama of sanitary reform' who

> Set to work everywhere washing and splashing, and twisting and rinsing, and sponging and sopping, and soaping and mopping till mankind began to fear a deluge of soap and water. It was a perpetual Saturday night and John Bull was scrubbed, and rubbed, and small tooth combed till the tears came into his eyes, and his teeth chattered, and his fists clenched themselves with worry.[2]

The new president of the reconstructed Board of Health, Sir Benjamin Hall, was an advocate of parochial responsibility and he refused to take any initiatives under the Public Health Act unless pressed by a majority of ratepayers. On the other hand, he was faced with the same problems as his predecessors in that, when he did find it necessary to intervene, he came up against slow-acting, sometimes hostile, local bodies. Once Hall got a taste for intervention, however, he began to revel in it. He discovered the sheer scale of the problems and began to criticise those who put obstacles in the way of reform. As one of the first businessmen to be appointed to ministerial office, he was concerned with making the administration of the state more efficient and free from patronage.

---

[2] *The Times*, 1 August 1854.

Hall stepped in and forced change in London, imposing a Metropolitan Board of Works, responsible for all sanitary concerns. He forced the local boards and vestries to accept an MOH. His Diseases' Prevention Act of 1855 gave the central state permanent powers to deal with epidemics. His Nuisances' Removal Act required the appointment of inspectors with the power to enter premises to eradicate nuisances such as horse knackeries or tripe boiling premises in the heart of cities. The definition of nuisances was extended to include excessive overcrowding. On the other hand, London's private water companies, often supplying unfiltered water from the Thames, were immensely powerful, with some 86 of their shareholders sitting in the Commons in the 1850s. They effectively dragged their feet on water improvement in the capital for half a century.

Unlike Chadwick, who thought it was sanitary engineers who mattered, Hall gave an enhanced role to the medical profession. The emphasis began to switch to preventive medicine. He turned to John Simon, who had been MOH of the City of London since 1848, for advice and Simon became the government's medical officer. A very different character from Chadwick, Simon believed that any reforms would have to be accomplished slowly and sensitively. He had, however, no doubt that 'it was the duty of a christian society to protect the poor against such [sanitary] evils by stringent legislative interference'. He found an ally in Hall's successor, William Cowper, Palmerston's 'stepson', who, like Palmerston, was an enthusiastic sanitary reformer.

They responded to further pressure from the medical profession to have proper medical inspection, rationalisation of the vaccine supply and control of the whole system by the medical experts of the Board of Health. But they came up against opposition in the Commons. Not that the anti-centralisers were in a majority, but in the fluctuating politics of the 1850s, a small group would block measures by threatening to vote down the government. It was not until the end of the 1860s that control over vaccine and vaccinators was finally gained by the Board of Health.

Where Cowper and Simon were successful was in getting some control over medical qualifications through the 1858 Medical Act. Until then there were at least 21 different sources of medical qualification within Britain and Ireland. The Act created the General Medical Council to supervise, to some extent, medical education and professional ethics. It began a medical register of qualified practitioners. Simon and his associates inundated the public with facts and figures about the state of the nation's health, confident that revelation of the realities would be enough to persuade authorities to act. The 1858 Public Health Act gave Simon power to initiate investigations and to create a department to carry out these. Although politicians were opposed to the centralisation of power, in reality, Simon and his department were steadily able to extend their power and influence over local authorities. There was very little decentralisation and local bodies had to turn to the medical officer's department for guidance. They were the people who could identify and publicise the problems and the experts who could offer the solutions. They had to approve of local bye-laws for public health and could ensure that there was a fair amount of uniformity in practice.

More and more discretionary power lay with permanent officials and they increasingly ensured uniformity of standards.

At the same time, most of the legislation was still permissive. It was up to local authorities to decide whether or not to implement measures. In his 1865 report, Simon pressed for an end to the permissive system, arguing that it should no longer be discretionary whether a town was kept filthy or not. Local authorities should be obliged to act to protect public health. With cholera appearing on the scene once again, the timing was fortuitous. Authorities were now obliged to act. They had to inspect their own districts and take action where necessary. A key clause 49 allowed *any* person to complain to the Home Secretary against authorities failing to perform their statutory duties and the Home Secretary could act, get work done and charge it to the local authorities. It was indeed a revolution in government, with the central power allowed to carry out work without being accountable to the local ratepayers.

The extent to which attitudes had changed in 20 years was nowhere more obvious than in *The Times*, which welcomed the fact that public health now stood 'upon the ground in which it ought to stand, enforcing the attention of local authorities to it, instead of leaving it to their option . . . instead of the will and pleasure of Town Councillors, we have the law of the land'.[3] By 1875, there were 1,206 medical officers of health in the country.

Despite the legislation, there was still something chaotic about the system. Another Royal Commission on Sanitation brought out the fragmentation of sanitary responsibilities. The Local Government Act of 1871 brought together the Local Government Act Office, the Registrar-General's Office, the Medical Department and the Poor Law Board under a single, powerful Local Government Board, and an 1872 Public Health Act created the basic local organisation. An important feature was the requirement for all local authorities to ensure a clean water supply and, even more importantly, it gave them the power to borrow money at low rates of interest to develop sewers and water supplies. Another Public Health Act of 1875 codified and consolidated the previous piecemeal legislation.

Simon could resign in 1876, confident that a huge amount had been achieved. That said, however, death rates continued to rise throughout the 1860s, something which at least kept up the pressure for action. But the approach was always a piecemeal one of adding new responsibilities to existing bodies. Because of the considerable resistance from a variety of directions at both local and national level, changes were slow and there was little new thinking about structures. The fact that public health and the Poor Law were so intertwined remained an insuperable barrier and placed limits on how the problems of public health were viewed. It took a long time for the public health measures to have an effect on mortality rates and to persuade people of the importance of cleanliness. Not until the last third of the century did mortality rates begin to decline significantly.

---

[3] *The Times*, 11 August 1866.

Factory and mines reform

Because the early cotton mills tended to be far from towns, labour had to be imported. The source of some of this labour was the poorhouses of the south. From these, pauper children were sent as apprentices to Lancashire. In the 1790s, a number of people began to expose the conditions in which many of these children had to work and live. The arguments tended to be practical ones, warning of the dangers of disease spreading from factories to the wider population.

In 1802, Sir Robert Peel, father of the future Prime Minister, and a hugely successful factory owner, successfully brought in the Health and Morals of Apprentices Bill, to protect pauper apprentices by limiting their working day to 12 hours and requiring that they be instructed in reading and writing. The evidence is that there was little attempt to ensure the Act was carried out. Few of the justices of the peace took any interest. With the coming of steam power, newer factories tended to be situated in towns, where they were much more in the public eye. Pressure for further reform began to grow, with demands for shorter hours of work for children. The main arguments against government interference were that any restrictions in hours would drive trade from the country and that leisure was the root of moral evil. A new Act, again driven by Peel, was eventually passed in 1819, by which no person under the age of 9 could be employed and children under 16 could work no more than 12 hours a day. It was confined to cotton mills and, once again, responsibility for checking its implementation was left to local JPs. Abuses and evasion of the Act continued.

It was from Yorkshire, where the woollen mills were not covered by the legislation, that a new public campaign for reform emerged in the 1830s (see Chapter 18). The first result came in 1833 after a Royal Commission (again with Chadwick as secretary), that the factory reformers very effectively used as a platform for exposing the most extreme examples of the exploitation of children within factories. The ministry was far from enthusiastic and it was individual MPs who tried to get a measure introduced. The government and opponents of reform, in many cases middle-class Radicals, saw the demand for restriction of children's hours as a cover for a general shortening of hours for adults. They argued that such restrictions would weaken the industry's competitive position, as well as being an unacceptable interference with labour just as the country was accepting the need for *laissez-faire*, a reduction in government regulation. The reformers' argument was that children and, they later argued, women were not free agents who could pick and choose where they could work. The state was, therefore, justified in protecting them. It was to combat reforming pressure that the government, having defeated a ten-hour bill with the help of many of the MPs from the newly enfranchised industrial towns of the north, introduced their own bill. This became the Factory Act of 1833 by which children aged 9 to 13 were restricted to eight hours' work, while 'young persons' between 14 and 18 were restricted to 12 hours'. By granting eight hours for the younger children, the government seemed to be outbidding the factory reformers; in practice, it allowed the use of children in shifts and enabled long hours for adults to be maintained.

One key feature of the measure was the establishment of an inspectorate to ensure that the Act was being adhered to. The Factory Commission had revealed that there was an unwillingness on the part of workers to report infringements of earlier acts because, in many cases, it was the adult workers themselves who were employing the children – usually from their own family – as their assistants. The workers, too, had a vested interest in evading the law. It was probably Chadwick who suggested that, rather than leave inspection to unpaid local magistrates, there should be specially appointed government inspectors, with the right to enter factories and the duty to report regularly to the Home Secretary. Although initially there were only four inspectors covering the whole country and they lacked the means of ensuring compliance, it was a system that gradually expanded.

The issue revived in the 1840s, with Peel's government in power. It now got caught up in the wider struggle between agricultural landowners and the manufacturing interest over the Corn Laws. Liberals attacked the advocates of shorter hours as 'pseudo-philanthropists', ready to be generous at the expense of industry but unwilling to do anything when their own pockets were affected. Meanwhile, the factory inspectors were highlighting the inadequacies of the legislation, particularly as regards the provision of schools, medical treatment and safety.

There was initial success on the part of the evangelical Lord Ashley in getting women and girls out of underground working in collieries with the Mines Act of 1842, helped by the belief that the roles of men and women in society needed to be kept separate. The legislation covering coal mining was steadily extended. An 1850 act provided for regular inspection (although with only a single inspector covering the whole area of the north of England and Scotland) and an 1860 one allowed miners to appoint a checkweighman to ensure that they got the correct payment for the loads they delivered. In 1844, the Home Secretary proposed fixing the hours of women and young people in textile factories to 12 a day, while children's hours (from the age of 8) were reduced to 30 a week, plus 15 hours of schooling. For the first time, dangerous machinery had to be fenced and accidents had to be reported. Again, the Act fell short of the aspirations of the 10-hour campaigners, although it did incorporate many of the recommendations of the inspectors, who were concerned to extend their interventionist powers.

In the election of 1847, the reformers ran a very effective campaign to pin down candidates. The result was an Act in 1847 restricting the hours of women and children to 10 per day and, three years later, the working day was fixed to between 6 a.m. and 6 p.m. Although there was no restriction on the hours of adult males, because of their dependence on child and female helpers, their hours quickly fell into line. The Act was strengthened by further legislation in 1850 and 1853. Between 1864 and 1878, protection was gradually extended from the textile industry to other non-textile factories and workshops, a position codified by an Act of 1878. A crucial factor was the reports of the factory inspectors, who encouraged legislation to deal with safety issues in mills. Very, very gradually over the next decades, employers were required to take responsibility for accidents on their premises.

Education

The debate about education grew from the debates over the place of children in the workplace. In England and Wales, schools were provided by the church societies, by individuals and by endowments. There were great variations in the amount and quality of education available in different areas, although there is evidence of relatively high levels of literacy among some groups of workers. By the 1820s, there existed numerous pamphlets and papers aimed at a literate working class. In Scotland, there was a rather complacent belief that a reasonable educational system existed thanks to the parish schools of the Church of Scotland. However, the complacency was dented by exposés that showed that fewer than half the children between the ages of 6 and 14 attended school and many of those who did attend were in private rather than national schools.

Concern about the lack of education amongst most children had been raised early in the century, with calls by Samuel Whitbread that at least two years' education should be provided by the parish. His call was countered by those who argued that, since there was no shortage of clerks, clerics or teachers, then there was no case for educating the poor. Some businessmen were beginning to argue that an ability to read would be useful, but anything more than that was likely to give workers aspirations beyond their station. Undoubtedly, the needs of industry were eventually to play a part in the rate of development of popular education, but in the early decades, that need was for a relatively unskilled labour force, including cheap child labour.

Church involvement in education in England and Wales came largely through the British and Foreign School Society, formed in 1808 to help build schools for Nonconformists, and the National School Society of 1811, financed by the established church. The fact that the churches provided a large part of the education of the working classes was to prove a major obstacle to state involvement. Every time there were proposals to extend education provision, sectarian battles ensued. Anglicans protested that the state should not be assisting Nonconformity, while Nonconformists were wary about accepting state aid lest it threaten their independence.

Once again, it was a variety of different pressures that persuaded the government to act. There was Christian pressure, which believed that children ought to have some religious education. There was radical pressure from those who believed that an educated population would be more reasonable and rational. There was conservative pressure which argued that schools would be able to exert some social control and produce a more respectable and more law-abiding population. In 1833, the state made its first grant of £20,000 to the two church societies to help with school building in the north of England. Since half the cost had to be found from voluntary contributions, the effect was limited. Grants to fund school equipment and teacher-training followed in 1843 and 1846.

The other route of government intervention was through the Factory Act of 1833, which required factory owners to provide two hours' schooling daily for their working children. This resulted in some good schools, but inspectors found that, in many cases, the requirement was being treated with contempt. An attempt in 1843 to extend the provision to three hours, with the local Anglican priest involved in inspection, and to make attendance compulsory, led to the inevitable protests from Nonconformists.

State grants to build schools increased steadily. A committee of the Privy Council was established under James Kay-Shuttleworth and, thanks to his pressure, the grant had grown to over half a million pounds by the 1850s, a large part of which went on the training of teachers. A Royal Commission under the Duke of Newcastle looked at the rising cost of education and, in 1861, agreed that state support should continue, but with a system of payment by results, under which schools were tested on how effectively they were teaching the basics of the three Rs and on the attendance of their pupils. It probably had the effect of narrowing the education provided but, since it offered some kind of measure of the effectiveness of teaching, the Revised Code, as it was called, continued in force until 1897.

From the 1860s, various groups were pressing for education to be separated from the churches. When it was found that, even where schools were available, many children were still not attending, there was a cry that education should be made free and compulsory. There were the inevitable protests about the demoralising effects on children and parents of both compulsion and no charges. Among Nonconformists there was a powerful 'voluntaryist' lobby that believed that private agencies were as capable as the state of providing education. A further pressure for change came with the 1867 franchise extension. Robert Lowe (see Chapter 16) declared, 'It will be absolutely necessary that you should prevail on your future masters to learn their letters', but it is far from clear that most politicians saw education as a necessary consequence.

The urgency of action became more apparent when a report from Manchester revealed that, despite massive voluntary effort, the provision of schools in the city was still hugely inadequate. At the same time, many industrialists were concerned about the scarcity of workers with the necessary literacy to cope with changing technology and there were unfavourable comparisons with what was happening in other countries. On the other hand, the conclusion of one historian is that the business community failed hopelessly to get the kind of educational programme that they wanted.[4]

The outcome was the Elementary Education Act of 1870. It failed to match the hopes of the reformers, since it left the church organisations as the main bodies to provide schools. Only where they were not meeting the requirements would locally elected school boards step in to provide schools, financed by local rates, and such schools would not be free nor would attendance be compulsory. Even at the end of the century, more than half of those in elementary schools were in church schools. Not until 1880 was attendance everywhere in England and Wales made compulsory up to the age of 10, raised in 1893 to 11 and in 1899 to 12. An act of 1872 dealt with the separate situation in Scotland, where, because of the rather better school provision and greater agreement between the churches, education was made compulsory and

---

[4] G.R. Searle, *Entrepreneurial Politics in Mid-Victorian Britain* (Oxford, Clarendon, 1993), pp. 267–70.

parish and most other church schools were transferred for no cost to directly elected school boards in every city and parish. Where parents could not pay the fees, the Poor Law authorities could provide. As with other reforms, the expansion of education came about partly in response to specific needs and partly from the pressure of particular groups. But the shape it took was affected by the bureaucratic pressures to extend control over a system that was perceived as overly diverse.

All these measures were concerned with education of the children of the working class. Their education was seen as something separate from the education of the middle and upper classes. In England and Wales, to a greater extent than in Scotland, the quality and quantity of education that the working class was to receive were assumed to be different from that that was required by other classes. The middle and upper classes had largely to depend upon private schools (the so-called public schools) and upon some endowed borough and grammar schools. Criticism of many of these increased as a more confident middle class became concerned about the quality and content of the education being provided and at the brutality associated with many of them. There was criticism of the narrow classical education on which the main private schools concentrated. Thomas Arnold at Rugby School in the 1840s had sought to lead the way with reform, but his priorities were 'first, religious and moral principle; secondly, gentlemanly conduct; and thirdly, intellectual ability'. A number of those influenced by Arnold went on to found or reform public schools later in the century.

It was accepted that the leading private schools were for the elite. An inquiry into them in the 1860s (when fewer than 3,000 children attended) assumed that they were for 'that small proportion of the youth of any country who are to become in the fullest sense educated men' and, although calling for some broadening of their curriculum, accepted that the classics should remain the core of the education of the nation's future rulers. Another inquiry, the Taunton Commission, looked at education for the middle classes. It recommended further social divisions, with three grades of school. Grade 1 schools were for the sons of parents of ample but 'confined' means, who could be expected to continue at school until the age of 18 and go to university. Grade 2 schools were for those who would leave at the age of 16 and go into the army or the professions – the bulk of the middle class, and Grade 3 for the sons of small tenant farmers, tradesmen and 'superior artisans'. On the commission's recommendations, schools that had once been free to the local community, financed by endowments, were turned into fee-paying secondary schools where entrance was by competition, but the fuller reforms that it recommended were not carried out.

There were numerous other areas where the state was intervening and challenging both the rights of property and individual freedom. A Railway Regulation Act of 1844 laid down that, if profits exceeded 10 per cent of capital, then the state could require new fares; the same Act required all new lines to provide a Parliamentary train, morning and evening, to take workers to and from their employment. 1866 saw discussion of possible nationalisation. 1860 brought an Act for Preventing the Adulteration of Articles of Food, making it an offence, among other things, to add arsenic to beer to give it a froth. The Alkali Act of 1863 was the first attempt to reduce atmospheric pollution (and smells) from chemical works. The Contagious Diseases Act of 1864 allowed the police in naval bases and garrison towns to require a woman to be examined to ensure that she was not spreading venereal disease. In 1869, in order to achieve an integrated national system, the state took over the telegraph system. The coming to power of a Conservative government, if anything, increased the extent of interventionism. The sale of foodstuffs was further regulated; public health legislation was tightened; local authorities were given power to clear slums, to control building standards and layout of streets and to build houses for artisans. Samuel Plimsoll's Merchant Shipping Act stopped the overloading of ships. Although almost all these measures fell well short of what campaigning reformers wanted, they nonetheless reflected huge changes in the perception of what the role of the state ought to be.

In half a century, the balance between the individual and the state and between local and central government had altered. One cannot argue for a direct line of policy – indeed, Gladstone and the Liberal governments of the 1850s and 1860s set as their goal the reduction of government expenditure. However, government was involved in many more areas by the end of the period and power was increasingly tilted away from the localities towards the centre. Advice to local authorities had altered by the 1870s to instruction, with, for example, boards of guardians who failed to carry out proper vaccination procedures getting a month in gaol, *pour encourager les autres*.[5] How did this come about? After the departure of Chadwick and Southwood Smith, one probably cannot identify any direct Benthamite influence. But change did not come about merely through administrative momentum. Inertia and the resistance of vested interests of factory owners, ratepayers, workers who wanted their children to go to work, people who objected to being scrubbed clean had to be overcome. Change required both the exposure of problems and the pressure of reformers – whether these were motivated by evangelical religion, Benthamite utilitarianism, general humanitarianism or career ambition. Reformers and action for social reform were not confined to one party. Broadly, however, Conservatives were more sympathetic to social reform, although wary of any threat to the sanctity of private property and of centralisation, while Liberals clung to the view that the best government was little government.

There was not a great deal of working-class pressure for reform, although trade unions did join in the campaigns for shorter hours – some of this perhaps motivated by a desire to prevent women from competing with men for jobs. But workers remained deeply suspicious of the state. A great deal of intervention was to curb the nastier habits of the mass of the populations and to bring a measure of social control. Thanks to evangelical pressure, bear-baiting was banned in 1836, and cockfighting in 1849. Public houses began to be regulated, starting in Scotland, where, in 1853, licensing hours were shortened and Sunday closing imposed. Police forces spread – first in London, with the formation of the Metropolitan police in 1829, then in the towns covered by the Municipal Reform legislation and then, in the 1840s, in rural areas.

---

[5] The Keighley Board of Guardians in 1876.

The Police Act of 1856 ensured that the system was universal and properly inspected. Even what on the surface might appear an unquestionable good, such as powers given to local authorities to act against overcrowding and to begin slum clearance, had a hugely detrimental effect on the poorest and caused overcrowding in other areas. Compulsory education meant fees and child earners taken out of the labour market. Suspicion of state power was perfectly rational. The working class accepted the Liberal argument that good government meant little government.

Further reading

Checkland, S., *British Public Policy 1776–1939* (Cambridge, Cambridge University Press, 1983)

Finlayson, G., *Citizen, State and Social Welfare in Britain 1830–1990* (Oxford, Clarendon Press, 1994)

Fraser, Derek, *The Evolution of the British Welfare State. A History of Social Policy since the Industrial Revolution* (Basingstoke, Macmillan, 2003)

Hardy, Anne, *The Epidemic Streets: Infectious Diseases and the Rise of Preventive Medicine* (Oxford, Clarendon Press, 1993)

Harris, Bernard, *The Origins of the British Welfare State. Society, State and Social Welfare in England and Wales 1800–1945* (Basingstoke, Macmillan, 2004)

Smith, F.B., *The People's Health, 1830–1910* (London, Weidenfeld & Nicholson, 1979)

Thompson, F.M.L. (ed.), *The Cambridge Social History of Britain 1750–1950: Volume 3: Social Agencies and Institutions* (Cambridge, Cambridge University Press, 1990)

18

Democratic pressures

The early Victorian period brought dramatic changes to the nature of political debate, and the political arena widened immeasurably. Public opinion came to include the working class and there was a recognition of the possibility of influencing politics by means of pressure groups and campaigns. Voluntary organisations proliferated, and they learned from one another the tactics of winning public support and influencing the politicians. Parliament found that it had to respond to the pressures. Certainly, they could not be ignored, and concessions had to be made or the campaigns countered.

Parliamentary reform

The arrival of the Whigs in office in 1830 pushed the issue of parliamentary reform to the forefront. A reforming spirit was in the air and Catholic Emancipation was only one sign that more and more politicians were coming to accept the inevitability of change. There were a number of factors that led up to the explosion of the reform movement. There was the surviving Whig tradition that dated back to Wilkes and Wyvill. There was a working-class movement, associated with Paine and the London Corresponding Society, that had carried on into the nineteenth century and was now intermingled with economic grievances. Thirdly, there were reform pressures from the middle classes, increasingly confident in their social standing, especially in the growing industrial towns. A growing sense of being a distinct class led them to look upon themselves as the key figures in society, the group who were bringing prosperity to the nation. Many of the middle class believed that they had attained their wealth through hard work, ingenuity and self-sacrifice, in contrast to a hereditary, parasitical landed class.

Among the aristocracy there were those who were coming to recognise that the new middle class were not a threat to property, but just as likely to defend the rights of property as the landed class. Where once middle ranks and workers had been banded together as 'the people', now there was an awareness that a division could be made in 'the people' between the middle classes and the mass of workers. Property could be defended with the aid of the new capitalists. The middle class in the industrial towns were partly concerned with getting an extension of the franchise, in particular so that they could push through reform of local government. But it was also about ensuring that their interests were adequately represented in Parliament by getting a redistribution of seats.

The news in March 1831 that the Reform Bill had passed its second reading in the Commons by a majority of one was greeted with popular celebrations. The government's defeat in committee in May and the subsequent general election unleashed a round of demonstrations, meetings and petitions. The structure of the reform movements varied in different parts of the country, depending often on the nature of social relationships. In Birmingham, still very much a city of small workshops and relatively close contact between employers and employed, the banker Thomas Attwood had set up a 'Political Union of the Lower and Middle Classes of the People' in December 1829 to campaign for reform. Veteran reformers were revitalised and the Birmingham model began to be followed in towns. In the factory towns of Manchester and Glasgow, where inter-class contact was rarer, separate reform associations emerged. Many of the industrial middle class, in particular, were fearful about stirring up agitation amongst workers, whose discontents about industrial developments were being expressed through their trade unions, but this was matched by fears that the working class would act on their own. In London, veteran campaigners, like Francis Place, went out of their way to discourage talk of physical force and to stress that 'the style of 1817 and 1820' was no longer applicable and that gradual constitutional change could be achieved without resort of violence.

In small towns, it was the gentry and businessmen and often the town councils and trade guilds that passed resolutions in favour of reform. Generally, the call was for an extension to 'a great proportion of the productive classes' or 'to give a voice to the real property, wealth, industry and intelligence of the country'.[1] Petitions flooded into Parliament from all parts of the country. It soon became apparent that any reform was likely to fall well short of the universal manhood suffrage that some reformers had been demanding for decades, but most went along with the view that any measure was best in the first instance.

When the Lords yet again rejected the Bill, protests were unleashed throughout the country. Newspapers appeared with black borders; the bells of Birmingham churches were tolled. The Birmingham Political Union called for the withholding of taxes. Elsewhere, there were assaults on the persons and property of known anti-reformers,

---

[1] Reports in the Whig *Scotsman* newspaper in January 1831.

and in Nottingham, Derby and Bristol, protests degenerated into riots. In Bristol, it ended with the burning down of a sizable portion of the town, the mansion house, the customs' house and the bishop's palace (21 bishops had voted against the Bill), but most protests remained orderly.

There is little doubt that the continuation of outside pressure, and its intensification at moments of crisis in the passage of reform, ensured that the Whigs persisted with the measure, despite the hostility of monarch and Lords, and doubts within their own ranks. The demonstrations were certainly unprecedented in size and brought new people into the political arena; there was talk of revolution. But, the middle-class leaders of the reform movement were anti-revolutionary and were generally able to maintain control. Perhaps most important of all was the fact that in the Whigs there *was* an aristocratic party that was prepared to bring reform. It meant that reform could come through constitutional means.

The factory movement

Working-class disappointment at the limitations of the 1832 reform was palpable, and, very quickly after 1833, disenchantment with the Whig government set in. The focus of discontent switched to specific issues. Even before the reform agitation had passed, the issue of factory reform was activating people in the industrial towns. One would not want to give the impression that it was only among working people that there were doubts about the direction of the new industrial society. There were many others, whose instincts were Tory, who disliked the trends. They saw the advance of *laissez-faire* as part of a liberalism that threatened tradition, the church and the landed class and would, in time, create anarchy. As against an image of society where each struggled for himself and where freedom was allowed to each individual to pursue self-interest, they believed that a stable society had to rest on mutual obligation. The ruling groups could only expect deference in return for accepting responsibility for those below, just as the squire and the parson accepted responsibility in an idealised rural village. It was such people who tended to support the campaign for factory reform in the 1830s and 1840s. For the 'Tory Radical' Richard Oastler and others, there was a danger of working-class deference being destroyed by the impact of unregulated industrialisation and a danger to the landed class if it aligned too obviously with the new industrialists. 'Cotton mills,' Oastler declared, 'are not a necessity – fields are.'

Conditions in factories – particularly the conditions in which children were employed – were a source of concern by the end of the eighteenth century. The poet William Blake was not alone in seeing factories as 'dark Satanic mills'. His fellow poet, Robert Southey, had written of 'a new sort of slave trade' and Wordsworth bemoaned the tyranny of the factory bell in once-tranquil villages. Calls for a ten-hour working day by three Bradford employers stirred Richard Oastler to pen his denunciation of 'Yorkshire slavery' in 1830. In Yorkshire, elements of the older system of domestic production still persisted and the hope was that regulation could restore some fairer pattern of competition. In Lancashire's cotton industry, the large factory dominated and here the demand was for government intervention to improve conditions. The leader of the Lancashire cotton spinners' union, John Doherty, led the way with short-time committees campaigning for a reduction in the working day for adults as well as children. It was partly as a result of pressure from a factory reform campaign, made up of industrial workers, together with sympathetic Tory squires and parsons, that the 1833 Factory Act was passed, keeping the focus firmly on children.

Many of those who had been campaigning for the Ten Hours Bill supported working-class protests against the Poor Law Amendment Act (see Chapter 17). The new system was seen as depriving the poor of their traditional rights and undermining the age-old interrelationship between social classes. To many working men, the new Poor Law was another example of the treachery of the Whigs. In the populous industrial cities of the north there was an awareness that workhouses offered no solution to the problems of cyclical unemployment in the factories. To many of the ratepayers there seemed to be cheaper and more effective ways of dealing with such unemployment through occasional doles rather than driving families to destitution before aid could be given. Public meetings of protest spread across Lancashire and Yorkshire in 1837 and 1838. Short-time committees that had been campaigning for factory reform turned their organisation to this campaign. However, the protest faded as the Poor Law Commissioners proved less interventionist than had been feared and much of the old pattern of poor relief continued. Radical protesters turned their attention to Chartism.

Chartism

For someone like the London campaigner Francis Place, the best hope still lay in achieving political rights. He and others like him believed that the working class could be reconciled to the new industrial society if they were given some political influence. There was a long-held commitment to political reform among groups of London artisans – a tradition that went back to the London Corresponding Society and that was kept alive by campaigners like Henry 'Orator' Hunt. Others among the middle class believed that assistance from elements of the working class was necessary if power was to be wrested from the landed class. It was essentially people from these three groups who contributed to the emergence in 1837 of the demand for the People's Charter.

In June 1836, the London Working Men's Association was formed, with William Lovett as secretary. It called for radical reform in the shape of universal suffrage, the ballot, annual parliaments, equal representation, abolition of Members' property qualifications and a repeal of the newspaper stamp duty. It was not intended as a mass movement, but was to be confined to 'the *intelligent* and *influential* portion of the working classes'. Propagandists were despatched to different parts of the country. Meanwhile, Feargus O'Connor, MP for Cork until 1835, when he parted company with Daniel

O'Connell, turned to Britain to find a new base. He began to campaign throughout the country on behalf of what was called the 'Great Radical Association'.

In Birmingham, a *petit bourgeois* group, associated with Thomas Attwood, who had continued to preach the message of class collaboration, revived the Birmingham Political Union in 1837. The Political Union proposed to launch a mass agitation that would lead to a national petition. Attwood announced his conversion to universal suffrage, declaring that 'the masses of the people constituted the only engine through which it was possible to obtain reform, and that mighty engine could not be roused into efficient action without the agency of Universal Suffrage'.[2] The London Working Men's Association and their political friends continued working on proposals and engaging in their propaganda activities and, in May 1838, 'The People's Charter' was launched. This called for: universal male suffrage for those aged over 21; 300 electoral districts with roughly the same number of inhabitants; triennially elected returning officers; annual parliaments elected by secret ballot; a salary of £500 for MPs.

The movement became national and had gained a powerful voice with the publication in November 1837 in Leeds of a newspaper, *The Northern Star*, edited by Feargus O'Connor. The Charter, simplified to its six points of: universal male suffrage; vote by ballot; annual parliaments; equal electoral districts; payment of members of parliament and no property qualification for MPs, was a restatement of those traditional Radical demands that dated back to the 1780s.

Chartism became, for a short time, a kind of catch-all movement, with the Charter acting as a rallying cry and differences of emphasis being blurred. The grievances of the excluded were many and varied, and the views of the kind of changes that would come about should the Charter be granted were also legion. Some felt that there were right-thinking reformers of all social classes who should co-operate to bring change by peaceful persuasion. Others believed that only a working class standing on its own could challenge both the political power of the landed class and the industrial and social dominance of the middle class. Some considered that reason, debate and argument would persuade politicians to bring change. Others held that only the threat of force would bring about concessions.

Debates on tactics became central to the discussions at the National Convention, held in London from February until June 1839. Delegates from all over the country attended. A few took to wearing red caps and *tricoleur* sashes and talked of the need to prepare for the seizure of power should the petition be rejected. For the Birmingham delegates and some others this was too much and they withdrew. A substantial number, however, argued that the right of freeborn Englishmen to arm, if necessary, should not be abandoned. At the beginning of July, the Convention moved to Birmingham, where there had been excited demonstrations. Even before the Convention arrived, the Home Secretary, not confident that recently elected magistrates in Birmingham

---

[2] Quoted in Clive Behagg, 'An Alliance with the Middle Class: the Birmingham Political Union and Early Chartism', in James Epstein and Dorothy Thompson (eds), *The Chartist Experience: Studies in Working-Class Radicalism and Culture* (London, Macmillan, 1982), p. 73.

were capable of maintaining order, had despatched a detachment of the Metropolitan police to the city. It was their actions in charging a crowd in the Bull Ring that led to riots in the city and the arrests of various Chartist leaders, including the mild William Lovett, who had done little more than act as secretary to the Convention and issue a protest condemning the arrests. He was sentenced to a year in gaol.

Focus on

Chartism

This is an extract from one of the Chartist newspapers, *The Chartist Circular*, from April 1840. There were many Chartist newspapers in different parts of the country. With the exception of Feargus O'Connor's *Northern Star*, which ran from 1737 until 1837, most of them were short-lived. *The Chartist Circular* was published in Glasgow between 1839 and 1841.

> But who, possessed of the least power of reflection, could expect that a parliament, composed as the present is, would ever effect any good? On a former occasion we declared that the Corn-Law Repealers though ten times more numerous and powerful than they are, would never annihilate that detestable monopoly, until there was a complete organic change in the representation of the country. Is it to be supposed, indeed, that a house, the majority of whom are returned by a hundred and fifty thousand monied clodpoles, and wealth-worshipping shopocrats – a house in which there are a hundred and sixty-seven officers of the army and navy – upwards of fifty placemen, and a host of aristocratic pensioners, would abolish the corn-laws, or in any other benefit the country, by opposing the interests of the great hereditary incurables, who possess the soil, and usurp the liberty of the people. . . . Therefore, if the Corn-Law Repealers are sincere, and we believe the inevitable ruin now threatening the commerce of the country, and which can only be averted by the abrogation of every restriction in trade, and a proportionate reduction in the expenditure of the state, has really made the moneyocracy somewhat serious, they must adopt the means to clean this Augean stable, in order to obtain redress of the nation's wrongs. The means are abundantly within their reach: they have only to raise the standard of universal suffrage – to unfurl the banner of rational liberty, inscribed with the motto of equal rights and equal laws, and their power, united with that of the unenfranchised millions will be invincible. The Corn-Laws will then be repealed – and not till then – the interest of the national debt will then be proportionately lowered – a corresponding reduction in taxes will be effected – an equitable adjustment of the various interests of society will be brought about – and the nation will be raised to greatness, prosperity, and glory; because its people will be free.

Source: The Chartist Circular, No. 30, 18 April 1840.

A few days later, the petition for the Charter with 1,238,000 signatures was ineffectually presented to the House of Commons by Attwood and duly rejected. The Convention returned to London soon afterwards amid some acrimony, with accusations that the leadership had failed to prepare what were called 'ulterior measures' should the petition be rejected. A small group began to conspire to organise uprisings or, at the very least, to threaten demonstrations. On 4 November 1839, John Frost, a former justice of the peace in Wales, who had lost his position because of his association with Chartism, led a group of Chartists and miners to the town of Newport in Wales. They were met by troops who opened fire and 20 or more Chartists were killed and about 50 wounded. The uprising followed on weeks of secret comings and goings, but attempts at co-ordinated protests failed. Frost and two of his colleagues were brought to trial and sentenced to death. This, in turn, led to further protests and attempted armed insurrection in various parts of the north of England. Mass arrests followed. While the attempted insurrections were easily put down, the extent of protest was enough to persuade the authorities to commute the sentences to transportation.

Many history books make a great deal of the division between 'physical force' Chartist advocates and 'moral force' ones. In practice, the language could alter, depending on the audience and the circumstances. There is little sign of any serious efforts at arming. The real division was between those who believed in co-operation with middle-class reformers and those who opposed it. The former wanted to show that the workers 'deserved' the vote because they were respectable, intelligent and politically aware. These were the ones who held peaceful meetings, often associated with the expanding temperance movement. On the other side, were those who argued that the middle classes, having obtained the vote in 1832, had then abandoned their working-class supporters. If the Charter were to be gained, then the workers would have to act on their own initiative and keep the focus firmly on their own demands. These refused to co-operate with the middle-class-dominated Anti-Corn Law League, and, indeed, discovered the very effective publicity tactic of disrupting anti-Corn Law meetings. At the same time, the social organisations of Chartism, such as Chartist churches, which were strong in Scotland and in the Midlands of England, Chartist soirées and social gatherings offered a sense of community in a world where old communities were breaking up. Many of the same people were attracted by O'Connor's Land Plan, which envisaged the setting up of farming communities, where people could work their own plots of land. All the groups attracted support from working people, such as shoemakers, tailors, weavers and other artisans, who were feeling the effects of a deepening trade depression at the end of the 1830s and early 1840s or suffering from the longer-term impact of the erosion of their status, their independence and their earnings as a result of industrial change. For these, the Chartist movement was a way of expressing their anger and frustration, in the hope that it would frighten the government and employers into a change of attitude. From the government's point of view, the movement seemed dangerous because it had that combination of economic and social grievances alongside its political elements. The Chartists had learned from the pre-1832 middle-class reformers to identify themselves in their speeches and publications as 'the people', the 'nation'. Link that with strikes through-out parts of Lancashire and Derbyshire among factory workers and miners, as there were in 1842 in the so-called 'Plug riots', it is little wonder that the government and their supporters believed that the danger was real.

The response was to make use of troops. New garrisons were set up throughout the country. General Napier, back from smashing Indian unrest, was sent in to give a show of force throughout the north of England. The authorities had, however, learned the lessons of Peterloo that the excessive use of force could be counterproductive and lead to a wave of sympathy. Most of the middle class believed that they were living in a state where liberal principles were spreading and where the working class would support such liberal principles if they were properly educated and kept out of the hands of agitators. The sending of troops to break up demonstrations was the kind of thing that reactionary, absolutist, continental governments did, not liberal constitutional ones. The authorities were well aware that a repetition of anything like Peterloo was likely to shatter that image and, perhaps, give the middle class a reason to think that the state was not as liberal as they had imagined. Therefore, generally, troops were displayed rather than used. There were no attempts to arrest Chartist speakers during mass meetings. The knock at the door tended to come early in the morning.

Why did Chartism fail? The customary answer has been: divided aims and divided leadership. Also, because it rained on 10 April 1848 as they tried to deliver yet another great petition to Parliament, the will to revolution was reportedly washed away. But Chartism did not fail because of its internal problems. Its aims remained very consis-tent and, although there were undoubtedly tensions, its leaders succeeded remarkably in maintaining co-operation. Chartism failed because those in power, backed by power-ful elements of the middle class, were determined to resist. If it had won its political demands, then the fear was that it would usher in an unwanted democracy. If it had won some of the social demands, then it would have been a threat to the advance of capitalism. There was real concern in April 1848 when the movement, revived after five years of relative quiet, came up with a third petition. Mainland Europe, after all, was afire with revolution. Special constables were recruited in their thousands to defend London. But the danger of revolution was always exaggerated and when it failed to materialise then the whole movement could be dubbed a failure or, pre-ferably, a laughing stock. The Treason Felony Act of July 1848 made it even more dangerous to talk of reform. Transportation for life could result

> [i]f any person whatsoever shall, within the United Kingdom or without, compass, imagine, invent, devise or to deprive or depose our Most Gracious Lady the Queen, . . . from the style, honour, or royal name of the imperial crown of the United Kingdom, or of any other of her Majesty's dominions and countries, or to levy war against her Majesty, . . . within any part of the United Kingdom, in order by force or constraint to compel her . . . to change her . . . measures or counsels, or in order to put any force or constraint upon her or in order to intimidate or overawe both Houses or either House of Parliament.

Figure 18.1 The great Chartist meeting in Kennington Common, 10 April 1848. This etching is based on an early photograph by William Kilburn of the huge Chartist demonstration held before the third Chartist petition was presented to the House of Commons. Note the mixture of social classes in the crowd and the fact that there are a few women attending.
Source: Alamy Images

The authorities broke the Chartist movement by intimidation, by the arrest of leaders, by the use of informants and by winning the propaganda battle. They were helped by the fact that the economic pressures were being reduced. After the bleak year of 1842, economic demand began to rise again and unemployment levels to fall sharply. Railway building gave a boost to the economy. But governments were also responding to some of the demands. Factory legislation had, at long last, brought the ten hours rule for children, and women and children were banned from coal mines.

There has been a powerful argument that it is wrong to see Chartism as principally a working-class movement – rather, it was a political movement that was still caught in the language of popular radicalism that went back until at least the 1780s. The movement certainly used the language of class, but, the argument goes, this did not reflect that class actually existed as a result of the experience of industrialisation, as E.P. Thompson argued. It was the language used which created a sense of class.

The historian Gareth Stedman Jones was at the forefront of this critique of older views. He pointed out that there was little evidence that those participating in

Chartism had any great sense of looking forward. Rather they were looking back and talking about older constitutional rights. The argument was not that they were being exploited by the employers and, therefore, needed political power. The argument was that the English constitution had been corrupted by some people and that if it could be restored to its earlier purity then all would be well. In other words, Chartism was not something new, but came at the end of radical movements which dated back to the eighteenth century. It used the language of class as a way of rallying support from excluded groups. The tendency was to talk about the industrious classes, which did not just mean workers, but included employers also. The industrious classes were seen in opposition to the idle aristocracy. Chartism faded when the state proved not to be totally corrupt, when it began to reform; when Factory Acts were brought in. Even as economic exploitation increased, radicals were not able to tap into this as a source of grievance, because they had not the language to do so. The enemy was the corruption of the constitution, not exploitative capitalists. By this argument, once there were enough signs that governments were less corrupt and at least trying to respond with the social legislation of the 1840s, then Chartism could only fade.[3]

It is true that Chartists leaders generally failed to provide leadership for the mass strikes of 1842 and 1848, but individual Chartists were perfectly capable of using both the language of politics and the language of class conflict. An important factor was, undoubtedly, that the new industrial society was bringing gains to many more people. Whereas in the early stages of industrialisation there were many more losers than gainers from change, by the end of the 1840s that was being rapidly reversed. But, despite the decline of the mass movement, a belief in the legitimacy of Chartist demands never disappeared.

The Anti-Corn Law League

The Chartists also had to compete with the ideological panacea being presented by the campaigners against the Corn Laws. Demands for the repeal of the Corn Laws grew out of the reform movements of the early 1830s. Anti-Corn Law associations appeared in Glasgow and London, but it was from the Manchester association, in October 1838, that plans for a nationwide Anti-Corn Law League emerged. It was dominated by Lancashire industrialists. The organising genius was a merchant, George Wilson, and the public face was provided by Richard Cobden, a calico manu-facturer, and John Bright, a cotton mill owner from Rochdale.

Learning from the experiences of earlier pressure groups like the anti-slavery movement, the League concentrated on the single issue of the Corn Laws and did not allow its efforts to become diversified in other reform agitations. The Leaguers took all

---

[3] Gareth Stedman Jones, 'The Language of Chartism' in James Epstein and Dorothy Thompson (eds), *The Chartist Experience: Studies in Working-Class Radicalism and Culture* (London, Macmillan, 1982), pp. 3–58.

the forces of right to be on their side, presenting the Corn Laws as morally, economically, politically, socially and intellectually untenable. Clergymen were called in to declare that the laws were sinful, 'violating the paramount law of God and restricting the bounty of providence'. The campaign, at moments, attained an almost religious fervour, with all who opposed it seeming to be on the side of the forces of darkness.

The League argued that the Corn Laws, by adding to the price of bread, restricted commerce and were responsible for economic distress. If corn could be imported from abroad, foreign countries would buy British manufactured goods, which would bring an increased demand for labour. At the same time, by freeing international trade, a permanent cause of dispute between nations would be removed. The opponents of the League argued that the real motive was the desire of manufacturers to have cheap labour, something that most Chartists suspected.

Focus on

The repeal of the Corn Laws

This extract is from a speech by John Bright at Covent Garden Theatre, London, in 1845. Bright (1811–1889) was a cotton spinning factory owner from Rochdale in Lancashire. A Quaker in religion, he was active on behalf of Dissenters. He, with Richard Cobden, was at the forefront of the Anti-Corn Law League and he was elected to Parliament in 1843. For Bright, repeal of the Corn Laws was merely a first step in the struggle against aristocratic dominance.

It is a struggle between the numbers, wealth, comforts, the all in fact, of the middle and industrious classes, and the wealth, the union, and sordidness of a large section of the aristocracy of this empire; and we have to decide, for it may be that this meeting itself may to no little extent be the arbiter of this great contest, – we have to decide now in this great struggle, whether in this land in which we live, we will no longer bear the wicked legislation to which we have been subjected, or whether we will make one effort to right the vessel, to keep her on her true course, and, if possible, to bring her safely to a secure haven. Our object, as the people, can only be, that we should have good and impartial government for everybody. As the whole people, we can by no possibility have the smallest interest in any partial or unjust legislation; we do not wish to sacrifice any right of the richest and most powerful class, but we are resolved that that class shall not sacrifice the rights of a whole people.

Source: J.E.T. Rogers (ed.), *Speeches on Questions of Public Policy by John Bright MP, Volume II* (London, Macmillan, 1868), pp. 145–6.

The League launched attacks on the landed aristocracy for clinging to protectionism and most members saw the campaign as part of a struggle against the power of
an aristocratic establishment. The leaders toyed with the idea of a mass lock-out
of their workers and a mass refusal to pay taxes. The idea was abandoned as too
dangerous, but when a series of mass strikes took place in Lancashire in 1842, many
Tories believed that the League was behind them. Certainly, some activists were not
averse to disorder as a means of frightening government. At the same time, Cobden
was able to present the moderate face of the League and reassure a majority within
Parliament that repeal would bring stability and even prosperity. Although Peel's
biographers tend to emphasise concern over the Irish famine as the crucial factor in
Peel's 'conversion', there seems little doubt that the League's campaign helped
persuade first the Whigs and then Peel that repeal had to be pushed through and the
agitation quietened.

Administrative reform

For Bright and Cobden and some others, repeal of the Corn Laws was always seen as
merely one step in a wider programme of reforms that would weaken the hold of the
landed class and the established church. To John Bright, the Crimean War was further
proof that the battle against aristocratic political power had still to be won. The Peace
Society – so important to Bright, with his Quaker faith – had been formed in 1847 to
build on the gains of 1846. Free trade, the Anti-Corn Law Leaguers had argued,
would remove one of the causes of conflict between nations and an industrial and trading society required peace. Since Adam Smith, the argument for free trade had always
had a moral dimension to it; the removal of protectionism and monopoly would make
both individuals and nations better. As revelations about the misconduct of the war
appeared, so criticisms mounted. By December 1854, *The Times* was claiming that the
expedition to the Crimea was 'in a state of entire disorganisation'. It blamed an army
and governmental system based on patronage and seniority as opposed to ability and
talent. The criticism was initially focused on the Prime Minister, Lord Aberdeen, who
had not hidden his lack of enthusiasm for the war, but, as the blunders continued, the
critique gradually broadened. The common factor seemed to be aristocratic rule –
Aberdeen at home and the Lords Raglan, Cardigan and Lucan in the Crimea – but
also the whole system of patronage by which appointments were made. Why was the
country still run by the old aristocracy when middle-class industrialists were obviously
responsible for its prosperity? Let the lessons and techniques of industry be applied to
the country.

Radical demands for an inquiry into the conduct of the war led to the fall of
Aberdeen's government and its replacement by one led by Palmerston – Bright's
'old charlatan'. An Administrative Reform Association (ARA) was formed, with the
wealthy hosiery manufacturer, Samuel Morley, as chairman, calling for efficiency in
government and with the motto 'the Right Man in the Right Place'. By the time the

committee of inquiry reported, however, victory was in sight and Palmerston was very effectively stirring patriotic fervour among the middle classes and taking the credit for victory.

The war had divided old Anti-Corn Law League allies, with few joining Bright and Cobden in condemnation of it. There had always been those among the Manchester middle class who were uneasy at the League's attacks on the aristocracy. The ARA never became a mass movement and tended to attract writers and professionals rather than industrialists. Bright (going through a nervous breakdown) and Cobden both paid the price of their opposition to the war by being defeated in the election of 1857. Although they were both back in Parliament within two years, they were not able to rebuild their old alliances. Prosperity and Palmerston's bellicosity, together with his political skills in communication, proved too appealing to most of the middle class.

Middle- and working-class demands continued to make themselves heard through a swelling number of newspapers and a variety of organisations. The mid-century decades brought a proliferation of voluntary associations, the main means through which the urban middle class shaped and influenced their towns. According to historian R.J. Morris, these voluntary societies 'provided an expression of social power for those endowed with increasing social and economic authority' but were still excluded from real state power. A study of 100 leading supporters of the teetotal wing of the very powerful temperance movement brings out very clearly the extent to which there was a network of campaigning pressure groups (see Table 18.1). Most were Nonconformists, many were in business and the largest group were textile manufacturers. The overlap with the Anti-Corn Law League is striking, as is the extent to which religion mattered. The Liberation Society in particular, formed in 1853, brought the issue of disestablishment of the Church of England to the forefront of politics. A broadly based liberal movement was emerging, which stood for free trade, the reduction of taxes on consumption, slashing military expenditure and a small, neutral state that gave no protection to particular interests, and believed in self-help and voluntarism.

The Second Reform Act

Chartism did not die completely in 1848. A few Chartists remained active throughout the 1850s and 1860s, and their ideas continued to be discussed and debated in political clubs and coffee houses. There was a sense of relief among the politicians that they had survived 1848 without revolution. But the possibility of mass action was always there. There were various views about what ought to be done. Some argued for limited reform before anything more was demanded. Others argued that nothing should be stirred up and that government should wait until a reform campaign reappeared. A third way, adopted by Bright, was to use and *control* a working-class reform movement to achieve middle-class goals of liberalisation of the state, with more

Table 18.1 Other reforming activities of prominent teetotallers: 1833–72

Prohibition	100	Home Mission Society	2
Anti-slavery	41	Financial reform	2
Anti-Corn Law League	40	Religious Tract Society	2
Peace movement	39	Anti-duelling	2
Liberation Society	36	Church Missionary Society	2
Mechanics' institutes	22	Society for the Diffusion of Useful Knowledge	2
Anti-Contagious Diseases Act	15	Climbing boys	2
Sunday schools	15	Governor Eyre committee	2
Bible Society	14	Hospitals	2
Chartism	12	Aborigines Protection Society	2
Animal cruelty	12	Lifeboat Society	1
Educational voluntarism	12	Soldier's Friend Society	1
Sanitary reform	11	Anti-air pollution	1
Complete suffrage	10	Lancastrian schools	1
Ragged schools	10	Administrative reform	1
Sabbatarianism	9	Early Closing Association	1
Co-operation	8	Anti-flogging	1
Support of North in American Civil War	8	Anti-gambling League	1
Factory regulation	8	Penitentiary movement	1
Anti-smoking	7	Anti-birth control	1
Free press	6	Church Pastoral-Aid Society	1
London Missionary Society	6	London Society for Promoting Conversion of the Jews	1
Public libraries	6	Phonetic Society	1
Sunday opening of museums	5	London City Mission	1
Penal reform	5	Baptist Missionary Society	1
Freehold land movement	4	Aged Female Society	1
Volunteer movement	3	Society for Bettering the Condition of the Poor	1
Freedman's aid movement	3	National Thrift Association	1
Reform League	3		
Pro-Garibaldi	3		
Y.M.C.A.	3		
Anti-opium trade	3		
Owenism	2		

Source: B. Harrison, *Drink and the Victorians. The Temperance Question in England, 1815–1872* (London, Faber, 1971), p. 174.

efficient government, more middle-class influence and a weakened church establishment. Bright and others were convinced by the violence of some of the Chartist language that, without class collaboration, a dangerously isolated and embittered working class would emerge.

Bright had a problem in trying to court the working classes. There was no love lost between the workers and the 'millocracy' of the Manchester School, which Bright stood for, with its commitment to unregulated *laissez-faire*. Bright and Cobden had always been vigorous opponents of factory legislation to shorten the hours of work. Nor had free trade been particularly popular amongst the working class. Most were not in principle opposed to the protection of their industries from foreign competition. An alliance between Bright and the politically active working-class leaders was not an obvious one. But the improved economic conditions of the 1850s were laying the foundation for the powerful narrative that Bright and Cobden were generating that prosperity stemmed from free trade.

Bright had worked since 1848 on forging links with working-class audiences. New attitudes began to emerge within trade unionism that favoured collaboration more than confrontation. Also, middle-class radicals and working-class leaders could unite on issues of foreign policy. There was widespread support for the Italian independence movement, with Garibaldi proving exceptionally popular on his visit to Britain in 1864. There was similar support for Polish independence and, on the whole, most working-class leaders, although by no means all, came round to supporting the Northern cause in the American Civil War. Working-class activists in London and in the provincial cities began sharing platforms with middle-class radicals on these issues and this confirmed Bright in the view that the trade-union leaders were Liberal in their attitudes and did not pose a threat.

A demand for the extension of the franchise slowly began to re-emerge among the working class, with the appearance of a new, younger generation of leaders. In 1862, the leaders of London unionism formed a Manhood Suffrage and Vote by Ballot Association and a working-class press – the *Bee-Hive* in London, the *Glasgow Sentinel* in Scotland – helped spread political consciousness. The campaign faded during the excitement of the American Civil War, but at the beginning of 1865 it was revitalised as the Reform League.

Bright had come to believe that there was a section of the working class – the respectable, better off, skilled 'aristocracy of labour', as they were sometimes called – who were different from what he dubbed the 'residuum' and others referred to as the 'great unwashed'. This better-off section of the working class could now be trusted with the franchise. Whereas Chartism had been about getting the vote in order to change society, now there was evidence of an acceptance of free trade and of the laws of supply and demand. Radicals began to talk of workers being worthy of the franchise and of having the necessary qualities for 'citizenship'. The Reform Union continued to campaign for a moderate extension of the franchise to £6 householders, but in London the Reform League demanded manhood suffrage and the ballot. It began to build a strong working-class base and to spread from London to other cities.

Gladstone's proposals of March 1866 were more limited than any reform proposal over the previous two decades, going no lower than householders whose houses had a rateable value of £7 per annum. The advice from most middle-class Liberals was that this should be supported as the best that could be achieved. But, even this moderate measure was too much for Lowe and the 'Adullamites'. Lowe rejected Bright's arguments that there was a respectable elite of the working class that could be managed. To him, trade unions were not proof of a working class ready for self-government, but evidence that the workers would act from class motives and would, in time, subjugate the minority that the middle classes would become. The Adullamites, in conjunction with the Conservatives, voted down the bill and the government fell.

It was clearly much easier for most reformers to demonstrate against a Conservative government than a Liberal one. Demonstrations reached a new intensity in July 1866, when the weight of the crowd pushed down the rusty railing of Hyde Park, to which they had been refused admittance. Three days of sporadic rioting followed before the League leaders persuaded the police to withdraw and they managed to restore order. Other impressive reform demonstrations followed in Manchester, Newcastle, Glasgow and Edinburgh, in all of which trade unions complete with banners were well represented.

Many trade unionists were still wary of getting their organisations too caught up in political activities, that were seen as potentially divisive. What changed that was the danger to trade unionism as a result of the Hornby *versus* Close case, which threatened the security of trade-union funds, and calls for legislation to restrict trade unionism in the aftermath of violent attacks on non-unionists in the so-called 'Sheffield Outrages'. A strong case could be made for trying to ensure that there would be sympathetic voices in Parliament. What also roused people were Robert Lowe's attacks suggesting that the working classes were not worthy of the vote because they were venal, ignorant and drunken. Accepting these would undermine the whole case for 'respectability' that the trade-union leaders had been building up.

Disraeli's Reform Bill of March 1867 proposed a very limited household franchise, hedged around with qualifications that would effectively have excluded most of the working class. It stirred little enthusiasm. In May, the Home Secretary's ban on a further meeting in Hyde Park was ignored, despite the presence of 13,000 special constables. The poet Matthew Arnold, for one, was horrified by these events, 'this vast residuum . . . marching where it likes, meeting where it likes, bawling what it likes, breaking what it likes'. The Home Secretary resigned, the government, according to Disraeli, 'having suffered some slight humiliation in the public mind'.

As in 1832, the popular demonstrations ensured that the politicians persisted with the measure. Within a fortnight of the Hyde Park demonstration, Disraeli had abandoned most of the 'safeguards' against democracy that he had originally proposed. It is doubtful whether the popular agitation or fear of revolution actually contributed much to the shape of the Act. That was much more due to parliamentary manoeuvring, as Disraeli was determined to ensure that the Conservatives remained in office and was prepared to make concessions to the Radicals in order to get their support and to keep the Liberals divided.[4] Perhaps Conservatives could be more relaxed about a mass franchise than Liberals. Liberals had gone with Bright in believing that there was a labour aristocracy that could be absorbed within Liberalism. Their debates lay over where the line should be drawn between the labour aristocracy and the 'residuum'. They were fearful of including the latter. The Conservatives had fewer concerns. As Robert Lowe feared, there were plenty of signs that the working class was conservative both in temperament and in politics. The future Lord Salisbury recognised that 'the poorer men are, the more easily they are influenced by the rich' and that 'the ruder class of minds would be more sensitive to traditional emotions'.[5]

The Second Reform Act did not usher in democracy or red revolution. Things went on much as ever. The fact that there was only a limited redistribution of seats meant that it could only have a very limited effect on the actual distribution of power. One might have expected much in the election of 1868 from the Reform League. It had managed to mobilise the trade unionists, and, with its 600 branches and 65,000 membership, there seemed to be the possible nucleus of a party. There was talk of working-men candidates and of using the power of the franchise to achieve 'the direct representation of labour in Parliament'. But no working-class representation resulted. Few reformers had thought beyond winning the franchise. There was little sense of the vote as a preliminary to a social programme. No working men were nominated for seats where there was any chance of winning. The League leadership were concerned to maintain their ties with the Liberal Radicals who had provided the funding for the League. They believed that it was only with Liberal support that they could get some of the trade-union reform that they wanted. What was envisaged was a reformed Liberal Party 'in which organization the working men shall be consulted and called into active political life'.[6] A few working-men candidates did stand in the 1868 election but the practical problems, not least the cost, of elections and of maintaining a member of parliament had not been faced.

Disenchantment with the Liberal government led to new campaigns. The anger of Nonconformist groups, like the National Education League, at the failure of the 1870 Education Act to bring all schools under state control and, even more so, to allow Poor Law boards of guardians to pay the fees of pauper children attending church schools, contributed to the defeat of Gladstone's government in 1874. To this was added trade-union anger at the Criminal Law Amendment Act, brought in at the behest of Liberal businessmen. In the election of 1874, 14 Labour candidates went to the poll. Two miners were elected, Thomas Burt in Morpeth and Alexander McDonald in Stafford.

---

[4] For this argument see F.B. Smith, *The Making of the Second Reform Bill* (Cambridge, Cambridge University Press, 1966) and Maurice Cowling, *1867. Disraeli, Gladstone and Revolution. The Passing of the Second Reform Bill* (Cambridge, Cambridge University Press, 1967).

[5] Gertrude Himmelfarb, 'Politics and Ideology: the Reform Act of 1867' in her *Victorian Minds* (New York, Knopf, 1968).

[6] George Howell, trade-unionist secretary of the Reform League, to the Liberal MP, James Stansfield.

It was Conservatism that won the day, however. In many constituencies, Conservatives were able to play up to popular Protestantism and to organise the working-class vote around anti-Irish sentiment. By 1874, there were at least 150 Conservative Workingmen's Associations around the country committed to 'resisting any attempt to subvert the Protestant faith or the Constitution of the Country; to protect the prerogative of the Crown and to defend the rights and privileges of the people'. At the same time, a number of Conservatives sought to emphasise the Party's traditional concern over social issues. The need for better working-class housing was pushed. Disraeli in 1872, in one of his best-known speeches, had talked of the state's responsibility to provide 'pure air, pure water, pure food, healthy homes and public recreation' – *Sanitas sanitatum omnia sanitas*. The Liberals liked to believe that it was the unpopular licensing of public houses that had done for them, 'carried away in a torrent of gin and beer'. There is little evidence that the brewers and publicans had yet associated with Conservatism. The Liberal problems were more fundamental ones.

It was easier to get Liberal unity over foreign policy issues, and Gladstone returned to the public arena in 1876 with an attack on the support that Disraeli was giving to the Turks, who were crushing a Bulgarian uprising with great ferocity. His pamphlet *Bulgarian Horrors* sold 40,000 copies in a matter of days. In the mass meetings of his Midlothian campaign which followed, he was able to, once again, stir radical and Nonconformist opinion to a new, almost religious enthusiasm, for policies driven by moral imperatives.

Further reading

Belchem, John, *Popular Radicalism in Nineteenth-Century Britain* (Basingstoke, Macmillan, 1996)

Chase, M., *Chartism. A New History* (Manchester, Manchester University Press, 2007)

Evans, E.J., *The Great Reform Act of 1832* (London, Methuen, 1983)

Hollis, Patricia (ed.), *Pressure from Without in Early Victorian England* (London, Edward Arnold, 1974)

Parry, J.P., *The Rise and Fall of Liberal Government in Victorian Britain* (New Haven and London, Yale University Press, 1993)

Phillips, John A., *The Great Reform Bill in the English Boroughs. English Electoral Behaviour 1818–41* (Oxford, Oxford University Press, 1992)

Walton, John K., *The Second Reform Act* (London, Methuen, 1987)

Wright, D.G., *Popular Radicalism. The Working-Class Experience 1780–1880* (London, Longman, 1988)

Timeline 1831–80

Year	Government and politics	War and empire	Economic and social	Cultural and intellectual
1831	First Reform Bill defeated in March; Whigs win election; Second Reform Bill defeated in October		Tithe war in Ireland; potato famine in Ireland; Game Act	
1832	Third Reform Bill passed in June		Cholera epidemic; Royal Commission on Poor Laws opens	
1833	Irish Coercion Bill		Abolition of slavery in empire; first education grant; Factory Act; Burgh Reform (Scotland) Act	*Tracts for the Times*
1834	Grey resigns; Melbourne Prime Minister till November; Peel Prime Minister from November		Grand National Consolidated Trades Union; 'Tolpuddle Martyrs'; Poor Law Amendment Act	
1835	Tamworth manifesto; Melbourne Prime Minister	Boer Great Trek	Municipal Corporations Act; Borough Police Act	
1836			Formation of London Working Men's Association	Total abstinence from alcohol movement founded; University of London founded
1837	Accession of Victoria			
1838	The People's Charter		Formation of Anti-Corn Law League	
1839	Resignation of Melbourne; Bedchamber crisis; return of Melbourne	Opium War with China; First Afghan War	Chartist Convention in London; Newport Uprising in November; County Police Act	Infant Custody Act

Year	Government and politics	War and empire	Economic and social	Cultural and intellectual
1840	Queen marries Prince Albert	First permanent colonists in New Zealand	Inauguration of the penny post	
1841	Resignation of Melbourne; Peel Prime Minister			
1842		Treaty of Nanking; China cedes Hong Kong; retreat from Kabul	Chadwick's Sanitary Report	
1843		Natal becomes British colony	Disruption in the Church of Scotland, creating Free Church	
1844			Bank Charter Act; Railway Act; Limited liability companies permitted	Independent Order of Rechabites founded in Salford
1845			Potato blight leading to Irish famine and Highland famine	John Henry Newman of Oxford Movement becomes Roman Catholic
1846	Repeal of the Corn Laws; defeat of Peel; Russell Prime Minister		Manchester starts five-year project to bring water from Pennines	
1847	Whig election victory		Young Ireland movement; Ten Hours Factory Act	Charlotte Brontë, Jane Eyre; Emily Brontë, Wuthering Heights
1848	Third Chartist petition; Karl Marx and Friedrich Engels, The Communist Manifesto		Cholera epidemic; Public Health Act	Elizabeth Gaskell, Mary Barton; T.B. Macaulay, History of England; J.S. Mill, Principles of Political Economy
1849		Annexation of the Punjab	Navigation Acts repealed	Cock fighting illegal
1850	Death of Peel	Gold Coast made British colony	Formation of Amalgamated Society of Engineers	Charles Dickens, David Copperfield

Year				
1851	Ecclesiastical Titles Bill; Palmerston dismissed as Foreign Secretary	Great Exhibition		
1852	Russell resigns; Derby Prime Minister February–December; Aberdeen Prime Minister	Gold discovered in Australia		
1853	Northcote–Trevelyan report		Compulsory Vaccination Act	Betting Houses Act for England and Wales; Forbes Mackenzie Act closed Scottish pubs on Sundays; Gaskell, *Cranford*
1854		Crimean War; battles of Alma, Balaclava and Inkerman		
1855	Aberdeen resigns; Palmerston Prime Minister		Nuisance Removal Act	Stamp Duty on newspapers abolished; *Daily Telegraph* published at one penny
1856		Treaty of Paris; Livingstone completes crossing of Africa; annexation of Oudh	Bessemer steel process	
1857		Indian rebellion; war with China; Irish Republican Brotherhood formed	Financial crisis; Divorce and Matrimonial Causes Act for England and Wales	Tom Hughes, *Tom Brown's Schooldays*
1858	Palmerston resigns; second Derby ministry February–June 1859	Government of India taken from East India Company	Removal of disabilities from Jews; Medical Act establishes General Medical Council	Transatlantic telegraph cable laid; Langham Place Group launch *English Woman's Journal.*
1859	Liberal unification; Palmerston Prime Minister			Volunteer Movement; Charles Darwin, *On the Origin of Species*; J.S. Mill, *On Liberty*; Dickens, *A Tale of Two Cities*; Samuel Smiles, *Self-help*
1860		Maori War	Cobden Free Trade Treaty with France; Food and Drugs Act	

Year	Government and politics	War and empire	Economic and social	Cultural and intellectual
1861	Death of Prince Albert	Amercian Civil War		Duty on paper abolished; Dickens, *Great Expectations*
1862			English Revised Code in education	
1863			Whiteley's department store opens; first underground railway in London	Football Association formed; rules of football codified; Charles Kingsley, *The Water Babies*
1864	Gladstone supports reform; Garibaldi in England		Contagious Diseases Act	
1865	Formation of Reform League; general election; death of Palmerston; Russell Prime Minister	Jamaica revolt		Lewis Carroll, *Alice's Adventures in Wonderland*
1866	Reform Bill defeated; Derby's third ministry; John Stuart Mill presents petition for women's suffrage		Financial crisis; 'Sheffield Outrages'	Queensberry rules in boxing
1867	Second Reform Act	British North America Act; Fenian rebellion		Church organ blown up in Walsingham; W. Bagehot, *The English Constitution*
1868	Disraeli Prime Minister Feb–Dec; Reform Acts for Scotland and Ireland; Gladstone's first ministry; Liberals win general election		Trades Union Congress first meeting	
1869	Disestablishment of Church of Ireland; women ratepayers get the vote in local elections	Opening of Suez Canal	National Education League; Charity Organisation Society formed	Matthew Arnold, *Culture and Anarchy*

Year				
1870	Butt's Home Government Association	Franco-Prussian War	Irish Land Act; Elementary Education Act for England and Wales	Married Woman's Property Act
1871		H.M. Stanley meets David Livingstone	Trade Union Act; Criminal Law Amendment Act	Darwin's *The Descent of Man*
1872	Ballot Act		Education (Scotland) Act; Licensing Act for England and Wales; National Agricultural Labourers' Union	First Scotland v England football match (score 0–0)
1873	Formation of Irish Home Rule League	Ashanti War; formation of Gold Coast		Moody and Sankey religious revival starts in Newcastle
1874	General election; Disraeli Prime Minister			
1875		Purchase of Suez Canal shares	Artisans Dwellings Act; Public Health Act; Conspiracy and Protection of Property Act	
1876	Queen made Empress of India; Disraeli becomes Earl of Beaconsfield		Merchant Shipping Act	Gladstone, *Bulgarian Horrors*
1877	Transvaal annexed			Wimbledon Tennis championship
1878		Congress of Berlin; invasion of Afghanistan; Cyprus acquired		
1879	Midlothian campaign; Parnell leads Irish Home Rule Party	Zulu victory of Isandlwana	Irish 'land war'; agricultural depression	
1880	General election; Gladstone Prime Minister	War with Boers	Employers' Liability Act; elementary education in England and Wales made compulsory	First Australia v England test match at cricket

PART 5

The imperial heyday
1880–1918

19

Britain and its Empire

Approaching empire and imperialism

Recent years have seen a revival of interest in empire and in the ideology of empire, imperialism. There is a general recognition that Britain cannot be understood without an awareness that it was the greatest of imperial powers from the eighteenth century until the middle of the twentieth. What is not agreed is what and who drove imperial expansion and how pervasive imperialist attitudes were within society at large. Nor is there a consensus amongst historians on the impact that empire had on domestic politics and domestic culture.

In the seventeenth and eighteenth centuries, empires had been justified in terms of mercantilism: colonies were necessary for the wealth of the mother country. By the early nineteenth century, however, there were growing doubts about mercantilism. The demand was for an end to restrictions and monopolies. The world's wealth was no longer seen as static, but as something that could grow by means of trade. For a Britain that was economically confident and dominant in manufactures, the philosophy of free trade made sense. In a free-trade world, colonies were of less value and, it is argued, British governments showed remarkably little interest in expansion in the half-century after 1820. Existing settlement colonies (where Britons had settled in significant numbers) were pushed towards self-government. Lord Palmerston, for one, believed that the value of colonies was overrated, declaring 'all we want is trade and land is not necessary for trade'. What Britain needed were markets and these did not require political control.

Such arguments were challenged by historians in the 1950s. Britain's concerns to ensure markets and supplies made her seek dominance and influence in as many areas as possible. This, the argument runs, was as much 'imperialism' as direct control was.

Over whole parts of the world, through economic dominance, Britain was able to maintain a hegemony without the use of force and create an 'informal empire'. If that did not work then they were quite ready to resort to force and assert political control.

Looking at the policies adopted towards the settlement colonies, it is possible to see much of the old pattern continuing through to the end of the 1840s. Emigrants from Britain headed for Canada and Australia in large numbers in the 1830s and 1840s and new areas of settlement were established in Western and Southern Australia and in New Zealand. However, by the end of the 1840s, Canada and the Australian colonies were moving towards responsible government. On the other hand, in the search for *new* markets there was an increasing readiness to use force. In India, the East India Company had lost its monopoly in 1813 and there was a huge expansion of both trade and political control over the next 20 years, culminating in the annexation of Sind, the Punjab and Kashmir in the 1840s. Attempts to push into Afghanistan ended in disaster and the wiping out of an Indian-British force of 165,000 soldiers and camp followers in 1842.

It was in response to pressure from trading interests in India that China was attacked in the Opium War of 1839–42 to force the Chinese government to open its economy to trade in opium and to cede Hong Kong. Further demands on China followed, with treaty ports to give privileged access to British goods. A policy of forceful intervention was pursued to spread markets. At the same time, piracy problems and merchant complaints led to steady encroachment on the independence of the Malay States. As a result of developments in tin extraction, the new Malay wealthy were not necessarily the traditional rulers. This created political instability, with European merchants backing rivals to get concessions. The breakdown of order encouraged further intervention until, by 1874, almost all the Malay rulers were obliged to accept guidance from British officials. There were huge opportunities for freebooters. The East Indian merchant James Brooke took control of an area of North Borneo in 1841 in order to suppress piracy and soon declared himself Rajah of Sarawak, a title which his sons and grandsons held until 1946.

Indian revolt, African scramble

Decades of policy contradictions and racial insensitivities in India generated grievances and simmering discontents that turned an army mutiny at Meerut in May 1857 into a much more serious rebellion that spread throughout Northern and Central India. The brutality on both sides was great. At Kanpur in June nearly a thousand Europeans, about half of whom were women and children, were massacred, and rumours of other massacres abounded. There was much talk of sexual assault by Indians on British women, talk that was to shape interracial attitudes for the rest of the time the British were in India. The lengthy siege of Lucknow, the capital of Oudh, which had only recently been annexed, provided the heroics to capture the public imagination in Britain. Despite the calls for restraint by the Governor-General, lampooned as 'Clemency' Canning, the military response against the rebels was brutal, urged on by politicians and press in Britain. Hundreds were hanged and many thousands shot on the spot. Most notoriously, some were strapped to cannons and blown to pieces, a punishment that had been practised by the Mughals.

Although most of the sepoys (Indian infantry privates) remained loyal, the effect of the rebellion on British thinking was traumatic. The East India Company's rule was brought to an end and the Crown took over its responsibilities, with a Secretary of State in London and a Viceroy and an all-British executive council in Calcutta. British India meant some 60 per cent of the subcontinent, with the remaining 40 per cent consisting of some 600 Indian states that ran their own internal affairs but recognised British suzerainty. The westernising assaults on Indian traditions were identified as a major cause of the unrest and, therefore, Viceroys resorted to more indirect rule through existing Indian elites. Educated Indians found their career opportunities blocked. Princes, once regarded as barbarous feudal anachronisms, now became traditional rulers and vital allies, who could rule with the guidance of British political officers or 'residents'. The proclamation of Queen Victoria as Empress of India in 1876, while in part a riposte to the centenary celebrations of independence in the United States, was also about giving a clear figurehead to the Indian aristocracy. The British rulers became, more than ever before, a separate ruling caste with all the pomp of the former Mughal emperors.

No area of empire caused so much trouble to the British as southern Africa, where racial and cultural differences between English and Boer and between black and white combined with economic and strategic problems. There were two settler colonies: Cape Colony, which had a majority of settlers of Dutch origin, and Natal, with fewer than 40,000 settlers scattered in isolated farms. Then there were the Boer Republics of the Transvaal and the Orange Free State, created by settlers trekking north to escape British domination in the Cape. The British claimed paramountcy over the Boer territories while accepting their right to self-government. Around these were various independent African communities whose peoples also spread into the areas of white settlement, their former homelands.

The 1840s to 1860s was what has been called a period of 'benign neglect' of Africa. By the 1870s, however, a policy began to emerge which implied a rather tighter hold on southern Africa, with the ultimate hope of creating a British-dominated federation. This involved trying to maintain amicable relations with the Boers and achieving stability on the frontiers. On the borders of the areas of white settlement there was pressure both for land and for labour and this, in turn, created pressure on the independent African states. Boer farmers were moving into Zulu lands in the constant search for farmland for the sons of large Boer families. Since they were not able to crush the Zulus on their own, there was pressure for British involvement. The independence of the Zulus under Cetshwayo and their readiness to resist white encroachments were an inspiration to other Africans to defy European pressure. The Zulus sought British mediation to curb Boer advances. It was in the aftermath of Boer defeats by Zulus that, in January 1877, the senior British official in Natal, the

Secretary for Native Affairs, led a small force into the Transvaal. It was justified by saying that the effectively bankrupt Boer state was incapable of defending its frontiers. His attempt to persuade the Boers to accept incorporation in a British South Africa was rejected and he announced annexation. He then turned on the Zulu Kingdom. Although the Zulus achieved a huge victory at Isandlawa, they eventually lost their political independence and much territory. The Zulu Kingdom was fragmented into petty fiefdoms and, although Cetshwayo was restored, he was no longer able to control the state, and civil war broke out. With the British entangled with the Zulus, the Boers felt confident enough to reassert their independence, which they gained after defeating a British force at Majuba Hill in 1881. It also encouraged freebooting Boer adventurers to push further into surrounding African kingdoms, once again adding to the instability on the frontiers.

Explanations of empire

Few issues have generated such debate as the reasons for imperial expansion and, particularly, the race for colonial expansion among European powers in the late nineteenth and early twentieth centuries. For a long time, many historians looked for economic explanations. Marxist historians favoured what is known as the Hobson–Lenin thesis, named after the economic journalist John Hobson, who first postulated it, and Lenin, who elaborated on it and popularised it for left-wing circles. This argued that imperial expansion was essentially a search for new areas of investment, coming at a time when returns from domestic investment were in decline, since capitalism, according to Lenin, was entering its last stages. Having invested, powerful financial interests then demanded that their investments be protected by government. While there were undoubtedly financiers who saw opportunities for better returns abroad, the biggest flaw in the Hobson–Lenin thesis is that most British investment did not take place in the new Empire that expanded from the 1870s, but in the old-established dominions and in the United States. Probably as little as a quarter of British investments went to the colonies in the last quarter of the nineteenth century.

A second economic explanation puts the focus on the search for new markets. As other countries industrialised, the competition for market share was intense, and sheltered colonial markets were attractive. Again, one can find evidence that shows that there was concern about the increasingly protectionist policies being pursued by other powers and worries that British goods would find themselves excluded from markets unless there were clearly delineated spheres of influence. On the other hand, aristocratic governments were not all that responsive to the needs of traders and remained very committed to the liberalisation of trade.

A third economic explanation emphasises the increasing importance of the search for secure supplies of scarce raw materials. Palm oil had become important from the late 1820s; by the 1850s, wool from Australia, tea and jute from India and tin from

Malaya were needed and, by the end of the century, rubber. Rubber was necessary, first for bicycles, which were gaining in popularity from the 1880s, and then, in the early twentieth century, for motor cars. It was also needed as insulation for the emerging electrical industry. After 1900, oil began to feature as a new, and increasingly vital, raw material, particularly once the navy began to convert. All of these intensified interest in the supplying regions in Africa, Asia, the Middle East and the Pacific.

Yet others have focused on strategic reasons for imperialism. Central to this is the place of India, 'the jewel in the crown'. Although economic factors were central to the initial expansion in India, by the late nineteenth century, other factors had come into play. India was a symbol of Britain's imperial greatness. It also meant that Britain was able to be a great military power, while still maintaining its traditionally small standing army at home. It gave Britain influence in other areas of Asia, like China and Indo-China. The route to India lay through the Suez Canal, opened in 1869, but also round the Cape of Good Hope, which remained of huge importance. Egypt and Southern Africa had to be kept out of the hands of other powers who might threaten the routes to the East.

Others have looked for sociological explanations, influenced by the ideas of the Austrian economist, J. E. Schumpeter. Schumpeter argued that the main social forces behind imperial expansion were atavistic ones – an aristocratic social class that saw its traditionally dominant role in society being challenged by the new financial and industrial middle class. They saw empire as a means by which their military and governing role could survive. In recent years, historians have latched on to the idea of 'gentlemanly capitalism', observing that powerful commercial, banking, shipping and trading interests in London had substantial imperial investments and close links with the aristocratic political class.

This brings us to political explanations of imperialism. The central argument suggests that all western European countries were facing major internal problems by the last quarter of the nineteenth century. A growing working class, increasingly organised in trade unions and in socialist parties, was posing a threat to the established political order, and was less and less willing to tolerate the fluctuations of the economic cycle. Imperial expansion offered a way of maintaining the standard of living of the European working class at the expense of the underdeveloped world. Colonies could also offer a safety valve for the unemployed and justify the maintenance of large armies. Finally, empire could appeal to crude instincts for domination and could persuade even those who were living in considerable poverty that they were still better off than those whom the best-known poet of imperialism, Rudyard Kipling, had labelled 'lesser breeds without the law'. Individual politicians learned to play the imperial card for their own advantage.

One has, of course, to distinguish between what shaped government policy and what motivated individuals. Racist perceptions of the superiority of western culture were everywhere. The historian Macaulay's view that 'a single shelf of good European literature is worth the whole of the native literature of India and Arabia' was widely adhered to. Thanks to the anti-slavery movement, the British liked to see themselves

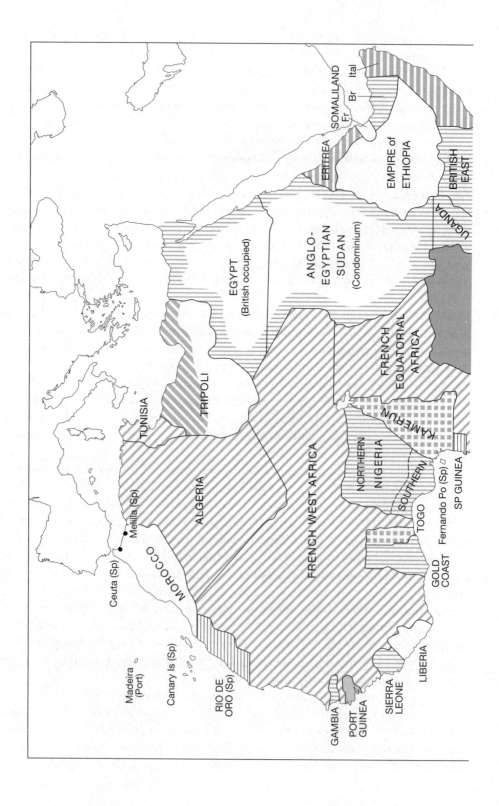

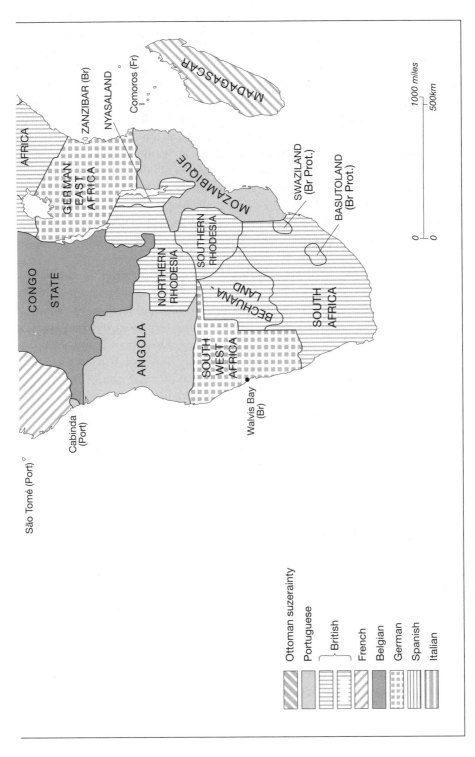

Map 3 Africa partitioned, *c.* 1914

as liberators from arbitrary government and barbarism. Traditional rulers in India, Burma, China and Africa were almost always presented as brutal to their subjects, while the British offered order and justice. Africa, in particular, by the second half of the nineteenth century, was regularly portrayed as 'in a savage state of nature'. The constant judgment was that other races were not like the British and that they needed to be taught to be the same. Only then would they be capable of governing themselves. British imperialists looked for evidence of loyalty, responsibility and diligence. The complaints against disloyalty were legion, with the enemy attacking in a treacherous manner, breaking truces, failing to play by the 'rules of the game'. Christian conversion was perceived as instilling a sense of loyalty in converts. The indigenous population were felt to lack a sense of responsibility; they could not be relied upon to do as was asked. Rudyard Kipling's *The White Man's Burden* talked of the cross he had to bear, to 'watch sloth and heathen folly, bring all your hopes to nought'. Diligence and a sense of time were also lacking – qualities which were essential if a reliable labour force, on which civilisation depended, was to be created.

It was believed that the world could be 'modernised' into a European mould by a combination of Christianity, civilisation and commerce. Christianity was seen as the foundation for other tastes and attitudes which, in turn, could lead on to economic development. However, 70 years of Christian missionary activity in India had proved remarkably unsuccessful. It is calculated that there were fewer than 2 million Indian Christians out of a population of around 254 million in 1881, and many of these were in groups that had been Christianised before the arrival of the British. Africa seemed to offer greater hope, and David Livingstone managed to link missionary activity with the campaign against slavery. He talked of a moral duty to establish a British presence in Africa to protect Africans from Arab slave raids. While earlier missionaries had tended to empathise with their flock, by the last quarter of the nineteenth century, most were more likely to adopt the prevailing racial attitudes on the inferiority of the black races.

Testing the explanations

The favourite area cited in support of the theory of capitalist imperialism is Egypt. Here one seems to have the right ingredients. Bankers and politicians, including Gladstone himself, had lent heavily to the Khedive (essentially the ruler, although in theory the country was still part of the Ottoman Empire) of Egypt. The British and French had already ousted one ruler in 1879 when he tried to get rid of European financial controllers, and replaced him by another who was expected to be more amenable. But there was a danger that, if the internal situation deteriorated, then he would renege on repayments; hence the need to restore financial order. In order to reorganise the finances, taxes had to be raised; these were put on the landed elite and funds to the Egyptian army were reduced. This prompted a rebellion by Colonel Ahmad Urabi's nationalist movement and demands for Egyptian participation in economic and financial decisions. These were seen by financial interests as pointing to 'disorder and anarchy' and threatening to challenge the system of dual control imposed by Britain and France. The bondholders called for more protection, leading in 1882 to direct military intervention.

For the British government, the dangers posed by nationalist success were three-fold. It might present a threat to access to the largely British-owned Suez Canal, opened in 1869 and the shortest and cheapest route to India. It might jeopardise the position of British creditors of the Egyptian government, of whom there were many. Thirdly, it might trigger similar nationalist movements in other areas of what was still nominally part of the Ottoman Empire. Britain had no desire to see an unregulated break-up of that empire.

Hopes of joint intervention by British and French forces were dashed when the French government fell and so the British forces acted alone. Alexandria, which the nationalists had been fortifying, was bombarded by the Royal Navy and Sir Garnet Wolseley crushed Colonel Urabi's forces at Tel-el-Kebir. The British found themselves in what, time and time again, was asserted to be *temporary* control of Egypt. Egypt was never formally annexed, but was to remain a real, if anomalous, part of the British Empire for another three-quarters of a century and until another nationalist revolt.

The other area that Hobson used to support his argument was South Africa. The South African War of 1899–1902 (dubbed the Boer War) was seen as having been carried out by Joseph Chamberlain on behalf of the South African mining magnates who were finding it difficult to get cheap black labour, because of the policies of the Transvaal government. This seemed to be confirmed in 1903, after the war, when Alfred Milner, the High Commissioner, allowed the importation of Chinese labour to work in the gold fields to solve cheap labour problems for the mine owners.

Economic interests had played their part in the move north from the Cape Colony. In 1889, the businessman and politician, Cecil Rhodes, formed the British South Africa Company, which was prepared to bear the cost of administration of the area south of the Zambezi river. By being willing to cover the costs, Rhodes overcame the British government's case against expansion. Germans, Portuguese and Boers all had interests in the same area, where there were hopes of gold discoveries, but Rhodes was able to mobilise pressure from the Cape to persuade the British government to declare a protectorate. Rhodes used charm, influence, contacts and bribery to sway opinion. He obtained his charter and the right to colonise and govern a huge area of southern central Africa, soon called Rhodesia. Similar things happened in other parts of Africa. In 1886, George Goldie, a trader on the River Niger, gained a charter for his Royal Niger Company and was given charge of the huge area around the upper river. In 1888, British interests in Kenya and Uganda were largely handed over to Sir William Mackinnon's Imperial British East Africa Company. Goldie, and others like him, generally had no desire to be subject to control by the British government. They wanted to be able to pursue their own activities without interference from the Colonial Office. It was not they, then, who were pressing the so-called new imperialism of metropolitan rule.

Some historians have tended to conclude that although financial interests could, on occasion, *influence* government, they did not actually *control* policy. Aristocratic governments were not pushed into imperial expansion against their will. The relationship of economic factors to imperialism is much more complex. Work on West Africa shows the social and political consequences of European involvement in particular areas. The key change in the economy of West Africa was the switch from external slave-trading to the production of vegetable oils. The former trade had been organised by large-scale entrepreneurs who were usually warrior chiefs. Vegetable oil production could be undertaken by small-scale producers, using family labour. The traditional warrior elite lost out. Drastic falls in the price of palm oil in the late 1880s created intense pressure on producers and traders. Tensions grew between old and new elites and between small and large-scale producers. At the same time, there was foreign competition for supplies and tensions over markets.

There were disputes between European creditors and African producers. African producers tried to push up prices by restricting supplies. Firms like Goldie's Royal Niger Company attempted to eliminate competition and cut out middle men in order to reduce costs. Competition between firms intensified. Merchants, who had once been suspicious of government intervention, now pressed for a more forward policy of imperial control. The demand was for the imposition of order in the hinterland to prevent the disruption of supplies. There was pressure for the abolition of internal tolls levied by African states and for more railway construction. Pressure on the Colonial Office from commercial interests to solve the economic, social and political problems caused by the growth of commerce led to the territory behind the trading stations on the coast being carved out more clearly. The advance of French interests from the north was a further complication. The boundaries of Nigeria were agreed with the French in 1898 and the government took over control from the Niger Company.

Elsewhere, the Empire was a sheltered environment for British exports at a time when British manufacturers were finding themselves squeezed out of European and United States' markets by both competition and high tariffs. India and other parts of the Empire were becoming a market for Lancashire textiles and for Welsh and Scottish iron.

There is no doubt that economic interests did play a large part in explaining imperial expansion in certain areas and at certain times. Cain and Hopkins have identified an interlocking elite of what they call 'gentlemanly capitalists' based mainly in the south-east of England – an elite that linked merchants, financiers, big landowners and government. These were people who had much invested in empire and were enthusiastic about it. But economic interests cannot solely explain imperial expansion any more than any other single factor and, of course, business activity with the developing world was seen not just as desirable in itself but as an agency of civilisation and modernisation.

Given the need to defend India, the routes to India also had to be protected. There were three routes; the first via Constantinople overland to the Persian Gulf – hence the policy of bolstering Turkey against Russian aggression. The second route was by way of southern Africa. The third, from the 1870s, was through the Suez Canal. A case can be made for seeing expansion in Africa as largely about defending the routes to India. The Cape of Good Hope remained of vital importance, since Suez was regarded as far too vulnerable in the event of war. Once it was decided that the Cape was indispensable then it had to be protected and the hinterland had also to be controlled.

Egypt, obviously, was vital for control of Suez. On the other hand, the invasion of Egypt should not be seen as the first stage in a grand partition of Africa. The British actually pulled out of the Sudan, which was an Egyptian protectorate, in 1885, after an Egyptian army under General Gordon had been annihilated by the forces of Mahdi Muhammad Ahmad and Khartoum captured. It was not until 12 years later, with concern growing that other powers might move into the area south of Egypt, that Britain came to feel it was necessary to control the headwaters of the Nile if Egypt and the canal were to be protected. That meant controlling the Sudan, and on 2 September 1898 an Anglo-Egyptian force under General Herbert Kitchener defeated the Mahdi's successor, Khalifa Addallah, at Omdurman. Modern technology overwhelmed the Dervishes. Kitchener lost 368 men in the battle while 11,000 of the Khalifa's forces fell under the machine-gun bullets. Kitchener's brutality in the Sudan and his desecration of the Mahdi's tomb were criticised in political circles, but his activities were publicised in the *Daily Mail* in such a way that he became the archetypal manly imperial hero. A week after Omdurman, Kitchener set off to confront a small French force under Colonel Marchand at the tiny settlement of Fashoda, south of Khartoum. After an overexcited few weeks in which war with France seemed possible, Marchand withdrew.

The need to protect routes could, of course, be extended to almost everywhere. It was easy to present any move by other powers as a potential threat to a British sphere of influence. But the almost total lack of British interest in an area like the Congo in the centre of Africa, that had no strategic importance – important though it was for raw materials such as rubber – would seem to support the argument that there was less concern for territory in which there was not a strategic interest. Relations with the Boers were, to an extent, governed by fears that they would allow Germany a foothold in their territory. The Boer attempts to break free from British hegemony – for example, by building a railway from the Transvaal to Portuguese territory to give them an outlet to the sea – were seen as dangerously independent. This made the Transvaal an area of growing alarm for the authorities in Cape Colony.

The people who were most aware of these strategic considerations tended to be the soldiers and the administrators on the spot rather than the government in London. Governments were pushed and pulled along, rather unwillingly, by colonials who got themselves into difficulties. This can be seen very clearly in India where an Indian government under the Viceroy could only be partly controlled by the Cabinet in London. Early on, much territory was seized by the East India Company against the wishes of the India Office and, indeed, some Governors-General were dismissed for pursuing expansionist policies. The threat to India was perceived as coming from

Russia, which had been steadily expanding its control over Central Asia. On the borders of India the so-called 'Great Game' was played out as the British sought to prevent Russian infiltration of the frontier areas, while the Russians were suspicious of British intentions in Central Asia. It is far from clear that either threat was a serious one but, nonetheless, it was used throughout the nineteenth century by the Indian government to justify a forward policy, meaning literally to get there before the Russians. The restraint most of the time came from London.

Concern about a Russian mission being received in Afghanistan in 1878 led to the second Afghan War and the imposing of a measure of British control at Kabul. Similar strategic considerations from an Indian perspective, this time about French advance in Indo-China, pushed the British into Burma. Another area of Indian concern was the Persian Gulf, a key trading area with India. Worries about Russian economic influence in Tehran arose in the 1890s, and there was pressure from India on London to take a tighter hold in Persia (Iran). Similar arguments were put forward for British involvement in Tibet and a force was sent there in 1902 – a move that was later repudiated by London.

Other examples can be cited where the government in London repudiated decisions made by colonial authorities that were in conflict with what, for the moment, were prior strategic considerations. As the settlements with France and Russia, and negotiations with Germany, in the early twentieth century were to show, there was a readiness to barter overseas territory for European considerations (see Chapter 25). The attraction of the emphasis on strategic considerations is that it presents the British as 'the reluctant imperialists', reacting to the activities of others. Russia threatened India, France West Africa and Germany South Africa and, therefore, Britain unwillingly had to take defensive action. The rest of the world did note, however, that, despite her reluctance, Britain did rather well out of the scramble for empire.

Political considerations

The argument that imperialism stirred up a popular nationalism to which politicians of all shades had to succumb is a powerful one. Disraeli saw how effective imperial slogans were in reviving Conservative fortunes in the 1870s. There was undoubtedly a great deal of propaganda in favour of imperialism. There were a number of influential books. J.R. Seeley, in *The Expansion of England* published in 1883, saw an indifference to empire, but, somehow, Britain had 'conquered and peopled half the world in a fit of absence of mind'. This could only indicate that there was some inevitable imperial destiny that had to be fulfilled, even though the English (the term used) had not fully realised that they were an imperial race. British civilisation was the model of the future that could be spread to the rest of the world. J.A. Froude in *Oceana or England and her Colonies*, which came out in 1886, argued that, without colonies, England would sink into insignificance, a mere trading community. Greatness was tied up with empire. The Empire could also offer some solution to the problems of the growing industrial towns with their large and unhealthy populations, suffering from 'physical decrepitude'. Empire would give space for the surplus population, but it would also provide a challenge, like the role of the frontier in the United States, saving 'the English race'.

Such books were aimed at the educated, but the ideas quickly found their way into popular acceptance. By the 1890s, popular imperialism was seen as something that would sell newspapers. A new, cheap, sensationalist press had emerged with the appearance of the *Daily Mail* in 1896. It could be argued that what they were tapping into was nationalism, as much as a desire for further expansion, but Seeley's idea that empire and nation should be synonymous had taken hold. By the 1890s, British society was well and truly saturated with nationalist and military images and ideas. The Queen, the army and the Empire all took centre stage, helped by the Queen's jubilees of 1887 and 1897.

There were other ways in which empire entered the consciousness of the British people. The word 'imperial' began to be used increasingly, with *imperial* companies and *imperial* conferences. There was a massive literature of tales from the Empire, such as Rider Haggard's *King Solomon's Mines* of 1885 and G.A. Henty's *With Roberts to Pretoria* of 1902 or *With Kitchener in the Sudan* of 1903. There was a powerful cult of the explorer, from David Livingstone through to H.M. Stanley, with masculinity largely being defined by adventure and militarism. Images of empire helped sell everything from toothpaste to coffee, tea, soap and bleach. The sense that the dominions were Britain abroad was further strengthened by tours by English and Australian teams with 'the Ashes' series dating from 1882. The New Zealand rugby 'All Blacks' had a very successful tour in 1905. An annual Empire Day was launched in 1904.

In his famous essay, *The Sociology of Imperialism*, published in 1919, J.A. Schumpeter argued that empire was not the product of new economic and social developments. It was the surviving elements of the pre-capitalist world, the soldiers and the aristocracy, who were the gainers. If empire mattered, then the conquerors and the administrators of empire remained vital. Part of the nationalist rhetoric was an emphasis on the heroic nature of British history. The heroes of the stories, men who were upper class, 'the best of the breed', tested their metal in Asia and Africa. The Empire offered power, challenge, a chance of a little wealth and, at least, a good pension, and it allowed the continuation in colonies of social hierarchies and structures that were, to an extent, being eroded in Britain. The generally aristocratic officer class took the same line and there were always promotion opportunities in imperial wars.

Whether the ordinary members of the public were quite so enthusiastic about imperial conquest is more questionable. Soldiers generally had a fairly low status within the working class. Where there was a sense of empire was with the old white colonies. Large numbers of emigrants had left Britain for Canada, Australia, New Zealand and, to a lesser extent, South Africa. The letters home from these immigrants produced a sense of a common community. This did not necessarily extend to a desire for conquest of new territory. It would be quite wrong to see British people unquestioningly swept up in a wave of imperialism. It is true that from 1886 until 1905 they voted for a Conservative Party that firmly identified itself with empire, but many continued to vote for a Liberal Party associated in many people's minds with anti-imperialism. In some ways, the sheer raucousness of imperial propaganda, particularly after 1884, perhaps indicates how difficult it was to persuade all that the Empire was a good thing. Certainly, the concern of right-wing nationalist organisations such as the Navy League (1894), the British Empire League (1896) and the National Service League (1906) was that the working class showed a marked indifference to anything beyond their daily existence. Against that, it can be argued, as by Edward Said and John MacKenzie, that the awareness of empire was so pervasive that it did not need to be spelled out. When the popular press and popular novelists wrote about adventure, heroes and military exploits, these were signifiers of imperialism.

Gladstone condemned Disraeli's policies in the 1870s. Gladstone was returned to power in 1880 on the back of a radical upsurge, rejecting Disraeli's apparently expansionist policies and yet, by 1885, Britain was deeply involved in the 'scramble for Africa'. There was no clear pulling back. Most significantly of all, Gladstone invaded Egypt. Despite this, as long as he remained leader, the Liberal Party was identified with anti-imperialism, but he led a party that was split on attitudes to empire. Lord Rosebery was the chief exponent of the argument that there needed to be a Liberal imperialism. He talked of imperialism in the language of Seeley: 'that greater pride in Empire which is called Imperialism and is a larger patriotism.' When Rosebery became Prime Minister in 1894, Uganda was annexed, although Gladstone had resisted it. What had been a Conservative policy had now become a Liberal one. A substantial number of radical Liberals opposed such a policy. They remained hostile to the new imperialism and saw it as the product of a vulgar, aggressive and immoral state of mind, which, as Gladstone had argued, it was the statesman's duty to curb. Many saw it as diverting attention from social problems at home.

When the Conservative government came back into power in 1895, Salisbury's Colonial Secretary was the former Liberal Joseph Chamberlain (see Chapter 23). He chose the Colonial Office because of a conscious belief in the importance of empire. He had come to believe in the need for an imperial federation, linking the white dominions – Canada, Australia, New Zealand and South Africa – in a common defence policy and an imperial customs' union. He probably envisaged that the dominions would remain mainly primary producers, while Britain would be the manufacturing country. Initially, he was restrained by Salisbury, but the kind of pronouncements that Chamberlain made encouraged expansionist colonialists. In a famous speech he indicated a shift in policy: 'I regard many of our Colonies as being in the condition of undeveloped estates, which can never be developed without imperial assistance . . . those estates which belong to the British Crown may be developed for the benefit of their population and for the benefit of the greater population which is outside.' Over the next few years, Chamberlain launched various schemes of irrigation and railway and harbour building in Africa, backed by government money. At every stage, however, he had to battle against Treasury resistance to such expenditure.

Focus on

Opposition to imperialism

This extract comes from an article by Robert Wallace (1831–99), Liberal Radical MP for East Edinburgh from 1886 until his death. He had previously been a Church of Scotland minister and editor of *The Scotsman* newspaper.

> Ever since the Queen's 'Diamond Jubilee' 'Empire-builders' have been having a high old time, which has grown higher and bolder since the great *coup* of Omdurman . . . The people to whom it is a positive intoxication to think of 'an Empire whose drum-beat, following the sun and keeping company with the hours, encircles the globe with an unbroken chain of martial airs' . . . to whom the conversion of home heathens and the civilization of home savages are dreary and insipid occupations compared with doing the same things among even more repulsive aliens, provided they are thousands of miles away and have never been seen by their Quixotic benefactors; the more or less consciously insincere people who profess that their real aim in depriving coloured races of their tribal or national independence is to work out what they call their 'destiny' – which they seem to have ascertained in many ways unknown to ordinary mortals – by getting the chance of 'educating' their victims, of delivering them from oppressors, of securing them the blessings of peace and justice, and not appreciably or at all to increase our wealth at their expense, or pamper our vainglory by the annexation of their territory, a view of matters credible, perhaps, to 'simple sinners' or 'the Marines', . . . all these classes of people have been swaggering about for months past brandishing the Imperial sword and beating the Imperial drum . . .
>
> The 'stricken field' of Omdurman and the 'Fashoda incident' and the wild and militant clamour which arose over them alarmed me into the belief that this Beaconsfield Imperialism, or Jingoism, had found its way into quarters where I had hitherto supposed it was an unwelcome stranger, and had even reached the utmost *penetralia* of the Liberal or Radical party, of which I am a humble member. . . . The Liberal Imperialist's emotion is a 'profound pride in the magnificent heritage of Empire won by the courage and energies of his ancestry'. I must confess this is not how the spectacle of Empire affects me. There is as much of regret as of pride in my feeling about it. . . .

Source: Robert Wallace 'The Seamy Side of Imperialism' in *Contemporary Review*, LXXV (1899), pp. 782–99.

Focus on

Joseph Chamberlain and the imperial mission

This is an extract from a speech by Joseph Chamberlain, the Colonial Secretary, to the annual Royal Colonial Institute dinner, 31 March 1897.

> But the British Empire is not confined to self-governing colonies and the United Kingdom. It includes a much greater area, and a much more numerous population in tropical climes, where no considerable European settlement is possible, and where the native population must always outnumber the white inhabitants; and in these cases also the same change has come over the Imperial idea. Here also the sense of possession has given place to a different sentiment – the sense of obligation. We feel now that our rule over these territories can only be justified if we can show that it adds to the happiness and prosperity of the people, and I maintain that our rule does, and has, brought security and peace and comparative prosperity to countries that never knew these blessings before.
>
> In carrying out this work of civilisation we are fulfilling what I believe to be our national mission, and we are finding scope for the exercise of those faculties and qualities which have made us a great governing race.

Source: http://www.wwnorton.com/college/english/nael/victorian/topic_4/chamberlain.htm

The South African War

Soon after Chamberlain came to the Colonial Office, Cecil Rhodes, the Prime Minister of Cape Colony, conspired to invade the Transvaal to overthrow the Boer state. The position of the Transvaal had altered dramatically with the discovery of gold in Witwatersrand in 1886. It brought resources to the Boer state that allowed it to be more assertive in its relations with Britain, and also pulled thousands into the boom town of Johannesburg. There was no way that a British government was going to let these huge gold resources fall into hostile hands. Initially, Chamberlain was quite happy with the idea that, should there be an uprising by the *uitlanders* (the white immigrant workers and businessmen involved in the gold mines but who had no political rights in the Transvaal), a force led by Rhodes' associate, Dr Leander Starr Jameson, would invade to 'rescue' them. In the end the rising did not take place, but Jameson's force still invaded on 30 December 1895. Chamberlain condemned the raid and demanded withdrawal. Jameson's troop pushed on, but within a couple of days was cut off by the Boers and rounded up. The Dutch in Cape Colony were extremely angry and dreams of South African unity were shattered. A House of Commons

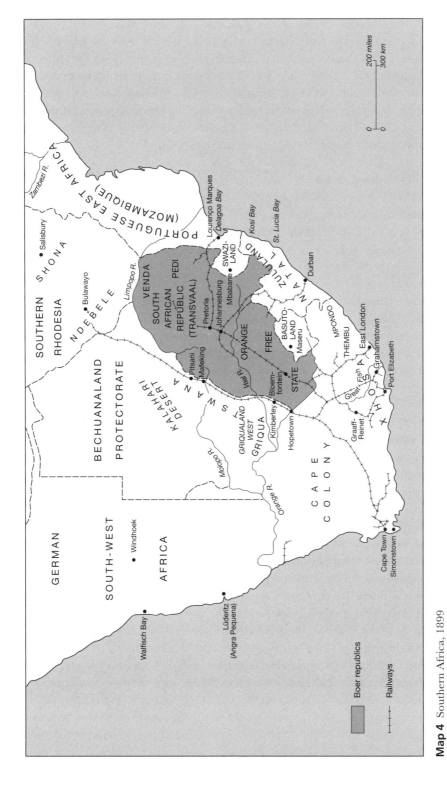

Map 4 Southern Africa, 1899

Source: Smith, Iain R., *The Origins of the South African War, 1899–1902* (Pearson Education, 1995)

inquiry on the question of complicity exonerated Chamberlain, but the vote was strictly on party lines. His first biographer says that he was lured by Rhodes. There does, however, seem little doubt that Chamberlain and the Colonial Office were involved to the extent of accepting Rhodes' assurances that an uprising was likely. Rhodes and the South Africans thought that Chamberlain was wholeheartedly supporting them. In the post-mortem on the raid, Chamberlain protected the South Africa Company's Charter in return for Rhodes ensuring the 'missing telegrams' between himself and Chamberlain conveniently disappeared.

A new High Commissioner, Sir Alfred Milner, was appointed, and relations with the Boers deteriorated rapidly. He had been sent to conciliate Dutch and British, but, as a firm believer in an Anglo-Saxon imperial mission, he was determined to force the Boers into a British-dominated union. There was something inevitable about the war which broke out in 1899, when the Transvaal demanded the removal of British troops from its borders. Most Liberals believed that Milner and Chamberlain had bungled negotiations with the Boers. Conservatives and Liberal imperialists, however, supported the war as something that had been forced on Britain by Boer intransigence and few had doubts about the strategic importance of the Cape. Among the Liberal radicals and Labour there was a group of pro-Boers who condemned Chamberlain and the war, arguing that Chamberlain had generated the conflict to help the investors and business interests in the Transvaal and in the largely British-owned mining companies. In fact, this is very doubtful. Chamberlain was concerned to retain British supremacy in southern Africa because of the Cape's vital importance as a naval base for imperial defence. He feared the emergence of a Dutch-dominated, republican federation, which seemed possible because of the rapidly increasing wealth of the Transvaal and the anti-British attitudes of the Cape Dutch after the Jameson raid.

The war, which went on until 1902, was a traumatic one in British history. Remarkably unprepared, the British found themselves surrounded at Mafeking, Kimberley and Ladysmith. In what quickly became labelled 'Black Week' in December 1899, British forces went down to defeat. But the tide gradually turned. Mafeking was relieved in February 1900, the news of which was greeted with wildly drunken jollification in London, repeated in May when Ladysmith fell. Pretoria, the capital of the Transvaal, was captured in June, but the Boers now embarked upon increasingly nasty guerilla warfare. The army found it difficult to cope with the unorthodox tactics adopted by the Boers. It made them resort to ever more violent reprisals. Boer farms were destroyed to prevent their being used as guerilla bases and the land was scorched. More than 111,000, people – mainly women and children from the farms – were incarcerated in prison camps and some 28,000 perished there from disease and malnutrition – 22,000 of them children under the age of 16. In the camps the policy of attempted anglicisation continued, with some 300 women teachers from Britain and the dominions recruited to work in the camps. Peace was eventually signed at Vereeniging in June 1902 and the Transvaal and the Orange Free State were annexed.

In the aftermath of the war, Chamberlain continued to pursue imperial dreams. In 1903, he launched a programme for tariff reform, with preference for colonial goods and protection against foreign goods. The Conservative Party was bitterly divided and the issue of tariff reform played a major part in bringing a Liberal majority in 1906. In other words, Chamberlain failed to find a popular response to his dreams of imperial unity. With the exception of Chamberlain, few leading British politicians had a clear commitment to imperial expansion and even he was basically following a policy of 'what we have we hold'. His stroke, which took him out of politics in 1907, removed a powerful imperialist voice (see Chapter 24).

The Liberals were in no sense opposed to the idea of empire. What they disliked was the jingoism that had dominated, as they saw it, the last 30 years, when empire as a moral force for progress had given way to rapacious exploitation and land grabbing. The introduction of indentured Chinese labour into the Rand goldfields was to the Liberal leader, Campbell-Bannerman, 'a system indistinguishable in many of its features from slavery'. In the view of Campbell-Bannerman and his associates in 1906, concepts of 'liberty' and 'justice' had to return to the centre of imperial activity. In southern Africa, the policy was one of trying to conciliate the Boers to achieve the long-wanted federation of southern Africa.

The price for reconciling the Boers and ensuring that the Cape remained loyal was to abandon any suggestion of racial equality. Article 8 of the Treaty of Vereeniging, which ended the South African War, had stipulated that the granting of the franchise 'to natives will not be decided until after the introduction of self-government'. Smuts, one of the Boer leaders who, in time, was most enthusiastic about conciliation with the British, talked of the need for 'a grand racial aristocracy' of whites to stand against an 'overwhelming majority of prolific barbarism', and the British government went along with this. Little was done to safeguard the rights of the black population, lest it cause friction with the whites. Nor were civil rights granted to the substantial 'coloured', largely Indian population in South Africa, since to do so might have raised the question of similar rights for the Indians in India. These issues were left to the future South African legislatures, undoubtedly with the hope that attitudes would change and a more liberal public opinion would emerge.

Self-government was given to the Transvaal in 1908 and to the Orange Free State in 1909 and Boer majorities were returned. The long-cherished Union of South Africa followed in 1910. In all, racist policies were firmly built in. In 1911, a Native Regulation Act imposed a rigid colour bar in employment and was designed to secure that blacks did not gain skilled jobs. A 1913 Land Act abolished land ownership for most black Africans, with the intention of forcing them into wage labour.

A policy of indirect rule was favoured with regard to other areas of Africa. While there does seem to have been an effort by the Colonial Office to curb overly aggressive tactics by people like Lord Lugard in northern Nigeria and to restrain the amount of white settlement in Kenya, in the event, words of reprimand were not likely to be an effective hindrance to those on the spot.

It is hard to find a clear or consistent pattern in British imperial expansion, other than to keep hold of territories it already possessed as well as any areas where there was a trading bridgehead. Certainly, there were commercial interests, to which governments would respond erratically. There were strategic concerns on the part of government as they saw other countries assert their interests in particular areas. There were religious and humanitarian groups, who sought to christianise. There were more ruthless, speculative interests, tycoons like Rhodes, who pulled in governments against their will. The interaction of all of these had succeeded in creating an empire that covered a third of the world by 1914.

Further reading

Cain, P.J. and Hopkins, A.G., *British Imperialism. Innovation and Expansion 1688–1914* (Harlow, Longman, 1993)

Cannadine, David, *Ornamentalism. How the British Saw their Empire* (London, Penguin, 2002)

MacDonald, Robert H., *The Language of Empire. Myths and Metaphors of Popular Imperialism, 1880–1918* (Manchester, Manchester University Press, 1994)

MacKenzie, J.M. (ed.), *Imperialism and Popular Culture* (Manchester, Manchester University Press, 1986)

Porter, Andrew (ed.), *The Oxford History of the British Empire, III: The Nineteenth Century*, (Oxford, Oxford University Press, 1999)

Porter, Bernard, *The Absent-Minded Imperialists. Empire, Society and Culture in Britain* (Oxford, Oxford University Press, 2004)

Rich, Paul, *Race and Empire in British Politics* (Cambridge, Cambridge University Press, 1990)

Said, Edward, *Culture and Imperialism* (London, Vintage, 1993)

Smith, Ian R., *The Origins of the South African War 1899–1902* (Harlow, Longman, 1996)

Thompson, Andrew S., *Imperial Britain. The Empire in British Politics, c.1880–1932* (Harlow, Longman, 2000)

Woollacott, A., *Gender and Empire* (Basingstoke, Palgrave Macmillan, 2006)

20

The late-Victorian and war economy

Economic contradictions

The mid-Victorian period from 1850 to 1880 was one of enormous success for the British economy. As we saw in Chapter 13, there had been tremendous growth in heavy industries (such as coal mining, shipbuilding, the iron industries, the railways); rising production and diversification across the whole economy; burgeoning investment both at home and abroad; and rising standards of living for the majority of the people. Poverty, poor housing, ill-health and many other social problems of a very severe nature persisted, but economic prosperity had marked the period.

The late-Victorian and Edwardian period from 1880 to 1914 was one of a rather different, though confusing, character. It was a period of apparent contradictions. On the one hand there is evidence of sustained growth in economic performance, particularly in those industrial sectors that had been pioneered in the previous 100 years. In heavy industry, Britain came to rule the world economy, supplying over a third of the world's ships, exporting massive quantities of coal, and supplying even the world's traditional textile nations like India with cheap cottons from the mills of Lancashire in England and finer cottons from Lanarkshire and Ayrshire in Scotland. Technologically and imperially, Britain seemed in many respects to rule the world. The Empire covered a third of the land mass of the globe, and, within that, the nation had a free-trade empire, providing a ready market for her products and places for investment. But British investment was not limited to the Empire and, indeed, most went outside it. Investors continued to pour millions of pounds into the burgeoning industries and into transport systems – notably railways and harbour development – of places like North and South America as well as India and Australia. This was an especially good period to be an investor, for there was money to be made on the back of the explosion in British economic dominance in the world.

The statistics of industrial production seem very impressive. In Table 20.1, it can be seen that all the major staple products were growing rapidly for most of the period. With steel production taking over from the older form of pig-iron, industrial production of these products reached a peak in 1913, the last full year of production before the outbreak of the First World War in August 1914. The textile industry was still importing growing amounts of raw cotton (around 80 per cent of it from the USA), illustrating that, even as the economy had moved increasingly into heavy industry, textiles remained a very important sector. But at the heart of the continuing industrialisation of the nation was the coal industry. Employing over a million workers by 1913, it was a vast enterprise, producing coal from places with major deposits stretching from Kent in the south-east, through South Wales, the Midlands, Lancashire, Durham and the north-east, into Ayrshire, Lanarkshire and Fife. The doubling of coal output from 129 million tons in 1873 to 287 million tons in 1913 is a significant indicator of economic growth. The year 1913 represents the all-time high point of coal output in Britain. Though much of the coal was burnt in the home, and a portion was being exported, British industry was heavily reliant on coal to power steam engines, steam locomotives and steam ships. It also powered the blast furnaces producing the rising output of pig-iron and steel which, in turn, was used in all manner of metal products, ranging from ships and locomotives to buckets and spades. The enormous growth in shipbuilding was particularly located on the rivers Clyde, Wear, Tyne and Lagan,

Figure 20.1 Launched in 1911 for the White Star Line, RMS *Titanic* hit an iceberg on its maiden voyage on 15 April 1912. Of the 2,227 passengers only 705 survived.
Source: Mary Evans Picture Library

Table 20.1 Industrial production in the UK 1853–1938: cotton, coal, pig-iron, steel and steam ships

Year	Cotton total imports (millions of lbs)	Coal (millions of tons)	Iron (millions of tons)	Steel (millions of tons)	Steam ships (number)	(thousands of tons)
1854/55	887	65	3.7	–	174	64.3
1863	670	86	4.5	–	279	107.9
1873	1,528	129	6.6	0.6	396	281.6
1883	1,734	164	8.5	2.0	806	621.6
1893	1,417	185	6.9	2.9	448	380.4
1903	1,793	230	8.9	5.0	695	586.8
1913	2,174	287	10.3	7.7	755	950.0
1923	1,357	276	7.4	8.5	313	375.7
1933	1,487	207	4.1	5.3	284	74.0
1938	1,324	227	6.8	10.4	454	489.5

Note: figures from 1923 exclude Irish Free State/Republic of Ireland.
Source: B.R. Mitchell and P. Deane (eds), *Abstract of British Historical Statistics* (Cambridge, Cambridge University Press, 1962), pp. 115–6, 131–2, 136–7, 180–1, 221–2.

though smaller yards elsewhere also grew, contributing to the country's dominance in both world shipbuilding and world shipping.

These data provide an image of economic growth for the period 1880 to 1913. This image is intensified by looking in Table 20.1 at the decline in production figures for 1913 to 1938. In this longer-term context, Britain's economic performance before 1914 looks extremely impressive.

There is, however, another image of the economy for this period. This second view is one of relative economic decline and, in certain respects, stagnation. What is the evidence for this? First, there was the start of a slowdown in overall economic growth. Growth in overall output, known as gross domestic product (GDP), showed a drop from 2.1 per cent per annum in 1873–99 to 1.4 per cent in 1907–13. Second, despite British dominance of the world economy for most of this period, there was a decline in its share of world markets. Between 1899 and 1913, the value of British exports grew by 48 per cent, but, as a proportion of all world exports, they declined from 36 per cent to 30 per cent (and continued to fall to 20 per cent by 1929).[1] Third,

---

[1] GDP figures from N. Crafts, 'Long-run growth', in R. Floud and P. Johnson (eds), *The Cambridge Economic History of Modern Britain: Volume II: Economic Maturity, 1860–1939* (Cambridge, Cambridge University Press, 2004), p. 13. Export figures calculated from data in C.K. Harley, 'Trade, 1870–1939: from globalisation to fragmentation', in ibid., p. 162.

British industry was succeeding well in traditional staple industries, but it was performing much less strongly in newer industries than other countries. It was especially poor in consumer and consumer-related goods – electricity production, electrical products, motor cars, pharmaceuticals and chemicals, as well as cheaper consumer products like pianos and trinkets of various kinds. Production, sales, and exports of these new goods tended to be rising much more steeply in the USA and Germany than in Britain. And fourthly, the dominance and cheapness of home coal was making the British economy difficult to modernise. Coal's cheapness made it uneconomic for many industrialists to move to electrical power, and this hindered the development of electrical products and electricity-powered production. It also reduced the speed with which Britain moved from coal-fired to diesel-powered ships.

Part of the story here concerns a downturn in economic performance in Britain in the first part of the period. Between 1873 and 1896 there was what was called at the time (and since) the 'great depression' in the British economy. This is especially associated with the performance of British agriculture, and the growing dependence on the importation of foodstuffs – including meat brought under refrigeration for the first time from New Zealand, Australia, South America and the USA. Although British agricultural workers and the British countryside were adversely affected by falling prices for food as imports rose, the bulk of the population, of course, gained greatly from this. Cheap, usually imported, foodstuffs more than made up for stagnating wage rates. Consumption of food, clothing and even luxuries went up. Chains of food shops – with names like Thomas Lipton's from Glasgow, Coopers in Liverpool, John Williams in Manchester, and John Sainsbury's in London, as well as Co-operative stores – spread in these decades, selling butter and margarine, bacon and ham, tea and biscuits to a growing working-class market. These multiple grocers offered cheapness and quality, hugely benefiting industrial workers and their families. So, whilst there has long been much debate about whether this depression existed or not, it is not possible to report that it was wholly detrimental to Britons.

However, there were also significant problems in the industrial sector. It is during this period that Britain's two big competitors – Germany and the United States – started to deprive it of both international markets and international growth and investment. The USA and Germany grew very strongly in those traditional heavy industries in which Britain had been a pioneer, but did so with the widespread application of new and efficient production techniques. In coal mining, for instance, those two nations developed their operations very dramatically, using mechanical coal-cutting equipment, moving railway extraction of coal, and fewer but more highly skilled and better-paid workers. By comparison, most British coal mines were owned by small, less well-capitalised firms, and retained manual coalface operations (men digging coal out with picks) and used lifts rather than moving conveyor belts in coal extraction.

Secondly, during the period between 1880 and 1913, the USA and Germany moved into the manufacture of new products. Amongst these were electrical goods, electricity generation, oil production, motor cars and synthetic chemicals and drugs. Now, on the face of it, Britain witnessed rapid growth in these products. Table 20.2 shows the

Table 20.2 Cars and goods vehicles on British roads 1904–38 (thousands)

Year	Cars	Goods vehicles
1904	8	4
1908	41	18
1914	132	82
1918	78	41
1928	885	306
1938	1,944	495

Source: B.R. Mitchell and P. Deane (eds), *Abstract of British Historical Statistics* (Cambridge, Cambridge University Press, 1962), p. 230.

growth in the numbers of cars and goods vehicles on British roads, and it looks impressive. However, the international comparison was less promising; by 1938 there was only 1 car for every 20 people in Britain compared to 1 car for every 9 in the USA.

In essence, Germany and the USA were starting to construct economies based on the production of consumer goods for the home and leisure, whilst Britain continued to specialise in the production of capital goods for industry and commerce – things like locomotives, ships and railway lines. On top of that, British production methods failed to modernise sufficiently. In addition to failure to move from coal power to the use of electricity for production, there was a failure to develop a high wage economy using skilled labour. In Germany and the USA, the labour force became more highly skilled and better paid and able to buy the consumer goods they were making. Thus, there was the development of a car culture in the USA even before the outbreak of the First World War.

By 1913, therefore, the British economy appeared to be extremely strong, still the largest exporting economy in the world, and with a free trade market in her colonies. London was the world's financial capital; the pound was the strongest currency; Lancashire dominated the world production of cotton textiles; South Wales was a massive exporter of coal; and the Glasgow area dominated shipbuilding and the making of marine engines and locomotives. But there were enormous problems looming, as indicated by the failure to modernise methods of production, products and the skill base of its workers. How do we account for Britain's problems and the failure to tackle them?

Did the late-Victorian economy fail?

The late-Victorian economic condition of Britain is a significant focus of attention for historians. This is because many of the roots of Britain's later relative economic decline are traced to the period 1880–1918. Economic historians have, since 1970, been divided over whether the economy failed and, if so, how it failed.

It is important to start by isolating the precise underlying development that gave rise to this debate. The dominant focus of inquiry into the British economy since around 1870 is its decline relative to many other countries (notably other industrial advanced economies such as the USA, Germany and most of Europe, Japan and elsewhere). The term 'relative economic decline' is very important, because it is distinguished from what would be an erroneous view – that the British economy was in (absolute) decline. Consequently, it is vital to acknowledge that the British economy continued to grow between 1880 and 1914, but whereas before 1880 Britain had outstripped most of its competitors, after 1880 its rate of growth was exceeded by these other nations. This is seen as an important turning point. During 1780–1880, Britain had been the world's leading industrial nation – the first to become industrial, and the strongest – but between 1880 and 1914 it lost its dominance to the USA, whilst Germany was close behind in many respects.

The 'late-Victorian economy failed' hypothesis concerns a failure to keep up, rather than an absolute decline and economic collapse. The question was first posed by McCloskey in 1970, and has been elaborated since then. A number of key propositions have been put forward by economic historians to make the case that the economy failed and to explain why it happened.

(a) The 'early start' thesis

This thesis holds that, because Britain industrialised first in the late eighteenth and early nineteenth centuries, ahead of places like Germany and the USA, it suffered the consequences. It became set in grooves of old technology, old working practices and old products from which it was very expensive to escape after 1870. It was cheaper to keep old equipment trundling along inefficiently than to scrap it and invest in new machinery. This situation was reinforced by labour being plentiful, less skilled and cheaper than the fewer, more skilled and more expensive workers needed to run new technology. Employers saw little reason to change their working arrangements. New technology also required new factory buildings or configurations of work processes. Moving production lines needed very different layouts from old-fashioned batch production of goods. In addition, in mining it was geologically impossible to adapt old mines to the needs of new machinery; mines had to be dug with coalface chambers suited to large machines rather than the low-ceilinged coalfaces used in manual digging, and sloping extraction shafts were needed for conveyor belt removal rather than vertical lifts.

The 'early start' thesis thus argues that economies that started industrialisation later were always going to be in a preferential position. Such nations could wait to see which technology worked the best, save on development costs, design infrastructure like railways after the mistakes had been sorted out by countries that industrialised first. The late starter was always going to be able to modernise and grow faster in the long term. Countering this is evidence that Britain's new industries were growing more rapidly in the 1890s and 1900s than staple industries. By 1907, 10 per cent of employment was in new industries – small, but still a significant innovation.

(b) The weakness of the imperial economy

A second thesis is that Britain suffered from reliance on a sheltered market, the empire. British goods and products remained weaker in design and uncompetitive in price terms on international markets because they were sold to colonies where they had considerable competitive advantage over products from other countries. In this way, British goods did not have to face the full impact of competition or respond to new types of product, new design, and the cost issues in production. As a result, British products and manufacturing processes remained inferior, and became increasingly so the longer this imperial reliance lasted. When the reliance on empire broke down during the First World War, it caused a crisis. India, for example, developed its own cotton industry and bought a smaller proportion of cotton goods from Britain, contributing to the start of a decline in the Lancashire cotton industry.

The imperial reliance thesis has had supporters for many years. But though some British merchants became lazy and uninterested in modernisation because of the security of profits from sales to the colonies, there are many observers who feel that the imperial economy was only a small part of the British economic experience, and that the country's products were performing better in other markets.

(c) Shortage of investment

This argument is that British investors – both private and banks – starved British industry of investment to upgrade production lines and products. Money was diverted overseas, where investors who felt 'safe' investing in railways, docks and transport could find good returns, reducing the risk from new-industry investment at home. Also, a deeply conservative banking system favoured longstanding clients and traditional sectors of investment at home in preference to new entrepreneurs and new products. Another element in this thesis is the reliance in Britain on cheap waged labour (compared, for instance, to the USA). The economic success of Scotland at this time, for example, is often attributed to the low wage rates paid to industrial workers (9–13 per cent lower than in England in the 1890s), who, as a result, lived in some of the worst housing in the industrialised world.[2] Low wages were a cheaper option for industrialists than investment in expensive machines, creating a heritage of under-investment and technological lag (for instance, in coal-powered batch production factories rather than electricity-powered moving production lines).

---

[2] R.J. Campbell, *The Rise and Fall of Scottish Industry 1707–1939* (Edinburgh, John Donald, 1980), pp. 191–4.

It is not yet known how effective banks in USA or Germany were by comparison. A long-held view of economic historians is that the German banks played a big part in investing in industrialisation in this period whilst British banks did not. However, a new view is emerging that British banks were not as inefficient or conservative as was previously thought, responding to investment requests when approached. As for wage levels, they did rise comparatively after 1900, though American workers continued to enjoy higher levels of pay.

(d) The climacteric argument

This argument proposed that there was a hiatus in British economic growth in the second part of this period – in the 1890s and after – caused by diminishing returns from investment in an already well-developed economy. The evidence of growth failure – a fall in GDP growth from 2.1 per cent per annum in 1873–99 to 1.4 per cent in 1907–13 – seemed to point unfairly to poor performance. It is suggested that British managers of industry were operating quite rationally in deciding, unlike American counterparts, that with cheap labour and lower demand for new products, modernisation was inappropriate. In this argument, the economy could not have grown any faster. The managers were facing an overpowering situation and were not guilty of failing to keep up. Certainly, by the late-Victorian period, the potential for growth was more limited than in the USA, with its opening up of bountiful natural resources, its rising and skilled immigrant population and its ability to borrow the best of start-up technology from Britain. It was also more limited than in European nations which bought in British firms and workers to start up industries and train their workers, and which were able to impose high tariffs behind which infant industries could be nurtured to size and profitability without British competition. Indeed, Britain's attachment to free trade in the 1880–1914 period was an important part of the nation's political and moral culture which other nations neither shared nor emulated. British investors may have been under-ambitious with respect to the types of industry into which they put their money. Railways remained the favourite, but main lines had all been constructed, so most of the 5,000 miles of new track between 1880 and 1900 were branch lines, which quickly lost money. This led British investors to move into overseas ventures – notably, still being under-ambitious in railway and transport investment – and into land in places as diverse as the USA, Australia and Argentina. However, it remains arguable how much this outflow of investment was the cause or the consequence of low investment needs at home.

Critics of this argument suggest that there are problems with the growth data, and that decline in growth was actually much smaller; in other words, British growth failure was minor. This would then diminish the suddenness of the change in British economic fortunes in the late-Victorian period. Indeed, it would tend to push the timing of any relative economic decline from the Victorian and Edwardian periods to the interwar period. Thus, critics suggest, that there was no essential failure before 1918.

(e) The failure of entrepreneurship

This argument lays the blame for the failure of British industry to keep pace with that of the USA and Germany at the door of the owners and managers of industry who did not innovate in new products, new production methods and new markets (especially outside the colonies). The evidence here relies on the slower growth rates, older capital products and out-of-date production methods. The failure is seen to consist in lack of risk-taking, not modernising management practices sufficiently quickly, relying on unskilled labour rather than science and new engineering, not carrying out good market-testing to find out what consumers wanted, and not learning about the new products.

Many economic historians react against this argument. First, there is much evidence of entrepreneurial success in this period, of managers taking risks, using new technology, winning new markets, and competing very successfully. This is obvious in the expanding retail sectors, but it also applies to firms in traditional staple industries which had to compete against newer companies overseas, with fewer shackles of old equipment and so on. Second, there is plenty of evidence of science education within British industry. The number of members of British engineering institutions rose from 4,000 to 40,000 between 1870 and 1914, and though the USA and Germany may have had a lead in science-trained personnel in industry between 1830 and 1880, British industry was closing the gap rapidly thereafter. Third, rather than the standardised output and processes pioneered in the USA, there was a strong tradition of craft know-how on the British factory floor, yielding the flexibility and customised product that British industry tended to offer.[3] Fourth, rather than individuals, institutions were responsible for a degree of 'failure', because institutional rigidity had crept into the mature British economy by the 1880s; this restrained choice and promoted existing economic elites (like managers) helping each other to survive against challengers. Fifth, there is the suggestion of 'path dependence' in which managers were limited in their choices because of infrastructure constraints, such as a failure to increase railway efficiency through using larger-sized coal wagons because loading and unloading facilities were prohibitively expensive to replace everywhere at the same time. In this way, a myriad of explanations to challenge the thesis are deployed.

---

[3] G.B. Magee, 'Manufacturing and technological change', in R. Floud and P. Johnson (eds), *The Cambridge Economic History of Modern Britain: Volume II: Economic Maturity, 1860–1939* (Cambridge, Cambridge University Press, 2004), pp. 92–5.

Focus on

Harry Gordon Selfridge

One of the important areas for entrepreneurs in the early twentieth century was retailing. With improved transport, rising disposable income and widening consumer products, shrewd business people could make or exploit dramatic changes to public taste.

One such was American-born Harry Gordon Selfridge (1858–1947), who, in 1909, opened his own magnificent department store in London. Selfridge's was located on what was then the unfashionable end of Oxford Street in London, but Selfridge had a feel for customer desires. He sensed the need for British shopping to break out of a certain feeling of austerity and restraint, and sought to make purchasing a pleasurable and exuberant experience. Having splashed London with advertisements for his store opening (including four large features in *The Times*), he opened the store on 15 March 1909 in some style. *The Times* reported:

The opening of Selfridge's

The great 'Store' which Messrs. Selfridge and Co have erected on Oxford-street, London, was opened yesterday almost literally with a flourish of trumpets, for a bugle sounded at 9 o'clock was the signal for the unlocking of the doors. Thenceforward until late in the evening the building was crowded with interested visitors. There was much curiosity manifested in this imposing American 'Store' which Messrs. Selfridge have created in the centre of London. The proprietors, besides scattering some 600,000 personal invitations broadcast throughout the land, extended a formal welcome through the newspapers to the 'entire public' to visit Selfridge's during the first week of its existence. The invitation was accepted yesterday by a vast number of people, and it was noticeable that women – whose enthusiasm for new shops, whether American or English, is of course irrepressible – by no means predominated unduly; the male sex was well represented. There were small crowds of potential shoppers outside the doors before 9 o'clock, and a rush was made for the honour of making the first purchase.

The elaborate decoration of the exterior with festoons of laurel and the flags of all nations, no less than the gala appearance of the shop windows – in which costumes were displayed, with flowers and painted panels for background – gave some hint of the sights that were in store for Messrs. Selfridge's visitors. The interior of the building presented the appearance rather of a fair than a mere shop. There were masses of flowers and foliage everywhere, while the two great 'wells,' which reach from the ground floor to the skylights in the roof, were filled with myriads of tiny globules suspended on threads, which reminded one of the snow that was falling outside. There were orchestras playing apparently at every corner. The glittering array of wares, seen to the best advantage in show rooms that are more airy and spacious – owing to the absence of dividing walls and partitions – than those which are familiar to London eyes, impressed one with their infinite variety. There appeared to be everything here that man or woman could desire to purchase. Apart, however from the open aspect of the rooms, there was bound to be little that was typically American about the 'Store,' except, perhaps, the lavish supply of telephones and the pleasant habit of the shop assistants in refraining from asking what they could do for one.

On the top floor the visitors found suites of restaurants. Adjoining the restaurants is a roof garden, where, in more sunny weather than was experienced yesterday, they may take coffee in the open air. Descending from the fourth floor to the one beneath it, the visitors discovered reception rooms decorated in different styles – known as the American, Colonial, French, and German rooms – together with galleries in which are displayed pictures and other works of art. An interpreter's room has been set apart for foreign visitors. There are also on this floor a 'rest' room for ladies and a room in which a trained nurse is constantly in readiness to provide 'first aid' to the sick. Railway and steamship ticket offices, a *bureau de change*, a library, information desk, post and telegraph office, and a theatre booking office all find places on the third floor, and a hairdressing saloon is at the service of customers.

Selfridge promoted 'the pleasure of shopping' – encouraging shoppers to browse in his store, when such freedom to walk around without buying was not generally encouraged in other shops, where assistants tended constantly to offer assistance. Shoppers, he realised, did not necessarily know what they wanted when they went shopping – something other stores were less likely to appreciate. He particularly targeted the female shopper, being one of the first department store owners to realise just how dominant women were in purchasing not just clothes, but household and consumer goods as well.

Selfridge himself was a flamboyant figure, given to several affairs with women, and he exuded the same style in dress and behaviour for which his store became famous. He walked his store for an hour each morning, encouraging staff to give him new ideas and boosting morale. In the interwar years, Selfridge became a spendthrift and gambler, but his store was initially easily successful enough to sustain his wants. However, by the later 1930s he was proving a drain upon the business, and in 1939 was ousted from the board with a small salary which he was forced to relinquish two years later, to live in a small house, dying in relative poverty at the age of 89.

Sources: Quotation from *The Times*, 16 March 1909. Additional material from Gareth Shaw, 'Selfridge, Harry Gordon (1858–1947)', *Oxford Dictionary of National Biography*, Oxford University Press, 2004 [http://www.oxforddnb.com/view/article/36010, accessed 22 May 2008]; L. Woodhead, *Shopping, Seduction & Mr Selfridge* (London, Profile Books, 2007).

(f) The decline of the industrial spirit (the Wiener thesis)

This thesis was made famous in the 1980s by an American historian called Martin Wiener. He argued that Britain went into relative economic decline, compared to Germany and the USA, because the British never really became imbued with 'the industrial spirit'. He claimed that, as Britain industrialised, and as there was a growth of industry and the capitalist ethos of working hard in towns and cities, in factories and in commerce, so industry actually remained extremely unfashionable amongst the British elites and in British consciousness as a whole. He cited the continued dominance of the landed elites and the ethos of the leisured classes in the countryside. He noted how British industrial millionaires wanted to give up working in industry as soon as they could, and bought into landed estates. This culture of the countryside, Wiener stated, was still visible in the 1980s. Moreover, he said, it was not visible in the USA and Germany in the same way. He argued that those two countries developed very thorough cultures devoted to industry, cities and the ethos of hard work. Engineers and getting oneself dirty in industrial work became accepted and prized in American and German culture, but not in British culture. In essence, according to this thesis, the economy of a nation is dependent on its culture.

In this account, the British educational system looms large. It is claimed that, even at the height of British industrial leadership in the world economy in the nineteenth century, the country's elite schools and universities nurtured a social snobbery against industrialism. This was especially true of Oxford and Cambridge Universities, where study of the classics dominated, ignoring large swathes of science and technology. In 1870, only 19 students graduated with degrees in science, maths or technology, and even in 1908 there were only 300 students in the whole of England enrolled for applied science degrees.[4] Though the Classics were seen as superior in Scottish universities, a much stronger science tradition existed there, stretching back to the eighteenth century. Most science education was going on in technical colleges and university colleges outside the golden triangle of Oxbridge and London.

There are many criticisms of this thesis. Firstly, it is seen as overly dependent on a cultural argument about economics, and based on inconclusive evidence – in other words, it is seen as an unfalsifiable argument. The role of religion in entrepreneurship is especially hotly debated, seemingly without resolution, with some historians alleging that Protestant Nonconformists were numerically significant as entrepreneurs, and others denying it. The claim of British cultural hostility to industrialism is seen as being overreliant on minor examples, rather than on systematic evidence. Indeed, economic historians produce examples of long-term innovation, entrepreneurship, economic renewal and world economic leadership. Finally, the Wiener thesis is seen as being the product of its particular political times – the late 1970s and 1980s – when

---

[4] G.B. Magee, 'Manufacturing and technological change', pp. 91–2.

the British economy was viewed as having been in decline for some decades. It was regarded as a 'basket case' by contemporary right-wing politicians, who read back into their understanding of the past British muddle, lack of innovation, spunk and risk-taking, and an overpowering trade-union tradition opposed to change and flexibility. This view has, with hindsight, proved to be at best overstated, and at worst plain wrong. The notion of Britain in decline in the third quarter of the twentieth century is now much changed (as we shall see in Chapter 27).

The answer to the claims of failure in the late-Victorian economy probably lies somewhere in the middle of all these arguments. Other countries were bound to catch up on Britain. There was little chance of one nation dominating a world economy forever. In general, the USA overtook Britain because it performed better in the services sector, with greater growth in retail and finance, and with improved productivity. Britain did not lose out so badly in terms of poor productivity in industry, though there were important trends here in which it did less well. Germany's growth lay more in tremendous development in industry, but its national performance was restrained by a poor agricultural sector (in which both Britain and the USA were more productive). Overall, the British position was not strengthened by having been first to industrialise, and having done so with fairly low levels of capital investment and reliance on low-level technology and cheap labour. Britain had too weak a heritage of high-capital investment. Yet, there was no collapse of British economic performance before 1914.

Rural society and economy

British rural society emerged from the 'Great Victorian Depression' by the mid-1890s, and from then until the 1920s new systems were established for the rural economy of many parts of mainland Britain. This was a period in which urban society and the British elites – more especially those of England – turned to the countryside to rediscover a lost golden age of values, including an essential national identity, communal values and spiritual renewal; this was exemplified in the Arts and Crafts Movement and the National Trust (founded in 1895). Yet, for rural elites all over Britain, there was challenge to status and privilege during the 1880s, and for the poor in many parts of rural Britain the prospect of destitution.

The 1880s witnessed anti-landlord agitation in Ireland, Scotland and, to a much lesser extent, in parts of England. The hold of the elites over rural populations was slackening all over Britain and Ireland. In post-famine Ireland, economic growth and stability returned, with modernisation in both agriculture and in industry. However, this was in part illusory, with these developments dependent on the sustained and large-scale out-migration of population to relieve poverty and inadequate resources. Many landlords went bankrupt from the 1870s, and some degree of security of land tenure came to small tenants, but this tended to freeze land-holdings and slowed down economic improvement in some parts. So growth was dependent on there being victims. In Scotland, too, emigration from the Highlands and Hebrides underlay continued poverty and social tension, but, with considerable Lowland sympathy, the Napier Royal Commission of 1885 granted crofters security of tenure. Meanwhile in England, tenant farmers formed strong organisations in Lancashire, leading to the creation in 1893 of the National Federation of Tenant Farmers. Tenants sought fixity of tenure, fair rents and compensation for improvements they made to farms. Landowners gave tenancies to new farmers from elsewhere in Britain – the Scots were especially mobile and innovatory – and they brought with them a harder tradition of facing up to landlord authority.

Many forms of grievance lay behind such moves. One was religion. In Ireland, the Catholic majority, mostly small-scale tenants, were in a longstanding opposition to the Protestant Ascendancy, contributing to a bitter 'land war' of the early 1880s; nationalist agitation was inextricably linked to the rural economy that would only be resolved in violent struggles of the 1910s (see Chapter 26). In the Scottish Highlands, the crofters were nearly all members of the Free Church in opposition to the landlords' Church of Scotland. In England and Wales, there was an increasing religious split as Nonconformity had been growing in the middle years of the nineteenth century amongst labourers and what were called 'the middling sort'. The Primitive Methodist and Bible Christians, groups which had left the increasingly middle-class Wesleyan Methodist Church, developed from the 1810s to the 1880s a distinctive religious culture which emphasised independence, self-worth and the development of preaching and organising skills which fed into the unionisation of the late nineteenth century. An ideology of equality, and claims to rights to free speech and freedom from deference to landed classes and their land stewards and estate managers, were taking hold quite fast.

Although there were attempts at unionism among agricultural labourers in the early 1870s, few of these survived, and trade unions always found it difficult to persuade poorly paid farm labourers, often in farms with a small workforce, to combine. By the mid-1890s, the worst of the Great Agricultural Depression was over, with prices and wages rising. But rural population continued to tumble from its peak in about 1860. From 1871 to 1911, the overall agricultural workforce in England and Wales fell from 1.6 million to 912,000. The cultivation of the land also fell; in 1872, 51 per cent of the cultivated area of Britain was growing crops; by 1913, this had contracted to 42 per cent, largely as a result of declining cereal production.[5] It was proving difficult to compete with the cheap grain from American's prairies, whilst dairy farming, though it grew significantly in the production of milk, failed (with the exception of Irish butter) to compete effectively with cheap margarine and imported Danish butter. As the workforce fell, mechanisation accelerated – especially as the migrant rural workforce for harvest (the Irish and the Scots especially) started to dry up. Reapers and binders joined the threshing machines which had been around since the 1830s,

---

[5] A. Howkins, *Reshaping Rural England: A Social History 1850–1925* (London, HarperCollins, 1991), p. 252.

and the life of the countryside started to change inexorably. Yet, jobs were easier to find in the countryside; labour was now in short supply, and as it was reported in north Norfolk in 1898, 'not a man, woman or child who is willing to work need be in want of a job'.[6]

From 1880 to 1914, railway branch lines extended further into the countryside of Britain. Many of these lines would never be economic, though some opened up new seaside resorts to expansion. But one thing they did was to bring the middle classes in ever greater numbers to both countryside and coast, whether on holiday or as residents. The rural social order of squire, parson, farmer and labourer was subverted by new wealth, which brought suburban-style estates of large houses, rising property prices, and the creation of new leisure facilities such as golf courses. The British countryside was starting to become an appendage of cities.

The war economy 1914–19

The four years of the First World War brought various consequences for the British economy. Firstly, Britain needed to increase output of war materials, including heavy industrial products for ammunitions and guns, and also textiles for uniforms. It also required the resurrection of food production to counter U-boat action around the British shores. So, a boost was given to the economy by government intervention. The principle of *laissez-faire* was ditched as the government directed both resources and people into war production, especially from late 1916 onwards when the Ministry of Munitions took virtual command of the British economy (see Chapter 26). The result was increased profits for many industries, full employment and a better diet for the British people as a whole, and greater security for investors. On the downside, however, Britain lost out in two ways. Firstly, the Empire was cut off, and during this four-year period many colonies (especially India) developed their own industries free from British imports. This ended reliance on British products (especially cotton textiles) and laid the basis for a crisis when the peace came. Second, British investment went into the maintenance of old equipment and production methods rather than into new technology, new products and new skills. Despite some innovation to meet fighting needs, the war gave a boost to the economy along old and familiar lines, and diverted much effort and attention from the possibilities of new ways of doing things.

Nothing was more serious in the long term than the war's deleterious effect on British overseas trade and the impact of monetary instability. Between 1913 and 1929, the British share of world trade in manufactured goods fell from 30 per cent to 23 per cent (even more serious than the fall experienced by European exporters). By comparison, the USA's share grew over the same period from 13 to 21 per cent and that of

---

[6] Quoted in ibid., p. 202.

Japan from 2.3 per cent to 4 per cent.[7] The impact of this was heightened by the collapse of the gold standard as the international system governing monetary exchange. This system favoured the greatest economy, that of Britain, which held the pound as a fixed value in the gold standard of $4.86 = £1. The system started to collapse when, on the outbreak of war, speculators moved their wealth from currencies in belligerent countries like Britain into gold. Not surprisingly, it was Britain's decision to come off the gold standard that caused the international exchange mechanisms to change. Increasing government issuing of currency and taking of loans to help pay the costs of war resulted in price inflation, making it more likely that British products would be expensive after the war. It also heralded greater difficulty in restoring confidence in British economic might by a return to the gold standard. In addition, the war required the selling off of a huge amount of British overseas investments, particularly in America, in order to finance borrowing to cover the cost of war, while revolution in Russia in 1917 led to huge losses in British investment there.

These monetary activities of the British government indicated how the war forced it to take a role in the economy that had previously been unthinkable. In the first place, the government not only took the country off the gold standard; it also raised income tax to unprecedented levels. In the second place, it had to place very large demands upon the economy to produce goods required for the war effort. This led during 1915–16 to the creation of a war economy in which the government increasingly directed what could be produced and where workers would be required by the armed forces or by key industries. And lastly, the war forced the government to take account of the vagaries of the free market in supplies – in particular food, which it had to ration during the later stages of the war. The government had to act not purely for economic reasons, but also had to consider the people's morale during very difficult periods of high casualties and depressed mood. In this way, the economy became for the first time geared to a national mission, and not merely to free-market forces. This was new both in practical and ideological terms and led both to the development of massive government bureaucracy capable of controlling the economy and to a presumption that at the end of the war there would be a return to 'normal' – to the *status quo ante bellum*. Not everything went to plan after the war, as will be shown in a later chapter.

Agriculture to a great extent boomed in the war. A rapid rise in prices in 1914 fostered extra cereal production, though this fell in 1915–16 because of soil exhaustion. With harvests poor in the USA, there was a food crisis by late 1916, and rapidly escalating prices, which hit working-class families very badly. This increased the state control of agriculture, and growing state purchase of food from overseas. Even from mid-1915, government had created the beginnings of state-directed food production and supply. Committees were appointed on a local basis to organise labour, food growing and food supply. The rural workforce expanded, through recruitment of

---

[7] C.K. Harley, 'Trade 1870–1939: from globalisation to fragmentation,' in R. Floud and P. Johnson (eds), *The Cambridge Economic History of Modern Britain: Volume II: Economic Maturity, 1860–1939* (Cambridge, Cambridge University Press, 2004), pp. 176–7.

both men and women – initially, those already in the countryside, but eventually, those from urban and industrial areas too. Late in 1916, the Women's Land Army was set up using volunteers, mostly middle-class in background. Wage controls encouraged the agricultural workforce to unionise rapidly between 1915 and 1921, with at least 270,000 members by 1919.[8] In all, more and more urban ways came to the countryside as a result of the war.

With hindsight, the war proved to be the end of British security in its staple industries. Britain lost its trade for four years; it saw long-term decline in its captive colonial markets; its industries were expanded beyond peace-time needs, and investment in new technology and plant was put on hold whilst companies luxuriated in fat government contracts for ships, munitions, uniforms, boots and all manner of things. The market mechanism stopped functioning, and the economy lost touch with the world economy.

Further reading

Campbell, R.J., *The Rise and Fall of Scottish Industry 1707–1939* (Edinburgh, John Donald, 1980)

Floud, R. and Johnson, P. (eds), *The Cambridge Economic History of Modern Britain: Volume II: Economic Maturity, 1860–1939* (Cambridge, Cambridge University Press, 2004)

Foster, R.F. (ed.), *The Oxford History of Ireland* (Oxford, Oxford University Press, 1989)

Howkins, A., *Reshaping Rural England: A Social History 1850–1925* (London, HarperCollins, 1991)

Trentmann, F., *Free Trade Nation: Commerce, Consumption and Civil Society in Modern Britain* (Oxford, Oxford University Press, 2008)

---

[8] A. Howkins, *Reshaping Rural England*, p. 268.

21

Intellectual ferment

Modernism

Between 1880 and 1918, there flourished key intellectual movements that were to be extremely influential during the twentieth century. These included Modernism, Darwinism, Marxism, Freudianism and feminism. Starting with art, this chapter explores their emergence. The 1890s, 1900s and 1910s were witness to some of the greatest artistic advances of the last 200 years, and from them were to emerge some of the leading movements to influence the writing, art and design of our world. As never before, art became a medium of exploration.

Modernism became the most trendy and the most daring art form. Modernism was a movement that, from the 1890s, sought to improve the understanding of the human condition in conjunction with science, social science and the overturning of tradition. In an expression of dissatisfaction with convention, previous 'norms' were to be cast aside in favour of incorporating into art new scientific discoveries and technology, as well as new understandings of society and of the mind. In the process, the attainment of any 'norm' was thrown into question and, indeed, the very existence of 'reality' too. The restraint on progress was to be removed, and everything that was progressive was to be encouraged.

Modernism was manifest in all forms of artistic endeavour. Impressionist painting of the nineteenth century evolved a style of representing reality in fuzzy strokes and ill-focused views which were evocative expressions of the world rather than detailed copies of it. Turn-of-the-century expressionist painting evoked emotion through distorted images, leading on to the adventurous Dadaists, Cubists and Surrealists, with painters like Pablo Picasso establishing non-realist styles of painting and sculpture that were to become influential in the interwar period after 1918.

Modernism in art was also to be influential in design and in architecture. The construction of buildings was to become more adventurous in these decades, characterised by bold straight lines, new materials like concrete and iron, and vertical construction using the technology of iron girders and concrete in skyscrapers. These trends were more muted in Britain than they were in Austria-Hungary, Germany or the United States, but international influence was strong in these years, and London attracted a nexus of new ideas on design and building.

In addition, there were also new forms of literature. Leading amongst these was the work of Joseph Conrad, whose novel *Heart of Darkness* (1904) turned the nineteenth-century narrative of European exploration from a grand story of Christian discovery and conversion into an almost gothic hell of man's fear of his own capacity for cruelty and horror.

In philosophy, a new breed of controversial thinkers was establishing a foothold in Europe, but with perhaps less influence in Britain during this period. Leading amongst these was the German Friedrich Nietzsche (1844–1900), who proclaimed in 1882 that God is dead. His work emphasised the importance of forces – what he called the 'will to power' – and raised doubt about the significance of facts and the very possibility of 'reality' and of 'truth'.

The interconnectivity between modes of inquiry and expression was the very life-spring of modernism as it drew in progressive liberals from many artistic and non-artistic backgrounds the *avant-garde* bohemians who could express the new world not just in a painting but in dress, lifestyle and even sexual orientation. Oscar Wilde (1854–1900), the Irish-born playwright and poet, was a famous figure on the London scene, best known for his play *The Importance of Being Earnest* (1895) – a comedy on Victorian seriousness which exemplified Modernism's challenge to social tradition. But in the same year, following a high-profile libel trial, Wilde was imprisoned for gross indecency (homosexual acts) resulting from his relationship with the son of the Marquis of Queensberry and others. The case brought into the public arena knowledge of the existence of gay clubs and circles that had hitherto been confined to metropolitan elites. After two years in prison, Wilde was ruined in wealth and health. His downfall was a *cause célèbre* not merely for the future gay rights movement, but for freedom of expression and ideas. Ideas were coming in many new shapes and forms, upsetting established modes of society, display and thought.

Modernism brought ideas and art, philosophy and literature together in a way rarely seen before. It was a movement that expressed the new, unconventional and innovative ideas untrammelled by the incubus of officialdom and rules. With international exchange getting faster through the intercontinental telegraph, the arrival of the movie film in 1896, and swift sea travel, the twentieth century opened with a sense of daring and threat to convention. The rule was that there were no rules. As a result, modernism was almost inevitably controversial, and likely to be criticised by the more staid and conservative forces in society. Yet, at the root of the social innovation of modernism was the place of science.

Darwinism and science

The work of Charles Darwin (1809–82) fostered an intellectual revolution that continued into the late nineteenth century. The world of science was being opened up by the spreading implications of his thinking, and by the advance of new technology.

In his famous book *On the Origin of Species* (1859), Darwin's core idea was the theory of evolution, whereby he overturned previous religious understandings of the origins of life forms with the notion that plants, animals and humans evolved, changing their characteristics as a result of experience, in a constant melting pot of modification governed by the survival of the fittest. There were tremendous advances made in the 1860s and 1870s in the world of science in which these ideas were worked on by botanists, animal behaviourists and others. Medicine, botany and zoology were transformed. Many churchmen changed their understanding of the Christian Bible to absorb the fresh thinking, adapting to the new theory.

In the last two decades of the century, new implications emerged. One of these was the impact in human sciences. These can be summed up by the term 'social science', in which the principles of evolution in animals and plants in terms of physical bodies were used as a method for examining the development of human societies. The 1880s and 1890s witnessed a surge of pessimism about urban life – its rising crime, poverty, alienation of working people from civil institutions, and the rise of socialist trade unionism. This led many intellectuals like the English socialist William Morris (1834–1896), the founder of the Arts and Crafts movement of architecture, art and song, and author of *News from Nowhere* (1890), to 'rediscover' the English countryside and its values of communality and harmony, and to idealise country living as a lost Utopia. This fostered a movement to 'green' cities, to bring rural structures, landscape and values to the rescue of a failed urbanism. Bolstered by Darwinist ideas, cities came to be seen in ecological terms as growing from smaller communities to larger ones, but with the need for spaces to be reserved for different functions. This led to zoning of areas for housing, industry, transport, civic life and leisure, with green spaces and parks, and gardens being seen as essential for every house. Town planning was born, founded by an inspirational book by Ebenezer Howard (1850–1928) entitled *Garden Cities of Tomorrow* (1898). The first new towns were constructed at Letchworth in 1904 and at Welwyn Garden City in 1919, and a further 31 new towns were designated by the government in 1944–70. So influential was Darwinism in town planning that even an alternative strategy, developed by botanist Patrick Geddes (1854–1932), to transform cities by organic change rather than wholesale demolition, relied on the evolutionary principle.

As well as the greening of cities, the rediscovery of rural utopias had other consequences. The countryside was not simply regarded as more beautiful and healthier than towns, but as stable, moral, and patriotic. The yeomen of England were ascribed with superior wisdom and an understanding of nature, values which could redeem the squalor and alienation of urban society. 'Merrie England' became a vision of lost glory to be recalled, promoting academic research into country customs, folk music,

Focus on

The garden city

In 1898, Ebenezer Howard published a pamphlet that from 1902 was republished in its influential title of *Garden Cities of Tomorrow*. This advocated solving the problems of overcrowded London through the construction of satellite cities designed to a regular plan that segregated industry, housing and civic areas, with spacious homes with front and back gardens, and with an intimate connection with the countryside. The city was to be governed by trustees who would restrict or ban public houses. From this vision, the whole of the town planning profession began, which between 1904 and 1970 led to the construction of new towns and peripheral housing estates to ease inner-city congestion. Here are extracts from the book.

The reader is asked to imagine an estate embracing an area of 6,000 acres, which is at present purely agricultural, and has been obtained by purchase in the open market at a cost of £40 an acre, or £240,000. The purchase money is supposed to have been raised on mortgage debentures, bearing interest at an average rent not exceeding £4 per cent. The estate is legally vested in the names of four gentlemen of responsible position and of undoubted probity and honour, who hold it in trust, first, as a security for the debenture-holders, and, secondly, in trust for the people of Garden City . . .

Garden City, which is to be built near the centre of the 6,000 acres, covers an area of 1,000 acres, or a sixth part of the 6,000 acres, and might be of circular form, 1,240 yards (or nearly three-quarters of a mile) from centre to circumference. (Diagram 2 is a ground plan of the whole municipal area, showing the town in the centre; and Diagram 3, which represents one sector or ward of the town, will be useful in following the description of the town itself . . .)

Six magnificent boulevards – each 120 feet wide – traverse the city from centre to circumference, dividing it into six equal parts or wards. In the centre is a circular space containing about five and a half acres, laid out as a beautiful and well-watered garden; and, surrounding this garden, each standing in its own ample grounds, are the larger public buildings – town hall, principal concert and lecture hall, theatre, library, museum, picture-gallery, and hospital. . . .

Passing out of the Crystal Palace on our way to the outer ring of the town, we cross Fifth Avenue – lined, as are all the roads of the town, with trees – fronting which, and looking on to the Crystal Palace, we find a ring of very excellently built houses, each standing in its own ample grounds; and, as we continue our walk, we observe that the houses are for the most part built either in concentric rings, facing the various avenues (as the circular roads are termed), or fronting the boulevards and roads which all converge to the centre of the town. Asking the friend who accompanies us on our journey what the population of this little city may be, we are told about 30,000 in the city itself, and about 2,000 in the agricultural estate. . . .

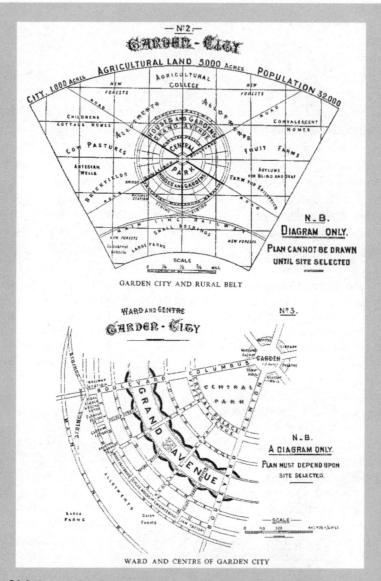

Figure 21.1 Garden city plans.
Source: E. Howard, *Garden Cities of Tomorrow*.

On the outer ring of the town are factories, warehouses, dairies, markets, coal yards, timber yards, etc., all fronting on the circle railway . . . The smoke fiend is kept within bounds in Garden City; for all machinery is driven by electric energy . . .

Source: E. Howard, *Garden Cities of Tomorrow* (London, Faber and Faber, 1946, 1965 edition), pp. 50–1.

drama, and religious ritual. This resulted in the formation in 1895 of the National Trust for Places of Historic Interest or Natural Beauty, in 1926 of the Council for the Preservation (later Protection) of Rural England, and in 1931 of the National Trust for Scotland. There was also an intellectual turn towards the poetry, music and song of the Celtic countries, with interest in Scotland in the Gaelic language and the bagpipes, and in Wales in the Welsh song and poetry of the Bards, male-voice choirs, and the institution of modern Eisteddfods (re-established in 1860). Even in small Orkney and Shetland, the folklore and language of the Norse heritage was rediscovered and embedded in education and schooling.

In these ways, Darwinist ideas came to be extremely influential from the 1890s in social reform, philanthropy and government. Increased attention fell upon social conditions with a growing recognition that these were the principal things to tackle in order to alleviate poverty, suffering and injustice. This type of thinking had wide implications. It deeply affected the Christian churches, where liberal-minded clergy became very concerned at housing and social improvement generally as vital to bringing more of the alienated people (especially the working classes) to the churches. Whereas the Christian churches had, in the Victorian period, tended to blame the individual poor man for his own condition, and insist that he rescue himself by giving up drink, saving more and becoming a 'good' person, from the 1890s many church leaders developed a strong sense of social justice which placed emphasis on government action over 'the social question' – especially housing and poverty.

Science did not rest on Darwin's achievements. In the physical sciences, tremendous theoretical work was done on the nature of the atom, leading in the 1900s to the work of nuclear scientists (especially at Cambridge University). The world of science was thus starting to show considerable influence in all forms of learning and government. Through the use of statistics to record human advance and the use of sociology in town planning and crime studies, the human condition came to be thought of as predictable. This was nowhere more influential than in the spreading sway of Marxism.

Marxism

Karl Marx (1818–83) was born in the Rhineland of German Jewish parents who had converted to Christianity. After university, where he studied philosophy, he met Friedrich Engels, and together they established in 1847 the Communist League dedicated to 'the overthrow of the bourgeois, the domination of the proletariat, the abolition of the old bourgeois society based on class antagonisms, and the establishment of a new society without classes and without private property'. In the following year, 1848, Marx and Engels wrote *The Communist Manifesto*, which ended with the famous slogan: 'The proletarians have nothing to lose but their chains. They have a world to win. Workingmen of all countries, unite!' In late 1848, both Marx and Engels were expelled from Belgium for their radical activities. Engels had business interests in

Manchester and Marx eventually settled in London, where he spent the rest of his life elaborating and refining his ideas, and being a focus for radicals' interest. His most famous book, *Das Kapital* (Capital), was only fully published after he died.

The essence of Marx's ideas was that history was a science that could be predicted. He divided the history of humanity into four ages: primitivism, feudalism, capitalism and, the ultimate state, communism. History was a progression from one to the other, driven by the inherent antagonism between social classes within each age. Thus, feudalism was dominated by the landed classes, but was overthrown by the middle classes with their own economic interests. This gave rise to capitalism, dominated by ideas of free trade and competition which, Marx predicted, was about to be overthrown at the end of the nineteenth century by the rising up of the oppressed working classes with their own economic interests, namely co-operation, unity and solidarity.

Marx's ideas were new and important in two respects. Firstly, he argued that the driving force of history was not, as previous philosophers like Hegel had claimed, ideas. They had held that ideas, introduced by leading thinkers and philosophers, changed the way people thought of and worked in the world. Marx rejected this. Instead, he argued that the reverse was true: history changed ideas. In his view, what drove history onwards were economic interests, the working out of conflicting economic interest groups who struggled for supreme power in each society – in short, historical materialism.

The second important aspect of Marx's ideas was how they related to working-class movements. Marx argued that working people would only attain justice by the over-throw of the capitalist system; this overthrow was inevitable, but could be hastened if the working classes developed a true consciousness of their subjugation by capitalists (or the boss class). In this way, Marx bequeathed to working-class movements from the 1880s onwards an apparently objective and coherent philosophy that seemed to amount to a science. His followers came to believe that they should agitate amongst the workers to convince them of their subjugation within the capitalist system. Trade unions should be urged not to work with employers for better wages and conditions, but to bring about the downfall of the capitalist system by continuous struggle with employers through strike action. The revolution became a goal to be hastened.

Even before Marx's death in 1883, his ideas gave rise to an international Marxist movement. Marx predicted that the first nation to experience a revolution of the workers would be Great Britain, merely because Britain was the first nation to industrialise. But that was not to be. Indeed, ironically, British workers and working-class move-ments became the least Marxist in Europe. It was in France and Germany that the workers were most successfully persuaded of Marxist goals, giving rise to the very serious prospect of revolutionary activity after 1900. Before that could happen, however, Marx's ideas had created a corps of deeply committed followers amongst Russian intellectuals who, from the 1890s, started to collect in London and develop their ideas of how an ideal society could be created. London became a hotbed of revolutionary camaraderie and intellectualism, and Russian émigrés started to plot the overthrow of the tsarist regime, making the first serious attempt at revolution in

1905 and moving on to the eventual October Revolution of 1917 that introduced the Soviet Union.

Marx had fostered an intellectual caucus around him in London in the third quarter of the century. London became a refuge for communists sheltering from oppression elsewhere in the world, and an important clearing house for ideas about the details of communist revolution and economic planning. Marx's daughter Eleanor Marx (1855–98) made a significant contribution to the movement in the 1880s and 1890s as a speaker and organiser for the first British Marxist party, the Social Democratic Federation. As her father's literary executor, she published his major works which were to inspire generations of Marxists and communists all over the world during the twentieth century.

The timing of the spread of Marxian socialist ideas was fortuitous since there was growing disillusionment with Liberalism and a questioning of the ability of the *laissez-faire* state to create the good society after which people strove. The dominant philosophy of individualism was being challenged. There had always been those who questioned it. Thomas Carlyle (1795–1881), an influential writer and critic, had long denounced what he called 'paralytic radicalism' – a belief that little could be done other than through individual effort. He was no democrat, but he believed that the ruling class had to take responsibility for the welfare of people. The economist and philosopher, John Stuart Mill (1806–73), in his essay *On Liberty*, published in 1859, had been concerned that the state should not become too powerful, but by the end of his life he claimed to be a socialist. How the condition of the people could be improved was what mattered, and the function of government was to deal with 'the curse of pauperism, the curse of disease, and the curse of the whole population bred and nurtured in crime'. Even more important was the art critic John Ruskin (1819–1900), who argued against a society that saw people as only economic beings and valued only things that could be turned into money. There was, he argued, no point in putting faith in the market if what it produced was bad. His fundamental doctrine was that 'Wealth is Life' – i.e. something that creates, restores, maintains and enhances life.

A further questioning of society's values and the role of the state came in the universities from British idealist philosophers. They distinguished between what they called negative freedom – freedom *from* something – and positive freedom – freedom *to do* something. If the market only provided a choice between 'gin shops on one side of the street and gin shops on the other' then perhaps the state had a role to create that truer positive freedom. According to philosopher T.H. Green,

> It is the business of the state, not indeed directly to promote moral goodness, for that, from the very nature of moral goodness, it cannot do, but to maintain the conditions without which a free exercise of human faculties is impossible.[1]

---

[1] Quoted in M. Richter, *The Politics of Conscience. T.H. Green and his Age* (London, Weidenfeld & Nicolson, 1964), p. 342.

Others carried this further and believed that individualism needed to be replaced by a society which emphasised community and co-operation – i.e. that the state had a moral function. There was a debate on the extent to which this end could be achieved.

Of course, there had been a huge extension of state power, with limited debate, over the previous 50 years, much of it at local level. There was a growing conviction that only community action could tackle effectively some of the most deep-seated problems of urban life. Linked with this was a growing admiration for and belief in public service. It created an administrative class who captured the 'high ground' of politics from the landed class and saw themselves as protectors of the 'national interest'.[2]

The challenge to individualism was also linked to the intellectual revolution that followed Darwinism. There was an acceptance that society too was a living organism that would evolve. The debate was over how such evolution would take place and whether intervention would distort or assist evolution. Should the environment be left to act like a sieve, separating the fit from the unfit and selecting those best adapted to their surroundings, or should it be manipulated to ensure that those who survived did so in a progressive environment?

Socialism came into this debate. The Social Democratic Federation, formed in 1884, was the main group directly influenced by Marxism, but the Socialist League, which broke away at the end of 1884, had among its members the poet and designer, William Morris, who was influenced by Ruskin. He denounced the ugliness of the world and blamed it on competition. Capitalism, he argued in 1883, produced nothing but unhappiness. Morris urged people to abandon making money for its own sake and turn instead to bringing about a new society. His *News from Nowhere* offered a dream of a rural utopia. A third socialist element in the 1880s was Fabianism, associated with the historians Sidney and Beatrice Webb and the Irish playwright Bernard Shaw. It offered an alternative to revolutionary socialism, a steady advance to a socialist, more efficient state that would evolve through the gradual permeation of socialist ideas.

It is perhaps ironic, then, that Britain was probably the least affected by Marxism of all the major European industrial nations. Though there were many radicals agitating in Britain, as elsewhere, during the first half of the twentieth century, British trade unions and working-class organisations were the least affected by communist ideas about fomenting revolution. Socialist groups in Britain tended to back what European Marxists dubbed 'revisionism', a belief that a socialist society could be created by peaceful means by winning control of the state through the ballot box. During the twentieth century, fewer communist candidates were to be elected to Parliament in Britain than in any other country and Britain seemed far removed from the prospect of a workers' revolution. Nonetheless, British intellectuals were quite strongly influenced by Marxism – notably writers and social scientists, including sociologists and

---

[2] J. Harris, *Private Lives; Public Spirit. A Social History of Britain 1870–1914* (Oxford, Oxford University Press, 1993), p. 194.

many historians. Indeed, the influence of Marxism in Britain has been highly visible in intellectual circles, including universities, and in the writing of history books.

The twentieth century was dominated by the outcomes of Marx's ideas – the Russian revolution, the rise of Stalin, the role of the USSR in the defeat of Nazism, the communist revolution in China, and then the cold war from 1945 until 1989. At its height, it is reckoned that Marxism defined the system of government for 40 per cent of the world's people. With the fall of the Berlin Wall in 1989, and the *de facto* collapse of the communist system in Russia in 1991 and its slide from favour in the new capitalism of China, only a handful of countries are now left with Marxist states – Cuba, North Korea and a few others. At the same time, Marxism as an intellectual tradition has suffered a great setback in the world's intelligentsia, including amongst British academics.

Freudianism

Sigmund Freud (1856–1939) was a physician, a neurologist, and the founder of psychoanalysis. Freud was driven by an intense desire to study natural science and to solve some of the challenging problems confronting contemporary scientists. After training as a doctor and doing his military service, he was appointed in 1885 a lecturer in neuropathology at the University of Vienna. In the 1890s, he started to study neurological disorders, and he was drawn to work on hysteria. He came to the conclusion that neuroses were caused by repression of memory and emotion. Freud saw repression as a means for the individual's mind unconsciously to conceal painful memory. He devised techniques of 'free verbal association' – slips of the tongue – to guide the therapist to the patient's hidden pains, whilst dream analysis could uncover infantile sexuality – the 'Oedipus complex' in which a boy had an erotic affection for his mother (and a girl for her father), and hostility towards the other parent. Freud's work forms the basis of the modern professions of psychology, psychiatry and various therapies.

Freud had a great deal to say about women. He postulated that many psychological problems had their origins in sexual repression brought on by society's values. Sexuality was repressed, especially by women, who were expected to be respectable, pure, virgins at marriage, and lacking knowledge of sex itself. Sex was the great taboo in the respectable classes of Europe between the 1850s and the 1950s. For a century and more, the members of the middle classes cultivated amongst themselves a culture of sexual oppression, enforcing as supposed norms patterns of behaviour that repressed instincts to pleasure and sexual gratification. It was unacceptable for women to think, talk or even know about sex. Breaking such a taboo in 'vulgar speech' or dress, or in lewd or libidinous behaviour, would almost inevitably lead to being socially ostracised.

Freud understood this and saw its adverse consequences. He began to argue that women had sexual identities and that women's sexuality should not be repressed.

Freud explicitly recognised that everyone – men and women – was a sexual being, with sexual drives from the moment of birth. Indeed, Freud considered that the phenomenon of hysteria, which was almost exclusively associated with women, was not a function of abnormality but was caused by the repression of women's sexuality. In his *Studies on Hysteria*, he argued that many women's psychological illness was due to the moral and sexual codes of the time. Moreover, Freud raised the notion that sexual identity was not fixed from birth but was shaped by experience, thus acknowledging homosexuality amongst women as well as men.

Freud was revolutionary in two ways. Firstly, he started to lay the intellectual and treatment foundations for new branches of medicine, those of psychology and psychiatry, which would later subdivide into other forms of therapy and counselling. Secondly, Freud founded the study of the mind very much upon women. Women were crucial to the emergence of each branch of psychology and psychotherapy, with a particular focus falling for several decades on the most common and observable abnormality, hysteria, as it applied to women. Freud published a study of Dora, a woman given to bouts of hysteria because of the effect of her father's influence upon her, and her guilt because of her attitudes towards him, and because of sexual repression in her lifestyle. This focus had both good and bad points. On the one hand, the condition of women, their plight and the burdens they had to bear came under close scrutiny, which resulted in a new appreciation that women were not necessarily inferior to men. This gave support to feminism, to the campaigns for female equality with males. It also exposed the extent to which the human mind was socially and culturally created, and how people could develop illnesses out of the pressures of life, and not merely out of biological or inherited factors. On the downside, the obsession with hysteria seemed in the short term to give support to deeply ingrained prejudices about female 'weakness'. Women, it seemed, could not handle pressure, and were prone to mental collapse. This approach angered many, notably women campaigning for equality, because it seemed to justify some people's prejudice against women.

Freud's influence, like that of Marx, has waned during the later twentieth and early twenty-first century, though not quite as spectacularly. Freud lived until 1939, and his influence was still strong in the 1950s and 1960s. But from the 1960s onward, his theories and methods came under relentless criticism. Especially critical were feminists, who regarded his attitudes to women as deeply flawed and biased, and a new breed of mental health students who formed an 'anti-psychiatry movement' that challenged the notion of madness and sanity as two mutually exclusive positions. Nevertheless, Freud's legacy was the therapy and counselling industry which is still booming, especially in the United States, but also in Britain.

Feminism

The period from 1890 to 1919 witnessed first-wave feminism. This is most strongly associated with the struggles to win women's right to vote, which was granted in two stages in Britain in 1918 and 1928. But feminism was broader and deeper than merely the suffrage cause. At stake was an ideology that women deserved equal rights to men in all areas of education, work and pleasure.

Personifying this ideology from the late 1880s was the 'New Woman'. Freud and feminists disagreed on many things, but they were united in the 1890s and 1900s in a recognition that women were capable of sexual feelings and that they should be liberated in order to enjoy physical sensation. Although today the ideas of Freud are criticised by feminists, at the time they had a great impact on the ways in which women's sexuality was perceived and understood. Freud questioned the view that women should be virgins upon marriage and pointed out that marriage could be a torment for some women. Feminists agreed and many started to reject traditional models of marriage, adopting alternative modes of life, living with men and/or women outside marriage. However, this kind of development was confined largely to women (and men) of the middle and upper classes, from bohemian and artistic groups, who either had less need to worry about moral condemnation or who turned their lifestyle into a form of protest, rather than a test of conformity. One such example was Karl Marx's daughter, Eleanor, who lived from 1884 with Edward Aveling, married but separated from his wife, and a distinguished scientist and Darwinist. The New Woman was considered daring, sexually adventurous, usually principled and, like Eleanor, a campaigner in the public sphere normally inhabited solely by men. As with Oscar Wilde at the same time, intellectuals and artists were experimenting with new forms of sexual relationships, and attracting the opprobrium of most conservative and church groups. This caused tension for Eleanor Marx, who committed suicide in 1898, apparently unable to stand the ridicule of her critics when Aveling cheated on her. Expressions of daring female sexuality were by no means confined to the refined and artistic classes, however. As we shall see in the next chapter, women's bodies were starting to be seen in many new ways.

On the practical level, there were a number of social changes which fostered the appearance of a new kind of woman. The first of these was education, with some middle-class women gaining increased access to higher education between 1880 and 1914 – though the subjects were restricted, and full graduation degrees were withheld by some colleges and universities. Yet, by 1900, women were being trained and practising in professional roles previously virtually unheard of – notably as medical doctors – and the trend to increasing access to university degrees and admission to professional ranks was to be sustained in the 1910s and 1920s.

The second area was employment: the world of paid work changed for many women in the 1900s. The emergence of a large service sector providing jobs as clerks, typists and shop assistants altered the experience of work for large numbers of women, although many of these were from the lower middle classes. After the 1914–18 war the standard of living rose for many young single women. They began to live more independent lives, spending more money on new clothes and fashions, make-up and toiletries (which became more widespread after 1900) and on entertainment (notably after 1910 on going to the cinema, a leisure venue dominated by women).

Third, in clothing and style, there were clear changes in the ways in which women dressed, particularly after the First World War. Although towards the end of the nineteenth century some women had abandoned their tightly laced corsets and their layers of petticoats, it was not really until the 1920s that hemlines rose significantly and clothing became looser and more functional. The war had a significant impact on women's dress: corsets and petticoats would have been dangerous while working in a factory, so they wore overalls, which some criticised as masculine. Women also began to use more make-up (without being labelled 'whores', as many were in the Victorian period) and cut their hair shorter (including the postwar 'flapper' style with its daring boyish look).

Fourth, women started to lead the development of what became known as consumerism. The spread of women's concern for dress signalled the rise of a consumer society in which both young and older women were the prime customers. New department stores appeared in the 1880s and 1890s, which tried to make shopping a pleasurable activity. These stores increasingly became a female space: both the assistants and the shoppers were primarily women, and store managers deliberately targeted female shoppers. The early stores in London included Whiteley's (1863), Barkers (1880), Peter Jones (1890), Harrods (1889), John Lewis (1900), and Selfridges (1909) while there were stores in provincial cities like Kendals in Manchester (which started in the eighteenth century), Bainbridges in Newcastle (from the 1830s) and Jenners' enlarged store in Edinburgh (1895). The retail revolution of the late nineteenth century was heavily dependent on the female middle-class market, but a wider evolution in the mass market for food and clothing was evident in the rise of packaged food and national name brands – again, targeted especially at female purchasers for family consumption.

And fifth, from the mid-nineteenth century, there was increased birth control advice made available through books and pamphlets – information on *coitus interruptus*, the safe period, sponges, douches and condoms. In 1877, Charles Bradlaugh and Annie Besant were tried for publishing a tract on family limitation; they were eventually found not guilty, and though still secretively distributed, more information became available to working-class as well as middle-class wives on how to control family size. Bradlaugh and Besant represented the linkage between secularism, socialism and feminism that opposed traditional church-framed ideas that a woman's life should be devoted solely to child-rearing. Marie Stopes' *Married Love* which, with difficulty, found a publisher in 1918, and which argued for an equal relationship between men and women within marriage, went through six editions in a matter of months. Her campaign for birth control clinics, the first of which she opened in 1921, gradually helped remove the stigma of discussing birth control and spread female knowledge of sexual matters. As a result, birth control to limit family size and to prevent pregnancy became markedly more widespread, reducing the numbers of children for working-class mothers from the 1920s. It was all very well for psychologists to talk about autonomous female sexuality, but this did not mean a lot to most heterosexual women without cheap and reliable birth control.

The 'New Woman', who was much talked about at the turn of the century, was thus a product of an intellectual revolution beginning in the 1880s and continuing through to the 1920s, and of major social changes on the practical level, giving women greater physical and psychological freedom. But the New Woman was regarded as a threat by some in society. She was seen as a challenge to traditional gender roles, traversing the boundaries laid down by Victorian morality and by the Christian churches in particular. She was seen by critics as sexually feckless and promiscuous, thus challenging the stability of society based on the family with its rigid role divisions. She challenged the state: particularly in respect of the birth rate. She was claiming to be an autonomous sexual being, capable of experiencing sexual pleasure, and threatening male sexual hegemony. And there was a longer-term fear: the realisation that these women who were beginning to challenge traditional notions of female behaviour would eventually make greater political demands.

Feminism has been the most resilient and, indeed, the most successful, of the three trends which emerged in the 1880s and 1890s. From bringing in the vote and the rights of women to education, the twentieth century would see the advance of thinking about women in all branches of life – something unthinkable to most contemporaries in 1900.

Further reading

Cherry, G.E., *Town Planning in Britain since 1900: The Rise and Fall of the Planning Ideal* (Oxford, Blackwell, 1996)

Cook, H., *The Long Sexual Revolution: English Women, Sex, and Contraception 1800–1975* (Oxford, Oxford University Press, 2004)

Cox, C.B. and Dyson, A.E., *The Twentieth Century Mind. History, Ideas and Literature in Britain 1. 1900–1918* (Oxford, Oxford University Press, 1972)

Fraser, W.H., *The Coming of the Mass Market 1850–1914* (London, Macmillan, 1981)

Hall, P., *Cities of Tomorrow: An Intellectual History of Urban Planning and Design in the Twentieth Century* (Oxford, Blackwell, 2002)

Hutton, R., *Triumph of the Moon: A History of Modern Pagan Witchcraft* (Oxford, Oxford University Press, 2001)

Laybourn, Keith, *The Rise of Socialism in Britain c. 1881–1951* (Stroud, Sutton Publishing, 1997)

22

People, society and culture

Social class

British society remained in its own perception dominated by the structure of social class. This was by no means a simple structure, but involved layers and confusions, overlaid with issues of region and religion.

The basis of social division remained economic inequality. Aristocratic wealth started to falter in this period, as rental income from farms fell, and some of the very largest country houses were in crisis in the 1900s, with some starting to suffer neglect and occasionally abandonment. Many country estates were kept afloat by sales of land for suburban expansion, or by judicious intermarriage with rich (occasionally American) families. Industrialists continued to buy into land and status, and the sense of a very wealthy elite ruling the country remained in place through the halcyon days of Edwardian Britain. For the middle classes, income levels rose significantly in these decades, with conspicuous consumption taking the form of larger houses, fine furnishings and the keeping of servants. However, the middle classes remained during this period fairly solidly house renters, not homeowners. Their numbers grew dramatically with expanding occupations – doctors, teachers, clerks, local-authority civil servants and the professions in general. Middle-class status grew in commerce and public service, with an ethos of respectability and duty.

Working-class real wages rose in the 1880s and 1890s, especially through falling food prices, but only slowly – if at all – from 1899 to 1913. The biggest increases were for workers in iron and steel industries and coal mining, whilst occupations dominated by women workers such as domestic service, clothing and textiles had the least increase. But trade depressions brought acute changes of fortune, as in the early nineteenth century; the recession of 1908–9 was especially severe, and led to major changes of attitude to poverty and how to deal with it. Social investigators like Charles Booth (who investigated London) and Seebohm Rowntree (York) showed that as much as 16 per cent of the people were in what Rowntree called primary poverty (that is without the income to sustain necessary food, heat and shelter), and a further 30 per cent were in secondary poverty (resulting largely from poor budgeting). For those in work, improving wages meant a significant increase in the range of consumption, but surprisingly little improvement in terms of health. For instance, there was little change in the weight and height of working-class people, so that in 1901 a panic erupted at the poor physical condition of army recruits at the time of the Boer War in South Africa. The cycle of poverty in many families, caused by old age, childbirth, injury at work and illness, unemployment and underemployment created instability in earnings, diet and health.

One of the distinctive ways in which the working class sought to deal with these problems was through friendly societies and benefit clubs by means of which, through regular savings, there were payouts in time of need. Some of these clubs had religious, trade-union or temperance connections, and had major social as well as financial roles. They provided a focus for class identity, as much as the burgeoning trade-union movement of the 1890s and 1900s. Class identity could come through all forms of organised clubs and societies – including sports organisations, which mushroomed in these decades.

At the same time, cities and towns were exploding in size with the construction of suburban housing of detached or semi-detached homes with gardens. This tended to make social segregation more pronounced, with suburbanisation of the middle classes, who increasingly commuted to work by train or tram. Meanwhile, manual workers generally continued to live near factories, in close-knit streets of terraced or tenement housing within walking distance of their work.

Yet, the extent to which social class divided British society needs to be put in perspective. There was an increasing sharing of experience between classes, with the developing leisure and pastimes of the period. In the music hall, which blossomed from the 1880s through to 1914, social classes mixed in many of the halls, and even seat segregation did not divide them. It became fashionable for some of the upper and upper-middle classes to be seen in the cheap 'pit' or standing area in front of the music stage, rather than in the balconies. More generally, the music hall embodied an ideal of the 'common people' of the country that attracted men and, to an extent, women from all social classes. Class was a malleable concept, not one with fixed boundaries. However, the rise of the trade unions and the labour movement after 1880 did have an important impact on perceptions of social class.

Trade unions and the labour movement

As the economy moved out of depression at the end of the 1880s, there was a new burst of trade-union organisation. This time it embraced many unskilled workers

Focus on

The music hall

Music hall was a hugely popular form of theatre which began in the 1830s and 1840s in the back rooms of pubs, but from 1860 to 1914 moved into purpose-built theatres. At its height just before the First World War, music hall entertained an estimated 25 million people and employed 80,000 artistes, promoters, stage and bar staff. It mixed genres of stage acting, comedy and acrobatic performing in a rolling programme that characteristically would start at 6 p.m. and continue until around midnight, with the audience coming and going from bar to seats, mingling in groups in conversation. The acts could vary from serious drama (doing an act from a Shakespearean play, for instance) to singalongs with songs old and new, to comedy 'turns' with mimicry of the leading politicians and royalty.

Here is a description of a night out in Glasgow in 1860, as a party of revellers move from hall to hall in the city centre:

[At the Britannia music hall] we were amused by the comic songs of Mr McGowan and the duos of Mr and Mrs Stephens. Mr McGregor Simpson electrified us with his Jacobite songs, Madame Henessier charmed us with a ballad, and the Misses Duvalli showed much proficiency in the terpsichorean art. Mr Spiers appeared to manage the musical affairs with much success. Crossing the street, we found ourselves in the Royal Parthenon, being much astonished by the impalement feats of a party of Chinese Jugglers and the graceful gymnastics of the Corelli family. Tom Glen gave us a hearty laugh by his rendering of an indescribably comic ditty, and Mr Burton seemed to have danced himself into the good graces of the numerous audience. Miss Kirby, Miss Howard and Mr E. Lyons proved that they were vocalists of no mean pretentions, and well worthy of public patronage. Having got the length of the Philharmonic, under the care of Mr Brown, we listened to many excellent songs from Mesdames Webb, Sinclair, Constance, Losebini, and Jackson. . . . We afterwards had a glass of Dunville's Irish Whiskey punch, with Mr Shearer of the Whitebait [Theatre], where we found Mr Lowick in the director's chair and the house in roars at the comicalities of Messrs Raymond and Warren, who were amusing the company with an election speech of immense power. The Misses le Brun then exhibited their pretty persons and many graces in a mazy dance, and were followed by a ballad from Miss Wilmott, who, in her turn, was succeeded by Mr Sellers in a comic effusion, and Mr Sanders in a more sentimental and serious one . . . Turning northwards, we arrived at the Milton Colosseum just as Professor Hall was giving a very good ventriloquial entertainment.

Music hall songs became national hits, establishing the basis of modern popular music. Here is the rousing song made famous by the Great (Gilbert Hastings)

Macdermott (1845–1901) from 1877 at the time of the Eastern crisis, and from which the term 'jingoism' (meaning patriotic chauvinism) emerged:

> We don't want to fight but by Jingo if we do,
> We've got the ships we've got the men, and got the money too.
> We've fought the Bear before, and while we're Britons true,
> The Russians shall not have Constantinople.

In the 1890s and 1900s, the most famous music hall artiste was the singer Marie Lloyd (1870–1922) whose bawdy songs and *double entendres* fostered a taste for acceptable naughtiness. Here is an extract from her signature tune, 'A Little of What You Fancy Does You Good' (1912, lyrics by George Arthurs and Fred W Leigh):

> I always 'old with 'avin' it – if yer fancy it,
> If yer fancy it – that's understood.
> And if drinkin' makes yer fat – I don't worry over that,
> 'Cos a little of what yer fancy does yer good!

Sources: music hall description from *The Era*, 22 April 1860, quoted in P. Maloney, *Scotland and the Music Hall, 1850–1914* (Manchester, Manchester University Press, 2003), p. 36. The Great Macdermott's song (composed by G.W. Hunt), quoted on http://www.victorianweb.org/mt/musichall/macdermott1.html. Marie Lloyd's song from Clarkson Rose, *Red Plush and Greasepaint* (London, Museum Press, 1964), p. 71.

rather than merely the skilled. Unions spread among dockers, seamen, gas workers and general labourers during 1889 and 1890 – groups that had hardly had any organisation in the past. Women workers, too, were caught up in the movement, with the strike of the match girls of the dangerous and unhealthy Bryant and May match factory in East London catching the public attention. There were numerous disputes in ports around the country in 1887 and 1888, but the month-long London dock strike of August 1889, which won the men a minimum sixpence (6d = 2.5p) an hour and a minimum work period of half a day, was widely publicised. This and many of the other strikes were assisted by socialists, who were keen to educate workers in an awareness of their exploitation. Because many unskilled workers were easily replaced and because few had the resources to sustain a strike, many of the strikes of the early 1890s involved bitter confrontation with strike breakers. Indeed, part of the success of the London dock strike was due to the fact that it was in August and the harvest had begun in Essex, so there was not an immediate pool of rural labourers that the dock employers could call upon.

In some ways, even more significant than the organisation among unskilled workers were the signs of new attitudes emerging amongst skilled workers. They were feeling the effects of increasingly cost-conscious employers and of new technology and new workplace organisation threatening some craft jobs. The new unionism of the 1890s was as much about a more confrontational attitude amongst old unions as about the rise of unions of the unskilled. Encouraged by socialist arguments, there was a readiness to look to the state for regulation of hours, with a growing demand for an eight-hour working day.

Employers fought back against the advances made by unions in the 1890s and many of those among dockers and general labourers more or less collapsed, but, overall, trade unionism began to grow. By 1900, membership had reached more than 2 million, probably about double what it had been in 1880. Although the first decade of the twentieth century was a difficult one, membership passed 3 million in 1910 and, by the end of the war in 1918, was approaching 7 million.

There were also signs of a growth in the political aspirations of the working class that the existing political parties were failing to meet adequately. Some socialists argued in pamphlets, in newspapers and at street corners that only a complete overthrow of the capitalist system would bring real change to the condition of workers. However, others claimed that, if workers had a stronger voice in Parliament, then they could get some of the changes that they wanted, particularly in respect of hours of work and safety. The Scottish miners' leader, Keir Hardie, formed the Scottish Labour Party in 1888 to get independent labour representation in Parliament. Other groups followed and, in 1893, Hardie and others were able to pull these together to form the Independent Labour Party. It contained a mixture of socialists and trade unionists and many of the latter were wary about some of the socialist language and demands. Many working-class people were suspicious of the idea of giving more power to the state, as socialists seemed to be demanding, to regulate hours of work and other aspects of people's lives. The state was traditionally seen as unsympathetic to the working class.

Hardie was briefly elected to the Commons in the election of 1892, but all the Independent Labour candidates went down to defeat in 1895. However, over the next few years, Hardie and others worked hard to win over trade-union support for Independent Labour and, in 1900, the trade unions backed the formation of a Labour Representation Committee to co-ordinate efforts to get Labour candidates elected. This eventually bore fruit in the election of 1906 when 29 were returned (see Chapter 24).

There were always tensions about how far trade unions should get involved in political campaigns or confine themselves to working to improve wages and conditions through their own efforts. In the years before 1914, there were groups of mainly younger trade unionists who believed that the leadership of many of the trade unions had become too complacent and that the Labour Party in Parliament appeared to be achieving very little. They called for a reliance on the industrial muscle of trade unions, urging the amalgamations of unions of different crafts into industry-wide organisations and working towards inter-industry links. Some were influenced by activities in France, where the syndicalist movement was working to achieve a general strike that could coerce the state. Few in Britain saw this as the ultimate aim of their activities, but there were signs of a much greater militancy among workers and, in the face of new management techniques transforming traditional work patterns, calls for much greater workers' control of industry.

The years of the First World War gave a boost to trade unionism. Although there was an industrial truce, workers were able to use their strong bargaining position to obtain advances from employers. The government was anxious to maintain industrial peace and encouraged employers to negotiate with the shop stewards, the union representatives in the workplace.

Signs of growing political awareness on the part of workers were apparent in most communities. Working-class candidates were getting themselves elected to school boards, parish councils and town and county councils. On these they pressed that contracts for work should only go to those firms that were committed to pay trade-union-agreed wage rates. They also joined some of the more radical Liberals, who were still the largest group on most councils, in supporting moves for municipal ownership of many public utilities, such as trams, gas and electricity supplies. The argument was that if there was to be a monopoly, then it should be a publicly owned one. Working-class representatives also pressed for local councils to do more to make available housing that was affordable to workers. There were signs before 1914 of middle-class rate-payers beginning to rebel against the rise in local rates to pay for improved facilities and local politics in many towns became polarised between middle-class ratepayers' associations and socialist-influenced labour groups.

The language of socialism increasingly came into the discourse of politics in the early twentieth century. Not all were agreed on what it meant. For some, it was about achieving a political and social revolution. For others, it was about gradually bringing improvements in the conditions of life for the mass of the population. For yet others, it was about the enhancement of state power to achieve eventually state ownership of the means of production, distribution and exchange. For many others, there was a Christian socialism which emphasised the ethical foundations of an equal society, in which injustice and social inequality should be regarded as unacceptable to God and combated through moral campaigns. Many clergy involved themselves in campaigns to improve the lot of exploited groups of workers, such as the women nail and chain makers in the Black Country who, because of the heat of furnaces, often had to work partially dressed. The challenge presented to traditional patterns by socialist ideas was one that all politicians were having to confront in the early twentieth century. Many undoubtedly feared that the ideas, in the long term, would pose a threat to private property and a challenge to the dominating elites. Much of politics is about responding to the challenge.

Women's lives

Men and women led very different lives. Women were subordinate to men in almost every aspect of economy and society, holding different positions and achieving different things. However, with rising feminist ideas about the 'New Woman' (see Chapter 21) the period from 1880 to 1918 witnessed the first major challenge to this state of affairs.

To be a woman in Britain between 1880 and 1918 was to be a second-class citizen. A plethora of laws, customs and conventions remained or came into force which restricted her life, ambitions, freedoms and rights. A woman was excluded from most areas of citizenship. In 1880, she could not vote or stand in elections to Parliament, in borough (or, from 1889, county council) elections, and only some minor elected organisations (such as school boards and parish councils) became open to the female vote and candidates. In 1880 a woman in England and Wales could only obtain a divorce from her husband if she was relatively wealthy, and she was then more likely than not to lose the custody of any children to her ex-husband; in Scotland, divorce was easier to obtain, but was still rare, and largely confined to the better off.

Women's role in society was strongly influenced by the way they were depicted in books, church literature, and in the expectations of family and women themselves. In those ways, women were marginalised in the structures of British society. They were encouraged (and encouraged each other) to restrain their own ambitions and to strive to perfect a very narrow range of characteristics. Women's magazines were one of the main means by which discourses on ideal women's behaviour and aspirations were circulated. Such magazines flourished during this period, many of them taking the form of 'family journals' that portrayed women in perfect roles, as the centre of the happy and contented family, dressed in highly feminine outfits, and essentially passive and confined, not worldly and active. Of course, the depictions were idealisations, and women and girls were anxious over how to negotiate difficult choices. Though aimed mostly at middle-class women, even working-class women came under strong pressure to conform to these ideals. Though work was an economic necessity, working-class women often had to give up jobs when they married – this marriage bar being imposed equally by employers, trade unions and women themselves.

But in the 1880s and 1890s, as the 'New Woman' challenged traditional notions of femininity, sexual relations with men became more openly acknowledged by women as important to their lives. The Prime Minister, William Gladstone, was told by his daughter in 1886 that, 'What is called "the American sin" [contraception] is now almost universally practised in the upper classes'.[1] Some feminists claimed sexual freedom. F.W. Stella Browne controversially asserted in an intellectual journal, *The Freewoman*, in 1912, that sexual experience was 'the right of every human being', though she acknowledged that the plight of poor women was linked to their having to feed and care for large families: 'our right to refuse maternity is also an inalienable right. Our wills are ours, our persons are ours; nor shall all the priests and scientists in the world deprive us of this right to say "No".'[2]

---

[1] Quoted in K. Gleadle, *British Women in the Nineteenth Century* (Basingstoke, Palgrave Macmillan, 2001), p. 180.

[2] Quoted in S. Bruley, *Women in Britain since 1900* (Basingstoke, Macmillan, 1999), p. 14.

In the popular arena, women's bodies and their sexual power were almost flaunted by dancers and actresses on the stage – such as Marie Lloyd, the most famous musical hall artiste of the 1890s and 1900s – and by many cinema actresses of the 1910s. Women's roles expanded in other ways. Indeed, music hall developed rapidly after the mid-1890s with a 'respectable' air as impresarios like H.E. Moss, who ran the large chain of Moss Empire music halls, moved their premises up-market with glamorous decoration and a stricter control of bawdy humour and language. After their emergence in the late 1890s, picture houses had also been down-market for a decade or so,

Figure 22.1 The arrest of Emmeline Pankhurst outside Buckingham Palace, May 1914. Mrs Emmeline Pankhurst (1858–1928), assisted by her daughters Christabel and Sylvia, founded the Women's Social and Political Union in 1903 and, from 1905, began to adopt militant and disruptive tactics to stir interest in their campaign for women's suffrage. The response of the authorities became increasingly violent.
Source: Mary Evans Picture Library

but in the 1910s started to emerge as places with superior narrative films that attracted women in greater numbers, and the premises improved in comfort.

Women were being seen more and more in both varied consumer and active roles. After the outlawing in 1883 of the use of paid canvassers, political parties started to use women as volunteers to knock on doors and seek men's votes, even though the women themselves had no right to vote. The issue of women's suffrage was on the political agenda from the mid-1860s, when John Stuart Mill first mooted it as part of parliamentary reform, and for the next four decades there was intense lobbying by women's groups, leading in 1897 to the formation of the National Union of Women's Suffrage Societies. Whilst suffragists campaigned strenuously but with a fairly conservative style for the female vote, a minority made their mark as militant suffragettes – so labelled by the conservative *Daily Mail* newspaper. Under the leadership of Mrs Emmeline Pankhurst and her daughters, Christabel and Sylvia, they left the NUWSS in 1903 to form the Women's Social and Political Union. The suffragettes challenged gender stereotypes with shocking tactics that overturned concepts of 'respectable' female behaviour – digging up golf courses, disrupting horse races, padlocking themselves to railings, throwing bricks at Post Office windows, and storming political meetings of men. This raised the profile of women's issues more generally, though the methods divided public opinion and contributed by 1910 to the growing sense of division in Edwardian Britain. All round the country, small acts of civil disobedience were committed by suffragettes, and though in no sense a challenge to civil stability, they showed that female members of the respectable middle classes were willing to engage in vigorous campaigning. Though working-class women were less likely to participate in those forms of action, they did take part in a wave of industrial strikes in the early 1910s.

The lives of many middle-class women changed during the 1890s and 1910s in a different way. Though British universities started to offer courses of study to women, only a narrow range of subjects (like teaching, nursing, languages and biology) was available. Medicine started to open up to women; after much struggle to be educated in various universities (stretching from Edinburgh to Berne), Sophia Jex-Blake (1840–1912) became in 1877 one of the first registered female physicians in Britain. However, medicine remained a problematic career for women. Although increasing numbers were admitted to study the subject, it was less easy for a woman to qualify and obtain a position as a doctor; some women were prevented from studying with men (in anatomy classes, for instance, which were deemed too embarrassing for persons of the same sex to look on a naked human body). Women's higher education received a fillip through the emergence of separatist, women-only colleges: Newnham College at Cambridge (1871), Lady Margaret Hall at Oxford (1878), and Queen Margaret's College in Glasgow (1883). But even after degree-level study, not all women students were allowed to graduate fully. Women at the University of London and in Ireland could obtain degrees from 1878–9, the four Scottish universities admitted women to all classes and degrees by 1892, and the University of Wales in the following year; but female students were not able to graduate in all subjects at Oxford until 1945 and at Cambridge until 1947, whilst other universities put severe restrictions on the freedom of women.

For working-class girls, however, career opportunities underwent less change. The arrival of state schooling in the 1870s led to compulsory education across Britain by 1880 for both boys and girls, but gender remained central to the system. Boys and girls were taught together in most classes, but remained segregated in the playground. Girls received special teaching to equip them for housewifely duties in adulthood, being taught domestic science (cooking, house cleaning, washing and other duties), whilst boys went to woodwork, metalwork and trades teaching that would lead them to the world of work. Few girls reached secondary school. More generally, girls had their expectations restrained by most schools and by either their father or mother.

In the First World War, women did experience new opportunities, filling the jobs that men vacated as they went for military service. For middle-class women, volunteering in war work ranged from making bandages and food parcels, to joining the Women's Land Army in 1916 and 1917 that sent volunteers to help in agriculture. For working-class women, unheard-of jobs appeared in munitions factories, in pithead operations at coal mines, and even in shipyards. Tens of thousands were recruited to fill the gaps in industry, transport, government and the postal service vacated by men in the armed forces. For the first time, they worked in large numbers in engineering works and in munitions factories like that at Gretna where an entire village was created to house the female workers sent from across the north of England and Scotland. In shipyards, too, women workers appeared, despite the fears of male trade unionists at this 'dilution' of their masculine skill. Male domains were invaded, much to the chagrin of many male workers, and women experienced an enormous transformation of their horizons and sense of self. Many taboos seemed to have been smashed. But the coming of peace in late 1918 brought most of this to an abrupt halt. Women were summarily dismissed from most occupations to make way for men returning from the war. Many women grumbled at this, but in truth there was a strong expectation of a return to supposedly 'traditional' feminine roles.

Men's lives

The simplicity of life for men lay in the fact that it was a man's world. It was the era in which the modern culture that still dominates Britain in the twenty-first century was shaped, and it was shaped largely by men for men. Men crafted modern institutions of sport and recreation; concepts of modern manhood and skill were to a great extent forged then, and the nature of the overt qualities that man should aspire to attain were largely set at that time. New technology – motor cars, telephony, electricity – shaped and provided the context for manhood, as did the growth of militarism in youth and adult organisations (the Boys' Brigade was founded in 1883, the Scout Movement in 1907 and the Territorial Army in 1908). The male penchant for organisation, committees, office-bearing and writing constitutions spread with the founding in the 1880s and 1890s of hundreds of football and other sports clubs, the popularisation of self-help friendly and building societies, and voluntary organisations of all kinds with the trappings of self-governing committees. This was the era of male bustle and bureaucracy as much as of patriotism and sport.

The middle-class man of the late-Victorian and Edwardian era aspired to very clear-cut values. He was a man who could marry the 'right' girl and produce a family, house them in a home (whether bought or rented) with at least one live-in general maid (more if they could be afforded, or 'a daily' maid if not), and provide for them completely from his earnings from a professional salary or business profits. In order for this to be possible, he tended not to marry until into his thirties, when he was established in a career. He would be aware that society recognised the vulnerability of men to temptations to drink, gambling, dissipation and (at its worst) womanising, including consorting with prostitutes. It was the role of his wife to build a good home where he felt able to partake of most pleasures. On Sundays, he would be strongly encouraged to attend church with his family, and lead them on a Sunday afternoon promenade in the public parks that mushroomed during this period.

The working-class man had much in common with richer men. Living in smaller and usually rented houses, he also negotiated the tension between temptations and male respectability, but often found this harder. As a manual worker in most cases, his sense of male strength came through waged labour and specific sources of pride and status within that, buttressed by a vigorous plebeian culture where drinking and football were prominent. Life was physically harder for the working man, with lower pay, poorer conditions and long hours of labour. Play in the pub or football park tended to reflect this in a great sense of release, and in the enjoyments of all-male banter in club, music hall or gambling there was a more vigorous participation, less encumbered by fear of loss of reputation. In manufacturing industry, which accounted for much of the working population of Britain at this time, there was a workplace culture in which apprenticeship and work experience allowed men to acquire a kind of property in their skill which was the equivalent of middle-class home ownership.

Sport became, and arguably remains today, the supreme expression, in a peaceful society, of what it is to be a 'true' man, a man of virility, physical strength, skill and determination. And men joined sports in their droves. In the 1860s and 1870s, sport developed overwhelmingly as a participant activity, with the men of the British skilled working class dominating the new soccer clubs. Most British football clubs that we have today were formed between 1870 and 1900, as clubs associated with working men and their communities. What was so characteristic of this period was the vast number of local football clubs. It was customary for streets – or even different sides of a street – to have their own teams. By the late 1880s, teams for young boys were common, with the Boys' Brigade and Sunday schools forming their own teams and holding their own knock-out competitions.

Spectator sport grew as fast as participant sport. In 1872, the first international soccer match between Scotland and England was played in Glasgow in front of 3,500 spectators. The numbers attending this fixture rose to 16,000 in 1876, 20,000 in 1878 and the same in 1892 and 1894. By 1900, the number was 63,000, with 102,000 in 1906 and 121,000 in 1908. Spectators expected to see players of quality and pressure for the professionalisation of football clubs grew. Battles between those who wanted to retain amateur status and those who saw the future in professional sport were won in football in favour of professionalism by the 1890s. The battles were often class ones between working people, who wanted value for their hard-earned pennies or who saw for themselves a future as a sportsman, and middle-class members of associations who saw sport as about moral improvement.

Drink was an even more common aspect of men's culture. Public houses were men's domain, and few women ventured in. Those that did quickly acquired a reputation as unrespectable and 'loose' women. Pubs were far more numerous than they are today, and the amount of alcohol drunk per head of population in 1900 was about twice current levels, although consumption was falling from the 1890s. The temperance movement was also very strong, especially amongst the upper working class and lower middle class, and their political clout led to very tight licensing laws which closed pubs early in the evening and most of the day, and all day on Sundays. Magistrates imposed extra demands upon publicans. In Scotland, pubs were almost universally required to be hidden from public view. Nobody was allowed to see into a pub from the street, and thus be enticed in, so pubs had windows covered to above head height and double doors which swung in different directions so that even when somebody entered, nobody on the street might see drink being consumed or served.

By 1900, manhood was rooted increasingly in patriotism, and one that had been heavily militarised. Boys brought up in the years after 1890 experienced uniformed youth organisations modelled on soldiering, imperial war games and hostility to German military growth. Baden Powell, in his *Scouting for Boys*, published in 1908, commented: 'Every boy ought to learn how to shoot and to obey orders, else he is no more good when war breaks out than an old woman.' This sense of manhood was to become evident in the extraordinary scenes in August 1914 when war was declared. Hundreds of thousands of young men turned up unbidden at recruitment offices for the army – entire factories of male workers; entire football teams; men's Christian groups; and groups of those merely known as 'pals' enlisted for service. But the experience of the war did much to change the nature of masculinity. Men were mown down by machine guns and obliterated by artillery bombardments in the intensity of trench warfare on the western front in France. The nature of the war was one of mass slaughter: on the first day of the battle of the Somme in 1916, 16,000 British soldiers died, sent 'over the top' to be shot to pieces by machine guns. Around 5.6 million British men were under arms in the war, and 705,000 of them were killed. British families were left without male breadwinners. And hundreds of thousands of men returned, wounded in body and in mind (see Chapter 26).

The Great War highlighted the vulnerability of maleness. Men's bodies were mutilated and disabled and disfigured on a massive scale – 31 per cent of those who served in the British army were wounded; more than 41,000 men had their limbs amputated;

and many who survived physically were irreparably damaged mentally. Shell shock was a medical/psychological condition brought on by the terrifying endless bombardments by explosive shells. It was responsible for up to 10 per cent of officers and up to 4 per cent of men of other ranks being sent home suffering from 'nervous shock'. Excluding men sent home wounded, shell shock accounted for one-third of discharges from the army. At the beginning of the war, most medical officers refused to believe men were suffering from legitimate symptoms – a misdiagnosis partially resulting from the long-standing belief that combat was part of the masculine persona. The result was that many shell shock victims were shot for cowardice. However, by 1917 military doctors began to accept that shell shock was a genuine illness.

War poets like Siegfried Sassoon or Wilfred Owen, or war novelists like Robert Graves, or Erich Remarque in his *All Quiet on the Western Front* (which was later turned into an anti-war film), wrote tortured explorations of maleness that came into public awareness in the 1930s. They did not see war as the quintessentially male experience. Many soldiers had expressed their feelings, and they did, despite censorship, write to friends and family at home to describe to them the horrifying conditions. And yet, when they returned home, they were to encounter uncomprehending family and friends who could never conceive of the horror they had experienced. Mothers, fathers and wives had seen fit and healthy young men leave; those who returned were often broken men. Men who had suffered mutilation returned to a country which did little to help them.

Ethnicity

Britain in the 1880–1919 period became more aware of migrant cultures. One which was already well known was that of the Irish – mostly Catholic Irish – although as many as a third in Liverpool and Glasgow were Protestant. But the 1880–1919 period witnessed large-scale Jewish immigration, and the beginnings of a significant non-white population, composed mainly at this time of Arabs from Yemen. In addition, London became a cosmopolitan haven for political and other refugees from many countries – such as Communists from Germany, Russia and Eastern Europe.

The Irish community of Britain was mainly concentrated in the larger cities – the disembarkation cities of Liverpool and Glasgow, but also Manchester and London. Here they formed mainly working-class communities, to be found in many poorer areas – in the East End and in north London; in Liverpool's Scotland Street and Vauxhall areas; and in Glasgow's Gallowgate. They worked mainly in unskilled jobs, labouring in the building trade and in the docks. In the late nineteenth century, the culture and self-confidence of the Irish Catholic community grew as Catholic churches were built and priests appointed, social clubs formed and as they claimed an ever-greater role in civil institutions. The trade-union movement, which rapidly spread into the unskilled working class in the 1890s, attracted many Irish Catholics, and the appeal of socialism and Marxism grew amongst them. Irish migrants formed football clubs which gave added pride and self-identity – Glasgow Celtic, Liverpool, Edinburgh's Hibernian and many other local clubs. Catholic firms and businesses developed. Many of these cultivated a strong role of trading with each other but, in general, they provided important economic opportunities to a mainly working-class community. Educational opportunities beyond school were limited and, indeed, probably the subject of religious discrimination. Certainly, discrimination in the workplace was rife, with Protestant employers openly rejecting Catholics in some industries. Despite this, the Irish community was becoming deeply embedded in British society, and it spread out slowly through the towns of mainland Britain, followed by its own churches and other institutions.

Jewish immigration resulted from large-scale pogroms in western Russia and eastern Europe. Driven out by bigotry, Jews travelled to Britain and, in some cases, to the United States to make a new life. Large numbers settled in London's East End, with other significant communities developing in Manchester, Glasgow and in seaside towns. The newcomers joined a well-established Jewish business community and many brought with them skills, especially in the furniture trades, in jewellery and in watch-making. They formed even more tightly-knit communities than the Irish, often ghettoised in a few streets, with rich and poor Jewish families living close together. With time, however, wealthier Jewish families moved to join the general suburbanisation of the urban elites. In London, wealthy Jews moved from the East End to Golders Green and, later, Finchley in the north; in Glasgow from the inner-city Gorbals to Newton Mearns in the south. To an important extent, Jews were unlike the Catholic Irish in developing a more languid form of religious faith; many Jews became secularised, many socialist, maintaining their Jewishness as a cultural and racial identity rather than a religious one.

The sharp rise in Jewish immigration in the 1890s led to demands for restrictions, often linked to deep-seated anti-semitism. The Aliens Act of 1905 came up with the concept, for the first time, of the 'undesirable alien', usually one who was apparently destitute, although there was still a place for those seeking asylum from persecution. War-time legislation against enemy aliens was extended in peace-time by an Act of 1919, which was largely aimed at reducing the number of foreign seamen in British merchant ships.

The 1880–1919 period witnessed much lower but still rising Muslim immigration to Britain. This had developed very slowly in the late nineteenth century, and continued in the First World War. Arab and Somali seamen had been very important to the British merchant marine during wartime, but most lost their jobs after the peace in 1919, causing widespread unemployment and poverty amongst them in the 1920s. British civil society was largely unsympathetic to their plight and enforced repatriation was introduced. Five hundred Adenis were deported from Cardiff alone by September 1921. Nonetheless, significant communities of Muslims existed – the largest being at Cardiff, Newport, Barry, Liverpool, Tyneside, London and Glasgow. This was the beginnings of what was to prove in the twentieth century a difficult transition for Britain to a multicultural society.

Inter-faith relations during this period were few. Protestant, Catholic, Jewish and Muslim religious bodies rarely communicated with each other, and there was a general feeling that Britain remained a Reformed Protestant nation in which other religions were inferior and, for many, unwelcome. Amongst churchmen, bigotry was more intellectualised than active or violently hostile. However, popular bigotry could be quite strong. In cultural organisations, there would be latent and sometimes real hostility, and there were incidences of violence and even riot – notable in Catholic and Protestant antagonism at football matches in the 1890s and 1900s. The strongest places of tension were in the Belfast, Glasgow and Liverpool areas. In Liverpool, the city police were widely regarded as dominated by Protestants, and after a particularly vicious riot in which the police used excessive violence, a Home Office inquiry was instituted that severely criticised the police. But in the main, bigotry was more economic and cultural – a denigration of the morality of minorities, and discrimination in employment. This was to remain a feature of British society for some time to come.

Further reading

Fraser, W.H., *A History of British Trade Unionism 1700–1998* (Basingstoke, Macmillan, 1999)

Holloway, G., *Women and Work in Britain since 1840* (London, Routledge, 2005)

Kent, S.K., *Gender and Power in Britain 1640–1990* (London, Routledge, 1999)

McIvor, A., *A History of Work in Britain, 1880–1950* (Basingstoke, Palgrave Macmillan, 2001)

McLeod, H., *Religion and Society in England 1850–1914* (Basingstoke, Macmillan, 1995)

Reid, A., *Social Classes and Social Relations in Britain 1850–1914* (Basingstoke, Macmillan, 1992)

Tosh, J., *Manliness and Masculinities in Nineteenth-century Britain* (Harlow, Pearson Longman, 2005)

23

Political change 1880–1901

The two decades after 1880 brought major political changes and saw the origins of further changes that were to mark the early decades of the twentieth century. Liberal dominance was challenged by a revived Conservatism. Liberal support within the working class had to face the threat from independent Labour. The drift was towards a politics based on class rather than religion. While the Empire continued to grow, Britain's dominant position in the world was being confronted by other powers and, closer to home, by nationalism in Ireland, and, to a lesser extent, in Scotland and Wales. This brought constitutional issues to the fore.

Irish unrest

The Liberals had a majority over the Conservatives and Irish Nationalists in the general election of 1880. The Queen went to great lengths to try to find an alternative to Gladstone as Prime Minister, but he refused to accept a subordinate office. Although he had returned to power in a torrent of radical oratory, this was not reflected in the Cabinet that he formed. Eight of his eleven cabinet colleagues were aristocratic Whigs. It was easy for Gladstone to lay down splendid principles, as he did in the Midlothian campaign which saw him back in Parliament as leader of the Liberals, but much less easy to carry them out. He had condemned Disraeli's expansionist policies but found it difficult to extricate the armed forces. The Boers in the Transvaal had to wrest their independence from the British by force, with their victory at Majuba Hill in December 1881. Far from leaving Afghanistan, the Indian army captured Kabul, only to withdraw rapidly in the face of a hostile populace. Revolt in Egypt brought an assertion of British control by force and an attempt to extricate Europeans from the Sudan led to Gordon's embarrassing death at Khartoum. (For imperial activities, see Chapter 19.)

Nearer home, the pressing problem was Ireland, where agricultural depression, as a result of American imports and local harvest failures, had unleashed a 'land war' – a rebellion of tenant farmers against rent levels. Farmers saw the gains of the relatively prosperous recent decades evaporating, while many landowners, who had invested heavily, were resistant to substantial rent reductions. In response to evictions, the land war quickly turned violent and led to a revival of Fenian activity.

At the end of the 1870s, a new voice had emerged within the Irish National Party – the charismatic, if aloof, Charles Stewart Parnell, a Protestant landowner with an American mother, who had entered Parliament in 1875. Parnell was able to link the politicians of the Home Rule Confederation and the land reformers of the Land League. In 1880, he was elected chairman of the Irish National Party and over the next few years he created a highly disciplined force. His MPs in Parliament were determined to keep the focus on the single issue of Irish Home Rule and prepared to disrupt the proceedings of the Commons to do so.

As the rural unrest grew worse, evictions were followed by ever more vicious agrarian outrages: cattle maiming; house-burning; hayrick destroying; and even murder.

Figure 23.1 Gladstone, Parnell and Chamberlain in the lobby of the House of Commons, 1880s. In the foreground left to right are Joseph Chamberlain, Charles Stewart Parnell, William Gladstone, Lord Randolph Churchill and Lord Hartington. Far left in the top hat is John Bright, facing Arthur Balfour also in a top hat.
Source: Mary Evans Picture Library

Parnell advocated boycotting (named after Captain Boycott, one of the earliest victims): refusing to pay what were regarded as unfair rents and refusing to take the farms of those evicted. The government responded with a mixture of 'kicks and kindness'. A Land Act in 1881 conceded some of what tenant farmers wanted: the three 'Fs' – fair rents fixed by tribunal; fixity of tenure; and free sale (the right to sell the 'interest' in a holding to an incoming tenant, but only to tenants who were not in arrears). It failed to quell the agitation amongst smallholders in the west of Ireland who wanted access to more land, while it left landowners with little incentive to invest in their estates.

A Coercion Act was brought in, suspending habeas corpus, appointing special magistrates and using troops to back up the armed Royal Irish Constabulary. The Land League was banned, and nationalist MPs were arrested. Parnell himself was interned in Kilmainham Jail for 'criminal incitement and intimidation'. By the end of 1881, there had been more than 800 arrests in Ireland for various acts of terrorism and incitement, and bombings spread to mainland Britain. After secret negotiations, in return for using his influence against the increasing number of violent outrages, Parnell was freed and, to all intents, arrears were written off. A new Chief Secretary for Ireland was appointed but, the day after his arrival, he and the Under-Secretary were assassinated in Phoenix Park by a terrorist group. The attack brought a new level of horror to a country where outrages against people and property had become commonplace.

Events in Ireland found milder echoes in Scotland, with numerous outbreaks of rural protest in the Highlands and the emergence of the Highland Land Law Reform Association and the more militant Scottish Land Restoration League. The Napier Commission of Inquiry of 1884 into conditions in the Highlands led in 1886 to the Crofters' Holdings Act, which made further clearance in the Highland counties illegal, appointed a land court to assess rents and gave crofters the right to hand on their holdings to their children. Events in Ireland and in Scotland pushed the issue of land reform to the forefront of radical programmes. The legitimacy of the existing system of land tenure was being challenged. The solutions devised also set important precedents for the state to intervene and to challenge the rights of property in order to create greater social equality.

The policy of 'kicks and kindness' was pressed by the most radical member of the Cabinet, Joseph Chamberlain, the President of the Board of Trade. He had encouraged the Kilmainham 'Treaty' with Parnell; he was, however, against Home Rule. Chamberlain wanted an extensive local government bill that would devolve control over aspects of local administration to county boards under a national council, not just in Ireland, but in Scotland and Wales also. It was part of a wider radical programme that he was beginning to devise. This included free primary education; financial reform; disestablishment of the Church of England; a further extension of the franchise; payment of MPs and land reform to make more smallholdings available – 'three acres and a cow', the catchphrase went – to free rural labourers from poverty and landlord control. To many on the political right, this seemed little short of socialism. His rhetoric, in which he called for the landed aristocracy – 'a class who toil not neither do they spin' – to pay a 'ransom' for their privileges, was seen as highly dangerous and infuriated the Whiggish elements in the government. But Chamberlain's concern, as a Birmingham industrialist, was to keep the focus on the landed class as the root of the nation's problems.

Major splits in the Cabinet bedevilled most attempts at serious reform and Gladstone's style of refusing to consult colleagues added to Chamberlain's frustrations. It was not just a Whig–Radical split. The Radicals were divided among themselves between staunch anti-imperialists and those who stressed the value of an imperial tie for what were referred to as 'backward peoples'. The influential but erratic Lord Rosebery, after a visit to Australia, had declared himself a Liberal Imperialist committed to 'a larger patriotism' and was attracting some of the brightest younger members of the party.

Parliamentary reform

The Franchise Act of 1884 put voters in the counties on the same basis as those in the boroughs – household suffrage for men. The Conservatives blocked the first proposals and there was a huge wave of protest throughout the country. Any measure, however, had to get past the Conservative-dominated House of Lords and a compromise was necessary. At Conservative insistence, the extension of the franchise was accompanied by a Redistribution Act. The Redistribution Act of 1885 was by far the more important of the two measures. It recognised, for the first time, that there should be some equalisation of the size of constituencies on the basis of population. Counties were divided into separate divisions and the gainers were the northern industrial areas. Lancashire now had 23 separate seats, the West Riding of Yorkshire, 19. The Act gave an increased number of seats to the largest cities and, even more significantly, these were, in almost all cases, single-member constituencies. Liverpool now consisted of 9 constituencies; Birmingham and Glasgow went up from 3 MPs representing the whole city to 7 separate divisions; Manchester had 6 and London had 58 instead of 19.

The simplistic assumption was that the newly enfranchised rural and mining working class in the counties would vote for the Liberals, and there was an expectation amongst many Radicals that an increase in urban constituencies was also bound to be to Liberal advantage. In fact, many of the latter went Conservative in the 1885 election. Single-member constituencies reflected the increasing class division of cities, with middle-class west ends separated from the working-class east ends. It was these new 'villa Tories', moving to the suburbs, who strengthened the Conservative position. However, the redistribution also encouraged demands for working-class people to represent predominantly working-class constituencies.

It would be wrong to assume, as it often is, that after 1884 there was more or less universal male suffrage. It was very difficult to get on the electoral register and it was very easy to be taken off. In theory, the vote went to all adult males. The vote was given to men who owned or were tenants of any dwelling house or portion of a dwelling house defined as a separate dwelling. This seems fine, but in practice it excluded tenants who had a landlord living in the same house. It excluded grown-up sons who still lived with parents. It excluded policemen and soldiers who lived in barracks. It excluded living-in servants. Assuming that a man had the necessary householding qualification, there were still problems. He had to have lived in the same house for a full year before the register was compiled. This was to exclude the 'unrespectable', who were assumed to be mobile. It has been estimated that 20–30 per cent of the electorate in towns moved every year.

There were other obstacles, such as disqualification for being in receipt of poor relief, and a voter had to have paid all local rates and taxes in full, not in instalments, before the date of registration. On the other hand, some people had two votes: the businessman for his residence and for his business, if they were in separate constituencies, and university graduates, who returned nine MPs for university constituencies – overwhelmingly in the Conservative interest.

Around 5 million adult males were excluded from the franchise. The vote went to just over 60 per cent of the adult male population and there were tremendous local variations. There is something of a debate over who exactly the excluded were. For a long time, there was an assumption that it was the poorest and, clearly, very many of these were disenfranchised. But many middle-class young men lived with their parents into their thirties. They married later than the working class and, because they were living at home, they had no vote. What is known for certain is that it was the young of all social classes who were excluded. Of the 21–30 age group, half were not on the electoral roll. 1884 brought universal suffrage to the middle-aged, which perhaps partly explains Conservative dominance in the 20 years after 1886. In none of these measures was there an acceptance of the idea that everyone had the *right* to vote. There was no concession to the principle of democracy. The idea was still that powerful Liberal one that the vote should go to 'capable citizens' – those who worked, paid their rates, had some education and were capable of reasoned judgments.

Gladstone's government of 1880–85 is a critical turning point in the history of Liberalism. There was evidence of disenchantment among some intellectuals, who began to look for alternative ways of creating the better world that they sought. These began to toy with the ideas of socialism that were emerging from continental Europe (see Chapter 21). There were also signs of disappointment amongst the working classes who had little to show for their loyalty to the Liberal Party and its 'Grand Old Man', as Gladstone had now become.

Gladstone struggled to hold his cabinet together. Tensions between Lord Hartington on the right and Chamberlain on the left were palpable at the rare Cabinet meetings that Gladstone called. He was isolated from both wings of his party and his decision to submit his government's resignation in 1885, when, with Parnell's help, a Tory amendment to the budget was passed, seemed to presage his retirement. Lord Salisbury came in as leader of a minority Conservative government and immediately called an election.

Salisbury's first ministry

After Disraeli died in 1881, there was no single leader of the Conservative Party. The rather colourless Stafford-Northcote led in the Commons and the Earl of Salisbury in the Lords. Within the party there was a young ginger group, the so-called 'Fourth Party' associated with the brash and arrogant Lord Randolph Churchill. They were highly critical of the 'double-barrelled mediocrities' and the 'gouty brigade' who dominated the party. These 'modernisers' sought to give more bite to the opposition and also to develop in the party an appeal to the new wider electorate. The creation of the Primrose League in 1883, as a vehicle of popular Toryism, was an attempt to do this. There was talk of 'Tory democracy', although the term was often ambiguous, implying an appeal to the masses but also intended as a response to the increasing number of business people who were drifting to the Conservatives and who sought to secure recognition within the landowner-dominated party. The Primrose League would tap into popular patriotism, deference and conservatism by creating a mass organisation, led by aristocratic Tories, but encouraging middle-class and even working-class participation. As Martin Pugh memorably put it, in 1900 there were more members of the Primrose League in Bolton than members of the Independent Labour Party throughout the whole country.[1]

The manifesto put forward by Gladstone in the election of December 1885 was very mild, with few commitments to Chamberlain's radical programme. He rejected Chamberlain's argument that the crucial thing was to respond to the new democracy. Gladstone said little about Ireland other than to hint at past injustices and so Parnell asked his supporters to vote for Conservative candidates. The Liberals lost all the seats in Ireland that they had won in 1880 and Irish Liberalism was largely destroyed. The Liberals made gains in county seats that had formerly been Conservative strongholds, but the results in the boroughs were less good, and Irish voters in Britain were blamed for some of the Liberal losses in English cities. The Liberals were still the largest party, but 86 Irish Nationalists held the balance of power in the Commons. It seems to have been the prospect of Irish Nationalists holding a threat over the other political parties that finally decided Gladstone that there had to be a permanent solution to the Irish issue. The problem was convincing those who were appalled at the idea of making concessions to Irish violence and who regarded Irish Home Rule as a threat to the whole future of the United Kingdom and the Empire.

Salisbury, still nominally the Prime Minister, was firmly against Home Rule: 'Ireland must be kept, like India, at all hazards; by persuasion if possible; if not, by force', and claimed, in an unguarded moment, that the Irish were as incapable of self-government as the Hottentots. His 'persuasion' involved the passing, in the Ashbourne Act, of Parnell's plan for Irish peasants to acquire land by purchasing their tenancies with the aid of a state loan paid back over 49 years.

---

[1] Martin Pugh, *The Tories and the People 1880–1935* (Oxford, Blackwell, 1985), p. 2.

Focus on

The Irish strategy in the general election of 1885

This is the Manifesto of the Irish National League to the Irish in Britain, 21 November 1885. The League was a highly centralised body formed in 1882 under the leadership of Parnell to campaign for Home Rule and agrarian reform. It was committed to constitutional action.

To Our Countrymen in England and Scotland

The Liberal party are making an appeal to the confidences of the electors at the general election of 1885, as at the general election of 1880, on false pretences. In 1880 the Liberal party promised peace, and afterwards made unjust war; economy, and its Budget reached the highest point yet attained; justice to aspiring nationalists; and it mercilessly crushed the national movement of Egypt and Arabi Pasha, and murdered thousands of Arabs rightly struggling to be free. To Ireland, more than any other country, it bound itself by most solemn pledges, and these it most flagrantly violated. It denounced coercion, and it practised a system of coercion more brutal than that of any previous Administration, Liberal or Tory. Under this system juries were packed with a shamelessness unprecedented even in a Liberal Administration, and innocent men were sent to the living death of penal servitude. Twelve hundred men were imprisoned without trial. Ladies were convicted under an obsolete Act directed against the degraded of their sex; and for a period every utterance of the popular press and of popular meetings was completely suppressed as if Ireland were Poland and the administration of England a Russian autocracy. . . . The Liberal began menacing the Established Church, and under the name of free schools made an insidious attempt to crush the religious education of the country, and to establish a system of State tyranny and intolerance, and to fetter the right of conscience, which is sacred in the selection of school as in the free selection of one's Church. The cry of Disestablishment has been dropped; the cry of Free Schools has been explained away; and the two last cries left to the Liberal party are the so-called Reform of Procedure and a demand to be independent of the Irish Party. Reform of procedure means a new gag, and the application to all enemies of Radicalism in the House of Commons of the despotic methods and the mean machinery of the Birmingham caucus . . . In every instance we earnestly advise our countrymen to vote against the men who coerced Ireland, deluged Egypt with blood, menaced religious liberty in the school, freedom of speech in Parliament, and promised to the country generally a repetition of the crimes and follies of the last Liberal Administration.

Source: Alan O'Day and John Stevenson (eds), *Irish Historical Documents since 1800* (Dublin, Gill and Macmillan, 1992), pp. 106–7.

Gladstone, meanwhile, was taking soundings with Parnell, and tentatively floating his ideas with colleagues. Before these were complete, his son, Herbert, probably with his father's collusion, announced in December 1885 his father's conversion to the idea of a parliament in Dublin. This so-called 'Hawarden kite' floated from Gladstone's country house in north-east Wales, stunned some Liberal supporters, although there had been radical support for Home Rule since Chartist days. Lord Hartington from the Whig right and Chamberlain from the radical left both condemned it. Gladstone, confident as ever that he was hearing the guidance of the Almighty, was happy to see the consternation of his rivals. Most recent work suggests that he was neither as knowledgeable about, nor as obsessed with, Ireland as was once thought. What did concern him was winning the internal struggle against those in his own party who he regarded as challenging him. He may well have hoped for the kind of bipartisan settlement that had pushed through Catholic Emancipation in 1829 and repeal of the Corn Laws in 1846, but Salisbury declined to play the role of Peel and split his party. The Conservatives from then on made unionism central to their party's policy.

The Liberal split

As soon as Parliament met, the Conservatives were defeated and Gladstone took office for the third time in January 1886. He announced merely an inquiry into the Irish Question and Chamberlain therefore joined the Cabinet. But, in March 1886, Gladstone proposed a scheme for a separate Irish assembly that would be subordinate to Westminster on matters of foreign policy, defence and many aspects of fiscal policy, although there would be no Irish MPs at Westminster. Gladstone argued that Home Rule would strengthen the union, although there were plenty who pointed out that it failed to respond to the aspirations of Wales and Scotland. Chamberlain resigned. He made contact with Lord Hartington and the Whigs and with the Conservatives through Randolph Churchill. The last had come to the conclusion that anti-Catholicism, 'the Orange card', was the one to play to attract popular support in Britain, declaring 'Home Rule is Rome Rule' and warning that 'Ulster will fight, and Ulster will be right'. Ulster Protestants viewed Irish nationalism as a threat to their economic position and feared discrimination in a Catholic-dominated Ireland.

The Home Rule Bill came up in June 1886. Ninety-three Liberals voted against it, the Bill was defeated and Gladstone called another election. A new Liberal Unionist organisation emerged around Hartington and Chamberlain. Chamberlain's thinking is quite difficult to discern. Gladstone's shabby and often insulting treatment of him was certainly a factor. Chamberlain was a man in a hurry who had a list of social reforms that he wanted to see implemented. Ireland did not particularly interest him, but it stood in the way of getting other things done. He was against Home Rule, because he knew that a majority in England was against it, and he believed that the party had to retain its support among the urban working class. He perhaps recognised that there was little chance of Gladstone's scheme getting through and he may have hoped that he was strong enough to force Gladstone's resignation. But Chamberlain also saw it as vital to maintain the integrity of the Empire, and Irish Home Rule could be a first step to its disintegration and could even pose a military threat to Britain.

The Whig rebellion is easier to comprehend. The great aristocrats who had once dominated the Whig party had been drifting away from the Liberal Party for decades. They disliked what they saw as the growing strength of middle-class radicals, like Chamberlain, within the party. They saw land reforms in Ireland and in the Highlands as a direct assault on landed property. They were suspicious of Gladstone's love of extra-parliamentary agitation and of his anti-imperialist instincts. Irish Home Rule brought the final 'passing of the Whigs' from Liberalism. From the Irish point of view, Parnell and his associates were now firmly tied to the Liberals as Conservatives hardened their hostility.

In the election of July 1886, anti-Catholic prejudice was played hard in many constituencies. The Liberal share of the vote held firm in Scotland and Wales, but England went overwhelmingly Conservative. Liberal strength now lay largely in what was dubbed the 'Celtic fringe' and in some of the English county seats. Even in Scotland there were signs of the better-off in the cities deserting the Liberal Party and voting Liberal Unionist. The Liberals, who failed to put up a candidate in 105 constituencies, were reduced to 191 seats, as against 316 Conservatives and 77 Liberal Unionists, while the Nationalists held their 86. Ulster was torn by sectarian violence in the shipyards and in the streets, with 32 deaths and nearly 400 injured.

Salisbury's second ministry

Chamberlain did not join the new Salisbury government. He still saw himself as a Liberal and he can at this stage have had few hopes for his own future. But the sudden and eccentric resignation of the Chancellor of the Exchequer, Lord Randolph Churchill, because he could not get cuts in defence expenditure, created a crisis and brought discussions of possible Liberal reunion. Chamberlain seemed keen and even seemed to be prepared to accept legislative authority in Dublin. What killed reunion was a revival of rural disorder in Ireland with a new campaign by evicted tenants. Parnell's attempts to get a bill to waive rent arrears were defeated. Salisbury's nephew, Arthur Balfour, became Secretary for Ireland and introduced a Crimes Bill, involving summary convictions without juries or with juries from the landowning class, to try to crush the agitation. Chamberlain and the Liberal Unionists voted for the Bill, pushed through the Commons by new procedures to guillotine debates. It was the end of the prospect of Liberal reunion.

The Queen's jubilee celebrations of 1887 unleashed a flurry of nationalistic sentiment into which the Conservatives tapped, presenting themselves as the patriotic party, and, increasingly as the English party, defending the institutions of monarchy, church and Empire against radical and Irish threats. Ireland still remained a central concern as disorder once again returned. 'Bloody Balfour', as he became in Irish demonology, pursued three years of coercive policies, refusing to regard Parnell and his associates as truly representative of Irish opinion, while at the same time making some concessions to remove land grievances. Parnell believed that the aim was to drive Ireland into open rebellion and to split the Liberals from Parnell. In fact it had the opposite effect, making most Liberals determined to bring about Home Rule.

What was clear was that the Conservatives had firmly set their face against Home Rule. The shooting to death by the police of three rioters who were resisting evictions at Mitchelstown, County Cork, and the quashing of any charges against the police entered nationalist martyrology. Protests at these events by Socialists and Irish in Trafalgar Square in November 1887, led to cracked skulls, two deaths and many other injuries on 'Bloody Sunday'. However, there was yet another Land Act to control rents and to encourage further land purchase by tenants – to Salisbury a price that had to be paid for union.

The exposure as forgeries of letters published by *The Times*, purporting to link Parnell with the Phoenix Park murders, confirmed Liberal support for him. But, in December 1889, Captain O'Shea filed for divorce, naming Parnell as co-respondent. Parnell's affair with Mrs O'Shea had started in 1880. It was known about by most members of the Irish National Party and was the subject of occasional gossip in Liberal political circles. When the case came to court it was undefended. Liberal Nonconformists were appalled, perhaps less at the fact of the affair than at the public revelation of it with all its prurient detail. Flouting conventional morality was not uncommon among the powerful, but it was not acceptable publicly to flaunt immorality and this was Parnell's sin. Cardinal Manning called on Gladstone to repudiate him and Gladstone eventually declared that Parnell's continuation in the leadership of the National Party would endanger the alliance with the Liberals. What finished Parnell was the widespread condemnation of him by the Irish Catholic clergy. Parnell clung on and his party split, with 45 against Parnell and 28 staying with him. His sudden death in October 1891 did little to heal the schism and only a handful of Parnellite members were returned in 1892.

The most far-reaching measure introduced by the Conservative government was the Local Government Act of 1888, something that Chamberlain found very attractive. For the first time, it established elected county councils in the historic shires of England and Wales, to replace the old, unelected Justices of the Peace Quarter Sessions, and an elected London County Council. While some Conservatives saw this as a step too far towards democracy, others saw the new councils as a useful check on the centralisation of power. The fact that the London County Council was captured by a 'Progressive Party' consisting of radical Liberals, trade unionists and socialists was a sign of changes in the air, but generally it was Conservatives who soon gained control of the county councils. Pressed by Chamberlain, the government also took up various social reform issues. Royal Commissions investigated tuberculosis, sewage disposal, epidemics and local taxation. Local authorities were encouraged to create allotments; school fees in elementary schools in England and Wales were abolished, those in Scotland in the same year (though it took four years to implement); and the new county councils were given responsibility for developing technical education. A Mines' Regulation Act brought some of the protection that miners had been demanding, but not the eight-hour working day that they sought, while a new Factory and Workshop Act responded to safety concerns.

Liberal divisions

The signs were clear by the end of the 1880s that Chamberlain was steadily moving closer to the Conservatives. He was anxious about the advance of socialist attitudes, reflected in organisations like the Social Democratic Federation and the Socialist League that had emerged early in the 1880s, and in the industrial unrest associated with the rise of new unionism (see Chapter 22). With Gladstone determined to persist with Irish Home Rule, there was little hope of getting from the Liberals the kind of programme that he felt was essential. The Liberal Party was in a bad way. As a result of the Whig exodus and the departure of many of the well-heeled middle-class, the party had lost its main financiers. But it had also lost its leading Radical. The dependence on Nonconformist Welsh and Scots was reflected in the programme adopted by the National Liberal Federation at Newcastle in 1891. At its head was Home Rule for Ireland; the disestablishment of the churches in Wales and Scotland; the abolition of entail, by which one generation could tie up an estate for the next two generations; the right of a local veto on public houses in an area; and the building of rural cottages. These were well-established Liberal measures, important to many of the party activists in the Celtic areas, but not exactly issues that were likely to galvanise the popular electorate in English cities. However, these were the only issues on which it was possible to get widespread party agreement. Imperial issues divided hopelessly and social reform measures were tricky, costing money and worrying to the middle class. The only nod in the direction of the urban working class was a vague promise of tidying up the male suffrage and an extension of employers' liability for accidents at work.

In spite of this, and thanks to overwhelming support in Wales and in Scotland, there was something of a Liberal revival. However, with 46 Liberal-Unionists in coalition with the Conservative Party, the Unionists as they now tended to call themselves, could command a majority of 43 over the Liberals. But with the 81 Irish Nationalists and the one Independent Labour Member, Keir Hardie, largely voting with the Liberals, the Queen was once again, and much to her unconcealed regret, forced to turn to Gladstone, the 'old, wild and incomprehensible man of 82 and a half'.

All the 1893 session was taken up with the Home Rule Bill. The 1886 proposals, which had entirely excluded Irish MPs from the Commons, were modified to allow 80 Irish members to sit in the Westminster Parliament, but to vote only on Irish and imperial matters. The Bill was passed by the Commons but went to inevitable defeat in the Lords by 419 votes to 41.

This was a talented government but it was unable to get past the egoism and intransigence of the 'Grand Old Man' and many of the working-class leaders despaired of making advances through Liberalism. It was no coincidence that an Independent Labour Party emerged in 1893. The differences over imperialism also deepened. A younger element around Lord Rosebery, and including a new political 'star', Henry Asquith, believed that only by identifying with popular enthusiasm for imperialism could the party hope to regain its domination.

Gladstone was tempted to have another dissolution after the defeat of the Home Rule Bill, but his colleagues were adamantly opposed, knowing the hostility or, at the very least, indifference to Home Rule in England. He retired in March 1894 after 61 years in politics, mostly at the forefront. The Queen snubbed him to the end, not asking his advice on his successor. She chose Rosebery, the Foreign Secretary. Lord Rosebery was no enthusiast for Home Rule and he quickly declared that it would only come about when a majority supported it in *England*, 'the predominant member of the partnership of the Three Kingdoms'. The House of Lords set its face against Liberal legislation for Welsh disestablishment and local option, and in the 16 months of Rosebery's government only the budget, with which the Lords could not interfere, brought a significant measure – the introduction of death duties. Rosebery disapproved of what he saw as a tax that fell heavily on the landowning class, but the measure, which future chancellors were to find an invaluable fund-raiser, went through. The money raised, however, did not go on social programmes like old-age pensions, as some Liberals had hoped, but on yet further naval expansion.

Conservatism triumphant

A defeat on a vote of censure of the War Office in the summer of 1895 was taken as an excuse for the government's resignation[2] and once again Salisbury returned to No. 10. He quickly called an election, which saw the Liberals go down to the worst defeat of any party since 1832, although their actual share of the vote went up. The Conservatives had made big advances in English cities. Only eight London seats returned a Liberal; only five in Lancashire; only two in Glasgow. The Conservatives and Liberal Unionists had a majority of 134 over all the other parties. It was clear that the Liberals had lost much working-class support as a result of their advocacy of Irish nationalism, temperance reform and church disestablishment, not, as is sometimes suggested, because of their failure to deliver social reform. ILP candidates too went down to defeat.

The Unionists played up English nationalism, regularly accusing the government of giving contracts to foreigners and failing to defend imperial interests. Also, as historian Patrick Joyce has argued: 'The Conservatives seem to have been better able to

---

[2] Rosebery himself was on the edge of a breakdown. In the press outside Britain his name was associated with the trial of dramatist Oscar Wilde because of his close attachment to Lord Francis Douglas, the brother of Wilde's lover, Alfred 'Bosie' Douglas. Francis Douglas took his own life in October 1894 and there were rumours of blackmail and homosexual activities.

respond to politics as participatory, local, convivial.'[3] In the Primrose League, which had about a million members in 1900, and in their workingmen's clubs, they had developed a social side to politics that was in marked contrast to the didactic, 'improving' tone that came from many Liberals. Conservatives were associated with the pub, the Liberals with temperance; the Conservatives tapped into deference, the Liberals still sought to appeal to reason; the Conservatives waved flags and banners at great outdoor rallies; the Liberals showed little enthusiasm for mass politics. Conservatives also gained from people identifying with their community – and that could be the town or the workplace – rather than their class. Politics remained strongly local and factory workers might vote in the same way as their employer because they had a sense that what was good for the firm was good for them. That belief could overcome any class sense at election time, even if at other times they might feel exploited by their employer. Perhaps most importantly of all, the Conservatives recognised the vital importance of organising their supporters and making sure that they turned out. A network of local party agents was beginning to emerge and although the Liberals, too, were trying to reorganise the party machinery, the Conservatives and Unionists had resources well beyond those of the Liberals.

They also were attracting more and more of the middle classes who resented rising taxation and saw too many concessions being made to the working class. The Liberals were no longer seen as defenders of individualism but as leaning towards collectivism. Salisbury was very specific – 'the chief object of Government in England at least, is the protection of property – property is the special object and care of the Conservative Party'. It was a message that was having a growing appeal amongst the better-off and the aspiring, anxious about democratic challenges.

Conservatives also had the advantage in many cities of an increasingly supportive regional press, where Conservatism could be presented both as a defender of property and of 'traditional' values, to appeal to a suburban middle class and, at the same time, as enthusiastic about the 'popular' culture of the pub, the racecourse and the football terrace, as against an 'improving', moralising Liberal party. To both social groups, it could present an image of the Empire as a glorious product of Britishness to which the Liberals were only doubtfully attached.[4]

Given a choice of leading offices, Chamberlain opted for the Colonial Office, full of schemes for imperial union. Salisbury concentrated on foreign policy. Further rights were given to Irish tenants to purchase their farms, in the hope that the creation of a conservative peasantry would stem nationalist sentiment. A Workmen's Compensation Act of 1897 provided government funds to compensate workers injured at work. But overall there was a desire to avoid anything that would push up taxation, which was already rising sharply to meet growing naval expenditure.

---

[3] Patrick Joyce, *Work, Society and Politics. The Culture of the Factory in Later Victorian England* (Brighton, Harvester, 1980), pp. 283–303.

[4] Matthew Roberts, 'Constructing a Tory World-view: Popular Politics and the Conservative Press in late-Victorian Leeds', *Historical Research*, 79 (February 2006).

Nonetheless, by the end of the 1890s there were many signs of disillusionment with the Conservatives and a fairly steady loss of by-elections. What saved them was the patriotic fervour stirred up during the South African War. The issue of how popular the war was remains contentious. The evidence seems to point to a deeply divided country. In places where there were military bases, not surprisingly, there was enthusiasm. The same is true in the shipbuilding areas of Glasgow, Tyneside and Merseyside. On the other hand, there were plenty of other areas where the critics of war were very successful. In Welsh-speaking parts of Wales, in east Scotland and in Ireland there was considerable sympathy for the Boer cause, but the Liberal divisions were apparent. The swing to the Unionists in Britain was only 1.3 per cent in the 'Khaki' election of 1900. It allowed the Conservatives and Unionists to maintain their majority and Salisbury formed a Cabinet well packed with associates of what became known as the 'Hotel Cecil Unlimited' – members by birth or marriage of his own family, the Cecils. Once the war was over, there was a growing sense of decline and much anxiety because of the weaknesses exposed by the war.

The death of the Queen in January 1901 also generated a powerful feeling of the end of an era and of the sense of stability and security that her 64 years on the throne had created. Her reign had done much to make the monarchy more secure after the discredited George IV and the colourless William IV. She had succeeded in making the monarchy respectable and created the idea of a royal family as part of a constitutional monarchy. Victoria created an image of being above party, although in private she never hid her distaste for Gladstone and Liberalism, finding Disraeli after 1874 much more to her liking. Disraeli managed to prise her out of her widow's seclusion and, in turn, he made extensive use of the royal prerogative to bypass Parliament. When Gladstone returned in 1880, Victoria did nothing to conceal her dislike. Despite it all, Gladstone remained extraordinarily loyal and tolerant of her interference. The Queen clung to her prerogatives on every possible occasion, even considering dissolving Parliament on her own initiative in 1893. She especially resisted challenges to what she regarded as her special prerogatives on foreign affairs, the church and the army.

Despite Victoria's efforts, monarchical political power did seep away and a measure of this was the extent to which royal ceremonial gained in importance. The symbolic aspects of monarchy came to the fore as political power waned. This was very much in line with what Walter Bagehot had predicted in his *English Constitution* of 1867, in which he had tried to get behind the myths to examine the real power structure. The more democratic the country became, he argued, 'the more we shall get to the state and show, which have ever pleased the vulgar'. To Bagehot, the monarchy was an essential element of what he called the 'dignified' as opposed to the 'efficient' part of the constitution. Monarchy was something that everyone could comprehend. A royal family appealed to people and provided a moral model, while a monarchy had a religious mystique associated with it that encouraged obedience to the laws. Most important of all: 'it acts as a *disguise*. It enables our real rulers to change without headless people knowing it. The masses of Englishmen are not fit for an elective government.'

There was the growing invention of traditions. Most of what is now regarded as traditional British ceremonial dates from the 40 years before 1914. Ceremonial uniforms ceased to change and as bicycles, cars and buses become the normal mode of travel, the royal family continued to use coaches. The 1887 golden jubilee of Queen Victoria's reign was an occasion for parades and splendour and an opportunity to wonder at the orderliness of it all. As the Archbishop of Canterbury noted, 'for days afterwards everyone feels that the socialist movement has had a check'. The diamond jubilee in 1897 was even grander, with the imperial theme dominant. A new popular press added to the adulation. The national anthem began to be played on more and more occasions and the composer Edward Elgar and others produced new ceremonial music. The monarchy had become central to British ceremonial 'tradition'.

Further reading

Blake, Robert, *The Conservative Party from Peel to Thatcher*, 3rd edn (London, Methuen, 1985)

Green, E.H.H., *The Crisis of Conservatism: The Politics, Economics and Ideology of the British Conservative Party 1880–1914* (London, Routledge, 1995)

Hamer, D.A., *Liberal Politics in the Age of Gladstone and Rosebery: A Study in Leadership and Policy* (Oxford, Clarendon Press, 1972)

Joyce, Patrick, *Work, Society and Politics: The Culture of the Factory in Late Victorian Britain* (Brighton, Harvester, 1980)

Lawrence, J., *Speaking for the People. Party, Language and Popular Politics in England, 1867–1914* (Cambridge, Cambridge University Press, 1998)

Pugh, Martin, *The Tories and the People 1880–1935* (Oxford, Blackwell, 1985)

Searle, G.R., *The Liberal Party. Triumph and Disintegration, 1886–1929* (Basingstoke, Macmillan, 1992)

Searle, G.R., *A New England? Peace and War, 1886–1918* (Oxford, Oxford University Press, 2004)

24

Edwardian politics 1901–14

The decade before the outbreak of the First World War was one of increasingly bitter political conflict, not only between but also within the main political parties. It reflected stresses that were becoming apparent in British society, as Victorian confidence receded in the face of domestic and foreign challenges. A sense of weakness emerged in the South African War, but there was also a sense of crisis in industry, as markets and profits shrank. The evidence of various social enquiries was that capitalism was not working for at least a third of the population. Progress was no longer certain. The landed class, too, was under threat as depression, death duties and curbs on property rights in both Ireland and Scotland bit deeply. All of this produced what the sociologist Durkheim called 'anomie', a lack of those clear markers on which people and groups depended. There was an often rather frantic search for solutions to a new range of problems. How far the solutions being offered would have proved lasting is impossible to know, because world war was to change so much.

Liberals divided

By the time of Rosebery's resignation in 1895, the Liberal leadership was in disarray. After the election, Rosebery walked away from the party leadership, but from time to time made speeches as if he were still leader. Gladstone died in 1898 and his passing re-opened the leadership issue. The choice was between Sir Henry Campbell-Bannerman and Herbert Asquith. Campbell-Bannerman, son of a Glasgow commercial wholesaler, was a conciliator trusted by all sections of the party and not identified with any of the many coteries with which it was bedevilled. Asquith, the son of a small businessman from Yorkshire, was 20 years his junior, a brilliant, hard-working man, polished by a Balliol education, a skilled debater, and early predicted for a leading role in politics. In 1899, he agreed to stand aside and to support Campbell-Bannerman as leader.

The Liberal Imperialists ('Limps' to their enemies), of whom Asquith was one, pinned their hopes on Rosebery and believed that it was necessary to rethink the philosophy and policies of Liberalism. Young, ambitious, university-educated professionals, they believed that, under Gladstone, the party had become too narrowly based, had become entangled with Irish nationalists and was out of touch with the sentiments and the needs of the rest of the country. They believed that a 'New Liberalism' needed to embark on social reforms that could offer an alternative to socialism for the working class. They also believed that the party had been losing the middle-class vote because of Gladstone's anti-imperialist tone, which made it seem unpatriotic.

Linked with their imperialism and with their concern about social reform was the Limps' call for 'national efficiency'. If the Empire was to be a success and if the nation were to survive in an increasingly competitive world, then the population needed to be healthy and well trained. There were signs of 'fatigue' in British industry and warning signals that it was less efficient than its European and American competitors (see Chapter 20). The leading Limps, therefore, interested themselves in educational reform and generally supported social improvements such as shorter working hours and better housing. This obviously involved taking one step away from traditional Liberal beliefs about self-reliance. The catchword was efficiency, *national* efficiency, and it made them ready to consider collectivist solutions, with the state playing a much more active role. It also put them in contact with more radical figures, such as Fabian socialists, who approached social reform from the political left. But the Limps were very moderate in their views, believing in state intervention as a final resort, when all else failed to provide a minimum of acceptable standards.

The South African War exacerbated the divisions in the Liberal Party. From the Limps point of view it was essential to be seen as 'patriotic'. On the other side were the 'pro-Boers', as they were dubbed, who saw the war as a capitalist war imposed on Britain by the mine-owners of the Rand and by the hawkers of armaments. The figure who emerged as the leading pro-Boer was the Welsh radical, David Lloyd George. The Limps and the pro-Boers were pretty evenly spread among Liberal MPs with another third and the bulk of the Liberal activists feeling that, whatever the rights or wrongs, the government had to be supported in a crisis. Campbell-Bannerman tried to lead from the middle. He supported annexation of the Boer states as a war policy, but only as a first step towards granting them self-government within a federal union.

The divisions within the party were pretty apparent and it is small wonder that they paid the price in the election of 1900. Soon afterwards, however, news of atrocities began to emerge. Emily Hobhouse, after a visit to South Africa, exposed the horrors of the concentration camps in which thousands of Boer women and children were dying from disease. She greatly impressed Campbell-Bannerman and, in June 1901, he attacked the 'methods of barbarism' being employed by the military in South Africa.

The Limps, responding to a rampant right-wing press, were horrified and more than ever committed to pushing out Campbell-Bannerman.

Emergence of Labour

One of the straws in the wind was the election in 1900 of Keir Hardie and Richard Bell as representatives of the Labour Representation Committee, recently formed by the Trades Union Congress and the Independent Labour Party. There had been trade-union backed MPs since 1874, when two miners' leaders, Alexander McDonald and Thomas Burt, had been returned. A number of other Lib-Labs, as they were called, were returned in 1880 and in 1885, mainly from mining districts. There were clear signs after 1885 that working-class political expectations were growing, but splits in local Liberal associations, a focus on measures like church disestablishment or temper-ance reform, which were not high on the list of working-class concerns, and often just a lack of resources, made it difficult for Liberal associations to select working-class candidates. Unsurprisingly, they were attracted by people who could fund their own election campaigns and even bring investment or philanthropy into the town. Also, there was a hardening of class attitudes in the years of a rather depressed economy in the 1880s and less willingness on the part of middle-class businessmen to empathise with trade-union expectations. The Liberal Party was failing to respond precisely at the time when there were growing aspirations amongst trade unionists.

The result was talk of the need to act independently of the Liberal Party. The mid-1880s had seen the appearance of socialism, partly growing out of intellectual disenchantment with Gladstonian liberalism and partly under the influence of Marxian ideas spreading from mainland Europe. In 1881, the Etonian Henry Myers Hyndman launched the Democratic Federation, which became the Social Democratic Federation in 1884. Other groups followed, like the Socialist League of the poet, painter and designer, William Morris and the Fabian Society, associated with Bernard Shaw and Sidney Webb, all believing that a radical or even revolutionary transformation of society was required – not only to tackle the problems of poverty and want, that were everywhere apparent, but also to create an environment for self-realisation. For many, socialism was an alternative to religious faith and there was talk of the 'religion of socialism'.

Socialism was not immediately attractive to most trade unionists. Early socialists tended, on the whole, to be middle-class and often contemptuous of what they saw as rather stodgy trade-union leaders. Many trade unionists believed that the working class had to devise its own solutions. Also, a socialist call for greater state intervention was not one that attracted most trade unionists. The state was not regarded as sympa-thetic. The state meant the law and the courts, which had shown themselves generally hostile to trade unionists; the state meant regulation and control of working-class lives and the imposition of middle-class values by unsympathetic bureaucrats; most of all, the state meant the hated Poor Law. In contrast, Conservative attitudes of enthusiasm for the monarchy and for the Empire, hostility to foreigners and the Irish, coupled with militant Protestantism, tended to be well received by many of the working class.

These were attitudes that were to take many decades to break down, but the demand for more Labour representation in local and national bodies continued to grow. There were signs of a gradual change in trade-union attitudes. Technological change and foreign competition were undermining the security of skilled workers, whilst, among the less skilled, more effective organisation was appearing. In 1888, the failure of the local Liberal Association to select the miners' leader, Keir Hardie, as its candidate for a by-election in the predominantly mining constituency of Mid-Lanarkshire resulted in Hardie standing as an independent. In the election of 1892, he was returned as Labour MP for the London constituency of South West Ham. The formation of a nationwide Independent Labour Party at Bradford in 1893 was intended to co-ordinate the numerous local assertions of independence from Liberalism that had begun to appear.

The timing of demands for independent labour politics varied from area to area and depended upon many factors: the energies of key local activists; maybe specific local industrial disputes; the responsiveness of local Liberals. The progress to a trade-union-based independent party needed more than the frustrated ambition of trade unionists or the pointed snubs of Liberal politicians. It needed direction, enthusiasm, hard work and a strong educational campaign outside the trade unions. This is what Hardie and his associates in the ILP offered. They had still to face powerful opposition from those within the trade-union movement who remained committed to the Liberals and in the 1895 election all 21 ILP candidates went down to defeat.

The next five years saw major setbacks for the trade unions. The powerful engineering union was defeated after protracted strikes and lock-outs in 1897. There were also some very hostile court decisions against trade unionists. Socialist campaigning began to have some impact, especially when the Liberal Party was tearing itself apart. In February 1900, a conference, called by the TUC to look at ways of getting more working-class representation in Parliament, formed the Labour Representation Committee. Pressed by Hardie, it was agreed that those elected would form 'a distinct Labour group in Parliament, who shall have their own whips and agree upon their own policy'. Ramsay Macdonald, a young journalist member of the ILP, was elected secretary of the new committee. In the 1900 election, the 15 candidates backed by the LRC garnered only 62,698 votes, but Bell of a railwaymen's union and Hardie were returned.

Liberals united

When Lord Salisbury eventually resigned in July 1902, he was succeeded by his nephew, Arthur Balfour. Balfour was immediately faced with controversy over educational policy. A bill to reform educational provision in England proved a powerful catalyst for Liberal unity. It was a measure that had much to recommend it for reformers, helping to deal with the glaring need for adequate secondary-school provision. Local educa-tion authorities replaced elected school boards and were now required to organise educational provision in secondary and technical areas, not just elementary. However, detached judgements on the value of the measure were not to be allowed. The enor-mity of the bill, in the eyes of the influential Nonconformist element within the Liberal Party, was that rate aid was to be given to Anglican schools and, worse still, to Roman Catholic schools. 'Putting Rome on the rates' stirred the rank and file from their disenchantment over divisions among the leadership. Liberal imperialist and radical Nonconformist could unite. Clergy denounced it, while leading laymen, especially in Wales and the West Country, refused to pay their rates and had their possessions impounded. Even before the bill became law, by-elections began to go to the Liberals, sometimes with massive swings.

The second great unifying issue for the Liberals came hard on the heels of the Education Act. In May 1903, Joseph Chamberlain announced his support for tariff reform and a breach with free trade. It was an issue that had been debated within the Midlands business community, which had felt the brunt of European competition, for more than 20 years. Chamberlain believed that Britain's greatness stemmed from her imperial might and the decline in her position since the 1880s was due to a failure to make the most of the imperial dominions. He came to the conclusion that the route to a unified Empire lay through economic co-operation, with free trade within the Empire and barriers against foreign goods.

A related problem was the need of government to increase its revenue-raising powers. Government expenditure had been increasing pretty steadily since the 1860s. There were the rising costs of bureaucracy, of new services such as education, and, from the 1890s, rocketing costs of defence. The Chancellor of the Exchequer in 1902 had already had to place a duty on imported corn to help cover the costs of the South African War. It was probably Chamberlain's hope that an imperial customs' union would in time lead to an Empire-wide military alliance that would reduce Britain's naval and military burden.

During the debates on the Education Bill, Chamberlain had been in South Africa. He returned filled with renewed enthusiasm for imperial unity. He was also increas-ingly conscious of working-class discontent and more aware than most politicians of the social problems that needed to be tackled: poor housing, unemployment, distress in old age. Admirer of Germany that he was, he saw that an effective response to the advance of socialism there had been Bismarck's social welfare measures. The usual Conservative anti-socialist rhetoric was not enough. A similar policy to Bismarck's was needed in Britain, but how to pay for it was the question. Increases in income tax were not acceptable – not just because they were electorally unpopular, but because they were seen as a tax on industry and initiative. Tariffs were the answer and would pro-vide the necessary resources to pay for old-age pensions and other social measures, protect British industries and, with imperial preference, help unite the Empire.

The bulk of Unionists were still committed free traders and the party split apart. Balfour saw his task as being to try to hold the government and the party together. He persuaded his ministers to declare a truce on speech-making on the issue, but he could not silence the rank and file. Chamberlain's young imperialist supporters, of whom there were many, and who, like their Liberal Imperialist counterparts disliked the domination of the party by the traditional elite, founded the Tariff Reform League to press Chamberlain's case in the country. On the other side, was the Free Food League to rally Unionist free traders. They battled for control of the grass roots of the party, gaining control of constituency organisations and making sure it was candidates favourable to their position who were selected. Balfour's efforts to find a middle way, often with convoluted arguments and elaborate manoeuvres, antagonised both sides. The Liberals had no doubt about the significance of what was happening. They could agree that free trade was sacrosanct and, in this they were defending the deeply entrenched and popular view that rising living standards over the previous half century had been the result of free trade.

Two other issues rallied Liberal backbenchers and supporters. There were proposals for reform of the licensing laws, to reduce the number of public houses, but with lavish compensation to the brewers, who, since the 1870s, had been a bugbear of Liberals with their open support of the Conservatives. Secondly, permission was given for the importation of indentured Chinese labour to work in the gold mines of South Africa. Even Asquith spoke against Chinese labour, particularly when it was revealed that Milner had given approval to the flogging of absconding labourers. Lloyd George joined in suggesting, disingenuously, that it had brought slavery back to the Empire. Not even South Africa could now divide the Liberal ranks.

That is not to say that the tensions were not still there. There was regular talk among the Limps of finding an alternative to Campbell-Bannerman. As it became clear during 1905 that Balfour's government could not last much longer, intrigues intensified. It was perhaps knowledge of these intrigues that persuaded Balfour to resign in December 1905 rather than to ask for a dissolution. In the end, the power of the prime ministerial office to distribute jobs meant that Campbell-Bannerman was able to see off moves to get him to go to the House of Lords. The leading Limps were well represented in the new government. Asquith accepted the Chancellorship of the Exchequer, Edward Grey the Foreign Office and R.B. Haldane was mischievously sent to the War Office, often the grave of political ambition. They held three major, and what proved to be crucial, offices of state. In defence and foreign affairs it was to be Liberal-Imperialist attitudes that were to prevail. To balance the Limps, the rising Welsh radical, David Lloyd George, became President of the Board of Trade.

The election was called in January 1906 and, as the results came in, there was mounting excitement at the evident size of the Liberal landslide. By the end, with a swing against the Conservatives of 10.6 per cent, the Liberals had gained 229 seats and had an overall majority of 88. In Scotland, the Liberals had 60 of the 72 seats and in Wales not a single Unionist was returned. Only the wealthier residential districts of London, Ulster and Chamberlain's Midlands hinterland remained loyal to Unionism. The campaign slogans were traditional Liberal ones, 'Peace, Retrenchment and Reform', with no aspirations spelled out in any detail. Everywhere there was the defence of free trade, with the argument that tariff reform would mean more expensive food. The opposition tried to raise the question of Irish Home Rule, but Campbell Bannerman made clear that it was not to be an issue in the new Parliament. The Liberals had been elected with few policy commitments and, those there were, were about undoing past Conservative actions rather than pointing to a future programme. At the same time, there was a sense of impending change. There were 310 new members of the House and there was much talk of getting things done.

There is no doubt that among what would now be called 'the chattering classes' – influential opinion formers from law, politics and journalism – there were fresh ideas around. There was much talk of 'progressivism' from young Liberals, Socialists, Fabians and others. Basically, they were arguing that Gladstonian Liberalism and traditional Radicalism were not adequate to deal with the problems of the age. There had to be collectivist solutions. Liberty could no longer mean merely 'the absence of restraint, but the presence of opportunity'. Central to their policy was the need to maintain good links with Labour, not with socialists, but with the trade-union-dominated Labour Representation Committee.

Between 1900 and 1905, the Labour Representation Committee had five victories in by-elections, four of them against Liberal opposition. There was obvious anxiety before the general election about splitting the left vote and letting in Conservatives. The Liberals felt that they needed Labour support to oust the Conservatives, while Hardie and MacDonald believed that, to make a real breakthrough, the LRC needed Liberal help. The result was a highly secret pact, arranged in 1903, by which Labour was given something like 50 constituencies to contest against the Conservatives without Liberal intervention. This paid off, with 29 Labour MPs elected, in all but three cases without Liberal opposition.

The public commitment of the Liberal Party to Labour was to reverse the decision of the courts in the Taff Vale case of 1901, by which trade unions had found themselves liable for damages for the action of their members during a dispute. This was largely delivered by the Trade Disputes Act of 1906 that gave trade unions immunity from prosecution for the actions of their members. It was a reflection of what was now referred to as a 'Progressive Alliance' of Liberal and Labour.

Unpicking at least some of the provisions of the 1902 Education Act had been a commitment to the Nonconformists, and it had loomed large as an issue in many constituencies. A bill proposed an end to any denominational teaching in publicly-funded schools. It passed the Commons by a majority of 169. The House of Lords, where Nonconformists were few in number, did not just block the measure, but turned it on its head by amending the bill to make religious instruction *compulsory* in any school receiving public money. The government was forced to abandon the whole bill. A similar fate befell the Licensing Bill, another measure dear to Nonconformists. Attempts at land reform and the valuation of land holdings were all destroyed or mutilated by the huge Unionist majority in the Upper House. Very quickly the Liberals were faced with the issue of what to do about the Lords.

Of the 602 Peers with the right to sit in the Lords, something like 490 were Conservative-Unionist, as opposed to a mere 88 committed Liberals. To the Conservatives, the Lords were a necessary check on democratic radicalism. Balfour reflected widely held attitudes of his class and party when he wrote in January 1906 that 'the Great Unionist Party should still control, whether in power or whether in opposition, the destinies of this Great Empire'. The strategy devised was that the Lords would only use their power on bills over which there was great controversy, which, in practice, meant bills that Liberals were unlikely to make an excuse for a dissolution. They passed the Trade Disputes Bill, because to do otherwise would cause an uproar and antagonise the organised working class. They rejected the Education Bill because, although it was an issue dear to Nonconformists, it was not one that was going to agitate the country at large.

The majority of Liberals accepted the need for a second chamber. Campbell-Bannerman certainly felt that delay and reconsideration were sometimes desirable, but that, in the last analysis, the will of the Commons had to prevail. As regards the composition of a second chamber, there was a recognition that one based on the hereditary principle and on land would always favour the Conservatives. But, there was a wariness of questioning the hereditary right, since it might lead to a challenge to the monarchy. Also, any measure of reform had to be approved by the King and would have to be tempered with caution. Most Liberals were probably against reforming the composition of the Lords, wary of creating a democratic chamber that would challenge the Commons. They believed that the attack had to be on its powers. It would be difficult to challenge the powers of a reformed House of Lords.

Asquith's governments

Campbell-Bannerman, his health declining, backed away from the mare's nest of Lords reform. In 1908, he resigned and was succeeded by Asquith, whose place at the Exchequer was taken by Lloyd George. Lloyd George was in many ways an old fashioned radical, a hater of privilege and of gentry and aristocracy. At the Board of Trade he had shown a determination for action and for making his name, pushing through a raft of measures on patents, bankruptcy and the merchant marine among other issues.

Although now Prime Minister, Asquith presented the budget that he had devised as Chancellor, in which old age pensions were first introduced – pensions of 5 shillings (= 25p, worth just under £19.00 at 2008 prices) a week for single people over 70 whose income did not exceed £30 per year (the equivalent of about £12,000 a year in 2008), and 7s 6d (37.5p) for married couples. The cost was to be met from general taxation. It was a break with the past in that a group of people was to receive cash aid from the state as a right and without any workhouse test. Not everyone was favourable. Some Liberals were wary about such a breach of *laissez-faire* principles. On the Unionist side, the tariff reformers were annoyed, because they had always argued that tariffs were necessary to pay for pensions. Now it seemed they could be met from taxation.

In 1909, the new Chancellor, Lloyd George, needed to raise £16 million extra to pay for old-age pensions and armaments. He also needed money to implement schemes for state insurance against sickness and unemployment which were being devised by Winston Churchill, his successor at the Board of Trade, and himself. No doubt he had also other reasons, like attacking the landed class and catching the eye of the electorate. There is, however, little evidence that he saw it as likely to provoke the House of Lords into rejection, since there was no reason to think that they would reject a budget. He proposed a graduation of income tax, increasing the level on incomes over £3,000 and introducing a further super-tax level on incomes over £5,000. Licensing legislation, so recently destroyed by the Lords, was squeezed in, with a tax on pub licences and increased duties on beer and spirits. Taxes on motor cars and petrol were introduced. Then he turned to the land. It was an old radical tradition to attack the landowning class – capitalism and labour united against the aristocracy. The maximum death duty was to be levied on estates valued at over £1.5 million instead of £3 million, as previously. A 20 per cent tax was to be levied on the increase in the value of land, every time it changed hands; a 10 per cent tax on the increased value of landed property on the renewal of the lease; and half a penny in the £ on the value of uncultivated land. None of these was likely to bring him huge resources, but there was always the possibility of their being ratcheted up.

The main outrage of the Conservatives was reserved for the land taxes, which they saw as going beyond what should be contained in a finance bill. There was particular resentment that it would involve registration of land ownership. It took from April till November to get the budget through the Commons. Lloyd George relished attacking what he called 'the Dukes' and, by the end of 1909, he seems to have been goading the Lords into rejection. Unionist peers declared that they were not bound to give their adherence to so radical a finance bill until it had been 'submitted to the judgement of the country'. From the point of view of Britain's vague constitutional law, it was possible to argue that the Lords had the right to reject a budget in circumstances of exceptional gravity, and some had been arguing that the Lords had the right to force an election (or even a referendum) on a government whose 'mandate' (a concept that was starting to appear) was running out. At the end of November, the budget was rejected in the Lords by 350 votes to 75.

What was to be done? The precedent looked to was 1832, when the threat to create sufficient Whig peers to get the Reform Act through had been enough to persuade a majority of the Lords to step back from confrontation. Asquith first had to persuade the King, however. Edward VII was a deep-dyed reactionary, instinctively opposed to any attack on the hereditary principle and hostile to radicals like Lloyd George and Churchill. He even found the smooth Asquith too common for his tastes. But he wanted a peaceful solution. He brought pressure to bear on the Unionist leaders to prevent rejection of the budget, but he refused to give a guarantee to create the necessary 300 + peers to get it through. He insisted that two elections were required. First, there would be an election on the budget and, assuming the Liberals still had a majority, the budget would be reintroduced. If the Lords still rejected it, then the government could introduce a scheme to overcome the Lords' veto. There would have to be a second general election on this. If the Lords again rejected that, and only then, the King would create the necessary peers. This was broadly the pattern followed, but it was a requirement that was very much to the disadvantage of the Liberals and Labour, neither of whom had the resources available to the Conservatives.

In the election held in January 1910, the turnout was just under 87 per cent, the highest ever in a general election. It was a measure of how excitement had risen on the issue. The Liberals lost 104 seats and their margin over the Conservatives was reduced to 2. They were dependent for a working majority on the support of the 82 Irish Nationalist and 40 Labour members.

Despite the figure, Labour had not done too well. At the dissolution there had been 46 Labour members. There had been by-election wins, but the 29 of 1906 had also been augmented by the decision in 1908 of 12 miners' MPs, elected without Labour Representation Committee support, to join the Labour Party. There were signs, particularly in Lancashire, where tariff reform was not at all popular, that working-class voters were swinging away from Labour and back to Liberalism, recognising the value of social reforms such as pensions, labour exchanges and trade boards that the government had brought in. Liberals and Labour were, in practice, competing for the same voters. Overall, the results looked like a massive defeat for the Liberals, reflecting a great deal of middle-class resentment at the rises in taxation and in local government rates.

The Irish MPs had disliked the budget and voted against it. They now demanded, as a condition of their support, that the Liberals commit themselves to bringing in a Home Rule Bill. At the end of April 1910, the budget was passed and the government immediately proceeded with the Parliament Bill, which focused on the power of the House of Lords, and only in the preamble suggested that the issue of its membership would be tackled in future. The Bill proposed to remove the Lords' veto on legislation and replace it with the power to delay for only two sessions. Asquith warned that he would only dissolve for a second time if he were certain that, after another election, 'the judgment of the people as expressed in the election will be carried into law' – in other words, he would have a guarantee about the creation of peers. The King might well have been coming round to this when he died and the resolution of the issue was delayed.

With the death of the King, there was a real constitutional crisis. Lloyd George worked hard for a compromise. He wanted the matter out of the way as quickly as possible to press ahead with a social reform programme. He even toyed with the idea of a coalition government. But an inter-party conference broke on the issue of Home Rule. The Unionists insisted that the Parliament Bill should not apply to Home Rule for Ireland until that had been approved by a referendum or a further election. The new King, George V, was eventually persuaded to concede that he would, if necessary, create a sufficient number of peers to get the bill through, if the Liberals won a second election.

The election of December 1910 still attracted a turnout of more than 80 per cent and the result was much the same as in January, with the Liberals losing another three seats and Labour gaining two. The Parliament Bill passed its various stages in the Commons in May. There was then a break for the coronation and battle resumed in early July. A group of so-called 'die-hards' was determined to go down fighting, but the Conservative leaders accepted that it was time to retreat. The final debates took place on 8 and 9 August 1911. The 'last-ditchers' remained irreconciled, but in the end, the measure was carried by 131 votes to 114, with 37 Conservative peers (plus 13 bishops) voting with the government and many abstaining. In the aftermath, the House of Lords continued to obstruct and the promise to tackle the composition of the second chamber was postponed for a century.

Irish Home Rule

The passage of the Parliament Bill cleared the way for a Home Rule measure. It was not just the dependence on Irish votes that brought about the bill. Most Liberals felt that a settlement was long overdue. The land problem in Ireland had, to a large extent, been settled by Wyndham's Act of 1903 that made it cheaper to borrow to buy land than to pay rent and which provided a state bonus to landlords in Ireland who agreed to sell their estates. To the Unionists, of course, Home Rule was anathema, although increasing numbers were prepared to consider new federal structures covering the whole Empire.

By the end of the nineteenth century, to the traditional religious division between a Protestant majority in Ulster and a Catholic one in the south were added the economic divisions as Ulster industrialised. A wealthy, manufacturing and commercial, Protestant middle class was determined to cling to the union with Britain, whilst amongst the nationalists remarkably little thought seems to have been given to Ulster. When the Parliament Act passed and Home Rule seemed probable Irish Unionists' clubs and Orange lodges began to harden their response.

The leader of the Ulster Unionists in Parliament from 1910 was Sir Edward Carson, one of the greatest advocates at the English bar and MP for Dublin University. He was, interestingly, a Dubliner, not an Ulsterman. It was not religion that drove Carson, but a view that the union with Britain had to be maintained and that Home Rule would inevitably lead to independence. Carson was also convinced that, without Ulster, Home Rule was not possible. After the passing of the Parliament Act, he spent increasing amounts of time in Belfast, enthusing a burgeoning popular movement.

A new element was added with the resignation of Balfour from the leadership of the Conservative Party in November 1911, after many months of antipathy from tariff reformers within the party, who no longer trusted him. Balfour's approach to Ulster was like his approach to many other subjects – apparently slightly detached. In his successor, Andrew Bonar Law, there was no such indifference. Law, who had emerged as a compromise candidate, was a staunch Presbyterian, brought up in Scotland, whose father had lived in Ulster. He quickly identified with the Ulster Unionists and encouraged their worst excesses. In September 1911, Carson, addressing a meeting in Ulster, denounced the Liberal government's plans as 'the most nefarious conspiracy that has ever been hatched against a free people', and threatened a unilateral declaration of independence should Home Rule be granted. The Liberals were never certain how far such rhetoric was bluff.

The measure introduced in April 1912 was very similar to Gladstone's 1892 proposal. There would be a two-chamber Irish parliament, with 42 Irish members still sitting at Westminster. Key issues of defence and foreign policy remained reserved for London. The language became more and more hyperbolic, with Law talking of Ulstermen being ready to lay down their lives in resistance. To force Ulster into a Home Rule Ireland, he told a Glasgow audience, would be 'to exercise a tyranny as unjustifiable and cruel as has ever been seen in the world'. At Blenheim, in July 1912, he declared that there was 'no length to which Ulster will go which I shall not be ready to support'. In language that was being used widely in right-wing circles, the government was portrayed as 'a Revolutionary Committee which has seized upon despotic power by fraud'. His speech finally concluded that even if the Bill were to become law, 'there are things stronger than Parliamentary majorities'.

There is no doubt that many Unionists firmly believed that the government had not gained a popular mandate for the measure and that the Parliament Act was unconstitutional and imposed at the behest of the Irish nationalists. Their language reflected the frustrations and sense of helplessness that many Unionists felt at what they saw as an impending disaster for not just the unity of the kingdom but for the Empire. Law and the Unionists, confident that Home Rule would be rejected by the electorate, believed that they were justified in trying to force Asquith to have an election on the question, since Home Rule had not been an issue at the 1910 elections.

On 28 September 1912 Carson launched the Solemn League and Covenant, deliberately playing on the parallels with seventeenth-century Scotland.[1] Nearly half a million signed on the first day and declared their determination to resist Home Rule. The Home Rule Bill passed the Commons in January 1913. Within a fortnight the Lords had rejected it. That same month, the Ulster Unionist Council established the Ulster Volunteer Force to resist Home Rule by force. High-ranking figures in military circles rushed to advise it; sectarian riots and house burning intensified. Not surprisingly, the southern nationalists responded by setting up the National Volunteers.

Churchill and Lloyd George, amongst others, had come round to the view that the way out of the crisis would be to exclude Ulster from Home Rule, at least temporarily. The King chipped away behind the scenes, trying to persuade Asquith to hold another election, and there was ominous talk of the army refusing to act in the event of civil

---

[1] A 1643 agreement with English parliamentarians to preserve and extend Presbyterianism.

Focus on

The Ulster crisis, 1913

Letter of the Conservative leader, Andrew Bonar Law, to Sir Edward Carson, the leader of the campaign in Ulster against Home Rule, 18 September 1913:

I had a long talk with the King, and he asked me to put in writing a summary of the conversation. I did so and enclose a copy of it for you which gives all the information so far as my talk with the King himself is concerned.

Churchill was there, and we had a talk about the whole situation in the course of which he told me that he had a letter from Asquith suggesting that he should speak to me.

My talk to Churchill was practically confined to this: I told him that it seemed to me the position was a desperate one for both political parties. I said it was bad for us; but it seemed to me to be much worse for them. I told him that if the thing was to go on their lines they themselves had taught us that no half measures were any use, and that it was certain that we would stick at nothing when it came to the point. I told him that it was idle to suppose that they could leave you alone and trust to your movement breaking down from its difficulties. I said to him that most certainly the moment the Home Rule Bill passed you would not only set up your provisional Government, but that you would allow no force of any kind in your area except the force appointed by you; that you would appoint your own police, and allow no other body to interfere with your action. He then spoke in a half-hearted way as if it would be possible to allow even this to go without interference by force. He spoke, for instance, of stopping railway communication, and stopping sea communication; but I pointed out the absurdity of this, as it would interfere not only with Ulster but the whole of Ireland and the whole of England and Scotland which traded with Belfast, and I think he realized that that was impossible. I told him also that here in England there would be no half measures; and I said to him, 'Suppose it comes to this: the whole of the Unionist Party say that Ulster is right, that they are ready to support them, and that if necessary all the Unionist Members are turned out of the House of Commons' – does he suppose that the army would obey orders to exercise force in Ulster! I said that in that case we should regard it as civil war, and should urge the Officers of the Army not to regard them as a real Government but to ignore their orders. I said to him also that of course we realized as clearly as he did not only the seriousness but the actual calamity of allowing things to come to such a point. I said also that I saw no way out of the difficulty . . .

Source: R. Blake, *The Unknown Prime Minster. The Life and Times of Andrew Bonar Law* (London, Eyre and Spottiswoode, 1955), pp. 155–6.

Figure 24.1 Carson speaking in Belfast, 1913. Sir Edward Carson (1854–1935) was a leading QC who had led the prosecution of Oscar Wilde. An MP, he became leader of the Irish Unionists in 1910 and was determined to prevent Home Rule for the whole of Ireland. He was not an advocate of a separate Ulster.
Source: Mary Evans Picture Library

war. Field Marshall Lord Roberts, closely associated with the Ulster Volunteers, had argued that, in the event of civil war, the question of the army's loyalty to the government of the day was irrelevant. By February 1914, Asquith had come to the conclusion that, despite the opposition of most in his party and of the Irish Parliamentary Party to any compromise, Ulster counties had to be given the option of excluding themselves for a term of years. It would make immediate rebellion on the passing of the Act difficult to justify. In March a group of officers of the pukka 3rd Cavalry Brigade, based at the Curragh barracks, made it clear that they would prefer dismissal rather than be forced to coerce Ulster. The government, in embarrassment, and threatened with more senior resignations should the officers be disciplined, caved in, assuring them 'it had no intention whatever of taking advantage of the right to crush political opposition to the policy and privileges of the Home Rule Bill'. By the summer of 1914, the question had come down to defining Ulster, since the counties of Fermanagh and Tyrone had pretty evenly balanced Catholic and Protestant populations, and to deciding for how long Ulster would be excluded from a Home Rule Ireland. By the end of

July the position had been reached that, to all intents, Ulster could exclude itself permanently.

By now, however, the European war had overtaken events. In September, the Irish Home Rule Bill passed through Parliament by means of the Parliament Act, with Bonar Law leading his party out of the House of Commons to show their disapproval. It covered the whole of Ireland, but was suspended until the end of the war. Asquith assured the House that there would be ample time given to discuss an amending Act. Carson confidently declared that Home Rule in Ulster would not survive the end of the war by ten minutes.

To some, Asquith's failure to deal with the threat of armed resistance in Ulster in 1913–14 was a huge political failure. In the view of others, his caution saved the country from civil war. What is clear is that the Liberals did not really appreciate the reasons for the violence of the Unionists on the issue. They showed a fundamental lack of understanding of the mentality of the right, some of whom, frustrated at every turn, were willing to go to any length to stop the government. To them, all institutions were being undermined by the Liberal, Socialist, Nationalist alliance – the Empire (concessions to the Boers); the Lords (emasculated); the monarchy (its prerogatives more or less disappeared); the Church (disestablishment of the Church in Wales also went through thanks to the Parliament Act); the land (Lloyd George's budgets and more promised); property (with taxes and the abolition of property votes); individual rights (compulsory insurance and trade-union privilege); and now the very union itself, with even the Welsh and Scots joining in demands for Home Rule. And all of this had been carried through by a minority government, becoming yet more of a minority through by-election losses.

Should the Liberals have acted differently? They might have called the Unionists' bluff and run the risk of civil war. They were not going to do this for nationalists (illiberal in all but their nationalism) whom, in many cases, they disliked. Asquith's tactic was to give way gradually under pressure, perhaps in the forlorn hope that some solution would somehow emerge and the Ulster Unionists accept the situation. Most of all, the Liberals wanted to get the whole issue out of the way. It had bedevilled British politics to the disadvantage of the Liberal Party for half a century. Most felt that there were other priorities. Few, if any, of the politicians realised how late in the day it was in Ireland.

Liberalism in 1914

How far the signs of the demise of the Liberal Party can be detected in the years before 1914 is still much debated. In a classic text of 1936, George Dangerfield wrote of *The Strange Death of Liberal England* amid the Labour, feminist and Irish unrest of these years. As against that, there was nothing inevitable about the rise of the Labour Party and, indeed, there were no real signs of a Labour breakthrough. It was still a relatively small fourth party. Lloyd George and others within the government were outlining an extensive programme of social reform. National insurance for health and unemployment had come in. There was a commitment to progressive taxation to bring some redistribution of wealth and in 1913 Lloyd George had offered an ambitious land reform programme. He seems to have accepted the possibility of pushing up income tax levels in order to fund increased state expenditure. This might have been more than enough to see off the challenge of Labour. By emphasising the social concerns of 'New Liberalism', Liberals were probably managing to check the advance of Labour. Religion, once the politically defining issue, was of less and less importance.

On the other hand, there were signs of middle-class revolt against rising taxation. It was particularly apparent in local government results, where the Conservatives were making advances in the largest cities on a programme of anti-socialism and anti-rates. Indeed, a rebellion amongst backbenchers forced Lloyd George to reduce the tax rises that he had planned in his 1914 budget. One can see the roots of post-war Liberal problems in the years before 1914. As class was becoming more important, and as politics, especially local politics, were becoming increasingly about socialism and anti-socialism, Liberal catchphrases had less appeal. Also Liberal organisations were crumbling, in line with the weakening influence of voluntary societies, that had been so central to the vitality of Gladstonian Liberalism. Local Liberal associations were fine for selecting candidates, but they were not effective in adjusting to new kinds of local politics.

Further reading

Bernstein, G.L., *Liberalism and Liberal Politics in Edwardian England* (London, Allen Lane, 1986)

Bew, Paul, *Ideology and the Irish Question. Ulster Unionism and Irish Nationalism, 1912–1916* (Oxford, Oxford University Press, 1994)

Brooks, David, *The Age of Upheaval. Edwardian Politics 1899–1914* (Manchester, Manchester University Press, 1995)

Green, E.H.H., *The Crisis of Conservatism: The Politics, Economics and Ideology of the British Conservative Party 1880–1914* (London, Routledge, 1995)

Jalland, P., *The Liberals and Ireland: The Ulster Question in British Politics to 1914* (Brighton, Harvester, 1980)

O'Day, Alan, *Irish Home Rule, 1867–1921* (Manchester, Manchester University Press, 1998)

Powell, David, *The Edwardian Crisis. Britain, 1901–1914* (Basingstoke, Macmillan, 1996)

Searle, G.R., *The Liberal Party. Triumph and Disintegration, 1886–1929* (Basingstoke, Macmillan, 1992)

Stewart, A.T.Q., *The Ulster Crisis* (London, Faber, 1967)

Trentmann, Frank, *Free Trade Nation. Commerce, Consumption and Civil Society in Modern Britain* (Oxford, Oxford University Press, 2008)

25

The British road to war

It was by no means obvious before 1914 that Britain and Germany were headed for war. Although there were those who talked about the threat posed by an overweening German state, it was largely after the war that the inevitability of the conflict was taken for granted. Parallels were drawn with the Napoleonic Wars and it was argued that, in order to maintain a balance of power in Europe and to prevent any one state dominating, Britain had to intervene. Historians now adopt a more questioning position on this, looking more critically at the case that Germany presented a threat to British interests between 1880 and 1914. Whatever the causes, there is undoubtedly a paradox in a Liberal government, which included many committed to non-intervention in Europe, taking the country to war.

Splendid isolation

During the Midlothian campaign of 1879, Gladstone had laid down that Britain 'should avoid needless and entangling engagements' (see Chapter 16). This was to remain something of a popular shibboleth in Britain over the next 30 years. Nonetheless, for a country with an empire and commercial interests that spanned the world, it was difficult not to get entangled in issues not always of Britain's own making. In reality, at the end of the nineteenth century, Britain was very much in a similar position to the one she had held in the years after 1815. Russia, Austria and Germany were united in the conservative *Dreikaiserbund*, while Germany, Austria and Italy had a military Triple Alliance. Britain had republican France as a potentially liberal support, but that possibility was shattered when the decision was made in 1882 to invade Egypt. France felt deeply offended by the British action. French politicians had long believed that 'if we lose Egypt we also lose our influence in the Mediterranean'. It was to remain the major barrier to any possible *rapprochement* between Britain and France. The result was that Britain was largely isolated in Europe.

The greatest threat to Britain's imperial interests, so heavily focused on India, was inevitably Russia, whose growing dominance of Central Asia was pushing towards British spheres of influence on the Indian frontier. The sense of isolation encouraged Salisbury to look for alliances; so much so, that there were soon rumours of Britain joining the Triple Alliance. This was never seriously on the cards. As Salisbury pointed out to the Ambassador in St Petersburg, 'no two Powers are less fitted for a mutual defensive alliance than England and Germany; for Germany's most dangerous enemy [i.e. Russia] is almost invulnerable to us'. But, he went on, there was a clear affinity with the central powers: 'England and Germany, and to a great extent Austria are "satisfied" powers. France and Russia are "hungry" powers.'[1]

An approach by Germany in 1889, proposing a treaty against a future French attack, was rejected by Salisbury, using what was to become a familiar argument, that Britain's democratic constitution would not allow alliances without the permission of Parliament. He also pointed out that Britain was a naval, not a military power like Germany. To confirm this, he persuaded Parliament to establish the 'Two Power Standard', by which the British fleet would be greater than any two continental fleets combined, and to embark on an extensive, and hugely expensive, shipbuilding programme.

The fear of Britain joining the Triple Alliance pushed France and Russia together in what has been seen as the 'fateful alliance'[2] – the Dual Alliance of 1893. This produced a very real sense of isolation in British government circles. France and Russia together posed a huge threat to British imperial interests. Their combined fleets were too strong for the British Mediterranean fleet. France was consolidating its North African empire, carving out territory that impinged on British West African interests. In Indo-China, French interests were adjacent to British India and Burma and the two countries were competing for influence in Siam (Thailand). In 1898, there was a real possibility of conflict with France over the French expedition to Fashoda in the Sudan, which seems to have been largely about exerting pressure on the British to leave Egypt.

Russia was always ready to take advantage of British vulnerability to extend its influence in Afghanistan and in Persia (Iran). In 1895, it was Russia, Germany and France, without Britain, that imposed a settlement on Japan in her war with China. At the end of 1895, the United States contemplated war with Britain over a border dispute between Venezuela and British Guiana. In 1896, the Kaiser's telegram to President Kruger of the Transvaal congratulating him on having foiled the Jameson raid seemed an indication that German enmity had also now to be considered (see Chapter 19).

---

[1] Salisbury to Robert Morier, Ambassador to St Petersburg, 1 February 1888.
[2] The term is George Kennan's *The Fateful Alliance. France, Russia and the First World War* (Manchester, 1984).

There is no doubt about the sense of frustration, weakness and isolation that these events produced. The phrase 'splendid isolation' was first used in the Canadian Parliament over President Cleveland's threats of war with Britain, and what had been the product of circumstances and ineptness was raised to the stature of a positive policy by some politicians and some journalists. But most in government viewed the extent of isolation and an exclusion from decisions in different parts of the world as dangerous. Joseph Chamberlain made some tentative approaches to Germany in 1898, but the Germans had no wish to be pulled into conflict with Russia, and German interests in East Asia were limited.

The Boer War brought out very clearly just how isolated Britain was. There was even talk of possible international intervention on behalf of the Boers. The fact that it proved so difficult to defeat a handful of farmers made the country traumatically aware of its weakness. Russia seized the opportunity to extend its influence in the north of China and in Persia. In France there was a wave of sympathy with the Boers, with even the *haute couturiers* creating Boer-style hats for the new season. As the French ambassador to London, Paul Cambon, remarked, the Boer War was of great significance for Britain in her relations with other powers, 'it made her wiser'.[3]

There was a growing awareness of the reality of Britain's weakness. The War Office was warning in 1899 that Britain was trying to maintain the largest empire the world had ever seen, 'with armaments and reserves that would be insufficient for a third-class power'. But, with increasing demands for social expenditure, there was no enthusiasm for substantially increasing military resources. Economically, Britain was no longer so dominant. Alternative strategies had to be sought.

It was to strengthen the British position in the East that the British turned to Japan. A memorandum from the Admiralty in 1901 had revealed that British warships in East Asia were inferior to those of Russia and France. An Anglo-Japanese Alliance was signed in January 1902, by which each was to support the other if attacked by two other powers. It allowed Britain to withdraw some of the fleet from eastern waters. The pressing need, however, was to alleviate any threat from France and Russia.

French relations

There were signs of changes in France. Fashoda had persuaded some in France to abandon hope of getting Britain out of Egypt and to look for 'compensation' in territory elsewhere, particularly Morocco. Britain had limited interests there, other than that Gibraltar should not be threatened. The French ambassador reassuringly stated that all France desired was the 'security of what she already possessed'. Efforts began to settle outstanding differences between the two countries. An official visit by King Edward – always partial to the corporeal pleasures of Paris – helped prepare

---

[3] Christopher Andrew, *Théophile Delcassé and the Making of the Entente Cordiale* (1968), p. 203.

public opinion for a change. Two months later, the visit was reciprocated by the French President. Lansdowne, the Foreign Secretary, worried about the impending outbreak of war between Russia and Japan, was anxious to see a settlement. Lord Cromer, the Consul-General in Egypt was keen to see the last remaining French involvement in Egypt removed so that he could press ahead with various administrative and financial reforms. Gradually, in the autumn of 1903, settlements were worked out over Morocco, Egypt, Siam, Newfoundland, Zanzibar, Madagascar, Nigeria and the New Hebrides, all long-standing areas of tension between the two powers.

In April 1904, the Anglo-French Convention was signed. The French agreed that they would stop asking the British to leave Egypt. The British recognised France's right 'to preserve order' in Morocco and 'to provide assistance for the purpose of all administrative, economic, financial and military reform which it may require'. In addition, there were five secret articles that, in the elliptical language of diplomacy, committed each to mutual support of planned changes in Morocco and Egypt.

Two years after the Anglo-Japanese alliance, an even more significant break with the past had been made. The two agreements were linked. Russia and France were allies and their fleets jointly presented the greatest threat to British interests. Imperial rivalry with these powers held out the most likely chance of conflict. There were two possible ways to respond to this. The Anglo-Japanese alliance was to deter France and Russia ganging up against British interests in the East. The second option was to remove the pressure on the Empire and this is what the *Entente Cordiale* was about. Britain saw the agreement as a colonial settlement and as sending a conciliatory message to Russia. The French Foreign Minister, Théophile Delcassé, however, sought much more – a political alliance: 'Just think! If we could lean on Russia and on England, how strong we would be in relation to Germany.'

Britain, in its negotiations with France, had paid little attention to Germany's interest in these developments. The problem was that Germany had business interests in Morocco. During the winter of 1904–05, unrest broke out in Morocco and the French began to exert pressure and threatened to take action 'to restore order'. In March 1905, the Kaiser landed from his holiday yacht at Tangiers and declared that he hoped that 'the peaceful competition of all nations' in Morocco would continue and that he regarded the Sultan as 'an absolutely free ruler'. It was, no doubt, a rather crass attempt to take advantage of French weakness (as a result of the defeat of Russia by Japan) to put France more firmly in its place.

German pressure on France was also seen as an attempt to prise apart the recent entente, and there certainly were some in French government circles, sympathetic to Germany, who believed that the French had been hoodwinked into playing the British game. At the resulting conference at Algeciras in January 1906, Germany found itself isolated. The secret clauses of the Anglo-French Convention came into play and, between them, France and Britain conciliated most of the other powers. Only Germany, Austria and Morocco voted against France being given oversight of reform in Morocco. The British did try to persuade the French to make some concessions to Germany, but, when this was presented as a sign of Britain deserting France, they eased off. The British position was that they believed that concessions ought to be made to Germany, but were not prepared to risk the entente to achieve these. Already, Britain's hands were far from free.

On 4 December 1905, Balfour had resigned and a week later the Liberals came to office and immediately called an election. The new Foreign Secretary was Sir Edward Grey. It was not at all certain what changes this would mean. Would there be a return to Gladstonian Liberalism and a backing away from involvement with other European powers? Campbell-Bannerman launched the election campaign by declaring his support for the *Entente Cordiale*, but also talking of a League of Peace with Britain at its head, accompanied by disarmament. Liberals had, as part of their policy, the improvement of relations with both Germany and Russia. But Grey was not a Gladstonian. He was a Liberal-Imperialist, opposed to any radical divergence from Conservative practice. The emphasis was to be on 'continuity'.

During the weeks of the transition of governments there seemed the possibility that Germany and France might actually go to war over Morocco. Lord Lansdowne, the Conservative Foreign Secretary, had told the German ambassador in November that if Germany were to attack France 'light-heartedly' (whatever that meant), then British public opinion would make it difficult for Britain to stand aside. On 3 January, with colleagues dispersed for the election campaign, Grey repeated this warning to Germany. The French ambassador was pressing for some stronger commitment. Would Britain 'be prepared to render France armed assistance'? Grey had the excuse of saying that since everyone was scattered for the election, he could not give a definite response, but, in his personal view, 'public opinion in England would be strongly moved in favour of France'. Meanwhile, Cambon, the French ambassador, said that informal communications between the Admiralty and War Office and the French and British naval and military attachés should continue. Grey did not dissent from this.

Whether Grey was aware of these military conversations before this time is uncertain. He was, at any rate, distracted by the tragic death of his wife in an accident early in December. Grey, Lansdowne, Haldane and others in their memoirs, written in the 1920s, all claimed that there had been contacts between the service chiefs and the French *before* the Liberals came to power. It is not clear that this was actually the case. Certainly, British military people were considering what might happen if war broke out. At the War Office, the assumption was that a British expeditionary force would be sent to France in the event of a German attack.

The first evidence of informal military contacts came in December. The central body for military planning was the Committee for Imperial Defence (CID), set up in the aftermath of the South African War. The Prime Minister was the only permanent member of this Committee, but there was an inner core of regulars who were influential, including Lord Esher, a friend of Balfour and close associate of the King. On 13 December, two days after the Liberals came into office, Esher met with Clemenceau, the French Minster of the Interior, who urged that there needed to be some understanding of what would happen in the first week of a war. An informal meeting of the CID, with Esher, Sir John French of the cavalry brigade and the Director of Naval

Intelligence, discussed some of the possibilities and approached the French military attaché with questions of what France might do. At no point had the government played any part. All this was done without authority and it was not until 9 January that Grey was informed. Three days later he met with Haldane, the Secretary for War, and told him to come up with a military plan to back up France in the event of war.

The question arises then, were the CID anxious about what many of them regarded as a dangerously radical government under the leadership of a much disliked Campbell-Bannerman, who had never been forgiven for his criticisms of the military in South Africa? To what extent was there a rush to get talks going to give Grey the impression that these had been going on for some time? They probably knew Grey's views well enough not to be overly concerned, but Campbell-Bannerman was less secure. Did they decide to keep him in the dark? It was nearly the end of January before he was informed and, by then, the military conversations had commenced. The Cabinet was not told. Campbell-Bannerman had doubts about 'the stress laid on joint preparations', but he went along with it. Only a handful of ministers apart from the Prime Minister – particularly Haldane at the War Office and Asquith – knew of the talks. When Haldane was later asked about the British expeditionary force which, together with the formation of the volunteer, territorial army, was part of the army reforms on which he embarked, he continued to imply that the most likely use would be on the north-west frontier of India to resist a Russian invasion. Radical members of the Cabinet knew nothing of the military talks until the crisis of 1911. Had they done so, they would undoubtedly have been appalled. It was not until August 1914 that Parliament was informed. Meanwhile, British officers made regular visits to France and the French military attaché made regular visits to the War Office, using the back door.

We have the situation then of the military and their associates keeping Grey in the dark until they had ensured his commitment; Grey keeping Campbell-Bannerman in the dark until he, too, was faced with a *fait accompli*; Campbell-Bannerman keeping the Cabinet in the dark until, again, it was too late to do anything.

German and Russian relations

While most of the military still saw Russia as Britain's most formidable threat, the navy did not. To them it was Germany that presented the most serious challenge. It was 1902 before the Cabinet considered the issue, following a memorandum from the First Lord of the Admiralty suggesting that the new German navy was 'being carefully built up from the point of view of a war with us'. With the appointment of the abrasive Admiral John Fisher as First Sea Lord in 1904, the focus on the German threat became even sharper. He set about the formidable task of trying to modernise the navy. Senior ranks were opened up to talent. Fisher introduced submarines, began the process of converting to oil power and, most significantly, formed a home fleet to operate in the North Sea. Overseas squadrons were reduced in order to strengthen those based in the Atlantic and the North Sea. Orders were placed for new battleships.

There was even wild talk of 'Copenhagening' the German fleet – a reference to the seizure of the neutral Danish fleet in 1807.

Evidence of a challenge to British naval dominance was easy to find. All the leading powers were impressed by the writings of the American Captain A.T. Mahan, who had argued that, in the future, it was sea power that would determine the political and economic hegemony of nations. German officers spoke openly of rivalry with Britain. Talk of German investment in railway construction in Turkey became elevated to the 'Berlin to Baghdad' railway and seen as further evidence of the German threat. In February 1906, the first of Fisher's new battleships, *HMS Dreadnought*, was launched – bigger and faster than anything that had gone before and with fire-power from its ten 12-inch guns equal to three older battleships. It was the new naval technology that other powers, including Germany, were obliged to follow. But other powers could also spend on mines, submarines and torpedoes, which quickly eroded British dominance. Battleships added huge new costs to naval building, since they were so very much more expensive to build and maintain than gunboats and cruisers. The 'naval race' was underway and Germany became the Admiralty's obsession.

The popular press and various works of popular fiction, such as Erskine Childers' *The Riddle of the Sands* of 1903 and William Le Queux's *Invasion of 1910*, serialised in the *Daily Mail* in 1906, helped generate public fears of a possible German invasion and painted an image of a country awash with German spies. A further 'naval scare' was generated in 1909 when Germany was seen to be capable of building ships as fast as Britain, and hysterical fears of invasion were played on by the less scrupulous politicians and press. A growing number of politicians succumbed to the anti-German mood. A new secret service bureau was established to deal with the 'extensive system of German espionage' that was believed to exist. An Official Secrets Act was pushed through all its stages in the Commons on a Friday afternoon in August 1911, when fewer than a sixth of members were present. It granted sweeping powers to act against those who were deemed to be 'prejudicial to the safety or interests of the state', including police powers to arrest, without a warrant, anyone committing an offence or being suspected of committing an offence under the Act.[4] By 1913, around a quarter of government expenditure was going on the navy. Expenditure on the secret service was not made public.

There were those within the British Cabinet who were keen to improve relations with Germany. Some, like Haldane, were admirers of many aspects of German culture; others had no desire to get involved with French aggression. There were still a few Gladstonian anti-war radicals, who believed that Liberal foreign policy ought to be different from that of the Conservatives. But, apart from the navy, there were not very many areas of British–German tension the settlement of which might have provided the stepping stones to an agreement. On the other hand, once it had been

---

[4] K.D. Ewing and C.A. Gearty, *The Struggle for Civil Liberties. Political Freedom and the Rule of Law in Britain, 1914–1945* (Oxford, Oxford University Press, 2000), pp. 39–43.

decided by Grey that the entente was central to his policy, the chances of a meaningful approach to Germany were very limited.

The hardening of attitudes within the Foreign Office was borne out in a famous memorandum of 1907 by an official, Eyre Crowe, 'On the Present State of British Relations with France and Germany'. Crowe concluded that either Germany was 'definitely aiming at a general political hegemony and maritime ascendancy, threatening the independence of her neighbours and ultimately the existence of England' or she was merely seeking to extend her commerce and culture. Whatever the reason, it presented a challenge and it needed to be made clear to Germany that there would be 'determined opposition at the first sign of British and allied interests being adversely affected'. Crowe's relatively detached analysis made precise perceptions that had been gaining influence for some years. It encouraged more vigorous anti-German sentiment

Focus on

Britain and the 'balance of power'

Memorandum of Mr Eyre Crowe on the Present State of Relations with France and Germany, 1 January 1907. Crowe (1864–1925) was in charge of the Western Department of the Foreign Office which was responsible for the states of Western Europe. His mother was German and he had a German wife, but he increasingly came to believe that Germany was seeking to establish a political hegemony in Europe that had to be resisted.

> History shows that the danger threatening the independence of this nation has generally arisen at least in part, out of the momentary predominance of a neighbouring State at once militarily powerful, economically efficient, and ambitious to extend its frontiers or spread its influence with the danger being directly proportionate to the degree of its power and efficiency, and to the spontaneity or 'inevitableness' of its ambitions. The only check on the abuse of political dominance derived from such a position has always consisted in the opposition of an equally formidable rival, or a combination of several countries forming leagues of defence. The equilibrium established by such a grouping of forces is technically known as the balance of power, and it has become almost a historical truism to identify England's secular policy with the maintenance of this balance by throwing her weight now in this scale and now in that, but ever on the side opposed to the political dictatorship of the strongest single State group at a given time.

Source: G.P. Gooch and H.W. Temperley (eds), *British Documents and the Origins of the War*, Volume III (London, 1928).

within the Foreign Office that was further strengthened when a coterie of new officials came along. Zara Steiner concludes that it would be wrong to think in terms of an organised group, but Grey 'received advice that was based on suspicion, if not hostile interpretation of German motives and the most able and influential men at the Foreign Office shared this view'.[5]

Meanwhile, moves were made to settle matters with Russia. France was pressing for this agreement and Russia was more amenable after her disastrous defeat by Japan in 1905. This was more difficult, since many Liberals regarded Russia as the epitome of despotism. There were four main regions of imperial rivalry between the two Powers: Central Asia, East Asia, Persia and the Ottoman Empire. Settlements were reached on three of these areas. Russia agreed to leave Afghanistan to British control and both agreed to leave Tibet to China. Persia was divided into two spheres of influence: a large Russian sphere in the north, including the capital, Tehran; Britain in the south, where, as fate would have it, the main oil deposits turned out to be. To keep the Russians out of Constantinople had been a cornerstone of British policy since the end of the eighteenth century. However, with Egypt occupied, Constantinople was seen as of much less strategic importance. The British indicated that they were quite relaxed about Russia trying to press other powers to be allowed to take her navy from the Black Sea through the Straits.

There was no great warmth for the Russian entente. In the public mind it never developed into a relationship comparable to the *Entente Cordiale*, although visits of Nijinsky and the *Ballets Russes* and the production of Chekhov's plays all helped alter perceptions of Russia. Military staff visited Russia and, by 1912, the press began to talk of the Triple Entente. As Grey later explained, although the ententes were not alliances, an assumption was building up that, in the event of war, the countries were likely to be allies. To further cement the new bond with Russia, much British investment began to flow into the country.

New tensions

Another serious Moroccan crisis blew up in 1911 when, as a result of a popular rebellion again the Sultan, who was a French puppet, the French seized the main cities. All the signs were that they were about to declare Morocco a French protectorate. The Germans demanded compensation and, in July 1911, despatched a gunboat, the *Panther*, to Agadir – ostensibly to defend their citizens but, in practice, to impede the impending French annexation of Morocco. It was also a useful way to exert pressure on the French to make some imperial concessions, and, indeed, it looked as if Germany and France would reach an agreement. Britain feared that

---

[5] Zara S. Steiner and Keith Neilson, *Britain and the Origins of the First World War*, 2nd edn (Basingstoke, Palgrave Macmillan, 2003).

this might include the concession to Germany of a port on the Moroccan coast. In November 1911, the Chancellor of the Exchequer, Lloyd George, regarded as being from the radical wing of the Cabinet, made reference to the crisis in his annual speech to the City of London. He warned that, where her interests were 'vitally affected', Britain would not allow herself to be treated 'as if she were of no account in the Cabinet of nations'. The press immediately took this up as a warning to Germany, but, as the historian A.J.P. Taylor pointed out, it can also be seen as a warning to France not to go ahead and reach any agreement with Germany without consulting Britain. Britain was determined to maintain the *Entente Cordiale* and feared being isolated by a new *rapprochement* between France and Germany.

As the crisis dragged on, the Committee of Imperial Defence agreed that, in the event of war between France and Germany, a British expeditionary force should be sent to France. In the end, the crisis blew over, as the Germans backed down. A new Franco-German agreement was signed, by which Germany recognised a French protectorate over Morocco in return for a piece of the French Congo. But the crisis had been of crucial significance. To many in Germany it was a humiliating climb-down. It made future retreat in the face of Anglo-French pressure more difficult. Britain had made it clear, yet again, that she was committed to the support of French interests, although there were no great British interests in Morocco. Indeed, Britain had helped ensure that there would be no Franco-German *rapprochement*.

It was only in the midst of the Agadir crisis that most members of the Cabinet heard about the military conversations with the French and Russians. While some were undoubtedly horrified about the extent of commitment, key radical figures, like Lloyd George and Churchill had shown themselves willing to go along with the pro-French sentiments. Indeed, Churchill, who became First Lord of the Admiralty in October 1911, needed little encouragement to adopt towards Germany the gung-ho attitudes of most of the senior naval staff.

After the crisis, there was one of the extremely rare House of Commons' debates on foreign policy. All the Liberal backbenchers who spoke were critical of Grey's foreign policy and of its lack of openness. The secret articles of the Anglo-French entente were published for the first time. There was concern about the influence of Foreign Office officials and at what was seen as the sacrificing of potentially liberal movements in Persia for the sake of an agreement with Russia. There were demands for a new approach to improve relations with Germany.

The one fluent German speaker in the Cabinet, Haldane, was sent in 1912 on what was hoped would be a secret trip to sound out German ministers. News of his visit got out and the right-wing press talked of a possible sell-out by a government that, because of domestic issues, they regarded as dangerously radical. Haldane's mission merely confirmed what were increasingly irreconcilable positions. Germany wanted Britain to declare that, in the event of a Franco-German war, Britain would remain neutral. Britain wanted Germany to cut back its naval building programme. Neither could deliver these without risking huge domestic consequences.

1912–14

A need to reassure France and also a reflection of a continuing sense of overcommit-ment led to a further co-ordination of the British and French defensive systems in 1912. The British withdrew their fleet from the Mediterranean and stationed it in home waters, while the French put their Channel fleet into the Mediterranean. It was agreed informally that military planning should assume collaboration in the event of war. Asquith and Churchill had little doubt that the naval deployments, in particular, were creating moral obligations, if not more, to defend the French Channel coast. Grey, however, continued to imply that Britain still had a free hand to decide what her actions would be.

During 1912–14 relations between Britain and Germany steadily improved. It soon became clear that, to all intents, Germany had given up the dreadnought race. Britain and Germany worked closely to localise the wars that broke out in the Balkans and to curb their allies. The British withdrew opposition to German railway-building in Turkey and the Germans recognised the rights of the British to develop the recently found oil resources in Persia and Mesopotamia (Iraq). A deal was worked out by which the British agreed to support German claims to some of the Portuguese colonies in Africa, should the Portuguese Empire fall apart. As the Permanent Secretary at the Foreign Office noted in May 1914, 'since I have been at the Foreign Office I have not seen such calm waters'.

War, when it came, came unexpectedly. There was general sympathy for Austria when news came through of the assassination of the Archduke Ferdinand by Serbian nationalists at Sarajevo. The expectation was that Britain and Germany might once again work together to keep the lid on the tensions in the Balkans. But Austria, for its own internal reasons, was determined to drive Serbia into subordination. Russia, with equally pressing internal concerns, had no option but to defend Serbia. Germany, unwilling to take the risk of losing its one reliable ally, did nothing to curb Austria's determination. France, for whom the alliance with Russia had been crucial to her escape from isolation, would certainly stand by Russia.

What would Britain's position be? Russia and France pressed Grey to bring pressure to bear on Germany by declaring unequivocally that, if war came, Britain would support France and Russia. Grey was unable to do this, because the Cabinet had not discussed the matter and he knew that many of the Cabinet were pacific. He also did not want to say anything that would encourage aggressive posturing by Russia and France. The Foreign Office officials had no doubt about the position: 'the whole policy of the Entente can have no meaning if it does not signify that in a just quarrel England would stand by her friends'. The Cabinet was split and fierce debate ensued: Grey and Churchill were for immediate intervention; Lloyd George wanted to wait and see; three others wanted to keep out of the situation. A number were uncommitted. Asquith, as Prime Minister, while sympathetic to Grey's position, was anxious to hold his Cabinet together. Grey's resolve was strengthened, as the Cabinet debated the issues all day on 2 August, by a letter from the Conservative leader, Bonar Law, promising Conservative backing for intervention on behalf of

France and Russia. Grey now told the French that Britain would prevent the German fleet coming down the Channel to threaten the French ports. John Burns and John Morley immediately resigned from the Cabinet.

The commitment to France was given before Germany sent its ultimatum to Belgium demanding right of passage. To most people's surprise, Belgium chose to resist. The news of this arrived a few hours before Grey was due to address the Commons on 3 August. In his speech, Grey revealed to the Commons, for the first time, the extent of the military and naval discussions with France and Russia, while still insisting that these involved no binding commitments. He then revealed the Cabinet's promise of the previous day to France. He ended by stressing that, if France were beaten, Germany would be left dominating the Continent. There was no vote, but there was little dissent. On 4 August, an ultimatum was sent to Berlin demanding withdrawal from Belgium and, when that was ignored, war was declared. No one else resigned from the Cabinet. The invasion of Belgium had given vacillating Radicals a suitable moral justification for going along with Grey and Asquith.

Focus on

The causes of the Great War

This is from the Independent Labour Party, *Manifesto on the War*. The ILP, led by Keir Hardie, was one of the bodies affiliated to the Labour Party.

It is not the Serbian question or the Belgian question that pulled this country into the deadly struggle. Great Britain is not at war because of oppressed nationalities or Belgian neutrality. Even had Belgian neutrality not been wrongfully infringed by Germany we should still have been drawn in.

If France in defiance of treaty rights had invaded Belgium to get at Germany, who believed we should have begun hostilities against France? Behind the back of Parliament and the people, the British Foreign Office gave secret understandings to France, denying their existence even when challenged. That is why this country is now face to face with the red ruin and impoverishment of war. Treaties and agreements have dragged Republican France at the heels of despotic Russia, Britain at the heels of France. At the proper time this will be made plain and the men responsible called to account.

We desire neither the aggrandisement of German militarism nor Russian militarism, but the danger is that this war will promote one or the other. Britain has placed herself behind Russia, the most reactionary, corrupt, and oppressive power in Europe. If Russia is permitted to gratify her territorial ambitions and extend her Cossack rule, civilisation and democracy will be gravely imperilled. Is it for this that Britain has drawn the sword?

Source: Independent Labour Party, *Manifesto on the War*, 11 August 1914.

Why war?

It was a sense of weakness that had driven British governments to seek settlements with their colonial rivals, France and Russia. Britain was no longer capable of defending all her imperial interests should France and Russia continue to exert pressure on them. Germany, with limited imperial interests, was not particularly interested in helping Britain defend her Empire and lacked the naval resources to do so. The ententes were the outcome. For Britain they were about relieving the pressure, but for France they were intended as the preliminary to an alliance. Should the ententes crumble, then Britain's weaknesses would become apparent. Anxious to prevent that, and always aware that there were those within French government circles who were suspicious of Britain and favoured improved relations with Germany, Grey had to concede to French pressure for ever greater commitment. He went as far as he could without having to bring the whole issue to Parliament – or even the Cabinet – until he had no option but to do so. In July and August 1914 there was no alternative policy other than maintaining the ententes, with the result that Britain had to go where France and Russia led.

One could hardly publicly base a foreign policy on an admission of weakness. The threat from Germany was a much simpler justification for the policies being pursued. Yet in so many ways Germany did not pose a threat. Her interests were not in areas of great British concern. There was little colonial rivalry between the two, but this meant that there was little to negotiate on. Far from causing war, imperial rivalries had proved to be the means for settling differences. Other people's lands could be carved up and redistributed. Germany was largely excluded from this and so there was not an easy basis for any deal. The German navy was an irritation rather than an immediate threat, but there were plenty who had a vested interest in exaggerating the German naval threat to encourage ever greater expenditure on warships. It was an issue that could be readily played to public opinion in the most simplistic terms. Organisations such as the Navy League, formed in 1895 and powerfully backed by a right-wing press, constantly harped on about the German threat. In practice, Germany at no point seriously challenged British naval dominance. In 1914 she had a mere 13 dreadnoughts to Britain's 22 and France's 14, 4 battlecruisers to Britain's 9. But within Germany the navy had become a symbol of Germany's emergence as a world power and, therefore, there could be no public repudiation of naval building without something big in return. That could only be a clear statement of neutrality by Britain, something that she could not do without its being seen as a betrayal by France.

None had any concept of the kind of war that was about to be unleashed. It was a measure of a world that was soon to disappear that, with war declared, Mrs Margot Asquith and her step-daughter, Violet, went to bid farewell to the German ambassador.[6]

---

[6] S. Koss, *Lord Haldane: Scapegoat for Liberalism* (New York, Colombia University Press, 1969), p. 16.

Further reading

Bartlett, C.J., *Defence and Diplomacy. Britain and the Great Powers 1815–1914* (Manchester, Manchester University Press, 1993)

Charmley, J., *Splendid Isolation? Britain and the Balance of Power 1874–1914* (London, Hodder & Stoughton, 1999)

Kennedy, P.M., *The Rise of Anglo-German Antagonism* (London, Allen & Unwin, 1981)

Steiner, Z., *The Foreign Office and Foreign Policy 1989–1914* (Cambridge, Cambridge University Press, 1969)

Steiner, Z., *Britain and the Origins of the First World War* (Basingstoke, Macmillan, 1977)

Strachan, H., *The Outbreak of the First World War* (Oxford, Oxford University Press, 2004)

26

The First World War

The coming of conflict

Even before it ended, the First World War had replaced the Napoleonic Wars as the 'Great War', and the images of it have shaped perceptions of warfare into the present century. The experiences of that war had a powerful influence on many opinion formers and political leaders through until at least the 1960s. Since the 1920s, historical perspectives on the war have been highly critical of the role of military leaders, who were held responsible for the scale of the slaughter in the trenches of the western front. The interpretation of 'lions led by donkeys' has long held sway and has only recently begun to be challenged. Military historians point to the rapid learning curve that had to be gone through to change from a tiny regular army whose experience had been largely confined to colonial police-keeping to a mass army of amateurs, and to the way in which new tactics were learned from disastrous mistakes.

Politically and administratively, the war was also of great significance, leading to the decline of the Liberal Party and to the extension of the state's role. The Liberal Party and the country entered the war with a fair level of unity. The invasion of Belgium proved a useful justification for many Radicals. Even the Labour Party went along with the decision for war. Only four Labour MPs voted against support, one of whom was the leader of the party, Ramsay MacDonald. But the Independent Labour Party, an autonomous organisation within the Labour Party, became the focus of anti-war activities. Socialists and Radicals were particularly appalled by the idea that Britain should be in alliance with autocratic tsarist Russia.

Most people expected the war to be relatively short, as recent European wars had been. Many probably did not even envisage a major land war, but expected the decisive battles to be at sea. Also, for a generation and more, a cult of militarism had been inculcated amongst the middle and upper classes, in the private schools in particular. There was also a huge literature of adventure tales that projected an image of the chivalrous and manly hero to which many aspired and for whom war would provide an opportunity. Initially, there was a sense that war was an extension of the games of school, or the exercises of the officer training corps at university, and an experience not to be missed. Herbert Asquith, one of the Prime Minister's sons, in his poem of May 1915, 'The Volunteer', saw the clerk 'who half his life had spent/Toiling at ledgers in a city grey' equally caught by the romance of war and, even in death, finding 'those waiting dreams are satisfied' as he 'goes to join the men of Agincourt'.

There was a remarkable readiness to put restrictions on people's liberty. The Defence of the Realm Act (DORA), passed four days after the outbreak of war, gave the government enormous powers to issue regulations 'for securing the public safety and the defence of the realm'. By the end of 1914, another two such DORAs had been passed, which included provisions for the use of courts martial against suspect civilians. The Acts allowed governments to make regulations without much parliamentary scrutiny. In time these allowed, among many other powers, the taking over of private property; the control of meetings; the restriction of people's movements; regulation of the press and other means of communication; and the suppression of political opposition to the war. Few made the transition to a war situation more enthusiastically than Lloyd George, although he did have some doubts. He knew from his contacts with the financial and business communities that most were appalled at the prospect of a war that would create havoc with trade and with the international credit system. But, as he wrote in his self-justifying *Memoirs*, he 'realised that the only safe way out was through the gates of victory, and that victory was only to be won by concentrating all thought and energy on making war'.

The German military onslaught nearly did succeed. Within two weeks, the German armies were in sight of Paris. The British contribution, as the War Office had planned, was to send a British expeditionary force of some 90,000 to France to support the French army on its left wing. They met the Germans at Mons and proceeded to retreat at speed, falling back 200 miles in 13 days. But the German advance was halted and, by mid-September, both sides had dug in and committed themselves to trench warfare.

Although Haldane, during his time at the War Office, 1906–12, had increased the size of the regular, full-time army and created a reserve 'territorial army', they were small compared with those of other countries, and Britain was the only major European power without conscription. The territorial army was poorly equipped and intended only for home defence, so any expansion of the army had to depend on new volunteers. But there were not the arms, the equipment, the training, the accommodation or the logistical planning available for the million recruits who came forward by Christmas 1914. It was also an army with an officer corps that was ill-prepared for a new kind of war. Military advancement generally came through contacts and through conformity to established patterns; there was little room for the unorthodox or even the modern. The tactics of the Napoleonic Wars were still taught rather than those of the technological Russo-Japanese War. There was even 'a psychology of military incompetence' that ensured that it was the least flexible and least imaginative who rose to the top.[1]

Although the Conservatives had made clear their support for the war, there was no possibility of a coalition government at this stage. Relations between the leaders of the two main parties had been too bitter in the months before the war, and the right wing of the Unionist Party continued to snipe at the government, accusing it of having left the country unprepared for a war which they (the right) had long predicted. The appointment of General Kitchener as Secretary for War was a shrewd way of reassuring the military leadership, most of whom had been violently hostile to everything that the Liberal Party stood for in the years before the war. It was also a response to persistent calls from the press for some heroic leader. Kitchener had made his reputation by his victory at Omdurman and during the South African War. He had been built up over the years in the pages of the *Daily Mail* as a great imperial hero and he was mistakenly believed to be an efficient organiser and tactician. Unfortunately, Kitchener proved to be largely devoid of both parliamentary and strategic skills, and bone-headed in his refusal to admit or to rectify mistakes. Nonetheless, he remained a popular figure with the press, as the 'strong man'.

Kitchener's initial task was to bring about the rapid expansion of the forces. The recruitment poster with his face on it, by Alfred Leete, declaring 'Your Country Needs You', came out late in 1914. Unlike most of his colleagues, Kitchener soon came to the view that the war was likely to go on for at least three years and he proved effective in getting recruits and moving them to France rapidly. By the end of 1914 there were around 300,000 volunteers coming forward each month; so many, in fact, that key industries, such as mining, were facing critical labour shortages.

In addition, Asquith's style of giving his Cabinet a relatively free hand was hardly suited to the colossal problems of running a war. Lloyd George, by contrast, quickly enhanced his reputation, and patriotic speeches about 'marching through terror to triumph' found him useful friends on the political right and gained him enthusiastic coverage in the *Daily Mail*. Within days he had made the changes necessary to prevent the collapse of the financial structure. Soon he was talking about the need for ever greater state regulation and was frustrated by Kitchener's failure to tell the Cabinet what was going on in terms of war supplies. Initially, there was no control over private armaments firms and the War Office and the Admiralty were often competing for supplies from the same producer. Lloyd George got agreement with the trade unions, the Treasury Agreement in March 1915, to bring in 'dilution of labour' – the use of unskilled workers and women workers to undertake tasks that had formerly been reserved for skilled, unionised workers. By the spring of 1915, he was well into a scheme for either prohibition or the nationalisation of the drink trade.

---

[1] See N. Dixon, *On the Psychology of Military Incompetence* (New York, Basic Books, 1976).

The government was divided between those who believed that the strategy should be to concentrate all available resources on a quick victory and those who believed in a more cautious approach to make sure that the country survived the war without too much damage. Of course, it was rather unfortunate for the government, that there were no victories. The Cabinet, frustrated by what seemed to be the generals' only strategy of slogging it out on the western front, began to look at the possibility of a second front. Lloyd George favoured a landing in Greece and into Serbia eventually to knock out Austria. Churchill at the Admiralty favoured seizing the Dardanelles, important for Britain's grain supplies from Russia and as a route for providing much-needed aid to Russia. There were also plenty like Churchill who saw the attractions of dismembering the Ottoman Empire in the Middle East, which had come into the war on the side of Germany in October 1914. Churchill won the argument and the outcome was the disaster of Gallipoli. The mistaken belief was that naval power alone could penetrate the Dardanelles. When, in March 1915, this failed because of Turkish fortifications, it was agreed to proceed with a landing on the Gallipoli peninsula. Fewer troops were sent than were asked for and they were quickly pinned down on the beaches by Turkish gunfire. Changes in command did nothing to solve the problem and, as the campaign dragged on for months, the casualties were huge. Some 43,000 British, nearly 12,000 from the Australian and New Zealand forces and 5,000 French perished, but there was a concern about withdrawing lest Britain be seen as running away from an Asiatic enemy. Not until the start of 1916 was the campaign abandoned.

Coalition government

As early as March 1915, there was talk of plots against Asquith, who was under fierce attack from the Tory press. On 12 May 1915, Asquith informed the Commons that a coalition was 'not in contemplation'. A week later it happened and the last Liberal government came to an end. The government was hit by two crises at the same time. The first was an outcry about a shortage of shells, with *The Times* claiming that success in the second battle of Ypres, where gas had been used, had been prevented by the lack of shells. The next day, Lord Fisher, the First Sea Lord, walked out of the Admiralty. He declared that such were his disagreements with Churchill over the Dardanelles' tactics that he could no longer work with him. Bonar Law now threatened to unleash his backbenchers on the government and force an election. To avoid this a coalition emerged. The coincidence of these events has led to suggestions that there was a plot. Churchill had never hidden his views that a coalition government was necessary and he may have encouraged *The Times* to take up the issue. Much more significant was the fact that Lloyd George and Bonar Law were talking and that Lloyd George had become convinced that the shell shortage was real enough and that Kitchener had been ignoring warnings on this for months.

On Saturday 15 May, when Fisher resigned, Asquith did not seem too bothered. When Bonar Law learned of it, however, he insisted that Churchill had to be moved out of the Admiralty. He also argued for a coalition at a time when great efforts were being made to get Italy into the war on the side of the allies. Asquith, meanwhile, was in a state of near mental paralysis. Over many years, he had developed a passion for a young woman, Venetia Stanley. He clearly had become besotted by her and letters to her poured from him, sometimes as many as two or three a day. On 12 May 1915, she had broken the news to Asquith that she was to marry his private secretary, Edwin Montagu. Asquith was devastated, openly declaring that he was heartbroken. Churchill's biographer, Martin Gilbert, believes that the Stanley affair affected Asquith's judgment. But even before the crisis there had been signs of a Prime Minister under stress. A coalition might also present the opportunity of getting rid of the increasingly obstructive Kitchener. On 21 May, the *Daily Mail*, trying to bring down the government, launched a highly critical attack on Kitchener, describing the shell shortage as his 'tragic blunder'. Not wishing to give the impression of being run by the press, Asquith decided to let Kitchener remain. In the end, it is hard not to see the coalition as anything more than a last-ditch effort by Asquith to hang on to office. The most significant move was to take the procurement of munitions out of the hands of the War Office and to set up a new Ministry of Munitions under Lloyd George. The cluster of other Unionists who came in – Carson, Curzon, Austen Chamberlain, Walter Long, and Lansdowne – had all been strong opponents of Irish Home Rule, an issue that was soon to regain the centre stage.

To many Liberals the coalition was the great betrayal, with a decade of Liberalism thrown away at the first muttered dissent from the Unionists. However, the coalition had preserved Asquith and, at least, projected an image of national unity. In any case, Asquith was probably aware that there were other issues looming that would put impossible strains on a Liberal government – not least conscription.

Lloyd George at the Ministry of Munitions was moving towards a huge transformation of the British economy. He pulled in fresh talent from outside Whitehall to create the new department. He made contacts directly with businessmen, by-passing the War Office. There was more and more intervention in the actual running of industry. He brought state control over the production of armaments and over the distribution of raw materials. The Munitions of War Act of August 1915 made strikes illegal, required the suspension of work practices that restricted particular tasks to skilled workers, and restricted the movement of workers by requiring them to have a leaving certificate from their previous employer. It strengthened the hands of employers, but the ministry also pressed for an extension of bargaining with trade unions and for radically improved social welfare measures in the workplace. Lloyd George was seen as the most effective of ministers and his appeal began to be above party. He started to attract many Conservatives as someone who could break out of what they saw as too *laissez-faire* an attitude to the pursuit of the war.

The need for manpower was insatiable. Adverts and white feathers were not enough to satisfy the demands of the generals. The war on the western front was largely a standoff in trenches. There were still only 28 British and Empire divisions there in August 1915, compared with 98 French ones. The need for some success because of the disastrous events in Gallipoli and also because of fears of a Russian collapse led to the first 'big push' at the end of September 1915 at the Battle of Loos. There was a shortage of munitions and of men and the British used chlorine gas as an attempt to compensate. After three weeks there were 61,000 casualties, including nearly 8,000 dead, many of them regular army Scottish units, while other new recruits were being thrown in straight from the boats. Pressure from Unionists for conscription had been mounting for some time and even a few Liberals were prepared to concede that it might be fairer. In October 1915, Lloyd George, together with a number of the Conservatives, threatened to resign if conscription was not introduced. A scheme to get all men to register their willingness to serve in the forces was a last effort to save the voluntary system, but the next stage soon followed. In January 1916, the first Military Service Act was passed, calling up unmarried men between the ages of 18 and 41. Lloyd George now pressed to get conscription extended to married men and showed little sympathy to conscientious objectors. Once again, Asquith conceded to the pressure.

The western front was being built up for another big offensive in June 1916 and the war in the Middle East was going disastrously wrong. At Easter 1916, a revolt broke out in Dublin, in small part over the threat of conscription there. Bad news continued when the British and German fleets at long last made contact on the last day of May. Admirals Beatty and Jellicoe failed to prevent the German High Seas Fleet making its escape. Honours were heaped on Beatty and Jellicoe, though in fact the British had lost the same number of ships in the Battle of Jutland as the Germans, but twice the tonnage, and Admiral Sheer's battle cruisers had proved themselves more than a match in both marksmanship and manoeuvring for the flamboyant Beatty's cruisers. It was a failed opportunity to bring the war to an earlier end by eliminating the German naval threat. On the other hand, the Royal Navy still effectively controlled the North Sea and was able to maintain the blockade of German trade, which was eventually to break the will of the German home front to continue the war.

In June 1916, the problem of Kitchener was solved when he went down with *HMS Hampshire*, which hit a mine while on its way to Russia. Lloyd George, now without a rival, took over the War Office. In July, the battle of the Somme began to help relieve pressure on the French. Douglas Haig, the commander of the British forces in France, had drawn the lesson from futile assaults in 1915 that what was needed was an attack along a broader front, to break the German lines to allow the cavalry to gallop through. After days of bombardment of the German trenches, 110,000 advanced – only to find that the Germans had emerged from their deep dugouts, where they had survived the bombardment. On the first day, 60,000 were killed or wounded, including 5,000 from the Ulster Division. Eventually, there were 360,000 casualties in the four months over which the battle raged. At sea, the Germans were building up their submarine fleet and its activities were beginning to tell on the British economy. The news from Gallipoli was of yet more losses.

There were some tentative moves afoot to put out feelers on a negotiated peace. The main protagonists for this were the former Foreign Secretaries, Lord Lansdowne and Sir Edward Grey, but even Asquith said that they had at least to consider the possibility of a compromise peace. Lloyd George and the Tory members of the Cabinet were violently hostile. The Americans were also pressing and there may have been concern that Asquith would be won over to the side of peace negotiation. On 25 November, Lloyd George and Bonar Law drafted a scheme for a small war committee of four, with Lloyd George as chair, and they threatened resignation if Asquith refused to accept it. Asquith took this as part of a plot to humiliate him and he insisted on remaining in charge. Lloyd George resigned and so did Asquith, fairly confident that no government could be formed without him, but unable to form a government that did not include Lloyd George or Law. Law declined the role of figurehead Prime Minister and there was no alternative but to appoint Lloyd George.

Asquith and his supporters, which included the majority of Liberal ex-ministers, were never to forgive Lloyd George's ousting of him and there is no doubt that Lloyd George did intrigue. But perhaps only intrigue could prise out someone as certain of their own indispensability as Asquith appeared to be. Yet, he had to go. His style, his attitudes and his fudging on so many issues meant that there was a lack of effective leadership as the war situation became critical. Lloyd George, the *petit bourgeois*, Welsh Nonconformist had started his political career as an old-fashioned Radical, but, increasingly, he had begun to use the language of national efficiency, of power and of imperialism.

Lloyd George's coalition

Lloyd George pushed ahead with his war committee: himself, Law, Curzon, Milner and the Labour leader, Arthur Henderson. The membership tells us much. Milner, who had been strongly advocating a more vigorous pursuit of the war, was instinctively opposed to democracy. He regarded his policies in South Africa as having been betrayed by the politicians. Curzon was the former Viceroy of India, a man of the grandest hauteur with few liberal instincts. Henderson was there to ensure that the organised working class stayed in line. To all intents, Lloyd George was creating a dictatorship. Even the established civil service was by-passed, with a separate secretariat of advisers operating from sheds in the garden at Downing Street – the so-called 'garden suburb', answerable only to the war committee. It fitted with the aspirations that had been apparent in Lloyd George, for a decade or more, that politics could be restructured on a non-party basis.

The style of interventionism that had worked effectively at the Ministry of Munitions now spread to the rest of the economy. New ministries of Food, Shipping, Labour and National Service were established, together with an Air Board. Mines, shipping, chemicals, medical supplies, dye-stuffs and liquor were all, in effect, placed under government control. A vast range of new economic controls were brought in on production, supplies, prices, commandeering stocks, centralising purchases and controlling exports. In farming, the Board of Agriculture took responsibility for production and brought an additional four million acres into cultivation. Prices, wages and rents all came within government control.

On the whole, business went along with these measures. Profits were good. Most of the time there was industrial peace and there were opportunities to impose new techniques and new organisational practices with the minimum of disruption. Something of a new mood of national unity began to appear. Labour generally welcomed the rationing of food and the control of prices and rents. Where there was dissent and anti-war sentiment it was pretty ruthlessly crushed. The Union for Democratic Control was regularly harassed by the police and socialist papers were raided and suppressed. Conscientious objectors were given neither sympathy nor protection: more than 6,000 suffered much ill treatment in prison at the hands of both prison officers and other prisoners.

Militarily, 1917 was an even worse year than 1916. The unrestricted U-boat campaign that the Germans had launched in February was causing severe hardship in Britain, which was dependent on supplies from North America. In April alone, half a million tons of British shipping were sunk and not until the following month could the Admiralty be persuaded to organise convoys for merchant ships. War expenditure was creeping up to around £5 million a day, not counting the loans that had been made to Russia, France and Italy. Only America's reluctant entry into the war in April 1917, after Germany's unrestricted submarine warfare had sunk American shipping, relieved the unremitting gloom. America's main initial contribution was to ensure that Britain's credit in the United States was maintained by covering payments due, and that supplies to Germany were blocked.

The second half of 1917 brought the third battle of Ypres or Passchendaele, which cost 400,000 British lives for an advance of less than five miles. Lloyd George, who had opposed the 1917 offensive, was thoroughly disillusioned with Sir William Robertson, the Chief of the Imperial General Staff, and with the commander-in-chief in France, Sir Douglas Haig, both of whom he felt lacked imagination. Both were uncompromising 'westerners' and committed to the defence of what they saw as the army interest against politicians. Lloyd George believed that Haig was squandering the lives of his troops in what he called 'western holocausts'. But it was difficult to oust commanders who had assiduously built up allies both at court and in Parliament. Haig also used the press to intimidate the politicians by blaming failures on the lack of political back-up. March 1918 brought a German offensive and a British and French retreat. The need for some co-ordination between British and French forces had long been apparent, but largely resisted. However, the German advance forced change and it was agreed, much to the chagrin of the British military, that the French General Foch should take on the task of co-ordination.

The military setbacks also had immediate political repercussions. Lloyd George decided to anticipate attacks on him by telling the Commons that the army in France was larger than it had been in 1917 – that the fault, in other words, lay with the generals, not the government. The generals hit back in the press and, through Asquith, hinted that the government was hiding the truth. On 7 May, Major-General Sir Frederick

Maurice, former director of military operations, published a letter in several news-papers accusing Lloyd George of having given inaccurate information. In a debate on the following day, Lloyd George demolished his critics by claiming that it was Maurice's own department that had supplied him with the figures, dishonestly hiding the fact that he had later been given amended figures. He made the issue a matter of confidence in the government. In the event, 98 Liberals voted with Asquith against the govern-ment, leaving only 71 supporting Lloyd George. It marked an irrevocable Liberal split.

Ireland

The fall of Parnell in 1890 had resulted in a deep and bitter split in the Irish Home Rule movement, both inside and outside the Irish Parliamentary Party. In 1900, a sem-blance of unity had been achieved under the moderate leadership of John Redmond. Although Redmond did occasionally make statements that appeared to threaten a violent uprising, in practice, he was firmly committed to the constitutional road to Home Rule. Outside the Parliamentary Party, there were stirrings of significance. There was the Irish Republican Brotherhood, which carried on the tradition of the Fenians in believing that nationalism was about the setting up of a republic. It revived in the 1890s, triggered by the centenary celebrations of the 1798 United Irishmen, and largely financed by the American Clan na Gael. In 1899, Arthur Griffith founded the *United Irishman*, a paper which advocated *Sinn Féin* (ourselves alone). He sought a measure of devolution, which he thought could be achieved through abstentionism, the boy-cotting of British institutions. In 1905, Sinn Féin was established as a political party.

There had also been a revival of interest in Gaelic culture. In 1893, the Gaelic League was formed, with the initial aim of reviving the Irish language by getting it into the educational system. League membership came pretty solidly from the Dublin pro-fessional middle class, but they tended to look to the rural west of Ireland, where the language was still spoken, and to romanticise life in that area. The dreadfully poor economic conditions were presented as a welcome anti-materialism and the com-munity and the Catholicism of the region were idealised. W.B. Yeats, J.M. Synge and others in the Irish literary revival of the early years of the century found spirituality amongst the peasantry of the west and added to nationalist sentiment. All of these movements were generating a growing demand for a break of some kind with Britain, although, in most cases, they were not calling for complete independence. What they had in common was dissatisfaction with the leadership of John Redmond and his associates in the Parliamentary Party.

Protestants in Ulster feared not only for their religion but for their trade, their jobs and their culture, and Irish nationalists made little or no attempt to reassure them. The synergy of Catholicism and nationalism was taken for granted and it was assumed that Ulster could be coerced into acceptance of a united Ireland. The resistance in Ulster to the Home Rule Bill between 1912 and 1914 did nothing to persuade the nationalist movement to give thought to the issue of minority rights.

With partition of Ireland decided, but suspended for the duration of the war, there was no sense of an Ireland poised for rebellion in 1914–1915 but, for a few nationalists looking to history, the adversity of war was Ireland's opportunity. Only a handful were actually pro-German, but Sinn Féin saw the war as a British one and launched an anti-recruitment campaign. In contrast, Redmond joined in offering full support for the war, and in this he probably reflected the attitudes of most of the Irish. Just as in Britain, there was an initial rush to the colours from both Protestants and Catholics. But the Sinn Féin campaign, in time, proved effective and recruitment in Ireland was relatively low compared with other parts of Britain. The prospect of conscription being extended to Ireland directly challenged this.

In April 1916, Sir Roger Casement, a former diplomat, was captured in the west of Ireland after landing from a German submarine. He had hoped to bring in German armaments, but the German supply ship had to be scuttled to avoid capture. On 23 April, Easter Sunday, the mystical Catholic school-teacher, Pádraig Pearse, who had been talking of bloodshed as 'a cleansing and sanctifying thing' and a necessary precondition of independence, together with some 1,600 supporters seized the Dublin post office in O'Connell Street and a number of other public buildings. The republic, 'a sovereign, independent state', was declared by a self-styled provisional government. For most people in Dublin and elsewhere, the uprising came as a complete surprise and, initially, seems to have been greeted with some amusement. A week later, 64 rebels and 200 civilians were dead, along with 132 police and soldiers. Another 2,614 people

Figure 26.1 Dublin after the Easter Rising of 1916. The nationalist rebels in 1916 seized the general post office in O'Connell Street and some of the surrounding buildings. The British army responded with heavy artillery, which resulted in considerable destruction of the surrounding buildings.
Source: Mary Evans Picture Library

were wounded and much of the centre of the city blasted by shells. Martial law was imposed, and, there were summary executions and other atrocities that antagonised moderate opinion. Courts-martial imposed death sentences on 90 participants and, although 75 of these were commuted, 15, including Pearse, were executed in early

Focus on

Ireland and conscription in 1918

This extract is taken from a letter of Sir Horace Plunkett to 'Colonel' House, 26 April 1918. Plunkett was a moderate, Protestant nationalist, a supporter of dominion status for Ireland, while Edward House was an influential adviser to the President of the United States, Woodrow Wilson.

. . . To-day all the Nationalists have been compelled to join in the organised resistance to conscription. Under clerical influence the women will make the passive resistance very effective, and I doubt whether any considerable levy can be effected without bloodshed, with untold consequences in the United Kingdom and abroad. Organised Labour is equally determined. The country now demands a settlement which will abolish the supreme authority of the Imperial Government over military service.

The moral justification put forward by the Roman Catholic Church and therefore likely to be repeated in America is as follows: Ireland claims and expects the President to support her right of self-determination. She demands the full status of a self-governing Dominion. The Acts constituting the dominions give them certain naval and military powers and control over the conditions of military service. Yet the Dominions have all voluntarily supported the Empire with their blood and treasure. Trust Ireland, satisfy her political aspirations and she will do likewise. The Irish Parliament is long overdue, and to accompany the concession of Home Rule for Ireland with conscription by England is a tyrannical act.

This claim for a Dominion status demanded by Sinn Féin as the nearest approach to complete independence has given fresh strength to the federalist idea. The activity of the Roman Catholic Church against conscription has hardened the opposition to Home Rule in England and in Ulster which now asserts its right of self-determination and its claim to exclusion. The new Irish demand for military powers, not even asked for in former attempted settlements, is objected to on the further grounds that they could not be conceded to the English, Scottish and Welsh Parliaments which are expected by many to be established immediately after the war. I hear it said that with so much pro-German activity in Ireland and amongst the American Irish, a concession which might open Irish harbours to enemy submarines would involve grave military risk.

Source: Alan O'Day and John Stevenson (eds), *Irish Historical Documents since 1800* (Dublin, Gill and Macmillan, 1992), pp. 164–5.

May. The executions were carried out separately over a couple of weeks and martyrs were created.

Attempts by Lloyd George and others, in the aftermath of the rising, to find a settlement were blocked largely by the intransigence of southern Irish Unionists who were well-placed in the coalition government, and by the realisation of the nationalists that the exclusion of Ulster would be permanent. Opinion in southern Ireland swung behind a broad coalition of nationalists backing Sinn Féin. By 1917, it was winning by-elections against Redmond's people and an alternative Irish 'parliament', the Dáil Éireann, was established.

The inclusion of Ireland in the Military Service Bill of April 1918 gave further impetus to Sinn Féin's advance. The condemnation of conscription was widespread in Ireland, with leaders of the Roman Catholic Church speaking out against it. There was a general strike and Redmond and the Irish Parliamentary Party abandoned Westminster, with most of their supporters finding their way into Sinn Féin. Its gains were cemented even more by the arrests of Sinn Féin leaders for, reputedly, being involved in a German plot and then by the declaration by Lloyd George in November 1918 that Home Rule would be postponed until conditions in Ireland had changed. In the election in December Sinn Féin candidates, now committed to complete independence, won 72 of the 101 Irish seats.

War and Empire

In contrast to Ireland, the rest of the Empire showed remarkable loyalty and a readiness to get involved in European power struggles. In August 1914, war was declared on behalf of the Empire by the British government with the minimum of consultation. Within four months of the outbreak of war, Australian and New Zealand troops, with Japanese allies, seized everything German in the Pacific. Anzac forces were then shipped to Europe and huge numbers perished on the beaches of Gallipoli. South African forces captured German South-West Africa and African, West Indian and Indian troops seized the other German colonies in Africa. The greatest contribution, however, came from India, which provided more than a million of the 3 million from the Empire who were eventually mobilised.

Moves against the Turkish Empire had begun badly, with an advance from Basra towards Baghdad ending in the disastrous surrender of some 13,000 troops at Kut-el-Amara in April 1916. However, moves into Palestine had been more successful and T.E. Lawrence had helped stir an Arab rebellion. The Middle East now had the added importance of oil supplies in Persia and Mesopotamia (Iraq). Since 1905, the Royal Navy had been converting from coal to oil and, given the collapse of the Ottoman Empire, the British were determined to stake their claim in its territory. It was a concern to avoid future tension between Britain and France in the Middle East that led to the notorious Sykes–Picot agreement of April 1916. By this secret agreement, the two countries earmarked areas of influence. Britain assumed she would have control of Palestine and most of what was to become Iraq to the Persian Gulf and the areas around the Gulf. France would have spheres of influence in Syria and the Lebanon. When the Russian Bolsheviks revealed the existence of this secret deal in 1918, the Arabs, who had been promised support for independence, regarded it as a great betrayal. The British defence was the usual one that the Arabs would need foreign assistance on the road to independence.

There was even greater inconsistency in November 1917 in what has been dubbed the Balfour Declaration. Balfour, the Foreign Secretary, reported in a letter to Lord Rothschild that the government 'viewed with favour the establishment in Palestine of a national home for the Jewish people'. It reflected 20 years of very effective lobbying by the Zionist organisation that had assiduously cultivated leading politicians. What was envisaged was not an independent Jewish state but a British protectorate, under which Jewish settlements would be allowed to develop. The British authorities were pretty confident that a substantial Jewish presence in the area would help maintain British domination. It was also a fairly cynical propaganda exercise to gain Zionist support in America and, perhaps, even Jewish support in Russia at a time when the British position in the war seemed fairly desperate. Whatever the justification, there was no way that betrayals were going to be avoided in the post-war settlement.

The xenophobia of war

The war years had quickly brought to the surface many of the more unpleasant aspects of British society. Attacks on Germans living on Britain and on people who had non-British names began almost at once. Prince Louis of Battenberg, the First Sea Lord since 1912, felt obliged to resign as early as October 1914 as a result of hostility to his German antecedents. Encouraged by some of the press and stoked by a decade or more of fictional accounts of war, there were regular spy scares. There were demands for the internment of all Germans and the seizure of their assets.[2] Stories of German atrocities were used to stir hysteria. The sinking of the Cunard liner *Lusitania* off the coast of Ireland on 7 May 1915, with the loss of nearly 1,200 lives, unleashed anti-German riots across the country. In Liverpool, some 200 businesses and houses were burned down by the rioters and 150 Germans were taken into police custody and sent to Scotland for internment. The socialist journalist, Robert Blatchford, denounced Germans as an 'insatiable race of savages' and called for 'something very near to extermination of the German people'.[3] Stock exchanges and restaurants excluded even naturalised Germans from their premises. Anti-Semitism was never far below the surface and the patriotism of Russian-Jewish socialists in London's East End was questioned. In 1917, royal dukes and princes, the Tecks and the Battenbergs and

---

[2] *The Times*, 15 May 1915.
[3] Paul Ward, *Red Flag and Union Jack. Englishness, Patriotism and the British Left 1881–1924* (1998), p. 125.

the princesses of Schleswig-Holstein dropped their German titles and adopted British ones. Battenberg became Mountbatten and the Saxe-Coburg family name of the immediate royal family was dropped in favour of Windsor.

Germanophobia was not something that grew spontaneously but was fomented by journalists and politicians who had axes to grind and grievances to avenge, merely continuing the racist anti-alien campaigns of the early years of the century. Most of the attacks were on people who were associated with the Liberal Party and continued the pre-war theme that the Liberal government, in the hands of the Irish, the socialists and pacifist radicals, was systematically betraying the country. One of the main victims of such vitriol was Haldane, the Lord Chancellor. Haldane had frequently in the past expressed his admiration for German culture, but his real crimes in the eyes of some was his rejection of the calls for the introduction of conscription when he had been at the War Office and his attempt to improve relations between Britain and Germany in 1912.

Labour and the war

Government needed the collaboration of national labour leaders to ensure an effective war effort and Labour MPs were brought into the government. There were, however, bitter divisions within the Labour movement. Some MPs were enthusiastically patriotic while others were co-operative, though with reservations about how the war had been brought about. However, there was also a substantial anti-war element and there were a few, particularly after the Russian revolution of 1917, who believed that war presented the opportunity for revolution and therefore called for active opposition to the war.

Labour political leaders were incorporated into areas of government. Arthur Henderson, the chairman of the Labour Party, joined Asquith's Cabinet in May 1915 as labour advisor and, despite deep suspicion of Lloyd George within the ranks of Labour, he accepted a place in Lloyd George's War Cabinet. Henderson tried to make some headway on plans for post-war reconstruction, but with limited success. He was, however, sent to Petrograd (St Petersburg) in 1917 to try to persuade the new Russian government to remain in the war. While there, he recognised that the Russian government was not likely to survive attacks from the Bolsheviks unless there was a prospect of peace. He therefore supported Labour attendance at an international socialist peace conference being held in neutral Sweden. For this he was sacked from the War Cabinet. Lloyd George thought that Henderson had caught a touch of 'revolutionary malaria' on his trip to Russia.

The effect of Henderson's exit from the Cabinet, however, was to allow the Labour Party and Henderson himself to come out more unequivocally in favour of a negotiated peace. There was also a determination to reaffirm a rejection of Liberalism by means of a socialist programme. In 1918, the Labour Party adopted a new constitution that included, for the first time, a commitment to socialism. This was Clause 4, which called for the nationalisation of the means of production, distribution and exchange.

The rapid withdrawal of Russia from the war in the aftermath of the Bolshevik seizure of power in November 1917 increased the pressure on the western front. There did seem to be a possibility of defeat in the spring of 1918 as a result of the German advance, but that seems to have brought a revival of patriotism and a renewed determination to see the struggle through. There is not a great deal of evidence that anti-war sentiment was gaining ground, despite grumbles about rising food prices – rather, there was a feeling that the sacrifices should not be in vain and that the struggle should continue. Unexpectedly, the German front and the fronts of their allies began to crumble in September 1918, as deprivation from four years of blockade had started to destroy civilian morale. Supplies and manpower were no longer available to the German armies, while the allied ones had learned many tactical lessons from the earlier disasters. Tanks and aircraft and better armaments were now being used and fresh American troops and supplies were beginning to appear on the battlefields. Berlin put out feelers to America's President Wilson about the possibility of peace. Germany was in the throes of revolution and already there were fears of the danger of Bolshevism spreading beyond Russia. Britain was prepared to accept less than unconditional surrender and an armistice was agreed on 11 November.

The impact of war

How far the war actually brought substantial and permanent social changes is problematic, although it certainly generated concern about conditions and enthusiasm for reform. The Ministry of Munitions had interested itself in the welfare of workers and had co-ordinated various welfare projects dealing with diet, health, holidays, housing and sanitary arrangements. The machinery of government was altered, resulting in the formation of a Ministry of Health and a Ministry of Labour. A Ministry of Reconstruction was set up in 1917 to try to bring together various piecemeal projects with the aim of creating a 'more harmonious social order'. Much was made of the sense of community generated by the war, the common sacrifices and suffering. In practice, service in the army had, if anything, strengthened social divisions. When necessity had required the opening up of the officer corps to a few of the lower middle class, they were dubbed 'temporary gentlemen'.[4] There were few signs of a new harmony or mutual understanding between social classes. There was always a tension between trying to create a new society and trying to get back to the world as it was in 1914, and both Liberals and Conservatives were resistant to handing more power to the state and to forcing powerful interests to co-operate.

However, the impact of the war needs to be measured not just in terms of the legislation that it produced, but in terms of the impact on people's minds. 6.1 million men served in the armed forces – 55 per cent of men between the ages of 15 and 49 – and

---

[4] Gerard J. De Groot, *Blighty: British Society in the Era of the Great War* (Harlow, Longman, 1996), p. 116.

another 2 million men, women and young people were in munitions' work. Never in British history had there been such a mobilisation. Three-quarters of a million died and it has been calculated that around 3 million Britons out of a population of fewer than 42 million lost a close relative in the war.[5] The death rate as a proportion of the population was comparable to that during the Napoleonic Wars, but concentrated in 4 years rather than 23. For every 9 men who went to the western front, 5 were killed, wounded or missing. 12 per cent of those who were mobilised were killed and the slaughter crossed class boundaries. The proportion killed among the officer corps was higher than amongst the rank and file. Asquith lost a son; Bonar Law lost two sons; five of the former Prime Minister, Lord Salisbury's ten grandsons were killed, along with Lord Rosebery's son. The war also left behind 240,000 amputees; 10,000 blinded by the enemy's and their own mustard gas; 73,000 suffering from disorders that were lumped under the name of 'shell shock', but included the effects of a variety of traumas. Perhaps another 500,000 had wounds of some kind.

To set against the horrendous costs there were gains. The life expectancy of those who remained in civilian work improved. There were signs that, in both health and in earnings, differences between the poorly paid and the better-paid narrowed. In the city slums, both infant and maternal mortality fell sharply. With better earnings, nutritional levels rose and, in spite of shortages, the quality of diet was maintained during the war. For some women, the war opened new horizons as they joined organisations such as the Women's Volunteer Reserve or the Women's Army Auxiliary Corps (WAAC). For others, there was work in munitions factories and as drivers, though generally at lower rates of pay than men. They were pushed out as soon as the war ended and there was a post-war reaction against what was seen as the subversion of traditional gender roles and panic about the independence of such women. It led to a strengthening of the ideal of motherhood as the 'correct' role for women.

How the First World War has been remembered and perceived has been the subject of much writing. Most see the war as a hugely significant watershed in European culture, ushering in the modern world. The certainties of an earlier age were overthrown and the authority of the old order was irrevocably undermined. Recent work emphasises how perceptions changed over time or how different perceptions could exist side by side. When the first Remembrance Day was celebrated on 11 November 1919, emphasis was still on the victory against German militarism and victory parties on armistice night continued to be held through until the mid-1920s. The two minutes' silence that was adopted in that first year was about remembering the sacrifice that had been made, but there were few doubts that the war had been a necessary defence of worthwhile values against a brutal challenge. The sacrifice had been a noble one and the wearing of a red poppy, which was adopted by the ex-servicemen's association, the British Legion, in 1921 helped survivors identify with the sacrifice.[6]

---

[5] Adrian Gregory, *The Silence of Memory: Armistice Day 1919–1946* (Oxford, Berg, 1994), p. 19.

[6] The symbol of the poppy came from a poem by the Canadian John McCrae, 'In Flanders' fields the poppies blow/Between the crosses, row on row', and had been adopted earlier by American veterans.

Memories begin to alter in the second half of the 1920s. With around 50,000 war memorials appearing in every town and village in the country over the next 20 years, the sense of the tragedy of war was powerfully implanted in plays, novels and poems. All brought out the brutality, waste and futility of war. How far the cynicism of poets and writers permeated much beyond literary circles is difficult to judge. The idea that this had somehow been a noble sacrifice reflecting courage, determination and patriotism probably remained the dominant sentiment. That the leadership had failed to match the courage and sacrifice of the ordinary soldier *did* gain ground and has remained one of the most powerful perceptions of the war.

Further reading

Gregory, A., *The Silence of Memory: Armistice Day 1919–1946* (Oxford, Berg, 1994)

Bond, Brian (ed.), *The First World War and British Military History* (Oxford, Oxford University Press, 1991)

Braydon, Gail and Summerfield, Penny, *Out of the Cage. Women's Experiences in Two World Wars* (London and New York, Pandora Press, 1987)

Burk, K., *War and the State: The Transformation of British Government, 1914–1919* (London, Allen and Unwin, 1982)

De Groot, Gerard J., *Blighty: British Society in the Era of the Great War* (Harlow, Longman, 1996)

Fussell, P., *The Great War and Modern Memory* (Oxford, Oxford University Press, 2000)

Robbins, K., *The First World War* (Oxford, Oxford University Press, 2002)

Turner, J., *British Politics and the Great War: Coalition and Conflict 1915–1918* (New Haven, Yale, 1992)

Winter, J.M., *The Great War and the British People* (Basingstoke, Macmillan, 1985)

http://www.bbc.co.uk/history/worldwars/ has an excellent collection of articles and images.

Timeline 1881–1918

Year	Government and politics	War and empire	Economic and social	Cultural and intellectual
1881	Death of Lord Beaconsfield	Boer victory at Majuba Hill	Irish Land Act	
1882		Occupation of Egypt; Phoenix Park murders		
1883				Andrew Mearns' *Bitter Cry of Outcast London*; Boys' Brigade founded
1884	Third Franchise Reform Act; formation of Fabian Society; formation of Social Democratic Federation		Royal Commission on the Housing of the Working Classes	
1885	First Salisbury ministry	Upper Burma annexed; death of Gordon at Khartoum	Housing Act	
1886	Third Gladstone ministry; Irish Home Rule Bill; second Salisbury ministry	Royal Niger Co. Chartered; gold discovered at Witwatersrand; foundation of Johannesburg; Indian National Congress		
1887	Victoria's golden jubilee			
1888	Local Government Act	British East Africa Co. in Uganda; De Beers Mining Corporation	Bryant & May matchgirls' strike	Invention of moving picture camera
1889	Formation of London County Council	British South Africa Co.	London dock strike	*Fabian Essays*
1890	Parnell/O'Shea divorce	Cecil Rhodes PM of Cape Colony		William Morris' *News from Nowhere*

Year	Government and politics	War and empire	Economic and social	Cultural and intellectual
1891	Death of Parnell		Free elementary education	
1892	Fourth Gladstone ministry; Keir Hardie and John Burns elected to parliament			
1893	Formation of ILP	Government take control of Uganda	National coal strike	Booth's *Life and Labour of the People of London*
1894	Resignation of Gladstone; Rosebery Prime Minister; married women ratepayers get the vote in local elections		Death duties introduced	
1895	Third Salisbury ministry	Jameson raid	Invention of internal combustion engine; London School of Economics founded	Oscar Wilde in Reading jail; formation of National Trust
1896				Launch of the *Daily Mail*; Olympic Games in Athens
1897	Queen's diamond jubilee; National Union of Women's Suffrage Societies formed	Milner becomes High Commissioner in South Africa	Engineering lock-out; Workmen's Compensation Act	
1898		Battle of Omdurman; Fashoda crisis; Curzon Viceroy of India		Ebenezer Howard, *Garden Cities of Tomorrow*
1899		South African War; Government take Nigeria from Royal Niger Co.		

1900	Formation of Labour Representation Committee; Unionist election victory			Launch of the *Daily Express*
1901	Death of Queen Victoria; Edward VII	Commonwealth of Australia	B.S. Rowntree's *Poverty: a Study of Town Life*	
1902	Balfour Prime Minister	Anglo-Japanese Treaty; Peace of Vereeniging	English Education Act	J.A. Hobson, *Imperialism*
1903	Chamberlain's tariff reform speech; Liberal-Labour pact; Women's Social and Political Union formed			
1904		Anglo-French Entente; Empire Day established	Letchworth Garden City founded	J.M. Barrie, *Peter Pan*; Joseph Conrad, *Heart of Darkness*
1905	Resignation of Balfour; Campbell-Bannerman Prime Minister; Sinn Féin formed	Moroccan crisis	Report of Inter-departmental Committee on Physical Deterioration	
1906	Liberal election victory	Algeciras conference; launch of *HMS Dreadnought*	Trade Disputes Act; school meals introduced	
1907		Anglo-Russian Entente	School medical inspection introduced	Boy Scout movement
1908	Asquith Prime Minister		Juvenile Courts formed; Old-Age Pensions Act	Olympic Games in London
1909	People's Budget		Trade Boards Act; Labour exchanges; Osborne judgement; Royal Commission on Poor Laws	
1910	General election – January; death of Edward VII; George V; general election – December	Formation of Union of South Africa		Girl Guides' Association formed

Year	Government and politics	War and empire	Economic and social	Cultural and intellectual
1911	Parliament Act: life of a parliament reduced to five years, payment of MPs introduced; Bonar Law Conservative leader	Agadir crisis	National Insurance Act	
1912		Haldane mission to Germany	Coal miners' minimum wage	Sinking of the *Titanic*
1913	Emily Davison, suffragette, killed by King's horse at Epsom Derby		Trade Union Act	Society of Psychoanalysis formed; D.H. Lawrence, *Sons and Lovers*
1914	Home Rule Bill passed	War with Germany 4 August; retreat from Mons		
1915	First coalition government		Treasury Agreement; Ministry of Munitions formed; rent strikes	Formation of Women's Institute
1916	Easter Rising in Dublin; second Coalition; Lloyd George Prime Minister	Battle of Jutland; Battle of the Somme	Conscription introduced; daylight saving introduced	Women's Land Army formed
1917	Establishment of Dáil Éireann	Balfour Declaration; Battle of Passchendaele; USA enters the war		
1918	Fourth Franchise Reform Act; Maurice debate; 'Coupon' election		Food rationing; conscription in Ireland; Education Act raises school leaving age to 14	Marie Stopes, *Married Love* and *Wise Parenthood*

PART 6

War and the end of empire 1919–63

27

The economy in peace and war

Boom and bust 1919–32

The fortunes of the British economy in the interwar period present enormous contradictions. Regeneration of industries sits alongside the collapse of staple industries, rising employment in new industries alongside large-scale unemployment, state intervention alongside the reapplication of *laissez-faire*, and the rise of the modern world of motor cars and radio alongside overcrowded houses with outside toilets. No single story can encapsulate such a period.

The end of the First World War in November 1918 brought a short-lived economic boom. In town and country, employment prospered as employers geared up for an expected massive rise in orders to replenish the economy and to return it to business as usual. Investment poured back into traditional industries, only to see little recapturing of markets and no prospect of a return on that investment. The result in 1920–1 was a severe recession with the loss of economic confidence, the collapse of staple industries, mass unemployment, and the prospect of tremendous political unrest with the growth of socialism and trade-union activity amongst the industrial working classes.

The international position did little to favour the economy. The First World War led to Britain's trading position weakening; overseas markets for British products fell sharply as many colonies developed their own industries (notably the cotton industry in India, which impacted badly on the Lancashire cotton industry). In 1919, the government was compelled to suspend the link between the pound and the gold standard, and this contributed to the onset of recession in 1920. But to keep faith with its imperial legacy and to maintain its former position of world economic leadership, the government fought hard to restore it again in 1925 at a value of £1 = $4.86. However, this was overvalued, leading to years of high interest rates and British products being too

Focus on

Unemployment

In 1938, the Pilgrim Trust, a charity, published an influential report called *Men Without Work* which gave the results of a detailed survey undertaken into the impact of depression on the communities, especially on the long-term unemployed. Here are two extracts.

One of the main differences between the 'working classes' and the 'middle' classes is the difference of security. This is probably a more important distinction than income level. If working men and women seem to be unduly anxious to make their sons and daughters into clerks, the anxiety behind it is not for more money but for greater security. Rightly or wrongly, they feel that the black-coated worker has a more assured position. The semi-skilled man is at the mercy of rationalisation. A week's notice may end half a lifetime's service, with no prospects, if he is elderly, but the dole, followed by a still further reduction in his means of livelihood when the old age pension comes. We take as an example a shoe laster from Leicester, who had worked thirty-seven years with one firm. 'When I heard the new manager going through and saying: "The whole of this side of the room, this room, and this room is to be stopped", I knew it would be uphill work to get something.' He went on to describe to us how he had not been able to bring himself to tell his wife the bad news when he got home, how she had noticed that something was wrong, how confident she had been that he would get work elsewhere, but how he had known that chances were heavily against him. For months and indeed often for years such men go on looking for work, and the same is true of many casual labourers. There were in the sample old men who have not a remote chance of working again but yet make it a practice to stand every morning at six o'clock at the works gates in the hope that perhaps they may catch the foreman's eye.

. . . in the Rhondda . . . there are thousands of fully employable men unemployed. An instance taken at random from this group in the Rhondda sample is a collier, aged 37, who served three years in the [First World] War and has now done no work whatever for five years. He is described as wiry and very fit, a 'great walker, who always does his physical "jerks" '. But unemployed men are not simply units of employability who can, through the medium of the dole, be put into cold storage and taken out again immediately they are needed. While they are in cold storage, things are liable to happen to them. In the case of this man what happened was that the 'will to work' had been affected; he 'seemed quite unconcerned about work'. And the other thing which it seems from the records may have happened (though in some cases it is impossible to say for certain) is that the health of one of his children had been seriously impaired by the low level at which the family has had to live.

Source: Men Without Work: A Report made to the Pilgrim Trust (Cambridge, Cambridge University Press, 1938), pp. 67, 144–5.

expensive in world markets. This contributed significantly to the poor state of British economic performance in the 1920s; investment was low and unemployment was over 10 per cent of the labour force, at a time when the US economy was performing well. Then, in October 1929, the Wall Street Crash occurred when investors in America lost confidence (especially in real estate property) and called back investment from outside of the USA, leading to a worldwide recession. This impacted very badly on Britain, forcing the country off the gold standard forever in 1931, and leading unemployment to a new high in late 1932 and early 1933.

Throughout the 1920s and into the 1930s, the industrial problem became one of overcapacity, of too many factories and production lines trying to survive poor trading conditions by competing with each other. This made matters worse rather than better. Slowly at first, the government started to intervene to reduce overcapacity in production by encouraging amalgamation of companies, the destruction of factory machinery, and the formation of cartels which could compete jointly with overseas manufacturers.

In the countryside, many tenant farmers had done well out of the war, becoming conspicuous consumers of expensive motor cars and constructing private leisure facilities (such as tennis lawns). Even rural labourers' wages had risen sharply since 1914, controlled by government wages' boards which fostered stability and assured incomes. But crisis came between 1921 and 1923. Minimum agricultural wages almost halved, hopes of land distribution for cultivation did not materialise, and labourers, angered by war profiteering by tenant farmers, began a strike in Norfolk in March 1923 against further proposed falls in wages. It was only the election of the Labour government of 1923, with its promise of wages' boards again, that quelled this unrest. However, although the countryside became stabilised, the importance of the rural economy had diminished, accounting in 1924 for a mere 4 per cent of the national income, compared with the 21 per cent it had been in 1850.[1] More fundamentally, the power of the rural elite, the Church of England and even of the dissenting chapel, had diminished sharply. The radicalisation of the rural labourers, the state-controlled food supply system, and the arrival of the urban middle classes undermined the unitary social system that had formerly underpinned the rural economy. With tourism, commuting, and increasing use of the countryside for retirement, the customary ways of thinking about and organising rural society and economy had, to a great extent, dissolved.

Recovery and war 1933–45

From 1933, there was quite significant economic recovery in Britain. Several key factors are attributed with playing leading roles in this: new industries, government policy and rearmament.

---

[1] A. Howkins, *Reshaping Rural England: A Social History 1850–1925* (London, HarperCollins, 1991), p. 288.

The international situation changed from the 1930s. Protectionism, not *laissez-faire* and the free market, came to rule the international economy. A general tariff, covering imports in general, was introduced in Britain in 1931, whilst the abandonment of the gold standard (followed by most countries) allowed the pound's value to diminish, and thus increase the overseas sales of British products. Government intervention in the economy was also important. The government became more agreeable than ever before to manipulating the economy for the benefit of private industry. Interest rates were slashed to around 2 per cent, where they stayed until 1950, leading to 'cheaper money' and higher investment in industry and cheaper mortgages in the now-booming market for housing. Meanwhile, to tackle unemployment, a regional economic policy emerged to encourage new industries to start up in depressed zones and industrial estates were created.

Action gathered pace to end the overcapacity in staple industries like textiles and shipbuilding. The government encouraged companies in these and other sectors with reduced trading positions to amalgamate or form cartels, with major financial incentives to permit the closure and destruction of plant, including the demolition of slipways in shipyards. This sought to make British industry more co-ordinated in its attempts to win overseas contracts, and allow it to modernise in technology and organisation. In many industries, this was assisted by the rearmament policy of the mid- and late 1930s. Government placed orders for military ships, munitions and other supplies ahead of another world war, and this brought renewed orders, employment and some prosperity to older industrial areas of the north of England, Scotland and South Wales. Acting under a new economic philosophy, government introduced gradually the concept of spending its way out of recession, a policy that was to stay more or less in place until the 1970s. However, there were some costs to this. The loss of market competition within British industry did little to improve productivity in many older industries; with overcapacity, it became cheaper to maintain old equipment and old work practices, contributing to the long-term slide from industrial innovation.

Moreover, it is important to recognise the social costs of the sustained depression in the staple industries between 1920 and 1939. Never less than 10 per cent of the British workforce was unemployed in these years, and even with reduction of overcapacity, families suffered severe hardship for years at a time. Middle-aged and older workers were especially badly hit, some losing jobs in their thirties in the early 1920s never to work again. To avoid problems, some companies took dramatic steps to adjust. In order to cope with the disappearance of suitable iron-ore supplies in Scotland in the early 1930s, the Motherwell steel firm of Stewart & Lloyd relocated its entire operation and workforce to the new town of Corby in Lincolnshire, only for that to experience severe decline and eventual closure some 40 years later.

At the same time, the 1930s witnessed the coming of age for some new products, many new factories and a shift in much manufacturing from the north to the south. In the mid- and later 1920s, high-technology production plants appeared in the south of Britain to manufacture cars, car components, electrical goods and pharmaceuticals. Factories arrived in the countryside, notably in the road corridors leading west and

Figure 27.1 Cowley car plant in Oxford, 1925 with the Morris Bullnose being made by
an early production line method. William Morris, later Viscount Nuffield (1877–1963), established
the Morris car company with a staff of 12 at Cowley in 1912, where it grew into one of the two
largest British car companies between the wars. It merged with the Austin car company in 1952.
Source: Topfoto

north from London. The Morris Motor Company set up in the rural village of Cowley
outside Oxford, and employed rural and village workers in the 1920s; in the 1930s it
expanded further, with the recruitment of unemployed South Wales miners. Electrical,
typewriter and car-component factories blossomed around the south and west
Midlands, and along the road corridor towards Bristol.

New industries were not totally divorced from older ones. In textiles, for instance,
there was a move from natural fibres like cotton to artificial fibres like rayon, combining
expertise in the chemical and textile industries. Yet, factories located in the south
(whether of new or old industries) seemed 'new' for several reasons. One was that they
relied on electricity rather than coal for power, so did not need to be close to coalfields,
as had been the case for much of major industrial innovation in the preceding 80 years.
Secondly, industries for consumer products could now locate closer to consumer
markets: the more prosperous middle and working classes of London and the Home
Counties. Thirdly, the labour for these industries was seen as suited to two types of
worker: unskilled women workers, dextrous in component assembly, and skilled (mostly
male) workers. Lastly, and more generally, the northern zones of the staple industries

of the north and north-east, south Wales and west central Scotland gained a reputation in the 1910s and 1920s for industrial militancy, and employers wanted to escape labour problems wherever possible and move south. It was there that the new optimism of the suburban south of England, with its generally wide streets, motor-car usage and innovatory social climate, signalled that the economic weight of the country was moving from the north for the first time since the eighteenth century.

The state was much better economically prepared for the Second World War than for the first. The biggest change of the war was transforming the economy from a mainly free-market system to a mainly centrally managed economy. In 1938, only 7 per cent of net national expenditure went on defence or war-related activities; by 1941, this had risen to 53 per cent, and in 1943, was still at 44 per cent. Consumer goods became restricted, money was raised through government bonds, and income tax was dramatically increased with the introduction of the 'Pay As You Earn' (PAYE) system in 1943 – or 'stoppages', as it was colloquially known – by which most British citizens still pay tax today. To finance the war, external funds were needed, mostly in the form of 'lend-lease' from the USA, which gave Britain access to American war materials; in all, this was valued at \$27 billion to Britain.[2]

The war reinforced many of the gains of the 1930s. Industries were given fresh government orders, employment became general, and there was full production in most sectors. It brought technological invention and spin-offs: radar, nuclear fission, the jet engine, computing and many smaller technical innovations resulting from wartime needs. There were losses, though. The trend to low investment and making-do with old machinery was exaggerated in wartime at a period of short supplies. Investment was low at the very time when production was high, and the cost would be six or seven years of lost renewal of machinery and production practices. Moreover, the need to sustain good labour relations during the war gave a strengthened hand to trade unions and, some argue, to industrial cartels, a strength that was sustained into peacetime. Once again, the economy was thrown into the loss of overseas markets as the United States and colonial nations experienced considerable expansion of their share of international trade. To a greater extent than in the First World War, Britain in 1939–45 faced the loss of overseas economic power, coupled with the mounting likelihood of losing the Empire entirely.

Agriculture was one sector of the economy that was in unremitting decline as a proportion of the national economy, and as a source of employment. Yet, it was revolutionised in the late 1930s and 1940s. Contingency plans were being laid for war with Germany. From 1935, government committees in each country prepared outlines of an agricultural policy for war – food growing, supply and labour. Preparations were laid for increasing cereal production, giving government grants to farmers for improved drainage and fertilisers, and subsidies were extended from wheat to cover oats and

---

[2] P. Howlett, 'The war-time economy, 1939–1945', in R. Floud and P. Johnson (eds), *The Cambridge Economic History of Modern Britain: Volume III: Structural Change and Growth, 1939–2000* (Cambridge, Cambridge University Press, 2004), pp. 1–2.

barley. Government bought and stored fertilisers, tractors and machinery, and grants were issued for the ploughing up of grassland during the four months before the outbreak of war in September 1939.[3]

When war came in 1939, the government put into practice many of the lessons learned more slowly in the First World War. The workforce, industry, agriculture and financial sectors were geared to the needs of war immediately. Conscription was introduced, both for military service and for key civil occupations. Civilians were recruited by conscription for things like mining (groups of young men known as the 'Bevin Boys' after the minister responsible for the plan), whilst women were called up for service in occupations ranging from post workers to air defence.

Did the interwar economy succeed?

The discussion in Chapter 20 left hanging the question: if there was some perceived slow down in the late-Victorian economy, was there greater success in the interwar period between 1919 and 1939?

It may seem strange that economic historians should see the period as one when the British economy performed relatively well. There were high levels of unemployment, economic suffering, deprivation, crime and ill-health, and the British share of world export trade in manufactured goods fell from 24 per cent in 1921–5 to 19 per cent in 1931–8.[4] It is true that many industries were in deep trouble, and that Britain's position in international trade worsened with the decline of the imperial market and the rise of the American and Japanese economies. Yet, there is significant evidence that the economy started to develop in ways that were to set it in the future on a course of stronger economic growth and improved standards of living for its people.

Between 1924 and 1937, output grew more rapidly than between 1873 and 1913, and, moreover, labour productivity grew only marginally more slowly than over the same period. This is the foundational evidence for there having been a real economic breakthrough. An important role was played by government, which moved away from reliance on the free market to an unprecedented degree of intervention in the economy, although initially, it failed to intervene quickly or vigorously enough to guide the closure of unprofitable industries and enhance the competitiveness of new industries. There is some merit in the argument that the maintenance of empire took much time and money, and directed attention from the development of a modern and vibrant economy. But the government attempt to reduce overcapacity was working by the early 1930s. Moreover, there is evidence that product innovation was improving as

---

[3] A. Howkins, *The Death of Rural England: A Social History of the Countryside since 1900* (London, Routledge, 2003), p. 116.

[4] S. Bowden and D.M. Higgins, 'British industry in the interwar years', in R. Floud and P. Johnson (eds), *The Cambridge Economic History of Modern Britain: Volume II: Economic Maturity, 1860–1939* (Cambridge, Cambridge University Press, 2004), p. 380.

research and development by British firms improved. The formation, encouraged by government, of Imperial Chemical Industries (ICI) in 1926, united four smaller chemical companies, creating the first major multi-division conglomerate in British ownership, and forming a leading high-technology company with considerable investment in new products.

Overall, the British economy was moving steadily from the primary end of production (mining and manufacturing) to the tertiary, to retail, professional and personal services, education, and recreation and tourism. Those working in the retail and wholesale trade, for instance, numbered some 1.99 million in 1901, but 3.09 million in 1938.[5] This reflected in part the development of a more consumer-orientated economy, in which improved travel and communications enabled swifter distribution of goods and greater social access to many products and services, as well as the emergence of new opportunities for employment – for instance, in the BBC, formed in 1927 as a public radio corporation.

Despite these strengths, there were ways in which the economy was not working well enough. For one thing, Britain was slow in the 1920s in modernisation of production. The spread of electricity did not take place in the 1920s in the way it did in many other countries, which completed their national grids in that decade. This allowed the USA to march ahead in manufacturing innovation and productivity. On the other hand, when the British national grid was completed in the mid-1930s, it was able to proceed more efficiently than other countries, learning the lessons of others' mistakes.

New industries used to be seen as being of enormous importance to the industrial recovery of the 1930s, but this is now debated. They employed only around 6 per cent of the total workforce, and though some performed very well by comparison with other nations (Britain exported more cars by 1938 than Germany, Italy or France[6]), compared to staple industries, the new industries did relatively poorly in penetrating overseas markets. So, staple industries remained vital to exports, employment and national income. But here, there remained problems of industrial leadership – including in large companies, where what has been described as a 'cosy amateurism' still prevailed.[7] And despite new products and improving productivity, there was too much reliance on British technology. Overall, technological inventiveness had long since passed from Britain: between 1876 and 1926, the USA accounted for 44 per cent of major inventions, Germany 18 per cent and Britain only 14 per cent.[8] Economic chauvinism was still a factor in the British boardroom, and there was insufficient

[5] M. Thomas, 'The service sector', in R. Floud and P. Johnson (eds), *The Cambridge Economic History of Modern Britain: Volume II: Economic Maturity, 1860–1939* (Cambridge, Cambridge University Press, 2004), p. 101.

[6] S. Bowden and D.M. Higgins, 'British industry in the interwar years', p. 380.

[7] Terry Gourvish, quoted in N. Crafts, 'Long-run growth', in R. Floud and P. Johnson (eds), *The Cambridge Economic History of Modern Britain: Volume II: Economic Maturity, 1860–1939* (Cambridge, Cambridge University Press, 2004), p. 22.

[8] G.B. Magee, 'Manufacturing and technological change', in R. Floud and P. Johnson (eds), *The Cambridge Economic History of Modern Britain: Volume II: Economic Maturity, 1860–1939* (Cambridge, Cambridge University Press, 2004), p. 89.

investment in American machines. This may have been compounded by the inability of shareholders to hold the managers properly to account.

A final issue is that the way in which 'economic success' has to be gauged changed significantly in the interwar years. In 1919, British government firmly believed in three pillars of economic thought inherited from the Victorian era and which it had, essentially, propagandised to the world. These were: first, to maintain the gold standard and London as the centre of the world financial system; secondly, to maintain free trade; and thirdly, to keep government spending small and always in balance with income.[9] By 1945, government had repudiated the gold standard, and the London Stock Exchange had lost considerable leadership to Wall Street in New York; free trade was replaced by protectionism and tariffs to protect both old and new industries against competition; and government economic intervention had mushroomed at both national level and micro-economic levels, with massive growth in expenditure. The principle of the managed economy had been created in the 1930s, in which economic signals to industry were backed up by heavy spending, grants and subsidies. At the same time, welfare policy had developed, which required the state to allow families to overcome cyclical recessions (through benefits for unemployment, illness, childbirth and death) and become better educated with more state schools and funded university places and grants. In this way, economic success was no longer judged on government's low level of economic intervention, but by how well government did the job of managing the economy.

From austerity to prosperity 1946–63

The period from 1945 to the early 1970s is now widely regarded by economic historians as 'the golden years' when British economic growth was strong, at an average of 3 per cent per annum. Economic recovery was regulated by the government, with economic advisors who encouraged a mixture of nationalisation and cartelisation to maximise efficiency. The coal industry was nationalised under the National Coal Board, iron and steel under the British Iron and Steel Federation, the rail network in British Railways, road haulage under British Road Services, and a number of other companies were fostered or created by government to run the economy on managed principles. This rescued staple industries, and brought nationalisation as the solution to industrial problems. Government loans (cheaper than commercial ones) paid for new investment in machinery or, in many cases, for the patching of old machinery. But, in the main, in the 1940s and 1950s, this policy seemed to work well.

However, the 1940s and 1950s witnessed economic problems. Up to 1964, productivity of British workers was not strong, and lost ground to the USA, Japan and France.

---

[9] J.D. Tomlinson, *Public Policy and the Economy since 1900* (Oxford, Oxford University Press, 1990), pp. 10–11.

Moreover, growth was cyclical. Until 1950, Britain sustained the 'cheap money' policy that had been introduced in 1931 and under which economic recovery had been nurtured. But this changed in the early 1950s with the introduction of the policy of 'stop-go' by which the government signalled by low interest rates and tax changes that the economy should 'go' for growth. By the time inflation and excessive consumption had been generated after 6 or 7 years, it signalled by high interest rates that the economy should 'stop', before starting the cycle again. This 'stop-go' cycle of 11–13 years had major shortcomings. Primarily, industry could not plan for long-term investment. An adverse balance of payments was an ever-present problem, because in times of 'go' for growth, industrialists and merchants substituted imports for domestic products, the production of which was stifled in the previous 'stop' period. As a result, investment lagged consistently behind other countries.

After the war, rationing did not end immediately; indeed, rationing became stricter. Furniture stayed rationed until 1948, clothes until 1949, and some food until 1954. Government policy laid emphasis on austerity and generated a *Zeitgeist* of gloom and restrictiveness. As late as 1951, the meat ration was cut, creating deep dissatisfaction with the Labour government, and contributing greatly to the election of Churchill's Conservative administration in the general election of that year. During the 1950s, food production was heavily controlled by the state, leading to some changes in response to consumer demand. Egg production rose with the introduction of first deep-litter sheds and then battery methods (with a pen for each hen) in large warehouses. Chicken production was also increased, so that it was transformed from being a luxury in the British diet to being a staple.

In the post-war years, a new geography of British agriculture emerged. The south and east of England re-emerged as the prosperous cereal-growing belt. Wartime emphasis on cereals, backed up by government subsidy and technical support, became a permanent policy in peacetime, and the government now regarded it as its duty to ensure the fertility of the land and maintain farms and farm buildings. Economic stability became the watchword, and, to this end, the Ministry of Agriculture created a powerful administrative system to provide a wide variety of subsidies, incentives and directions to farmers by pumping large amounts of money into the rural economy. Large cereal producers did best – in Kent, East Anglia, Cambridgeshire and Lincolnshire, especially. Smaller, mixed farmers, notably in upland areas of the north of England, Wales and Highland Scotland, fared much less well from this subsidy regime. Part of the transformation was the shift in the 1950s and 1960s towards machine-based farming in which labourers were replaced very rapidly by mechanisation. This was partly because workers found more lucrative employment in new industries or in towns, but partly also because the costs of labour (often including tied houses) became too much for farmers to sustain.

By 1963, the sense of economic austerity was slackening as consumer choice and spending grew, as taste and diet modernised in the post-war world. Economic horizons were rising, though difficult issues still lay ahead.

Workers and trade unions

The interwar period was a difficult time for millions of British workers. The downturn in the economy, and the severity of depression in the heavy industries, mining and in textiles caused wide-scale unemployment. Money wages were hit by the decline in trade, reaching an interwar low in June 1933 in the shadow of the Wall Street Crash. But during the 1930s, conditions improved slowly, with hours of work shortening, holidays lengthening, and, with the Holidays with Pay Act of 1938, there was the prospect of paid holidays for all workers (except agricultural workers and domestic servants), albeit delayed by the war. For those in work, standards of living were generally rising, and overall conditions for families were improving in the 1930s as a result of state intervention – not just on paid holidays, but also on minimum wages for most low-paid workers. The state intervened in regulating wages in road haulage, and wage regulation boards operated in many industries. Government became more accessible to workers' organisations, and the state became more proactive in regulating conditions and pay. Workers benefited from other government policies, including rearmament from 1933, and from rationalisation of industries like cotton.

The British trade-union movement experienced fluctuating fortunes during the period. Unions emerged strengthened from the First World War. They had grown rapidly during wartime, defending workers in heavy industries from deskilling and dilution (when unskilled, non-unionised workers were introduced to push forward the war effort). The need to maintain industrial peace in wartime assisted the cause of unions, and in the mining, shipbuilding and engineering industries they were dominant by the early 1920s. At the same time, socialist ideas gained ground, as reflected in the rapid advance of the Labour Party. Trade unionism boomed between 1917 and 1920, culminating in 48.2 per cent (8,253,000) of British workers being trade-union members in 1920 – a density higher than at any time again until 1974. British trade unions were hit hard by the world recession of 1921–2, and again, although less severely, by that of 1931–3, reaching a low point of membership density of 22.9 per cent (4,350,000) of workers in 1933. Yet, unions during the 1930s recovered their membership strength, but not so much their ability to force industrial conflict. Strike action decreased, especially in England. Indeed days lost through strikes hit a low point in 1933–9 only matched by the 1990s, with coal mining accounting for 48.6 per cent of the loss – of which 46 per cent took place in Scotland and a further 24 per cent in South Wales.[10] Things improved thereafter, though slowly, to reach a membership of 8,603,000 (43.0 per cent) in 1946.[11] Unions experienced highly volatile fortunes, with the interwar period being both a high point and a low point.

---

[10] C. Wrigley, *British Trade Unions since 1933* (Cambridge, Cambridge University Press, 2002), p. 11.

[11] Ibid., pp. 7, 18.

Trade unions were overwhelmingly for male workers, and were to remain so until late in the twentieth century; by 1945, still only 16 per cent of female workers were in unions, compared to 39.3 per cent of male workers. Militancy was often stronger where the influence of the Communist Party was greatest, notably in mining areas. The coal industry was racked by many industrial disputes, with major strikes in 1921 and 1925–6, the latter leading to the general strike when, for six days, the Trades Union Congress called all workers out in sympathy with striking miners. The general strike bitterly divided the nation, with large numbers of striking transport and other workers being replaced by bands of organised strike-breakers, led by members of the middle classes. The strike did not succeed, and for the miners the bitterness of these years lasted well into the 1940s, when they remained the most likely to strike.

In the Second World War, men and women were conscripted not just to military service but to other forms of essential war work. From December 1941, all men and women (other than those looking after children) were made liable to national service, and the unions gave assistance to government in agreeing to restrict strikes without warning in return for concessions on rationing and subsidies. The result was extended collective bargaining between unions and employers, with greater constructive planning and sorting out of problems, thereby strengthening unions for the post-war world. Among the expected concessions was the creation after the war of the welfare state (see Chapter 32). In this sense, one of the great victories of the Labour movement was the product not of industrial action but of wartime emergency.

Further reading

Floud, R. and Johnson, P. (eds), *The Cambridge Economic History of Modern Britain: Volume II: Economic Maturity, 1860–1939* (Cambridge, Cambridge University Press, 2004)

Howkins, A., *Reshaping Rural England: A Social History 1850–1925* (London, HarperCollins, 1991)

Howkins, A., *The Death of Rural England: A Social History of the Countryside since 1900* (London, Routledge, 2003)

Tomlinson, J.D., *Public Policy and the Economy since 1900* (Oxford, Oxford University Press, 1990)

Wrigley, C., *British Trade Unions since 1933* (Cambridge, Cambridge University Press, 2002)

28

Political change 1919–39

The 1920s and 1930s still tend to be looked upon as the bleakest decades of the twentieth century, when industrial depression, unemployment and class conflict seemed to dominate. The political leaders are viewed today as having been of second rank, and are generally perceived to have failed both in tackling domestic problems and responding to international ones. Historians have tried to modify such views by emphasising the constraints under which politicians had to work and recognising the huge task that recovery from the effects of the First World War involved. Against the collapse of many of the traditional heavy industries needs to be set the growth of new ones providing the consumer goods for a growing middle class (see Chapter 27). Perhaps most striking was the ability of the country to survive economic difficulties without a depression on the scale of that of the United States, without class conflict of the level apparent in France, and without the resort to fascism that came in Germany, Italy and other parts of central Europe.

Adjusting to the peace

The armistice ending war took effect on 11 November 1918, and Parliament was dissolved three days later. The election of December 1918 was fought under a much extended franchise, that now gave the vote to all men over 21, instead of confining it to householders. It also gave the vote to women over 30. Actually, more women than men gained the vote in 1918. The Reform Act of 1884 had not given Britain a democratic franchise (see Chapter 23). Indeed, amongst those countries that had representative government, Britain was the one that fell furthest short of universal suffrage. Studies of the electorate in 1911 find that something like 4.5 million men who would have had the vote under a system of manhood suffrage failed, for a variety of reasons, to be included on the electoral register. Electoral reform in 1918 changed that, with an electorate that rose from under 8 million in 1910 to over 21 million in 1918. This had major implications for politics and required new approaches and different organisation.

The Conservatives, even before 1914, had recognised the value of organisation and of symbols, co-opting the flag, patriotism and Empire into their rituals, and they very successfully made an appeal to property owners and to the deferential working class. The Labour Party, too, gained. The majority of the new voters were young and working-class, many organised in trade unions during the war, when union membership grew. Firmly identified as the trade-union party, Labour was able to tap into a growing class consciousness amongst industrial workers. The Liberal Party, rent with internal division, was slower to adapt to the new mass electorate.

Conservatives also gained from the vote going to women over 30. The argument for women getting the vote had been going on since before 1832. They came up against the claim that women needed to be protected from the public world of politics and to be seen as part of a family in which a man – father, husband or brother – mediated between them and the state. When feminists began to challenge this, they were met with ridicule or anger. There were also party-political arguments that stood in the way. Although Liberals were, in principle, in favour of a gradual extension of the franchise, their experience in the aftermath of 1884 was that the gainers from such an extension were the Conservatives. They feared that the same would happen with women voters. Women were generally believed to be more under the influence of the churches and, therefore, more conservative. Before 1914, campaigns for votes for women won support from some men in all political parties, but in no party did it have a high priority.

The weight of opinion amongst historians now seems to be that the influence of Mrs Emmeline Pankhurst and the direct action of the Women's Social and Political Union, formed in 1903, has been exaggerated. It is generally claimed that the violence of their union did not shift public opinion in their favour, even when they were forcibly fed during hunger strikes in prison. Rather, it had the reverse effect. Most recent work suggests that the behind-the-scenes efforts of moderate groups such as the much larger and more representative National Union of Women's Suffrage Societies, formed in 1897 by Mrs Millicent Garrett Fawcett, was much more effective in winning influential converts.

The fourth Representation of the People Act emerged in 1918 from a conference set up to deal with the problem of drawing up a new register. Who was going to vote? The existing residential qualification would have excluded heroic soldiers and sailors but admitted 'shirkers'. It would have excluded those key industrial workers who had moved to work in the munitions' factories. The old measures of who was 'fit' to vote could no longer be applied and universal enfranchisement seemed the only option. The conference proposed a shortened period of residence to qualify. Only at the end did the conference turn to the issue of women. An equal franchise was rejected lest it result in more women than men voters, and, instead, it was proposed that the vote

Focus on

The Labour Party in 1918

From *Labour and the New Social Order*, January 1918. Drafted by the Fabian intellectual, Sidney Webb and by Arthur Henderson, MP this Labour Party Statement of Policy contained the first commitment by the Labour Party to an extensive socialist programme.

What we now promulgate as our policy, whether for opposition or for office, is not merely this or that specific reform, but a deliberately thought out, systematic, and comprehensive plan for that immediate social rebuilding which any Ministry, whether or not it grapple with the problem, will be driven to undertake. The Four Pillars of the House that we propose to erect, resting upon the common foundation of the Democratic control of society in all its activities, may be termed, respectively:

(a) The Universal Enforcement of the National Minimum;

(b) The Democratic Control of Industry;

(c) The Revolution in National Finance;

(d) The Surplus Wealth for the Common Good.

. . . All these laws purporting to prevent any Degradation of the Standard of Life need considerable improvement and extension before they can fulfil their purpose of securing to every worker, by hand or by brain, at least the prescribed Minimum of Health, Education, Leisure, and Subsistence, whilst their administration leaves much to be desired. . . . The Labour Party stands not merely for the principle of the Common Ownership of the nation's land, to be applied as suitable opportunities occur, but also, specifically for the immediate Nationalisation of the Railways, Mines and the production of Electrical Power . . .

For the raising of the greater part of the revenue now required the Labour Party looks to the direct taxation of the incomes above the necessary cost of family maintenance; and for the requisite effort to pay off the National Debt, to the direct taxation of private fortunes both during life and death.

. . . One main Pillar of the House that the Labour Party intend to build is the future appropriation of the Surplus, not to the enlargement of any individual fortune, but to the Common Good. It is from this constantly arising Surplus (to be secured, on the one hand, by Nationalisation and Municipalisation and, on the other, by the steeply graduated Taxation of Private Income and Riches) that will have to be found the new capital which the community day by day needs for the perpetual improvement and increase of the various enterprises, for we shall decline to be dependent on the usury-exacting financiers . . .

Source: Labour and the New Social Order (Labour Party Statement of Policy), January 1918.

should go to women occupiers or the wives of occupiers over the age of 30. In the changed politics of 1918, Liberals, Tories and Labour members who had supported women's suffrage could unite to defeat the anti-suffragists, while others were anxious to ensure that the militant movement did not revive. Fewer than 60 MPs voted against the measure.

The election of December 1918 was dubbed by Asquith the 'coupon' election, as Lloyd George and Bonar Law, keen to maintain a coalition, endorsed those Conservatives, Liberals and Labour on whose support they could hope to count, and punished those Liberals who had voted against the government in the Maurice debate (see Chapter 26). In the patriotic fervour of victory, 483 'couponed' members were returned, consisting of 145 Lloyd George Liberals and 333 Conservatives plus some independents. Asquithian Liberals were reduced to a mere 36 MPs, with all the leaders, including Asquith, losing their seats. Labour had 60 MPs and, thanks to better organisation and more candidates, nearly twice as many votes as the Liberals. Ireland returned 72 Sinn Féinners (including the first woman MP, Countess Markiewicz) who declined to take their seats. The real gainers were the Conservatives. Lloyd George was not intent on throwing in his lot with the Conservatives, but he believed that new structures were necessary for a novel situation. In one way, of course, he was reflecting that coalition mentality that he had shown before 1914. It was a powerful government. Bonar Law and Lloyd George complemented each other and they were surrounded by people, like Churchill and Balfour, who were often slightly detached from their party.

There was an attempt to pick up some of the social reform policies that had been pushed before the war. The Ministry for Reconstruction came up with ambitious plans for new housing; for the abolition of the Poor Law; for improved health provision; for the expansion of education; for land settlement for demobilised soldiers; for better industrial relations. An Education Act of 1918, that made secondary education compulsory to the age of 14, promised a new school building programme, encouraged technical education, extended evening classes and dramatically improved teachers' salaries. A Housing Act for the first time required local authorities to provide housing. The promise of 'homes fit for heroes' had a powerful resonance with returning soldiers. Unemployment insurance was extended from the specific industries to which it had been confined in 1911 to all workers who were insured for health, and the level of old-age pensions was raised. Industrial councils were established to try to iron out problems in industrial relations. There was a strong hope that a new era of social relationships was about to emerge.

The hopes were soon quashed. Powerful vested interests put obstacles in the way of reform. Local authorities were slow to seize the opportunities offered by the Housing Act. Unions were resistant to the concept of industrial councils. The middle classes were increasingly critical of the costs of reform. It was not long before the Conservatives began to rebel against what they saw as lavish state expenditure. The immediate post-war economic boom had come to an end, profits were harder to get and there was a demand for tax cuts. The balance was now tilted strongly against the supporters of social reform in all parties. By the autumn of 1921, the reform plans were being ruthlessly axed. The housing programme was curtailed, education expansion halted and teachers' salaries cut.

Talk of social harmony faded when trade unions, with membership much enhanced, pressed for concessions. Lloyd George increasingly hardened his attitudes, arguing that the state had to defeat strikes: 'Failure to do so would inevitably lead to a Soviet Republic.' After the formation of the Communist Party of Great Britain in July 1920 from an amalgamation of earlier socialist groups, overexcited reports from the Special Branch saw a Bolshevik threat in every industrial dispute. The fact that many of the most bitter disputes were in the crucial coal industry made the government concerned about maintaining supplies and the Emergency Powers Act of 1920 incorporated many of the features of the war-time DORA, allowing the government to declare a state of emergency and to use troops to maintain supplies.

The Irish treaty

In Ireland, outside Ulster, Sinn Féin MPs had set up a provisional government with ministries paralleling the official ones. The policy was to make British government impossible by creating maximum disorder. The government responded by sending in an ill-disciplined, auxiliary force largely made up of ex-soldiers – the 'Black and Tans' – and by often arbitrary arrests and reprisals, the effect of which was to increase support for the IRA. In November 1920, in a spectacular *coup*, the Irish Republican Army (IRA) assassinated 12 Special Branch officers in Dublin. Later that day, the Black and Tans opened fire on a crowd at a football match, resulting in 12 deaths. Martial law was imposed. Such actions alienated British as well as Irish public opinion, but failed to crush the IRA.

A recognition by some in the IRA that the British would not be driven out by force alone, and a growing concern in Britain at the cost in lives and at the international (particularly American) criticism of its Irish policy, led to a truce in the summer of 1921 and negotiations began. The Government of Ireland Act had already been passed at the end of 1920, partitioning the country between north and south until unity by consent could be achieved. By it, there would be devolved parliaments in Belfast and in Dublin, linked by a Council of Ireland. The hope of most British politicians was that Ulster's separation from the rest of Ireland would be temporary, but, by insisting on there being only six, as opposed to the traditional nine, counties, in what was now called Northern Ireland, Ulster Protestants ensured that there would be a Protestant majority for the foreseeable future.

The Union ended for all but the six Ulster counties in December 1921. Attempts to persuade James Craig and his government in Northern Ireland to accept some all-Ireland arrangement were blocked by Bonar Law's determination that there could be no coercion of Ulster. The Irish Free State, as the rest of the island became, was to have fiscal autonomy, a parliament and its own army, in return for an oath of fidelity to the British Crown (which for many republicans proved an impossible stumbling block) and the retention of a naval base. To the Irish negotiator, Michael Collins, the treaty gave Ireland 'the freedom to achieve freedom', but it was rejected by Eamonn De Valera and a group of irreconcilables who could not swallow the oath of fidelity. In the end the treaty was accepted by the Dáil Éirann by a majority of only seven, and the new state embarked on a bitter civil war between those who accepted dominion status and those who wanted nothing less than a republic.

Meanwhile, in the new Northern Ireland, some initial attempts to conciliate Catholics came up against resistance from the Protestant working class. There were fears that if such populist sentiments were not responded to then the working class would turn to socialism. With the Free State increasingly emphasising its Catholic nature, Sir James Craig declared that 'we are a Protestant Parliament and a Protestant State'.

End of coalition

Lloyd George and Bonar Law spent a great deal of 1919 in Paris at the peace conference, largely putting constraints on President Wilson's grander ambitions, but failing to prevent the fragmentation of much of east and central Europe. The Treaty of Versailles that emerged in June 1919 was a harsh one, but, thanks to Lloyd George, it was more moderate towards Germany than the French would have wished, although the level of reparations being demanded was still unrealistic. Fairly quickly, the European arrangements began crumbling and Britain found itself increasingly isolated. The United States had withdrawn into isolation, refusing to participate in the League of Nations. Tensions with France were persistent as the French sought to obtain reparations from Germany, while Britain was ready to waive some of these for the sake of restoring normal economic relations. Lloyd George even found himself at odds with the Dominions when he seemed to be ready to enter a war with Turkey alongside the Greeks.

Failures in foreign policy undermined Conservative confidence in Lloyd George. Many Conservative backbenchers had found it difficult to swallow the Irish settlement, granting power to a government in the south whom they regarded as terrorists. Also, there was still a strong tariff-reform element in the party and they felt that the coalition Liberals were standing in the way of reform. The style of leadership did not help. The government majority was too large for the leadership to have to pay attention to the rank and file, and decisions were made with little effort at consultation. Furthermore, an air of corruption began to gather around the government as stories of the selling of knighthoods and baronetcies to boost Lloyd George's election chest became commonplace.[1] Bonar Law was persuaded to return to active politics and to break with the government. The chief advocate for this was the little-known Stanley Baldwin, President of the Board of Trade since 1921. Lloyd George resigned and Bonar Law became Prime Minister, but survived only six months. Of all the Conservatives

---

[1] The Order of the British Empire had been Lloyd George's invention in 1917.

who had been in office under Lloyd George, only a handful were willing to enter Law's Cabinet. The others remained faithful to Lloyd George, regarding Baldwin and his associates as nonentities with 'second-class brains'.

An election was called right away and the Conservative platform was 'tranquillity and freedom from adventures at home and abroad'. They gained a majority of 88 over all the other parties. Baldwin was Chancellor of the Exchequer and so had the unenviable task of trying to settle the issue of Britain's war-loan debt to the United States. The United States was pressing for agreement on levels of interest and length of repayment period. Britain was owed more by her former European allies than she owed the United States, but the former were refusing to pay until reparations were forthcoming from Germany. Baldwin's deal eased the British terms of repayment to the United States, but nonetheless accepted the necessity of beginning repayment right away.

When, in May 1923, Bonar Law resigned, due to terminal cancer, it was Baldwin who succeeded him, rather than the 'coalitionist' Lord Curzon, as some expected. He was faced with two party problems. The first was to get the leading Conservative coalitionists back into the fold; the second was to tackle the perennial issue of tariff reform – or protectionism, as it was now called. His solution was to call another election and to commit the party to protectionism, an action which some thought was 'suicide during a fit of temporary insanity'. There was growing concern about the rising levels of unemployment, with warnings of the dangers these posed to political stability, and Baldwin had concluded that protecting the home market was one way of stemming the rise.

The election of December 1923 produced a stalemate; no party could form a government without the help of another. The result was, however, a rebuff for protectionism since the Conservatives lost 86 seats. The majority of commercial, financial and manufacturing interests, together with the Labour movement, remained firmly wedded to free trade. Asquith and Lloyd George fought the election under the same free-trade banner and there was a slight revival in Liberal fortunes, with 158 MPs. The real gainers were the Labour Party, which jumped to 191 seats and a higher percentage of the vote than the Liberals. When Parliament assembled in January, Baldwin was defeated on a vote of confidence. Asquith supported Labour, believing that he was acting strictly within the constitution, since Conservative policies had so obviously been rejected. But he also held the view that if there were to be a Labour government then it should be tried under the safest of conditions, when it was in a minority and could be voted out of office at any time.

Labour government 1924

Politics had become very firmly about class. Since 1918, Conservatives had blamed Labour – always described as socialism – and the trade unions for pushing up wages, undermining the nation, lowering productivity and threatening property. Labour blamed the Tories for exploiting the workers. Both ignored the Liberal Party. Indeed, Ramsay MacDonald, again and again, indicated his deep dislike for and distrust of the Liberals. The last vestiges of Lib-Lab co-operation had disappeared and the Liberals, who could not appeal to the loyalties of any social class, went into near-terminal decline.

Labour had been steadily gaining ground since the war. Between 1918 and 1922, Labour Party organisation was streamlined and, with the Irish issue out of the way, Catholics in Britain swung to Labour. The party had a steady income from the political levy on trade unions and local Labour parties had been established in most constituencies. Ramsay MacDonald, who had been returned to the Commons and elected as leader in 1922, was invited to form a minority government. A few on the left of the party argued against accepting office, but MacDonald was convinced that Labour had to prove that it was capable of government. There was a debate within Labour about the policies to pursue. Should they opt for a cautious policy in order to remain in power as long as possible or should they embark on a full socialist programme and achieve what they could before being put out? MacDonald's instincts were always towards caution. He did not believe in the inevitability of class warfare. He did, however, believe in the inevitability of socialism by evolutionary means.

The government was faced, as were all governments of the interwar years, with the question of what to do about unemployment. It was a double problem of how to remove the cause and how to relieve the unemployed. On the former it did little because ministers did not know what to do. They blamed capitalism, but had no idea how to alter the system, and even where there was widespread agreement, such as on nationalisation of the coal mines, there was no way that such a measure was going to get through. Philip Snowden, the Chancellor of the Exchequer, was one of the most conservative and unimaginative of Labour ministers and quickly succumbed to control by the mandarins of the Treasury.

What caused disquiet in Conservative circles was the decision to recognise the Soviet Union, to give it 'most favoured nation' trading status and to grant it a loan. Despite the moderate actions of the government, there were still those who saw it as little removed from communism, despite the fact that the Communist Party of Great Britain had been constantly refused affiliation to the Labour Party. It was this suspicion that finally brought down the government. The editor of the communist *Workers' Weekly* was arrested and charged under the Incitement to Mutiny Act of 1797 for an article calling on the army never to open fire on the workers. After protests by Labour backbenchers, the case was dropped and the Conservatives claimed that illicit pressure had been applied on the legal authorities. In a vote of confidence in October 1924, the Liberals (perhaps increasingly disgruntled by MacDonald's failure to consult them) and the Conservatives defeated the government and MacDonald called an election.

Just before the election the *Daily Mail* published the notorious Zinoviev letter, purportedly from the secretary of the Communist International, plotting subversion with the left in Britain. It was probably a fabrication by crazed elements in the secret service who saw no difference between Ramsay MacDonald and Lenin, but it fitted with a campaign that tried to present the Labour government as marching at the orders of Moscow. In fact, Labour's share of the vote increased. It was the Liberal vote that collapsed, giving the Conservatives a majority of 149 over all other parties. The Liberals had shrunk to 40 MPs and had largely disappeared from urban England.

Conservative government 1924–9

Stanley Baldwin was a shrewd politician who passed himself off as an easy-going country gentleman, and who sought to model himself on Disraeli, emphasising what came to be called 'one-nation conservatism'. With unemployment continuing to rise, there were demands for more positive action by the state, but most on the right considered that the way out of depression was to reduce state expenditure. The decision by Churchill, who had, rather surprisingly, become the Chancellor of the Exchequer, to return sterling to the gold standard in 1925 was in line with the advice that he was getting from all the powerful financial interests. It also tied in with a Churchillian desire to return Britain to its pre-war standing. Only the economist Maynard Keynes pointed out that the effect of an overvalued sterling would be to depress the economy, squeeze profits and generate more unemployment (see Chapter 27).

Baldwin favoured moderate social reforms with little ideological packaging and, compared with more modern governments, his lack of action is remarkable. However, in 1926, he drove through a bill that gave a Central Electricity Board the monopoly of selling electricity and the task of creating a national grid, which, it has been argued, 'was quite possibly the most important single Act passed between the wars'.[2] Baldwin's hopes of a period of industrial peace were quickly dashed by mining disputes. The mine owners were demanding wage cuts, longer hours and the abolition of the minimum wage. Faced with a threat of a general strike, the Cabinet buckled to pressure and agreed to continue the wartime subsidy to the industry for a further nine months to allow a Royal Commission under Lord Samuel to look at the situation. The government used the time while the Samuel Commission was sitting to prepare contingency plans should a miners' strike again ensue. Emergency powers were put in place and, in October 1925, nine leading members of the Communist Party were locked up. The Samuel Commission recommended wage cuts, but not longer hours, and urged that steps be taken to rationalise the industry by bringing together some of the many small companies into larger, more efficient units.

The end of the subsidy led first to a miners' strike followed by a sympathetic general strike in May 1926. The evidence is of substantial solidarity in sympathy with the strike amongst workers, and equal solidarity in hostility to it amongst the middle classes. Despite protestations to the contrary, there was a powerful class-war element in the attitudes exposed. The TUC leadership was taken aback by the vehemence of the response of ministers like Churchill. Government preparations to maintain supplies

---

[2] K. Middlemas and J. Barnes, *Baldwin: A Biography* (London, Macmillan, 1969), p. 394.

Figure 28.1 General strike, 1926. Strike breakers at St Enoch's Station, Glasgow. There were plenty of volunteers ready to break the strike. Some were non-union workers, others were railway company managers, while some were businessmen and university students.
Source: Science & Society Picture Library

were well in hand; the preparations of the TUC for such an eventuality had been minimal. After nine days, with signs of solidarity cracking, the TUC called off the general strike and the miners were left on their own, battling on until the end of 1926.

There were demands for a curb on trade unions and the TUC in their negotiations with government had done nothing to obtain guarantees against victimisation of activists, which was widespread. The 1927 Trade Disputes and Trade Union Act outlawed general strikes, the legal eight-hour day in mining was suspended and trade unionists were specifically to opt in for payment of their union's political levy in support of the Labour Party rather than, as previously, opt out if they were against it.

Alongside this, however, there was some social legislation coming from the former Liberal Unionist tradition of the party. The son of Joseph Chamberlain, Neville Chamberlain, the Minister of Health, brought in a Contributory Pensions Bill, that included widows' and orphans' pensions and pushed up the rate of payment for old-age pensioners. In one sense, it was a completion of Lloyd George's pre-war schemes, but it was also different. Lloyd George's pension had been funded from taxation. The

Conservatives had reduced both income tax and super tax and now pensions would have to be financed from flat-rate insurance contributions. The trend towards graduated taxation which had come gradually from the early twentieth century was halted.

There was still an attempt to finance unemployment benefit from unemployment insurance. But this was impossible in a situation where more than a million were unemployed, many of them not insured. A number of Labour-controlled councils and boards of guardians were paying higher wages and higher rates of poor relief than those approved by the Ministry of Health. In 1926, Chamberlain moved against these. When boards had overspent, the ministry was empowered to replace elected guardians by nominees of its own choice. The Unemployment Act of 1927 removed more of this problem by allowing many who had hitherto been on poor relief to qualify for unemployment benefit.

Chamberlain then turned to local government in which, as a former mayor of Birmingham (like his father before him), he was a great believer. There had been no alteration in local government boundary areas since 1888 and 1894, despite substantial changes in the size and location of population. On top of this, different official bodies covered different areas. The 1929 Local Government Act, one of the major pieces of twentieth-century legislation, created fewer but larger authorities. Most major services were to be concentrated under the county councils and county boroughs. The boards of guardians, that had administered the Poor Law since 1834, were abolished and their powers transferred to the public assistance committees of the county councils. Chamberlain was largely left to do as he liked. Baldwin played little part in shaping policies and many on the right were not entirely happy. Baldwin's motto, both at home and abroad, was 'safety first', but he also had to face the realities of a party where business was well represented in both Parliament and in the constituencies. They were showing signs of disenchantment with a government that had, despite its sentiments, failed to reduce expenditure and taxation.

Labour government 1929–31

Yet another Representation of the People Act preceded the 1929 election. No sooner was the 1918 Act passed than the illogicality of confining the vote to women over 30 became apparent. By the Equal Franchise Act of 1928, the vote was given to women between the ages of 21 and 30, bringing them into line with men. The electorate increased by more than 7 million, with women outnumbering men. The Conservative press reflected concerns about giving the vote to young women, dubbed 'flappers', who, with their short skirts, bobbed hairstyles and tastes in music seemed to be casting off the patterns of the older generation. Many Conservatives would have been happier with a minimum age of 25 for both sexes, but there was a recognition that there could be no question of taking the vote away from young men and, against the opposition of Churchill, there was an acceptance of the inevitable and an optimism that even young women would be Conservative.

In spite of some clever appeals to women and dire warnings of the threats to society from socialism, the Conservatives lost out badly. Labour became the largest party for the first time, but still a minority. They came to power in May when there seemed to be shoots of improvement. Exports were going up slightly and there was even a slight fall in the unemployment figures. Industrial spokesmen were urging the government to do nothing to threaten the improvement, to avoid any further social legislation and maintain curbs on the trade unions. Lloyd George and the rump of the Liberals with a programme of public works would have supported Labour in efforts to reduce unemployment, but to most on the left, any collaboration with Lloyd George was unthinkable. From within the ranks of the Labour government, Oswald Mosley proposed active government intervention: bringing in tariffs to help restore the home market; controlling the banks to stop overseas investment at the expense of domestic investment; raising pensions and the school leaving age to take people out of the labour market; interfering in industry; and establishing public work schemes. But the Parliamentary Labour Party rejected the plan by 210 votes to 29. They looked rather to persuading other countries to reduce tariffs to stimulate trade.

The hopes of early 1929 vanished in the blizzard brought by the collapse of the stock market in America in October 1929. Commodity prices plunged and the consequences of this were felt round the world in the next two years. Although the value of exports nearly halved between 1929 and 1931, the home market initially remained fairly stable. The government embarked on an extensive legislative programme. The Coal Mines Act shortened miners' working hours to seven-and-a-half a day and imposed a measure of rationalisation on the owners. Christopher Addison, once a reforming coalition minister and now a Labour one, brought price fixing to farming through agricultural boards. The powerful London Labour leader, Herbert Morrison – in many ways the most successful of ministers – helped bring some order to the largely chaotic road traffic situation with a Road Traffic Act, which, among its many provisions, brought in licensing for different kinds of vehicles; made third-party insurance compulsory; introduced the Highway Code; regulated the hours of work of lorry drivers; and gave local authorities the right to run buses and trams. He also laid down plans for the creation of a publicly owned London Transport, run by an appointed board.

However, unemployment began to climb relentlessly from 1.5 million in January 1930 to over 2.75 million in December. To meet the drain on the unemployment fund, the government had the choice of cutting benefits, increasing contributions or borrowing. It chose the last. In May 1931, a committee under Sir Peter May was set up to report on the size of the expected deficit and the expenditure cuts that would be required to balance the budget. By the summer of 1931, when the May Committee reported, the deficit was estimated at £120 million. The committee was highly critical of government policies, which, it argued, had produced inflation, and called for cuts in public expenditure. Borrowing to pay the costs of unemployment had to be halted and, instead, £67 million had to be cut from unemployment payments. It led to a run against the pound and the nation's gold reserves shrank. To support the pound, further borrowing was required from French and American bankers. They looked for evidence of cuts being made in government spending and that meant cutting payments to the unemployed.

To the mounting crisis over government spending was added in early August 1931 a City of London crisis, as a result of the collapse of banks in central Europe. Once again, speculators lost confidence in the pound and converted to gold. With further loans required, the right-wing press made the cutting of unemployment payments the symbol of the government's willingness to tackle the crisis. During 19 and 20 August, the Cabinet set about trying to make economies and managed to agree on savings of around £56 million. Philip Snowden, the Chancellor, tried to persuade them to agree to a further £20 million, part of which would come from a 10 per cent cut in employment benefit. On Saturday 22 August, MacDonald, at a hastily summoned Cabinet meeting, made clear that a loan from New York bankers, essential for maintaining British creditworthiness, could only be achieved if the budget were balanced to the satisfaction of the opposition parties. The Cabinet split, with 11 going along with Snowden and 9 refusing. The government's resignation was inevitable.

National governments

MacDonald handed in his government's resignation on the morning of 24 August 1931 and emerged from the meeting with the King with the news that he was to form a 'national' government. The King and his private secretaries had had such a government in their sights for some time and it seems to have been they who proposed that MacDonald remain as Prime Minister. Some in the business community saw a national government as a way of restoring confidence and Baldwin and Neville Chamberlain came round to the idea of supporting a MacDonald-led government, which they saw as preferable to a Conservative government with Liberal support having to impose the cuts. To many people in the Labour Party, however, this was to become MacDonald's great betrayal of the movement that he had helped build, and the result of vanity. But the stance that MacDonald took was consistent with his earlier views that Labour had to show that it was fit to govern and could cope with crises. What he initially envisaged seems to have been a Labour government expanded to incorporate some people from other parties, perhaps for a relatively short period. It was to be an emergency government, not as a coalition, and the assumption was that, in the ensuing general election, there would be a return to the party position.

The formation of the national government had the required effect of steadying nerves and persuading the bankers to provide a loan. The new government went no further in the way of cuts than the £70 million over which the Labour government had split. Once in power, Conservative ministers determinedly resisted cuts in their own departments. The navy was less fortunate and a protest over pay and allowance cuts in September soon built up into the 'Invergordon mutiny', that drew comparisons with the mutinies of 1797. Financial confidence was again shaken and a run on the pound resumed. A week after the Invergordon incident the pound came off the gold standard again.

The Conservatives insisted on an early election, by now determined to implement tariff reform, and, in October, Parliament was dissolved. The decision was made to fight the election as a national government, which the bankers urged should continue, and MacDonald asked for a 'doctor's mandate', with little detail on policies. Although the actual number of votes for Labour did not fall dramatically, its seats fell to 52. It held on only in a few of the industrial heartlands and it was bereft of its leaders. George Lansbury, an elderly pacifist, took the leadership until 1935, when he was succeeded by his apparently colourless deputy, the middle-class Clement Attlee. Once again, it was the Liberals who suffered even more, and the Conservatives dominated with 470 MPs and 55 per cent of the popular vote.

The national governments that survived until 1940, first under Ramsay MacDonald, then Stanley Baldwin and then Neville Chamberlain, can be seen as examples of the British art of compromise. They avoided the internal traumas that tore apart most European countries in the 1930s, leading to the rise of extreme fascist and communist parties. These were not lacking in Britain, but both the far right and the far left were tiny, and parliamentary government survived. On the other hand, the national governments can be seen as a fairly disastrous series of governments that failed to respond to the economic crisis and pursued what proved to be a mistaken foreign policy of appeasement. There was no New Deal to tackle the problems of economic depression, such as Franklin Roosevelt brought to the United States. There was no improvement of the transport infrastructure, such as Hitler's autobahns in Germany, or great hydro-electric schemes in Scandinavia. There was inadequate intervention in industry to make it more efficient or to respond to the distress of mass unemployment (see Chapter 27). Rather the policy was one of drift.

Bits of both analyses stand up to scrutiny. It is worth bearing in mind that the British economy was less badly hit by the crisis than were the economies of the United States and most European countries (see Chapter 27). The economy was helped by the protection for industry that the Conservatives pushed through in the face of opposition. On 1 March 1932, Britain abandoned more than 80 years of free trade with a general import tariff of 10 per cent. The end of free trade, demanded by the majority of Conservative backbenchers, caused surprisingly little comment. Throughout the 1920s, it had come to seem irrelevant to the problems of the age. It did little to help the economic situation and it had lost its moral element with the war. *Laissez-faire* no longer seemed an option in the face of persistent unemployment. Hopes that tariffs would be a step towards greater imperial unity with empire free trade, pushed hard by Lord Beaverbrook and the *Daily Express*, came to little. The dominions had their own industries to protect.

There *were* those who called for more radical changes in the political and economic system than could be accomplished by parliamentary methods. On the political right there was the British Union of Fascists. Disenchanted by the rejection of his 1930 memorandum by Labour, Mosley sought to attract a cross-party group who would support his policies. When that failed to attract support, he launched the New Party, but found few who were willing to make the break with their old parties. No longer with a voice in Parliament, and with the prospect of a political realignment shattered, Mosley moved towards fascism. His body of uniformed 'blackshirts' were largely financed by Sir William Morris, the later Lord Nuffield, and other industrialists and, at a later stage, by Lord Rothermere, owner of the *Daily Mail*. Increasingly, communism was identified as the greatest threat and fascist violence intensified.

The Communist Party of Great Britain attracted growing support after its formation in 1920. Battles for the soul (or, at any rate, the policies) of the Labour Party continued throughout the 1930s in all the various parts of the wider labour movement. Weak in Parliament, the battles took place in pamphlets, local constituencies and in conferences. Although, from 1935, the leadership of the Labour Party was firmly in the hands of the studiously moderate, there were always elements who wanted a more rapid transition to a socialist society. Some considered they should collaborate with the Communist Party, which was organising hunger marches of the unemployed through the National Unemployed Workers' Movement. To most of the leaders of the Labour Party, however, the communists were a dangerous and divisive group determined to infiltrate the party. For others communism was a part of a wide spectrum of the Labour movement. Some sought a united front of the working class against the national government. There was particular concern at the failure of the Labour Party to reject the government's policy of non-intervention in the bitter civil war in Spain. The USSR was able to recruit future spies amongst some of the disenchanted young at the University of Cambridge and elsewhere.

Baldwin and Chamberlain

MacDonald resigned as Prime Minister in June 1935 and his place was taken by Baldwin, who had been the effective leader of the government since 1931 and increasingly openly as MacDonald's intellectual powers declined. But Baldwin too, in the eyes of many, was 'too old, too tired, too bored'.[3] A general election was held in November 1935 and it was the Parliament so elected that survived until 1945. Labour recovered somewhat, with a share of the vote comparable to what it had achieved in 1929, but with only 154 seats. Some of the most important figures in the party regained the seats that they had lost in 1931. The Liberal Party, outside the coalition, was down to a mere 20 members. But it was Baldwin's triumph helped by signs of economic recovery.

The big event of 1936 was the abdication. King George V died in January. Despite a cold and severe personality that probably did considerable damage to his offspring, he had succeeded in steering the monarchy through various constitutional crises and,

---

[3] R.R. James, *Bob Boothby. A Portrait* (London, Hodder and Stoughton, 1991), p. 157.

judging from the silver jubilee celebrations in 1935, had generated considerable loyalty. He was succeeded by Edward VIII who, in occasional statements, had given the impression of having a social conscience, although there had been little curbing of a frivolous life in London's high society on his part and that of his brothers. The British press kept the news of the new King's affair with the already once-divorced wife of an American businessman out of the papers, but the issue became public when Mrs Simpson secured a divorce from her husband at Ipswich, where it was hoped, perhaps, that the case would pass unnoticed. As one American paper put it succinctly, 'King's Moll Reno'd in Wolsey's Home Town'.

Gradually, more and more titbits on the affair began to appear in the press. Various schemes were put forward for a morganatic marriage, but these proved unacceptable to the governments of the dominions. Baldwin, reflecting widely held views, gave the King a choice between Mrs Simpson and the Crown. Churchill, ever the romantic monarchist, made a futile attempt to generate a King's party, but, in the end, Edward abdicated and left the country as Duke of Windsor and his brother, hitherto Albert, became George VI.

It was Baldwin's last major act. He retired almost immediately after the coronation and took an earldom. Baldwin's successor was Neville Chamberlain, who continued to press ahead with some social legislation, even nationalising mining royalties. But he was now faced with major foreign policy problems on which his experience was limited. His policy of appeasement of Hitler (see Chapter 29) ended in tears when, on 1 September 1939, Hitler invaded Poland and two days later, on 3 September, Britain declared war. Leaders who had generally proved cautious and unadventurous in domestic policy were now faced with the immeasurable complexity of organising for war. Thanks largely to Labour's attacks on the *Guilty Men* during the war and Churchill's self-justifying account of the 1930s, *The Gathering Storm* in 1948, the reputation of both Baldwin and Chamberlain was low until more balanced accounts began to appear in the 1970s with the release of public records. Both contributed to Britain's coping with economic depression better than many other countries and the extent of preparation for war was much greater than was once believed.

Further reading

Ball, S., *Baldwin and the Conservative Party* (New Haven, Yale, 1988)

Ball, S., *The Conservative Party and British Politics 1902–1951* (London, Longman, 1995)

Powell, D., *British Politics and the Labour Question 1868–1990* (Basingstoke, Macmillan, 1992)

Pugh, Martin, *Electoral Reform in War and Peace 1906–18* (London, Routledge and Kegan Paul, 1978)

Thorpe, A., *A History of the British Labour Party* (Basingstoke, Palgrave Macmillan, 2001)

29

The Second World War

The Second World War drew Britain into a dangerous confrontation with Germany and Italy in Europe and with Japan in South-east Asia. It was to stretch British military endeavour to near-breaking point, undermine its economy, threaten its empire and require an unprecedented mobilisation of the whole of British society. The outcome was in doubt, at least until 1942, when the tide began to turn, with the USSR driving back German forces in eastern Europe and huge resources in men and materials arriving from the United States.

The search for peace

The hopes of 1919, that the League of Nations would lead the way to a new international order, were quickly shattered when the United States' Congress refused to endorse it. Nonetheless, considerable faith remained that the League could help provide what came to be called collective security. In 1925, Britain and Italy became guarantors of the Treaty of Locarno, a non-aggression pact between France, Germany and Belgium. The British hoped that it would be the end of the continuing post-war tensions between France and Germany and would lead to German economic revival and the nation's restoration as a 'normal' European state.

The Nazis came to power in Germany in 1933 – something that the British initially tended to see as an unfortunate revival of Prussianism rather than as a new threat. However, surreptitious rearmament by Germany was speeded up. With Germany rearming, the choice before Britain and other powers was to use force to prevent this or to give up the idea of disarmament and let events take their course. Attitudes towards Germany were confused. There were those among the military who respected

the Germans for their efficiency and bellicose qualities. Some industrialists and politicians compared favourably Nazi success in generating employment and reforming the
economic infrastructure with the failures of British economic policy in the depressed
areas. Figures on the left of the Labour Party were more concerned with the potential
for the rise of fascism at home and suspected the anti-democratic instincts of the Tory
right-wing. There was a wide consensus that the Treaty of Versailles had been unjust
to Germany and therefore, an unwillingness to listen to Churchill's warnings against
German rearmament. By the autumn of 1935, the Labour Party conference recognised
'that there might be circumstances in which the government of Great Britain might
use its military and naval forces in support of the League to restrain an aggressive
nation', but it still voted against plans for increased expenditure on the Royal Air
Force. The Conservative Party was split too. Churchill, in the wilderness, thundered
against the German menace, but because of his extreme anti-communism and his
obsessive opposition to moves towards Indian self-government, his judgements were
seen as deeply flawed and he had little support in Parliament.

The government had the further problem that, even if it did decide to defend the
country against Germany, it was not clear how this was to be done. Experts produced
horrifying figures of likely casualties in British cities from aerial bombing in the belief
that 'the bomber would always get through'. It was expected that, in a matter of
months, there would be 600,000 dead and 1,200,000 wounded from bombing. The
only deterrent seemed to be counter-bombing of Germany cities, with the result
that RAF bomber command was built up at the expense of expenditure on the navy,
the army and fighter aircraft. These were also imperial politicians concerned equally,
if not more so, with the threat to the Empire from Japan and Italy. There were also
economic arguments from the Treasury that too-rapid rearmament, especially if it was
based on further borrowing, would undermine the position of sterling, and slow down
economic recovery.

Civil war broke out in Spain in 1936, when General Franco, backed by support
from both Germany and Italy, attempted to overthrow the elected Republican government. This persuaded some on the political left that fascism had to be resisted and
some 2,300 volunteers joined the British Battalion of the International Brigade, but
most in Britain had no wish to get pulled into a general European war for which the
country was ill-prepared. Also, the government did not want to be seen to be backing
the losing side or to get into conflict with Italy, lest it threaten British Mediterranean
interests. By the time the civil war ended with Franco's victory in 1939, the rest of the
world had largely pushed it out of mind.

From 1937, the Labour Party was calling for rearmament and warning of the
coming struggle with fascism, while the Conservative leadership pursued its policy of
appeasement. Neville Chamberlain became Prime Minister in May 1937. His reputation has undoubtedly suffered from a contrast with his successor, Winston Churchill,
and from the latter's seizure (through speeches and his own writings) of the narrative of
the Second World War, where appeasement of Hitler was presented as a disastrous
betrayal of Britain's interests and of its moral standing. From the 1960s, there was

some attempt by historians to understand and defend the policy as a realistic one in the circumstances. As early as 1933, Chamberlain had noted the German danger and had been a strong supporter of rearmament. His mistake was to believe that he had the ability to influence Hitler and, if error it was, to do everything possible to prevent another European war. He went to great lengths to court Mussolini, the Italian dictator, whom he was convinced could be rescued from Hitler's clutches, and whose country bestrode Britain's Mediterranean and imperial trade routes.

In March 1938, Austria was incorporated into the German Reich and Hitler now turned up the pressure on Czechoslovakia, one of the new states that had emerged in the aftermath of the First World War. Chamberlain refused to give any guarantee of support to the Czechs and, instead, along with the French government, pressed them to conciliate Hitler by making concessions to the substantial German minority in the Sudetenland. He recognised the failings of the Treaty of Versailles and saw no British interests involved in 'a quarrel in a far-away country between people of whom we know nothing'. He recognised that, with Austria now incorporated in Germany, there was little that could be done to aid Czechoslovakia. Chamberlain sought a solution that would satisfy Hitler, basically arguing that any solution was better than unleashing another long, devastating war. He made three flights to Germany in September 1938 (the first time a British Prime Minister had flown) culminating in the infamous Munich meeting, where France and Britain agreed that the Sudetenland should be transferred to Germany. Chamberlain returned, waving a piece of paper and claiming at the airport that it promised 'peace for our time'. This was greeted across the country with great enthusiasm, but very quickly guilt replaced that enthusiasm; a feeling that the most democratic of post-war states had been betrayed. Czechoslovakia lost all its western defences and six months later German forces were in Prague.

How far Munich was an unforgivable betrayal of a small nation in a vain attempt by Britain and France to protect themselves or how far it was a sensible and pragmatic piece of diplomacy will continue to be debated. According to some, as he announced 'peace with honour' on his return from Munich, Chamberlain said to those nearby: 'We must have time – time is what we need.' In this he was reflecting what he saw as the reality of the situation. The new RAF fighter-building programme, embarked on in 1936, would not be ready until 1939 and views within government were that the situation had to be held until at least that date.

The problem with that line of argument is that Chamberlain did not seem to use the time particularly effectively. Armaments output did increase, but that was the result of decisions made earlier. The government wanted to avoid a repetition of 1914 and not until February 1939 were plans made to expand the armed forces and, once again, to create an expeditionary force to fight on mainland Europe. Any enhancement of defence capability needed to be deployed in the Empire, not in Europe. We know now that the German military was much less prepared for war in 1938 than they claimed, and an extra year gave time to Hitler, as well as to the British, to prepare for war. Conceivably, there was little that could be done to assist Czechoslovakia, since it was too far away, but the same was true of Poland. The British and French gave guarantees of support to the Poles in March 1939 – guarantees, it should be noted, of their independence, not of their frontiers and which were pretty meaningless without getting an agreement with the USSR. But the Poles would not tolerate any Soviet involvement in their defence.

Appeasement was largely abandoned in March 1939 with the seizure of Czechoslovakia, but its advocates remained in control. An offer from the Soviet Union of an alliance was rejected, and Stalin, suspecting that Britain and France were not above coming to terms with Hitler at the expense of Russia, signed a non-aggression pact with Hitler. German pressure on Poland mounted through the summer and Hitler seems to have been persuaded, almost to the last, that Britain would abandon Poland, just as it had the Czechs. Poland was invaded on 1 September and on Sunday 3 September, Chamberlain announced that Britain and Germany were at war.

Britain's war

By early 1939, there was a wide acceptance that war with Germany had to come. There was a mounting sense that the sacrifice or betrayal of Czechoslovakia had been a rather shameful act in which the British had failed to live up to their self-image as a moral nation different from dictators like Hitler and Mussolini. There were those who argued that the 'dishonour' of Munich had undermined the belief in British excep-tionalism and would threaten the hold on empire. There was concern that German demands in the Near-East could threaten British interests, particularly if Germany acted in cahoots with the USSR. There was also the historical perception that Britain had a particular role in the world to stand up to the domination of the continent by a single power.

There was no great enthusiasm for war, with none of the flag-waving that had happened in August 1914, but there was general agreement that the cause was a just one. Few thought that Britain had some responsibility for its outbreak, as had been the case in 1914. The Communist Party and the rump of the ILP came out against the war, calling for 'revolutionary defeatism', although a year earlier they had been the loudest critics of appeasement. Not until 1941, when Hitler invaded Russia, did the war cease to be an imperialist war in the eyes of the Communist Party.

Some of the errors of the First World War were avoided. Conscription was already in place. On 3 September 1939, all men aged between 18 and 40 became liable for call-up. There was some serious scarcity of equipment, particularly for the army, but the output of aircraft was greater than that of Germany. On the other hand, it took a long time to create an effective mechanism to co-ordinate war needs and there was a continued wariness about regulating private industry. Not until March 1940 was Winston Churchill, who went to the Admiralty on the outbreak of war, put in charge of a committee for co-ordinating the war effort.

Building on the experience of the First World War, there were immediate calls for a coalition government, but neither the Labour Party nor the Liberal Party would serve under Chamberlain. The first few months were dubbed the 'phoney war' and the first war budget in 1940 saw very little effort to raise taxes to cover future costs. Not much appeared to be happening and secret negotiations continued to try to limit the conflict, with many in government hopeful that economic sanctions would be enough to deter Germany. Bombers flew over Germany, dropping leaflets rather than bombs, assuring the Germans that the war was with Nazism, not with the German people. While no assistance was sent to Poland, there were serious plans to come to the aid of Finland, which was invaded by Soviet troops. One way of aiding Finland was through neutral Norway and Sweden and this would have the added effect of securing their important iron ore deposits. The government debated the issue but was wary about openly breaching neutrality, although Norwegian coastal waters were eventually mined. Hitler lacked such reservations and, in April 1940, Denmark and Norway were captured. It was all over in a couple of days. A British and French attempt to seize Narvik and other parts of northern Norway came too late and too ineffectually, and the troops had to be evacuated.

Pre-war governments had been perceived as complacent when it came to dealing with social problems. Now the government seemed complacent in fighting the war. Demands for Chamberlain's resignation came from his own backbenchers. In an emotional speech to a highly charged House of Commons, the elderly Conservative, Leo Amery, quoted Oliver Cromwell's words to the Parliament of the 1640s: 'You have sat too long here for any good you have done. Depart, I say, and let us have done with you. In the name of God, go.' Two days later, on 10 May 1940, German forces invaded Belgium, the Netherlands and Luxemburg. Chamberlain resigned and the King sent for Churchill, although there were moves within the ranks of the Conservative Party to block his appointment. To Rab Butler at the Foreign Office he was 'the greatest political adventurer of modern times', while to Lord Halifax, he and his immediate cronies were little better than 'gangsters'.[1] In the eyes of the public, however, he was seen as the man who had had the measure of Hitler in the 1930s, and both Labour and Liberals made it clear that they would not serve under anyone other than Churchill. A coalition government was formed, with the Labour leader, Clement Attlee, as Churchill's deputy.

The beginnings of the coalition were hardly propitious, and Churchill's position was far from secure. By 20 May, the Second German Panzer division had reached Abbeville, effectively cutting the British forces off from the main French army and from their supplies and bases. British, French and Dutch forces were trapped on the beaches of Dunkirk by the advancing *Wehrmacht*. The German advance was slowed in a week of fierce battles, particularly by the French, on the perimeter of Dunkirk. For reasons that are far from clear, the Germans delayed the final assault. The commanders of the Panzer divisions probably needed time to refit before turning for the final assault on Paris. In the end 338,226 troops were evacuated, 225,000 of them

---

[1] Anthony Howard, *RAB, The Life of R.A. Butler* (London, Jonathan Cape, 1987), p. 94.

British. The disaster was presented as some kind of major triumph of defiance. On the radio, the novelist J.B. Priestley created a powerful image of the 'little ships' that had snatched 'glory out of defeat' as they 'made an excursion to hell and came back glorious'.[2] For the 51st Highland Division, further down the coast at St Valéry-en-Caux, there was no such rescue and many felt that they were abandoned in a vain attempt to persuade the French government to continue the fight. Meanwhile, the War Cabinet contemplated suing for peace. On 22 June, with Paris occupied, France surrendered; the British strategy since 1919, of depending on the French to halt a German advance, had failed.

From then through to September, what Churchill dubbed 'the Battle of Britain' took place in the skies over southern England. Invasion was awaited and the Home Guard, formed in May, stood to (usually ancient) arms. The blitz of London started on 7 September, after the RAF had bombed Berlin, and continued for 57 successive nights, killing more than 20,000 and leading to considerable unrest at the lack of adequate shelters. The Spitfires, operational since the summer of 1938, were, however, more manoeuvrable than the slower bombers of the Luftwaffe and able to bring greater losses than they sustained. Young men were rushed into training as pilots to replace British losses and, by the middle of September, more aircraft were emerging from factories than were being downed in the air battles. The British had the crucial advantage of radar and they had succeeded in deflecting the radio direction beams on which German aircraft depended.

By the end of October 1940, Hitler had postponed any plans he had for the invasion of Britain, but bombing spread from London to provincial cities. Coventry, Birmingham, Bristol, Sheffield, Portsmouth, Southampton, Exeter, Cardiff, Swansea, Belfast, Liverpool, Manchester, Hull, Greenock and Clydebank were all heavily bombed. Two powerful images emerged from the battle. The first was of the valour of 'the few', the young pilots who flew the Spitfires, many just out of school or university. The second was the sense of island Britain 'standing alone' against the might of the German army – which from one perspective was inaccurate since, as in the First World War, Canada, Australia, New Zealand, South Africa, and, most of all, India eventually contributed thousands of soldiers.

The whole character of the war was altered in June 1941 when Hitler invaded the Soviet Union and Churchill learned to say nice things about Stalin. There was an idealisation, even in the right-wing press, of the Soviet people's bravery and resilience. On 7 December, Japanese planes bombed the American fleet at Pearl Harbor in Hawaii and the Americans entered the war. But bad news predominated. Three days later Britain's only two capital ships in the east, the *Prince of Wales* and the *Repulse*, placed as tokens there to defend what was already recognised as an indefensible Singapore, were both sunk by Japanese warplanes. On Christmas Day, the Japanese captured Hong Kong and launched an assault on the Malayan peninsula. An army of

---

[2] J.B. Priestley, *Postcripts* (Wednesday 5 June 1940) (London, Heinemann, 1940), pp. 1–4.

Figure 29.1 Coventry after the bombing raid of November 1940. Coventry, a major industrial centre in the Midlands, was heavily bombed by the Luftwaffe on the night of 14–15 November 1940. Around 500 were killed and about the same number injured, while among the destroyed buildings was the medieval cathedral. Some controversy exists as to whether the government had prior warning of the raid from the code breakers.
Source: Science & Society Picture Library

130,000 in Singapore surrendered to 23,000 Japanese in February 1942, shattering British prestige in Asia and any lingering belief in the idea of European invincibility. What can only be seen as a racist underestimation of the military ability of the Japanese meant that there was little preparation for resistance to their speedy advance. Conscription was extended, with the age limit raised to 51, and single women between 20 and 30 were required, for the first time, to do some kind of war service. Britain was the only country in which women were conscripted.

Churchill had for many months been in regular communication with President Roosevelt, trying to persuade the United States to enter the war. There was talk of swapping British bases in the West Indies for ships and planes. In March 1941, the American Congress had passed the Lend-Lease Act that empowered the President to provide goods and services to those countries whose defence was seen as vital to the interests of the United States. In practice, this meant Britain and, later, the USSR. In August, Roosevelt and Churchill issued the Atlantic Charter that laid down a joint declaration of peace aims, abrogating any desire for territorial expansion, committing themselves to making any territorial changes subject to the desires of the people concerned and pledging themselves to 'respect the right of all people to choose the form of government under which they will live'. In spite of this, Churchill still found it inconceivable that 'the Natives of Nigeria or of East Africa could by a majority vote choose the form of government under which they live'.[3] Arguably, Churchill's greatest achievement was to persuade Roosevelt to join the war and to make the defeat of Germany a priority. The huge American resources made victory against Germany inevitable in the long term. By 1944 there were around a million American troops based in Britain.

It was some time before the tide of war turned; up to that time, criticism of the government grew, with talk even of replacing Churchill. There were two major turning points. In May 1942, the advance of German and Italian forces towards Egypt and the Suez Canal was halted at El Alamein, a mere 70 miles from Alexandria. Crucial to success was the fact that code-breakers at Bletchley Park, in the highly secret Ultra project, had succeeded in breaking the German and Italian army and navy ciphers. Secondly, in December, the Russians halted the German advance into Russia at the battle of Stalingrad. There were calls for the opening of a second front to help take the pressure off the Russians, but, with the bulk of American troops still undergoing training, Churchill was not going to risk the depleted British forces or withdraw troops from India threatened by Japanese advance.

After American entry and Stalingrad it was largely a matter of time, effort and sacrifice. Although there were heavy losses of merchant ships transporting supplies across the Atlantic, by the end of 1942, British and American shipyards were building ships faster than they were being sunk by U-boats. In July 1943, American, British and Canadian forces invaded Sicily and moved on into Italy. Although an armistice was signed in September with the Italian government that had replaced the ousted Mussolini, the German army took control of Rome and the north of the country. It was not until June 1944 that Anglo-American troops entered Rome. German forces continued to hold the north until the end of the war.

On D-Day, 6 June 1944, the long-planned invasion of France was launched in Normandy by British and American forces. A week later, the first unmanned 'flying bombs' or 'doodlebugs' landed on London and some 5,000 fell on the city over the

---

[3] M. Gilbert, *Finest Hour. Winston S. Churchill 1939–1941* (London, Heinemann, 1983), p. 1163.

next three months. In August, Paris was liberated and, in September, the American first army crossed the German frontier, while another army landed in the French Riviera and quickly moved up the Rhone valley. In retaliation, rocket-propelled bombs, the V1s and V2s, were launched against London. A mainly British attempt to outflank the Germans by an airdrop at Arnhem proved a costly disaster and the Germans were able to create a dangerous bulge in the American lines in the Ardennes in December before being pushed back.

But German ability to engage in sustained warfare had been much weakened. Since the start of 1944, there had been intensive bombing of all parts of Germany. Over 1,000 German planes were destroyed in January 1944 alone and by the beginning of 1945 there was little of the Luftwaffe left. The vital machine factories of the Ruhr had been regularly pounded, although they showed remarkable ability to recover and renew production. Destruction was not confined to industrial or military targets, however. Since 1942, there had been an agreed British policy of what was called 'terror' bombing of German cities, intended to destroy civilian morale. In February 1945, a raid by 773 bombers was made on the medieval city of Dresden, a city largely undefended and with no significant military or industrial targets. Its normal population of 650,000 had been swollen by an influx of refugees fleeing the advancing Red armies from the east. After the initial British bomber raid with 12,000 lb 'blockbuster' bombs, American bombers followed up with another two days of destruction. The resulting firestorm made it impossible to count the dead and estimates range from 35,000 to more than 100,000.

By May, the Russian army was in Berlin and VE Day was proclaimed in Britain on 8 May. Ominously, the victorious allies, Britain, the United States and the USSR could not agree on the date to declare the end of the war. They had, however, already agreed on how Europe would be carved into spheres of influence. At conferences in Moscow and at Yalta, it was decided that the USSR would have the predominant influence in most of eastern Europe, while Britain was to predominate in Greece. Germany and Berlin were to be divided into Soviet, British, American and French sectors.

On 15 April 1945, British and Canadian troops entered Bergen-Belsen concentration camp and, for the first time, saw some of the horrors of Nazi policy against Jews, churchmen and women, trade unionists, communists, homosexuals and gypsies. Reporters and film crews eventually followed and gradually brought evidence of the enormity of the slaughter, particularly of Jews. While stories of the atrocities of the enemy are commonplace in war, by the summer of 1942, information was coming through of the systematic extermination of the Jewish population in Germany and Poland. There was, however, an unwillingness to believe what were often seen as exaggerated rumours and there was no attempt to publicise them in propaganda broadcasts. By the end of 1942, the allied governments were aware of the situation, but there was no serious talk of rescue of any from Vichy France or from the edges of Hitler's Reich. The formidable campaigner, Eleanor Rathbone, tried to catch the public's attention on the issue and to persuade the government to find ways of aiding Jews to escape from Europe, but there were only token relaxations of refugee policies. The post-war trials of Nazi leaders at Nuremberg brought knowledge of the Nazis' genocidal policies to the public and, gradually, the fact of the systematic slaughter of some 6 million Jews – what from the 1950s came to be called 'the Holocaust' – registered.

The war against Japan had still some months to run. In the six months after Pearl Harbor the Japanese had overrun the Philippines, the Dutch East Indies, Malaya and Singapore, French Indo-China and Burma. Hundreds of Pacific islands had been occupied and the threat to Australia had only been halted by American ships and planes in the battle of the Coral Sea in May and June 1942. From 1943, the Japanese were experiencing huge naval losses and were being driven out of the Pacific islands. By the summer of 1944, after resisting a Japanese assault in north-east India at Imphal and Kohima, forces led by the Australian General Slim were pushing back into Burma in fierce fighting. After May 1945, the whole of American air might was turned on Japan itself. The remnants of its navy and industry were destroyed and battleships were able without hindrance to bombard Japanese cities. Isolated and with infrastructure and morale largely shattered, Japan was moving towards surrender when atomic bombs were dropped on the cities of Hiroshima and on Nagasaki in August.

The emergence of atomic power was the culmination of decades of scientific work on the nature of matter. Between the wars, work on the atom continued and in 1938 in Berlin, two chemists split the nucleus of the uranium atom by bombarding it with neutrons – what was called nuclear fission. This held out the possibility of bomb making, although there were still considerable doubts as to whether it was really feasible. British scientists remained fairly sceptical about what could be done. After December 1941, when the United States entered the war, more resources were poured into nuclear research and British expertise and scientists moved to America to collaborate in what was called the 'Manhattan project'. From then it became essentially an American project, with little feedback to Britain. In July 1943, Churchill and Roosevelt, by the Quebec Agreement, settled the basis of future collaboration. In return for handing over a huge amount of technical information, the British understanding was that the Americans would share their future findings, but it was only to be on American terms.

The Manhattan project gradually moved to completion in the early months of 1945, as Germany went down to defeat. Some scientists believed that there was no need to complete it, but the Americans had already switched their focus to the post-war world and to their relations with the USSR. The attraction of using the atomic bomb was to end the war quickly, since the prospect of invading the Japanese islands was looming and there were estimates of anything up to a million possible casualties. Some suggested a demonstration of the bomb's effect would be enough, but the concern was that it might not explode, and there were only three bombs built. The first was successfully tested at Los Alamos, New Mexico, in July and the other two were used at Hiroshima and Nagasaki, deliberately chosen as cities that, to date, had suffered little bomb damage. At least 70,000 died in the former, 40,000 in the latter. The world had entered a new era.

A political consensus?

The tendency of most writers has been to see the war itself as some kind of turning point in British society. The war, it is suggested, brought people together in a magnificent communal effort, particularly in the early years when the outcome was far from certain. As Britain 'stood alone' in 1940 and 1941, a new mood of national solidarity was created. This is the argument of what Paul Addison calls a 'massive new middle ground' emerging from the war – what he refers to as 'Mr Attlee's consensus'. The dominating narrative of the war years is that there was a sense of common sacrifice, with everyone pulling together and everyone experiencing rationing to ensure fair shares all round. Much is made of children being evacuated from the slums of cities to small towns and villages and people, in what we would now call prosperous 'middle England', suddenly realising the huge problems of housing, health and education that existed in their midst. The better-off were willing to accept higher taxes, to redistribute wealth in society and to create a more equal post-war world. It was a cosy, heart-warming image that made the nation feel good about itself. Out of this, the argument goes, there arose another consensus that there should be no going back and, therefore, an acceptance that the state should play a much bigger role. There was now a belief that the state should act to ensure that there would be no repetition of mass unemployment, by means of managing the economy and social engineering – that poverty could, in fact, be eradicated.

Very much more than in 1914–18 there were concerns about the kind of society that was to be created in the post-war world. In January 1941, the popular *Picture Post* magazine talked of a 'new Britain' for which the country was fighting and outlined 'a Plan for Britain'. Within a month of the Dunkirk evacuation, a national milk scheme was introduced to supply milk at a reduced price, with free milk for mothers and children. While preparations were being made to resist invasion, old-age pensions were supplemented. In 1942, the Beveridge Report offered a possible blueprint for post-war reconstruction of social welfare (see Chapter 32). The ideas were broadly adopted, put into place by the Labour government after 1945 and generally accepted by successive Conservative governments. Here was the consensus in action.

But this rather comfortable view has been challenged and, writing in the 1990s, one social commentator suggested that the problem in Britain since 1945 was the lack of consensus, with confrontational politics, confrontational industrial relations and confrontational class relations.[4] There is plenty of evidence of the persistence of class tensions and the contestation of different interest groups throughout the war. London's East End did not quietly sit out the blitz without anger and protest at the lack of provision for those bombed out. Strikes, although illegal, did not disappear. Churchill, on more than one occasion, declared that he was fighting for 'the values of traditional England', on other occasions for the British Empire – not for some egalitarian world.

---

[4] Will Hutton, *The State We're In* (London, Jonathan Cape, 1995).

To Churchill, the war was won by the old order, by individual effort and by traditional leadership. That was not the view of everyone. For those who saw the war as part of an international struggle against fascism, it had been won by a democratic society that had rallied in a collective way – a people's war, not Churchill's war.

Churchill did not like the Beveridge Report and he told his colleagues early in 1943 that he had no intention of promising its implementation after the war. The Conservative Chancellor of the Exchequer was adamant that there ought to be no post-war commitments and the Labour leaders in the coalition had similar reservations. The coalition government was pushed into endorsing the Beveridge proposals by Labour backbenchers and activists outside Parliament who mobilised public opinion. Teachers and lecturers in the forces, running classes for troops, pushed the idea of a new, more equal society being created. Socialist-influenced pressure groups in the medical profession and elsewhere pressed their ideas for radical reform. Enthusiasm for welfare reform gathered momentum in spite of government. The war, by this argument, did not produce a consensus, but a rather uneasy compromise. An examination of the white papers on reconstruction produced during the war shows that they are often vague and ambiguous and not an agreed programme for action.

What may have happened, however, is that the wartime expansion of the state brought new people into the heart of government, who tended on the whole to be left-wing in their politics, or, at any rate, not strongly Conservative. The kind of people, for example, who ran the Ministry of Information were often active in the world of culture, and they used their talents to propagandise the kind of welfare planning articulated in the Beveridge Report. Keynes and academic economists influenced by him sold the idea that the state could regulate the economy, while socialists argued that the effectiveness of wartime controls on the economy confirmed their commitment to the continuation of central control in the post-war world.

The extent to which the war fundamentally changed attitudes on class is very doubtful; after all, the traditional ruling order had a relatively successful war. It has been suggested that the war altered the position of women in society. More women came into and remained in the workplace and married women began to go out to work. By 1943, 46 per cent of women between the ages of 14 and 59 were in paid employment, a higher proportion than in Germany or Russia. It contributed significantly to the growth of equality between the sexes. Sex discrimination in work began to break down and there were moves towards equal pay for men and women. It may be that, as they became involved in military work, joining the WRNS and the ATS, women gained confidence and independence, although they were excluded from carrying arms when they were eventually and grudgingly admitted to the Home Guard. On the other hand, there was no great social revolution. Women certainly moved into some new industries and white-collar jobs, but at least half of them were squeezed out after the war. Trade unions were determined that demobilised men should be given priority. There were, however, more job opportunities for women. It is not that they moved into areas of men's work, but that there were more jobs available. As always, however, war probably strengthened traditional sex roles, with man as

Focus on

Socialism and the war, 1941

This extract is taken from George Orwell, 'The Lion and the Unicorn. Socialism and the English Genius' (February 1941). George Orwell (1903–50) was the literary pseudonym of Eric Blair, a left-wing journalist and essayist. He had fought on the republican side in Spain and was strongly opposed to Chamberlain, but in this essay he developed the case for left-wing patriotism. His best-known work, *Animal Farm*, was completed in 1944, but not published until after the war in Europe had ended.

The swing of opinion is visibly happening, but it cannot be counted on to happen fast enough of its own accord. This war is a race between the consolidation of Hitler's empire and the growth of democratic consciousness. Everywhere in England you can see a ding-dong battle ranging to and fro – in Parliament and in the Government, in the factories and the armed forces, in the pubs and the air-raid shelters, in the newspapers and on the radio. Every day there are tiny defeats, tiny victories. Morrison for Home Security – a few yards forward. Priestley shoved off the air – a few yards back. It is a struggle between the groping and the unteachable, between the young and the old, between the living and the dead. But it is very necessary that the discontent that undoubtedly exists should take a purposeful and not merely obstructive form. It is time for *the people* to define their war-aims. What is wanted is a simple, concrete programme of action, which can be given all possible publicity, and round which public opinion can group itself.

I suggest the following six-point programme is the kind of thing we need. The first three deal with England's internal policy, the other three with the Empire and the world:

1. Nationalization of land, mines, railways, banks and major industries.
2. Limitation of incomes, on such a scale that the highest tax-free income in Britain does not exceed the lowest by more than ten to one.
3. Reform of the education system along democratic lines.
4. Immediate Dominion status for India, with power to secede when the war is over.
5. Formation of an Imperial General Council, in which coloured peoples are to be represented.
6. Declaration of a formal alliance with China, Abyssinia and all other victims of the Fascist powers.

The general tendency of this programme is unmistakable. It aims quite frankly to turn this war into a revolutionary war and England into a Socialist democracy.

hero and woman as homemaker, and welfare legislation was often about nurturing motherhood and families.

Did the war bring about a more equal society? There was certainly much talk of the need for this to be an outcome, but there was no consensus about what that actually meant. For some it meant an equality of contributions, such as the flat rate of the insurance proposals. Others saw it as being about a redistribution from the rich to the poor. There is little evidence to support the view that the tax system brought a redistribution of wealth; indeed, more people among the less well-off were forced to pay tax.

In some ways the nature of victory was a problem. The old social order and the traditional institutions had adjusted remarkably well. Churchill himself was a product of a bygone, aristocratic age. George VI and Queen Elizabeth had done well, staying in London (or at least Windsor) and having Buckingham Palace bombed. Parliament seemed to have worked and the BBC's reputation was much enhanced. The code breakers of Bletchley Park who had broken the German secret codes were the elite products of Oxford and Cambridge. The officer corps had performed well and the slaughter of war had been small compared with that in most other countries and certainly compared with the First World War, with around 300,000 soldiers and 60,000 civilians killed. Unlike in most other European countries, there did not need to be a major rebuilding of institutions or trust.

General election 1945

The election was held in July 1945 after Labour ministers, under pressure from their backbenchers, had broken with the coalition. They themselves might have been tempted to stay on, but, since 1931, Labour activists were opposed to the idea of coalition government. The Labour manifesto, *Let Us Face the Future*, emphasised the party's commitment to nationalisation of coal, electricity, transport, iron and steel. Few believed an early Gallup poll that pointed to a Labour victory. In the event it was a landslide. Labour had 393 seats in the new parliament, compared with 213 Conservatives and a mere 11 Liberals. For the first time, the party had an overall majority of 148. To most in Britain it was a surprise. Churchill had confidently predicted in private a majority of anything between 30 and 80 seats for the Conservatives.

The election was won not on foreign affairs, but on housing, employment and other social issues. A number of factors came together to bring victory. Labour had managed to get itself firmly associated in people's minds with the Beveridge Report that had so caught the popular imagination. For once, the Labour leaders were well-known and experienced. In many ways, they were better known than many of the Conservative ministers because they had controlled the home ministries. Attlee had run the government when Churchill was out of the country. Ernest Bevin had been a very high-profile Minister of Labour and seemed to have made a difference to conditions in the workplace, such as forcing employers to deal with trade unions. Herbert

Morrison had been in charge at the Home Office. No one could claim that Labour were not fit to govern.

There was also a determination that there should be no return to the conditions of the 1930s, which were presented as a terrible time of unemployment and appeasement, both of which were blamed on the Conservatives. A key factor in the election result seems to have been a determination to keep out the Conservatives. But the political environment had also changed substantially. Socialism had lost the taint of terror with which it had been associated since 1917 and the Bolshevik Revolution. The USSR had been the great and victorious ally, with communism apparently having worked to rally the nation to the tremendous sacrifices that the Soviet people had made. Churchill tried the old smears, claiming, in a notorious party-political broadcast that a Labour government would bring the Gestapo to Britain. It was a dire miscalculation. There was a massive weight of propaganda, usually coming from left-wing film makers who, while certainly pushing images of the indomitable will of the British people, at the same time also presented images of an older, class-ridden world, the world of Colonel Blimp, which stood in the way of progress.[5]

The war had brought a belief in planning. There were plans for victory and planning was associated with the socialist left, as opposed to the individualism of the right. If peace were to be successful then it too had to be planned for. War had produced a confidence that things could be done and changed quickly. It had been done with aircraft production and shipping, why not with housing and welfare?

Labour for the first time won votes across the country, not just in its old industrial heartlands. A breakthrough in southern England and among the middle class came in 1945. The swing to Labour in London was 17 per cent, compared with less than 10 per cent in Scotland and a national swing of 12 per cent. For the first time, Labour attracted middle-class voters in substantial numbers, particularly the professional middle class – 22 per cent of the middle class voted Labour. They also gained the support of most of the young – those voting in the first election since 1935. After all, in this new world of planning and state intervention that they held out, who were to be the gainers? Clearly there was going to be a need for more civil servants, more teachers, more architects, more planners, more doctors, more social workers. The new world was a lower-middle-class dream.

What there was not was a great groundswell for socialism. Labour won only 47.8 per cent of the votes cast. Forty per cent of service personnel did not vote. There was some apathy or weariness. Gallup polls, which were just coming into use, showed that most people actually favoured a coalition government – not the existing one, since there was suspicion of Churchill's attitudes, but a least party collaboration. The electoral system, however, allowed Labour to win a substantial number of former Conservative seats with small majorities.

---

[5] Colonel Blimp was a cartoon character drawn by David Low in the *Evening Standard*, but also used in Powell and Pressburger's 1943 film *The Life and Death of Colonel Blimp*. Blimp was presented as clinging to an outdated form of unthinking patriotism.

Further reading

Addison, P., *The Road to 1945* (London, Pimlico, 1994)

Calder, A., *The People's War* (London, Pimlico, 1992)

Charmley, John, *Chamberlain and the Lost Peace* (London, Macmillan, 1989)

Donnelly, M., *Britain and the Second World War* (London, Routledge, 1999)

Fielding, S., Thompson, P., and Tiratsoo, N., *'England Arise': The Labour Party and Popular Politics in 1940s Britain* (Manchester, Manchester University Press, 1995)

Gardiner, J., *Wartime Britain, 1939–1945* (London, Headline, 2004)

Kushner, T., *The Holocaust and the Liberal Imagination: A Social and Cultural History* (Oxford, Blackwell, 1994)

McDonough, F., *Hitler, Chamberlain and Appeasement* (Cambridge, Cambridge University Press, 2002)

Milward, A.S., *War Economy and Society 1939–45* (Harmondsworth, Penguin, 1977)

Robbins, K., *Appeasement* (Oxford, Blackwell, 1997)

Rose, S.O., *Which People's War? National Identity and Citizenship in Wartime Britain 1939–1945* (Oxford, Oxford University Press, 2003)

Smith, Malcolm, *Britain and 1940. History, Myth and Popular Memory* (London, Routledge, 2000)

30

People, society and culture

Social class

For most of this period, social class was a vital ingredient in individual identity. However, there were important changes to the way in which it was viewed, with significant attempts by the state to diminish class differences, and with a growing belief that a democratic society should imply an erosion of social inequality. However, increased working-class political militancy (in strike action and notably in the general strike of 1926) emphasised class division.

Until the 1940s, the British had a sense that they were being ruled by the upper class. This was probably also a reality. In 1922, the Conservative Cabinet contained 8 aristocrats and 8 members of the middle class, and none of the working class; 14 had gone to public school (8 of them to Eton), 13 had gone to university (all to Oxford or Cambridge). In 1945, the Labour Cabinet contained 8 middle-class and 12 working-class members, and no aristocrats; 5 had gone to public school (but only 2 to Eton), and 10 had gone to university (only 5 to Oxford or Cambridge). In 1963, the Conservative Cabinet had only 5 aristocrats but now 19 middle class (though still no working class), 21 had been to public school (11 to Eton), and all the 17 who had been to university had been at Oxbridge.[1] By 1963, aristocrats were becoming more and more the butt of jokes, their presence an embarrassment to many, even in the Conservative Party.

Though the titled classes were diminishing in proportion to the rise of middle-class meritocracy in government, they had an influence beyond mere numbers. The

---

[1] Data from D. Butler, 'Electors and elected', in A.H. Halsey (ed.), *Trends in British Society since 1900* (London, Macmillan, 1972), p. 247.

monarchy still gave an elegant sense of a natural order to society, even when its power was sharply diminished, or when King Edward VIII abdicated in 1936 because of his desire to marry a commoner and divorcee. The Royal Family headed a social system that still acknowledged the manners and deportment of the landowning class and, until 1957, they continued to grace the London 'season', when debutantes, mostly the 18-year old daughters of the well-to-do, moved round a mêlée of balls and parties. The House of Lords still contained the old aristocracy (and, until 1958, no women), but they were dying out, replaced by new peers created from the political classes. With every Labour government, new Labour peers were appointed to give a working majority in the House of Lords, and no practical steps were taken to abolish the House. But aristocrats remained present in the Commons, and their influence extended deep into traditional banking, investment and business firms. The upper classes continued as a functioning social set in London and, increasingly, on an international social scene that took in the French Riviera, New York and various corners of the Empire. Aristocratic wives were often hostesses, entertaining the 'smart set'. They became glamorous, started associating with film stars and the offspring of new money (occasionally marrying both), and fostered their credentials as the class of celebrity. It was given to be a class of scandal, exposed in papers like the *News of the World* for sexual misdemeanour or dishonest commercial dealings. In time of war, this made the upper class prone to unpopularity, and many believed that it was only because the shy King George VI and his alert wife, Queen Elizabeth, stayed in London during the blitz, making a well-publicised tour of the working classes in the bombed-out East End, that the British people continued to acquiesce to the upper class.

Cities and suburbs were the real crucible of class relations in Britain. Cities offered both shared and segregated spaces where classes were defined, given boundaries and occasionally clashed. The middle classes were the middle-income groups, who could vary between wealthy bankers and figures in the financial city of London, to the lower middle classes of teachers, clerks and accountants. This was a wide range, and they were generally schooled separately, as well as living in different qualities of housing. But they tended to be united in the workplace, being mostly on the management side of industrial relations. In their dreams and aspirations and, to an extent, their recreations and ideals, they had some broad similarities. By 1900, middle-class family size had fallen significantly, and it continued to do so in the twentieth century. This helped to foster prosperity. Having mainly been a class that rented houses before 1914, they turned to the private ownership of housing in this period, aided by the spread of mortgages from building societies. Indeed, though a significant minority still rented homes, between the 1930s and early 1960s home ownership became the hallmark, and the new central aspiration, of the middle classes of Britain. The houses they bought were increasingly located in outer suburbs, on side roads, and had larger gardens front and back. For the wealthier amongst them, a motor car was a leisure option to be considered. City centres became areas that, except for work and shopping, the middle classes generally desired to avoid. Their lives became focused on the home. The house and garden were their new recreation; the increasingly well-equipped kitchens, with gas or even electric cookers and refrigerators, were the places for most meals; and the radio – and, from the early 1950s, the black-and-white television – the centre of home entertainment. The British middle classes rarely dined out in the evenings before the 1960s, and only a small proportion would go to select public houses.

The middle classes in the twentieth century continued to be defined, as in the nineteenth century, by adhering to virtues of hard work and effort, of self-reliance and family values, and sobriety and respectability. They tended to be strong church members, even if in this period their church attendance was declining and becoming very much less than weekly. Indeed, their churchgoing habit was in marked decline over the period 1919–63, but this was offset by pretty strict observance of church baptism, marriage and funerals, and, until the late 1950s, by sending most of their children to Sunday schools. Some things were changing, however. More and more, the middle classes were university graduates and members of professions, with certificates and diplomas as credentials of skill and effort. By the 1950s, they were sending not just their sons but also their daughters to university. The few who continued to have live-in servants in the 1920s found these disappearing in the 1930s and 1940s, although daily domestics who came for a morning or two per week continued. But status was no longer being defined by servants and separateness from working-class mores. The middle classes shared the benefits of the welfare state with the working classes – notably the arrival of the National Health Service in 1948 which ended the need for private health insurance (see Chapter 32).

Working-class experience was even more varied than that of the middle classes. The city centres were theirs, as were industrial suburbs, but many lived in housing that was deteriorating fast in this period. This was often described at the time as 'slums', terraced housing or, as in Scotland, multi-storey tenement housing of brick or stone. Gardens were rare; yards were common, as were inadequate outside toilets, damp and lack of heating. Housing was a priority for social improvement by the late 1940s and 1950s, with massive state building programmes of up to 100,000 houses per year, coupled with mass slum-clearance programmes. Coal fires abounded, which contributed to the smog that hung over cities and caused poor health; a dense smog in London in 1952 caused around 4,000 deaths immediately and even more in the longer term, leading in 1956 to the Clean Air Act that within 15 years brought about the burning of smokeless fuel in city homes. Health was poor amongst the British working class, and the arrival of the welfare state in the late 1940s introduced measures that did much to improve the conditions of life.

Economic experience varied enormously during this period (see Chapter 27). In the UK as a whole, unemployment never dropped below 10 per cent of the labour force between 1919 and 1939, but it was as high as 40 per cent in some of the worst places, such as Merthyr Tydfil in Wales and parts of Lanarkshire in Scotland. Entire communities were 'on the dole', and the social relief systems were viewed with suspicion because of the 'means test', where inquiry into family circumstances could cause embarrassment and shame. Poverty carried a stigma, and applying to alleviate it could cause even more of a stigma. Social class became sharpened during this extended period of depression, as too did industrial strikes. The general strike of May 1926 brought out the depth of social divisions. For six days, the nation was bitterly divided between a radical working class and their small number of middle-class intellectual supporters, and the middle and upper classes who staffed transport systems, newspaper publication and various services. Though the acrimony subsided afterwards, miners remained embittered and quite radicalised, determined to pursue with great vigour future industrial disputes over pay and conditions.

From the 1930s, social inequalities started to diminish in a variety of ways, one being leisure and holidays. The working week was reduced through legislation from 1919, and paid holidays were enacted from 1938 for all bar agricultural workers and domestic servants. More generally, there was a sense developing that access to leisure and free time were marks of a democratic society – the rights of being a citizen. To this end, provision of public leisure facilities increased. Youth and community centres, village halls, playing fields for football and other sports, playgrounds for children, and even the simple device of allowing cul-de-sacs and other safe areas of urban streets to be used for play, developed under government support. Sport for all became a policy of the government from 1937, and Fitness Councils were set up for each of the home countries which would lead at the end of the Second World War to the greater promotion of sport, the creation of sports facilities, the training of coaches and the provision of national sports centres. Healthy recreation was seen as important to both the physical and general wellbeing of the people.

Poverty diminished with the outbreak of the Second World War in 1939. The government stepped in to control the distribution of resources in a system of rationing that extended from food (including children's sweets) to clothes (including thread), furniture, wood and virtually all the products consumed by the nation. Each man, woman and child in the country was entitled to rations of each product, including a set amount of meat, bread and butter, and ration books had to be shown when making purchases. The beneficial side of rationing was that it guaranteed a good wholesome diet to all, with nutritionists ensuring the best distribution of vitamins and nutrients, and this fostered a strong healthy cohort of children born in the 1940s and 1950s. In a wider way, it tended to equalise access to material goods, reducing the sense of class difference. This was especially important during the war, when the state was keen that national unity be fostered to sustain morale in the dark years when defeat and invasion were seen as real possibilities. The levelling effect of rationing continued after the war ended in 1945, as rationing was maintained by the Labour government because of the poor financial situation in the country.

The sense of erosion of class difference was encouraged during the war by propaganda. In some ways, the very experience of war was socially levelling. Though the divide between officers and enlisted men continued, promotion was based more on merit than social background than had been the case in the First World War. The home front was also levelling in some ways. German bombing afflicted all social classes, and people of different backgrounds might share communal air-raid shelters or tube stations. However, this must not be overstated. Many of the middle and upper classes lived in outer suburban areas that were less bombed than the working-class terraces of East London, Coventry and Hull, or the tenement flats of Clydebank. Working-class housing tended to be closest to key military and economic bombing targets, and middle-class households with their own gardens usually had their own air-raid shelters. Yet, the sense that class should not be a definer of such things grew during the war. With planning for the welfare state and the Beveridge proposals of 1942 (see Chapter 32), there was a general national consensus emerging that social class might still exist, yet efforts should be made to decrease its material manifestations.

This feeling that class was being eroded was to some extent emphasised in the late 1940s and the 1950s by the continuation of rationing, and a wider sense of shortage. Towns heavily bombed by German wartime raids left an air of disorder and ruin. In the midst of this there was a moral as well as material austerity that valued thrift, restraint, mild manners and the absence of showiness, all of which tended to encourage a social levelling. People were essentially prevented from spending much money. Rationing reduced household expenditure, whilst even foreign holidays were restricted because of exchange controls that limited the amount a person could take out of the country to £50 (a limit remaining in force until the 1970s and the equivalent of about £1,250 at 2007 prices). Though car-ownership expanded in the 1940s and 1950s, this was greatly restricted by the control of credit (or hire purchase as it was then called) which forced a buyer at certain points in the 'stop-go' cycle of economic policy to put down a one-third deposit and pay off the debt within two years. The late 1940s and 1950s are recalled by many as years of drabness and conformity – drabness in clothes, and drabness in the colour of cars. Yet, with new housing being built, the creation of 30 government-designated new towns from 1947 onwards, and the rebuilding of many city centres, city life was starting to be transformed in the 1950s.

Life in rural Britain was also being transformed, but not always in the same ways. For most of those who worked the land and the seas in Britain – the agricultural labourers, many forestry and wood trades, and fishermen – the 1920s and 1930s were not a prosperous time. Rural workers in 1937 had half the average weekly wage of urban skilled workers, and 30 per cent less than urban labourers.[2] But there were rural people who had rising fortunes, as the suburbanisation of the countryside advanced. Bungalows and middle-class homes spread along the lanes and roads outside many towns and cities, notably in the south of England, where car as well as rail transport made commuting quick and easy. Rural life became the ideal for large numbers of the middle classes. English identity was being ever more rooted in a fantasy of bucolic charm, but now composed of private detached or semi-detached houses, hedged and manicured, nestling amidst a landscape of open fields and scattered trees.

The counties around London – Surrey, Middlesex, Kent and Essex – became very suburbanised. Far from being backward and isolated, the completion of the national

---

[2] A. Howkins, *The Death of Rural England: A Social History of the Countryside since 1900* (London, Routledge, 2003), p. 95.

electricity grid in the early 1930s and the tarmacking of country roads made the countryside – certainly in the south and the Midlands of England – fill up with the consumer durables and leisure items of the time: motor cars, bicycles, telephones and household goods. The expansion in the size of local government and the welfare state increased work, both in white- and blue-collar jobs. New rural factories for consumer goods brought high and secure wages to the countryside, with work both for women and men.

The coming of the Second World War shook up the social structure and complacencies of neighbourhood and narrow communities. From 1 September 1939, two days before war even broke out, children were evacuated to the countryside, creating family trauma and confrontation as children of poor city dwellers were billeted on the comfortable rural middle classes. There was shock at sometimes unruly, even wild children from the East End of London arriving in quiet country areas; but children were traumatised, wetting beds and terrorised by unfamiliar ways and accents (and those who went to Wales were confronted by a language they did not understand). With the war not really starting for many months, refugees drifted back home, only to move out again during the blitz years of 1940–3. The countryside changed even more after the war, when the policies of government favoured farmers but not so much landowners. Many country houses were requisitioned by the military, while some others were largely abandoned, the landed class finding less and less income or even social purpose to living in the countryside in large mansions. The great days of the rural elites had passed, and although some still remained, it was increasingly through the move into tourism (with country houses opened to the public). Many properties were taken over by the National Trust and the National Trust for Scotland in advantageous deals that could preserve some toehold for the gentry in their former lands or houses.

Yet, on the surface, it still seemed, even in 1963, that an old social order was in place in Britain. The monarchy was healthy, challenged by few, and, if criticised at all, the aristocracy were mocked more than hated. The coming of the welfare state, of massive council-house building programmes, and the expansion of secondary and university education during the 1950s, offered opportunities to all which, ironically, tended to reinforce middle-class power, wealth and status. For, if anything, it was the middle classes who benefited the most from the welfare state, preserving not just their wealth but their ability to access opportunity, and still able to get the management and promoted posts in the workplace. Working-class work and home life remained insecure and sometimes of poor quality, with many living in areas scarred by bomb sites all through the 1940s and 1950s. Community spirit was still strong, but starting to suffer through slum clearance and dispersal to outlying estates. Sociologists were finding by the end of the 1950s that traditional family networks, based on proximity of mothers' and married daughters' homes in inner-city areas, were being eroded by new housing estates. Material benefits were coming, but the fragility of staple industries, and the continued shortage of educational and professional opportunities, made the working-class experience tough. Above all, social class still seemed in place as a definer of British society. The middle classes were still 'the salaried classes', paid monthly direct to bank accounts, and employing tradesmen to fix and fit their houses. By contrast, the working classes were still the 'waged class', paid weekly in pay packets, and worrying about 'stoppages' for national insurance and tax, and keeping homes fit to live in through trading skills with each other in a 'moonlighting' economy. In these respects little had changed since 1919.

Men, women and youth

Many men came home from the First World War in 1918 and 1919 with their masculine identity in a vulnerable state. The crisis of masculinity on return to 'Blighty' was heightened by the economic crisis that emerged after 1919. High unemployment removed for many the remaining prop of masculine pride. Scarred by war, the working man could no longer rely on a job.

The effects of long-term unemployment for men were exacerbated by the changing nature of work. The restructuring of the economy was leading to the long-term decline of heavy industry and of skilled jobs in engineering and mining. In their stead, moving production line methods were spreading mechanisation, automation and deskilling. Though economically more efficient, deskilling meant the subdivision of production into several simple operations for less skilled staff, while at the same time taking the technical knowledge out of the hands of the worker and placing it in the hands of the employers. This meant that skilled labour could be replaced by cheaper, unskilled workers. This hit male workers much more than female workers; indeed, in many cases, it was unskilled women workers who replaced skilled men. Taken together, war, unemployment and the rise of women's work were displacing many men from the position of sole breadwinner in many households. Indeed, many families were relying in the 1930s on women's income.

Even in the middle classes, there was crisis. Teachers were made redundant in large numbers in the 1930s to cut the nation's wage bills in the midst of recession, and opportunities in banking and finance faltered. Yet, expectations remained that men would be economically and physically strong. When men felt that they were not fulfilling their expectations of themselves, various things resulted. Domestic violence rose dramatically in the 1920s and 1930s, noticeably rising to a peak on Saturday nights after football and heavy drinking. Court cases where men had beaten up their wives and children became very common in industrial areas. The popularity of gambling rose tremendously in the 1920s and 1930s, despite the economic recession. Outside of licensed race tracks, virtually all forms of gambling were illegal, but it was so widespread that it could not be halted by the police. The football pools escaped the law by claiming to be a game of skill, not chance, but other forms of betting in clubs and shops, including on horse and greyhound racing, were illegal, though enormously popular. Gambling was also lucrative to bookmakers and operators of one-arm bandits – also known as fruit machines – which spread from the 1910s. So confident were bookmakers that, by the 1950s, some were openly operating out of shops, paying rates and installing televisions so punters could watch races on Saturday television. The government wanted to have gambling officially recognised and properly controlled so that it could be taxed for revenue, but the churches opposed this on moral and religious grounds during the 1940s and 1950s. Only in 1960, after popular pressure and the rising opposition by liberal intellectuals to the state restricting private pleasures, was off-course betting legalised. As a result, betting shops appeared all over the country, and tax became payable on bets or winnings.

This was one important step in the decriminalising of mainly male popular culture. Public houses were men's domain; few women ventured in before the 1970s (and those who did often acquired poor reputations). Pubs were numerous, almost entirely in working-class areas, but they were regarded with suspicion and disliked by churches and moral campaigners, and were closely monitored by local licensing courts. To restrict their influence, especially over children and young people, they had short opening hours (generally closing at any time between 9 p.m. and 10.30 p.m., and only opening for two hours over lunch). Sunday opening was banned in Scotland and Wales, and admission of children was strictly prohibited. In some parts of the country, the middle-class hostility to pubs was very strong. The church-based temperance movement that had been founded in the Victorian period remained influential in the 1920s, and though it weakened thereafter, the churches kept up pressure on political parties through the 1940s and 1950s to enforce strict licensing laws. For instance, in Scotland, between 1920 and 1976, local communities were given the right to vote for the closure of all pubs, and around 40 districts did so until the 1940s, including industrial villages, some districts of Glasgow, and fishing villages on the east coast. It was women who, in the main, voted to close public houses, while most working men voted in such plebiscites to keep pubs open. From the 1930s, the temperance ideal started to lose its popularity, and by the 1960s there was pressure across Britain for the liberalisation of licensing law, longer pub hours, and a new standard of public house suitable for women and middle-class drinkers.

The restrictive environment for drinking and gambling until the 1960s was indicative of the strength of the Christian churches. Women continued to be the more strongly religious sex. They made up in the region of two-thirds of churchgoers, and heavy pressure was put on young girls to be religiously observant. In a 1947 opinion poll, 54 per cent of women claimed to be churchgoers (compared to 44 per cent of men), whilst in 1951, in another survey, 58 per cent of women claimed to say prayers daily (compared to only 31 per cent of men).[3] Probably half of British children went to Sunday school in the 1950s, many of them led there by mothers. The Christian religion dominated many aspects of life, and imposed a strong moral code upon women. Single girls and women who gave birth were the subject of tremendous criticism and stigmatisation by family and community, and the churches ran homes

---

[3] G. Gorer, *Exploring English Character* (New York, Criterion Books, 1955), pp. 270, 453.

for unmarried mothers where these unfortunate females were 'retrained' and their children usually taken from them and put up for adoption. Sexual freedom was low for women. Periodic moral panics were created by the Conservative press and the state, including during the Second World War when American soldiers and airmen arrived. In the quite conservative moral climate of austerity in the 1950s, the number of children born out of wedlock reached a low point of under 5 per cent of births.

Focus on

Getting pregnant out of wedlock

To be a single mother in the 1950s was to break massive taboos about sexual purity before marriage. The consequences were dire, including for family relations. In Shropshire, Lorna Sage became pregnant in the late 1950s at the age of 16. She recalled:

> It was so unthinkable that when I felt ill, bloated, headachy, nauseous and, oh yes, my period hadn't come, I stayed in bed and we called out our new doctor, a pale, prim man in his thirties, Dr Clayton. After taking my temperature, asking about bowel movements and looking at my tongue, he looked out of the window at the copper beech tree, cleared his throat and asked could I be – um – pregnant? No, I said, feeling hot suddenly, No. He recommended a urine test anyway. Meanwhile I took aspirins for my aches, but they didn't go away and although school had started and I'd finished Virgil, I spent days at home. One of them Dr Clayton turned up again, embarrassed and puzzled. How old was I? Sixteen. He'd heard I was a clever girl, doing well at school, didn't we ever have biology lessons? I must have known what I was up to . . . From his first words and his tone, which had weariness and contempt in it, I knew it was true, just absolutely as until that moment I knew it couldn't be.
>
> I'd been caught out, I would have to pay. I was in trouble, I'd have no secrets any longer, I'd be exposed as a fraud, my fate wasn't my own, my treacherous body had somehow delivered me into other people's hands. . . . My mother came upstairs and opened the door, her face red and puffed up with outrage, her eyes blazing with tears. . . . For a minute she says nothing and then it comes out in a wail, *What have you done to me*? Over and over again. I've spoiled everything, now this house will be a shameful place . . . I've soiled and insulted her with my promiscuity, my sly, grubby lusts.

In the event, Lorna married her boyfriend and avoided being put in a Church Home for Unmarried Mothers.

Source: L. Sage, *Bad Blood: A Memoir* (London, Fourth Estate, 2001) p. 236. © 2001 Sage, L., HarperCollins Publishers Ltd (UK); courtesy of Faith Evans Associates (Europe); copyright © 2000 by Lorna Sage, reprinted by permission of HarperCollins Publishers (USA and Canada).

Until the 1960s, women's place in British society was still resolutely perceived by many in the middle classes, in government and in the newspapers to be in the home. As late as 1961, a female columnist in *Woman's Own* magazine advised its readers:

> You can't have deep and safe happiness in marriage and the exciting independence of a career as well . . . It isn't fair on your husband. I believe [any man] would tell you that he would rather his wife stayed at home and looked after his children, and was waiting for him with a decent meal and a sympathetic ear when he got home from work.[4]

This was a powerful message, enforced not merely by a male-dominated society; middle-class women themselves had cultivated a domestic-based notion of the respectable and moral woman. For working-class women, both before and after marriage, work was often an economic necessity, especially during times of high male unemployment. The types of jobs open to them remained restricted, however: retailing, work in textile factories, component assembly, and domestic service and cleaning. For many working- as well as middle-class women from the 1880s to the 1950s, the 'marriage bar' came into operation, imposed equally by employers, trade unions and women themselves, whereby a woman who married was expected to give up her job. For a woman in the civil service until the 1940s, to sustain a life-time career meant she had to stay single, and to sacrifice having a family.

Little by little, it was women who started to change the definition of womanhood. Professional careers remained limited until the 1960s – in teaching (into which as much as 70 per cent of all women graduates went in the 1920s and 1930s), pharmacy, medicine and nursing. For working-class women, the consumer boom of the 1930s brought new factory-working opportunities, whilst in the war years and in the 1950s they found in the time of labour shortage a welcome from employers in aircraft manufacture, food processing, laboratory work, office administration and component assembly. From 1945 to 1963, the main growth of women's employment was in part-time work; as many as 90 per cent of all part-time employees were women, and their role in the economy was designed at this period to sustain their domestic and family responsibilities.[5] In this way, there was much less change than the growth of female work might suggest to the fundamental role of women in British society. A woman's main role was to remain in the family, prioritised as reproducers rather than as workers. Sir William Beveridge, the architect of the welfare state, held the conviction that,

> The attitude of the housewife to gainful employment outside the home is not and should not be the same as that of the single woman. She has other duties . . . In the next thirty years housewives as Mothers have vital work to do in ensuring the adequate continuance of the British Race and of British ideals in the world.[6]

---

[4] Monica Dickens in *Woman's Own*, 28 January 1961, quoted in C.L. White, *The Women's Periodical Press in Britain 1946–1976* (London, HMSO, 1977), p. 11.

[5] A. McIvor, *A History of Work in Britain, 1880–1950* (Basingstoke, Palgrave Macmillan, 2001), p. 191.

[6] W. Beveridge, *Social Insurance and Allied Services (The Beveridge Report)* (CMD 6404) (London, HMSO, 1942), paras 114, 117.

Figure 30.1 Mothers with their babies waiting to be seen at a child welfare clinic in Glasgow in the 1950s.
Source: RCAHMS Enterprises

Yet, there were signs of pressure building for gender equality. One such pressure was coming from leisure and recreation. Until the 1910s, organised leisure for women was limited in scope, much of it based in the family, the church or community sharing. The cinema was the main engine of change. By 1920, half of the British population went to the cinema at least once a week, more than two-thirds of them female, and most films were aimed at women, dealing with themes of romance. The culture of the film was supported by film magazines and their focus on the celebrity of the screen stars. With the arrival of the films with sound – the 'talkies' – in 1927, cinema started to move up-market and the new Odeon picture houses were characterised by art nouveau architecture and plush seats. This made them even more welcoming to women, turning most cinemas into a strongly feminised environment. Through democratising recreation for women, the cinema became an engine of social change, though, ironically, it was where women saw traditional role models on screen who hankered after love and marriage, home and domesticity. Cinema-going quickly became the greatest organised leisure pursuit. At its peak in 1946, there were 1.6 billion cinema attendances per year, but it started a slow decline thereafter, fuelled from the mid-1950s by the rising popularity of television.

The expansion of leisure and recreation was an important way in which democratic Britain developed in these decades. For both women and men, the working classes and the middle and upper classes, access increased and diversified. With the opening up of the countryside by train, bus and especially the motor car, the interwar period witnessed a dramatic increase in visits by both middle- and working-class families for leisure. Men and women were attracted to rambling and cycling, and the more adventurous were to be seen mountaineering. Day-trippers were joined by weekenders and holiday makers, staying at bed and breakfasts, public houses and small hotels. Political issues could be involved. Rights of way and pathways brought urban folk deep into the countryside, fostering some resentment, cultural clash and sometimes disputes over access rights. The Derbyshire hill, Kinder Scout, became the focus of attention into the issue of access rights after the landowners forbade entry. A mass trespass in April 1932 by ramblers of the communist-inspired British Workers' Sports Federation led to the arrest of six people for unlawful assembly and breach of the peace (of whom five were jailed), but laid the basis for access legislation in 1938 and 1940 and the formation of national parks in England and Wales in the 1950s.

The appeal to family life was uppermost in the image of women and men enjoying culture and leisure – never more than in the 1951 Festival of Britain on the banks of the Thames in central London, which showed off in a mass of displays new design and style in home design, kitchens and fashion – the things that austerity made it difficult for Britons to enjoy. One of the reasons for a renewed emphasis on family life was a new panic about the youth problem. Concern for juvenile delinquency was not new in Britain, with the 'hooligan' issue of the late 1890s, and juvenile crime rose in the depression years of the 1930s. The novelty by the 1950s in many places was the youth gang, roaming loose in jumbled bomb sites and along city streets, jostling passers-by with an insouciant hard machismo. The fears were presciently exploited in the 1947 film version of Graham Greene's pre-war novel *Brighton Rock* (1938), which depicted this combination of youth, male bravado and crime in even a well-to-do coastal resort. But in cities like Glasgow, gangs became a moral panic in the 1950s and 1960s, with sociologists making inquiry of the habits and dangers they presented.

The gangs seemed to relate to wider youth development. The teddy boys of the early- and mid-1950s, dressed in a pastiche of Edwardian-era suits, were followed by rockers of the mid- to late 1950s, inspired by Elvis Presley and rock 'n' roll. Music was starting to be very important to youth culture in a novel way. Until the mid-1950s, sheet music outsold old shellac 78rpm recordings because of the latter's high cost, but the coming of cheaper vinyl records enabled mass sales of singles and then LPs (45rpm singles and 33rpm LPs respectively). This was the technology that generated the youth revolution. Music and fashion for young people had, until the 1950s, differed little from that of adults; youthful aspiration was to dress like adults and emulate their orchestral dance music. But things started to change. In music, the skiffle bands of 1957–9 introduced many (including John Lennon of The Beatles) to making music, whilst stars like Cliff Richard and Tommy Steele started a British version of American rock and pop. A new youth culture based on juke boxes in coffee bars swept Britain and, by the early 1960s, music sales and fashion were starting to foster a widespread pop culture of town-hall dances, whilst orchestra-based dancing declined sharply. In the face of signs of increasing sexual activity and an explosion in youth crime after 1957, the nation – including the Conservative Party – was starting to see the need for a liberalisation of British institutions to keep pace with a rapid transformation in youth and popular culture. Britain was on the verge of the sixties' revolution.

Ethnicity

The ethnic composition of Britain changed dramatically between 1919 and 1963. From being an overwhelming white nation, divided by Christian denomination and class, Britain had, by the end of this period, become a society where race was to be a new point of division.

The 1920s witnessed a rising tide of awareness of racial and religious minorities in Britain. The Jews, the Irish and the Muslims each became the victims of bigotry. The worst examples of racial and ethnic tension were in Northern Ireland. With the formation of the Irish Free State in 1922 which partitioned the island (see Chapter 28), the remaining six counties in the north were formed into a province of the United Kingdom, and sectarian tension between Protestant and Catholic was intense and at times bloody. This was an area of Britain where religion mattered very deeply. Not only did it divide communities, Christian church observance was exceptionally strong. It is likely that over half of the population attended church on a weekly basis, and the symbols of Protestant loyalism and Catholic-dominated republicanism ran throughout the state. It was also an armed society, with guns acquired through legal and illegal means. Protestants outnumbered Catholics by over two to one in the province, dominating its political, civil and police institutions. Protestants also dominated in the commercial and business community, and there was widespread discrimination against Catholics in employment. Even more, there was suspicion and hatred over the desire of Catholics to become part of the emerging republic to the south. The result was endemic violence, especially in the early 1930s, with over 300 dead in street clashes in 1933 alone. Sectarian clashes quietened in the later 1940s and 1950s, but the essential division in Northern Irish society remained.

Sectarian conflict between Protestant and Catholic was also felt in mainland Britain, though never with the bloody consequences or the institutional divide to be found in Northern Ireland. In Scotland, the 1920s and 1930s witnessed the Catholic Church starting to acquire some influence and status in civil affairs – notably with the foundation from 1919 of state-funded Catholic schools. A reaction set in almost immediately, with hostile Protestant public opinion rallying to the supposed danger of 'Rome on the rates', and, by the late 1920s, small political parties of extreme Protestants were gaining elected councillors in Edinburgh and Glasgow. In Liverpool, the peak of sectarian rivalry occurred in the 1890s and 1900s, but in the interwar period, as in other towns like Manchester, Preston and London, as well as in Scotland, the Orange Order kept alive Protestant identity and hostility to Catholic intrusion, and discrimination in employment tended to restrain Catholics from getting promotion to skilled jobs. In the 1940s and 1950s, however, sectarianism became more and more marginalised from civil life in mainland Britain. Council housing reduced sectarian discrimination, though this was accomplished, mostly by common consent, in Northern Ireland and some Scottish towns by segregation of Catholic and Protestant housing estates. Full employment and prosperity opened up more skilled and professional jobs to Catholics (notably in local government). Anti-Catholicism declined most in England, but in Scotland it held an entrenched position in both education and in the enmity between some fans of Rangers and Celtic football clubs, which each attracted rival support in Northern Ireland.

Ethnic and religious riots of one stamp or another started to become a feature of British experience. One of the most politically charged was the so-called Battle of Cable Street in the East End of London in 1936, when some 200,000 Jews, communists, and members of socialist and Labour organisations rallied to head off a march against British Jewry by 3,000 British fascists led by Oswald Mosley. With hindsight, this was a tipping point when the fascist threat was faced down in British popular culture. Though anti-Semitism was a significant feature of Britain (especially in the south of England), it lacked the potency that it had in Weimar and Nazi Germany and elsewhere in interwar Europe, where fascist parties were fostered on the back of rising popular opposition to Jewish business and ghettos. Nevertheless, religious bigotries between Catholics and Protestants, and against Jews, were part of the social climate in Britain, as elsewhere in the interwar period. The Second World War did much to reduce these, and especially after the revelation of the Jewish Holocaust in the 1940s, the position of Jews in Britain was never likely to become again the subject of organised and mass bigotry.

Until the late 1940s, Britain remained a nation almost totally white. But black, middle-eastern and Asian migrants started to change perceptions during the 1950s. There had been small numbers of blacks and Asians in Britain in previous centuries, many brought as servants or freed slaves of British landowners in the Empire. But in the depression of the 1920s there was a perceived 'flood' of Muslim immigration – some Yemeni and Arab seamen, as well as Indian pedlars in Glasgow, Liverpool and elsewhere, who travelled the country selling textiles and other products. White opinion turned against them, especially in dock cities like Cardiff, South Shields and Glasgow, leading to the government's 1925 Special Restrictions Order that tried to control immigration through an alien certification system. Council housing, built and rented out by local authorities to improve the housing of the working classes and the poor, became subject to deliberate racist management. For instance, Cardiff town council apparently amended by-laws to prevent Muslims from obtaining council-housing tenancies outside of a designated ghetto area of Bute Town. Immigration of Muslims did grow in the 1940s and 1950s, but remained relatively low. Much more numerous in the 1950s was the migration of black Caribbeans, who were predominantly Christian, coming to work in Britain. Starting with the arrival of the *HMT Empire Windrush* at Tilbury in June 1948 with 492 passengers from Jamaica and Trinidad, the numbers arriving rose dramatically during the 1950s, encouraged by government in order to make good the labour shortage. Between 1948 and 1962, there was no legal difference between British and colonial citizens and so entry was open to migrants from the colonies. Racist reaction developed quickly, particular in Birmingham and London, where the early Afro-Caribbean migrants settled. Periodic disturbances and assaults on black lodging houses were reported in the early 1950s, and the British fascist leader of the interwar period, Oswald Mosley, attracted renewed political support in Birmingham. In Notting Hill in London on August Bank Holiday 1958, several days of riot and disturbance were started when some white youths attacked a mixed-race couple. Race issues continued to escalate, culminating in a reversal of immigration policy in 1962, from which point entry to Britain was made progressively more difficult for colonial citizens. The race issue was then projected to the top of the political agenda for the remainder of the 1960s.

By 1963, Britain was transforming into a multiracial society. The way in which this was achieved, and the implications for migrants and British society, will be examined more closely in Chapter 35.

Further reading

Benson, J., *Affluence and Authority: A Social History of Twentieth-Century Britain* (London, Hodder Arnold, 2005)

Brown, C.G., *Religion and Society in Twentieth-Century Britain* (Harlow, Pearson Longman, 2006)

Carnevali, F., Strange, J.-M., and Johnson, P., (eds), *20th Century Britain: Economic, Cultural and Social Change* (London, Longman, 2007)

Hill, J., *Sport, Leisure and Culture in Twentieth-Century Britain* (London, Palgrave Macmillan, 2002)

McKibbin, R., *Classes and Cultures: England 1918–1951* (Oxford, Oxford University Press, 1998)

Smout, T.C., *A Century of the Scottish People 1830–1950* (London, Fontana, 1997)

31

From Attlee to Macmillan
1945–63

The period from 1945 until 1963 saw the country face huge challenges as it adjusted to a post-war world where it was, to all intents, bankrupt; where parts of many bombed towns and cities had to be rebuilt; where an empire was no longer sustainable; where hot war gave way to cold war; and where there was great uncertainty about where Britain's future interests and role in the world lay. The remarkable thing is how much was achieved, despite the huge difficulties.

Labour in power

The extent of Labour's victory was a surprise even to the Labour leaders. To many of the rank and file, the first majority Labour government presented the opportunity to implement aspects of a programme that socialists had been debating for more than half a century. Central to this was nationalisation, taking into state ownership 'the means of production, distribution and exchange', as clause 4 of the Labour Party's constitution of 1918 had it. The ultimate goal would be the eventual elimination from industry of private capitalists, with the profits going back to the community rather than to shareholders.

The Bank of England was the first major institution to be taken under the new government's control. This was hardly revolutionary and merely recognised the role that the Bank had been playing as the nation's central bank since the early nineteenth century. The governor and the deputy governor stayed in office. The really symbolic act of nationalisation was that of the coal mines – the sweet revenge for defeat in the 1926 strike, many miners thought. On 1 January 1947 notices went up announcing, 'This colliery is now managed by the National Coal Board on behalf of the people.' It was not just ideology. Reports before and during the war had recognised that much of the industry needed modernising. The units were still too small and there had been a lack of investment in the equipment available for getting and hauling coal and in facilities for workers (see Chapter 20). There was no great unwillingness to see the government take it over and the compensation to the coal owners was good. The structure of putting an appointed board in charge was one that Herbert Morrison, the Home Secretary, had developed in 1930–1 when extending state control of electricity production and laying the foundations of London Transport. It fell short of the kind of control of industry by workers that had been talked about before 1918.

The start for the Coal Board was not auspicious. Three weeks after nationalisation, the country was faced with the worst winter since 1881 – a winter that went on and on. There had been a failure to build up adequate reserves and coal shortages were followed by power cuts. The people in their nice new 'prefabs' (prefabricated buildings, asbestos-built, in many cases) found that they had neither electric fires nor coal to burn. The Royal Family wisely decided to take a trip to South Africa on the newly completed, but already obsolete, battleship, *HMS Vanguard*, while the remnants of the British Raj arrived home from India to a cold, austere land, where both coal and servants were lacking.

Next on the list for nationalisation was transport. Two national airline companies were created – the British Overseas Airways Corporation (BOAC) for long hauls and British European Airways (BEA) for domestic and European – both flying out of the new London airport at Heathrow, where the check-in area was initially in a tent. The four railway companies that had existed since 1923, but had been under government control during the war, were merged into British Railways, while long-distance road transport, that had also been tightly controlled and, to an extent, co-ordinated during the war, was nationalised in 1948 as British Road Services. The communications network of Cable and Wireless and the gas industry were also taken into public ownership, both seen as monopolies that were central to the national interest.

As nationalisation proceeded, Conservative opposition to it mounted and came to a head with the proposal to nationalise the iron and steel industry. Unlike most of the others, this was not an ailing industry that needed to be bailed out. It was a clear case of nationalisation in principle. Whereas the coal industry and the railways had for decades been the subject of extensive government intervention, steel was modern and profitable and the owners and their Conservative allies were willing to fight against nationalisation. Also, whereas nationalisation had been central to the demands of mining unions since at least 1917, the steel unions were not very keen on it. It was blocked by the House of Lords, using the argument that there had to be a general election to test the public view. Steel nationalisation was delayed by the House of Lords until after a new election and eventually went ahead in 1951.

One of the strongest cards that Labour played in the election was its commitment to the reform of welfare provision as spelled out in the Beveridge Report of 1942. This was a vital part of the 'New Jerusalem' that some held out to voters. The burden on government to push these measures through was great and so too were the costs, requiring the maintenance of austerity measures throughout the government's life and adding to the financial problems.

The fact that the country was bankrupt in 1945 and dependent upon an American loan on harsh conditions meant that financial difficulties cast a perpetual shadow over what the Labour government could achieve. A week after the end of the war with Japan, to the consternation of the Cabinet, lend-lease abruptly came to an end, and Britain had to find the resources to pay for imports. A loan of just under $4 billion had to be negotiated, repayable over 50 years, amid concerns from the American Congress that the money would be used to subsidise socialism. The need to keep public expenditure in check and to curb imports was great. Bread rationing, which had been avoided during the war, was introduced in the summer of 1946. With the American loan exhausted by the summer of 1947, and a condition of the loan that sterling had to become fully convertible into other currencies coming into force, the crisis became more acute. A flight from sterling into dollars gained momentum. Convertibility had to be suspended within a matter of weeks.

There were also tensions over nationalisation. Not all the Cabinet were committed to nationalisation of iron and steel, but a compromise proposal that fell short of complete nationalisation met with a furious outburst from the left of the party. There were conspiratorial moves to replace Attlee, but the coterie of leaders who had been in government since 1940 were all showing signs of wilting under the strain. Sir Stafford Cripps became Chancellor in 1947 and his austere demeanour was a timely accompaniment to the austerity budgets that he introduced. Taxes were raised, control over public spending was tightened and the unions were persuaded to accept a wage freeze. He succeeded in getting the economy back on an even keel, with inflation kept in control, and the coming of Marshall Aid from the United States helped pay the unexpectedly high costs of the welfare reforms. A new financial crisis in the autumn of 1949, however, resulted in the dramatic devaluation of the pound by some 30 per cent, from £1 = $4.03 to £1 = $2.80.

From the summer of 1947 there is clear evidence of a loss of faith among the ranks of ministers in state planning of the economy and industry that had seemed to work so well during the war. They responded to pressure from business for an end to restrictions, with Harold Wilson, at the Board of Trade, promising a 'bonfire of controls'. Nonetheless, with hindsight it is possible to see the immense achievements of Attlee's government. There was no return to the unemployment that had blighted the lives of so many in the two decades after the First World War. Surveys showed that levels of poverty had been dramatically reduced from the almost one in three before 1939 to something like one in 20 or less in 1950.

Britain in the world

It was Attlee and the Foreign Secretary, Ernest Bevin, who appeared at the resumed Potsdam Conference at the end of July 1945 – no doubt to the surprise of Stalin and the new American President, Truman. There were those who had hopes of a change in foreign policy to something more 'socialist', but neither Attlee nor Bevin were the men to bring this about. The former was the product of that most imperialist of public schools, Haileybury, while Bevin, as a trade unionist, had developed an almost pathological hatred of communists. Both were determined that Britain would show that it was still capable of being a 'great power'.

In spite of the dire economic and financial state of the nation, the government was anxious to present itself to the world as still a power to be reckoned with across the globe. The Treasury pressed for drastic reductions in the armed services, but arguments about the need to assert British prestige through the maintenance of global imperial commitments carried the day. Conscription was retained, despite its costs, and despite a big rebellion by Labour backbenchers, with all 18-year olds or those who had completed higher education being required to undertake two years of military or 'national' service.

Attlee's decision to push ahead with the manufacture of Britain's own atomic bomb in early 1947 was about prestige, not defence, and was carried out without the knowledge of Parliament. Bevin had no doubt that the country had to have the bomb, no matter what the cost, and 'with the bloody Union Jack flying on top of it'.[1] But the decision also stemmed from a realisation that the United States, despite the war-time Quebec Agreement, was not going to share its nuclear information.

At the Foreign Office, Ernest Bevin, who had once believed that 'Left could talk to Left' and that Britain could act as a mediator between the USA and the USSR, soon abandoned the idea and increasingly aligned himself with American attitudes. In 1946, at Truman's home town of Fulton, Missouri, Churchill kept true to his deep-seated antipathy to communism, and identified an 'iron curtain' dividing Europe. Bevin, who had spent three decades battling communist influence within the Labour Party and the trade unions, found it not too difficult to adjust to the Truman Doctrine of containment of a totalitarian USSR by means of aid to democratic countries. Little effort was made to conciliate the critics of Bevin's policies from what became the 'Keep Left' wing of the party. One reward was the remarkable offer in June 1947 from the new American Secretary of State, George Marshall, of economic assistance to Europe. Bevin had the sound instinct to seize-the opportunity with both hands and to ensure that Britain, France and West Germany, at least, came up with a plan, even if the Soviets rejected it as a capitalist plot. Britain received around £700 million of the aid, a vital contribution to its economic recovery.

Dependence on American goodwill meant a desire to avoid too frequent divergence on policy. This was most strikingly apparent in Palestine, where American pressure forced a modification of British restrictions on Jewish immigration (see Chapter 33). With growing suspicion of Soviet intentions, it also meant the return of bases for American bombers in Britain. Bevin, determined to get American commitment to European defence and fearful of a return to the American isolationism that had followed the First World War, also played a major role in the emergence of the North Atlantic

---

[1] A. Bullock, *Ernest Bevin, Foreign Secretary 1945–51* (Oxford, Oxford University Press, 1985), p. 352.

Treaty Organisation (NATO) in April 1949. This was in response to the Soviet blockade of West Berlin – itself an attempt to prevent the creation of a separate West German state from the three non-Soviet sectors of occupied Germany. By the North Atlantic Treaty, an attack on any one of the 12 members that eventually were included would be regarded as an attack on all. The increase in military commitments from 1948 onwards did more than anything to create the economic difficulties that the Labour government faced. The desire to remain a 'world power' and the failure to recognise the reality of Britain's changed position in the world was to bedevil the next half century and more.

By 1949, there was a strong sense of a government running out of steam. Bevin had already had a heart attack and Attlee, Morrison and Cripps had all spent time in hospital. The government was finding that it was coming up against growing obstruction of its aims from the City of London, from business interests and from some of the civil servants. People were tired of nearly a decade of austerity and relations with the trade-union movement had deteriorated. Attempts to introduce a planning element into wages met with fierce union resistance. A wages policy was seen as a threat to the authority of the trade-union movement. With a high demand for labour in coal and at the docks, union leaders, still tied by the wartime rules that, to all intents, banned strikes, found it difficult to curb unofficial action by their members. The Conservatives had regained confidence and had expectations of a return to power.

The defeat of the Conservatives in 1945 had stimulated a massive reorganisation of the party. Policies were being reshaped by younger members to put the party in tune once again with 'the spirit of the age'. Conservative policy statements revealed a concern with social issues that, to some, had seemed markedly absent in the 1930s. There was an acceptance of a mixed economy, with elements of public ownership and with no attempt to undo all of Labour's nationalisation measures.

Nearly 1.5 million more people voted for Labour and its allies in the election of February 1950 (when there was a turnout of 83.9 per cent) than had done so in 1945, but the votes were generally in places where Labour already had large majorities. The redrawing of boundaries by the 1948 Representation of the People Act, which reduced seats in some of the cities and reorganised London constituencies, cost Labour some 30 seats. The south was swinging away from Labour and the Labour majority tumbled to only 6 over all other parties. The Liberals clung on with a mere 9 members, having greatly assisted the Conservatives by putting up candidates in only 109 constituencies.

The government itself was in disarray. Stafford Cripps was dying and the Chancellorship went to Hugh Gaitskell, not to the leading left-winger in the government, Aneurin Bevan, who had piloted through the new National Health Service (see Chapter 32). It began a process of disenchantment on Bevan's part with the leadership and a bitter personal antipathy towards Gaitskell that was to harm the party for a decade. The contrast was striking. Gaitskell was a Hampstead intellectual, the voice of the professional middle classes, 'a desiccated calculating machine' in Bevan's eyes. Bevan was from a mining background in the Welsh valleys, all emotion and socialist rhetoric, although with an extravagant lifestyle.

The government was immediately faced with yet another financial crisis, exacerbated by the war that broke out when communist North Korean forces, in June 1950, crossed the 38th Parallel into South Korea after the Americans, who had occupied the country since 1945, had pulled out. The government had no doubt that Britain had to back the American response, in what was called a 'police action' under the banner of the United Nations. The argument was that it was necessary to halt the North Koreans to deter Soviet aggression elsewhere, but the real concern was to ensure that America did not once again turn its back on Europe. There was initial success; in October, the invaders had been driven back across the 38th Parallel and, despite warnings from Mao Zedong's new Communist regime in China, there was talk of reunification.

Chinese forces now appeared on the scene. The British government was appalled at the American talk of bombing China. Attlee flew to Washington to try to restrain the Americans in their fervid anti-communism. There is little evidence that he had much effect, but he helped counter the voices from the Republican Right in Congress who were emphasising that America's primary interests lay in Asia rather than Europe. Anxious to do nothing to undermine Truman, Attlee's government fell into line with the Americans and with this came a doubling of defence expenditure in less than two years. To pay for this, Gaitskell introduced charges on dental and ophthalmic services, an action which gave Bevan a reason to resign. Many saw his resignation as the result of personal pique on Bevan's part at having been passed over for the chancellorship, but, as Peter Hennessy and others have argued, Bevan's case against rearmament was a powerful one and the cost put a strain on the economy just when recovery was getting underway.[2]

The Labour government of 1950–1 struggled on for 20 months of dreadful scenes, with the sick and dying being carried through the voting lobbies to maintain the government's narrow majority. Crisis followed crisis, with the Conservatives using every tactic to grind down Labour and keeping the House sitting for endless hours. The one bright spot was the highly successful Festival of Britain on the London South Bank, intended to signal Britain's revival after the war, by displaying new design, art and technology (see Chapter 30).

A new election was called in October 1951. Once again, the Labour vote went up, with the party polling more votes than ever before or since, and, once again, getting more votes than the Conservatives. Nonetheless, the Conservatives had an overall majority of 17, with the Liberals reduced from 9 seats to 6. Liberal votes went to the Conservatives, reflecting a middle-class disenchantment with austerity.[3] The country entered 13 years of Conservative rule and the Labour Party began to tear at itself.

There is still a fierce debate over the achievements of the Attlee government. Could more have been achieved in creating a better and fairer society, by using the opportunity of a huge Labour majority? Or, was too much spent too quickly on welfare measures, at the expense of rebuilding and modernising industry? The government was driven by a determination that conditions for the mass of the population would be very different from what they had been before 1939 and in this they undoubtedly

[2] Peter Hennessy, *Never Again: Britain 1945–1951* (London, Jonathan Cape, 1992), p. 418.

[3] Peter Hennessy, *Having it so Good: Britain in the Fifties* (London, Allen Lane, 2006), p. 191.

succeeded. The extent to which a broader socialist programme could be introduced was limited by the resources available, the weariness with war and austerity and a dependence upon American goodwill and aid.

Winston Churchill as peace Prime Minister

Churchill at 77 was, by 1951, really too old for government, although the accession of a young and photogenic Queen Elizabeth early in 1952 contrasted well and led to talk of a new Elizabethan age. Churchill lacked the energy to do very much and played the role of war statesman, interesting himself in foreign affairs. But even in this field, most of the work was left to the Foreign Secretary, Anthony Eden. Domestic affairs were largely in the hands of R.A. Butler, the Chancellor of the Exchequer, and he encouraged the development of the social policies worked out in opposition. His policies seemed so similar to those of his Labour predecessor, Gaitskell, that there was talk of 'Butskellism'. Relations with the trade unions remained better than they had been during the last years of the Labour government. The Conservatives committed themselves to building 300,000 houses per year – more than Labour had ever achieved. Under Harold Macmillan at the Ministry of Housing, this figure was reached in 1953 and, in the following year, some 347,000 homes were completed, although at the cost of capital projects in education and health. Its contribution to solving the worst of housing problems was limited, since the houses being built were more tied to the demands of middle-class commuters than to the needs of those being cleared from the slums.

There was a gradual slackening of Labour controls. Wartime food subsidies were cut and rationing was gradually brought to an end. In 1953, 6d (2.5p) was slashed from the basic rate of income tax. Another step on what was dubbed 'the Conservative road to freedom' was denationalisation. Few saw much chance of a market for the coal mines and the railways, but steel was sold off, together with parts of road transport, although it took many years before the privatisation process was completed. By 1954, the government could look back on a fair amount of success: prices had been stable since 1952; there was a favourable balance of payments; industry was growing rapidly and levels of employment were high. In February 1955, the decision was made that Britain should produce its own hydrogen bomb to supersede the atomic bomb that had been tested in 1952. The public argument was that such a bomb was needed to deter the Soviet Union from an attack on Britain. Once again, as Churchill made plain, the main motivation was to maintain the status of Britain as a great power and he and his successors in government through until the end of the 1980s continued to spend a higher proportion on the military than any other European state.

In 1953 Churchill had a major stroke, but the extent of his illness was a well-kept secret, unreported in the press. Throughout 1954 the Cabinet more or less ran without him, and not until April 1955, after some persistent pressure from colleagues, did Churchill retire. He was succeeded by his patient heir apparent, Sir Anthony Eden – a man whose good looks and patience had got him far but whose vanity, indecision and irritability (to a large extent brought about by persistent ill health) were to prove a major handicap.

Eden's government

Eden's ministry had a good start. Butler's tax cut contributed to an election victory in May 1955 that saw a Conservative gain of some 23 seats, giving them a majority of 59 over all other parties. He won the election against a bitterly divided Labour Party, with Bevan and his supporters demanding a stronger commitment to socialism and an anti-American rhetoric in foreign policy. However, though Eden was experienced in foreign affairs, his lack of experience in office in a domestic department was a disadvantage.

Crisis hit almost at once. In the aftermath of the election, sterling came under pressure and the balance of payments went into the red. Industrial relations were deteriorating, with a rash of unofficial strikes. 1955 saw the largest number of disputes since records began in 1893 and the largest number of days lost through strikes for more than 20 years. There were also worrying signs of inflation and of a country whose commitments were overextended and which was living beyond its means. The result was an autumn emergency budget when taxes on purchases, but not on income, were sharply increased and economic stagnation set in, which it took more than two years to shake off.

Discredited, Butler was shunted out and Harold Macmillan came in as Chancellor, faced with shrinking gold and dollar reserves as confidence in the pound slipped. Public spending was squeezed, including defence expenditure. Indecision was obvious in many of the government's actions and even a sympathetic press was calling for the 'smack of firm government'. War was not what they had in mind, but it was what they got with the Suez affair of August 1956 (see Chapter 33). Aware of the accusations of weakness and, indeed, treachery that had been thrown at him from within his own party in 1954 when he had agreed to withdrawal of troops from Egypt, Eden was determined to have his 'finest hour' by ousting Nasser. He saw the Egyptian president as a dictator who must not be appeased. In practice, Eden showed great indecision when faced with a huge public outcry, signs of mutiny among some of the reservists called up, and American pressure. Macmillan, who had supported intervention provided it was hard, fast and effective, was the first to appreciate that there was no option but withdrawal when the Americans, deeply concerned at the risk of the oil-rich Middle East falling under Soviet influence, applied financial pressure and there was an imminent danger of the sterling financial area collapsing. The Suez war brought a gradual awareness of the limitations now of British power.

Eden's career crumbled in illness and ignominious failure and in January 1957 he resigned. Macmillan was his successor. Many expected Butler to succeed, but he had had a bad press for his failures at the Treasury. Also he had always been seen as someone with liberal leanings within the party and these were confirmed by his barely concealed opposition to the Suez invasion.

Labour found it difficult to capitalise on Conservative difficulties. The party had not used the time since 1951 to come up with fresh ideas. Bevan formed an anti-American left-wing ginger group which, by fair means and foul, fought for control of constituency parties and for domination at conferences. Generally, the recurring issues were over policies that seemed to align Britain too closely with the United States. The rearmament of Germany to bring it into NATO caused fierce debate in 1954. This was followed by concern that Britain might be pulled into America's increasing involvement in Indo-China, which Attlee declined to condemn. But, strong arguments were emerging from some of the younger MPs that the party had to move away from seeing socialism as largely about nationalisation. Attlee, too, clung to office rather too long and a great deal of the trouble stemmed from the battle for succession between Hugh Gaitskell and Bevan.

The Macmillan years 1957–63

It was a diminished, divided and depressed nation that Macmillan took over. Beneath an outward image of a slightly decadent Edwardian was a man of intellectual ability and political shrewdness, with great energy when it came to the exercise of power. In spite of the fact that Suez marked the symbolic end of British power in a world sense, Macmillan was determined to reassert Britain's role alongside the United States. Relations with the United States were helped by the fact that, under Macmillan, the Empire was shed with some speed (see Chapter 33).

Economically, things were fairly bleak throughout 1957. This caused an industrial crisis, with widespread strikes and a hardening of attitude towards trade unions. Since 1951, relations between the government and the trade unions had been remarkably good, but in 1957 they went sour, with calls for curbs on union power. Key trade-union leaders rejected all calls for 'wage restraint' and such was the fervid atmosphere that there was talk of a general strike. Relations were not helped by the Rent Act of 1957 that removed rent controls that had been in place since 1917 and allowed rent increases to some 5 million houses. Perhaps the most significant policy was the announcement in the Defence White Paper that conscription would come to an end in 1960, together with the decision that nuclear weaponry would be central to the country's defence. Nuclear armaments were seen as cheaper than conventional weaponry and the threat of retaliation the only viable defence against attack. The USSR was perceived as the threatening aggressor, although why the Soviets might want to attack Britain was never made clear. What was behind the policy was a determination to restore the so-called 'special relationship' with the United States, which Macmillan, who knew President Eisenhower well from the war years, felt he had a particular ability to strengthen.

With economic difficulties continuing at the end of 1957, the Chancellor of the Exchequer, and the Treasury ministers recommended further sharp reductions in public expenditure. But Macmillan, anxious about industrial unrest and concerned about rising unemployment, was resistant to the demands for further savings in the area of welfare. The Chancellor and his two junior ministers resigned, a decision that

Macmillan *en route* for a six-week tour (hardly conceivable these days) of South-east Asia and Australasia sought to brush off as 'little local difficulties'.

On his return, Macmillan confidently pushed for reflation of the economy and the second half of 1958 into 1959 saw an economic boom stimulated by a budget that encouraged increased consumption. Import prices fell and exports and production rose. Wages also rose and, with them, domestic consumption. The government chopped 9d off income tax, 2d off beer and cut purchase tax. In the autumn of 1959 came the election and yet another Conservative victory, with the Conservatives gaining 20 seats from Labour, although losing ground in Scotland. Gaitskell had promised that a Labour government would not increase income tax, but this could not compete with Macmillan's reassurance that the country had 'never had it so good'. The Tories had an overall majority of 100.

Attlee had retired soon after the election of 1955 and was succeeded by Hugh Gaitskell. Surprisingly, this brought a measure of peace with the Bevanites, presumably because Bevan accepted his defeat and had an eye on future office. Throughout

Focus on

The Conservative Party in 1959

This is taken from the 1959 Conservative Election Manifesto, *The Next Five Years*:

The British economy is sounder today than at any time since the first world war. Sterling has been re-established as a strong and respected currency. Under Conservative governments we have earned abroad £1,600 million more than we have spent. Our exports have reached the highest peak ever. Overseas, mostly in the Commonwealth, we are investing nearly double what we could manage eight years ago. Capital investment at home, to build for the future, is over half as large again. To match this, and make it possible, people are saving more than ever before.

The paraphernalia of controls have been swept away. The call-up is being abolished. We have cut taxes in seven Budgets, whilst continuing to develop the social services. We have provided over two million new homes and almost two million new school places, a better health service and a modern pensions plan. We have now stabilised the cost of living while maintaining full employment. We have shown that Conservative freedom works. Life is better with the Conservatives. . . .

By raising living standards and by social reform we are succeeding in creating One Nation at home. We must now carry this policy into the wider world where the gap between the industrialised and the underdeveloped nations is still so great. This can be done by individual service, by increased trade and by investment, public and private.

Source: http://www.conservativemanifesto.com/1959/1959-conservative-manifesto.shtml

the 1950s, Bevan had stood for unilateral nuclear disarmament by Britain, but in 1957 he announced his belief that for Britain to abandon the hydrogen bomb was to send a British Foreign Secretary 'naked into the conference chamber'. It was a blow to the left of the party, which lost its most charismatic figure. Bevan died in 1960, leaving behind myths and what has been called a 'sentimental' notion of socialism[4] to which sections of the Labour Party felt it necessary to pay homage for the next 30 years.

Efforts at rethinking Labour policy were going on, with most of the new ideas coming from people on the right of the party. Gaitskell's allies argued for a jettisoning of some of the old shibboleths. Anthony Crosland's *The Future of Socialism*, published in October 1956, rejected the Marxist argument, held by most on the left, that capitalism would inevitably collapse under the weight of its own contradictions. He argued that the ownership of industry was irrelevant and that what mattered was who managed it and how it was managed. Crosland called for the abandonment of Clause 4 of the party's constitution, with its commitment to nationalisation. Instead, he focused on how to create a more equal society through education and welfare, and a more liberal society by making divorce easier and repealing laws on censorship and homosexuality. Crosland's book influenced the next two political generations, but, meanwhile, it unleashed another spate of internecine struggle within the party. To the defence of Clause 4 was added the demand for nuclear disarmament and behind that banner marched the swelling ranks of the Campaign for Nuclear Disarmament, formed in February 1958 by a group of Quaker pacifists and leftish intellectuals.

The Labour Party fought the 1959 election with high expectations of victory. With defeat, the splits and bitterness intensified. Gaitskell could barely hide his contempt for what he saw as an emotional irrationality in CND and he detected communist infiltration behind the demands for unilateral disarmament. When, in 1959, a motion in favour of unilateral disarmament was carried at the Labour Party Conference, Gaitskell refused to accept the conference decision and declared that he would 'fight, fight and fight again' to overturn it. This he succeeded in doing in 1960, when unilateralism was rejected and the party began to seek a compromise between socialism and Crosland's revisionism. To a great extent, the party began to emerge revitalised from these struggles and something of a political truce with the left persisted. For the first time, Gaitskell seemed to be getting across to the public as a personality. His hostility to moves for Britain to join the European Common Market, was in tune with most on the left, although a few of his former allies parted company with him (see Chapter 39). Not all had Gaitskell's faith that the Commonwealth could be turned into some alternative world bloc. Suddenly, however, early in 1963 he died, aged only 56, to be succeeded by Harold Wilson, who had the credentials for the left of having been associated with Bevan in his resignation over health charges in 1951. He proved to be an extremely effective leader of the Opposition as the Conservative government began to weaken.

The years 1959–60 were portrayed in the cartoons of 'Vicky' (Victor Weisz) as the era of 'Supermac' and 'MacWonder'. Politically secure at home, Macmillan sought to

---

[4] J. Campbell, *Nye Bevan: A Biography* (London, Hodder & Stoughton, 1987), pp. 373–5.

Focus on

The Labour Party in 1960

This extract is from the writings of Anthony Crosland (1918–77), MP for Southampton and later South Gloucestershire, who was on the moderate left of the Labour Party and its leading intellectual. His influential book *The Future of Socialism* was published in 1956.

Next, the Party must rid itself of the image of being pro-austerity and anti-prosperity. To the extent that this is a hangover from the post-1945 period of rationing and controls, it will soon disappear of its own accord. Unfortunately it is constantly being refurbished by Labour speakers, and notably by those moralists in the Party who repeatedly condemn the whole affluent society as rotten and evil. They fail to distinguish between the fact of affluence, which is to be welcomed unreservedly since it widens the range of choice and opportunity to the average family, and certain avoidable attributes of the society, such as the distribution of the affluence, the neglect of social spending, the vulgar commercialisation of culture, and so on. This confusion of the whole with the part creates a most harmful impression of hostility to economic progress, and allows the Tories to appropriate the sole kudos for being the party of prosperity. In consequence, they remain in power, and so frustrate all possibility of reforming the society; for, as Samuel Lubell once remarked, only God can create a tree, but only Government can create a park.

The anti-prosperity image is fed from another source. Many Labour speakers decry the present prosperity as 'bogus' or 'phoney', alleging that it must either collapse under the excessive weight of hire-purchase or be engulfed in an inevitable slump. There is no warrant for either of these views. Consumer debt per head of population is three times as high in the US as in Britain, and half as high again as a proportion of personal income; yet the system has not collapsed, and prosperity continues to increase. And despite the certainty of minor recessions, something approaching full employment will be maintained in Britain – if only because the Conservatives know that a failure here would lead to certain defeat at the polls. Without doubt, the prosperity is badly distributed, as performance, in terms of growth and investment, is pitifully poor by international standards. But the fact that the prosperity could be greater does not make it any less real; and to be always nagging at it is simply to give the impression of disliking and resenting it.

Source: From C.A.R. Crosland, *Can Labour Win?* (Fabian Tract, No. 324, 1960).

play the role of world figure, the mediator between the USSR and the USA. When Kennedy became American President in 1960, Macmillan tried to build a close relationship, presenting himself in Britain as the wise uncle of the young president. He worked for a summit conference in the hope that it would lead to a détente between the two superpowers. But much of it was illusion. While the deeply unpopular compulsory national service came to an end and defence expenditure was reduced, the 'independent' nuclear deterrent was retained. Until February 1960, this was to be the British-made Blue Streak missile, but spiralling costs meant that it ceased to be viable as a military project (though the civilian use of Blue Streak in a project to launch British satellites, then as part of a European programme, continued until that, too, finally ceased in 1970). The government then turned to the American Skybolt missile until that also was abandoned by the Americans in November 1962 as 'a pile of junk'. In desperation, Macmillan, under attack from the right within the Conservative Party, persuaded Kennedy, against the advice of the Pentagon, to allow Britain to buy the Polaris submarine missile in return for giving the Americans a base in the Holy Loch, on Scotland's west coast. There was no serious consideration of whether it made sense for Britain to remain a nuclear power on the basis of total dependence on the United States. It was seen as the ill-affordable price that had to be paid for maintaining a place at the 'top table'. It confirmed France's General de Gaulle in his hostility to Britain's entry to the European Common Market and within weeks he had vetoed the British application for membership (see Chapter 39).

Economic problems returned, with an adverse balance of payments and wage rises that were well above the rate of growth. No answer to the problems was found and, with government expenditure increasing, there was a financial crisis in the summer of 1961, and the threat of devaluation. The response was to apply strongly deflationary measures, with a huge rise in taxes on consumption and a pause on public sector pay that quickly produced recession. By early 1962, the government was clearly very unpopular, particularly among public-service workers. Industrial unrest was mounting and there were defeats in by-elections by the resurgent Liberals, who were the first of the parties to grasp the importance of the relatively new medium of television for politics. Macmillan's dramatic response was to sack seven of his Cabinet colleagues in July 1962, including the Chancellor. It was an extraordinary, if slightly desperate exercise in prime ministerial power, dubbed 'the night of the long knives', showing the Prime Minister's readiness to 'lay down his friends for his life', as the future Liberal leader, Jeremy Thorpe, quipped. It did, however, bring new, clever, younger men to the fore. It looked briefly as if Supermac had done it, culminating with the successful conclusion of a ban on the testing of nuclear bombs in the atmosphere in 1963.

But, in the autumn of 1962 there was a spy scandal at the Admiralty, where an official had been blackmailed for his homosexual activities. In January 1963, the 'third man' in the affair of the Cambridge spies, Guy Burgess and Donald Maclean, who had escaped to the Soviet Union in 1951 just before being exposed, was confirmed; he was Kim Philby, for long a leading figure in the secret services, who turned up in Moscow. In the spring there were rumours of an even bigger scandal at the War Office, when information about the affair of John Profumo, the Secretary for War, with a 19-year-old aspiring model, Christine Keeler, appeared in the press. Keeler had also had an affair with an attaché at the Russian embassy. Profumo had to resign after admitting that he had lied to the Commons in trying to bluff his way out of the embarrassment.

Figure 31.1 Supermac cartoon from the *Evening Standard*, 26 June 1959. In the late 1950s the cartoonist Vicky (Victor Weisz) regularly portrayed Macmillan as Supermac. Quintin Hogg, Lord Hailsham, is sitting at the desk, with R.A. Butler standing beside him. The golf player in the frame is President Eisenhower, while Supermac's opponent in the big fight is Hugh Gaitskell.
Source: British Cartoon Archive, University of Kent, www.cartoons.ac.uk

Macmillan survived Profumo's resignation in June 1963, but in September he was struck down by illness and forced to resign, in the middle of the party's annual conference. The result was a free-for-all for the succession between Rab Butler, Viscount Hailsham and the fourteenth earl of Home. Macmillan worked to block Butler's succession and, although he seemed to favour Hailsham originally, recommended Home, the Foreign Secretary.[5]

---

[5] Thanks to a prolonged struggle by Anthony Wedgwood Benn, Viscount Stansgate, it was accepted in 1964 that a hereditary peerage could be renounced. Lord Home took advantage of this to become Sir Alec Douglas Home, only to revert in 1974 to the title Lord Home, but this time with a life peerage, nine years after he gave up the Conservative leadership.

While it is easy to be cynical about 'MacWonder', scathingly lampooned by the highly original TV show *That Was the Week that Was*, Macmillan had achieved much. He had contributed to lowering some of the tensions of the cold war. He, with Home, had helped negotiate a test ban treaty. Most spectacularly of all, he had managed to get Britain out of its empire with less trouble than might have been feared. What he failed to do was to find a new role for Britain that recognised the reality of its position. His weakness was in managing the domestic economy, but this partly stemmed from a dislike of the social consequences of too harsh deflation. As Britain moved through a cultural revolution from the 'traditional' fifties to the 'swinging' sixties, the Macmillan years managed to generate the illusion that Britain was still a major power influencing the rival super-powers.

Further reading

Barnett, C., *The Lost Victory. British Dreams, British Realities 1945–1950* (London, Pan, 1996)

Childs, D., *Britain since 1945: A Political History* (London, Routledge, 1997)

Dutton, D., *British Politics since 1945: The Rise and Fall of Consensus* (Oxford, Oxford University Press, 1991)

Hennessy, Peter, *Never Again: Britain 1945–1951* (London, Jonathan Cape, 1992)

Hennessy, Peter, *Having it so Good: Britain in the Fifties* (London, Allen Lane, 2006)

Jefferys, K., *Retreat from New Jerusalem: British Politics 1951–64* (Basingstoke, Macmillan, 1997)

Lenman, Bruce P., *The Eclipse of Parliament. Appearance and Reality in British Politics since 1914* (London, Edward Arnold, 1992)

Morgan, K.O., *Labour in Power, 1945–1951* (Oxford, Clarendon Press, 1984)

Morgan, K.O., *The People's Peace: British History since 1945–1989* (Oxford, Oxford University Press, 2001)

Tiratsoo, N., *The Attlee Years* (London, Pinter, 1991)

32

The welfare state

Origins

The term 'welfare state' was defined by historian Asa Briggs as:

> a state in which organized power is deliberately used (through politics and administration) in an effort to modify the play of market forces in at least three directions – first, by guaranteeing individuals and their families a minimum income irrespective of the market value of their work or their property; second, by narrowing the extent of insecurity by enabling individuals and families to meet certain 'social contingencies' (e.g. sickness, old age, unemployment) which lead otherwise to individual and family crises; and third, by ensuring that all citizens without distinction of status or class are offered the best standards available in relation to a certain agreed range of social services.[1]

It was the commitment to provide 'the best standards available' and to 'all citizens' that differentiated the welfare state from what has been called a social service state. It moved away from minimum standards to optimum standards, which should be available to all. The term 'welfare state' is generally attached in Britain to the period from the 1940s until the 1970s. In these decades, the extension and maintenance of a system that provided security 'from the cradle to the grave' became central to the policies of all governments. From the 1970s belief in the idea weakened, with a renewed emphasis on individual responsibility to meet the crises of life and the pejorative term 'nanny state' came into the vocabulary.

---

[1] A. Briggs, 'The Welfare State in Historical Perspective' in *Archives Européens du Sociologue*, 2 (1961), p. 228.

Welfare in the nineteenth century was largely the responsibility of families, charities, churches, voluntary organisations of various kinds and mutual-aid organisations, like friendly societies and trade unions. Local authorities played a part in dealing with the destitute by means of the Poor Law and with the poor sick by the provision of municipal hospitals. The central state's role was largely one of cajoling and facilitating local authorities.

A change came with the measures brought in by the Liberal governments of 1905–15. These included the provision of school meals for needy children and of old-age pensions for the indigent aged. Concerned not to have to raise taxation, the government latched on to the system of insurance as pioneered in Germany and New Zealand. By this, the individual, the employer and the state all contributed to an insurance scheme to cover some of the emergencies of life. The National Insurance Act of 1911 formed the basis of health insurance for all manual workers and of unemployment insurance for some groups, with payments being made through what were called approved societies – private insurance companies like the Prudential and friendly societies, like the Oddfellows or the Free Gardeners.

The principle of insurance was further extended after the First World War, when most workers were brought into the unemployment insurance scheme, and, in 1925, a contributory old-age and widows' pension scheme was introduced. With the pension payable at the age of 65, the concept of a retirement age gained ground. The great attraction of insurance was that it seemed to strengthen the virtue of self-help, with people contributing and getting assistance as of right. Against it was the fact that it was a flat rate that all paid, no matter how well-off they were, so it contributed nothing to the redistribution of wealth. Also, as Winston Churchill said, it depended for its success, like all insurance schemes, on 'the magic of averages' – on the fact that most people would not need to draw on it. With unemployment soaring in the interwar years, the insurance scheme could not cope and various temporary expedients had to be applied to prop it up. Since so much of the unemployment was long-term, many had used up their entitlement to relief through insurance and had to look to the state. Only in 1934 did the state accept that it had a responsibility for the long-term unemployed and established an Unemployment Assistance Board. Payments were not 'as of right' and were only made after a means test had shown that all other possible sources of help, including the extended family, had been used up. In the depressed areas of the country, the means test became one of the most disliked aspects of the social services.

By 1939, there were widespread complaints about many other aspects of the services. Responsibilities for hospitals, education and welfare were divided between local authorities, the national state and voluntary organisations, with the result that there were huge variations in what was available in different parts of the country. Where once local variation was seen as something to be valued and encouraged, the demand was now for uniformity throughout the country. Although after 1934 unemployment benefit included a dependents' allowance, this was not so for those on sickness benefit under the health insurance scheme. This was one of the main complaints. Another concerned the involvement of commercial 'approved societies' within the state scheme.

They, too, offered different benefits for the insurance paid. The biggest complaint of all was that health insurance did not cover hospital treatment or specialist services. The latter were very piecemeal, with county councils running the maternity services, and the TB sanitoria, voluntary charity hospitals, county council hospitals and still half the hospitals run under the Poor Law. After 1929, local authorities had power to exercise a co-ordinating control over all of these but there was no unified service – something that the medical profession was pressing for.

The half-century since the end of the nineteenth century had seen a considerable transformation in social thought and policy. The state had come to accept a responsibility for individual crises such as sickness, widowhood, orphanhood, unemployment and for old age. What was still debated was how far such a responsibility should go. There were various pressures for continuing change. The depression of the interwar years had revealed the extent of poverty and the vulnerability of families in many parts of the nation. A humanitarian concern with the plight of the most needy was one factor. A second was the belief, current since the end of the nineteenth century, that there ought to be some kind of minimum standard in a civilised society, below which no one should be allowed to fall – a concern that, in what was still one of the wealthiest of nations, people ought not to be allowed to starve or die untended. There was also popular pressure from below, as reflected in the Labour Party and the trade unions demanding improvements for the nation's working people. Governments responded to these democratic pressures. There was also middle-class pressure, because they were the ones who often had to pay the full costs of medical treatment and were loath to draw on charities. Finally, there was, as always, administrative pressure for co-ordination of services, uniformity between regions and a comprehensive system.

Beveridge and after

All of these factors came together during the Second World War. There was a determination that the aftermath of war should bring a more civilised, more equal, more socially efficient society. Various committees were formed to think about the post-war world. A key one was the Interdepartmental Committee on Social Insurance and Allied Services under Sir William Beveridge, who was a Liberal academic administrator and former civil servant. It resulted in the Beveridge Report of 1942 that came to symbolise reconstruction. Its timing was perfect. It came out a week after the victory of El Alamein – 'not the beginning of the end, but the end of the beginning', as Churchill said. Its aim was to deal with the known causes of want and to abolish these by extending the system of insurance that had been introduced before the First World War. Beveridge talked of conquering the five 'giants' of idleness, ignorance, squalor, disease and want. By continuing to base payments at times of sickness and unemployment on insurance it was intended to avoid a means test for benefits. Everyone would pay their contributions at the same flat rate and get benefits as of right. The plan was also to rationalise the various social welfare services into a coherent structure.

Focus on

The Beveridge Report 1942

The following extract is taken from the Beveridge Report.

> The first principle is that any proposals for the future, while they should use to the full the experience gathered in the past, should not be restricted by consideration of sectional interests established in the obtaining of that experience. Now, when the war is abolishing landmarks of every kind, is the opportunity of using experience in a clear field. A revolutionary moment in the world's history is a time for revolutions, not patching.
>
> The second principle is that organisation of social insurance should be treated as one part only of a comprehensive policy of social progress. Social insurance fully developed may provide income security; it is an attack upon Want. But Want is only one of the five giants on the road to reconstruction and in some ways the easiest to attack. The others are Disease, Ignorance, Squalor and Idleness.
>
> The third principle is that social security must be achieved by co-operation between the State and the individual. The State should offer security for service and contribution. The State in organising security should not stifle incentive, opportunity and responsibility; in establishing a national minimum, it should leave room and encouragement for voluntary action by each individual to provide more than that minimum for himself and his family.

Source: From the *Report of the Committee on Social Insurance and Allied Services*, Cmnd 6404 (1942).

Forced on a rather reluctant government by an all-party revolt of backbenchers, a white paper of 1944, *Social Insurance*, accepted the principles that Beveridge had enunciated as essential for the success of his scheme. There had to be a health service; there had to be full employment; and there had to be family allowances. Social security was not merely about dealing with the emergencies of life – unemployment and sickness – but with the normalities of birth, families, reßtirement, old age and death. There needed to be maternity benefit, family allowances, retirement and old-age pensions, and funeral benefit.

Beveridge had argued for benefits to be at subsistence level, but remnants of older attitudes persisted. The white paper put the minimum at below subsistence level. Benefits were still seen as an addition to personal savings. Even retirement pensions were never at subsistence level and increasing numbers of people had to depend on what was called national assistance, outside the insurance system. A National Assistance

Board was for the final relief of people 'without resources to meet their requirements or whose resources must be supplemented in order to meet their requirements', providing means-tested benefits. At every turn there was some cheese-paring of the Beveridge proposals as the costs began to be calculated. Parts of his proposals, such as industrial retraining for the unemployed and working-class life assurance, were quietly dropped. However, a Ministry of National Insurance was established in 1944 and the scheme came into effect in July 1948. All workers paid their insurance stamp and, in return, received an extensive measure of social security. It was a state service, with the system of approved societies abolished.

It had long been recognised that family size was closely linked to poverty. In 1924, Eleanor Rathbone's Family Endowment Society had begun the campaign for financial help for children, whether there was a breadwinner in work or not. It received support from both the right and left, with Conservatives arguing that healthy children were a prerequisite for healthy manhood to meet the nation's military needs. The Family Allowance Act of 1945 provided 5 shillings (around £7.00 at 2008 prices) a week, considerably less than reformers had been urging, for a second and further child. The allowance rose to 8 shillings in the 1950s and to 18 shillings (about £11.00 at 2008 prices) in 1968, when child tax allowances were reduced. A means-tested family income supplement in 1970 brought back memories of the eighteenth-century Speenhamland system, since it was available to low-paid workers who were actually in work, but it was not very successful.

Inseparable from national insurance was a national health service. Ill-health too had long been identified as a cause of poverty. Another 1944 white paper spelled out the goal of 'a comprehensive cover for health provided for all people alike'. Just as people were accustomed to look to the state for essential facilities like a clean and safe water supply, declared the white paper, so they should now be able to look for proper facilities for personal health. It envisaged a reorganisation and rationalisation of all the medical services in the country, providing a unified service in contrast to the pre-war mixture. In fact, this had already been largely achieved. In preparation for the expected casualties of bombing, the Emergency Medical Service had been established before the war, with the government already controlling most aspects of the hospital services.

The man largely responsible for getting the recommendations of the white paper into legislation was Aneurin Bevan, the Minister of Health. The result was the National Health Service Act of 1946 (with a separate Scottish Act in 1947), which set up a comprehensive scheme of medical care and treatment free to all, whether insured or not. It was to be financed largely from taxation. The insurance contribution was always little more than 10 per cent. Bevan had the same problems with the doctors that Lloyd George had in 1911. They were determined not to become civil servants, a state salaried service that the 1944 white paper had proposed. Just as in 1911, there were threats to strike and to refuse to come into the new service. But, just as in 1911, the doctors capitulated, with consultants, as Bevan reputedly declared, having 'their mouths stuffed with gold' and given the freedom to maintain private practices. The service faced a huge initial demand. Five and a half million pairs of spectacles were issued within the first year and there was a lack of capital investment in hospitals to deal with the major reconstruction required. Nonetheless, the aim was to provide a universal service of high-quality medical provision 'free at the point of delivery' and this quickly became the central part of the new welfare state, since it was used by all social classes. The founders assumed that, with a healthier population, there would be an eventual fall in demand. In practice, a healthier population with longer lives required more and more from the service.

Closely associated with the provision of social welfare was educational reform. It was the Conservative minister of education, R.A. Butler who pushed through educational reform before the end of the war. He had to do it against the opposition of Churchill, who wanted no educational controversy during the war, and Butler had to rely largely on support from Labour ministers. The measure was eventually given the go-ahead, as an alternative to Beveridge. As the Chancellor, Kingsley Wood, bluntly stated, rather 'money for education than throw it down the sink with Sir William Beveridge'.[2]

The Butler 1944 Education Act (followed by a less radical Scottish Act in 1945) made state education entirely free, raised the school leaving age to 15 with no exemptions and pointed to a later rise to 16, which came in 1969. At one end, nursery schools were to be made available where needed and, at the other, there would be part-time education available in working hours up to the age of 18 and local authorities had responsibility for expanding technical and adult education. The Act retained voluntary church schools incorporated within the state system and, most significantly of all, an existing tripartite system of secondary schools with grammar schools, secondary moderns in England (senior and junior secondary in Scotland) and a small number of technical schools, with selection based on the result of the 11-plus examination or the Scottish Qualifying Examination. The loss of nearly 400,000 potential workers between the age of 14 and 15 at a time of manpower shortages made Butler's reforms problematic, but they were carried through nonetheless and there was a huge expansion of education, doubling as a proportion of public expenditure over 40 years. The demands were enormous. There had been little expenditure on the maintenance of schools during the war years and many had been damaged by bombing. The wartime and immediate post-war baby boom meant that the numbers coming into school in the 1950s took a great leap. Investment in education never matched the needs.

By the mid-1950s, there was also growing criticism of the divisive nature of the educational system, with career prospects largely decided by the results of one examination at age 11. Resources tended to be directed towards grammar schools to a greater extent than to secondary moderns. Middle-class parents began to join educationists in criticising the system. Labour conferences began calling for comprehensive secondary schools and for the incorporation of some of the public schools into the

---

[2] A. Howard, *RAB: The Life of R.A. Butler* (London, Jonathan Cape, 1887), p. 133.

state system. The Labour government of the 1970s launched moves towards comprehensive mixed-ability schools and the policy was continued by the Conservatives until it began to be questioned in the 1990s.

Another of the 'giants' to be slain, that Beveridge had identified, was squalor. Between 1919 and 1939 over 4 million houses were built, almost a third of them by local authorities. But the housing shortage in 1939 was greater than it had been in 1919 and the years and destruction of the Second World War added to the problem. Half a million houses had been destroyed by bombing and another 3 million severely damaged. The Town and Country Planning Act of 1944, based on the Uthwatt Report, gave important powers to local authorities to purchase land compulsorily and to redevelop areas of cities. The firms that had made the Mulberry Harbours for D-Day were turned over to the production of prefabricated houses. However, the post-war years saw major shortages of building materials and ambitious building programmes had to be cut back. There were also differences of opinion about priorities. Were the homes for returning heroes, the industrially skilled or those with greatest need? In 1951, there were still three quarters of a million houses short. Harold Macmillan, the Conservative minister of housing, committed the government to a target of 300,000 houses, a target which was surpassed in 1954, but only at the cost of a huge reduction in the size and standard of council housing. Social housing remained the responsibility of local authorities, who decided how many to build. As a result, houses were not always built in the right place, at the right time and for the most needy people. Cost was always the main consideration, rather than need. The dual problem of providing enough houses and providing them at rents that the poorest of the population could afford was never satisfactorily solved. Labour had mistrusted private building firms to deliver what was needed and municipal building expanded. There were calls for all privately rented accommodation to be brought under the control of local authorities. In contrast, the Conservatives encouraged more private house building and stressed the aim of creating a 'property-owning democracy'. By 1959, there was more private house building than public and a growing feeling that municipal housing in huge suburban estates had become unimaginatively uniform.

Further encouragement to private ownership was given between 1974 and 1989 by tax concessions on mortgage payments and, from 1980, tenants of municipal and social housing were given the right to purchase their properties at discounted rates. Whereas, in 1945, only around 40 per cent of the population owned their own property, by 2007, the figure was coming close to 70 per cent.

A third wartime white paper, *Employment Policy*, committed the government to 'the maintenance of a high and stable level of employment'. It reflected the extent to which the economics of J.M. Keynes had become economic orthodoxy. It accepted that it was possible to plan against unemployment and that public expenditure and capital expenditure by private enterprise could be manipulated and controlled to hold off economic depression. Over the next 30 years, economic management, coupled with a worldwide demand for goods to replace what had been devastated by war, succeeded in keeping unemployment below 3 per cent of the insured population.

Taken together, these measures made up what came to be called the welfare state. In 1950, Seebohm Rowntree returned to York for a third survey. In 1899, he had found that 15.46 per cent of the working-class population were living in primary poverty, lacking the necessary resources to meet the most basic of needs. In 1936, he calculated that the figure had fallen to 6.8 per cent and in 1950 it was down to 3 per cent. The 1940s seemed to have made a difference.

In the 1950s, all the major political parties outbid one another in claiming to be the true authors of the welfare state, but by the 1970s there were signs that the consensus on welfare was beginning to break down. With both death rate and birth rate falling, there were already worries in the 1950s about an ageing population. The fact that full retirement pensions were paid from the start rather than, as Beveridge had wanted, after 20 years of building up an insurance fund, had immediately breached the insurance system. The social insurance system that had been envisaged was never fully developed and benefits were paid out of current revenue rather than out of an accumulated fund.

Concerns about funding led to the introduction of charges for dental and ophthalmic services in 1951 and then on prescriptions in 1952. There were accusations that the health service was extravagant – a charge that a committee in 1956 found unjustified. In fact the health service's share of GDP did not increase greatly and much less was being spent on medical services than in most of the rest of western Europe, where the introduction of welfare services was central to the restoration of states devastated by war and fascism. There were huge successes. Tuberculosis was largely eradicated as a result of mobile X-ray vans identifying the illness early and new drugs dealing with it. The cases of children's diphtheria fell from 47,000 in 1939 to 6 in 1970. Thanks to vaccines, polio had largely disappeared by 1970 and measles, too, looked as if it were on the way out until panic over the side effects of a vaccine set in. Voices from the political right began to argue, however, that extensive welfare measures were depriving sections of the population of the qualities of thrift, self-reliance and industry and creating a culture of dependency.

From the 1970s, unemployment was allowed to creep up. There had been a price to pay for the concern to keep unemployment low. Inefficient industries were propped up; businesses were encouraged to go to areas where unemployment was high, but where the skills and communications were lacking; and there was little attempt to direct investment into areas that would improve the country's low levels of productivity. The result was increasingly high levels of inflation, a failure to modernise and the steady loss of competitive international markets. By the mid-1970s, even a Labour government was arguing that it was no longer possible for the state to spend its way out of a recession. Between 1979 and 1986, under the Conservatives, the number of unemployed trebled and manufacturing industries were allowed to collapse in many parts of the country.

There were also concerns that, despite the welfare state, poverty was not disappearing. Insured benefits after 1945 were reviewed at five-yearly intervals, but, with prices and wages rising sharply in the 1950s, there was a decline in the purchasing

Figure 32.1 X-raying for tuberculosis, Glasgow, 1957. Throughout the nineteenth and first half of the twentieth century, tuberculosis was a widespread disease not confined to any particular social class, but prevalent in the poor housing conditions of many cities. A mass X-ray campaign in the 1950s to identify the disease at an early stage largely eradicated it, although there are signs of its recurrence.
Source: Science & Society Picture Library

power of these benefits, which were never high enough to keep people out of poverty. This meant that more had to turn to means-tested public assistance to make ends meet. A study in 1954 found that 8 per cent of the population were living in households under a poverty line, taken as 140 per cent of the basic national assistance scale. These were around 4 million people, of whom 1,150,000 were children. Of those, 600,000 were living below the *basic* national assistance scale. In 1960, another study found that 14 per cent, or 7.5 million people, were living below the poverty line, with 2 million below the level of basic supplementary benefit (as public assistance had become).

The poorest remained the poorest because of their lack of basic assets. There were those on low earnings who were often caught in a poverty trap, by which any increase in earnings led to a greater loss in means-tested payments. Work incentives were reduced by taking virtually a pound off benefits for every pound earned. Among the poorest were the aged – particularly women, who had only state pensions – and large families. These were the same categories of the poorest that Charles Booth and Rowntree had identified at the beginning of the century. Added to these were one-parent families, as patterns of family life altered in the 1960s with the rising acceptance of divorce. The social insurance system was not designed to cope with this new generator of poverty and such families had to rely upon means-tested benefits.

The attempts to deal with these problems involved an extension of selective means-tested schemes. Increasingly, the criticism was of the notion of universality, which implied that benefits and, to some extent, contributions should be equal and available for all. This was largely about trying to cut costs, but there was also an ideological element, which was determined to puncture the collectivist approach. The argument was that, just as competition in industry provided a more efficient and cheaper service, so choice in welfare would do the same. But there was also an argument for concentrating state help on those who were really in need rather than providing benefits for people who could afford to make their own provision.

As the problems of the system grew, the attempts to deal with it became more complex. Studies began to show that it was not necessarily the poor who benefited from public services. In practice, more middle-class than working-class people utilised the educational services and health services. Many of the poorest failed to qualify for subsidised municipal housing or were obliged to leave it for more expensive, privately rented housing, since local authority housing tended to go to families where the head of the household was in work.

By the 1970s, there was a widespread debate on welfare, as the issue of controlling public expenditure became more pressing. Costs in education and health, in particular, were increasing disproportionately fast. There were arguments that the rise in personal incomes was now such that individuals were perfectly capable of providing for themselves. The state's role was to prescribe standards, but otherwise, individuals ought to be allowed the choice of contracting out of state services and paying for private services in the open market. This would ensure that there were more resources to deal with remaining pockets of poverty through means-tested benefits. Local authorities and national authorities frequently operated different measures of need. To counter demands for cutbacks in welfare commitments, sociologists argued that increased national wealth made possible the extension of social services. They cautioned against selectivity on the grounds that it reinforced the condition that it was supposed to alleviate. It was necessary, they claimed, to get away from the concept of the minimum, to redefine poverty and to recognise that it needed to be tackled in the round. People required the housing standards, the physical assets, the environmental and occupational facilities, as well as the cash incomes, to participate in what is seen as normal for average members of society.

The end of the welfare state?

From 1979, one of the most dramatic changes was in home ownership. The 'Right to Buy' granted to council tenants (see Chapter 34) met the aspirations of many, to whom ownership had once been a dream, and also met the Conservative aim of curbing municipal power. By the early twenty-first century, eight out of ten homes were owner-occupied, with less than 20 per cent in the social housing sector. Private land-owners and housing associations were encouraged to take over council housing estates. The need for housing remained as high as ever, to provide for the increasing numbers of divorced, elderly and single households as well as for key workers in areas of rapid population growth. By the late twentieth century, the rising costs of buying houses led to huge cultural changes, as young couples generally had to maintain two incomes in order pay their mortgages. One result was delay in the timing of having children.

Beveridge and Bevan had both believed that an effective health service would, in time, reduce the demand on its services as the population became healthier. In practice, as expectations grew, as the population aged, and as advances in medical technology pushed up costs, the National Health Service devoured an ever-growing share of public expenditure. While the great scourges of the pre-1945 years – polio, tubercu-losis, scarlet fever, diphtheria, whooping cough and measles – were gradually controlled, new ones – cancers, heart-disease, strokes, the products of modern lifestyles – took their place. Expenditure on the health service rose from just under 5 per cent of GDP in the 1970s and 1980s to over 8 per cent in the early twenty-first century, coming somewhere near the European mean. But, with demand seemingly insatiable, the rationing of care had become essential.

All governments have tried to find ways of controlling the cost of the health service. The Conservatives in the 1980s began a process of reorganisation, privatising areas of the health service by contracting out areas of work. In the 1990s, they sought to apply market forces by giving GPs their own budgets with which to purchase services from hospitals. From 1997, Labour took up with enthusiasm the Conservatives' Private Finance Initiative, by which the building and management of hospitals (and schools) was contracted to private companies, and they increasingly brought in private health care companies to take over some of the routine aspects of the service and to ration some treatments. Both undertook a number of reorganisations of the service, seeking to bring in the management techniques of private industry and to ration the expendi-ture on drugs. But it was hard to see how rising demand for increasingly costly health care could be met from public funds, given the apparent resistance to tax increases. In education, there was increased government intervention in the actual content of school curricula and, as in other areas, a demand for public accountability to be based on defined targets and performance league tables.

The insurance principle was largely abandoned as insurance benefits were cut and replaced with means-tested ones. In 1982, pension payments ceased to be linked to earnings and instead were linked to prices, which generally rose more slowly. Companies were encouraged to develop occupational pension schemes and individuals encour-aged to invest in personal pensions. The better-off and those in public services gained from a huge growth in these occupational pensions. The problem of the poorest in society remained. Something like 25 per cent of households continued to live below the poverty line, including nearly 30 per cent of children. The main effort to deal with this has been through the introduction of a system of tax credits for children and to supplement low incomes. By supplementing earnings there is a sense in which the

Focus on

Reforming the welfare state 1985

Here the Secretary of State for Health and Social Security, Norman Fowler, is indicating in a Green Paper of 1985 a move away from the Beveridge model of universal welfare provision. Among its main proposals was the abandonment of a State-provided retirement pension scheme to one based upon compulsory private insurance.

Much has changed in the forty years since then [1942]. The ability of most people to make more of their own provision has substantially improved. For instance, the spread of home ownership among those previously relying on public provision of housing underlines the wish of most people for greater independence.

1.9 Yet the scope and scale of state social security has extended greatly. The decision at the outset of national insurance to pay pensions at once rather than after a build-up of entitlement substantially changed Beveridge's concept. The later development of earnings-related benefits and contributions was a further step away from the 1942 report.

1.10 We should not be deceived about the nature of national insurance today. It is *not* the same as private insurance and owes little to normal insurance principles. It is a pay-as-you-go scheme. Today's contributions meet the costs of today's benefits. As for tomorrow, the most we can do is to create a liability to be met by our children . . .

1.11 Forty years on from Beveridge there is little point in seeking to replicate private insurance arrangements inside the state organisation. We should certainly recognise the debt we are building up for the future. But the better course is to distinguish between what can and should be organised by individuals and their employers and what can and should be organised by government. This is what the twin pillar approach seeks to do. It recognises the importance of state provision but it seeks to define its limits.

1.12 In developing this approach the Government believe that three main objectives must underlie the reform of social security.

First, the social security system must be capable of meeting genuine need. . . .

Second, the social security system must be consistent with the Government's overall objectives for the economy.

Thirdly, the social security system must be simpler to understand and easier to administer.

Source: From the Green Paper, *Reform of Social Security*, Cmnd 9517 (1985).

system has restored aspects of the eighteenth-century poor law. While this has undoubtedly brought help to the poorest in society, the most striking feature of the last decade has been the growth of inequality, with a widening gap between the comfortably-off and those who are just under a relative poverty line. Despite the introduction of a minimum wage in 1999, the evidence points to increased physical segregation between rich and poor areas and increased exclusion of many from participation in aspects of life that the comfortably-off regard as the norm. There is growing evidence of the tension generated by this leading to social breakdown on the edges of deprived areas. Hopes of the 1940s to eradicate poverty have given way to schemes for controlling the impact of it through anti-social behaviour orders and increased incarceration.

Further reading

Barr, N. et al. (eds), *The State of Welfare: The Welfare State in Britain since 1974* (Oxford, Clarendon Press, 1990)

Harris, Bernard, *The Origins of the British Welfare State. Society, State and Social Welfare in England and Wales 1800–1945* (Basingstoke, Macmillan, 2004)

Lowe, R., *The Welfare State in Britain since 1945*, 3rd edn (Basingstoke, Macmillan, 2004)

Thane, P., *Foundations of the Welfare State* (London, Longman, 1996)

Timmins, N., *The Five Giants: A Biography of the Welfare State*, rev. edn (London, HarperCollins, 2001)

33

The end of empire

The concept of Commonwealth

The aftermath of the First World War saw the British Empire extended to its greatest extent, covering a quarter of the Earth's surface and a quarter of its population, as Britain took control of former German and Ottoman territories. The quarter-century after 1945, however, saw the rapid shedding of that empire, so that all but a handful of small dependencies had gone. The disappearance of the British Empire was part of a wider reaction against colonialism that also brought to an end the empires of France, the Netherlands, Belgium and Portugal. What is debated is whether the British withdrawal from empire was carried out more peacefully and with less trauma than that of other imperial powers.

It was Lord Rosebery on a visit to Australia in 1884 who declared that, while Australia was now a nation in its own right, this did not imply separation from the Empire, 'because the Empire is a commonwealth of nations'. The concept was rather overshadowed, though, by the talk of Joseph Chamberlain and others from the 1880s about a much more integrated imperial federation. The term 'Commonwealth' appealed to Liberals, who had qualms about imperialism, and socialists, like the Fabians, who referred to a 'commonwealth of communities flying the British flag'. In 1907, 'dominion' formally replaced the word 'colony' to describe Australia, New Zealand, South Africa and Canada at imperial conferences. The term 'Commonwealth' also began to be used more widely to differentiate British concepts of empire from those of Germany and France.

The idea was further advanced during the First World War, by the establishment in 1917 of the Imperial War Cabinet, which dominion ministers could attend. A further attempt to define the position came with the Balfour Report produced by the 1926 Imperial conference, which referred to 'autonomous communities within the British

Empire', with equality of status. By the Statute of Westminster of 1931, it was accepted that the views of dominion parliaments took precedence over those of Westminster and no dominion law could be declared void even if it conflicted with a Westminster statute. Governors-General now acted on the advice of dominion governments, not of London.

The Colonial Office still tended to see Empire and Commonwealth as synonymous, but the beginning of the end of Empire came with the Second World War. Paradoxically, the outbreak of war saw evidence that the Commonwealth did mean something. Most of the dominions joined, but, in contrast with 1914, only after a decision was made by the dominion governments. Only Eire – as the Irish Free State was known from 1938, when it became, to all intents, a republic within the Commonwealth – declared for neutrality.

The war brought issues of independence for the remaining parts of the Empire to the forefront. Although Churchill was still saying that he was not in office 'to preside over the dissolution of the British Empire', it was difficult to talk about freedom in Europe and not to see its implications for Empire. There was also the further fact of the United States, that prided itself on its anti-imperialism and was particularly influenced by events in India.

South Asia

Although demands for self-government in India went back at least until the 1880s, when the Indian Congress Party was formed, the First World War greatly accelerated the growth of nationalism. The emergence of new nation states in Europe did not go unnoticed in India, and the League of Nations gave its blessing to the concept of self-determination. The war, and, even more so, the 'loss' of Ireland, undermined the belief in the moral superiority of the British. They could certainly be resisted, even if they could not be beaten. There was also considerable resentment on the part of many Moslems at the way in which the Indian army had been used to expand the Empire in the Middle East at the expense of Turkey. Anxious to at least mollify nationalist demands, the Secretary of State for India in 1917 made the first formal commitment to 'the progressive realisation of responsible government in India as an integral part of the Empire'.

At the same time, there was always a readiness to resort to force in moments of crisis, such as in the Sikh holy city of Amritsar in 1919, when troops opened fire on a crowd of demonstrators hemmed in a park, killing perhaps as many as 500 (the official figure was 379) and wounding around 2,000. The Amritsar massacre horrified liberal opinion in Britain. The British authorities could not cope with the tactic of passive disobedience, which was being adopted, under the influence of Mahatma Gandhi. The imperial self-image was that the British were the ones who brought order and peace to violent nations. How to cope with people who were not violent but were still protesting was a problem they never solved and, indeed, it often produced a frustrated violence on the part of the authorities.

Concessions were made in the interwar years, including granting the Indian government fiscal autonomy. This allowed the imposition of tariffs against cotton goods, with

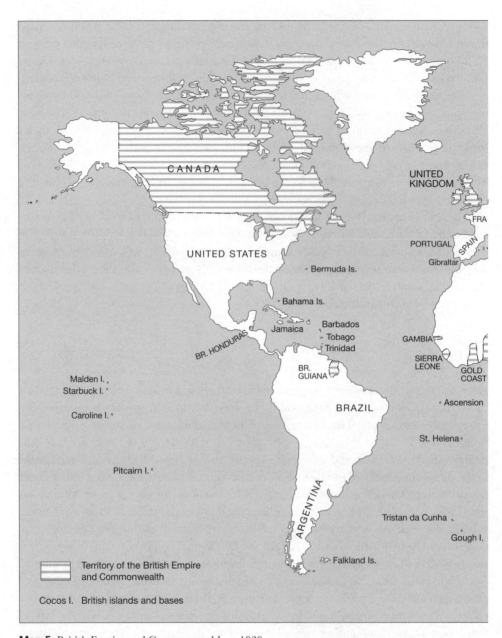

Map 5 British Empire and Commonwealth, *c.* 1939

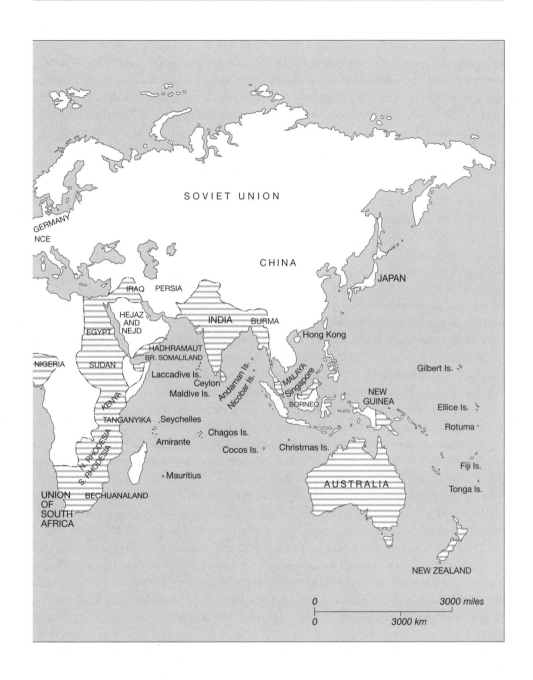

disastrous effects on the Lancashire cotton industry. Political reforms established the principle of diarchy (double government). In each of the Indian provinces, a British governor and his officials were responsible for finance, police, justice and labour matters, while an elected legislature was responsible for education, health, agriculture and public works. The electorate however, was incredibly narrow, based on property and education. Only 5 million out of a population of over 300 million could vote.

Many in the national government in the 1930s were keen to bring in some measure of self-government to India, but moves in this direction came up against obstruction from those, like Winston Churchill, who were opposed to almost any transfer of power to Indian hands. Despite such opposition, a huge Government of India Act was passed in 1935, that proposed a federation of British India and the 600 or so princely states. The franchise was widened and there was to be some measure of responsible government at the centre for everything except foreign affairs and defence. Nationalists in the Congress Party made huge gains in the elections to the provincial councils, and there were signs of a growing acceptance that independence had to come.

On the outbreak of war in September 1939, the Viceroy declared war without any consultation with Indian representatives. Congress proposed that support should be conditional on clearly spelled out assurances that, soon after the war, a constitution for independence would be framed and that, meanwhile, Indians would be brought into central government. To some, all this was more evidence of the treasonable nature of the nationalists. No concessions were made and, by the end of October 1939, all the Congress governments in the provinces had resigned and direct rule had been imposed and many of the nationalist leaders locked up.

At the same time, there was a growing need to ensure that India did not explode in nationalist unrest. In August 1940, under pressure from the Labour members of the War Cabinet, the offer was made of dominion status after the war 'with the least possible delay'. But when, in 1941, Roosevelt and Churchill's Atlantic Charter declared that the war was about 'the right of all people to choose the Government under which they live', the latter made it clear that this applied only to Europe, not to the Empire.

With the Japanese threat coming closer to India, Congress leaders were released from prison. They now argued for co-operation with the British for the defence of India against the Japanese, and large numbers of Indians volunteered for service. Although filled with distaste at the prospect of any concessions to nationalism, Churchill had no alternative but to try to mollify Indian opinion. India was offered dominion status and an elected constituent assembly immediately after the war to decide on a constitution, with any province having the right to remain outside the dominion. But this was still seen as too imprecise by most nationalists and, as some said, why negotiate when the British might go anyway? As Ghandi put it, 'Why accept a post-dated cheque on a bank that is obviously failing?' Instead, Ghandi launched a 'Quit India' campaign, calling for immediate surrender of control to Indians. Once again, with the prospect of open rebellion, nationalist leaders found themselves locked up and protests were suppressed with a great deal of violence. With the moderate leadership in prison, wilder spirits turned to sabotage; there were attacks on railway stations and post offices, and administrators identified as collaborators with the British were assassinated.

The situation deteriorated further in 1943, when the worst famine in Indian history hit Bengal. The loss of rice imports from territories under Japanese control, a scorched-earth policy to halt the Japanese advance out of Burma and the outbreak of disease in home-grown crops led to serious shortages and to as many as 1.5 million deaths from the effects of malnutrition. There was a growing sense of an inability to control events. The Indian Civil Service and the police were short of recruits and barely able to maintain either the administration or law and order. With more than 2 million Indian volunteers under arms there were worries about post-war loyalties.

The war in the East ended in August 1945, by which time the Labour government was in power. It was a government with people in it who had campaigned against imperialism throughout their political lives, but, even if they had not been there, expediency demanded a quick solution in India. With troops anxious for repatriation and the British economy largely dependent on American aid for survival, there were never going to be the resources to suppress open rebellion in India. There was a recognition that there was no option except withdrawal, although an assumption remained that British influence would stay strong within an independent India. The charismatic Lord Louis Mountbatten was sent to carry out the process and, reputedly, to try to reconcile the growing tensions between the Moslem League and the Hindu-dominated Congress – although how far the British government was really concerned to maintain the unity of India is highly debateable. To try to concentrate minds, and with an increasingly desperate desire to reduce imperial commitments to an affordable level, the government announced a deadline of June 1948 for Indian independence.

Surprisingly, the announcement of the end of the Indian Empire, so long seen as 'the jewel in the crown', was not viewed in Britain as the momentous event that one might have expected. With austerity still operating and the country suffering the coldest weather for over a century, with even bread and potatoes rationed and coal in short supply there were other concerns. Even government ministers were distracted.

It quickly became obvious that a speedy solution meant partition between Moslem-dominated areas and those where Hindus were in the majority. With growing communal violence in mixed areas – particularly in the Punjab – Mountbatten made the fateful (and some say disastrous) decision to bring forward the date for departure. The last thing he wanted was for British troops, keen to get home after six years of conflict, to be caught up in a civil war. He was also anxious to conciliate the Congress to ensure that India remained within the Commonwealth, which was seen as vital for reasons of prestige, strategy and the maintenance of sterling. In June 1947, he announced that the transfer of power would take place ten months earlier than planned, on August 15 – the second anniversary of the Japanese surrender that he had received. Vanity played its part.

There were to be two successor states and a one-man boundary commission quickly set about drawing frontiers. What emerged was a divided Pakistan[1] (the name adopted by the Moslem part), divided into a western and an eastern area separated by a thousand miles of Indian territory. There was a frantic dividing up of the assets of the civil

---

[1] An artificial construct coming from P for the Punjabis, A for the Afghans, K for Kashmiris, with the whole meaning roughly 'land of the pure'. The eastern part broke away in 1971 to form Bangladesh.

Figure 33.1 Jawaharlal Nehru with Lord Louis and Lady Edwina Mountbatten on Indian Independence Day, 15 August 1947. Mountbatten (1900–1979), who had been Supreme Allied Commander in South-East Asia during the war, was the last viceroy of India, whose controversial decision it was to speed up the handover of power to India and Pakistan. Nehru (1889–1964) was the first Prime Minister of independent India.
Source: Press Association

service, the army and the police. As independence day approached, communal conflict escalated – particularly in the Punjab and Bengal, which were themselves being partitioned. Uncertainty and instability were aggravated by the fact that the boundaries between the new states were not to be revealed until after independence. 7.4 million moved from what was to be Pakistan to India, while 7.2 million moved in the opposite direction. No one knows how many died as whole trainloads were massacred, villages wiped out and tens of thousands of others perished in the makeshift refugee camps. Figures range from 200,000 to over a million. The princely states were given the right to opt for which of the new countries to join. The fact that the Hindu ruler of Kashmir, which had a large Moslem population, opted for India left a festering wound that was soon to lead to war between the two countries.

Withdrawal from other parts of Asia followed Indian independence. Ceylon (later Sri Lanka), where there had been a peaceful nationalist movement gained its independence for the asking in 1948, but with a legacy of communal division that the British had made little attempt to heal. Burma was more problematic. Nationalist movements had existed amongst the student population since the 1920s. In the 1930s, the British

faced workers' strikes, student protests, peasant marches, often responding with considerable violence. Although the nationalists had initially welcomed the Japanese invasion, the racist attitudes of the invaders had, by 1944, produced an anti-Japanese
alliance of different nationalist groups, and in the post-war election Aung San and the
nationalists won an overwhelming victory. The British, shocked by the strength of
nationalism, agreed to immediate independence. The new state in January 1948 opted
to be a republic outside the Commonwealth, but Aung San and five of his colleagues
were assassinated and the new state soon plunged into civil war.

The Malayan Peninsula ought logically to have moved to independence in the
wake of India and Ceylon. That this did not happen was partly because, with its tin
and rubber resources, it was economically very valuable to meet Britain's post-war
needs. There was also a substantial settler community on the rubber plantations. The
communist insurrection which broke out in 1948, mainly among the rural Chinese
community, seemed to make the case for staying overwhelming. The departure of the
Japanese had led to economic disruption with food shortages and industrial unrest,
often met with great harshness. Support for the Malayan Communist Party gathered
pace. Although the British insisted that what was involved was merely an 'emergency',
in fact what they faced was 12 years of guerrilla jungle warfare before it was suppressed, helped by the fact that insurrection had limited popular support among the
Malay population. The British government was concerned to ensure that the rubber
and tin supplies remained in friendly hands and, once that had been achieved, they
were happy enough to leave power to a relatively feudal Malay aristocracy. Malaya
became independent in 1957 and the island of Singapore, with its majority Chinese
population, became self-governing in 1959, after considerable internal unrest. It joined
the new Federation of Malaysia, but withdrew in 1965. The process of withdrawal
continued, with the Maldives and Mauritius given up. In 1968, British troops were
withdrawn from Singapore and the British presence in East Asia was confined to a
small Hong Kong garrison, which came to an end in 1997.

Africa

The pace of change in Africa from the early twentieth century had been extraordinarily
rapid. The economies of East and West Africa depended on vulnerable commodities
like palm oil and cocoa. Prices for these were relatively good throughout the 1920s.
New areas were opened up and roads and transportation improved. The collapse of
commodity prices in 1929 proved disastrous, bringing real distress to many producers.
But there was a wider significance. So much land had been brought into cultivation for
export crops that there was not enough left to grow food. The tendency, however, was
to blame food shortages on the 'backwardness' of African farming methods. Government officials did not see economic development as part of their role; the emphasis
remained on what was called 'trusteeship' over native rulers. Attitudes remained highly
paternalistic and this sometimes led to the blocking of commercial developments.

The governor of the former German colony of Tanganyika in the 1920s saw his aim as 'to develop the native on lines which will not westernise him and turn him into a bad imitation of a European'. In Uganda, little encouragement was given to European settlement, and British governments were committed to maintain Uganda as an 'African' country under trusteeship. Kenya, as the East African Protectorate lying between Uganda and the sea was renamed in 1920, was very different. Just before 1914, white settlers had discovered the Kenya Highlands and set out to attract others to what was billed as another New Zealand. Soon a European landholding class, separate from the colonial administrators, pursued a life of notorious hedonism in 'Happy Valley', with drink, drugs and sex promiscuously on offer. Official policy was to try to protect the native Kikuyu and Masai, but what the white settlers wanted was their own parliament to run the place, free from Colonial Office interference.

The place where settlers did get their own way was Rhodesia, north and south of the Zambesi. In the southern part there were, by 1918, some 30,000 white settlers, who had mainly come from South Africa. The northern part had few European settlers and, when the charter of the British South Africa Company ran out in 1923, the north became a Crown colony, as Northern Rhodesia. There was little attempt to impose London rule on Southern Rhodesia and it was treated, more or less, as a dominion.

Africa, too, had felt the forces of nationalism during and after the Second World War. There was still a tendency to see Africans as unlikely to be able to aspire to the running of their own affairs for decades to come, and attitudes in Britain failed to keep pace with the aspirations of emerging nationalist movements. In Kenya, a Kikuyu Central Association had been pressing for land reform. In West Africa, some young Nigerians and Gold Coasters, educated in the United States, had brought back Pan-Negro ideas emanating from the West Indies and amongst American Blacks. Some British officials were aware of the changes and pointed to the growth of an African middle class in some territories that was no longer content to tolerate the authority of the native rulers through which Britain's indirect rule operated.

There was no sign that the Labour governments of 1945–51 wanted to do much constitutionally in Africa. Colonial Office talk was of partnerships in economic development, although there was always a dichotomy between development for the sake of the local population and development because of British needs for raw materials. Large numbers of technical experts came into the colonies to 'develop' them and there was an expansion of education for Africans. Such development plans all operated on the assumption that partnership would continue for many decades. Particularly after economic crisis hit Britain in 1947, there was an assumption that the priority should be to provide the commodities that Britain needed for recovery. The Board of Trade, for its part, was anxious to restore markets for British goods. The Treasury, on the other hand, faced with recurring sterling crises, was wary about colonial reserves that backed up the currency, being spent on imports. It was the immediate economic needs of Britain that took precedence.

Black ex-servicemen found it difficult to get jobs, and it was a protest of these in the Gold Coast in February 1948, during which the police opened fire, killing two protesters, which brought Kwame Nkrumah to the forefront of Gold Coast politics. Educated at universities in Britain and the United States, Nkrumah had been inspired by the Pan-African Congress held in Manchester in October 1945, which had called for independence for black Africa. He left the educated-middle-class United Gold Coast Convention that wanted self-government 'in the shortest possible time' to form a mass movement in the Convention People's Party to agitate for immediate independence.

A boycott of British imports led to shootings and arrests, but, within nine years, the Gold Coast had become the independent state of Ghana. In the midst of growing cold war tensions, there were fears in Britain about the spread of communist influence and anxieties about the cost of maintaining order. A British committee recommended a rapid advance to self-government, with the introduction of universal suffrage, irrespective of the low levels of literacy (around 10 per cent) that existed. Influenced by the techniques used in India (the Indian independence movement became a symbol for colonial subjects everywhere), Nkrumah launched a campaign for 'positive action' and called a general strike. He was duly locked up, but, in the elections of 1951, his Convention People's Party won the majority of seats. To go back on commitments to popular election the British government would have had to use substantial force, which the United States would not have tolerated and which would have offered massive propaganda opportunities for the Soviet Union. As a result, there was little option but to offer Nkrumah, in prison, the title of 'leader of government business'. A year later, he was given the title 'Prime Minister' and became the first African minister in a British colony.

The coming to power of a Conservative government brought no change of policy. In 1957, dominion status was granted to Ghana. The move to independence seemed to have been accompanied with the minimum of violence and to have led to no massive disruption of relationships. British politicians began to see this as the way of the future, about which Britain could be proud: a relatively peaceful transfer of power, in marked contrast to the French, who were using force to try to maintain their empire in Indo-China and Algeria. On the other hand, France had, in 1958, set a new pace by pushing French West African colonies to independence and to membership of the United Nations, giving France a very powerful bloc there.

Inevitably, the much larger territory of Nigeria was influenced by what was going on with its near neighbour. A strike in Lagos in 1945 was a portent of discontent, with various nationalist groups largely organised on ethnic lines. In this huge country there were different large ethnic groups, as well as religious differences between a Moslem north and the rest. The British attempts to deal with these by means of a federal solution were resented by some of the younger nationalists, who saw it as a British tactic to divide and rule. Once again, strikes and protests were suppressed with considerable brutality by the colonial authorities, giving propaganda victories to the nationalist parties, No party was able to obtain an overall majority in the elections of 1959 and the relationships between different regions were far from solved. Nonetheless, in October 1960, Nigeria became fully self-governing and declared itself a republic in 1963. By 1966, the ethnic tensions had burst into civil war. Once Ghana and Nigeria were independent, there was no way that Britain could retain Sierra Leone and the Gambia. Sierra Leone, also racked by ethnic tensions, became independent in 1961, while the Gambia followed in 1965.

West Africa at least had the good fortune to be without a substantial European settlement. In Kenya, there were long-standing grievances amongst the African population against the white settlers who had seized their land. There was a European population of around a quarter of a million among 6.8 million blacks. Nationalists were able to mobilise the land discontents among the Kikuyu and to unite educated Africans with rural traditionalists. The British government feared that the white settlers in Kenya might make a unilateral declaration of independence, rather than see concessions being made to the black population.

In the 1950s, with little progress being made towards African rule, armed revolt broke out. The Mau Mau was based on Kikuyu secret societies, but included organisers who had seen service in the armed forces. Although it emerged from internal tensions about land and inheritance within Kikuyu society, it instituted attacks on white settlers. It started gradually in 1950–1, but the trouble escalated as the authorities tried to repress the growing discontent. As a guerrilla struggle intensified, a state of emergency was declared, which lasted from 1952 until 1960. African political parties were banned, civil liberties suspended and the more radical African leaders, including Jomo Kenyatta, arrested. Kenyatta was charged with having organised the Mau Mau and, on the basis of almost no evidence, was sentenced to seven years' imprisonment. It did not get rid of the Mau Mau, and, indeed, probably widened the armed revolt. More and more troops had to be sent in to deal with the guerrillas. Now these were mainly British troops, not Empire troops that had played this kind of role in Africa in the past, although a loyalist African 'home guard' was established. The expulsion of many thousands of Kikuyu families from European-controlled farms and the removal of 30,000 from Nairobi generated recruits for the Mau Mau. On the other hand, the British authorities managed to keep the armed struggle largely confined to the Kikuyu areas and to undermine Mau Mau claims to reflect nationwide demands. They successfully gave encouragement to the emergence of new, moderate African politicians.

With 32 white settlers killed, the repression became harsher. Special forces were sent in to eliminate key Mau Mau leaders. At the request of the Governor, summary justice was used, including the death penalty for anyone administering the Mau Mau oath. Communal punishments were imposed on areas where there were incidents. Some 1,090 Africans were hanged – in some cases in public, 20,000 were killed and anything between 160,000 and 320,000 passed through Kikuyu prison camps, while others were hemmed in within fenced villages.[2] Tales of brutality, torture and sexual violence began to seep out from the camps. Such actions did not fit the British self-image of the peaceful transition from empire. Church leaders and others spoke out against what was being done. Revelations of atrocities by British troops at Hola Camp, where, in 1959,

---

[2] The true figures are uncertain since the British government went to great lengths to hide the extent of the repression. There was something of an attempt to air-brush the whole campaign from historical memory, something that is only now being exposed by non-British historians, see Caroline Elkins, *Imperial Reckoning. The Untold Story of Britain's Gulag in Kenya* (New York, Holt & Co., 2005).

11 detainees were beaten to death by warders after a riot, led to a denunciation by the young Conservative MP, Enoch Powell, of the repressive measures being used.

A solution was desperately sought. In 1957, a legislature was established, with an equal number of Europeans and Africans, plus some elected Indians and Arabs, together with nominated officials. Two Africans were admitted to the executive council, but they refused to take their seats until Kenyatta was released. But the hatred of Kenyatta was deep among the white population and there was a refusal to accept his importance as a potential leader.

Change was, however, on the way. In London, Ian Macleod had been appointed as Secretary of State for the Colonies, with the remit to decolonise. With colonialism being condemned at the United Nations and in the United States, as well as by liberal opinion at home, defending empire was becoming impossible. With the cold war between the West and the Soviet Union at its most intense, the fear was always that failure to respond to nationalist demands would drive the third world, as the new non-aligned states came to be called, towards communism. The Prime Minister, Harold Macmillan, talked of 'a wind of change' blowing through Africa, although he was unprepared for the speed with which Macleod acted. Kenyatta was released and in December 1963 Kenya became independent with Kenyatta as Prime Minister. The new government sought to reassure the white population, but many of these had already moved out to Southern Rhodesia.

In 1962 Uganda became independent, with Milton Obote, a young building company executive, as Prime Minister. The third element of what, it was hoped, might become an East African Federation, was the trust territory of Tanganyika, a former German colony. United Nations pressure, rather than internal agitation, encouraged moves towards independence there. Julius Nyerere, a young, Edinburgh-educated teacher, had begun to create a national movement that very effectively appealed to world opinion through the United Nations' committees and, in 1961, achieved independence after only a year of self-government.

A federal structure was the preferred solution in official circles for the three central African territories of Northern Rhodesia, Nyasaland and the largely self-governing Southern Rhodesia. The Conservative government was keen on federation and they played down African objections. The white government in Southern Rhodesia enthused about a partnership which they claimed would be a close one – comparable to that of a rider with his horse!

In spite of all the warning signs, federation was pushed ahead, and in 1953 a Central African Federation was established, headed by the leader of the Northern Rhodesian whites, Roy Welensky. The federal government was elected by a largely white electorate, with over half the members of the legislature coming from Southern Rhodesia. The vision was of continuing British dominance in Central Africa and this was allowed to override the objections from every section of African opinion. In 1957, the British government refused to intervene when a bill was brought in by the federation Parliament to reduce African parliamentary representation from an already derisory low level. Welensky's favourite line was that government had to remain in the hands of the 'civilised and the responsible'. An attempt by the Prime Minister of

Southern Rhodesia to give Africans a modest say in government resulted in his being ousted. White settlers, increased by growing numbers who had emigrated from Kenya, were determined to retain the very comfortable lifestyle that they had established.

In Northern Rhodesia and Nyasaland, nationalist movements grew, despite the imprisonment of leaders and the shooting of protestors. A British commission of inquiry had been unable to find any black representative who was in favour of the federation. It was not what the British government wanted to hear, but the existing situation was no longer defensible to Commonwealth opinion and the federation was unsustainable. Nyasaland was granted African majority rule in 1960, but Northern Rhodesia, with some 66,000 white settlers and valuable copper deposits, proved more problematic. Nevertheless, on 1 January 1964, Nyasaland became independent as Malawi and North Rhodesia as Zambia.

That left the situation in Southern Rhodesia exposed. Concessions to the black populations in the North had pushed the Southern Rhodesian electorate further to the right. There was constant talk of 'betrayal' by the British government. In December 1962, the Rhodesia Front Party, based on farmers and white industrial workers, ousted the former middle-class leadership, who were seen as too liberal. The Front demanded complete independence. The British government took the line that, before that happened there had to be safeguards for Africans, but did little to bring this about. The arrival of a Labour government in 1964 convinced white Rhodesians that they could only lose out and, on 11 November 1965, the Rhodesian premier, Ian Smith, unilaterally declared independence. It was illegal and treasonable and caused much soul-searching in military, legal and civil service circles in Rhodesia, but the possibility of the British government taking action was never high. Very quickly the case was made that it was inconceivable to attack 'kith and kin'. A rather ineffective boycott was imposed. In 1970, a republic was declared and it survived unrecognised, but secretly supplied by South Africa and other boycott breakers, until civil war and American pressure brought it down in 1980, when Zimbabwe emerged.

The Mediterranean and the West Indies

The British had the League of Nation's mandate to run Palestine. Ever since 1919, they had faced problems of trying to balance Arab interests against those of the growing Jewish presence. Elsewhere in the British sphere of influence in the Middle East, First World War commitments to the Arabs had – to an extent – been met by the creation of the kingdoms of Iraq and Transjordan. Palestine was much more problematic and, from 1928, there were regular explosions of unrest amongst the Arab population against Jewish settlement and the British presence. According to an historian of British policy in the Middle East, 'among the huge majority of Arabs, the grievance about Palestine destroyed every shed of regard for Britain'.[3]

---

[3] E. Monroe, *Britain's Moment in the Middle East 1914–1971* (London, Chatto and Windus, 1981), p. 123.

The aftermath of the Second World War focused attention on the Jews and, undoubtedly, many saw the establishment of a Jewish homeland as a slight recompense for the guilt of the Holocaust. Zionist influence was particularly strong in the United States. But the British had the problem of trying to regulate immigration, and were responsible for the unedifying spectacle of survivors of the Nazi concentration campaigns illegally trying to enter Palestine and finding themselves locked up in British prison camps in Cyprus. The British Foreign Office was traditionally pro-Arab and was anxious to limit Jewish immigration. There was also anxiety to maintain British bases in Palestine as an alternative to the now very hostile environment of Egypt. Against that, the Labour Party had adopted a Zionist position and talked naively of the Arabs being encouraged to move out to make way for Jewish settlers.

The existing Jewish settlers in Palestine were now very effectively organised, economically, politically and militarily. There were a number of terrorist groups, that ruthlessly used terror tactics against both Arab and British. This, in turn, led to counterterrorism. The blowing up of the British military headquarters in the King David Hotel in Jerusalem in July 1946 by Jewish terrorists, killing 91, and the hanging of two British sergeants from a tree in August 1947 led to counter atrocities by the British occupying forces and to attacks on Jews in Britain. Enthusiasm for maintaining the Palestinian mandate evaporated. The pressure from America to admit more Jewish settlers was intense and the government feared that their negotiations for an American loan would be blocked unless concessions were made.

There were schemes for partition of the land and for a federal structure that came to nothing since they could only be accomplished by the use of force. A bankrupt Britain could no longer afford to maintain its dominant role in the Middle East. The British, faced with huge American pressure to throw open Palestine to unrestricted Jewish immigration, and unable to persuade the Arabs to accept any significant increase in immigration, announced to the United Nations in September 1947 that they would give up their Palestine mandate in June 1948. The United Nations, by the narrowest of majorities, voted for partition. As the British mandate ran out, so attempts to control matters on the ground were largely abandoned and open war between the two communities broke out. On the eve of the British withdrawal, Jewish settlers declared the independent state of Israel.

The withdrawal from Palestine made Egypt more important. Egypt had always been something of an anomaly and was never fully incorporated within the Empire. Since 1882, there had been numerous British statements that their presence there was temporary. Only in 1914 was it proclaimed a British protectorate. This was officially ended in 1922, when Egypt was declared independent. However, the British presence remained paramount, with a large garrison of troops, and, on numerous occasions, British troops were used to crush nationalist unrest. Under a treaty in 1936, a British garrison was to stay in Egypt until 1956, the argument being that only in this way could the Suez Canal be defended. In 1952, in the aftermath of an upsurge in nationalist feeling, an Egyptian army coup ousted King Farouk. The inspirer and eventual leader was Gamal Abdel Nasser. As so often, the British authorities failed to appreciate the extent to which his nationalism reflected Egyptian views.

Faced with growing hostility and attacks on troops, the British in 1954 agreed to withdraw the beleaguered garrison, but retained the right to return in the event of a serious threat to the Suez Canal. It was to make sure that it did not join Egypt that the British now encouraged independence moves in the Sudan, still nominally an Anglo-Egyptian condominium. There was no settler class, little real strategic value, apparently, few natural resources and so little resistance in Britain. In 1955, Sudanese notables in their Parliament voted for an independent republic, outside the Commonwealth, which was formally established in January 1956.

Ten months later the British were back in Egypt. In September 1955, Nasser announced that Egypt was to purchase armaments from the Czechs, having fruitlessly negotiated with both the British and Americans. As part of a vision of modernisation, he was also negotiating for funding for a high dam in Aswan on the upper Nile. Having made little progress with Britain and the United States, he turned to the USSR and made clear Egypt's non-alignment in the tension of the cold war. When America abruptly broke off negotiations about funding and Britain followed, Nasser nationalised the canal, owned by the Suez Canal Company, in which the major shareholders were the British and French governments. Overnight, the Company's installations were seized and Egyptians moved in. Contrary to nearly a century of British expectations, the Egyptians proved quite capable of managing the technicalities of the canal.

To Anthony Eden, now the Prime Minister, there were various issues. First there was a belief that he had perhaps pulled out of Egypt rather too readily in 1954. He came under great pressure from the 'Suez group' on the right of his party to maintain imperial authority. Secondly, he developed a perception of Nasser as a dictator, comparable to Hitler or Mussolini, who must not be appeased. The British and the French were both suffering from a post-war sense of lost influence and, with anxieties about their remaining empires, they began planning an attack on Egypt. The problems were substantial, since neither country had the necessary resources to sustain a long struggle. They secretly colluded with Israel and, on 29 October 1956, Israeli troops invaded Egypt. Eden, as planned, publicly expressed shock at this action and announced that, to protect the canal and to separate the combatants, British and French forces would have to invade. By the time the invasion fleet had sailed from Malta, Nasser was able to block the canal by scuttling ships in it.

The invasion went ahead, but Britain was condemned throughout the world and the country was deeply divided. Most of the members of the Commonwealth voted at the United Nations in condemnation of the invasion. In the end there was a run on the pound and the American government, which had made clear its hostility to the use of force (after all, a presidential election was pending in November), warned Eden, in the bluntest terms, that there would be no financial backing unless the British withdrew. In considerable humiliation, the decision to do so was made. The result was a loss of what remaining influence Britain had in the Arab world and an oil crisis. The loss of confidence and the powerful sense that the country could no longer control its own foreign policy is crucial to understanding the rapid shedding of empire in the late 1950s and 1960s.

Focus on

The Suez crisis, 1956

This is the editorial in *The Observer*, 4 November 1956 – the first newspaper to oppose the British–French invasion of Suez.

> We wish to make an apology. Five weeks ago we remarked that, although we knew our Government would not make a military attack in defiance of its solemn international obligations, people abroad might think otherwise.
>
> The events of last week have proved us completely wrong; if we misled anyone, at home or abroad, we apologise unreservedly. We had not realised that our Government was capable of such folly and such crookedness.
>
> Whatever the Government now does, it cannot undo its air attacks on Egypt, made after Egypt had been invaded by Israel. It can never live down the dishonest nature of its ultimatum, so framed that it was certain to be rejected by Egypt. Never since 1783 has Great Britain made herself so universally disliked. That was the year in which the Government of Lord North, faced with the antagonism of almost the whole civilised world, was compelled to recognise the independence of the American Colonies.
>
> Sir Anthony Eden's eighteenth-century predecessors succeeded in losing us an empire. Sir Anthony and his colleagues have already succeeded in losing us incalculable political assets. So long as his Government represents this country, we cannot expect to have a good standing in the councils of the nations. . . .
>
> Ever since 1945, there have been two cardinal features of British external policy. The first has been to uphold the rule of law with special reference to the United Nations. The second has been a steady progress away from imperialism, exemplified in the full emancipation of Burma, India, Pakistan, West Africa and the West Indies. Neither of these cardinal features of our national policy were sincerely endorsed by the Conservative Party, as we now see. In the eyes of the whole world, the British and French Governments have acted, not as policemen, but as gangsters. It will never be possible for the present Government to convince the people of the Middle East and of all Asia and Africa that it has not been actively associated with France in an endeavour to reimpose nineteenth-century imperialism of the crudest kind.

Source: *The Observer*, 4 November 1956.

Yet, there were still lessons to be learned. Following the withdrawal from Egypt in 1954, Cyprus was identified as the new permanent base in the Mediterranean. The government bluntly declared that Cyprus was one of those strategic territories which 'owing to their particular circumstances can never expect to be fully independent'. Among the Greek-speaking population, the nationalist demand was for *enosis* (union with Greece), and an increasingly violent guerrilla war broke out. Once again, the executions, floggings, torture and imprisonment of suspects, that were the response to the rebellion, undermined Britain's self-image. The religious leader, Archbishop Makarios, was built up into a sinister figure of evil and, in the spring of 1956, he was exiled. However, exile only enhanced Makarios's prestige amongst his compatriots and, in 1957, he was released and the British began to negotiate a withdrawal. Again, the right wing of the Conservative Party protested violently, but, in 1959, it was agreed that Cyprus become independent, though with the British retaining what were called 'sovereign military bases'.

Malta, too, had strategic importance in the Mediterranean and, as the Second World War had proved, incredibly valuable port facilities. In 1955, there was talk of actually incorporating Malta in the United Kingdom, with representation at Westminster, but it came to nought. There followed a period of protests and riots against British rule until, in 1961, internal self-government was achieved and in 1964 Malta became an independent dominion.

Yet another federation was created in the West Indies in 1956, after a decade of discussion, but its survival was brief. The larger islands of Jamaica, Trinidad and Barbados had no desire to see scarce resources shared with the smaller ones and they were anxious about too many people coming from the smaller islands in search of work. Independence was agreed for May 1962 and, when it was clear that Jamaica was opposed, the federation was dissolved. Jamaica and Trinidad and Tobago became fully independent in August 1962, with Barbados following in 1966. Attempts to retain a federation of some of the smaller islands gradually broke down.

Why the end?

The rapidity with which all but a few small dependencies were shed in the years after 1945 can only be explained by taking into account a variety of different factors. Most of all, it reflects the decline in British power that had been going on for more than half a century but was speeded up by the Second World War. Britain did not have the resources to maintain either the administration or the defence of the Empire. With India and Burma gone, the strength of the huge Indian army was no longer available to operate in Asia and there were no longer the strategic arguments for maintaining the routes to India. As had been apparent in India, the requirements to maintain control in the face of determined nationalist movements were beyond what any government could seriously consider. Put more crudely, as the historian Corelli Barnett has pointed out, there was a 'squeamishness at the harsh realities of colonial government'.[4] Exhausted by the war, demoralised by austerity, with old assumptions challenged and undermined the will and the sense of mission to persist with imperial projects had evaporated. Those few politicians who tried to play the imperial card found little popular response.

---

[4] C. Barnett, *The Collapse of British Power* (London, Eyre Methuen, 1972), p. 20.

Given the lessons of India, there was hope that the mistakes would not be repeated in Africa. In fact, most of the mistakes *were* repeated, with nationalist leaders branded as terrorists and popular protests forcibly crushed, only for the realities to be recognised and the nationalists released and placed in office. There was the problem, in many colonies, of finding people to whom to hand power. As more than one nationalist pointed out, there had always been a paradox in the claim that colonies were being prepared for eventual self-government when most blacks were systematically excluded from experience in government and, indeed, from access to education. The timing in a few cases, therefore, depended upon finding enough people with the necessary education to take over power. There was also the huge pressure of international opinion that was making colonialism, in the traditional sense, unacceptable. Pressure came especially from the United States, which saw itself as anti-colonialist and certainly could not persuade most of its population to get involved in a war if they thought it was about defending European empires. With an acceptance of a post-war dependence on American goodwill and financial support, plus a view that only a close 'special relationship' with the United States could give Britain some kind of 'great power' role, withdrawal from empire was inevitable.

The surprising thing is that the shedding of empire seemed to cause so little debate within Britain, outside Parliament. But a survey carried out by the Colonial Office in 1947 had revealed an astonishing level of ignorance about the Empire. Most people's perception of the Empire did not extend much beyond the 'white dominions' and, even in the 1960s, with frequent royal tours, many were still happy to think of these as still part of the Empire. However, there was also very effective selling of the idea that the Empire had been a great success in that it had led 'subject peoples' to a position where they were now capable of self-government. It was presented as another British success story and evidence of Britain's exceptionalism. In practice, Britain's last days of empire were as brutal as those of most of the other imperial powers and only a combination of colonial resistance, world opinion and lack of resources had forced governments to accept that there was no alternative to withdrawal.

Further reading

Anderson, D., *Histories of the Hanged: The Dirty War in Kenya and the End of Empire* (London, Weidenfeld & Nicolson, 2005)

Brown, J.M. and Louis, W.R., *The Oxford History of the British Empire, IV: The Twentieth Century* (Oxford, Oxford University Press, 1999)

Darwin, J., *The End of the British Empire: The Historical Debate* (Oxford, Oxford University Press, 1991)

McIntyre, W.D., *British Decolonisation, 1946–1995: When, Why and How did the British Empire Fall?* (Basingstoke, Macmillan, 1998)

Reynolds, David, *Britannia Overruled. British Policy and World Power in the 20th Century* (Harlow, Pearson Education, 2000)

Timeline 1919–63

Year	Government and politics	War and empire	Economic and social	Cultural and intellectual
1919	Dáil Éireann set up; Lady Astor first women to take seat in House of Commons	Government of India Act; formation of Northern Ireland; Amritsar massacre	Sankey Commission in coal industry	
1920		League of Nations formed	Unemployment Insurance Act	
1921	Anglo-Irish Peace Treaty			
1922	Lloyd George resigns; Bonar Law Prime Minister; Conservative election victory	Egypt independent		British Broadcasting Company established
1923	Death of Bonar Law; Baldwin Prime Minister; general election (December)			Divorce on grounds of men's adultery granted
1924	First Labour government; Ramsay MacDonald Prime Minister; Conservative election victory (October); Baldwin Prime Minister			Baird television invented
1925	Plaid Cymru formed		Return to gold standard; Contributory Pensions Act	
1926			General strike	Penicillin discovered
1927			Trade Disputes and Trade Union Act	BBC formed as public corporation; first talking film 'The Jazz Singer'

1928	Fifth Franchise Reform Act	
1929	Labour election victory; MacDonald Prime Minister; Margaret Bondfield first woman cabinet minister	Wall Street Crash	Virginia Woolf, *A Room of One's Own*
1930	Ghandi's salt march	
1931	Formation of national government; national election victory	Off the gold standard	
1932	Statute of Westminster	Protective tariffs introduced	Aldous Huxley's *Brave New World*
1933		Unemployment Insurance Act	
1934	Scottish National Party formed		
1935	Baldwin Prime Minister	Jarrow hunger march	J.M. Keynes, *General Theory of Employment, Interest and Money*; first TV broadcasts
1936	Death of King George V; abdication of Edward VIII; George VI		
1937	Resignation of Baldwin; Neville Chamberlain Prime Minister		
1938	Resignation of Eden as Foreign Secretary	Munich Agreement	Virginia Woolf's *Three Guineas*
1939	Declaration of war (3 September)		
1940	Winston Churchill Prime Minister	Germany invades Low Countries and France; Dunkirk evacuation; Battle of Britain	

Year	Government and politics	War and empire	Economic and social	Cultural and intellectual
1941		Conscription of women		Death of Virginia Woolf
1942		Surrender of Singapore; Battle of El Alamein; 'Quit India' campaign	Beveridge Report	
1943		Allied landings in Sicily		
1944		D-Day landings; Battle of Imphal	Butler Education Act (England); National Health Service White Paper	
1945	Labour election victory	Victory in Europe; Victory over Japan	Family Allowances introduced	Evelyn Waugh's *Brideshead Revisited*; George Orwell's *Animal Farm*
1946			Nationalisation of Bank of England; National Insurance Act; Employment Policy White Paper; New Towns Act; bread rationing introduced	Marriage bar in Civil Service abolished
1947		Indian independence; withdrawal from Greece	Coal industry nationalised; Town and Country Planning Act; sterling crisis	'New Look' for women's fashion
1948		British Nationality Act; withdrawal from Palestine; Burma independent; Ceylon (Sri Lanka) independent; state of emergency in Malaya	National Health Service established; British Railways formed; electricity industry nationalised; Marshall Aid	Olympic Games at Wembley

Year				
1949		Formation of NATO; Ireland withdraws from Commonwealth	End of clothes rationing; devaluation of sterling	Orwell's *1984*
1950	Labour election victory	British troops in Korea		
1951	Conservative election victory; Churchill Prime Minister	European Coal and Steel Community formed	Charges for teeth and spectacles introduced	Festival of Britain
1952	Death of George VI; Elizabeth II	British atomic bomb in Australia	Prescription charges introduced	
1953		Central African Federation		Crick and Watson discover structure of DNA
1954		Withdrawal of troops from Suez Canal Zone	End of food rationing	
1955	Churchill retires; Anthony Eden Prime Minister; Conservative election victory	Gold Coast becomes independent Ghana		
1956		Sudan becomes independent; attack on Egypt		John Osborne's *Look Back in Anger*; Bill Haley's 'Rock Around the Clock'
1957	Eden resigns; Harold Macmillan Prime Minister	Malaya independent; British hydrogen bomb test; Treaty of Rome creates European Common Market		
1958	Chancellor of the Exchequer and two ministers resign over rise in government expenditure		Founding of CND	Race riots in Notting Hill

Year	Government and politics	War and empire	Economic and social	Cultural and intellectual
1959	Conservative election victory			
1960		Nigeria independent; Cyprus independent	End of compulsory National Service; creation of European Free Trade Association	Court case over publication of D.H. Lawrence's *Lady Chatterley's Lover*
1961		Sierra Leone independent; Tanganyika independent; Kuwait independent		Contraceptive pill
1962	Macmillan sacks a third of the Cabinet; Gaitskell comes out against Common Market	Uganda independent; Jamaica, Tobago, Trinidad independent		Launch of *Private Eye* and of *That Was the Week That Was*
1963	Death of Gaitskell; Wilson becomes leader of Labour Party; Profumo affair; resignation of Macmillan; Sir Alec Douglas-Home Prime Minister	Kenya independent; Borneo independent; Sarawak independent; Singapore independent	French veto British membership of Common Market	New universities opened

PART 7

The reshaping of Britain 1964–2007

34

Economic modernisation

The free-market economy

The 1960s witnessed the last ten of Britain's so-called 'golden years' of strong economic growth (at 3 per cent per annum). From 1973, there was considerable change, and this is usually presented by economic historians as a significant crisis. Though this interpretation has been challenged recently, on the basis that what happened in that decade was a short-lived crisis that deviated from long-run trends, this section focuses on the crisis and explanations of its cause.[1]

From 1973, a series of major events and changes impacted on the British economy. These were: major increases in oil prices by the Arab-dominated Organisation of Petroleum Exporting Counties (OPEC); the abandonment of free-trade agreements originally set up in the 1940s; an apparent abandonment of Keynesian economic theory, and the onset instead of free-market economic theory, especially under the Conservative government of Margaret Thatcher from 1979–90. The result was slower growth rates (of around 2.3 per cent per annum) until 2000, which really started to affect the economy from around 1973. This was accompanied by the rise of unemployment and inflation, compounded everywhere by the collapse of the international monetary system. What followed was a sharp decline in world trade, impacting on exports – notably of British manufactured goods. This hastened the steady collapse of most staple industries, and put pressure on government to bail out with subsidies to large nationalised industries like coal, shipbuilding and steel. Public spending was high and, by the end of the 1970s, the economy seemed in a downward spiral.

---

[1] J. Tomlinson, 'Tales of a death exaggerated: how Keynesian policies survived the 1970s', *Contemporary British History*, 21 (2007), pp. 429–48.

Figure 34.1 The first British Concorde supersonic aircraft coming into land on its maiden flight, April 1969. Heavily subsidised by both governments, this British-French co-operative venture symbolised what Prime Minister Harold Wilson was attributed with calling 'the white heat of the technological revolution', but which in reality never returned on the investment. The last Concorde aircraft were withdrawn from service in 2003, partly as a result of a crash at Paris in 2000, which killed 113 people.
Source: Science & Society Picture Library

In the 1970s and 1980s, the favoured explanation for these woes was the rising cost of production and, importantly, the cost of wages. The prosperity of the 1960s fuelled demands funnelling through trade unions for improvements in real wages, for substantive gains to people's standards of living, leading initially to an income policy under the Labour governments of 1964–70 and 1974–79 which allowed wage increases in line with cost of living rises. This became a recipe for ongoing inflation in the 1970s, prompting wage demands from many workers in excess of 25 per cent per annum.

The systems of checks and balances that had been constructed by the British state in the 1940s and 1950s, through demand management by means of rationing, stop-go policies, and nationalisation, appeared to be in tatters.

This state of affairs gave rise to a major policy shift in economics in Britain, the USA and the West generally. Keynesianism fell out of favour, at least temporarily, and in its place came monetarism. Rather than controlling the economy through demand management, as Keynes had argued, monetarists held that inflation – price rises generated by an excessive money supply – was at the root of economic problems. If government printed too much money, and gave too much freedom to trade unions to demand higher wages for workers and welfare benefits for the unemployed, monetarists argued, the result was the decline of economic growth. The late 1970s witnessed the gradual rise of a monetarist philosophy that advocated strict control of the money supply, opposition to wage increases, no subsidies to ailing industries, and cutting back on welfare benefits. The Labour government signalled from 1975 that it was abandoning attempts at demand management and control of unemployment, but failed in the late 1970s fully to implement this new philosophy. A so-called 'winter of discontent' in late 1978 and early 1979 resulted from large numbers of public-sector workers coming out on strike with demands for huge wage increases. Most notoriously, some gravediggers in Liverpool and Tameside (Manchester) came out on strike, leaving bodies unburied. This contributed to massive press hostility and to a fall-off in public confidence in Labour economic management. The result was that the Labour Party lost the general election of 1979.

The Conservative Party, led by Margaret Thatcher, swept to power in 1979 and set about a brutal monetarist policy to squeeze inflation out of the economy. This involved large-scale unemployment on a level not witnessed since the 1930s; massive trade-union unrest (notably the miners' strike of 1984–5, which the miners lost, leading to the effective demise of deep mining in Britain in the following five years); and an increase in poverty as welfare benefits were cut and spurious claimants (called 'scroungers') were ruthlessly pursued. This introduced a period of sharp division between traditional working-class political representatives of the left and the revivified Conservative Party and its supporters in industry and financial markets. Individualism in politics, economics and personal philosophy became the order of the day.

One of the major developments of the Conservative governments of Margaret Thatcher during 1979–90 and of her successor, John Major, during 1990–97 was deregulation. Nationalised industries were sold off to the private sector, including not just manufacturing concerns such as shipbuilding, iron and steel, and the coal industry, but also key utility companies, which it had previously been thought were 'natural' monopolies that should be under public control. These industries included the railways; the ownership of gas and electricity; most major airports; the national airline British Airways; British Telecom (BT, previously part of the Post Office); the electronics and communications firm Cable and Wireless; and a whole host of other enterprises which had formerly been owned or controlled by the state. These were sold off in a bonanza of market flotations, often at much less than estimates of value. This was ostensibly intended to create a nation of small shareholders, but in reality fostered massive wealth for companies and for many entrepreneurs. In addition, even in parts of the economy still run by the state, market operations came to dominate, including in the National Health Service, local government and the prison service, where the 'market mechanism' was perceived as the way forward to improve the efficiency of contracts for work done. Outsourcing, contracting out, internal markets, targets and incentivisation (with bonuses) became the catchwords of both economy and government.

More widely than this, the Thatcher years brought deregulation and encouragement for private business and individual economic advancement on all sorts of levels. Many of these were initially in traditional sectors of the economy, but in the 1990s the revolution spread into new business opportunities – notably in banks and financial work, in retail, electronics, mobile phone technology, and online. The way commerce operated was perceived to change, with the rise of financial incentives in the form of massive bonuses for young and go-ahead workers in the business world. This was viewed not just as an economic change, but as a change of British economic culture, in which risk-taking was rewarded. This bonus-led culture itself spawned new business in and around the world of work – new catering and restaurants, gymnasia and health clubs, new magazines and holiday opportunities. In this way, the influence of monetarism was seen to extend beyond free-market economics to create a free-market individualism, the like of which Britain had not entirely seen before.

This reached its peak of symbolic significance in home ownership, encouraged by the Thatcher government through the sale of council (state-owned) houses to sitting tenants. To own a home became in Britain, more than almost any other nation outside of North America, an expression of individualism and citizenship, resulting in a sustained long-term property boom. To an extent, British popular culture became in the 1990s and 2000s obsessed by houses, their purchase, improvement, and money-making potential. Equally, the property market in Britain and other nations was a key element of the world economy in terms of investment and the construction industry. But it was the most vulnerable point for both national and global economic stability and growth, and was the cause of several financial panics in the early 1990s and late 2000s.

In these sorts of ways, the monetarist revolution of the 1980s came to fruition in the 1990s and 2000s. After Thatcher left office in 1990, her successor as Conservative Prime Minister, John Major, retained essentially the same economic policy. To many eyes, so too did the New Labour governments of Tony Blair (elected in 1997) and that of Gordon Brown, who succeeded him in 2007. Yet, public spending rose faster under Chancellor of the Exchequer Gordon Brown between 1999 and 2007 than ever before in peacetime, raising questions as to how far monetarism had, in fact, triumphed over Keynesianism. Nonetheless, a monetarist culture survived, even escalated, under New Labour. The creation of monetary stability, low inflation and a growth culture based on targets and incentivisation spread across all sectors of life – not just in the private sector and government businesses (such as they remained), but also in education, health care and local government work. The economic philosophy that generated the succeed-or-collapse rule for business paralleled the educational philosophy that emerged in the 1990s of high levels of testing of students and closure of 'failing' schools. The free-market revolution seemed to seep throughout British life, with money at the root of most decision-making. However, evidence of interventionism by the state, and of rising spending, led some commentators to believe that the older economic philosophy of Keynesianism was a discreet survivor in economic policy.

The role of government intervention reached an unprecedented scale in 2008–9 as Prime Minister Gordon Brown encouraged world leaders to fend off recession and the danger of world depression through massive state spending (mostly to shore up the banking system with the provision of credit facilities). The 'credit-crunch' crisis of 2007–8 was an international phenomenon, partly attributed to the excessive lending of banks to the American 'sub-prime' mortgage market (of poorly secured low-income house buyers). British banks, encouraged by deregulation under first Conservative and then New Labour governments, became overexposed in the American sub-prime market, and in a spiral of declining confidence, income, demand and employment led to rising mortgage default and British banks with the most dangerous lending practices collapsed and required government bail-out. This led in 2008–9 to the nationalisation of the Northern Rock bank and the Royal Bank of Scotland, and emergency government-engineered takeovers of Halifax Bank of Scotland by Lloyds TSB, and of Dunfermline Building Society by the Nationwide Building Society. The cost of handling the crisis forced British national debt into a planned rise to £1.4 trillion over 2009–14, with the prospect of further cost if stability did not return.

Economic decline or transformation?

There are two major opposing judgements on the economic history of Britain since 1964. The first is that the British economy was in serious decline and crisis in the 1960s and 1970s because of the economic failure of Keynesian policy, and that it recovered spectacularly as a result of the brutal surgery of Thatcher's monetarist policy of the 1980s, sustained by ensuing Conservative and Labour governments. The second view is that, though the 'golden age' of British growth between 1945 and 1964 came to an end, what followed in the 1960s and 1970s was a period in which Britain performed relatively well, in trying international conditions, in contrast to European, American and even East Asian economies. Moreover, despite, or possibly because of, economic management and Keynesianism, this laid the basis for spectacular economic growth in the 1990s and early 2000s.

The first judgement is associated especially with right-wing economic historians. They point to the improvement in productivity in the 1980s as evidence of the failure of Keynesianism and the success of monetarism. They point more generally to the rise of a free-market liberalism that created an 'enterprise culture' which was self-evidently beneficial for innovation, incentive-led economic growth, and the decline of over-manning and restrictive trade-union practices that had grown since the 1940s to be a restrictive yoke round the neck of the economy. Above all, in this view, the economy needed to be modernised away from staple industries (coal, iron and steel, shipbuilding, textiles and engineering) which, although already diminished in importance, remained in 1979 a drain on the public purse, infused a left-wing dependency culture throughout society, and restrained the free movement of labour into growth sectors. In their place, emphasis was put on British expertise in the financial and services sectors of the economy, including intellectual property development (such as software, design and architecture). For the architect of this shift in culture, Mrs Thatcher, the 1980s had to undo the supposed damage of the 1960s which had combined a rampant socialism with an undermining of traditional family and moral values.

Focus on

The British economy 1937–99

Table 34.1 Economic performance of British manufacturing 1951–99

	Growth of output (% growth per annum)	Growth of labour productivity (% growth of output per worker)
1951–73	4.4	4.3
1973–79	−0.8	0.4
1979–99	0.8	3.3

Source: Data from S. Broadberry, 'The performance of manufacturing', in R. Floud and P. Johnson (eds), *The Cambridge Economic History of Modern Britain: Volume III: Structural Change and Growth, 1939–2000* (Cambridge, Cambridge University Press, 2004), p. 59.

Table 34.2 Shares of world exports of manufactures 1937–99 (%)

	1937	1950	1964	1973	1979	1999
United Kingdom	22.3	24.6	14.0	9.1	9.2	6.9
United States	20.5	26.6	20.1	15.1	16.3	17.8
Germany	16.5	7.0	19.5	22.3	21.6	14.2
France	6.2	9.6	8.5	9.3	10.0	7.4
Japan	7.4	3.4	8.3	13.1	13.1	12.2

Source: Table 3.5 in S. Broadberry, 'The performance of manufacturing', in R. Floud and P. Johnson (eds), *The Cambridge Economic History of Modern Britain: Volume III: Structural Change and Growth, 1939–2000* (Cambridge, Cambridge University Press, 2004), p. 64.

Table 34.3 Home ownership in Britain 1938–2003

	Percentage of homes owned by occupants
1938	32
1945	40
1980	56
1985	62
1990	66
2003	68

Sources: http://www.tutor2u.net/economics/content/topics/housing/home_ownership.htm; survey by Roger Burrows, University of York cited at http://www.jrf.org.uk/knowledge/findings/housing/113.asp, accessed 7 September 2007.

The second judgement is most strongly associated with a post-Thatcher consensus of revisionist economic historians. In this view, the British economy in the 1960s and 1970s performed slightly less well than in the 1950s, but still very strongly when compared with some leading competitors. Britain in the 1960s and 1970s closed the productivity gap with the world's leading economy, the USA, and though some other nations in Europe and the Far East, such as Japan, were improving productivity faster than Britain, the gap with some (such as Germany) had been nearly closed by the early 2000s. Thus, in this analysis, the productivity increase of the 1980s is downplayed; it was less than half the rate achieved in 1964–73, and it is explained as the product of forced redundancies in overmanned industries, the withdrawal of government subsidies and economic closures rather than the product of rising output. At the same time, the massive benefits of oil and gas discovered in the British sectors of the North Sea in the 1960s, and tapped by drilling rigs in the 1970s and 1980s, failed to push output and productivity improvement faster and were, in comparison to some similarly oil-rich countries (like Norway), largely wasted. Manufacturing received insufficient state support in the 1980s, causing the premature collapse of some industries which, in other nations, were supported through cyclical depression.

Thus, the first judgement characterises the 1950s, 1960s and 1970s as a period of British decline, and the 1980s, 1990s and 2000s as a time of success being snatched from failure. By contrast, revisionist scholarship moves away from a narrative of British decline in economy (and society) in the 1960s and 1970s, and reduces the emphasis on a massive contrast between the earlier and later periods. The second view is one that is coming to dominance amongst historians. The story of Britain as being of 'decline followed by failure' is now regarded with scepticism. Despite problems of the 1950s and 1960s (like loss of empire, overmanning and stop-go monetary policy), these decades witnessed no greater economic fluctuations than in most other countries.

In either analysis, the period from the mid-1990s onwards is seen as one of exceptional stability and good performance in the economy. From being the economic lame duck of Europe, Britain emerged as the most dynamic economy, with a rising competitiveness, productivity and entrepreneurship. This dynamism is seen to have been especially strong in the non-manufacturing sectors. In design, electronics, software development, mobile phone technology and internet business, Britain was performing especially well. This was demonstrated in the 'dot com' revolution in online business that marked the very strong shift after 2000 in retail business from the high street to online. The consumer society has been a major driver of growth and innovation, with a seemingly insatiable desire for fashion and innovation in clothes, cars and personal technology items (mobile phones, organisers, MP3 players, PCs, laptops, computer games and television technologies).

One result was the sustained flux in manufacturing sectors. Some of the major staple industries had a topsy-turvy history in relation to government after 1945. For instance, the iron and steel industry was nationalised by a Labour government in 1950, denationalised by a Conservative one in 1953, renationalised by Labour again in 1967 and finally privatised in the Conservative government's sale of state enterprises in 1988. For all that, the output of iron and steel continued to grow until 1973, but then declined 39 per cent by 1999.[2] Coal and shipbuilding declined even more severely, losing most of their productive capacity in Britain. By the 1990s, the nation had, in effect, lost its staple industries.

New industries developed with new products, though on a much smaller scale than the staples being lost. Moreover, product innovation led to great instability, as did the drive for competitiveness, with a continuous search for lower production costs. One result was the movement of some industries overseas to exploit cheaper labour. This applied in textiles, shoe-making, vacuum-cleaner manufacture, and also to new retailing systems like call centres. These developed in the 1990s, initially in British cities (and staffed by large numbers of part-timers from the student population), but, by 2000, were moving 'offshore', notably to India. Though trends in these sectors were often reversible, manufacturing came to rely increasingly on nontraditional patterns of recruitment and settlement. No longer were industries formed in particular towns to remain for decades or centuries, as happened from the late eighteenth century to the mid-twentieth century. Manufacturing came to be an international undertaking, dominated by global brands in computers, clothes and telephones (such as Dell, Hewlett Packard, Nike and Nokia) which, in the search for the lowest costs, kept moving production from country to country (such as Romania, Indonesia, Malaysia and, above all, China). Between the 1980s and 2000s, Britain became less and less a

---

[2] S. Broadberry, 'The performance of manufacturing', in R. Floud and P. Johnson (eds), *The Cambridge Economic History of Modern Britain: Volume III: Structural Change and Growth, 1939–2000* (Cambridge, Cambridge University Press, 2004), pp. 70–1.

place where things were made, and more and more a place where things were designed and consumed.

Agriculture (along with fishing) was one especially troubled sector of the economy. The arrival in the late 1980s of BSE (bovine spongiform encephalopathy, popularly referred to as 'mad cow disease') posed a major problem that was not over until 1997, by which time 170,000 cases had been found in cattle. This was followed in 2001 and again in 2007 by foot and mouth disease (FMD). Collectively, these made the British farming industry seem in the eyes of the British electorate to be a moral as well as economic problem. The 2002 FMD outbreak was especially debilitating to the upland and mixed farming areas of Britain; British beef was banned from the rest of the EU (after being only freed from BSE restriction in 1998). The government farming ministry (MAFF, later DEFRA) was slow to respond to FMD, and the result was that it spread to many areas of England and led to a mass culling policy that decimated livestock. Even with compensation, the loss of cattle, sheep and pigs was devastating to many farmers; some went out of business, and others took years to replenish their stocks. By 19 September 2001, 3.88 million animals had been slaughtered, incinerated and buried in mass pits, and more followed in later years.[3] With massive taxpayers' compensation on top of regular subsidies to farmers (larger farming estates gained up to £1 million per year), agriculture seemed to be kept afloat only by the political influence of landowners and the National Farmers' Union. Two other factors were EU policy and globalisation, each of which we examine below.

The change to the British economy in the last 40 years of the twentieth century was extraordinary. In the mid- and late 1960s, one important public and political reaction to the notion of economic decline was a massive campaign to 'Buy British'. But by the 1990s, this notion was almost impossible to sustain because many products were produced from component parts manufactured in different countries and then assembled elsewhere, whilst the companies owning them were in charge of major brands from different nations. In the 1960s and 1970s, there was serious concern in Britain over the collapse of volume car manufacturing companies – notably British Leyland, which had previously swallowed up major British brands like Austin, Rover and Hillman. Britain had been a leading exporter of motor vehicles, accounting for 52 per cent of all world exports in 1950, but this then fell to 24 per cent in 1957–62 and to 19 per cent in 1963–7.[4] By the 1990s, car production in Britain had stabilised, but through international companies with branch factories – Ford, Honda, Peugeot. In this way, it became harder and harder to recognise an easy way to a patriotic economic policy that could favour home-grown manufactured goods.

The British economy between 1964 and 2007 cannot be described as experiencing any overall absolute decline and, in comparative terms, its position has been one of

---

[3] A. Howkins, *The Death of Rural England: A Social History of the Countryside since 1900* (London, Routledge, 2003), p. 230.

[4] S. Broadberry, 'The performance of manufacturing', pp. 66–7.

extremely good performance during a period when the economic centre of the world economy has been gravitating towards developing nations (particularly China and India). In this sense, Britain's economy has been transformed and modernised and, in most respects, has been a significant success.

The European Union 1974–2007

In 1973, Britain joined the European Economic Community (EEC), which became in 1992 the European Union (EU). The EEC grew from an agreement over iron and steel production in 1951 to become at its foundation (in the Treaty of Rome of 1957) a group of only six nations (France, Germany, Italy, Belgium, Holland and Luxembourg), expanding to nine nations in 1973 and 17 in 2007 (see Chapter 39). The central concepts of the Union were, firstly, that member states formed a free-trade area in which goods, finance and labour could move freely; secondly, that a Common Agricultural Policy (CAP) could provide a production-managed regulation of practically all farm produce (including grain, livestock, dairy and wine); and thirdly, that iron and steel production should be regulated and controlled to maximise benefit by reducing competition. From 1968, tariffs between member states were removed, but a wider single European market was not implemented until 1992.

Underlying this growing role was what is now known as 'the European project', in which economic integration extended to social regulation, moving towards a federalist state with government powers over member states. Under the Maastricht Treaty of 1992, a common currency was planned and finally introduced as the Euro in 2002, and during 2004–7 attempts were made to form a common constitution which would further bind the member states into a kind of 'united states of Europe'. With power exerted through its own Brussels-based executive (the European Commission, headed by the European President) and by the European Parliament (sitting rotationally in Brussels and Strasbourg), the EU by the 1990s and 2000s had developed a myriad of extremely influential institutions, including the European Central Bank, the European Court of Justice, and bodies regulating many aspects of life on the continent. Britain sought membership from 1963, but was blocked (largely by France) until 1973. The British electorate remained divided over the merits of the EU, and this was reflected in considerable Conservative Party and Labour Party opposition. In the 1980s and 1990s, this led to constant pressure to obtain for Britain rebates on money put into the EU, and to stay out of certain aspects of the Union. Thus, in 1992, Britain remained outside of social integration plans (over things like work practices), and in the same year pulled out of the Exchange Rate Mechanism that sought to harmonise European currencies. In 2002, Britain stayed out of the Euro currency. But these things aside, the EU developed an important role in the British economy. The removal of border restrictions led to many Britons moving to France and Spain, whether to work, retire or establish second homes. British exports to Europe grew significantly, whilst trading with former colonies, already declining, diminished further. One of the important effects was in labour migration to Britain. In the 1990s and 2000s, the numbers of Europeans settling in Britain increased; young French people, thwarted by employment difficulties at home, started to come in large numbers to work in restaurants and shops, whilst after the 2004 accession of east European states, even larger numbers of migrants (especially Poles) came to work in the same sectors, as well as in agricultural labouring.

The EU had a considerable impact on agricultural, rural and fishing communities. The Common Agricultural Policy (CAP) was a cornerstone of the EU, fostered especially by the French to protect their politically powerful lobby of small and medium farmers, and this affected Britain too. The CAP worked by guaranteeing a Europe-wide price for farm products, leading to the EU buying and storing of excess. Food production – especially cereals – grew in Britain, as in the rest of the EU, outstripping European demand and resulting in the creation of large 'food mountains': warehouses of cereals and refrigerated plants for beef. By 1988, there were 1 million tonnes of butter, 5 million tonnes of wheat, 4 million tonnes of barley and 800,000 tonnes of beef (not to mention 'lakes' of French and German wine) being held in storage and, basically, never being sold or eaten. As much as 60 per cent of the EU budget by 1990 was spent on the CAP, though the policy (and the mountains) were reduced.[5] But most farmers, notably large farmers, benefited from this. Farming and commercial forestry fell increasingly into the hands of investment companies which moved the industry towards contract ploughing, planting and harvesting, using mobile hired workers. Heavy use of fertilisers and machinery meant that field sizes grew as hedges and walls were destroyed; rotation systems were often abandoned; and the flatlands of Britain became vast grain prairies. This did much to destroy wildlife habitats, hitting wild birds and insects. Pesticide use was intensified. A reaction to this set in the 1990s and 2000s, with a growth in organic farming and foodstuffs, government grants to sustain wildlife habitats at field margins, and some grants to restore drystone walls and hedging, but it could not make up for the damage done.

The fishing industry in Europe was in sharp decline from 1945. This was caused by sharp falls in most stocks of fish through overfishing as techniques of catching improved; the ability developed to spread nets over up to quarter of a mile wide and up to 100 miles in length that could remove fish from the floor bed as well as the surface areas. The EU sought, from the 1970s, to control the extent of fishing, imposing negotiated bans on types of net (especially narrow-holed nets that caught the young as well as mature fish), on periods of fishing, and on particular areas of the North Sea. In Britain, this led to the collapse of both inshore and deep-sea trawling industries in many ports, especially on the southern and Irish Sea coasts. From the 1970s, the major east-coast ports like Hull, Grimsby, Aberdeen and Lerwick started to contract, leaving in the 1990s only Peterhead and Fraserburgh as large-scale fishing centres. But, in the 2000s, these too suffered severe contraction, aided, as everywhere, by EU grants to scrap boats.

---

[5] A. Howkins, *The Death of Rural England*, p. 157.

Against this pressure to contract farming and fishing, the EU remained strongly influenced by the agricultural sector, especially the powerful political forces in France, Italy, Spain and Portugal. As a result, major grant-aid came to rural and coastal areas to ease the pain of economic loss; areas such as the Scottish Highlands, Hebrides and Northern Isles, north and central Wales, Northern Ireland, and upland England benefited from investment money to build new roads, finance start-up industries and invest in schemes of social benefit (including heritage and nature projects). In such ways, the European Union became increasingly important to both economic contraction and its off-setting with regional economic aid.

Work, education and trade unions

The second half of the twentieth century witnessed important changes in the workplace. Industry and jobs were changing, and the nature of trade unionism changed at the same time.

The sustained growth of the economy in the 1950s and 1970s, combined with the advent of the welfare state, brought significant rises in the standards of living for all social groups. By 2000, the average Briton was about three times better off than in 1949. However, there were victims. From the 1960s, unemployment started to rise slowly and, from 1979, much faster, leading to almost a tripling in the numbers in relative poverty during 1979–90.[6] Much of the unemployment and poverty was due to economic adjustment, the decline of staple industries, the shift from manufacturing to retailing and service sectors, and the collapse of many local staple-dependent economies (such as coal pit villages, shipbuilding communities and textile towns where too few alternative forms of employment developed). At its worst, regional levels of unemployment and poverty were very high during the 1980s, and some towns and cities (like Liverpool, Middlesbrough and Merthyr Tydfil) had not by the 2000s fully recovered their economic vibrancy. Yet, many other former zones of decline bounced back with urban regeneration (cities like Glasgow, Manchester and the docklands area of east London), to join London and the south-east generally in enjoying a boom in employment opportunities.

One of the main features of the period leading up to the 1980s was the unremitting contraction of many traditional sectors of the economy. Jobs in shipbuilding, coal-mining, engineering and especially textiles slimmed down sharply to the point where, by the end of the century, these sectors were a mere shadow of their former importance. This contraction was matched by the growth of other sectors of the economy – the banking, financial and retail sectors; electronics and electrical; tourism and leisure

---

[6] P. Johnson, 'The welfare state, income and standards of living', in R. Floud and P. Johnson (eds), *The Cambridge Economic History of Modern Britain: Volume III: Structural Change and Growth, 1939–2000* (Cambridge, Cambridge University Press, 2004), p. 213.

industries; computing; and education. In general, jobs were becoming less manual and unskilled in nature. The artisan jobs which had dominated the British industrial experience since the early nineteenth century – the engineers, boiler-makers, wrights, carpenters – were being replaced by workers at desks, component manufacture, or in software design and management. White-collar workers (those in administrative and professional jobs) made up only a third of the workforce in 1951, but a half by 1979. This also signalled a shift from male to female workers, and an increasing number of part-time workers. Between 1951 and 1991, the number of female workers rose from 7.1 to 22.9 million, and part-time workers increased from 779,000 in 1951 to 3,781,000 in 1981. Female workers were also tending to work longer, to have an older average age, and to work after marriage – something largely frowned upon until the 1950s. Moreover, mothers with school-aged children rarely worked in 1960 (only 20.2 per cent did), but by 1991 the majority did (58.4 per cent).[7] Women were becoming absolutely central to the economy.

One of the major features of British (and indeed most developed nations) in the second half of the century was the rise of higher education. There were only around 20,000 university students in Britain in 1900, and still only 82,000 in 1954. The numbers rose to 190,000 in 1966; 1,195,000 Higher Education Institutions (HEI) in 1991/2; and 2,086,080 (HEI) in 2001/2. An increasing proportion of students were women, with a trend discernible in the 1980s and 1990s for girls to outperform boys at almost all levels of education.

The years from the end of the Second World War to 1979 were good for the British trade-union movement. The period witnessed sustained growth in union members – from 8,603,000 in 1946 to 12,639,000 in 1979 – a rise from 43.0 to 53.4 per cent of workers. A most notable aspect of the rise was much improved unionisation of female workers, of whom 39.9 per cent were in unions by 1980 (compared to only 24.3 in 1946).[8] But things then deteriorated very sharply. The Conservative government led by Margaret Thatcher from 1979 to 1990 was very hostile to unions, and took on the militant miners in a prolonged strike in 1984–5 over pit closures, which the miners lost, resulting in the swift collapse of practically all deep mining in Britain. With it, the fortunes of the trade-union movement generally declined; membership slumped to 8,939,000 (or 39.0 per cent of workers) in 1989 and to 7,295,000 (28.8 per cent) in 2001. It was clear that trade unions did better during periods of political favourability (notably during Labour governments of 1964–70 and 1974–9), and also when the inflation rate was high, forcing workers to unionise in defence of their standard of living. Equally, strike activity was greatest during key periods; there were waves of strikes in 1957–62, 1968–74, and 1977–9, the last widely seen as contributing to the downfall of the Labour government at the 1979 general election. Britain was regarded in the 1960s and 1970s as being prone to strikes; it was called 'the British disease' as union activity here was compared unfavourably to the more sedate trade unions of

---

[7] C. Wrigley, *British Trade Unions since 1933* (Cambridge, Cambridge University Press, 2002), pp. 23–5.

[8] Ibid., pp. 18–19.

the rest of Western Europe (though the USA, Canada, Italy and Australia had more strikes than the UK between 1946 and 1976).[9]

One of the few bright spots in trade-union organisation at the end of the twentieth century was the growing influence of women. By 2000, women were approaching equality in some areas of work and unionisation. Some 28 per cent of women workers were union members by 1999, compared to 31 per cent for men.[10] In both education and work, women were outperforming men in many areas of life, though still being held back from high posts in many sectors through the so-called 'glass ceiling' on promotions. Nevertheless, with labour shortage and the sheer growth in numbers of women in jobs requiring high levels of skill and education, the age of women dominating the economy cannot be far away.

Globalisation

One of the important features of the modern world is globalisation. This is a view of the world that grew from the 1950s, starting with a comment of a Canadian theorist, Marshall McLuhan, that 'the world is now a global village'.[11] Initially, this was demonstrated by the ability of modern transport (especially air flight) to free up movement of people (or at least those who could afford to travel) as tourists, bringing awareness of other cultures and exposure to different ways of life. Accompanying this was apparent merging of some consumption patterns (with global brands in food, clothing and electrical goods), and supposed narrowing in matters of taste and style. Popular culture was merging, with the worldwide availability of modern music via radio, television and records. From the 1990s, the internet forged patterns of taste and culture that were no longer simply defined by physical borders between countries or continents, but by groups of people defined by race, age and simple taste – groups that were to be found stretched over many parts of the globe. In turn, in economic terms, globalisation is seen to mean the availability of goods and services on a world scale, facilitated by the freeing up of restrictions on the import and export of goods on account of the removal of tariffs. This process is by no means complete: the United States, for instance, has tariffs imposed upon imports of some products like iron and steel so as to protect native industries. But the global economy is seen to be much freer than before, the volume of goods being traded internationally has mushroomed, and the extensive specialisation of national economies is seen to be a product of a global market. This may be composed of smaller sub-markets – the European Union being the strongest example – but undeveloped nations have been drawn into manufacture and global trading to an unprecedented degree.

---

[9] Ibid., pp. 19–20, 41–2, 52.

[10] Ibid., p. 31.

[11] McLuhan interview on CBC, 18 May 1960, at http://archives.cbc.ca/arts_entertainment/media/clips/342–1814/, viewed 13 April 2008.

It is hard to overemphasise the extent to which business, including foodstuffs, became transnational during the late twentieth century. Globalisation brought increased exchange of goods, services, labour, finance and ideas across the planet. International air travel made it easier for both labour and products to be shipped quickly. Food products started to be transported very long distances in quantities never seen before, as new techniques allowed crops to be grown in previously unsuitable climates (for instance, under polythene covers – 'poly tunnels'). Manufactured products became increasingly dominated by consumer items of all sorts, and produced by firms which might have a nominal location in one country or another but which, in reality, were increasingly international in finance and shareholding. Globalisation represented one of the most important features of the modern world, and in an environment where free trade was the widely accepted strategy of major governments, this meant that industries had to remain constantly competitive, with improving productivity, innovation and labour education.

In addition to economic change is the idea that the globalisation of the world leads to globalisation of values – that people start to share the sense of belonging to one human race, with ideas of tolerance, multiculturalism, and interchange between people of different races, religions and identities. One product of this is the notion of multiple identities – that humans have become, by the early twenty-first century, the products of an international cultural milieu in which the individual may find much in common with somebody from a faraway country. For Britons, this might mean that they were no longer linked, as in the past, simply by where British peoples – so called kith and kin – had traditionally settled, often in the former colonies. So, in this way, British people were no longer seen to interact solely with peoples in the USA, Canada, Australia and New Zealand, but increasingly with those of France, Spain and Italy, where hundreds of thousands of Britons have settled permanently in the 1990s and 2000s. Indeed, there are many intellectuals who assert that there are now distinctive European values and a European sense of identity held – although not abrasively and chauvinistically – across much of the continent, embracing Britain as well. Such values include tolerance; a belief in the secular nature of the state; hostility to zealous nationalism (in part because of our experience of it in two European wars); and an opposition to torture, excessive punishment and capital punishment.

However, globalisation theory has its limits. For one thing, creation of global markets for goods and services did not completely undermine international tension and conflict. In the 2000s, superpower relations between the USA, Russia and China still remained fraught. For another thing, globalisation has not meant a free movement of peoples everywhere. Indeed, as global transport has increased, the degree of free movement has tended to become more limited. Nations like Britain, along with the USA, have severely curtailed immigration, and closed borders continue to exist for people even if they are more open for goods.[12] With the attack by Al-Qaeda on the

---

[12] R. Hansen, *Citizenship and Immigration in Post-war Britain: The Institutional Origins of a Multicultural Nation* (Oxford, Oxford University Press, 2000), p. 23.

World Trade Center in New York on 9/11 (11 September) in 2001, and subsequent attacks in many countries, security issues put a brake on the unhindered development of global freedom for people to move.

Further reading

Floud, R. and Johnson, P. (eds), *The Cambridge Economic History of Modern Britain: Volume III: Structural Change and Growth, 1939–2000* (Cambridge, Cambridge University Press, 2004)

Howkins, A., *The Death of Rural England: A Social History of the Countryside since 1900* (London, Routledge, 2003)

Peden, G., *British Economic and Social Policy: Lloyd George to Margaret Thatcher*, 2nd edn (London, Philip Allan, 1991)

Tomlinson, J., *The Labour Governments 1964–70: Volume 3: Economic policy* (Manchester, Manchester University Press, 2004)

Wrigley, C., *British Trade Unions since 1933* (Cambridge, Cambridge University Press, 2002)

35

Black Britain: ethnic minorities and multiculturalism

The background to 1963

Until 1945, Britain was a country whose people were overwhelmingly white. Most were Christian or Jewish, or families whose heritage lay in those religions. But Britain has a long history of contact with peoples of colour.

White Britons had played a leading part in the slave trade, transporting between 1600 and the 1770s millions of black Africans to the colonies of the Caribbean and what became the southern states of the USA. Slavery contributed significantly to the commercial growth of Britain in that period, and to the capital investment in other trade and manufacturing thereafter. White Britons were principal colonisers of the areas where slaves were made to work in the cotton, tobacco and sugar trades, and in ancillary tasks to the economies of those areas. The slave trade and slavery itself were viewed in Britain largely as justified. Until the later eighteenth century, there was general acceptance of the economic utility of slavery, based on the many widespread presumptions about the inferiority of native peoples. But from the middle of the eighteenth century, there was a slow development of opposition to these practices, led by many evangelical Christians who developed a mission to convert the world to Christianity and believed that all men and women were equal in the eyes of God. After a long and vigorous campaign by William Wilberforce and others, the slave trade in the British Empire was abolished by Act of Parliament in 1807. This was followed by the abolition of slavery itself in 1833, although, in reality, slavery persisted through influence and exception in many British colonies for decades more.

Most parts of the British Empire were formed either free from slavery or where it was much less numerically significant than in the Caribbean. During the eighteenth, nineteenth and twentieth centuries, Britain used military conquest and economic power to establish imperial rule over peoples of different ethnic and religious backgrounds across the Middle East, India, Malaya and Singapore, parts of China, and many parts of Africa. Moreover, trading extended British contact elsewhere, including to the East Indies (what is now Indonesia). Native peoples were swamped by white immigrants to Canada, Australia and New Zealand, which between 1867 and 1907 formed the first independent dominions – states largely free from British control, but still within a Commonwealth headed by the British monarch. Britain governed much of the globe between 1750 and 1945, determining the fortune of many millions of people of colour.

Between 1947 and 1969, the British Empire came to a fairly sudden halt. Starting with independence for India (and its partition into Muslim-dominated East and West Pakistan on the one hand, and Hindu and Sikh-dominated India on the other), the colonial peoples threw off the incubus of imperial domination in a wave that had many ramifications for Britain. But more importantly, it granted to these peoples self-determination, freedom from economic and social controls, and the growth of indigenous culture and democracy. The British Empire had ruled largely through diktat, rarely through any kind of true democracy, so the imperial legacy gave way to new forms of political development. For Britain, in the 1940s and 1950s, there was increased immigration from these countries.

After 1945 the most numerous immigrants to Britain were initially black Afro-Caribbean migrants from the West Indies. They were attracted from 1947 by deliberate government policy, engrossed in the Nationalities Act of 1948, to admit people from British colonies and former colonies to make up for the domestic shortage of labour during post-war reconstruction. This 'Windrush' generation (named after the ship *HMT Empire Windrush* that brought the first large group of migrants in 1948) were predominantly men, recruited by organisations like London Transport. From the British colonies of Jamaica, Trinidad and Tobago, tens of thousands migrated to Britain in search of work. Gradually, in the 1950s, more came from India, Pakistan and Bangladesh, and other blacks and ethnic Asians from Africa from the 1970s. Men came mostly, and some young single women to work in key occupations. The majority came initially expecting to return. Indeed, through the 1950s, this expectation remained strong, and, coupled with racist refusal by landlords of other forms of housing, most migrant men lived in crowded lodging houses in London, Birmingham and some other Midlands towns. Competition for housing and scare stories of single black men seducing or attacking white women became the greatest flashpoints for racist bigotry. In May 1948, 200 white men stoned a house in Birmingham where newly arrived Indians were staying, and by the mid-1950s the level of immigration was high enough for Oswald Mosley, British Fascist leader in the 1930s, to be campaigning again in the city on anti-immigration issues. By the end of the decade, British society was starting to appear deeply divided after a race riot in London's Notting Hill when white working-class youths chased 'niggers' over five days of the August bank holiday in 1958.

The Notting Hill riot, more than any other single event, awakened Britain to the 'race issue', and with mounting tension over the emergence of civil rights in the

American South, the British state started slowly to edge away from segregation and laws that might end up being racially discriminatory. But gradually, the population settled, migrants' families joined them and, by the early 1960s, government started a long succession of immigration controls to try to control what opponents regarded as a 'flood'. Racial tensions rose as well and, by 1964, with the election of the Labour government, race relations were high on the agenda for political action.

Focus on

Immigrants' stories

These are extracts from the Birmingham Black Oral History Archive, recorded in 1990–2.

Avtar Singh Jouhl (arrived from Punjab in India in 1958)

We came to Smethwick, my brother's house, it was in Oxford Road, Smethwick. There were many people, I thought maybe waiting for me to come, but when everybody went away there was still fifteen or sixteen people, Indians, staying at the house. In the front room, two double beds, in the bedroom upstairs, each bedroom two double beds and in the small room, one three-quarter bed and those beds with the metal springs and big wooden headboards. No carpets in the house, it was lino in all rooms. The food was kept under the beds and in the kitchen there was electric cooker and this – not the present-type steel sinks, but was this china-type big sink. No hot water system, the toilet was outside, there was a tin bath tub. It was a surprise to me to see the house, a villa-type house, small one, much smaller than my own house in Jandiala, much smaller than that.

Carlton Duncan (arrived from Kingston, Jamaica in 1961)

Fortunately I didn't have, like many of my compatriots, I didn't have to go house-hunting, find a room to let, that alone would have really killed me off. Because on my journeys to and from college, I used to pass these shop windows and I'd see 'ROOMS FOR LET – SORRY NO COLOUREDS, NO IRISH, NO DOGS', this kind of thing, and I couldn't understand that you know, we were in the 'Mother Country'. I was finding that very difficult to come to terms with.

Frank Santlebury (arrived from Barbados in 1955)

All the firms then were glad for workers. They weren't getting rid of people and giving us their jobs, they were glad for workers. They were only too glad to get people to do the work and that's why people were coming to the United Kingdom at the time. But in spite of that although it was so easy to get employment at that time, one could leave a job today and you could walk into a job tomorrow, leave it and you would find it was easy to get another job. There was no difficulty in finding employment at that time.

Esme Lancaster (arrived from Wilmington, Jamaica in 1950, returning there several times)

You see, one thing about it is that over the Caribbean, people are very Christian-minded – Christian more Christian then. And the thing is that surprise me is that we looked in England when we were children to be for Christianity, the root of Christianity as such, the missionaries were all white, coming to our country telling us about God, telling us about this and the other, you know. And we saw so many things, you know, and believe them that this country was all for Christianity. And when you come you'd be accepted as a Christian you know. And when we came here the difference is that it is not so . . . I was a member of the Anglican Church in Jamaica, and from a child sang on the children's choir, . . . I sang in the cathedral choir in Spanish Town where we met the Queen when she came on 1952. . . . Then, after that, I came back [to Birmingham] and now, when I came to this Church [St. Michael's, Handsworth] I came with my transfer [certificate] and that is supposed to be [for] the nearest Anglican Church. And then I went there and had taken my transfer cards and my Mother's Union card and whatever. I was told by the vicar that I should come back. And each time I go back, 'he's busy', I should come back. And then one Sunday that was St. George's Day, and he went in the pulpit preaching, and he was saying: 'I don't know why for the life of me you people are leaving this country, going away, and others are coming and enjoying it and you are leaving.' And he went on and then at the end of the service he came to the door, shook hands, and then said to me – he didn't shook my hand anyway – he said to me: 'I'm asking if you could find another church to worship because I don't want to lose my parishioners.' And he told me of Hockley Brook, a church in Hockley Brook, that would take me.

Ranjit Sondhi (arrived from Ferozepur, Punjab in 1966)

There was discrimination in those days, people wouldn't lend money to immigrant families, particularly Afro-Caribbean families, with the result that a lot of them had to resort to council housing. So eventually I think, both Afro-Caribbean communities and Asian communities did what was the only option available to them. They grouped together, bought houses in common, pooled their incomes and their savings, formed little co-operatives of their own, indeed some of the earliest co-operative movements were among black people in Handsworth, and bought houses . . .

Then when I went to university it all flourished. I think in the first year there was a demonstration against Enoch Powell, who had made his 'Rivers of Blood' speech and incidentally at that point really racism wasn't a word in my dictionary but he had made his 'Rivers of Blood' speech, he was due to come back there and we had organised a demonstration. The students had not liked it and I saw here a bunch of white,

> university students, largely white, protesting against a man who was making comments about black people and I thought this was something, I really must get involved, and I did and I was in the front line and I remember being punched by a policemen in the stomach, very coolly and very calmly. The policeman came while my hands were pinned behind my back by other demonstrators; I got punched in the stomach. Now this infuriated me and that fury lasted for many years, I couldn't talk about the incident without really feeling very angry about that but it had most important impact upon my thinking.
>
> *Sources*: D. Price and R. Thiara (eds), *The Land of Money? Personal Accounts by Post-War Black Migrants to Birmingham* (Birmingham, Birmingham City Council, 1992), pp. 13–15, 24; C.G. Brown, *Religion and Society in Twentieth-Century Britain* (Harlow, Pearson Education Ltd, 2006), pp. 212–14.

Patterns of migration, work and settlement

The numbers coming to Britain from the 'New Commonwealth' (principally the West Indies, India and Pakistan) grew rapidly in the 1950s, from an estimated 4,000 in 1953, rising to 42,650 in 1955, and then to 136,400 in 1961.[1] Encouraged by active recruitment by some employers (notably London Transport) and poor economic opportunities at home, those who travelled were often skilled workers, including graduates and professionals like engineers, chemists and teachers. Some travelled for advanced education, such as those from India and Pakistan, where the textile and allied industries were seeking skilled scientists. But, for the majority, the jobs on offer in the UK were semi-skilled or unskilled – jobs which, in many cases, British-born workers would not take. The migration then slowed down after 1962 with a succession of Acts of Parliament: the Commonwealth Immigrants Act 1962, which limited right of entry to those with job vouchers; the Commonwealth Immigration Act 1968, which sought to stop immigration by Kenyan Asians and inadvertently closed entry to all Commonwealth citizens; and the Immigration Act 1971, which effectively allowed entry by mostly white Commonwealth citizens, but not those who were black or Asian. Despite the effect of these laws, the majority of immigrants to Britain in the 1960s and 1970s were people of colour. Many were wives and children of men already working in Britain, and, as families expanded, the non-white population of Great Britain increased from estimates of 30,000 in 1951 and 400,000 in 1961, to 1.4 million in 1971, 2.1 million in 1981, 3.0 million in 1991 and 4.6 million in 2001.[2]

---

[1] Net migration (after deducting emigrants to those countries); Z. Layton-Henry, *The Politics of Immigration: Immigration, 'Race' and 'Race' Relations in Post-war Britain* (Oxford, Blackwell, 1992), p. 13.

[2] Commission for Racial Equality, http://www.cre.gov.uk/downloads/factfile02_ethnic_minorities.pdf, accessed 13 August 2007.

The largest flows of people came from Asia, the Caribbean and Africa, but their peak flows varied. From 1953 to 1961, 240,650 came from the West Indies, 69,800 from India and 42,250 from Pakistan (including East Pakistan, which in 1971 became Bangladesh).[3] But in the 1960s and 1970s, the proportions coming from Pakistan, India and Bangladesh increased, as did the numbers from Africa. It was this increase from the mid-1960s that prompted the change in government immigration policy. In 1968, the Kenyan government was pursuing what it officially called a policy of 'Africanisation' whereby Asians in the country were to be excluded. Some 200,000 Kenyan Asians – an ethnic group that had lived in Africa for centuries – booked flights to Britain, only to be turned away after the change in immigration policy. The same situation occurred four years later with Ugandan Asians, expelled by Idi Amin in a process that would later be called ethnic cleansing. After much debate, the UK government agreed to take and resettle 28,608, with some other Western nations taking smaller numbers.[4] After that year, the numbers of migrants stabilised until the end of the century at a government-controlled level of around 27,000–50,000 per annum from the New Commonwealth countries (out of a total of 50,000–80,000 immigrants from all places).[5] In 1981, a distinction was drawn between the citizenship of Commonwealth and UK people for the first time since 1948, by granting British nationality to the latter only. The numbers entering Britain were heavily restricted to close family and vetted asylum seekers. But, with natural increase, the numbers of black and Asian residents rose. By 2001, Asians made up 4.1 per cent of the British population; blacks 2.0 per cent; 1.2 per cent were of mixed ethnicity; Chinese 0.4 per cent; and others 0.4 per cent.[6]

In the main, black and Asian immigrants were forced to take jobs in Britain with lower status and skill levels than they had held prior to coming to Britain. Downward social mobility was a fairly common experience. Black migrants from the Caribbean came in the late 1940s and early 1950s to work, especially in the transport industry. Arriving mostly by ship at Southampton, they found jobs in London Transport and on the corporation bus services in Birmingham, Leicester, Coventry and other towns and cities of the Midlands, Lancashire and Yorkshire. The jobs they obtained were overwhelmingly unskilled. On the buses, blacks worked mostly as conductors, taking fares, as white union members regarded being a bus driver as a more skilled and better-paid job. In factories, blacks worked mostly in unskilled or semi-skilled work. In the hospitals and local government, many worked as cleaners or road sweepers. Even

---

[3] Figures calculated from data in Z. Layton-Henry, *The Politics of Immigration: Immigration, 'Race' and 'Race' Relations in Post-war Britain* (Oxford, Blackwell, 1992), p. 13.

[4] V. Robinson, 'The Ugandan Asian Programme 1973', at http://geography.swan.ac.uk/refugeedisp/drVR.htm

[5] R. Hansen, *Citizenship and Immigration in Post-war Britain: The Institutional Origins of a Multicultural Nation* (Oxford, Oxford University Press, 2000), p. 267.

[6] Figures from or calculated from Commission for Racial Equality, http://www.cre.gov.uk/downloads/factfile02_ethnic_minorities.pdf, accessed 13 August 2007.

by the early 1980s, movement out of low-status work was slow. Some 83 per cent of Caribbean males and 73 per cent of Asian males were in manual work (compared to only 58 per cent of white males), with Pakistani and Bangladeshi groups most concentrated in the lowest job levels. Interestingly, Asian women achieved almost the same level of penetration of professional and management positions as white women.[7]

Black and Asian workers were slow to join trade unions in Britain. The record of the unions was rather mixed between the 1940s to the 1970s; there was often considerable worker hostility to the employment of non-British-born labour, to blacks and to Asians. From the mid-1970s, the TUC and several unions campaigned against racism, and from 1998 there were TUC-run Black Workers' Conferences. Yet by the early 1980s, 56 per cent of black and Asian workers were members of trade unions (compared with 47 per cent of employees as a whole). However, during recession, levels of unemployment were especially high amongst black workers, reaching 24 per cent of Caribbean men in 1982.[8]

The unionisation of black and Asian workers attained the status of a *cause célèbre* in August 1976, when 137 largely female and Asian workers walked out of the Grunwick film processing plant in Willesden in north-east London, after the employer refused union recognition to the Association of Professional, Executive, Clerical and Computer Staff (APEX) which was trying to negotiate over what it saw as low wages and poor conditions. Amidst allegations of intimidation and violence, the factory became the object of picket lines during a two-year dispute. The Labour government inquiry that followed, under Lord Scarman, recommended the reinstatement of the strikers and union recognition, but in a House of Lords' legal judgement the employer's right not to recognise the union was upheld. The employer attracted support from some Conservative party politicians, and, although he was Anglo-Indian, this seemed to reinforce the impression of right-wing hostility to the black and Asian population.

The Asian immigrants established two distinctive areas of work. One was in the restaurant trade, with the development especially of Indian curry houses that initially catered for the Asian population but, from the early 1970s, attracted significant numbers of white people – especially students and young people. A second area was the corner shop, distinguished by long opening hours and provision of a wide range of merchandise. Originally, these shops suffered because white people would only buy goods from white-owned premises, forcing the Asian shop owners to stay open into the evening in order to attract more trade. Initially regarded with great racist hostility, they quickly became features of all towns and cities throughout Britain.

Settlement very quickly started to segregate black from white immigrants. Many West Indians arriving in London obtained temporary accommodation near to the employment exchange in Brixton, and after some obtained jobs on the buses, London

---

[7] H. Goulbourne, *Race Relations in Britain since 1945* (Basingstoke, Macmillan, 1998), p. 84.

[8] C. Wrigley, *British Trade Unions since 1933* (Cambridge, Cambridge University Press, 2002), p. 30; H. Goulbourne, *Race Relations in Britain since 1945*, pp. 84–5.

Transport opened its own recruitment office in nearby Camberwell. As a result, LT became the largest single employer of West Indian immigrants, and the black community of Brixton started to grow into the largest in the UK. In Birmingham, settlement started in the early 1950s in Handsworth, where cheap lodging houses opened for male migrants. Other areas of black settlement developed, such as Notting Hill and Southall in London, and Wolverhampton in the West Midlands.

Initially, immigrants tended to rent housing in often poor-quality terraced housing in the private sector. But, very quickly, the migrant population moved into home ownership. By 1971, 50 per cent of both Caribbean and white homes in England and Wales were privately owned, though for the Asian community this reached 76 per cent. Numbers in local authority housing were lower than for the overall population – only 4 per cent for Asians and 26 per cent for Caribbeans (compared to 28 per cent for the white population). This is one piece of evidence that, despite being less affluent than most white families at that stage, and despite the larger size of migrant families, they were doing remarkably well in self-supporting financial terms, especially as mortgages were hard to come by for people of colour.[9]

Levels of racial segregation have been sustained and, in some places, increased in the last quarter of the twentieth century. In London and Birmingham, the initial zones of settlement have sustained strong black and Asian populations, whilst many cities and towns in the Midlands and in West Yorkshire, ranging from Leicester and Coventry to Bradford, have very significant populations. At the same time, the black and Asian populations in some parts of Britain have remained low – Northern Ireland being one important area.

Multiculturalism and resistance to it

From 1948 to 1962, the British government conducted one of the most liberal immigration policies in the world. Lacking public support at home, it nonetheless granted citizenship to hundreds of millions of people in British colonies across the globe. This allowed the rapid immigration of black, south-east Asian and other peoples who transformed Britain in a remarkably sudden process into a multicultural society. At its peak in 1961, 136,000 people immigrated to Britain. But between 1962 and 1971, the open door to immigration was progressively closed, ending by the 1970s almost all privileged access held by Commonwealth citizens. The result has been that, from 1962 until the early 2000s, the number of immigrants has remained largely constant at around 70,000 per annum.[10] This is far fewer than the numbers that wanted to come to Britain.

In 1963, racial discrimination and racism were not illegal in Britain. A housing landlord could legally refuse accommodation to black people; hotels and shops and

---

[9] Goulbourne, p. 79.
[10] R. Hansen, *Citizenship and Immigration in Post-war Britain*, pp. 16, 21.

public houses could refuse service to black people; and there was no law preventing different wages, conditions of service, facilities or even education to people of colour. In the event, levels of discrimination in Britain were not institutionally as high as in South Africa or the southern states of the USA where, over very many decades, the civil states had created discriminatory policies against black people, with segregated schools, buses (and seats on buses), segregated public toilets for white and black, and limited voting rights for blacks. Those forms of racial separation had not had time to develop in Britain. However, informal discrimination was rife – not just by employers and landlords but, notoriously, by the police, the armed services and by many officials of local government and the judiciary. Unequal pay and opportunity were standard experiences for people of colour.

During the period 1963–2007, there was a tension within British society over attitudes to its ethnic development. A right-wing attitude of hostility to immigration and to the impact of black and Asian cultures developed. This was best articulated in what became a famous (indeed, for many, an infamous) speech in 1968 by a leading Conservative party politician, Enoch Powell, who was reacting against Labour Party legislation to outlaw racial discrimination. In what became known as the 'Rivers of Blood' speech, he warned of the likelihood that Britain might follow the example of the USA in developing civil breakdown along race lines. His view was that

> In 15 or 20 years, on present trends, there will be in this country three and a half million Commonwealth immigrants and their descendants. That is not my figure. That is the official figure given to Parliament by the spokesman of the Registrar General's Office. There is no comparable official figure for the year 2000, but it must be in the region of five to seven million, approximately one-tenth of the whole population, and approaching that of Greater London. Of course, it will not be evenly distributed from Margate to Aberystwyth and from Penzance to Aberdeen. Whole areas, towns and parts of towns across England will be occupied by sections of the immigrant and immigrant-descended population.

'The discrimination and the deprivation,' he said, 'the sense of alarm and of resentment, lies not with the immigrant population but with those among whom they have come and are still coming.'

> They found their wives unable to obtain hospital beds in childbirth, their children unable to obtain school places, their homes and neighbourhoods changed beyond recognition, their plans and prospects for the future defeated; at work they found that employers hesitated to apply to the immigrant worker the standards of discipline and competence required of the native-born worker; they began to hear, as time went by, more and more voices which told them that they were now the unwanted.

In a passage notorious for what is widely regarded for its racist and denigrating language, he quoted a letter from a constituent in Wolverhampton who described the experience of an elderly white lady being victimised by black children:

She is becoming afraid to go out. Windows are broken. She finds excreta pushed through her letter box. When she goes to the shops, she is followed by children, charming, wide-grinning piccaninnies. They cannot speak English, but one word they know. 'Racialist', they chant. When the new Race Relations Bill is passed, this woman is convinced she will go to prison. And is she so wrong? I begin to wonder.

Powell concluded with a warning of civil unrest on a large scale. He said: 'As I look ahead, I am filled with foreboding; like the Roman, I seem to see "the River Tiber foaming with much blood".'[11]

For this speech, Enoch Powell lost his position in the Shadow Cabinet, and eventually resigned his seat to become an MP for a Unionist party in Northern Ireland. The conservative, alarmist view that he represented split opinion amongst Conservatives, although the party remained generally hostile to immigration. But from the 1970s, two other parties with extreme views on immigration, and opposing cultural integration, came into being – the National Front and the British National Party. These were widely viewed by critics as being racist, because they fought amongst other things for the ending of black immigration, repatriation of black people, and the protection of the white culture of Britain. The British National Party and the National Front were always small parties in electoral terms, never gaining any MPs in Parliament but securing a few local councillors in some parts of east London and the north of England. Pursued by anti-racist organisations like the Anti-Nazi League, confrontations arose with demonstrations and counter-demonstrations, including the death at the hands of the police of anti-racist marcher Blair Peach during a march against the National Front in 1979.

Urged on by trade unionists and recruits from ethic minorities, the Labour and Liberal Parties favoured a more open immigration policy and a policy of cultural integration. The formation of a multicultural society became the official state policy, supported by legislation. It led to the creation of an ethos in British education, in social work, and in youth and community work, that sought to promote the integration of peoples of different races within British society, to ensure equal opportunities and end discrimination, and to seek acknowledgement, as the rest of Europe did, that the future lay in racial integration.

Discrimination and rights

The civil state in Britain was slow to react to the rights of the immigrant peoples and their offspring. The Race Relations Acts of 1965 and 1968 made certain specific actions illegal. The first outlawed barring entry to a person because of their skin colour to hotels, swimming pools and places of general public use, and created a rather

---

[11] Speech at http://en.wikisource.org/wiki/Rivers_of_Blood

weak Race Relations Board to investigate instances of discrimination, and the second made it illegal to discriminate on the basis of a person's colour in the vital areas of housing and employment. But the third Race Relations Act, of 1976, was the most important, outlawing racial discrimination for the following 30 years. It established the Commission for Racial Equality (CRE), which had stronger powers of inquiry into individual and generic cases, but also had powers to promote racial equality. The Act made it illegal to discriminate on the basis of 'colour, race, nationality or ethnic or national origins', or to segregate on racial grounds, and applied this principle to a wide range of activities in British life: in state organisations, trade unions, voluntary organisations, sports, schools, in legal partnerships, professional bodies, in provision of goods and service, and in advertisements. Both individuals and corporate bodies could be found guilty under the Act, and, in a major advance, it protected from victimisation individuals who sought redress under it, or gave evidence in cases brought under it.

From the mid-1970s, the fight against racism became one that moved from merely legal action to educational and training activities. Racism was seen to survive in public life, in popular culture and in the culture of many jobs, and the CRE led the way, with black and equality groups amongst teachers and other groups, to re-educate white British people to an awareness of the underlying racism that persisted in culture and language. Sensitivity to the language of denigration and prejudice arose (with key words like 'nigger' and 'paki' being targeted for abandonment in daily speech). Job discrimination was more difficult to tackle. Blacks and Asians were underrepresented in most organisations and professions such as the law, the police, academic life and the fire brigade. By the 1990s, however, there were larger numbers of lawyers and university graduates and postgraduates from the Asian community, and significant numbers started to enter the middle ranks of academia.

But the police and fire services were more difficult problems. Not only was the recruitment of ethnic minorities well below expectations, there were clear cases of racism in the investigation of crime. This reached a high point in the case of a 19-year-old black man, Stephen Lawrence. In April 1993, he was attacked in Eltham, in south-east London, by a gang of white youths, and after being called 'nigger', was stabbed twice and bled to death. An initial police prosecution was abandoned amidst claims of racism, and a private prosecution by the parents failed after the judge disallowed key eyewitness testimony. The *Daily Mail* newspaper named five suspects as the murderers, challenging them to sue for libel, which they did not. Meanwhile, the Police Complaints' Authority in 1999 exonerated officers of racism, but this was contradicted in the same year by a government public inquiry under Sir William Macpherson that concluded that the Metropolitan Police investigation had been incompetent and that the force was 'institutionally racist'.[12]

The Lawrence case highlighted the issue of institutional racism in other bodies which Macpherson directed should be explored, including the National Health

---

[12] http://en.wikipedia.org/wiki/Stephen_Lawrence

Service, local government and the civil service. Indeed, cases of discrimination persisted in many civil bodies and, in one sense, discrimination was driven underground into the locker rooms and the private thoughts of many racists. Even when there was no overt racism, there was clear evidence of the lack of thinking about the needs of ethnic groups. For instance, some medical conditions were more common amongst migrants, such as blood conditions like sickle cell anaemia in the black population, and thalassaemia amongst those from the Indian sub-continent and southern-European peoples, and their specific needs were not being met by British health authorities. Few sectors of the state were exempt from their unpreparedness for the needs of non-white immigrants and their children. Sometimes, there were differences which appeared irreconcilable. In one town in the north of England in the late 1980s, white parents argued that because the local school had a majority Asian roll, their children were denied a traditional English education.[13] This was not necessarily a racist position, but a perception of cultures clashing. Presumptions about what is 'British' culture became open to debate, and resolution of difficulties may not always have been possible.

None of this was to deny the persistence of racism, and the need to combat it. By the end of the twentieth century, there were perceptions of the need to consolidate the fight against discrimination and prejudice in a more holistic manner. In 2007, the CRE was replaced by the Commission for Equality and Human Rights, merging issues of gender and racial equality, and also with new legislation outlawing discrimination on religious grounds (which, prior to 2007, had only existed in law for Northern Ireland). Henceforth, racism, sexism and other ways in which essentialist attitudes fostered loss of human rights and dignity were to be tackled together.

Religious identities

In the 1950s, the bulk of the migrants to Britain had been Christians from the Caribbean islands. But from the 1960s to the early 2000s, a greater proportion of immigrants came from non-Christian backgrounds, mostly from Asia or Africa; foremost amongst these were the religions of Islam, Sikhism and Hinduism. However, from 2004, immigration became dominated by east Europeans, and especially the predominantly Roman Catholic Poles, who came to work in low-income jobs in agriculture and industry as a result of the expansion of the European Union from 15 to 25 nations and the free movement of labour from the east this permitted.

The majority of Christian immigrants from Jamaica and other islands were Anglicans – members of the Church of England – with most of the remainder being Methodist, Presbyterian and Pentecostal. This reflected the influence of British church missionaries that had converted slaves and their offspring from the seventeenth century onwards. Those who migrated to Britain in the 1950s and 1960s spoke of the

---

[13] H. Goulbourne, *Race Relations in Britain since 1945*, pp. 92, 97.

influence of their churches in nurturing their optimistic view of British culture – one which they had been taught was the cradle of Protestant Christianity, high morality and respectability. But many migrants were shocked on arrival in Britain to discover racism in some congregations which they were entitled to join, particularly in the Church of England, where some vicars openly asked black people to leave and not return as their presence was 'upsetting' the white worshippers. This led to the phenomenal growth in the Pentecostal congregations in urban Britain, especially in London and Birmingham, which came from the 1970s onwards to represent much of the black Christian community. Black Pentecostalism thrived; between the 1960s and the 2000s, their churches were the only significant source of growth in churchgoing and church membership during the collapse of Christian culture in Britain. By 1998–2005, non-white Christian churchgoers (predominantly black) were growing in number at the rate of almost 3 per cent per annum, compared to a decline in overall churchgoers (predominantly white) of just over 2 per cent per annum.[14]

Non-Christian religions amongst immigrants initially grew more slowly. In the early 1950s, there were about 30,000 Muslims, mostly Pakistani, of whom only 2,000–3,000 were in East London and less than 1,000 in Birmingham. Though Islam started to get organised earlier – notably with the foundation in 1936 of the Alawi order which established *zawiyas* (religious centres or lodges) in Cardiff, South Shields, Hull and Liverpool to serve the families of Yemeni and Somali seamen – there was a general lack of mosques until the later 1960s and 1970s because of the poverty of migrants and an expectation that most would return to their countries of origin. To begin with, this meant that Islamic religious observance was conducted in the home; only for the large Eid festival was a hall hired so everybody could pray together.[15] But as the permanence and prosperity of migrant Muslims and their children started to grow, so did organised religious worship; in 1960 there were only 9 Islamic mosques, by 1986 there were 200.[16] The same happened with Sikh gurdwaras, Hindu temples and Buddhist shrines. By 2001, most Britons (71.6 per cent) described themselves as Christian, but 2.7 per cent identified themselves as Muslim, 1 per cent as Hindu, and 0.6 per cent as Sikh.[17]

Language and religion made the Pakistani and Bangladeshi communities even more isolated than English-speaking black Christians from the Caribbean, and this was accentuated by clerics or imams who tended to encourage the retention of cultural distinction, rather than integration, as a means of sustaining the faith. Much the same applied to other faith groups, like the Sikhs, who experienced a unique form of

---

[14] Figures calculated from data in P. Brierley (ed.), *UKSH Religious Trends No. 6 2006/2007: Analyses from the 2005 English Church Census* (London, Christian Research, 2006), pp. 5.19, 12.2.

[15] H. Ansari, *'The Infidel Within': Muslims in Britain since 1800* (London, Hurst & Co., 2004), pp. 40–4, 107, 118, 130–50.

[16] Numbers registered with local authorities. K. Knott, 'Other major religious traditions', in T. Thomas (ed.), *The British: Their Religious Beliefs and Practices 1800–1986* (London, Routledge, 1986), p. 140.

[17] Census 2001, National Statistics, website www.statistics.gov.uk.

discrimination in the 1960s, when bus companies in Wolverhampton and other cities refused to employ men wearing turbans. Equally, Sikh men refused to wear crash helmets on motorbikes, a situation only reformed by special exemption in 1976. Although a few Hindus arrived from India in the 1950s and early 1960s, the main immigration occurred in 1965–72 during an exodus resulting from the so-called 'Africanisation' of East Africa (of Kenya, Tanzania and Uganda) by the governments there. The development of the faiths did not merely result in a sense of separation from the white population of Britain, but led to religion emerging as a strong factor for diversity *within* these communities. Indeed, in many cases, the faiths accentuated the cultural distinctiveness of ethnic groups, with first- and second-generation migrants encouraging the retention of strong links to parts of India, Pakistan and Bangladesh, with emphasis placed on the cultural rituals of dress, language, food and occasions such as weddings.

Between 1990 and 2007, there was a significant rise in religious militancy, notably among young men. Religious conservatism developed a new potency, and was common to most faiths, including Christianity. This was characterised by three things: first, growing fundamentalism, in which the core beliefs and scriptural command of each faith tended to be emphasised; second, militancy, in which forms of observance of faith like dress were pushed to the fore; and third, in some cases, violent extremism, such as in the rise of Islamist beliefs. British Islamism drew on the worldwide rise of hostility to Westernism. In 1989, Muslims publicly demonstrated against the publication of Salman Rushdie's book *The Satanic Verses*, which they regarded as blaspheming the Prophet Mohammed. Many young Muslims in Britain were attracted to forms of conservative Islam that emphasised separateness from the West, and unity, or *ummah*, with Muslims in other parts of the world. From about 1990, young Muslim men in increasing numbers adopted conservative beliefs, whilst some young Muslim women took to wearing the hijab (head veil) and a small number the burka (full body and face covering) to express their faith through avoiding enticing non-family men by the female form. Radical Muslim clerics became the object of media attack in Britain for allegedly encouraging young Muslims to join terrorist groups training in Pakistan and fighting with Muslim groups in Bosnia, Iraq and Afghanistan, reaching a crescendo of panic after the attack by Al-Qaeda which, in 2001, destroyed the World Trade Center in New York. A small number of Muslims undertook terrorist campaigns in Britain; four attacks on tube trains and a bus in London on 7 July 2005 left 56 dead (including the four bombers) and 770 injured; this was followed on 21 July by a failed attack again on the London underground, whilst in June 2007 a car-bomb attack in London and a petrol-bomb attack on Glasgow airport failed.

In the early twentieth-first century, religious identity seemed to become a more bitter source of social division in Britain than race. This was ironic in a country in which religious practice was amongst the lowest in the world. Indeed, from the 1960s, Britain had developed into a highly secular society with low Christian churchgoing, diminishing church membership, and rapidly falling levels of religious marriage and child baptism; in the late 2000s, it was noticed that the Roman Catholic Church had become the largest in Britain by dint of its acquiring hundreds of thousands of new Polish immigrants. Despite overall decline in church numbers, from the 1990s, there were increasing attempts by Christian churches to reassert influence upon government policy and party politics in areas such as education, abortion and censorship. This led to instances of ecumenical co-operation with Muslims and others to promote the influence of what became called the 'people of faith'. But despite rising religious identity amongst minority blacks and Asians, there was no evidence in the 2000s that suggested an overall change to the decline of the role of religion in the daily lives of the vast majority of Britons.

Further reading

Brown, C.G., *Religion and Society in Twentieth-Century Britain* (Harlow, Pearson Longman, 2006)

Gilroy, P., *There Ain't no Black in the Union Jack: The Culture, Politics and Race of a Nation* (London, Routledge, 1992)

Goulbourne, H., *Race Relations in Britain since 1945* (Basingstoke, Palgrave Macmillan, 1998)

Hiro, D., *Black British, White British: A History of Race Relations in Britain* (London, Grafton, 1991)

Holmes, C., *John Bull's Island: Immigration and British Society 1871–1971* (Basingstoke, Macmillan, 1988)

Solomos, J., *Race and Racism in Britain*, 3rd edn (Basingstoke, Palgrave Macmillan, 2003)

36

Media, youth and society

The media explosion

Britain in 1964, like most of the western world, was in the midst of a media revolution. First, access to television and to recorded music was exploding, with vast consumer purchasing of television sets, vinyl records and record players. Second, existing media were being reformed by technical innovation and experimentation, including pirate radio stations with mass audiences that took to the air in that year. Equally important was the development of satellite transmissions of television pictures from around the world, which allowed the 1964 Olympics in Tokyo to be transmitted live and, within two years, news events – for instance, from the front line in the Vietnam War – were brought to British screens within a few hours of their happening. Third, media (both new and old) were developing radical new symbolic meanings in the politics of the decade, with content transformed by a youth culture of pop music, risqué television drama and news of student rebellion in Europe and the USA. At the same time, there was a wider international revolt represented by the media – a revolt against deference, cultural staidness, and the influence of the generation of the Second World War.

These three aspects were given contemporary resonance by the Canadian philosopher Marshall McLuhan. In 1957, McLuhan first used the term 'global village' which, with 'globalisation', became an important, if contested, expression of political rhetoric in the last 30 years of the twentieth century. By this phrase, the world has come to understand a number of things. One is the rise of the idea of a free world economy, with the rapid and generally free movement of goods from one continent to another – not only by ship but also, in the case of perishable goods, by air. People were increasingly consuming the same things, in part with the same consumer products licensed worldwide by large business interests, like Levi jeans, Coca-Cola and record labels like EMI (see Chapter 34). Globalisation also referred to the way in which people in different countries, and increasingly more people within the same country, were consuming an ersatz culture that some regarded as a 'dumbed-down' literacy. This was best expressed in a book by the English social commentator Richard Hoggart, *The Uses of Literacy* (1957) in which he castigated the rise of English tabloid newspapers and the creeping disintegration of the literate culture of Shakespeare through mass culture:

> It may well be . . . that working-class people are in some ways more open to the worst effects of the popularisers' assault than are some other groups. Those who today, after the considerable sifting carried out by the educational system, perform the mass of work which is not intrinsically interesting and which makes only small critical and intellectual demands, are politically and economically freer than ever before. They have more money to spend than ever before; there are plenty of people more able than ever before to provide for them at the level of the lowest common denominator of response. In many parts of life mass-production has brought good; culturally, the mass-produced bad makes it harder for the good to be recognised.[1]

A lowest common denominator was coming to rule, according to Hoggart, often Americanised in character, and able to cross boundaries through the growing ubiquity of English as the world's *lingua franca*.

In 1964, McLuhan gave the world a second memorable phrase to understand what was happening – that 'the medium is the message'. By this he meant that until then, the media (writing, speeches, books, newspapers) for the previous four centuries had been transmitted with typographic technology that had imposed 'principles of continuity, uniformity and repeatability', generating an idea amongst educated elites especially that these media were in themselves conveying a message of rationality and high culture in Western society. Media had previously been dominated by high learning and useful knowledge. But, what he called 'electric media' – the radio, television, and vinyl records – of the 1960s were capable only of replaying other media (music, plays, speech), and in the process rationality was becoming increasingly marginalised by popular culture, entertainment and revolt. The result, he wrote, was that: 'In the electric age man seems to the conventional West to become irrational.'[2]

The significance of McLuhan's comments seemed to grow as the 1960s wore on. Young people were thwarted in listening to the latest music because of the BBC's state monopoly of radio broadcasting; the BBC's radio music station, the Light Programme, played little youth pop music, and its broadcasts featured stuffy, ageing presenters who failed to resonate with young people. The result during 1964–7 was pirate radio – stations based on anchored ships three miles off the British coast, outside the territorial

---

[1] R. Hoggart, *The Uses of Literacy*, (Transaction Books, 1998), p. 131.
[2] M. McLuhan, *Understanding Media: The Extensions of Man*, orig. edn 1964 (Cambridge, MA, MIT Press, 1994), pp. 10, 15, 299–300.

waters, where young disc jockeys played the latest records of emerging bands, together with commercials for youth products. Stations like Radio Caroline, Radio City, Radio London and Radio Scotland became the medium of choice of the 1960s generation of teenagers and 20-somethings, establishing a leap in youth culture from localised and regionalised to national self-consciousness. The pirate stations also encouraged record sales, giving the musical underground of the decade a firm economic base. This resulted in popularity for innovative records, including, by the mid-1960s, the long-playing albums (LPs). Especially novel was the market for fusions between different genres of music – American black blues music with British pop (in bands ranging from the Rolling Stones and the Beatles to Led Zeppelin and Deep Purple); folk music with both country and western and pop music (with artists like America's Bob Dylan, and Britain's Donovan and Fairport Convention). There was also a growing taste in white culture for black music like ska and reggae (in bands like Jimmy Cliff and later Bob Marley), and Eastern music like sitar sounds (in bands like The Beatles and Tyrannosaurus Rex). The government were forced to concede that a revolution in taste was underway, and it effectively outlawed pirate radio in 1967 whilst encouraging the BBC to revamp its approach with the launch of Radio 1 as a pop music station (which employed many ex-pirate DJs). This was followed in 1973 by the licensing of local commercial radio stations to broadcast around Britain.

Throughout the 1970s and 1980s, the music revolution grew as genres multiplied, as new generations constantly emerged, and as the youth of the 1960s became the new adult generation. Sales of LPs peaked in 1975 (at 91.6 million), whilst their replacement audio-cassette tapes rose to their peak (of 83 million sales) in 1979. The next technology, CDs, first registered popularity in 1983, and reached 219 million sales in 2001, demonstrating just how much the industry had grown. Within four years, however, conventional sales were replaced by internet downloads – both free and purchased – to be played on the personal MP3 player and iPod. The growth in dissemination of popular music seemed unlimited.

This applied equally to television. Growth in this market was constrained, like radio, by government restriction from diversifying as fast as in countries like the USA, where a generally free market had operated since the 1940s. Television in Britain was distinctive in being a medium reserved by the state to unite national culture. From 1948 until 1955 there was only one television channel (what is now BBC1), and from 1955 until 1964 there were only two channels (with ITV broadcasting through regional commercial television companies). In 1964, BBC2 started, in 1982, Channel 4, and in 1997, Channel 5. But these terrestrial channels each conformed to fairly rigid regulations; until the mid-1970s, daytime and night-time broadcasts were restricted to mostly educational items, but this changed with gradual deregulation under the Conservative government of the 1980s. Then, in 1989, satellite and cable transmissions commenced by the Sky and BSB networks, later merging under the banner of BSkyB, providing over 500 channels with decreasing regulation and increasing diversity of content. This meant that there was a long-term shift from the 1950–80 unity of viewing experience of the British people to the much more disunited viewing of the 1990s and 2000s. Competition for different types of viewer resulted in specialist channels on both radio and television which catered for ethnic and linguistic minorities. Programmes from India and Pakistan, as well as for Welsh-language viewers, assisted in the sense of multiculturalism in Britain. This process accelerated in the 2000s with the rise in digital broadcasting and the development of internet broadcasting. In this way, the advent of new technology in media made the culture of the country fragmented – nowhere more so than among teenagers and young people.

Youth culture

From the mid-1960s onwards, young people have been increasingly divided by the development of ethnic and taste identities around particular genres of music and dress – pop, mods, rockers, folk, rock, disco, punk, ska, reggae, rasta, grunge, goth, rap – an almost never-ending list of genres. In addition, there emerged ethnic and religious identities around Islamic, Sikh, and also Christian youth groups. This was a process of ceaseless division and emergence of new forms appealing to new audiences. In these cultural subgroups, there was a diversity not just of TV programmes, but of music, dress, comportment and activities. From the 1960s to the 2000s, youth identities became ever more unique and marked by cultural associations of incredible complexity. And with these developments in taste there followed commercial development. Capitalism was never far behind in providing sales to each group. In this way, a tremendous proportion of modern culture was closely linked to business.

Young people's leisure was one of the major growth areas of the British economy. It became one of the perennial problems for television broadcasters in the 1960s and 1970s that, although very young children of up to about 14 years of age came to watch television for many hours per week, those above that age were not attracted to the programme output on TV and turned instead to music and drinking. One of the victims was cinema-going, which declined in popularity. After a marginal fall during 1946–54, there was a massive decline over the next two decades: admissions fell from 1,276 million in 1954 to a mere 154 million in 1970, and then less sharply to 53 million in 1984, before starting a slow recovery to 141 million admissions in 2001.[3] Cinema gave way to a more variegated – and, in many ways, less controlled – youth experience.

The 1950s and 1960s saw the beginnings of a series of moral panics amongst the press, politicians and the public about youth culture. In the 1950s, territorial gangs seemed to terrorise parts of many major cities, including, most notoriously, Glasgow. Here the problem became the object of much sociological and government inquiry, reaching a fever pitch in 1968 when the pop singer Frankie Vaughan became involved

---

[3] Cinema admissions, 1951–1998: Social Trends 30, Office for National Statistics, accessed online at www.statistics.gov.uk on 19 September 2007; *British Film Institute Handbook, 2005.*

in organising an amnesty for gangs and their weapons in the massive Easterhouse council estate. Meanwhile, battles between Mods and Rockers in 1964–5 on English bank holidays at Margate superseded the earlier concern over the Teddy Boys, and the Hell's Angels of the later 1960s and early 1970s became a new object of public anxiety. By then, there was a wider concern that British youth was getting out of control.

To begin with, youth fashions were seen as interesting and daring – no more so than the rising hemlines of women's mini-skirts of 1964–8, followed by hot-pants. Daring dress seemed to symbolise daring sexual activity, for boys as well as girls. Boys were wearing effeminate long hair and outlandish fashions by the late 1960s, seemingly linked to the appearance of the hippies and drop-out generation of the later 1960s and early 1970s. Conservative commentators feared moral degeneration. This was accentuated by the rise of drug-taking, with the use of cannabis, LSD, amphetamines and, later on, heroin and ecstasy. The rise of punk during 1974–80 produced renewed alarm in the elites for its anti-authoritarianism, wild excesses, and what was seen as the anti-monarchical sentiments of the Sex Pistols' 1977 song 'God Save the Queen'. The later 1980s brought more concern over Generation X and rave culture. This contributed to the Criminal Justice and Public Order Act 1994, which sought to outlaw unauthorised music festivals. The mass music festivals, which had started with an event in 1970 on the Isle of Wight, had developed in the 1990s and 2000s into large and highly commercialised affairs (such as at Glastonbury, T in the Park, and the Reading festival). Opposition to youth culture was unremitting. In the 1960s, The Beatles and other pop stars were relentlessly pursued by police officers for drug offences. Most famously, Mick Jagger of The Rolling Stones was sentenced in 1967 to three months in prison, for alleged illegal drug possession, but released after an appeal. He attracted enormous sympathy from even conservative but libertarian commentators.

A major part of the opposition to youth culture came from the British churches. From 1963–7, there was a sudden and extremely sharp fall in church membership, accompanied by decline in attendance, baptisms and religious marriage ceremonies. Alienation from the churches was seen to be most strong amongst the young, and central to many of the concerns was the turning against organised religion by teenage girls and young women. This was linked by many churchmen to a mixture of rising sexuality, drug-taking, gay liberation and women's liberation. The proportion of marriages that were religiously solemnised fell in England and Wales from 70 per cent in 1962 to 60 per cent in 1970, going on to a mere 36 per cent in 2000; in Scotland they fell from 80 per cent in 1962 to 71 per cent in 1970, and then to 54 per cent in 1996. Meanwhile, parents were also becoming less church-oriented; infant baptism in the Church of England declined from 60 per cent of all English births in 1956 to 47 per cent in 1970, before tumbling to 20 per cent in 2000.[4] The conventional British churches seemed in freefall caused by a haemorrhage led by the alienated young.

---

[4] Data from figures in C.G. Brown, *Religion and Society in Twentieth-century Britain* (Harlow, Pearson Education Ltd, 2006), pp. 33–4.

Focus on

Mick Jagger

In 1967 the lead singer of The Rolling Stones, Mick Jagger, was found guilty of possessing a small quantity of a drug illegal in this country, but bought legally in Italy for travel sickness. He was sentenced to three months' imprisonment. This was widely seen as grossly punitive. So much so that even conservative commentators objected – including William Rees-Mogg, editor of *The Times*, who wrote a famous editorial extracted below. In the event, Jagger was released after a few days.

Who Breaks a Butterfly on a Wheel?

Mr Jagger was charged with being in possession of four tablets containing amphetamine sulphate and methyl amphetamine hydrochloride; these tablets had been bought, perfectly legally, in Italy, and brought back to this country. They are not a highly dangerous drug, or in proper dosage a dangerous drug at all . . .

In Britain it is an offence to possess these drugs without a doctor's prescription . . . This was therefore an offence of a technical character, which before this case drew the point to public attention any honest man might have been liable to commit. If after his visit to the Pope the Archbishop of Canterbury had brought proprietary airsickness pills on Rome airport, and imported the unused tablets on his return, he would have risked committing precisely the same offence . . .

One has to ask, therefore, how it is that this technical offence . . . was thought to deserve the penalty of imprisonment. In the courts at large it is most uncommon for imprisonment to be imposed on first offenders where the drugs are not major drugs of addiction and there is no question of drug traffic. The normal penalty is probation . . . It is surprising therefore that Judge Block should have decided to sentence Mr Jagger to imprisonment, and particularly surprising as Mr Jagger's is about as mild a drug case as can ever have been brought before the Courts.

It would be wrong to speculate on the Judge's reasons, which we do not know. It is, however, possible to consider the public reaction. There are many people who take a primitive view of the matter, what one might call a pre-legal view of the matter. They consider that Mr Jagger has 'got what was coming to him'. They resent the anarchic quality of the Rolling Stones' performances, dislike their songs, dislike their influence on teenagers and broadly suspect them of decadence, a word used by Miss Monica Furlong in the *Daily Mail*.

As a sociological concern this may be reasonable enough, and at an emotional level it is very understandable, but it has nothing at all to do with the case. One has to ask a different question: has Mr Jagger received the same treatment as he would have received if he not been a famous figure, with all the criticism and resentment his celebrity has aroused? If a promising undergraduate had come back from a summer visit to Italy with four pep pills in his pocket would it have been thought right to ruin

Figure 36.1 Mick Jagger and Keith Richards of The Rolling Stones leave Redlands, the house in which they were allegedly caught using drugs, for the first day of their trial in June 1967. *Source*: Topfoto

his career by sending him to prison for three months? Would it also have been thought necessary to display him handcuffed in public?

There are cases in which a single figure becomes the focus for public concerns about some aspect of public morality . . . If we are going to make any case a symbol of the conflict between the sound traditional values of Britain and the new hedonism, then we must be sure that the sound traditional values include those of tolerance and equity. It should be the particular quality of British justice to ensure that Mr Jagger is treated exactly the same as anyone else, no better and no worse. There must remain a suspicion in this case that Mr Jagger received a more severe sentence than would have been thought proper for any purely anonymous young man.

Source: The Times, 1 July 1967.

Yet, there was also religious innovation. For one thing, the black and Asian communities arising from post-war immigration were giving strength to black Christian churches, Muslim mosques, Sikh gurdwaras and Hindu temples. For another thing, the youth culture of the 1960s included a surge of curiosity about New Age religions, many inspired by Buddhism, Hinduism and Eastern mysticism generally. Pop stars like The Beatles, the Rolling Stones, Donovan, Lulu and others took a major interest in swamis and gurus (teachers) from the East. Some, like George Harrison with his singles 'My Sweet Lord' and 'Hare Krishna' did much to publicise this amongst young people, and helped to lay the basis for the rise of yoga, transcendental meditation and a whole host of spiritual and health movements in successive decades.

One important element of youth culture was its political implications. From the mid-1960s, a small but vocal minority of British students took a particular interest in supporting US students in opposing the Vietnam War, leading to demonstrations such as at the US Embassy at Grosvenor Square in 1968. Student revolt was also inspired by the student occupation of the University of the Sorbonne in Paris in 1968, fostering some similar but smaller British occupations during 1968–73, notably at Hornsey Art College, the University of Essex and the LSE. Students at the new universities of the period became caricatured in the press as constantly in revolt, and certainly the range of issues that students supported were wide, from opposition to the wars in Biafra and Vietnam to high student accommodation rents. One of the longest-lasting and ultimately influential protests was against apartheid in South Africa which, through boycotts of South African goods and investors like Barclays Bank, and disruption of South African sports' tours, was an important element in a worldwide campaign from 1968 to 1994. Over the decades, student protesting diminished in vigour although there were important peaks, over the overthrow of the Marxist Allende regime in Chile in 1973 and the poll tax in 1990 (see Chapter 38). But it is clear that by the mid-1990s, concern to obtain degrees and careers became more vital for the increasing student population, and the radicalism of the 1960s seemed to have gone.

Whatever happened to class?

The election of the Labour government of Harold Wilson in 1964 was, in one sense, the victory of a working-class-backed party over a middle-class-backed Conservative Party in the turnabout nature of British politics. But in another sense, this was a marker of a long process in which social class became less significant in British identity, culture and politics. One part of this process was the erosion of clearly defined class allegiance to the Labour and Conservative parties after the 1970s; associated with this was the simultaneous decline in the membership and influence of trade unions. Another part of the story was the rise of national identities in Wales and Scotland and ethnic and religious identities. But at the same time, social class started to diminish in importance. In the 1950s, social class seemed to be deeply embedded in Britain, having been an important source of identity since the late eighteenth century. What happened to it?

The rise of youth culture was an important fuel that consumed class. The young of the 1940s and 1950s were still strongly divided in their cultures: the Teddy Boys and the 'varsity' crowds were class-defined to a major degree. This slowly diminished from the late 1950s as pop stars started to come from all social groups and as their audiences began a process of developing a classless music culture. This was not a universal development by any means. The hippy culture, centred around 'progressive rock bands' of the mid- and late 1960s, was strongly middle- and upper- class in tone, whilst conventional rock and pop tended, to an extent, to attract working-class popularity. But, from 1970, it becomes more difficult accurately to describe bands as one social class or another. Punk had a proletarian edge, but it was one that became fashionable amongst many fee-paying public-school youths. To an extent, it had always been 'cool' for the rich to join in the common pastimes; they did this in horse racing and gambling in the eighteenth century and in the rougher music hall of around 1900, and wilder rock music of the 1980s. But the significance was much greater after 1960. Overall, it is fair to say that youth culture destabilised the older certainties of class division in culture and consumption.

One important aspect in change to British society was the decline of the ways segregation defined social class. In the second half of the twentieth century, the welfare state did much to eradicate inequalities in health and diet, and – although with less clear-cut success – in housing, education and opportunity. The expansion of subsidised council housing in the 1950s and 1960s, coupled with slum clearance, took the edge off extremes of poor housing, although it left deep segregation between council estates and private housing. But in the 1970s and 1980s, the expansion of home ownership through wider availability of mortgages to young people, followed by the 'right-to-buy' policy extended to council house tenants, led to more fluidity in the housing market and a common mania for home improvement. Access to opportunity in careers was facilitated by the expansion of higher and further education from the 1960s. Add in the collapse of staple industries, in which class division was severe between manual and non-manual workers (sometimes called white-collar and blue-collar workers respectively), and the structural underpinnings of social class were being significantly eroded within British society.

The media revolution also contributed to this. Initially, the expansion of terrestrial television between 1953 and 1989 fostered a sense of shared national viewing and, to a great degree, values. Even if people watched different programmes much of the time, there were commonly shared habits of viewing – religious programming in the 1950s and 1960s, news bulletins, and major sports events like international rugby and the FA and Scottish FA cup finals. This dissipated with the multiplication of television chan-nels in the 1990s and 2000s, allowing for diversity of viewing choices, and it is difficult to discern the re-establishment of a vigorous sense of class-based television viewing. Leisure pursuits in general became more commonly accessible, with children leading parents from all social backgrounds to the same kinds of organised commercial leisure venues; this might be described as the 'McDonaldisation' of leisure and eating out. Similarly, rich and poor adults tended to go to the same supermarkets in a way that was less common before 1970. Social levelling was also evident to some extent in entertainment, with clubs, restaurants and multi-screen cinemas having an attraction for people from most social groups.

One of the factors that formerly underpinned class identity was religion. But the de-Christianisation of Britain was felt across the social classes. The vast majority of people in white Britain lost formal connection with organised religion between 1964 and 2007; church membership collapsed by as much as 45 per cent between 1975 and 2000 alone, especially amongst the casual churchgoers. In a series of Christian-run censuses, weekly churchgoing was shown to have almost halved from 11 per cent of English and Welsh people in 1979 to 6.3 per cent in 2005.[5] Those going to Christian churches were increasingly from the black population of the country; by 2000, half the Christian church attendees in London were from ethnic minority groups. These trends removed the older class division of religion, where individual denominations had strong class identities (notably branches of Methodism in England and Wales and different Presbyterian churches in Scotland). Where formerly religion had been the great marker of class status in industrial and rural congregations, this was no longer the case. Secularisation and the decline in basic Christian beliefs were now transcending social class.

Religion mattered in Northern Ireland, and mattered more deeply than social class. It was the one part of Britain that had confessionalist politics – that is, people voted according to their religion, with the majority Protestants voting for Unionist parties that believed in remaining with Britain, whilst the minority Catholics voted for nationalist parties that favoured breakaway from the UK and absorption in a united Ireland. This continued through this period, underpinned by strong religious adherence and churchgoing during the era of the violent 'Troubles' between 1969 and 1998 (see Chapter 38). To be a Catholic or a Protestant was almost an unavoidable identity in Northern Ireland; in 2001, 97 per cent of adults claimed a religious identity, compared to under 85 per cent in the rest of Britain. And the intensity of expressing that identity was far stronger in Northern Ireland, with parades by opposing flute and pipe bands of the Orange Order (Protestant) and Ancient Order of Hibernians and republican marches (predominantly Catholic) during the marching season between March and August each year. Every aspect of life from education to housing, employment to leisure (where Catholics tended to supported Glasgow Celtic Football Club and Protestants supported Glasgow Rangers Football Club), seemed to be measured on a religious scale. All of this placed manifest social inequalities in a secondary political role in Northern Ireland. Social differences did transcend the religious divide; there were working-class Catholics and Protestants, sharing the same forms of relative deprivation. But, in Northern Ireland, social class was mediated by religion, which,

---

[5] Figures for churchgoing obtained from www.christianresearch.org.uk

in matters political and cultural, educational and economic, almost invariably took precedence.

Social class also diminished in Britain in the later twentieth century with the rise of issue-based politics, for instance, focused on environmental, rural and animal welfare issues. The countryside continued to be an important part of British culture. With fewer people working in agriculture, the countryside became increasingly a place in which to live and holiday, and the old significance of class division between landlords, tenantry and farm labourers dissolved after the 1950s, with mechanisation, depopulation and the rise of farm ownership. The growth of leisure was leading to the British countryside being used for second and third holidays after a 'main holiday' abroad in France or Spain. This meant that the countryside was, by the 1960s, being penetrated intensively by urban dwellers – mostly in cars, given the decline of the rural rail network under the railway cuts instituted by the Beeching plan of 1963. Tourism was, by 2000, more important economically to many areas of the countryside than farming.

The British love affair with the countryside turned out by the late twentieth century to be more and more classless, but turned increasingly against farming. The agriculture sector's use of fertilisers and destruction of animal habitats led to loud conservation complaints, with bird and animal charities (like the Royal Society for the Protection of Birds) leading the way in lobbying for active conservation of field margins, hedgerows, and an end to poisoning of raptors (like eagles, hen harriers and the reintroduced red kites). Animal charities and animal liberation radicals fostered growing public disquiet with animal husbandry – notably intensive factory farming of chickens, turkeys, pigs and other animals. The transportation of live animals (including cattle) within the EU, encouraged by the creation in 1993 of the Single European Market, led to campaigns and protests at docks – many by middle-class families unused to such forms of activism. The Conservative government of the early 1990s had to acknowledge the extent of middle-lass opposition to these practices, and the increasingly sophisticated ways in which the news media were exploited to maximise embarrassment to private shipping and farming companies. Opposition to animal testing led to the University of Oxford undergoing long-term protest for its laboratory work with animals. Single-issue campaigning was creating 'a politics of the cause', largely divorced from politics defined by social class.

However, the decline of social class should not be regarded as a complete collapse. Social inequality in income and wealth remained, notable by the dramatic improvement in the economic position of the rich and of middle-income families. Segregation in culture still remained. Though the majority of people might own televisions, they watched different programmes, often defined by social class. More working-class people watched soap operas and reality television, whilst professionals watched more news, factual and serious drama. Social groups also tended to watch different channels, with more working-class families having cable and satellite television to access pay-for-view live football and movie channels (which some professional classes tended to regard as both vulgar and expensive, preferring the free-to-air Freeview and Freesat platforms). Similarly, British people holidayed in different places, defined very strongly by social class; working-class people had stronger propensities to holiday in Spanish seaside resorts than middle-class families, who favoured France, Italy or the British countryside. These divisions remained irrespective of income levels, with well-off families originating in working-class backgrounds continuing to seek 'sun, sea and Shangri-La', suggesting very much that there was a resilience to cultural patterns of social class.

In one important sense, social class was greatly reduced by 2000 compared to 1960. The *language* of class was less frequently spoken, and acts and speech of social deference were much rarer. There were fewer remarks made about social difference in daily conversation, in part because it became less morally acceptable to define, and pass comment upon, people in this way. The morality of equality had, by the 2000s, come to dominate British consciousness. Just as it was less acceptable to highlight racial, ethnic, gender or religious differences between people, or to pass comment about the disabled, so it had become much less acceptable to appear to judge or even describe people in tones that suggested social difference and superiority. Rising incomes, especially in the 1980s and 1990s, had permitted working-class people to express an equality of taste for high-status marques of motor car, designer clothes and domestic furniture. Most children and young people dressed in socially indistinguishable ways by the 2000s, with a blend of uniform items, such as jeans and trainers, and culture-specific adornment, such as grunge or goth. The ubiquity of the mobile phone added to the ways in which social class was difficult to discern in everyday life. Whilst not invisible by any means, social class had become less marked, and remarked upon, in British life. And this trend may have had a bearing in the 1990s and 2000s upon the invigoration of national consciousness within the separate countries of the UK, and upon the decline of class-based party politics (see Chapters 38 and 39).

Further reading

Brown, C.G., *Religion and Society in Twentieth-century Britain* (Harlow, Pearson Longman, 2006)

Donnelly, M., *Sixties Britain* (Harlow, Pearson Longman, 2005)

Hewison, R., *Too Much: Art and Society in the Sixties 1960–75* (London, Methuen, 1986)

Marwick, A., *The Sixties: Cultural Revolution in Britain, France, Italy and the United States, c.1958–c.1974* (Oxford, Oxford University Press, 1998)

Obelkevich, J., and Catterall, P., (eds), *Understanding Post-war British Society* (London, Routledge, 1994)

Springhall, J., *Youth, Popular Culture and Moral Panics: Penny Gaffs to Gangsta Rap 1830–1996* (Basingstoke, Macmillan, 1998)

37

The gender revolution

Women's liberation

The twentieth century witnessed an extraordinary gender revolution. 'Gender' is the term applied to mean the social construction of women's and men's identities, which change with different historical epochs. In this regard, the nature of what it meant to be a woman and to be a man altered to a greater degree than in any previous century. Much of the transformation was crammed into the last 40 years of the century, and the central change – by far the most extensive – was to the social and political role, work and education, and sexual and life freedoms of women. The most important time was the period 1968–78, commonly referred to as the period of 'second wave feminism' and of the Women's Liberation Movement.

As earlier chapters have discussed, there were already major alterations to women's place in British society between 1880 and 1964. The 'New Woman' of the 1890s had broached the idea of feisty women seeking daring sexual relationships and career openings, but the numbers claiming to be fully 'new' were probably very limited and the extent of change was sharply limited by society's oppressive disproval. The suffrage movement, culminating in the final extensions of the vote to women in 1919 and 1928, was accompanied by a longer-term growth in opportunities in education and in an expansion of work for women. However, the changes underway had severe limitations. Firstly, in education, the opportunities offered to women were generally in the study of subjects thought 'suitable' for their gender – at school, domestic science, biology and languages, and in higher education, arts subjects (again dominated by languages and English literature), medicine, nursing, pharmacy and associated professions. In each case, these subjects were seen, in great measure, as extensions of what was perceived from the writings of Rousseau from the 1760s onwards as the biologically natural 'caring' roles of women, or considered suited to the creation of 'rounded' wives who supported professional men in their milieu.

Secondly, women's greater role in the workplace was heavily confined to what was regarded as 'women's work' – particularly assembly or highly repetitive jobs where women's supposed manual dexterity and suitability for recurring tasks were prized. In most cases, women were preferred because they would work for lower wages than men and were less prone to industrial action. How little changed in women's work can be seen from the fact that it was mostly married women who started to work more, and they worked mostly part-time rather than in career-making jobs. As can be seen from Table 37.1, only 11 per cent of married women in 1931 were in waged labour; this rose to 26 per cent in 1951, to 35 per cent in 1961, and to 49 per cent in 1971 (and continuing to 66 per cent in 1991). This was a very significant social revolution for women, and contrasted with a small decline in male participation in work (caused in part by more men reaching retirement age). But much of this was not full-time working. In 1943, only 7 per cent of working women were part-time, but this rose to 12 per cent in 1951, to 29 per cent by 1964 and to 35 per cent by 1973.[1] So, the middle decades of the century witnessed a revolution in female work, but although women in professions

Table 37.1 Men and women at work in Britain 1901–91 (%)

Year	Men Aged 15–64	Women Aged 15–59	Married Women Aged 15–59
1901	96	38	10
1911	96	38	10
1921	94	38	10
1931	96	38	11
1951	96	43	26
1961	95	47	35
1971	92	55	49
1981	90	61	57
1991	87	68	66

Source: T. Hatton, 'Women's work in Britain, 1911–1971: a regional perspective', Table 1, unpublished paper 1998. Used with permission of the author.

---

[1] P. Howlett, 'The war-time economy, 1939–1945', in R. Floud and P. Johnson (eds), *The Cambridge Economic History of Modern Britain: Volume III: Structural Change and Growth, 1939–2000* (Cambridge, Cambridge University Press, 2004), pp. 23–4.

like teaching, medicine and pharmacy were not uncommon, the revolution in general was confined largely to an erosion of the marriage bar in low-paid manual work.

In many ways, more important in the long-term revolution for women in education and work was what did *not* change. Women's place in society was conceived in British culture at the start of the 1960s as, in some respects, little altered from the Victorian period. A woman was seen as biologically suited to motherhood, and to domestic duties in support of a working husband. The natural state for an adult woman after about 20 years of age was married, and those who did not were still widely regarded as 'being on the shelf' and destined through 'spinsterhood' to being 'old maids'. Such representations of women were common in literature, on television and radio programmes, and also in government policy, which provided tax allowances for married men to better support their wives, and in which the welfare state was designed on the presumption of a woman's dependence upon a man. A woman's place remained resolutely in the home. For the single woman, British culture expected virginity before marriage or, if a single woman became pregnant, that she would be married before the birth. Thus it is no surprise that levels of sexual activity were low, and the illegitimacy rate was under 5 per cent of all births in 1958.

Come the 1960s, all of this started to change with extraordinary speed. Those who grew up in the post-war decades had often felt constrained or restricted. The novelist Angela Carter said: 'I grew up in the 50s – that is, I was 20 in 1960, and by God, I *deserved* what happened later on. It was tough in the 50s. Girls wore white gloves.'[2] A series of things developed that together revolutionised what it was to be a woman. Three main developments may be identified, demographic change, change in the cultural representation of womanhood, and political change.

Demographic change was the first to be noticeable. This comprised rapidly rising sexual activity, especially for young single women in their mid- and late teens; the decline of marriage before childbirth; and, after a short surge in marriages, from the early 1970s there was a reduction in the number of marriages. Sexual activity amongst single women was remarkably low in 1964. In a medical survey in that year, only 15 per cent of girls of 16 and 17 years of age said that they had had sexual intercourse. In 1974–5, a follow-up survey found that this had increased to 58 per cent, an extraordinary change in sexual habits in such a short time. However, the figures for boys in the same years showed a much smaller rise, from 40 per cent to 52 per cent. Illegitimacy rates (proportion of births taking place outside marriage) were already showing a significant, if small-scale, rise between 1958 and 1964 (from 4.9 per cent to 7.2 per cent in England and Wales, and from 4.1 per cent to 5.4 per cent in Scotland), which climbed in the next four years (to 8.5 per cent in England and Wales and to 7.4 per cent in Scotland). But this was only the small beginning of the revolution in births and marriage, with illegitimacy rising very steeply and unstoppably; figures between 1975 and 2002 rose from 9.1 per cent to 40.6 per cent in England and Wales,

---

[2] Quoted in S. Rowbotham, *A Century of Women: The History of Women in Britain and the United States* (London, Viking, 1997), p. 338.

and from 9.3 per cent to 44 per cent in Scotland. In Northern Ireland the figures rose from 10.9 per cent in 1985 to 33.5 per cent in 2002.[3]

As part of the demographic revolution, UK marriages declined by over a third during 1970–2000 – from 470,000 to 305,912 – whilst the proportion of those marriages that were religiously solemnised (mostly in Christian churches) fell from 62 per cent to just under 40 per cent.[4] So marriage was declining in popularity, marriages that did take place were often after families had been started, and weddings were markedly less traditional in character. These developments indicate how much the sexual revolution was instigated by changes in women's behaviour, and how much of the sixties sexual revolution was down to single women. Married women's sexual activity was changing over a longer period, noticeably with the arrival of the oral contraceptive pill from 1961. However, for moral reasons doctors would not prescribe the pill to single women until 1968, and even then access was difficult for many. In this way, the statistical evidence on sexual activity and illegitimacy indicate that more single women were having sex before the pill arrived.

The reason for this lay in the changing understanding of womanhood, especially for young women and the expectations of maturing teenage girls. Accompanying the sexual revolution was a wider cultural revolution, particularly amongst young people (see Chapter 36). Young women dispensed with a great deal of traditional dress and moral codes, and redrew the nature of the feminine self. Cultural representations of women and femininity had to change in response, notably in magazines for teenagers and young women. Out went images of prim and virginal young women in skirts and cardigans, and carrying handbags; in came pictures of 'swinging' young women in hip jeans and flowery T-shirts hanging out with boys. With this change, the expectation of marriage before sex for women disappeared from most popular literature. Even more fundamentally in the late 1960s and early 1970s, the common understanding that teenage girls were merely grooming themselves to find a husband dissipated, as university degrees and careers became the rising anticipation. The nature of 'womanhood' was being recrafted in a remarkably sudden surge of both professional and sexual freedom. The universal concept of the 'respectable woman' of domestic confinement, happy wifely subordination and motherhood that had dominated British culture for almost two centuries was overturned for much of the younger generation.

The cultural representation of women became the object of a revolt by young women against stereotypes of their behaviour, their clothes and their attitudes towards sex. From 1964, women's clothing was radically transformed, starting with the increasing sexualisation of dress with the arrival of the mini-skirt, which became shorter and shorter over the next six years, revealing an extent of leg which even in 1960 would

---

[3] J. Lewis and R. Kiernan, 'The boundaries between marriage, nonmarriage, and parenthood: changes in behaviour in postwar Britain', *Journal of Family History*, xxi (1996), pp. 372–87 at pp. 373–4; illegitimacy figures calculated from data at www.gro.gov.uk, accessed 17 November 2006.

[4] Figures calculated from data at Scottish, NI and England & Wales websites at www.gro.gov.uk, accessed 17 November 2006.

Figure 37.1 Isle of Wight pop festival, August 1970. Regarded as 'Britain's Woodstock', and with a larger attendance, the stunning line-up included The Who, Jimi Hendrix, Joni Mitchell, The Doors, Donovan, Chicago, Free, Jethro Tull, The Moody Blues and Leonard Cohen.
Source: Getty Images

have been considered little short of lewd. From 1966, there was a move towards less conventional forms of dress and decoration, with a trend away from the skirt-and-sweater combination towards flamboyant and colourful dresses, blouses and T-shirts, the arrival of the jeans as standard wear for younger women, and longer and unstyled hair. A small number of young women, the hippy generation of 1965–68, were seen in the press and on television dancing with few or no clothes at pop concerts and so-called 'love-ins'. The British establishment of church, politicians and traditional moral guardians were outraged, but attempts to denigrate such women as slatternly, promiscuous and immoral failed to carry the pejorative weight amongst the young that they used to. Such behaviour may not have been widespread, but young people were less willing to censure or criminalise such freedoms, and an increased liberty for women to openly express their sexuality rapidly entered British culture.

Focus on

Feminism in the 1960s

There was no single guiding ideology for this inchoate movement but a number of feminist writings were extremely influential – for example, Simone de Beauvoir's *The Second Sex* (1949) and Betty Friedan's *The Feminine Mystique* (1963), and Germaine Greer's *The Female Eunuch* (1970).

De Beauvoir's work, *The Second Sex*, was probably the most influential analysis of the female condition for the post-war feminist generation. She was the leading French intellectual of her day and she started with the proposition that women are not born but made – that is, femaleness and womanness was not something innate but constructed. She argued that women's basic freedoms had been limited by men who saw themselves as the norm. She wrote:

> A man is in the right in being a man; it is the woman who is in the wrong. It amounts to this: just as for the ancients there was an absolute vertical with reference to which the oblique was defined, so there is an absolute human type, the masculine. Woman has ovaries, a uterus: these peculiarities imprison her in her subjectivity, circumscribe her within the limits of her own nature. It is often said that she thinks with her glands. Man superbly ignores the fact that his anatomy also includes glands, such as the testicles, and that they secrete hormones. He thinks of his body as a direct and normal connection with the world, which he believes he apprehends objectively, whereas he regards the body of woman as a hindrance, a prison, weighed down by everything peculiar to it. 'The female is a female by virtue of a certain lack of qualities,' said Aristotle; 'we should regard the female nature as afflicted with a natural defectiveness.' And St Thomas for his part pronounced woman to be an 'imperfect man', an 'incidental' being. This is symbolised in Genesis where Eve is depicted as made from what Bossuet called 'a supernumerary bone' of Adam.
>
> Thus humanity is male and man defines woman not in herself but as relative to him; she is not regarded as an autonomous being. Michelet writes: 'Woman, the relative being . . .' And Benda is most positive in his *Rapport d'Uriel*: 'The body of man makes sense in itself quite apart from that of woman, whereas the latter seems wanting in significance by itself . . . Man can think of himself without woman. She cannot think of herself without man.' And she is simply what man decrees; thus she is called 'the sex', by which is meant that she appears essentially to the male as a sexual being. For him she is sex – absolute sex, no less. She is defined and differentiated with reference to man and not he with reference to her; she is the incidental, the inessential as opposed to the essential. He is the Subject, he is the Absolute – she is the Other.'
>
> The category of the *Other* is as primordial as consciousness . . .

Source: S. de Beauvoir, *The Second Sex* orig. edn 1949 (translation by H.M. Parshley). Reprinted by permission of the Random House Group Ltd (UK and Commonwealth, excluding Canada) and Random House Inc. (USA and Canada). Introduction available at http://www.marxists.org/reference/subject/ethics/de-beauvoir/2nd-sex/index.htm

The final ingredient in the gender revolution for women – the politicisation of the women's movement – had been developing to an extent in intellectual circles since the early 1960s, but it really only became a pronounced public development in 1969–70. This drew on a long strain of feminism that argued for recognition that women were historically subordinate to men, understanding of the underlying reasons for this, and action to change and correct it. In the shorter term in the late 1960s, the Women's Liberation Movement (WLM) – also known as second-wave feminism – was born out of developments in Europe (especially Paris), and on the east and west coasts of the United States. The student revolt across Europe in May 1968 included the development of a feminist consciousness that accompanied the development of post-colonialism and the anti-authoritarianism of student revolt. Though the WLM eschewed the cult of the personality, focusing instead on local consciousness-raising groups, leading figures of feminism in Britain in this period included Germaine Greer (who wrote an influential book *The Female Eunuch* (1970)); Erin Pizzey (who opened the first women's refuge in London in 1971); Rosie Boycott (who co-founded the influential magazine *Spare Rib* in 1972); and Sheila Rowbotham (a socialist feminist and historian). By the early 1970s, the WLM had developed into a loose affiliation of feminist organisations across Britain, Europe and North America that campaigned for legal and societal changes on a wide range of issues. These included an end to sexual harassment and sexualised representations of women in popular and official culture; women's rights to contraception and abortion; acceptance of lesbian women; action on domestic violence (including the creation of refuges for victims); an end to discrimination against women in work and education; equal financial rights for women (for instance, in getting mortgages, which they often could not without a male partner); and equal pay and promotion rights. Feminist action was undertaken through consciousness-raising groups; in public 'reclaim the streets' campaigns; self-help creation of women's refuges; demonstrations against 'Miss World' and other beauty contests; and the storming of male-only public houses. In one of the most famous actions in 1968, a small group of women sewing machinists, who made car seat covers at the Ford car plant at Dagenham in Essex, went on strike to oppose regrading of their jobs which amounted to loss of pay compared with male workers. With the support of the Labour Employment Secretary, Barbara Castle, they won, also instigating Parliament passing the Equal Pay Act of 1970.

Political lobbying led to strong Labour Party and Liberal Party support for many feminist causes. Indeed, the Abortion Act of 1967 which legalised medical termination of pregnancies was passed before the WLM had really been formed. Acts similar to anti-racial discrimination legislation were passed, including the Sex Discrimination Act of 1975, which created the Equal Opportunities Commission – a government agency that prosecuted and lobbied against institutional discrimination. However, issues of equality and equal pay remained active into the twenty-first century. Like racism, sexism has not been something that has been immediately or easily removed from society, partly because its forms are so diverse, and partly because it has been deeply embedded in most institutions – notably in the armed forces, the police and in many private clubs and sports. But also, from the 1990s, there was a notable diminution in the strength of the feminist movement, with growing hostility to the 'feminist' label amongst the next generation of young women. Women in their teens and twenties at the turn of the century had a tendency to accept that they *were* equal to men in key matters. They argued that there were in place reasonably effective anti-discrimination laws, equality of opportunity in education and most careers, and freedom to enjoy a newly sexualised form of femininity evident in popular culture, media and entertainment. In response, some older activists were alarmed at what they regarded as weakening of resolve, and called for a 'third-wave feminism' to fight anew for women's rights.

One of the unifying features of second-wave feminism in 1969–79 was the belief that 'the personal is the political' – meaning that women's experiences should be recognised as valid issues concerning policy and social behaviour, and should be acted upon. This, in turn, meant that subjects that had previously been regarded as unmentionable in the political sphere suddenly became issues for political debate: abortion, birth control, domestic violence and rape. Though WLM started out as a movement of university students and intellectuals, with no real mass support, its interest base did extend beyond that elite to encompass working women on issues such as equal pay.

The masculinity crisis

While women's fortunes have risen, men's have fallen. As women have taken advantage of economic trends and improved educational opportunities and, perhaps most importantly, have redefined what it means to be a woman, men since the 1950s have seen the very foundation of their masculine identity eroded.

In the 1950s and 1960s, British manhood had continued to experience some of the problems of defining masculinity. Work remained an important source of male identity, yet this had been a difficulty during the depression years of the 1920s and 1930s, and from the 1940s became a problem as female access to the labour market started to make inroads into a previously all-male world of skilled work. Soldiering had been an important source of identity that had been smashed in the slaughter and maiming of trench warfare in 1914–18, and though the death and injury rates were very much less in the Second World War, soldiering had been reduced to a source of boredom and mockery by the two years' national service which from 1949 to 1960, all healthy males of 18–26 years had to undertake (18 months in 1949). During both war and national service, the armed services became increasingly the object of derision for incompetence, delay and the pointlessness of 'square-bashing' (marching on the parade ground), or duties like guarding warehouses of copper pans. However, many national servicemen saw active service in the contracting British Empire, usually fighting communist or nationalist insurgents in places like Korea, Malaya, Borneo, Cyprus, Aden, or in the British-French military invasion of Suez in 1956. But even in warfare, Britain's military acquired a poor reputation amongst men. Many British comedians, such as Spike Milligan, Michael Bentine, Alan Bennett, and Michael Palin, and comic writers like Michael Frayn and Leslie Thomas, were graduates of the military and their comedy work repeatedly lampooned British military life in the 1950s and 1960s, displacing the warrior man as a readily available icon. With it went the former reverence for militaristic youth movements like the Scouts and Boys' Brigades which went into numerical decline in Britain in the 1960s. Older virtues of manhood seemed to be waved aside.

From the 1960s, the nature of manhood changed in the cultural flux of the times. On the one side, women were making great inroads into skilled and professional jobs. Traditional male identity as sole breadwinner or as sole worker in key occupations, was crumbling in the face of large-scale female action for equality of opportunity. This was perhaps most starkly seen at first in the middle classes with massive female recruitment to the new universities of the mid- and late 1960s, with women entering courses in languages, arts and social sciences, and quickly achieving success after gaining degrees in graduate entry to business, management, the civil service and expanding media. Though they were slower to develop success in the sciences, there was, by the 1990s, and 2000s, a considerable increase in the proportion of women in medicine, life sciences and even engineering, as they outperformed men in school leaving certificates and as men showed declining interest in physical sciences. In working-class occupations, female workers were demanding equality of pay and opportunity with men. The Ford women's strike of 1968 laid the basis for increased trade-union support for female workers, but at shop-floor level in traditional industries this caused great disquiet to both workers and shop-stewards. As the staple industries like engineering and ship-building contracted, men were finding their positions in alternative employment threatened by women workers, whilst male-only occupations, like coal-mining, from which women had been excluded by Victorian social-reform legislation, were disappearing rapidly.

This came to a head in the recession of the 1980s, when staple industries were involved in disputes, and as newer industries like electronics employed more women than men. The result was that men's traditional dominance of the labour market was rapidly being eroded. A stark image of breakdown in traditional working-class masculinity came in the coal strike of 1984–5 when, after a lengthy and intense dispute, the miners lost and the pits closed in the following few years, leaving the men in many cases in tremendous despair about work and manliness. This was ably explored in the film *Billy Elliot* (Dir: Stephen Daldry, Universal Studios, 2000) about the reaction of former coal miners to a teenage boy training to be a ballet dancer – the very antithesis of traditional masculinity. What it was acceptable for a 'real man' to do in life and culture was being constantly re-explored in the late twentieth century.

If men's employment was under renegotiation, the period opened up the nature of masculinity even more fundamentally in cultural terms. A man's appearance had changed little in British culture for 120 years: short hair, dark, baggy suit of jacket and trousers, and for most formal work and leisure occasions, a white shirt and tie. Even the young men of the 1950s had made little change to this, with the teddy boys aping the suit style of the Edwardians, and viewing the beards of the Victorian era with disfavour as a sign of scruffiness. But in the early 1960s, pop stars like the Beatles first experimented with slightly longer hair (albeit still groomed), then in the later 1960s with very long hair, beards and an explosion in experimental and eclectic clothes, flowery shirts and smocks, the ubiquitous T-shirt, afghan coats and recycled military coats, all adorned with shoulder bags and body jewellery. Hair-dressing, a profession considered female-dominated and alien to masculinity, was developing from the late 1960s as a new masculine world, led by men like Vidal Sassoon and explored in films like *Shampoo* (Dir: Hal Ashby, Columbia Pictures, 1975). The fashionable male form changed appearance (from staid to flamboyant) and symbolic meaning (from disciplined manliness to fluid sexuality) with incredible rapidity between 1964 and 1969, bringing a national chorus of complaint from political and church leaders and derisive attitudes from the older generation generally. To them, maleness in such costumes appeared to be becoming compromised with femininity, and they objected that it was difficult to tell young men and women apart.

This was the start of what would develop into a more throughgoing exploration of the nature of masculinity during the next 30 years. The notion of the 'new man' arose, distinguished from the 'old man' in at least two respects. First, in domestic affairs, new man was seen to be willing to participate much more than before in domestic duties like cleaning, washing clothes and cooking. The notion of equality in the home became an ideal for new man, though in most cases it seems it was an ideal more than a reality, as women continued to undertake more domestic duties than men. Second, new man shared being the earner; increasing numbers of young couples were delaying having children until their 30s or even their 40s, and both partners were going out to work. But just as important as changes in role were changes in attitude. Though there was a surge of marriages in the late 1960s, from the early 1970s the marriage rate started to fall very substantially and the proportion of traditional church weddings fell sharply by 2000. In this regard, the traditional married couple with traditional values was rapidly becoming less common in British society, and this was impacting greatly on what was expected of a man. In the 1960s, large numbers of men – probably the majority – considered it unmanly to be seen caring for their children, even to the extent of not being willing to push a baby pram in public. But this changed almost universally in the 1970s, 1980s and 1990s, with men taking increasing pride in child care in public, and with an icon of 'new manhood' like the footballer David Beckham causing a minor revolution amongst celebrities by carrying his young son Brooklyn onto the football pitch during big games. Such scenes were by the early 2000s standard fare, but were a very stark change to ideals of male behaviour from the 1960s.

The sexual revolution

The late twentieth century is synonymous with a sexual revolution in the Western world and one of the consequences has been a fundamental change in relations between and within the sexes. This revolution started with the availability of the oral contraceptive pill from 1961, but also encompassed the legalisation of abortion (in Britain the abortion rate increased from 2,300 officially performed in 1961 to 170,000 in 1973); the liberalisation of divorce law (in England in 1969, Scotland in 1976 and Northern Ireland in 1978); and the decriminalisation of male homosexuality.

It was not until the introduction of the oral contraceptive pill that women were truly able to take control of their reproductive sexuality. In the past, women were seen as being determined by their biological nature, focused on their wombs. With the pill, it seemed, this was no longer the case. It is difficult to exaggerate the significance of this one medical development for so many women and men from the 1960s onwards. It changed women's lives very dramatically. As one young woman from the 1960s said later: 'Sex was not a big risk anymore and nor were men . . . I was allowed to have what I liked and did not have to be frightened of sex because it could trap me into things. I didn't have to be punished.' For Angela Carter, the pill was inherent in women's liberation, making the year 1969 feel like 'year one'. She said that 'the introduction of more or less 100 per cent effective methods of birth control, combined with the relaxation of manners that may have derived from this technological breakthrough or else came from God knows where, changed, well, everything'.[5] The outcome was a new freedom for both men and women to choose when and in what circumstances they first had sex. The restraint of the state, of the family and, despite their best efforts, of the churches, fell away with great speed.

This new-found freedom extended to gays, a term applied by and to homosexuals from around 1970. During the later 1940s and 1950s, the cultural oppression of homosexuality in Britain was extremely severe. To be in a homosexual relationship was regarded in 'respectable' society (especially of the working and middle classes) as the most shameful and criminal of states. The prejudice against homosexuals was severe, with accusations of 'poof' and 'queer' used as the worst possible insult to men regarded as enemies, deviants or effeminate, irrespective of their sexuality. For this reason, criminals were active in discovering homosexual men, then blackmailing them for money in the face of threats of informing wives, employers and the police. The result was that police pursued both homosexuals and blackmailers. The Metropolitan Police in London was regarded by the gay community as particularly assiduous in its methods, using *agents provocateurs* to entrap gays by waiting to be sexually approached in men's lavatories (a favourite place where homosexuals were forced by the oppressive law to carry on dating, called 'cottaging'), and then arresting and prosecuting them. Many men in public life – lawyers, actors, military men, and Members of Parliament – were caught up in this oppressive atmosphere. Significant numbers were convicted and jailed for homosexual offences (one estimate is 1,000 men a year), and many more faced public exposure, ruined marriages and lost careers. It was all made worse by the excessive interest of the popular press which, as with heterosexual adultery and pre-marital affairs, revelled in exposing the sexual peccadilloes of the rich and famous.

A turning point was reached in 1954 when a member of the House of Lords, the third Baron Montagu of Beaulieu, was prosecuted for alleged homosexual sex with two other men, one of whom was journalist, novelist and playwright Peter Wildeblood. Montague and the third accused denied the charges, but Wildeblood became one of

---

[5] Quoted in H. Cook, *The Long Sexual Revolution: English Women, Sex and Contraception 1800–1975* (Oxford, Oxford University Press, 2004), p. 271.

the few men in the decade to declare in open court that he was a homosexual. After being sentenced to 18 months in prison, he became a campaigner for homosexual rights, defending the moral rightness of gay sex, and publishing a book *Against the Law* (1955) that helped a campaign that led to the setting up of the Home Office Wolfenden Committee. This, in its 1957 report, recommended the decriminalisation of homosexual activity in private between two consenting adults over 21 years of age. In the public mood of the 1950s, this was impossible, and it was not until 1967, in the midst of the liberalisation of so much of British life and law, that the Sexual Offences Act was passed. By then, public acceptance of the persecution of gays was diminishing, and police action was becoming seen as sordid, unacceptable and the ruination of perfectly law-abiding citizens, especially elite members of the civil establishment.

This led from the mid- and late 1960s to the emergence of an openly gay culture in Britain – including for lesbians and those of transgender – with the development of places where gay people might meet, gay pubs, clubs and special festivals like those organised by the campaigning Stonewall group. Groups like the Gay Liberation Front campaigned strongly in public in the later twentieth century for the acceptance of gays and lesbians by urging freedom from discrimination by sexual orientation to be preserved by employers and service providers alongside gender, race, religion and disability. But campaigning against gay sex continued amongst conservative church people, particularly in the Church of England, where it was an especially divisive issue in the 1990s and 2000s, leading to the cancellation of the appointment of a gay bishop, Revd Dr Jeffrey John in 2003. Gay sex was also perceived as a problem in the armed forces, where, after a case brought by four ex-service personnel in the European Court of Human Rights found against it, the Ministry of Defence accepted in 2000 that 'sexual orientation is a private matter'. Gay marriages, known as civil partnerships, became legal in 2005, and many long-term gay couples made use of the facility. Though homophobia is far from gone in Britain, the extent of the public acceptance of gays by the 2000s could not have been predicted in 1967.

So, gay liberation extended the gender revolution. Taken together, the period after 1964 witnessed an extraordinarily rapid freeing of sexual activity from both legal and discriminatory constraint. The display of all sexualities and most sexual activities in theatre, television, film, and later on the internet was freed from most censorship constraints, with the abandonment in 1968 of theatre censorship by the Lord Chamberlain which had governed stage plays since 1737. However, some social commentators and politicians regarded these trends as having baleful effects on public morality and social discipline, leading to social problems such as single-parent families and teenage pregnancies; according to a UNICEF report, the UK had the highest teenage conception and birth rates in Europe in 1998, with 30.8 births per 1,000 15–19-year-olds.[6] In this regard, many politicians looked upon the decline of the traditional family as a detrimental outcome of the gender and sexual revolution that started in the 1960s.

---

[6] http://www.unicef-icdc.org/publications/pdf/repcard3e.pdf

Whether it is regarded as a good or bad thing, the gender revolution of 1964–2007 has been one of the most marked developments of the last three centuries. Constitutional, political and ideological change is common and indeed pretty constant, and easy for us as historians to understand as part of the continuous process of historical change to the nation. Economic change arising from new technology, entrepreneurship, the drive for efficiency, and competition with other countries is also conceptually familiar to us, as we ourselves live through dramatic shifts in economic fortunes and opportunity. However, the nature of moral change is generally held to be slower, often imperceptible, and perhaps in some regards we tend to think of some issues of human behaviour, moral rightness and social acceptability as being unchanging. So, some may resist acknowledging just how much of the moral world which we inhabit has been transformed between 1964 and 2007. The gender revolution, with its liberation of women, crisis of male roles and performance, and freedoms for sex and sexualities, must be looked upon as one of the most profound sets of changes of the last three centuries.

Further reading

Bruley, S., *Women in Britain since 1900* (Basingstoke, Macmillan, 1999)

Cook, H., *The Long Sexual Revolution: English Women, Sex and Contraception 1800–1975* (Oxford, Oxford University Press, 2004)

Kent, S.K., *Gender and Power in Britain 1640–1990* (London, Routledge, 1999)

Rowbotham, S., *A Century of Women: The History of Women in Britain and the United States* (London, Viking, 1997)

Weeks, J., *Sex, Politics and Society: The Regulation of Sexuality since 1800*, 2nd edn (London, Longman, 1989)

Zweiniger-Bargielowska, I., *Women in Twentieth-Century Britain: Social, Cultural and Political Change* (London, Longman, 2001)

38

Politics from Wilson to Brown

The last 40 years of the twentieth century saw swings in government between Tory and Labour, reflecting a volatility in voting behaviour. Old patterns of party political allegiance, largely based on social class, broke down and new issues shaped political attitudes. Thirteen years of Conservative rule came to an end with the election in 1964 of a Labour government. There was a brief Conservative interlude between 1970 and 1974, with Labour returning to office until 1979. The Conservative victory in the 1979 election presaged 18 years of Conservative domination, to be followed in 1997 by a decade and more of Labour. During these 40 years the policies and programmes of both the main parties changed in response to rapidly altered circumstances.

Labour again 1964–70

In 1963 it was easy for the Labour leader, Harold Wilson, to paint the Conservative Prime Minister, Sir Alec Douglas-Home, as a fourteenth earl who was out of touch with experiences of ordinary people. Since the main issue of politics was becoming who could most successfully manage the economy, Wilson, the economist, was more than able to outmatch a Prime Minister who admitted that his financial skills were limited. Also, television came into its own in the election and the skeletal features of Sir Alec proved less than televisual. The remarkable thing, however, is how close the Conservatives came to winning the general election in October 1964.

The result of the 1964 election, giving Labour an overall majority of only four, was not the landslide for which many on the Left had hoped. Not since 1847 had there been so narrow a victory and the difficulties were immense. The post-war world economic boom had come to an end and there were signs of the economy overheating.

But Wilson had managed to create a sense that a new, more modern Britain was possible, making use of scientific and technological skills, which the 'Edwardian' and aristocratic nonchalance of Macmillan and Home had failed to utilise. The talk was of 'thirteen wasted years' of Conservative government. In contrast, Labour could offer what Wilson called 'the white heat of the technological revolution'. Labour was no longer presenting itself as a social democratic alternative to capitalism, but as able to manage capitalism with greater technological efficiency.

A national plan for economic regeneration was drafted by a new Department of Economic Affairs, but the refusal to devalue the pound in order to provide a boost to exports doomed the plan. There were fears that devaluation would disrupt the working of the economic system in which sterling still played a major role, but, more powerfully, there was a dread of Labour being once again labelled as the party of devaluation. Central to the planned regeneration was education and a huge reform of secondary schooling was launched, that was intended to replace the divisive selective system of grammar schools and secondary modern schools in England and Wales with an all-inclusive comprehensive system. Educational reform was to be at the forefront of the assault on social inequalities. By 1970, around 30 per cent of English children were in comprehensives; ten years later it was 80 per cent. Talk of incorporating the private schools into the state system, however, came to nothing.

In higher education, following the report of Lord Robbins in 1963, there was a huge expansion, with six new universities being built and older universities being encouraged to grow. Alongside these, Crosland, the Minister of Education, encouraged what was called a binary system of more vocationally oriented polytechnics run by local authorities. Some 30 of these were created. Amongst the most far-reaching achievements was the setting up of the Open University, to provide access to higher education opportunities for adults by making use of television. Controversy over the effect of the educational reforms remains, but there is little doubt that the late 1960s began a huge extension of educational opportunity. By 1970, for the first time ever, expenditure on education was exceeding that on defence.

At the end of 1965, Roy Jenkins became the youngest Home Secretary since Winston Churchill in 1910. He gave a fair wind to reforms that fundamentally altered many aspects of British society, but also reflected the huge social changes that had been taking place over the previous decade (see Chapters 36 and 37). One of the most significant reforms had pre-dated his appointment when a private member's bill brought the end of capital punishment. But, in less than two years at the Home Office, Jenkins became one of the great reforming Home Secretaries, although he was damned by his later critics as the person responsible for unleashing the 'permissive society'. He supported measures that began as private members' bills to remove the illegality of homosexual acts between consenting adults,[1] and to make abortion of

---

[1] The 1967 Act decriminalised homosexuality in England and Wales. The law in Scotland and Northern Ireland was not brought into line until 1980 and 1982.

foetuses legal in certain circumstances. The Home Office itself brought in measures that allowed divorce on the grounds of an irreparable breakdown of marriage and that removed the Lord Chamberlain's powers (dating from the eighteenth century) to censor theatrical productions. There was also prison reform, including the abolition of corporal punishment. The result was a liberalising of British social mores that had enormous implications for the shape of personal relationships and the kind of society that developed over the next 40 years.

An election in 1966 gave Labour a majority of 97 and the opportunity to bring some of its measures to fruition. But the government had little time to relish power before the economic problems intensified. A bitter strike of seamen in May 1966 led to a run on the pound. There were cuts in public expenditure and a wages' freeze. A debate over devaluation led to a Cabinet crisis of deep proportions in July 1966, with talk of a change of Prime Minister, and it left Wilson deeply suspicious of many of his colleagues.

The fundamental problems of the economy did not go away. Beleaguered by sterling crises, the government attempted to impose an incomes policy in 1967, 1968 and 1969 but met with limited success. Devaluation of the pound from $2.80 to $2.40, which James Callaghan, the Chancellor had been resisting since 1964, came in November 1967. Wilson lost a huge amount of his credibility and confidence. He was no longer able to prevent the divisions within both the government and the party from emerging in public and the government began to drift.

Relations with the trade unions were already soured by government attempts to impose wage restraint by the time Barbara Castle, the Minister for Employment, came up with *In Place of Strife*, to reform the structure and operation of trade unions. The aim of the policy was to weaken the influence of what were perceived as militant and manipulative shop stewards by requiring a ballot before strikes. The unions rebelled, using their voting power within the Labour Party. The government had little option but to capitulate and accept a face-saving declaration from the Trades Union Congress to discipline unions that failed to negotiate properly before strikes. One important measure, passed in the final hours of the Parliament in 1970 was the Equal Pay Act that allowed women to claim the same level of pay as men for the same or a closely related job.

Economic considerations also forced a curtailing of Britain's military role in the world. A defence white paper announced that forces 'east of Suez', in Singapore, Malaysia and the Persian Gulf would be halved by 1971 and then withdrawn. Wilson had found himself treading an increasingly delicate path over America's war in Vietnam. While open support for the war would have split the Labour Party, Wilson had no doubt that there could not be condemnation of it. American financial assistance was indispensable and there was a secret deal to remain east of Suez in return for getting American backing for sterling to try to prevent devaluation. When that failed, there was no option but withdrawal, especially since there was still a determination to retain Britain's position as a 'world power' by maintaining nuclear armaments in the shape of Polaris missiles. Wilson and most of his colleagues were attracted by the idea that

Britain could still retain its 'world role' by influencing American policy and by acting as a conduit to the leaders of the Soviet Union. Other areas of defence expenditure had to bear the brunt of the costs.

Heath's government 1970–4

Douglas-Home had resigned as Conservative leader in the summer of 1965, to be succeeded by Edward Heath, who was presented as a new meritocratic Conservative leader from outside the former aristocratic charmed circle. The Conservatives were deeply divided by issues of immigration and race, and by policies for Africa. After months of trailing in the public opinion polls, Labour seemed to nudge ahead in the spring of 1970 and this encouraged Wilson to call a snap election. However, the immigration issue, the struggles over wages policy and the rising cost of living told against them. Labour paid the price in the election of June 1970, which brought the Conservatives under Edward Heath to power with a majority of 32.

In a pre-election Selsdon Park[2] declaration in January 1970, Heath and his colleagues had announced that there would be no more state intervention to assist failing industries and no more price and wage control. Market forces would dominate. Picking up some of the policies outlined in *In Place of Strife*, the Industrial Relations Act of 1971 made collective bargaining agreements between employers and unions legally binding. There had to be a 60-day cooling-off period before a strike and the right not to belong to a trade union was enshrined in law. Fines for unions and imprisonment of some shop stewards merely embittered industrial relations and, by 1974, most commentators viewed the Act as a failure for having tried to do too much too quickly.

Heath began to lose the support of a substantial section of his party when he was determined to get Britain into the Common Market, a goal achieved in 1973, with the support of 69 Labour MPs (see Chapter 39). Powerful forces also resented the way in which Sir Edward Boyle and his successor as Secretary of State for Education, Margaret Thatcher, continued the earlier policy of eradicating most of the grammar schools and replacing them with comprehensives, allowing Thatcher to boast that she had approved more comprehensive schemes than all previous education secretaries put together.

Heath also seemed to be abandoning the Selsdon policy, by providing state assistance for the near-bankrupt Rolls-Royce Company and a short-lived rescue package for the even lamer Upper Clyde Shipbuilders which shop stewards occupied in a high profile sit-in in the summer of 1971. With unemployment rising above 1 million in 1972, there were signs of a loss of nerve to press ahead with the agreed policies. There were also major strikes – many of them unofficial – in the car industry, the Post Office and the docks. There was particular bitterness in coal mining, where earnings,

---

[2] A hotel where the shadow cabinet held a week-end conference.

Focus on

The growth of Conservative anti-statism, 1973

This is taken from the Manifesto of the Selsdon Group of Free Marketeers, September 1973.

> As members of the Selsdon Group we wish to see a change in the direction of Government policy. We want the Conservative Party to devote itself to the cause of personal freedom and to embrace economic and social policies which extend the boundaries of personal choice. We want the Government to abandon its present ragbag of authoritarian collectivist policies which have so often been discredited in the past . . .
>
> A policy for freedom requires a relatively low level of public expenditure. The smaller the government's share of the national income the smaller will be the total of resources allocated as politicians and civil servants see fit. At present the State takes unto itself over half the national product although private industry produces six sevenths of the nation's wealth. The level of public expenditure has soared under this Government. As a result the State's control over the decisions affecting our lives has increased, while in economic terms this growth of public expenditure has produced a huge net borrowing requirement which has been the root-cause of our present inflation. Drastic cuts in public spending are an essential requirement of a return to financial solvency and economic health . . .
>
> The common theme that runs through this policy statement is our conviction, as Classical Liberals, that only a policy of economic freedom can give the individual the degree of choice and independence essential to his dignity. We do not for a moment believe that the search for efficiency is the be-all and end-all of economic policy. The fundamental purpose of our economic liberalism is the protection of individual rights and the widening of opportunities upon which the achievement of all our non-economic ends depend.
>
> The private sector in industry must be expanded if resources are to be allocated rationally, i.e. by competition. Left to themselves, experience shows that politicians are only too likely to waste huge sums of public money subsidising inefficient industries and financing prestige projects which cannot justify themselves commercially and which often have damaging effects on the environment. High-minded talk of the 'national interest' is in these cases just a smoke-screen disguising the fact that the public has previously demonstrated no support for these projects through the market.

Source: http://www.selsdongroup.co.uk

in comparison with those of most other workers, had been failing to keep pace. In January 1972, the National Union of Mineworkers launched the first national strike of miners since 1926. A state of emergency was declared and there were restrictions on the use of power, but a government that was totally unprepared conceded a 20 per cent pay rise. Other groups pressed for comparable rises and a statutory incomes policy was imposed. In September 1973, with oil prices increasing fourfold after the Arab-Israeli Yom Kippur War, the miners submitted a new bid. An overtime ban quickly bit into scarce supplies and Heath announced a nationwide three-day working week. Power cuts soon followed and, in February 1974, the miners called an all-out strike. Before the strike started, Heath called a general election on the issue 'Who governs Britain?' – a foolish question which merely emphasised the government's weakness.

Although the Conservatives had the largest popular vote, rather to his surprise, Wilson, in February 1974, found himself back in power, albeit in a minority government. A second general election in October improved the position for Labour only slightly, giving it an overall majority of three. But Wilson was leading a party that was bitterly divided over Europe and over the whole direction of policy, with the party conferences still calling for public ownership of leading industries.

Labour government 1974–9

By the summer of 1975, inflation had reached 26.9 per cent and the rather vague concept of a 'social contract' between trade unions and government, of which Wilson had talked, gave way to demands from the Treasury for the implementation of a strict pay policy. The need to bring about drastic cuts in public expenditure inevitably produced tensions within the Labour movement. On the left, Tony Benn was arguing for nationalisation and increased state interventionism. On the right, Roy Jenkins and others saw this as precisely the direction of policy that Crosland's *The Future of Socialism* had been arguing against (see Chapter 31). Divisions came out most strongly in the campaigns before the referendum on continued membership of the EEC, but on 5 June the country gave an overwhelming endorsement of continued membership.

To the surprise of the public and of most political commentators – although not to his immediate entourage, who had been discussing a departure date for at least a year – Wilson resigned in March 1976. Various people searched for a conspiracy behind the resignation, but the reason seems to have been Wilson's recognition of his own failing powers and a weariness with the job. The avuncular James Callaghan was elected as his successor. He faced huge financial difficulties. Although inflation was beginning to fall, the Treasury overestimated the government's borrowing requirements and precipitated a financial crisis in the summer of 1976. It led to a perception that public expenditure was slipping out of control, with the result that the pound lost almost a quarter of its value. Wildcat strikes in the motor industry and the calls from the National Executive of the Labour Party for the nationalisation of banks and insurance companies all added to concerns in the international financial community.

In what was presented by some as a national humiliation, the government had to borrow from the International Monetary Fund in order to prop up the reserves. The IMF insisted on stringent terms for cutting government expenditure. The effect was gradually felt, with falling inflation, a strengthened pound, reduced unemployment and the resumption of economic growth, but it was too gradual. The beginning of the end of faith in the Keynesian post-war solutions was marked by a Callaghan speech in 1976, declaring that it was no longer possible for the country to spend its way out of recession by boosting government expenditure.

With union membership growing, unions seized the opportunity to press for wage increases well above the inflation level. The miners gained a 35 per cent increase in 1975, postmen received 38 per cent and power workers over 50 per cent. Railwaymen rejected a 27.5 per cent arbitration award on the grounds that it did not maintain their position in the league of earnings alongside the miners. By the winter of 1978–9, the voluntary 'social contract' between unions and government, that allowed the government to impose a measure of wage restraint, was dead and lower-paid public workers struggled to catch up with their better-paid brethren. What the press quickly dubbed a 'winter of discontent' left rubbish uncollected and, in one extreme case, the dead unburied.

A pact with the Liberals kept the government in power for some 18 months and opinion polls in the autumn of 1978 still indicated substantial support for them. However, that was eroded by the disruption and chaos of the winter. An election was forced in May 1979 after the government, by a single vote, lost a censure motion put down by the Scottish Nationalist MPs, after attempts to introduce devolved government in Wales and Scotland had collapsed (see Chapter 39). The country went to the polls with the experience of the 'winter of discontent' firmly in mind and with unemployment remaining high. The celebrated Conservative poster showing a queue outside a job centre and the caption 'Labour isn't working' proved highly effective.

The governments of Wilson and Callaghan had made some significant advances on issues of race and gender equality and had done much to improve health and safety legislation, but, they were seen, even within the Labour Party, as having largely failed. For some, the conclusion was that they had not been sufficiently socialist and had antagonised their core supporters. For others the conclusion was that a failure to confront trade-union power had fatally lost the party support. There were signs that older voting patterns, largely shaped by social-class loyalties, were giving way to more volatile patterns, governed by short-term concerns over prices and earnings. More and more skilled workers were being pulled into the tax system and resentment at this was building.

Margaret Thatcher 1979–90

Inevitably, there were concerns in Conservative circles about Heath's judgements in the aftermath of the 1974 elections and his difficult personality did little to soothe the divisions within the Conservative Party. Different Conservatives drew widely different conclusions from the experience of the Heath government. Moves to oust Heath became centred around a group of free-market Conservatives, who wanted a huge reduction in the state's involvement in all aspects of the economy and even in welfare. They backed the shadow Minister of Education, Margaret Thatcher, who was elected as leader in February 1975. The Conservative Party continued the reformulation of its policies, abandoning most of the features of consensus on how the economy should be run that to a greater or lesser extent had existed since 1945.

There is general agreement that 1979 marks a watershed in British political history. Not only was the first women Prime Minister elected, but she was elected on a programme that promised radically to alter the policies of the previous half century. She sought (at any rate with hindsight) to 'change the way we look at things, to create a wholly new attitude of mind'.[3] The manifesto promised to reduce inflation and curb the trade unions – a programme that had a stronger appeal in the south of England than in the industrial north of England and in Wales and Scotland.

The 1979 election gave the Conservatives a majority of 43, but with a smaller proportion of the electorate than Heath had obtained. Thatcher was cautious, initially retaining leading Heathites in her cabinet, despite her distrust of them. But her rhetoric was abrasive. The government made clear that its priority to reduce inflation came well above maintaining full employment. The first budget reduced income tax levels, cutting the higher rate from 83 per cent to 60 per cent, while indirect taxes,

Figure 38.1 'Labour isn't working', Conservative election poster, 1979. Designed by Saatchi and Saatchi, this Conservative election poster proved to be very effective in the general election of 1979. It later transpired that most of those pictured in the poster were young Conservatives.
Source: Alamy Images

---

[3] M. Thatcher, *The Revival of Britain* (London, Aurum Press, 1989), p. 98.

particularly VAT, were increased. Public spending was squeezed, despite what was the worst recession since the war. Unemployment that had been 1.4 million in 1978 rose to 3.2 million by the summer of 1982, thus seriously weakening the trade unions' bargaining position. Inflation fell from 23 per cent in early 1980 to 5 per cent in 1983. Thatcher made it clear that there would be no 'U-turn'. Acts were passed banning the closed shop and sympathy strikes by unions, and making unions liable for damages, both from workers and employers. She made clear her determination to break the power of organised labour and to challenge the attitudes of what she perceived as a liberal establishment in the media – particularly the BBC – and in the churches and universities.

Opinion polls by 1981 indicated that the popularity of the government was waning. What changed the situation was the launching of a war against Argentina after its seizure of the Falklands Islands in April 1982. The military Junta that ran Argentina had clearly misjudged the signals coming from Britain over some decades that it was not averse to some arrangement over the Falklands.[4] When the fishery protection vessel was withdrawn for economic reasons, the Argentines read more into this than was justified. They seized the opportunity to reassert their claim to the Malvinas, as they called the islands. In an emergency Saturday morning meeting of both Houses of Parliament on the day after the invasion, in a fervid atmosphere of humiliated patriotism, the government's plans to send a task force to recover the islands received backing from most of the Labour Party. American mediation, which would have involved Argentina having some say in the future running of the Falklands, although attractive to the Foreign Office, was vigorously rejected by Thatcher. The torpedoing, outside the exclusion zone that the government had declared around the islands, of the Argentinian ship, the *Belgrano*, with the loss of 368 lives, ensured that the war was to be a shooting one. Two days later, an Exocet missile sank *HMS Sheffield*, with the loss of 22 lives and many injuries. The invasion of the islands began at the end of May and on 14 June the Argentines surrendered. It had cost the lives of 255 British soldiers and 777 injured. The speedy victory, that involved the navy having to hire ships from private companies, allowed the government to claim that Britain was still a power to be reckoned with in the world and Mrs Thatcher to tap into popular jingoism as she called an election.

She also faced a Labour Party, now under the leadership of Michael Foot, long identified with the left of the Party. Labour were, all too obviously split over nuclear disarmament, nationalisation, Europe and the future direction of the party. Those on the left of the party wanted a siege economy of import controls and public ownership, including withdrawal from the Common Market. Faced with this, a group from the right of the party, Roy Jenkins (who for the previous four years had been president of the European Commission), David Owen, Shirley Williams and Bill Rodgers – all

---

[4] Since the 1960s, Foreign Office attempts to negotiate a deal with Argentina on the future of the islands had been blocked by an influential Falklands lobby.

former Labour ministers – formed the Social Democratic Party (SDP), which they claimed would 'break the mould' of British politics by creating a new centre ground. Twenty-five Labour MPs eventually joined the new party; Foot's achievement was to ensure that the haemorrhaging was not worse. But the infiltration of constituency parties by those associated with the Trotskyite Militant Tendency, demanding commitment to revolutionary socialist policies, meant that there were endless internal battles. It was in this atmosphere that the party went into the election of June 1983, with a manifesto outlining the left policies that the Labour conferences had sanctioned – what one Labour politician called the 'longest suicide note in history'.[5]

Few seem to have doubted that defeat was inevitable. There was a swing of more than 4 per cent to the Conservatives, who received 43.5 per cent of the vote, compared to Labour's 28 per cent and the Liberal–SDP Alliance's 26 per cent. The Alliance was an uneasy one between Liberals and the former Labourites, with personal animosities, inflated egos and struggles for leadership never far beneath the surface. The Conservatives were returned with a majority of 119 over all other parties.

Thatcher emerged from the Falklands War with an enhanced reputation for courage and firmness. She had stridently played up British nationalism during the conflict and in almost all her pronouncements on the European Community. She aligned Britain even more closely with the United States, building up a warm relationship with President Reagan and had no hesitation in purchasing the Trident successor to Polaris nuclear missiles. She had already succeeded in pushing out those whom her supporters described as 'wets', who still strove after consensus in domestic policy, and had replaced them with people who were seen as 'true believers' in the policy of pulling back the state's role. Her remarkably calm response to the attempted assassination of herself and her Cabinet by the IRA at the party conference in Brighton in October 1984 further enhanced her reputation for leadership. A readiness to resist those she regarded as the 'enemies within' was the main feature of her second administration.

Many within the Conservative Party still harboured a sense of humiliation and bitterness at the part played by the miners in the defeat of the Heath government in 1974. There was a determination that there would be no repetition of such an occurrence. The opportunity came in March 1984 with the decision of the National Union of Mineworkers, under a new president, Arthur Scargill, to resist further pit closures. The government had prepared well by ensuring that the power stations had good supplies of coal, while the miners had done little to ensure the backing of other unions. Once again, there was talk of using the strike to bring down the government, although the union had failed to secure the legitimacy of its actions by means of a national ballot. As the strike dragged on for months, attempts to prevent coal and coke supplies reaching power stations resulted in increased violence. Mass picketing was met with mass policing and mass arrests and there were bitter and bloody confrontations. By the end of 1984, however, more and more miners, reduced to penury, were drifting back

---

[5] Gerald Kaufman.

to work, creating deeply divided families and communities. Not until March 1985 did the miners' conference overrule Scargill and agree to a return to work. Pit closures followed rapidly and communities that had once had a vibrant culture went into rapid decline.

It was during Thatcher's second government that the policy of denationalisation – or privatising companies – got underway with vigour. By its end, nearly 50 major enterprises had moved out of state ownership. There was also the populism of forcing municipalities to sell off their housing stock at knock-down prices, leaving the poorest to struggle to find homes in the worst, and therefore unsold, accommodation. Very effective Downing Street public relations ensured that Mrs Thatcher was presented as the one who was pushing through these changes against the opposition of an instinctively 'socialist' establishment.

Although the unions were mauled and the Labour Party, now under Neil Kinnock's leadership, was still split, divisions within the Conservative Party were also becoming more open. There were reservations at the seeming unconcern on the part of the government at the growth of social inequality. Unemployment, in the areas where the now decimated staple industries of coal, steel and manufacturing had been, reached huge levels. In contrast, the reform of the financial sector of the City of London and its opening up to foreign investment banks generated fortunes for a small minority. Taxes on the richest part of the population were reduced from as high as 83 per cent on earnings and 98 per cent on savings to 40 per cent. There was talk of a 'loadsamoney' culture, where easy credit, materialism and conspicuous consumption held sway for a few 'yuppies'. The inequalities in society widened markedly and there were signs of the emergence of an under-class that barely participated in the world of the majority. Nonetheless, there was still little sign that those of the working-class electorate in England who had swung to Thatcher in 1983 were ready to abandon the Conservative Party. Many had gained a capital asset for the first time by being able to purchase their council house cheaply. Others had received a few shares in demutualised building societies, while the better-off had high hopes of returns from the now privatised public utilities. The election of 1987, helped by a pre-election economic 'boom', convincingly renewed her mandate, although there was clear evidence of a growing North–South divide, with the Conservative Party in Scotland in a rapid downward spiral.

When the economy again hit difficulties and interest rates and inflation once move began to rise, however, disenchantment began to appear. Thatcher was determined to renew her radical credentials. The community charge, quickly dubbed the 'poll tax' because it was a flat rate on all adults, was brought in to replace local rates, which had taxed the property value of houses. The level of hostility to the new scheme took most by surprise. Introduced in Scotland in 1989, it came to England in the following year. Thatcher saw it as a way to bring discipline into local government finance and as a way of coping with a threatened middle-class revolt when the value of their houses was belatedly reassessed. In fact, riots and widespread refusal to pay – at least until the final summons – sabotaged the administrative system. Thatcher found herself more and more isolated in Cabinet, as those who had risen on her patronage dropped out.

She increasingly lived in a state of mutual antagonism with her Chancellor, Nigel Lawson, and her Deputy, Geoffrey Howe.

The Chancellor resigned in October 1989, wearied by the alternative financial advisers to whom she turned, but it was the resignation of her Deputy Prime Minister, Geoffrey Howe, in November 1990 that destroyed Mrs Thatcher. Howe, was the last surviving member of her 1979 Cabinet, and, in his resignation speech, he revealed her increasing unpredictability and denounced her anti-European obsession (see Chapter 39). Challenged in a leadership election later in the month she failed to win a clear victory[6] over the former Defence Secretary, Michael Heseltine, and on 22 November she made a tearful exit from Downing Street.

Thatcher left a very great legacy – not least ideological. The roots of what, from about 1981, was dubbed 'Thatcherism' lay in the discussions of groups of right-wingers, many of whom who had always resented the consensus politics that they perceived as having operated since 1945. To these ideologues were added others who were appalled by the failure to curb trade-union power, by the level of inflation and the weight of taxation. The need for alternative economic and social strategies involving a huge cut-back in the role of the state was advocated through 'think tanks' like the Institute for Economic Affairs from the 1950s, but it was in the second half of the 1970s that they began to feed into the thinking of important Conservative politicians. Sir Keith Joseph is generally regarded as the conduit through which such ideas were introduced to Mrs Thatcher. Since 1974, he had been arguing that the only way to control inflation was through a tight money supply and a flexible labour market and that this might require increases in unemployment.

Between 1979 and 1983, the focus was on achieving financial discipline through 'monetarism' – namely, keeping tight limits on the supply of money (see Chapter 34). The price to be paid was unemployment rising to what, in the previous three decades, would have been regarded as unacceptably high levels. There was also an acceptance of the collapse of whole areas of manufacturing industry. Companies, it was argued, had to compete in the free market with no subsidy from the state and, if they could not, then they should disappear. To assist them, they would be freed from the limitations and restrictions imposed by trade unionism. A free market in labour, it was argued, was as essential as a free market in goods. In terms of economic recovery, the effects of this were limited, if not negative. There was little evidence of the creation of an entrepreneurial spirit. Many good manufacturing firms went under, as well as poor ones, and more and more manufactured goods were having to be imported, while fewer were there to be exported.

The term 'Thatcherism' also came to incorporate other elements. After the Falklands War there was a new emphasis on English nationalism and an aggressive assertion of Britain's role in the world, particularly sharing the virulently anti-communist stance of the United States. Accompanying this was a barely concealed dislike of many European

---

[6] The rules required a majority plus 15 per cent of Conservative MPs. She fell 2 short.

partners and of the trends detected in the European Community towards a federal Europe. There was much talk of making Britain 'Great' again. Reality, however, forced its way through, with concessions to Dublin on the future of Northern Ireland (see below) and the acceptance that Hong Kong could not be retained after the lease on the New Territories, that dated back to 1898, ran out. After much persuasion, Thatcher signed the agreement in 1984 to return Hong Kong to communist China. Finally, just beneath the surface, was a desire for moral improvement, for a return to what were called 'Victorian values', never very carefully defined. It was doubtful, however, whether such a moral transformation could really be achieved by a non-interventionist state.

In practice, of course, despite the ideological rhetoric, Thatcher was a pragmatic politician. In her middle period, at any rate, she tapped into populist sentiment. Policies that received a good response were played hard, while those that produced negative reactions were quietly dropped. By 1990 – privatisation aside – there had been no 'rolling back of the state', that she had once claimed to be the goal of her policies. Instead, as other institutions of civil society were attacked and weakened, the power of the central state grew as never before in peacetime. The autonomy of local government, particularly if it came up with the wrong election results, was greatly reduced, despite a rhetoric to the contrary. By the time of her resignation in November 1990 Thatcherism had become, as her Cabinet colleagues increasingly complained, little more than what Mrs Thatcher wanted. When that seemed to be an electoral liability, her colleagues ousted her.

John Major 1990–7

Mrs Thatcher's successor in 1990, John Major, had risen almost entirely on her patronage. His selection as Conservative leader was a surprise but it reflected back-bench and party hostility to more influential figures who were deemed to have betrayed Thatcher.

Major ditched the poll tax and relaxed the curbs on public spending, but he carried through the ill-thought-out scheme for the privatisation of British Rail. His broad aspirations were encapsulated in a much-derided Citizen's Charter, whereby he hoped to improve the quality of public services, by offering citizens greater choice and performance indicators on which to base that choice. The general election was left until almost the last possible moment in April 1992, with all the polls, after three years of economic recession, pointing to a Labour victory. However, suspicion that the Labour Party had not changed, despite the traumas of the 1980s, together with the hostility of a right-wing popular press, did nothing to help Labour.

The Conservatives were returned with a majority of 21 over all other parties. Major was immediately faced with the difficulty of holding together a party divided at all levels over relations with the European Community. To this was added a financial crisis, when speculation against the pound in September 1992 led to some £15 billion of reserves disappearing in a single day: 16 September, 'Black Wednesday'. The Chancellor of the Exchequer had to announce that Britain could no longer remain within the European exchange rate mechanism, to which it had been attached in October 1990, and that the pound would be allowed to float freely – essentially a devaluation.

Throughout his premiership, but especially after 1992, Major found himself treated with considerable contempt by some in his own party and the small majority gave the relatively tiny group of diehard Euro-sceptics inordinate power to obstruct. Meanwhile, the chaos of 'Black Wednesday' had undermined the traditional public view that the Conservatives could be 'trusted' on the economy. Labour, under Tony Blair's leadership from 1994, began to move ahead on the opinion polls. Sexual philandering and financial corruption within the government, lumped together by the media as 'sleaze' seemed in particularly sharp contrast to the call at the 1993 Conservative Party conference for a return in society to core values – 'Back to Basics' – and added to Major's difficulties. His greatest accomplishment was perhaps to lay firmer foundations for peace talks in Northern Ireland. He appears to have accepted his defeat in the 1997 election with considerable relief.

The 'Troubles' in Northern Ireland 1969–98

In the 1960s the tensions in Northern Ireland had begun to impinge upon the politics of the mainland, with mounting violence from the provisional wing of the IRA and growing protests from the minority Catholic population at the blatant discrimination against them in work and, even more particularly, in housing. Little was done to respond to Catholic grievances and a Unionist old guard clung to power at Stormont. When a new Prime Minister, Terence O'Neill, did try to institute reforms, particularly in the field of housing, and attempted to move away from sectarianism, he quickly faced protests from more hard-line Unionists, led by Dr Ian Paisley, and what became the Democratic Unionist Party.

At the same time, O'Neill's moves encouraged the emergence of a campaign for civil rights, echoing the language of the civil rights movement amongst Afro-Americans in the United States. Its roots lay amongst educated Catholics who had gained a university education, but still found themselves excluded from senior positions. There was also particular resentment at the almost exclusively Protestant auxiliary police, the B-Specials. During 1968, marches by the Civil Rights Association came under attack from the Royal Ulster Constabulary, themselves increasingly victims of IRA assassins. Seen on television, the street battles in Londonderry and elsewhere brought an awareness of Ireland that most of the mainland had previously avoided. O'Neill's success in the election of February 1969 was limited and, faced with growing criticism within his own party, he resigned. By then, however, the levels of violence from the IRA – soon to face schism with the breakaway of the most violent into the Provisional IRA – and the intimidation of Catholic families by Protestant paramilitaries was such that, in August 1969, the government sent in troops to try to restore some semblance of order.

After a heavy IRA bombing campaign in Belfast, the Northern Ireland government introduced internment. But, for internment to be successful, high-quality intelligence is required, so that only the key figures are picked up. In this case 342 nationalist leaders of all shades of opinion were interned without trial, thus adding to the tensions. With attacks on soldiers increasing, a civil rights march in Londonderry on Sunday 30 January 1972, in defiance of the ban on marches, was met by shooting from the troops, which resulted in 14 deaths and many injuries.[7] 'Bloody Sunday', as it was quickly labelled, was followed by widespread rioting, the burning of the British embassy in Dublin and by international condemnation.

After a bomb at the Parachute Regiment's Aldershot HQ and the attempted assassination of a Stormont minister, the Northern Ireland Parliament was suspended and direct rule from London was imposed in March 1972. By the end of the year, 445 people had lost their lives in the 'Troubles'. A referendum in March 1973 confirmed that a large majority of the population (58 per cent of the electorate) wanted to remain within the United Kingdom. Elections for a new Northern Ireland Assembly were held in June, when the result was that the official Unionists were still the largest group, but they needed support from dissident Unionists to get a majority.

The announcement in December 1973 of what was called the Sunningdale Agreement (after the hotel in which the discussions were held) on the composition of a power-sharing executive and plans for an All-Ireland Council led to further splits in the Ulster Unionist Party. Protestant opinion was outraged by negotiations with the IRA and, in May 1974, a two-week political strike, organised by the Protestant Ulster Workers' Council, and a bomb outrage by Protestant paramilitaries in Dublin, killing 28 people, followed quickly. By then, Labour was back in office and they gave in to the Protestant violence and replaced the power-sharing executive with direct ministerial rule. Internment was ended in June 1974, but the attacks on the mainland increased, with IRA bombings hitting civilians rather than the military. After bombs in pubs in Guildford and Birmingham, a Prevention of Terrorism Act, pushed through in 18 hours, among other things allowed the exclusion of Northern Ireland citizens from the mainland.

The late 1970s were years of relentless security struggle in Northern Ireland. One measure of this was the degree to which the normal checks and balances of democratic society were suspended. From 1976, trials involving members of paramilitary groups were heard before judges without juries, in a system known as the Diplock Courts, designed to circumvent the intimidation of jurors. In addition, in an attempt to tarnish members of republican military units as criminals rather than as political freedom fighters, those convicted of paramilitary offences were denied political status in the conditions of imprisonment. This angered republicans especially, with some 500 prisoners initiating a 'blanket protest' (refusing to wear prison clothes). A hunger strike

---

[7] A judicial enquiry into the events of that day was set up in 1998 and, after ten years of gathering evidence, a report is still awaited.

followed, which led to the death in March 1981 of Bobby Sands, the first of seven members of the Provisional Irish Republican Army (PIRA), and three members of the Irish National Liberation Army to die, igniting huge community violence. The stakes had been raised further in 1979 by two audacious assassinations by the Provisionals – in March of one of Margaret Thatcher's closest confidants, Airey Neave, in the car park of the Houses of Parliament, followed in August by that of the Queen's cousin, Lord Mountbatten while fishing in Ireland. Although Mrs Thatcher showed little sympathy with nationalist aspirations in Northern Ireland, the security vulnerability of major British figures, together with the horror of what was happening in the Maze prison, may have been crucial in persuading both British strategists and elements within the Provisional IRA and its political wing, Sinn Féin, to edge forward the slow process of moving from the gun to the ballot.

American pressure played its part in persuading Thatcher to allow Ireland some participation in trying to settle the Troubles in the North. It was agreed to form an Anglo-Irish Intergovernmental Council and there was talk of the prospect of an eventually united Ireland, should a majority in the north agree. Nonetheless, the sectarian divisions remained deep. In elections for yet another assembly in 1982, Sinn Féin won a third of the nationalist vote, using the slogan 'the gun *and* the ballot', while, on the other side, Dr Paisley's DUP had as many votes as the official Unionist Party.

In October 1984, the IRA launched an attack on the British Cabinet. It bombed the Grand Hotel, Brighton, where the annual Conservative Party conference was in progress. Thatcher narrowly missed assassination, but five other people were killed. Despite this, the government signed the Hillsborough Agreement of November 1985 with the Irish government. There would be co-operation on security and a recognition that Dublin would have a consultative role in Northern Irish affairs. Between 1992 and 1994, the IRA stepped up its bombing campaigns on the mainland. There were, however, indications in 1993 that the Provisional IRA was ready to bring the conflict to an end. Once again, secret talks were initiated with Sinn Féin, and the British and Irish governments promised an imaginative response if the violence ceased. A new cease-fire was agreed, only to be broken by bombs in London Docklands and at the Arndale Centre in Manchester in 1996. However, negotiations continued.

The foundations were laid by the Major government, but it was under the new Labour government that, in April 1998, the Good Friday Agreement was reached by all the Northern Ireland parties. There would be a new assembly; a release of prisoners; a review of policing and the administration of justice in the province; and regular North–South ministerial conferences. The Unionists were at last persuaded that the price of the IRA disarming had to be a sharing of power with Sinn Féin, while republicans accepted that a united Ireland would have to wait.

Nine years of discussion followed before Ian Paisley's DUP could be persuaded to accept power sharing with Sinn Féin. Ironically, it became possible when there were no other political groupings to challenge the domination of Sinn Féin and the DUP. Relative peace brought demands from the electorate for the parties to deal with 'normal' issues. The middle classes in the North began to see attractions in being associated with the now prosperous economy of the South. In March 2007, Paisley and Martin McGuinness of Sinn Féin agreed to co-operate in a new executive.

Blair and Brown from 1997

Younger members of the Labour Party were keen to continue the 'modernisation' of Labour policies that Neil Kinnock had begun and his successor, John Smith had continued. There was talk of finding a 'third way' between Conservatism and Socialism so that Labour could break into areas in the south of England that had formerly been Conservative fiefdoms – the so-called 'Middle England'. Labour became 'New Labour', mimicking Bill Clinton's 'New Democrats' in the United States. Tony Blair and Gordon Brown were at the forefront of this and, reputedly, Brown had agreed that Blair, with his flair for public presentation and communication, would go for the leadership and would, at some time unspecified, pass it on to Brown. Whatever the basis of the deal, Blair was duly elected leader of the party in 1994 and one of the most remarkable of political partnerships and rivalries was established. In an early speech, Blair declared the central policy of his government to be 'education, education, education'. In this there were echoes of Crosland, but there the resemblance ended. With 'New Labour' the emphasis was on the market, on labour flexibility and on globalisation. Where equality featured, it was equality of opportunity, not redistribution of wealth in order to achieve equality of outcomes. In a move of great symbolic importance, the party agreed in 1995 to abandon Clause 4 of its constitution, that had existed since 1918, committing it to the common ownership of the means of production, distribution and exchange. Nationalisation was at an end. There was also much talk of the modernisation of the country's institutions and of creating a 'new progressive alliance in British politics' with the Liberal Democrats and even with some pro-Europe Conservatives, but such ideas barely survived the election.

Even the most optimistic of Labour supporters were taken aback by the scale of the Labour victory in the election of May 1997 – a majority of 177 over all other parties. Expectations on the part of many supporters that aspects of Thatcherism would be dismantled were quickly dispelled. It became clear that Blair was determined to hold on to the centre ground of politics from which he had won. Gordon Brown, the Chancellor of the Exchequer, had already indicated that the first term would be one of financial 'prudence' and an early gesture was to pass to the Bank of England the responsibility for setting interest rates. The primacy that Thatcher had given to maintaining low inflation continued to be Brown's policy, with the Bank target set at 2.5 per cent.

There was talk of bringing an 'ethical dimension' to foreign policy. It was questionable how far the urging of NATO intervention in Kosovo and the bombing of Serbia to halt the 'ethnic cleansing' of the Moslem majority fitted such an aim, but Blair now began to talk of the need for Western powers, and especially the United States, to play a more interventionist role. He seems to have persuaded an unwilling American president to go along with it and he talked of democracies using force against regimes identified as wicked. Intervention in the civil war in Sierra Leone followed quickly.

A Welsh Assembly and a Scottish Parliament went ahead in May and July 1999, but reform of the House of Lords was more half-hearted, with the number of hereditary peers reduced, but 92 remaining. Perhaps the most striking constitutional innovation, however, was the marginalisation of the Cabinet and, to an extent of the House of Commons, and the concentration of decision-making in the hands of a relatively small circle of Downing Street advisers in the Prime Minister's private office.

Although there was evidence of disenchantment amongst traditional supporters at the policies of the government, much talk of 'spin doctoring' and a number of unpleasant scandals, the huge majority of 1997 was scarcely dented in the election of June 2001. When the World Trade Center in New York was destroyed in September 2001 by a shadowy group called Al-Qaeda the American declaration of a 'war on terror' brought immediate support from Blair. Within weeks, British planes were in action against the Taleban in Afghanistan, which was accused of having sheltered the terrorist inspirer, Bin Laden, and his Al-Qaeda supporters. It gave Blair another evil regime to confront and, thanks to his efforts, a widely based coalition was formed alongside the Americans. A decade later, the struggle against Taleban insurgents was continuing, with little sign of resolution. At home, stringent anti-terrorist legislation was brought in, reflecting an increasingly authoritarian ethos emerging from the Home Office. Civil liberties were eroded, detention without trial was introduced and the prison population soared to unprecedented levels. Only the courts seemed to stand in the way of further state infringement of traditional liberties.

The most fateful decision of the second term was undoubtedly the decision in March 2003 to join the Americans in an attack on Iraq to change the regime. Although the Americans would have been prepared to go it alone, Blair was determined that Britain should be involved in direct fighting. As had been apparent earlier, he had a belief that there was a moral responsibility to overthrow dictators. Britain's largest political protest ever took place in February 2003 against the war, but Blair was unmoved. He was confident in the rightness of the cause and oblivious to the reservations coming from within Britain and from most European leaders. It quickly became obvious that the Iraqis did not have the weapons of mass destruction that had been the 'excuse' for the war and it soon became apparent that there was no clear strategy either for creating a reformed Iraqi state or for ensuring an early exit for foreign troops. The decisions to go to war and the failures of that war were shadows over Blair's government from then on and contributed to a huge loss in his political standing and in his moral authority. Not until 2009 were British combat troops withdrawn.

As Chancellor, Gordon Brown presided over a period of economic stability such as the country had not experienced. The high levels of employment and the relative prosperity allowed huge increases of expenditure in the health services, transport and in education – all areas that had been starved of investment in the Major years. But, much of the capital investment was through controversial private finance initiatives or public-private partnerships, by which the building of hospitals and schools was handed to private developers. The attraction for the Chancellor was that this kept down the level of public borrowing, but the long-term costs and efficiency are still widely debated. Party protests that this amounted to nothing more than the privatisation of public services tended to be quickly quashed and economic success gave Brown and the Treasury an unprecedented dominance over most aspects of government policy.

At the election of May 2005, Labour lost more than 100 seats and had the lowest share of the votes for a winning party in modern times, but the majority of 66 seats was a comfortable one by past standards. Blair's announcement that he would not serve for the full term of Parliament further weakened his authority. The news on 6 July that London had won the competition to stage the Olympic Games in 2012 lifted (some) national spirits, only for these to be shattered on the following day, when suicide bombers attacked three London underground trains and a bus, killing 52 people and maiming many more. Once again, the response was the introduction of more limitations on individual liberty. The government in a decade introduced some 50 acts dealing with aspects of crime and extending police powers, with Blair trying to extend the period during which people could be held without charge from 14 to 90 days. A backbench rebellion blocked this, but a 28-day period received approval. The government found it hard to escape from minor scandals and from the more serious accusations of the selling of honours in exchange for party funding. The tensions between Blair and Brown, as the latter waited to take over as Prime Minister, came much more into the public arena.

Despite huge majorities, Blair's governments had shown themselves to be remarkably cautious. Increased government expenditure was accompanied by endless administrative changes, which seemed often to lack a clear outcome. Blair's excessively close relationship with an unpopular United States' President lost him influence in Europe. The constitutional changes were largely unfinished and social inequality widened to an extent that it had not done in half a century. The Labour Party was much weakened, haemorrhaging members. As so often with political leaders, Blair's departure was too long delayed.

Brown quickly faced difficulties from Blairites who believed that he had conspired to oust Blair and from a right-wing press that disliked his Scottishness and resented his failure to call an election in the autumn of 2007 or to agree to a referendum on the Lisbon Treaty for reform of the European Union. A worldwide financial crisis led to the near-collapse of a number of banks and their part-nationalisation. Brown was attacked both as indecisive and as leaning towards the attitudes of 'old Labour'. His reputation as an efficient manager of the economy as Chancellor of the Exchequer since 1997 was undermined by the growing financial crisis, rising unemployment, and the threat of recession moving into economic depression. All parties were searching for a response to an unprecedented crisis and trying to find alternative policies to those that had dominated over the previous three decades. This, however, was overtaken in 2009 by revelations in the press of how Members of Parliament were using parliamentary expenses for furnishings, for gardening and, most notoriously, to provide a floating duck house. Public faith in the parliamentary system was undoubtedly badly undermined.

Further reading

Boyce, D.G., *The Irish Question and British Politics 1868–1996* (Basingstoke, Macmillan, 1996)

Charmley, J., *A History of Conservative Politics 1900–1996* (Basingstoke, Macmillan, 1996)

Coopey, R., Fielding, S. and Tiratsoo, N. (eds), *The Wilson Governments 1964–1970* (London, Pinter, 1993)

Hattersley, R., *Fifty Years On: A Prejudiced History of Britain since the War* (London, Little Brown and Company, 1997)

Hennessy, P., *The Prime Minister: The Office and its Holders since 1945* (London, Penguin, 2000)

Leese, P., *Britain since 1945: Aspects of Identity* (Basingstoke, Palgrave Macmillan, 2006)

O'Hara, G. and Parr, H. (eds), *The Wilson Governments 1964–1970 Reconsidered* (London, Routledge, 2006)

Seldon, A. (ed.), *Blair's Britain 1997–2007* (Cambridge, Cambridge University Press, 2007)

Tiratsoo, N., *From Blitz to Blair: A New History of Britain since 1939* (London, Phoenix, 1997)

39

Fragmentation and Europeanisation of Britain

Since the 1960s there have been huge challenges to the concept of a United Kingdom. These came most strongly from Northern Ireland, where most of the Roman Catholic community favoured union with Ireland, and some were prepared to challenge the authority of the British state by force. But in Scotland and Wales, there was a rise in nationalist sentiment without the same religious and community fracture, and this resulted in the devolution of some powers to a Scottish Parliament and to a Welsh Assembly. By 2007, all political parties were in favour of some further devolution of responsibilities; the debate was on how much. At the same time, membership of what was at first referred to as the Common Market, then the European Economic Community, then the European Community and finally (in 1992) the European Union (EU) involved a sharing of British national sovereignty. Not surprisingly, these developments caused intense and long-running debates within Britain.

Wales and Scotland

The incorporation of Wales into England from the fourteenth century was much more complete than the Scottish experience. There were almost no distinctly Welsh institutions. It was only in the second half of the nineteenth century that things began to change. An anglicised landed gentry was increasingly out of touch with a Welsh-speaking peasantry and with the growing industrial population, many of them migrants from England. A sense of social separateness was intensified by the religious revivals that strengthened the churches outside the Anglican establishment. By 1851, some four-fifths of the population attended Nonconformist churches, usually referred to as chapels. The sweeping denunciation of Welsh popular culture by the Royal

Commission on the State of Education in Wales in 1847, that blamed what they saw as moral degeneracy and brutalism on Nonconformity, caused outrage, and the Liberal Party was able to tap into Nonconformist indignation, making huge gains from the extended franchise after 1867. The 1888 Local Government Act initiated a social revolution, with Liberal Nonconformists supplanting the gentry who had previously run county government.

Scotland in 1707 had retained its own established Church of Scotland, its own legal system and its own educational system and, after initial resentment at the union had faded, in the late eighteenth and early nineteenth century there were many Scots as well as non-Scots who routinely referred to Scotland as 'North Britain'. However, the emergence of a National Association for the Vindication of Scottish Rights in 1853 revealed the resentment amongst a small number at the extent to which a Scottish identity seemed to have been totally incorporated into a North British identity. A wider patriotism became evident in the erection of Victorian monuments to national heroes like William Wallace. There was also the practical concern that it was very difficult to get specifically Scottish issues discussed in Parliament. Conscious of the levels of discontent in Ireland, and under pressure from the Scottish aristocratic elite led by Lord Rosebery, the government set up a Scottish Office with a Cabinet seat for a Secretary for Scotland in 1885. The founders of the emerging movement for independent Labour in Scotland in the 1880s consisted of socialists and supporters of Home Rule and many within the ranks of Liberalism agreed with their position. A Scottish Grand Committee to allow for occasional discussion of Scottish matters was created in 1894.

In Wales, the focus of nationalist sentiment at the turn of the twentieth century was on the issue of disestablishment of the Church of England in Wales and was also expressed through the cultural nationalism of Welsh-language activities. There was little demand for political separation. The young David Lloyd George made his mark in the 1890s by calling for a measure of Home Rule for Wales, but such demands were muted. The expectation was that Welsh grievances, like those in Scotland, could be met within the British system. Nonconformist demands for disestablishment of the Anglican Church in Wales gathered momentum in the aftermath of a great religious revival in Wales in 1904–05, but there was little chance of a measure getting through before the House of Lords was reformed. Disestablishment was eventually conceded in the early weeks of the First World War and came into force in 1920, with the creation of a separate Church in Wales. The removal of the disestablishment issue allowed a new form of nationalism slowly to emerge.

Plaid Cymru (the Party of Wales) was formed in 1925, merging some tiny nationalist groups. Its base was largely in the rural areas of north Wales and the focus of its president, Saunders Lewis, was on making Welsh the official language of the Principality. Despite something of a cultural renaissance in Scotland in the 1920s, the lack of a serious language issue meant that cultural nationalism was always weaker than in Wales. The formation of the National Party of Scotland in 1928, uniting disparate groups of Home Rule and nationalist organisations, reflected a growing sense that the Labour Party was no longer interested in supporting moves towards Home Rule. Two nationalist candidates stood in the election of 1929 and five in 1931. Although the best they did was 14 per cent of the vote in one constituency, they were able to lose at least one leading Labour figure his seat. The result of this and other by-election interventions was to antagonise those within Labour who were sympathetic towards limited Home Rule.

The merger of the National Party of Scotland and the more right-wing Scottish Party led to the formation of the Scottish National Party (SNP) in April 1934. Once again, however, the new party made little electoral impact and, for the rest of the decade, it acted as little more than a pressure group. In the 1940s, John MacCormick, the SNP leader, worked towards achieving a united front in favour of Home Rule. The effect of this, however, was to split the party in 1942. MacCormick wanted a broadly-based Scottish Convention, but a majority in the party remained committed to Scottish independence. Taking advantage of the wartime electoral truce, the SNP candidate, Robert McIntyre, defeated Labour in a by-election in Motherwell and Wishaw in April 1945, but he did not hold the seat in the July general election.

Calls for neutrality during World War II lost Plaid Cymru support, and internal divisions weakened the nationalist parties in both countries. At the same time, the continued hostility to Home Rule on the part of the Labour Party ensured that the nationalist parties were able to offer a distinct alternative. Although there was little political success in the 1950s, cultural nationalism gained ground, with the language issue still at the forefront in Wales, while in Scotland there was a literary and folk-song revival.

Economic pressures also helped to generate nationalist sentiment. Post-war invest-ment had helped bring near-full employment and a substantial rise in incomes, together with improved health and housing. When the improvements began to lag in the 1960s and there was a sense in both Wales and Scotland that they were less well-off than most parts of England, alternatives became more attractive. Aware of the signs of discontent, the Labour government gave Wales a Secretary of State in 1964, but this was not enough to prevent the Plaid Cymru leader, Gwynfor Evans, winning Carmarthen in 1966, followed by massive swings in the Labour strongholds of Rhondda West and Caerphilly in 1967 and 1968. In Scotland in 1967, Winifred Ewing won a spectacular by-election victory against Labour in Hamilton, demonstrating that the SNP could penetrate Labour's industrial heartland. Membership rose from around 4,000 in 1967 to over 100,000 two years later. Even the Conservative Party felt the need to react and came up with proposals in 1968 for a Scottish Assembly.

The collapse of shipbuilding on the Clyde, the end of empire, the steady rise in unemployment and the discovery of North Sea oil at the end of 1970 brought both disenchantment and hope in Scotland. Protests at the decline of traditional industries and campaigns to save particular firms could quickly acquire a nationalist tinge in their rhetoric. The SNP came up with the slogan, 'It's Scotland's Oil'. The Labour govern-ment responded by setting up a Royal Commission on the Constitution under Lord Kilbrandon, but it did not report until the autumn of 1973, by which time enthusiasm within Labour had again waned. What altered attitudes was the election of 11 SNP MPs in the election of October 1974. Tensions began to appear within Scottish Labour, with 2 MPs leaving to form a separate Scottish Labour Party, committed to socialism and to devolution. An attempt in 1976 to get through a bill to bring a measure of devolution to Scotland and Wales was defeated by a revolt of Labour backbenchers. But since the government was dependent on SNP support to maintain its majority, there was another attempt with two separate bills. The government agreed to an advisory referendum in Wales and Scotland to test support for assemblies in the two countries, but, as a result of an amendment, with a requirement that 40 per cent of the electorate had to approve.[1] Although there was a narrow majority in Scotland in March 1979 in favour of devolution, it fell well short of the 40 per cent mark, while in Wales the proposal for an assembly was heavily defeated. It was the SNP that moved the vote of no confidence that brought down the Callaghan government.

Mrs Thatcher and her government showed no interest in the issue and perhaps assumed that it had gone off the agenda. The fact that the nationalist parties were making little advance in the number of MPs they were getting elected encouraged inertia. However, the withdrawal of state subsidies and the massive de-industrialisation that Thatcher's policies produced led to a mounting hostility to the Conservative Party.[2] From 22 Scottish MPs in 1979 the party had fallen to only 10 seats in 1987. A decade later, it had none. There was a growing sense in Scotland that the Conservative administration was out of tune with Scottish sentiment. Key figures amongst Scottish Tories, who had once shown some sympathy with devolutionist sentiment, now toed the Thatcher line, but demands for constitutional change gathered momentum in other parties. A broadly-based group, involving academics, trade unionists, churchmen and Labour MPs formed the Campaign for a Scottish Assembly, which, in 1989, led to a Scottish Constitutional Convention. The aim was to ensure that whatever emerged would be a Scottish scheme rather than one handed down from Westminster. With a mixture of political and independent representation, it sat for six years, financed by the Scottish local authorities, and laid the foundations of the Scottish Parliament. The SNP, for its own internal reasons, refused to participate in calling for something that fell short of independence, while the Conservatives stood apart. Hopes of a huge nationalist vote in the election of 1992 proved an illusion, with despondency and recrimination the response. But there were slow undercurrents of change.[3] Conservative legitimacy in Scotland was undermined by the fact that they had only 11 seats and the focus switched to demands for new structures that would reflect democratic aspirations.

---

[1] Although the mover of the amendment George Cunningham sat for Islington, his background was in north-eastern England, where hostility to Scottish devolution was strong.

[2] Since the end of the nineteenth century, Scottish Conservatives had preferred to use the name Unionist, but in 1965 they reverted to Conservative.

[3] J. Mitchell, *Strategies for Self-Government: The Campaigns for a Scottish Parliament* (Edinburgh, Polygon, 1995), p. 130.

Focus on

Scottish devolution

This is taken from a report produced by the Scottish Constitutional Convention in 1990. The Convention was made up of representatives of the Labour Party, the Liberal Democrats, the Scottish Green Party, the Scottish Trades Union Congress, most of the Scottish churches and various business groups. It was boycotted by the Scottish National Party and the Conservatives. Chaired by Canon Kenyon Wright, it laid down a blueprint for a devolved Scottish Parliament that formed the basis of the Scotland Act of 1998.

A decision was taken to seek challenging and fundamental reform of the structure of government in the United Kingdom. A Scottish Parliament securely based on legislative power will give responsive and direct government to the Scottish people while retaining essential links with the rest of the country. It will put an end to the unacceptable situation in which policies radically affecting education, housing or health can be imposed by Ministers out of touch with Scottish opinion. The friction that can result is bad for Scotland and the United Kingdom as a whole. Reform will give a sense of involvement in the political process that is presently lacking.

What self-evidently flows from this decision is that other parts of the country have a direct interest in the scheme, its form and how it is implemented. We are convinced that the passing of power to areas in which people live is right and has relevance for every part of Britain.

Any change can and ought to be based on agreement and assent. Scotland is not seceding, nor attempting to dictate terms or to impose a uniform settlement on other parts of the country. The aim is to strengthen the United Kingdom by establishing that our constitutional structure is sufficiently flexible to accommodate Scotland's needs. We expect Westminster to act because we expect Westminster to listen, recognise the need for reform, and acknowledge that the United Kingdom Parliament must take account of the diversity that exists within the United Kingdom.

The Scottish experience will stimulate debate and movement in other parts of the country. The North of England, Wales and the South West of England have suffered as certainly as Scotland from the centralization of power.

Source: *Towards Scotland's Parliament. A Report to the Scottish People by the Scottish Constitutional Convention,* 1990.

Commitment to a Scottish Parliament and a Welsh Assembly was built into the Labour Party manifesto in 1997, although Blair's vision of what would be involved was a great deal more limited than that of most of his party in Scotland. A referendum confirmed how far support had grown within Scotland, with every region voting in favour. The first election to the new Scottish Parliament took place in May 1999 and the formal opening was on 1 July. There was a narrow majority in favour of a Welsh Assembly in the referendum of 1997 and, in the first elections for the new Assembly, Plaid Cymru made advances in some of Labour's heartlands.

The early years of the Scottish Parliament suffered from hostility within sections of the Scottish press and from too many members of the Parliament (MSPs) whose route to power had been via the narrow confines of west of Scotland local government. An outcry about the escalating cost of the new Parliament building at Holyrood proved a useful weapon for those who were opposed to devolution. The sudden premature death of the First Minister, Donald Dewar, in 2000, deprived the Parliament of a powerful national voice. His successor, Henry McLeish, was ousted from his position largely because of machinations within the Scottish Labour Party and Jack McConnell, the rival who ousted him, was careful to do nothing that was out of line with Westminster. Scottish Labour began to haemorrhage members. In the third election, in May 2007, the SNP gained an additional 20 seats, mainly at the expense of the Greens and the Scottish Socialist Party, but the Labour vote also fell and the SNP became the largest party, with one more seat than Labour. With the Liberal Democrats refusing to form a coalition, the SNP formed a minority Scottish government, with Alex Salmond as First Minister.

There were also teething troubles in the early years of the Welsh Assembly. The First Secretary had to resign after a minor sexual scandal. Downing Street was determined to impose its own man as successor, against the wishes of the Labour Party in Wales, but in time local sentiment forced his replacement by the more popular Rhodri Morgan. Although Plaid Cymru had hopes that it would advance with the setting up of the Assembly, it lost ground in 2003, though it began to make inroads into traditional Labour seats. In 2007, it increased its representation from 12 to 15 and, with Labour lacking an overall majority, after long, drawn-out negotiations, Plaid Cymru came into coalition with Labour.

With devolution firmly embedded in Scotland and Wales, with devolved government in Northern Ireland restored and with nationalists in government in all three countries, questions about the future came to the forefront. For some, devolution was to be the means of bringing long-term stability. For others it was merely the first steps towards further constitutional change. Liberal Democrats favoured a federal system, with English regions having their own devolved Assemblies – a federal state within a federal Europe. Labour moves in this direction were set back in November 2004, when a referendum on an elected regional assembly for north-east England overwhelmingly rejected the idea. For others, particularly in Scotland, devolution was merely a transitional phase that would lead on to the more radical change of independence. The result was much discussion of Britishness: what it meant and how it might be strengthened. While most people in Scotland were still cautious about independence, support for further devolution continued to grow. In 1992 only 19 per cent of Scots claimed to feel more Scottish than British, but by 2007 this had grown to 78 per cent. At the same time, there was evidence of a rise in English nationalism distinct from Britishness. Such issues could not be separated from the crucial issue of the future of Europe and Britain's place in it.

The new Europe 1956–63

Amongst the countries of mainland Europe in 1945 there was a powerful desire to find the most effective means of bringing about economic recovery and also of preventing the recurrence of the conflicts of the first half of the century. Many in Europe were anxious about the ability of both France and Germany to escape entirely from their troubled past without some outside authority. The Americans, confronting the mess that was post-war Europe and anxious about the spread of communism, saw European integration as a way out, and American money helped fund the European movement that gained ground in many countries in the aftermath of the war. The British, who had had none of the trauma of occupation, had a very different perspective but were by no means unsympathetic. There was a strong desire to see recovery in Europe and to ensure that France had the necessary security against any future German threat. Bevin, the Foreign Secretary, took the lead in drafting the plans for the most effective use of Marshall Aid by the setting up of the Organisation for European Economic Co-operation in 1948.

Churchill, in a powerful speech in Zurich in September 1946, had spoken of the need for a 'United States of Europe' to ensure that there was never war within Europe again. It was, however, mainland Europe to which he was referring. With France, Italy and partitioned Germany in economic, social and, to an extent, political chaos, he and others saw the United States and the Commonwealth as the only possible allies. There was only limited interest in the proposals for an Anglo-French economic union, as a buffer against German revival. When Jean Monnet, the French Planning Commissioner, and Robert Schumann, the French Foreign Minister, came up with the plan for a European Coal and Steel Community in 1951, it was to Germany that they turned. German heavy industry would be controlled by a new overarching body, thus ensuring that it could not be diverted into war production again. Attlee and his associates, like generations before, men who thought in terms of the Empire rather than Europe, refused to come in. Britain's main trading partners were still within the Commonwealth, not in mainland Europe.

Whether this was a great mistake will continue to be debated. It did, however, reflect the realities of Britain's very different war experience from the countries of the mainland. It also recognised that the arena of British interests was still a worldwide one and there was no desire, as yet, to narrow the horizons to Europe. There was plenty of enthusiasm for inter-governmental co-operation but little for the loss of sovereignty that the European enthusiasts favoured. The six countries that committed themselves to further co-operation in 1952 – France, West Germany, Italy, the Netherlands, Belgium and Luxemburg – began to recover economically, thanks to what was dubbed the 'German economic miracle'. Encouraged by the Americans, who were now very conscious of the threat from the Soviet Union, there were dreams of even greater European co-operation, although proposals for a multinational European army did not get very far and were voted down by the French Assembly, while most British politicians saw the recovery of Germany as a challenge rather than an opportunity.

In 1955, there was talk of moving towards a wider European common market. Britain was invited to attend the crucial talks of the Six at Messina in June 1955, but Macmillan at the Foreign Office declined. Doubtful about the ability of the Six to maintain unity, he believed little would come of the talks, so only an official of the Board of Trade was sent to observe. Yet, it was out of the Messina talks that there emerged the commitment to the creation of 'a united Europe by the development of common institutions, the progressive fusion of national economies, the creation of a common market and the progressive harmonisation of social policies'. This was the basis of the Treaty of Rome in March 1957, establishing the European Economic Community, but committed to 'an ever closer union among the peoples of Europe'.

Most British politicians and officials still talked of the Common Market and saw it as a threat to Commonwealth trade and to the role of the sterling area, but their main concern was with the sharing of sovereignty that the new Community implied. Their response was to look for an alternative that was based on inter-governmental collaboration. The result was a European Free Trade Association (EFTA), that would not venture beyond trading links into political collaboration. It embraced Sweden, Norway, Denmark, Switzerland, Austria and Portugal along with Britain and came into being in January 1960. It was of little economic advantage to Britain, whose trade with these countries was limited. Attempts to seduce France and Germany into accepting the association of EFTA with the EEC had come to nothing. It was seen as an attempt to force change on the nature of the EEC, to delay the moves towards political union. With the economy of the Six growing two or three times faster than the British economy, there was little to recommend it.

Conscious of Britain's weakness, made even more apparent by the forced abandonment of Britain's independent missile programme and the dashing of hopes of acting as an intermediary between the United States and Soviet Russia, Macmillan's government in 1961 decided that there was little alternative but to apply for membership of the EEC. There was also pressure from America, anxious about the signs of France's resistance to American influence. But Britain now faced a relatively cohesive EEC, angered by what were seen as British attempts at sabotage and not prepared to grant the exemptions and adjustments to suit Britain's different agriculture and global trading interests that would have been possible before the Rome Treaty. The British wanted something quite different from the Treaty of Rome and, despite being supplicants, wanted a Community focusing only on trade, evident in the stubborn clinging to the term 'Common Market' by press and politicians. They were preoccupied by the issue of national sovereignty and an unwillingness to surrender any of it to a supranational body. Despite the rapid demise of empire, there was still a deep attachment to the white Commonwealth and concern that these countries should not lose out. But special treatment for the Commonwealth, which might have been gained easily before 1957, was not possible under the Community's Common Agricultural Policy, devised to protect the farmers of the Six.

In January 1963, France's President de Gaulle vetoed the British request for membership. Partly, it was because the British were asking too much, but, perhaps more than anything, it was because of his deep suspicions of the extent to which Britain was tied to the United States and his resentments at his treatment during the war. Paradoxically, De Gaulle's vision of the EEC as *Europe des patries* was not so very different from the British one, but he was not a man to let new visions overcome old grievances.

Labour and Europe 1964–79

Within the Labour Party, there remained powerful hostility to Britain's participation in the EEC, both among MPs and the trade unions. The Community was seen as strengthening capitalism and as politically dominated by Christian Democratic parties, to the exclusion of socialists. Nonetheless, Wilson's government, after the financial crisis of July 1966, came round to the view that only membership of the EEC would safeguard Britain's role in the world. While still very much a Commonwealth man at heart, Wilson recognised that the ties with the old dominions were fast being loosened. What was always referred to as the 'special relationship' that Britain had with the United States was cooling as Wilson determinedly avoided involvement in the Vietnam War. Wilson probably came to believe that membership of the EEC was economically necessary for Britain, if some structural changes could be made.

Faced with the immense problem of keeping the Labour Party together and keeping his leadership, Wilson won over his Cabinet to make a new application for membership without laying down preconditions. Having come to this conclusion, he set out to court the leaders of the Six. Once again, De Gaulle was not charmed and again vetoed the British application, warning the other five members, who were supportive of Britain's entry, that to press it would break the Community.

When Edward Heath, who had led the original negotiations in 1962–3, became Prime Minister in 1970, he was determined to take Britain into Europe. With De Gaulle gone, this now seemed possible. His successor was much more amenable towards British membership, as a counterweight to the Federal Republic of Germany's now overwhelming economic strength. Terms for Britain's entry were agreed in June 1971. There was little in them that recognised British needs and Britain would quickly become a major net contributor, since it would gain little from the Common Agricultural Policy. Although the government's public relations played on the economic benefits that would stem from membership, Heath and his ministers had little doubt of the political implications. With the Empire largely gone and America increasingly looking towards Germany and Europe, Britain was in danger of being isolated. Heath faced a vocal group of anti-Marketeers within his party and 39 of them voted against acceptance of the terms in October 1971. On 1 January 1973, Britain, together with Denmark and Ireland, joined and the Six became the Nine. Labour hostility towards what had now become the European Community (EC) had, if anything, hardened. The Labour Party conference voted five to one against entry. However, there was also a vocal pro-Europe group, led by Roy Jenkins, 69 of whom voted with Heath and gave him the majority that ensured that Britain joined. As a way of papering over the divisions in the party, Wilson proposed a renegotiation of the terms of Britain's entry, followed by a referendum.

The issue split the Cabinet and the party. 145 Labour MPs voted against membership, with only 137 in favour. Consequently, the campaign for the referendum produced strange bedfellows. Wilson, Thatcher and Heath campaigned for continued membership. Roy Jenkins led the Britain in Europe Campaign, with the Conservative deputy leader, William Whitelaw as his vice-president. On the other side, the Labour Cabinet members, Barbara Castle and Tony Benn, were at the forefront of the 'No' campaign, together with a clutch of Conservatives. The referendum of 5 June 1975, against the indications of earlier opinion polls, gave an overwhelming two to one majority in favour of continued membership. But scepticism remained powerful within the Labour Party, a major factor in persuading a group around Jenkins to break with the party and to form the Social Democratic Party (see Chapter 38).

Neither Callaghan nor Foot, Wilson's successors, showed any enthusiasm for the kind of Europe that was being envisaged by French and German politicians. Callaghan, in particular, was determined to revitalise the supposed 'special relationship' with America. When Neil Kinnock became Labour leader, in 1983, he wanted to pull out of Europe. On the other hand, his deputy, Roy Hattersley was an enthusiastic 'European'. However, Kinnock gradually began to modify his views and the support in other European countries for a social charter that would include the protection of workers' rights overcame some of the deep-seated trade-union hostility towards European integration.

Towards the European Union 1979–2007

From 1979 onwards, there were moves towards a unified currency in a European Monetary System that culminated in the introduction of the Euro in 2002. Britain and Denmark stayed out of it. The prospect of monetary union became the focus of much political hostility towards Europe within Britain, with the loss of the pound sterling being presented as the ultimate loss of national sovereignty. But there was also a realisation that the terms negotiated by Heath, and slightly modified under Wilson, were not particularly favourable to Britain. The Common Agricultural Policy built into the Treaty of Rome was about protecting the powerful groups of farmers in France and Germany from cheap imports, and maintaining relatively high prices. Britain, on the other hand, imported much of its food from outside the EC and, for more than a century, had argued that free trade was about cheap food. Also, the fact that the Community received 90 per cent of the duties on imports meant that Britain, a major importing nation, contributed a disproportionately high proportion of the Community's funds, whilst getting little back through agricultural subsidies. It was easy to blame an almost anthropomorphised 'Europe' for many of Britain's economic difficulties at the end of the 1970s. Certainly, it seemed to have failed to deliver the prosperity that the pro-Marketeers had promised.

When Mrs Thatcher came to power in 1979, she, with a deep suspicion of foreigners (other than Americans), was determined to get an adjustment to Britain's contribution to Europe. For her first three years in office, her relationships within the EC never got much beyond a demand for 'her money'. Worn down, her fellow leaders eventually conceded a rebate of the difference between 66 per cent of Britain's contributions to the EC through VAT and what it received from the Community. With the budget issue settled, it was possible for more conciliatory voices from within the government to emerge. There was now an enthusiastic demand for the removal of all internal obstructions to trade by the creation finally of a single market without exchange controls or restrictions on the free movement of labour and capital. What Mrs Thatcher was not prepared to agree to was monetary union and minimum uniform standards on social policy.

The 1986 Single European Act laid down the free movement of goods and services throughout the Community from 1992, very much in line with the British government's demands. However, accompanying it were changes for which Britain had no enthusiasm. This included the introduction of majority voting in the Council in a small number of areas, as opposed to the requirement for unanimity. The Act also looked forward to greater unification, much more integration and to the creation of a European Union.

Despite what had been gained in terms of British demands, the relationship with Europe constantly presented by Thatcher was of Britain as a reluctant European, valiantly standing up for British interests against a conspiracy of foreigners. Having cultivated a warm relationship with President Reagan, she believed that she had succeeded in re-establishing a 'special relationship' with the United States. She never learned to cultivate allies within Europe, nor to play by the necessary rules of Europolitics. As a result, decisions were constantly made into which Britain had only a limited input. Her ministers forced her to accept a measure of monetary co-operation at the Madrid conference in 1989, but they quickly paid the price. Howe was moved out of the Foreign Office and the Chancellor, Lawson, was marginalised until he resigned. Thatcher, ever more shrilly, preached against 'Brussels', as the EC was increasingly personified. She encouraged the Eurosceptics within her party to become more vocal. These ranged from those who were genuinely sceptical about aspects of European policy to a diehard core who found almost any collaboration with the EC anathema.

Thatcher's successor, John Major, had been the Chancellor who had pushed her to accept the pound's involvement in the European Exchange Rate Mechanism – a stepping stone to the introduction of a single currency. Soon after becoming Prime Minister, in 1990, he declared that he saw Britain's place as being 'at the very heart of

Focus on

Mrs Thatcher on Europe

This is an extract from the speech by Prime Minister Margaret Thatcher to the College of Europe, at Bruges, 20 September 1988.

We British have in a special way contributed to Europe. Over the centuries we have fought and died for her freedom, fought to prevent Europe from falling under the dominance of a single power. Only miles from here lie the bodies of 60,000 British soldiers who died in the First World War. Had it not been for that willingness to fight and die, Europe would have been united long before now – but not in liberty and not in justice. It was British help to resistance movements throughout the last War that kept alive the flame of liberty in so many countries until the day of liberation came . . . I want this evening to set out some guiding principles for the future which I believe will ensure that Europe does succeed, not just in economic and defence terms but in the quality of life and the influence of its people.

My first guideline is this: willing and active cooperation between independent sovereign states is the best way to build a successful European Community. To try to suppress nationhood and concentrate power at the centre of a European conglomerate would be highly damaging and would jeopardise the objectives we seek to achieve. Europe will be stronger precisely because it has France as France, Spain as Spain, Britain as Britain, each with its own customs, traditions and identity. It would be folly to try to fit them into some sort of identikit European personality. Some of the founding fathers of the Community thought that the United States of America might be its model. But the whole history of America is quite different from Europe. People went there to get away from the intolerance and constraints of life in Europe. They sought liberty and opportunity; and their strong sense of purpose has, over two centuries, helped create a new unity and pride in being American – just as our pride lies in being British or Belgian or Dutch or German . . .

Let Europe be a family of nations, understanding each other better, appreciating each other more, doing more together but relishing our national identity no less than our common European endeavour. Let us have a Europe which plays its full part in the wider world, which looks outward not inward, and which preserves that Atlantic Community – that Europe on both sides of the Atlantic – which is *our* greatest inheritance and our greatest strength.

Source: http://www.brugesgroup.com/mediacentre/index.

Europe'. Years of isolation meant that this was difficult, and a French-German axis was pushing forward towards monetary and political union. It was at Maastricht in 1991 that the treaty was signed which created a European citizenship, allowing for free movement of labour between member states, and committing what was now the European Union to move towards consolidation of foreign policy, of justice and of social policies. The last, the so-called social charter, was the one which caused greatest difficulty for many Conservatives, who feared that it would lead to the unpicking of many of Thatcher's anti-union reforms. In the end, Britain negotiated a temporary opt-out from the social charter. But this was not enough for Thatcher and the Eurosceptics within the Conservative Party and 22 Conservatives voted against the bill to ratify the Maastricht Treaty in May 1992. When a Danish referendum rejected the Treaty, an even larger number seized the opportunity to demand a renegotiation.

A financial crisis soured relations further. The linking of the pound to the Exchange Rate Mechanism (which essentially meant to the German Mark) had been made at the wrong time and at the wrong rate, with the pound overvalued. A speculative run on the pound in 1992 forced a precipitate withdrawal from the ERM on Black Wednesday, 16 September. Although the events revealed how little control Britain had in a global market, they greatly strengthened Euroscepticism within Britain, particularly since, in the aftermath of withdrawal, the economy seemed to move out of recession. The Conservative Party tore itself apart on the issue. Major had to battle with hundreds of obstructive amendments to the Treaty ratification bill. The English tabloid press indulged in the crudest of xenophobic rants, particularly aimed, as ever, at Germany. When Major resigned in the immediate aftermath of his defeat in the election, his successor, William Hague, made the saving of the pound from the single European currency his main policy.

Blair, Brown and Europe from 1997

Tony Blair came into office in 1997 with the reputation of being strongly pro-Europe. The very fact that he seemed to be able to speak French with reasonable fluency was taken as a sign of his commitment. The European Convention on Human Rights was incorporated into British law and most of the social chapter from which the British had opted out at Maastricht was adopted. Gordon Brown, the Chancellor, showed an innate caution about relations with the EU. He was backed by the powerful popular daily papers, the *Sun* and the *Daily Mail*, and by a majority of the Labour Party who were, if anything, hostile to the idea of interest rates being set by a central European bank. Blair, fearful of unleashing the kind of internecine warfare that was dividing the Conservatives, found that he had to choose his words with care and he became increasingly circumspect. Much as he revelled in the European arena, he constantly read the opinion polls that indicated deep hostility to Brussels. Little effort was made to alter that. When, in 2002, the euro became the new currency, Britain, along with Sweden and Denmark, opted out. Blair also clearly saw Britain as still having a global role and rejected the idea of trying to create a European third force that might challenge American hegemony.

In October 2004, the now 25 members of the EU agreed to a new constitution for the Union to try to streamline decision making. It included the appointment of a permanent President to replace the six-monthly circulation of the post among heads of government and it proposed the appointment of a Foreign Minister who could speak for the union. The new constitution was dependent on ratification by Parliaments and, in the case of France and the Netherlands, by a referendum. The British government, too, had promised a referendum, but this was not put to the test after the French and Dutch voted against acceptance.

In the first decade of the twenty-first century, British public opinion seemed, on the surface, to be no nearer accepting the progress to a united Europe that membership of the EU implied. Whole sections of the popular press continued to tap into perceptions of British exceptionalism and to pander to the cruder aspects of xenophobia. Yet, the extent of Europeanisation had been huge. Across the Union national barriers had steadily come down to allow movement of Europe's peoples to work, to holiday, to purchase property and to use public services. Cheap air travel had brought access to other parts of Europe within reach of the mass of the population. Integration of economies, laws, judicial systems, and universities with the rest of Europe continued. With lingering aspirations to play a world role still powerful among many politicians, and a clinging to the idea of a British 'special relationship' with the United States, the two main political parties have been wary about providing the leadership that might change perceptions of 'Brussels'.

Further reading

Aspinwall, M., *Rethinking Britain and Europe: Plurality Elections, Party Management and British Policy on European Integration* (Manchester, Manchester University Press, 2004)

Daddow, O.J., *Britain and Europe since 1945: Historiographical Perspectives on Integration* (Manchester, Manchester University Press, 2004)

Harvie, C. and Jones, P., *The Road to Home Rule: Images of Scotland's Cause* (Edinburgh, Edinburgh University Press, 2000)

Moon, J., *European Integration in British Politics 1950–1963: A Study of Issue Change* (Aldershot, Ashgate, 1985)

Parr, H., *Britain's Policy Towards the European Community: Harold Wilson and Britain's World Role 1964–1967* (London, Routledge, 2005)

Robbins, K., *Britain and Europe 1789–2005* (London, Hodder Arnold, 2005)

Taylor, B. and Thomson, K. (eds), *Scotland and Wales: Nations Again* (Cardiff, University of Wales Press, 1999)

Young, J.W., *Britain and European Unity, 1945–1999* (Basingstoke, Macmillan, 2000)

Timeline 1964–2009

Year	Government and politics	War and empire	Economic and social	Cultural and intellectual
1964	Labour win election; Harold Wilson Prime Minister	Northern Rhodesia (Zambia) independent; Nyasaland (Malawi) independent; Malta independent		Beatlemania; foundation of *Jackie* magazine; first Rolling Stones album *The Rolling Stones*; Radio Caroline
1965	Ballot of Conservative MPs introduced for selection of leader; Campaign for Democracy in Northern Ireland	Southern Rhodesia declares UDI; The Gambia independent	National Plan	Death penalty abolished; miniskirt in fashion
1966	Labour election victory	Basutoland (Lesotho) and Bechuanaland (Botswana) independent; Barbados independent; British Guiana (Guyana) independent		
1967		Aden independent	Abortion Act; homosexuality decriminalised in England and Wales; devaluation of the pound	
1968	Grosvenor Square demonstration against Vietnam War; Enoch Powell, 'Rivers of Blood' speech	Mauritius independent; Swaziland independent	Financial crisis	Oral contraceptive pill available for single women
1969	'The Troubles' start in Northern Ireland; Bernadette Devlin elected to House of Commons; voting age reduced to 18.	British forces east of Suez being withdrawn	*In Place of Strife*; Divorce Reform Act in England and Wales	
1970	Conservative election victory; Edward Heath Prime Minister		Equal Pay Act	Germaine Greer, *The Female Eunuch*

Year	Government and politics	War and empire	Economic and social	Cultural and intellectual
1971		Bahrain independent	Decimal currency introduced; Family Income Supplement	Women's Liberation march in London
1972	'Bloody Sunday' in Northern Ireland; direct rule in Northern Ireland	Expulsion of Asians from Uganda	Unemployment above one million; miners' strike	
1973	Sunningdale talks on future of Northern Ireland	IRA bombing campaign in Britain; Bahamas independent	Britain joins EEC; oil prices rise by 70 per cent; miners ban overtime; Cod War with Iceland	
1974	Election defeat of Conservatives in February; Harold Wilson Prime Minister; strike by Protestant workers in Northern Ireland against 'power sharing' executive; second election in October; Labour victory	Grenada independent	Health and Safety at Work Act; three-day week; miners' strike	
1975	Thatcher leader of Conservatives; referendum on membership of European Community		Sex Discrimination Act; Cod War with Iceland; inflation reaches 24 per cent; first oil from North Sea	
1976	Wilson resigns; Callaghan Prime Minister; David Steel replaces Thorpe as leader of the Liberal Party		Race Relations Act; sterling crisis; government borrows £2.3 billion from IMF	
1977	Lib-Lab Pact in House of Commons			Sex Pistols, 'God Save the Queen'; Death of Elvis Presley
1978	Scotland Act	Dominica independent		

Year				
1979	Devolution referenda; Conservative election victory; Thatcher Prime Minister; Scotland Act repealed	St Lucia and St Vincent independent	Newspaper strikes in Murdoch press	
1980	Michael Foot leader of the Labour Party	Southern Rhodesia becomes Zimbabwe	Council tenants given right to buy; homosexuality decriminalised in Scotland	
1981	10 dead in IRA hunger strikes; formation of Social Democratic Party	Antigua independent; British Honduras independent	Race riots in Brixton and Toxteth; right to buy council houses introduced	
1982		Falklands War	Homosexuality decriminalised in Northern Ireland; unemployment above 3 million	
1983	Conservative election victory; Neil Kinnock leader of Labour Party	IRA bombings on mainland; St Kitts and Nevis independent		First woman Lord Mayor of London
1984	Attempted assassination of Thatcher at Brighton	Brunei independent	Miners' strike	
1985	Neil Kinnock begins to reform Labour Party; Anglo-Irish Agreement		Brixton riots	
1986	Single European Act; Michael Heseltine resigns from Cabinet		Start of privatisation programme; Social Security Act	
1987	Conservative election victory		Stock market crash	
1988				Lockerbie bomb; Salman Rushdie's *Satanic Verses*
1989	Community charge (Poll Tax) in Scotland; resignation of Chancellor of the Exchequer, Lawson	Fall of Berlin Wall		World Wide Web invented

Year	Government and politics	War and empire	Economic and social	Cultural and intellectual
1990	Resignation of Thatcher; John Major Prime Minister		Poll tax riot; BSE disease in cattle erupts as a major health panic for humans	
1991		First Gulf War		
1992	Conservative election victory; John Smith Labour leader; first woman Speaker of House of Commons, Betty Boothroyd; Maastricht Agreement		'Black Wednesday'; Britain leaves ERM	
1993	Conservative election victory; European Union		Council tax replaces poll tax; single European market	
1994	Death of John Smith; Tony Blair leader of Labour Party		Channel tunnel opened	First women priests in Church of England; National Lottery launched
1995				
1996				
1997	Labour election victory, Tony Blair Prime Minister; Scotland and Wales vote for devolution	Restoration of Hong Kong to China	Britain accepts EU social chapter	Death of Diana, Princess of Wales; Dolly the cloned sheep
1998	Good Friday Agreement on Northern Ireland; Scotland Act and Wales Act		National Minimum Wage Act; Human Rights Act	
1999	Openings of Scottish Parliament and Welsh Assembly; reform of composition of House of Lords	Bombing of Serbia by NATO planes		

2000		
2001	Labour election victory	9/11 terrorist attack on Twin Towers, New York; American, British and eventually NATO entry into Afghanistan to fight Taleban	Foot and mouth disease outbreak
2002		
2003	Election for Scottish Parliament – Labour/Lib-Dem coalition	American/British invasion of Iraq	
2004			10 new countries join EU
2005	Labour election victory	7/7 Terrorist attack on London tube and buses, 52 dead	Kyoto Protocol on climate change Civil Partnership Act
2006			Equality Act
2007	Blair resigns. Gordon Brown Prime Minister; SNP win power in Scottish Parliament		'Credit crunch' financial crisis starts
2008			Crisis continues: nationalisation of Northern Rock Bank
2009	Scandal of MPs expenses	Withdrawal of combat troops from Iraq underway	Crisis continues: nationalisation of Royal Bank of Scotland after losses of £24 billion

Index